Principles of Macroeconomics

FIFTH EDITION

PART FOUR   Money, Banking, and Stabilization Policy

CHAPTER 20   Environmental and Energy Problems   436

PART SIX   International Economics

CHAPTER 21   International Trade   459

CHAPTER 22   Exchange Rates and the Balance of Payments   485

Preface

Any principles text must keep current with the state of economic knowledge, especially as it applies to the economic issues of the day. The fifth edition of *Principles of Macroeconomics* does this, in ways I outline below. But the most fundamental change in this edition is not one of organization or style: it involves a new emphasis which, I believe, will lead to far greater understanding and retention of the core material of the introductory course.

To students, perhaps the biggest defect in most textbooks is their failure to sift through the many details, and present a reasonably small number of basic propositions that should be given central attention. Thus students find it difficult to separate the essential and basic from the less important, and a few years after graduation their recollection of economics is often a smudge.

Almost as formidable a barrier to learning is the tendency of textbooks to treat each topic as a separate entity, with the connections among them either unstated or mentioned in passing. Because the topics are not brought together, the student is like a chef who has the ingredients spread on the counter but lacks the recipe for blending them.

The fifth edition attempts to remedy the twin problems of excessive detail and missing linkages:

Basic Ideas. To provide direction finders through the text, the present edition focuses on 46 Basic Ideas, two highlighted per chapter, which students are encouraged to think through carefully. One can reasonably expect these 46 Basic Ideas to stick with students. If so, their time will have been well spent, because these ideas really constitute the heart of elementary macroeconomics, stripped of frills and details. Based on classroom experience, this simple pedagogical aid helps students to see (and remember) the forest, as distinct from a hodgepodge of trees. (Besides presenting each of these 46 Basic Ideas in the relevant chapters in the text, a summary of them is printed in the front and back inside covers of the book, where students can readily refer to them.)

Cross-Chapter Cases. To make connections clear—connections not only between aspects of theory but also between theory and the uses to which it is put—this edition introduces five Cross-Chapter Cases. Appearing near the end of each part (other than the introduction), each takes up a major issue cutting across material contained in various chapters of the part. Among the issues developed in detail are the pros and cons of America's adopting an industrial policy, the accuracy of the economic forecasts of 1984, an account of a meeting of the Federal Open Market Committee, and the debt problems of Argentina, Brazil, and Mexico. These Cross-Chapter Cases are not mere appendages. They require students to draw on a number of tools and techniques to which they have just been exposed in the entire part.

Other New Material. While the 46 Basic Ideas and the Cross-Chapter Cases are the principal innovations in the Fifth Edition, much else has been changed. New inserts, for example, come in two varieties: some on new developments in economics while others deal with mistakes and fallacies. In addition, new materials have been introduced on such aspects of the current policy scene as tax reform, the strong dollar, the balance of trade deficit, the federal budget deficit, the B-1 bomber, and protectionism. Also, the IBM Corporation is now used to explain the operation of a giant corporation, significantly one with a strong entrepreneurial bent, in Chapter 6. Additional space is also devoted to relatively new theoretical developments such as the rational expectations hypothesis.

Glossary of Terms. Another new feature of the Fifth Edition is a Glossary of Terms, which is placed at the end of the book. I am grateful to Nariman Behravesh, who supervised much of the work underlying this glossary, for permission to include it here. This new section should make it easier for students to refresh their memories concerning the definition of economic terms.

Emphasis on Doing Economics. Most textbooks do not encourage the student to get involved in the subject. They simply lay out the material, leaving the student to absorb it passively. In the previous edition, I invited students to *do* economics in order to understand it better. Scores of examples were provided, each describing a real (or realistic) situation and then calling on the student to work through the solution. Within each chapter there were two problem sets, both designated "Test Yourself," that enabled students to check their comprehension of what they had just read. The reaction of instructors and students was very favorable, and the emphasis on doing economics is maintained in this Fifth Edition. One new feature is that the answers for the odd-numbered Test Yourself questions are now provided at the end of the book. Many students and instructors urged me to include them in this way.

Organizational Changes. Although many new features have been included in the present edition, the book is shorter than the previous edition, due to a tough (even ruthless) editing process. A very determined effort has been made to drop extraneous material and to keep the number of words to a minimum. This has led to a reduction in the number of chapters and to shortening in such areas as how banks create money. This edition, while leaner than its predecessor, manages, I believe, to be clearer, both theoretically and empirically.

Updating. All of the empirical and policy-oriented chapters have been updated. Since a text should reflect current conditions and concerns, the government policies in all the major economic areas—fiscal, monetary, incomes, farm, energy, environmental, and international—are reviewed in depth. The latest data available have been incorporated in the tables, diagrams, and discussions, while revisions in sections on economic forecasting, reserve requirements, and a variety of other topics have brought them into line with current developments.

As supplements to this text, I have prepared both a book of readings and a study guide containing problems and exercises. The book of readings is *Principles of Macroeconomics: Reading, Issues, and Cases,* fourth edition. It provides a substantial set of supplementary articles, carefully correlated with the text for instructors who want to introduce their students to the writings of major contemporary economists. It is designed to acquaint the student with a wide range of economic analysis, spanning the spectrum from the classics to the present-day radicals. The emphasis, as in the text, is on integrating theory, measurement, and applications.

The *Study Guide,* fifth edition, contains, in addition to problems, review questions, and tests, a large number of cases that require the student to work with quantitative material in applying concepts to practical situations. In practically every chapter of the study guide, a new case study has been added. Both students and instructor have reported that such cases are important in motivating students and illuminating economic theory.

An *Instructor's Manual* has been prepared by Michael Claudon of Middlebury College to accompany the text. A *Test Item File,* prepared by Herbert Gishlick of Rider College, is available both in printed form and on computer tape. *Transparency Masters* are also available to instructors who adopt the text.

Finally, it is a pleasure to acknowledge the debts that I owe to the many teachers at various colleges and universities who have commented in detail on various parts of the manuscript. The first, second, and third editions benefited greatly from the advice I received from the following distinguished economists, none of whom is responsible, of course, for the outcome: Wallace Atherton, California State University at Long Beach; Bela Balassa, Johns Hopkins; Robert Baldwin, University of Wisconsin (Madison); Arthur Benavie, North Carolina; Lee Biggs, Montgomery College; Donald Billings, Boise State; William Branson, Princeton; Martin Bronfenbrenner, Duke; Edward Budd, Penn State; Phillip Burstein, Purdue; Wade Chio, U.S. Air Force Academy; Michael Claudon, Middlebury; Warren Coates, Federal Reserve; Richard Cooper, Yale; Alan Deardorff, Michigan; William Desvousges, Missouri (Rolla); F. Trenery Dolbear, Brandeis; Robert Dorfman, Harvard; James Duesenberry, Harvard; William Dugger, North Texas State University; Richard Easterlin, University of Southern California; Jonathan Eaton, Princeton; David Fand, Wayne State; Judith Fernandez, University of California (Berkeley); David Gay, University of Arkansas; Howard A. Gilbert, South Dakota State University; Gerald Goldstein, Northwestern; Robert Gordon, Northwestern; Edward Gramlich, Michigan; Herschel Grossman, Brown; William Gunther, Alabama; Jerry Gustafson, Beloit; Judith Herman, Queens College; Alan Heston, University of Pennsylvania; Albert Hirschman, Harvard; Ronald Jones, Rochester; John Kareken, Minnesota; Ann Krueger, World Bank; Robert Kuenne, Princeton; Simon Kuznets, Harvard; William Leonard, St. Joseph's; Richard Levin, Yale; Raymond Lubitz, Columbia and the Federal Reserve; John F. MacDonald,

Illinois (Chicago Circle); Sherman Maisel, University of California (Berkeley); Leonard Martin, Cleveland State University; Thomas Mayer, University of California (Davis); William McEachern, University of Connecticut; Joseph McKinney, Baylor; Edward McNertney, Texas Christian University; Steven Morrison, University of California (Berkeley); John Murphy, Canisius; Arthur Okun, Brookings Institution; Lloyd Orr, Indiana; R.D. Peterson, Markenomics Associates (Fort Collins); E. Dwight Phaup, Union College; Roger Ransom, University of California (Berkeley); Charles Ratliff, Davidson College; Albert Rees, Princeton; Edward Renshaw, State University of New York (Albany); Anthony Romeo, University of Connecticut; Vernon Ruttan, Minnesota; Warren St. James, Nassau County Community College; Steven Sacks, University of Connecticut; Allen Sanderson, William and Mary; David Schulze, Florida; Edward Shapiro, University of Toledo; William Shugart, Arizona; Paul Sommers, Middlebury; Nicolas Spulber, Indiana; Charles Stone, Swarthmore; Richard Sutch, University of California (Berkeley); Frank Tansey, City University of New York; Michael Taussig, Rutgers; Thomas Tidrick, Clayton Junior College; Fred Westfield, Vanderbilt; Simon Whitney, Iona College; William Whitney, University of Pennsylvania; and Harold Williams, Kent State University.

Among the teachers who contributed comments and suggestions for the changes in subsequent editions are: Otis Gilley, University of Texas at Austin; Marvin E. Goodstein, University of the South; William Keeton, Yale; Walter Misiolek, University of Alabama; and Jennifer Roback, Yale.

I would like to thank Elisabeth Allison of Harvard University for contributing the inserts that appear (over her initials) in various chapters, Donald S. Lamm and Nancy K. Palmquist of W. W. Norton for their efficient handling of the publishing end of the work, and Edward D. Mansfield and Elizabeth D. Mansfield for editorial help. As always, my wife, Lucile, has contributed an enormous amount to the completion of this book.

Philadelphia, 1985.   E.M.

PART ONE

Introduction to Economics

CHAPTER 1

Economic Problems and Analysis

A recent national survey concluded that "the American public's knowledge of basic ... economic facts of life is sadly deficient." This is a disturbing discovery, but it is not altogether surprising. Most of us grow up unaware that economics enters into nearly every activity that we engage in. To help you understand the pervasive importance of economics, we begin by looking at a sample of the major problems economists deal with. Each of these problems could have a big effect on your life.

Economic Problems: A Sampler

UNEMPLOYMENT AND INFLATION

The history of the American economy is for the most part a story of growth. Our output—the amount of goods and services we produce annually—has grown rapidly over the years, giving us a standard of living that could not have been imagined a century ago. For example, output per person in the United States was about $15,000 in 1984; in 1900, it was about $3,000. Nonetheless, the growth of output has not been steady or uninterrupted; instead, our output has tended to fluctuate—and so has unemployment. In periods when output has fallen, thousands, even millions, of people have been thrown out of work. In the Great Depression of the 1930s over 20 percent of the labor force was unemployed (see Figure 1.1). Unemployment on this scale results in enormous economic waste and social misery.

Figure 1.1

Unemployment Rates, United States, 1929–84 *The unemployment rate has varied substantially from year to year. In the Great Depression, it reached a high of over 24 percent. In 1984, it exceeded 7 percent.*

The first of our sample of economic problems is: *What determines the extent of* **unemployment** *in the American economy, and what can be done to reduce it?* This problem is complicated by a related phenomenon: The level of prices may rise when we reduce the level of unemployment. In other words, inflation may occur. Thus the problem is not only to curb unemployment, but to do this without producing an inflation so ruinous to the nation's economic health that the cure proves more dangerous than the ailment. Consequently, another major accompanying question is: *What determines the rate of* **inflation** *and how can it be reduced?* As Figure 1.2 shows, we have experienced considerable inflation since 1929; the dollar has lost over four-fifths of its purchasing power during this period. Moreover, in the 1970s and early 1980s, our economy often has been bedeviled by "stagflation": a combination of high unemployment and high inflation.

During the past 50 years, economists have learned a great deal about the factors that determine the extent of unemployment and inflation, and about the ways in which the government can promote high employment with reasonably stable prices. Any responsible citizen needs to know what economists have learned—and to be aware of the differences of opinion among leading economists on this score. To understand many of the central political issues of the day, and to vote intelligently, this knowledge is essential. Also, to understand the fallacies in many apparently simple remedies for the complex economic problems in this area, you need to know some economics.

THE PRODUCTIVITY SLOWDOWN AND THE COMPETITIVENESS OF U.S. GOODS

Labor productivity is defined as the amount of output that can be obtained per hour of labor. All nations are interested in increasing labor productivity, since it is intimately related to a nation's standard of living. Many factors, including new technologies like microelectronics and biotechnology, influence the rate of increase of labor productivity. Historically, labor productivity has increased relatively rapidly in the United States.

However, beginning in the late 1960s, U.S. labor productivity rose at a slower pace. At first, it was unclear whether this slowdown was only tempo-

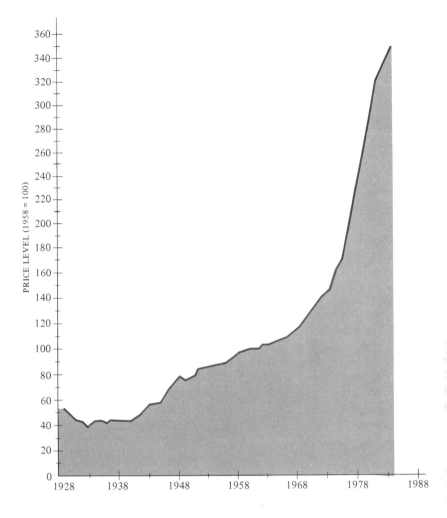

Figure 1.2

Changes in Price Level, United States, 1929–84 *The price level has increased steadily since the 1930s, and is now over eight times as high as it was in 1933.*

rary, but during the 1970s the situation got worse, not better. Between 1977 and 1980, labor productivity in the United States actually declined. (In other words, less was produced per hour of labor in 1980 than in 1977!) During the early 1980s, productivity growth picked up, but whether it would reach its old level—and stay there—was by no means obvious.

Many observers regard this productivity slowdown as being a very ominous sign for the U.S. economy. Moreover, they worry too about the fact that labor productivity in the United States has been increasing less rapidly than in many other countries like Japan and West Germany. For this and other reasons, there are questions regarding the ability of American firms to compete with their foreign rivals in industries like autos and machine tools.

Our second example of an economic problem is: *What determines the rate of increase of labor productivity? Why has this productivity slowdown occurred in the United States? What measures can and should be adopted to cope with it?* Economics provides a considerable amount of information on this score. Not only does economics tell us a good deal about the broad factors influencing national productivity levels; in addition, it provides rules and principles that are useful in increasing the productivity and efficiency of individual firms (and government agencies).

GOVERNMENT REGULATION OF BUSINESS

The 100 largest manufacturing firms control about half of all manufacturing assets in the United States (and their share of total assets seems to have increased since World War II). In certain industries, like automobiles, the 4 largest firms have accounted for over 90 percent of the market (see Table 1.1) Nonetheless, although the large corporations obviously wield considerable power in their markets, the American economic system is built on the idea that firms should compete with one another. In particular, the producers of steel, automobiles, oil, toothpicks, and other goods are expected to set their prices independently and not to collude. Certain acts of Congress, often referred to as the antitrust laws, make it illegal for firms to get together and set the price of a product.

Our third example of an economic problem is: *Why is competition of this sort socially desirable?* More specifically, why should we be in favor of the antitrust laws? What reasons are there to believe that such laws will result in a more efficient economic system? (And what do we mean by "efficient"?) To a business executive, lawyer, government official, or judge, these questions are very important, since it is likely that at one time or another these people will be concerned with an antitrust case. But these issues also matter to every citizen, because they deal with the basic rules of the game for firms in our economy. Of course, one reason why Americans have traditionally favored competition over collusion, and relatively small firms over giant ones, is that they have mistrusted the concentration of economic power, and obviously, this mistrust was based on both political and economic considerations. But beyond this, you should know when competition generally benefits society, and when it does not.

One way that society has attempted to control the economic power of corporations that dominate an entire industry is through ***government regulation.*** Take the case of radio and TV. The Federal Communications Commission, a government agency, monitors the activities of broadcasting stations and networks to prevent misuse of the airwaves. Other regulatory commissions supervise the activities of the power companies, the telephone companies, and other industries where it has been felt that competition cannot be relied on to produce socially desirable results.

During the late 1970s and early 1980s, there was a notable movement in the United States toward deregulation. At first, the movement was confined largely to the airlines, but then it spread to railroads, trucking, oil, and other industries. In part, this movement reflected a widespread feeling that the regulatory commissions tended to be lax or, worse still, to be captured by the industries they were supposed to regulate. In addition, it was felt that many aspects of regulation have contributed to inefficiency, both in the regulated industries themselves and in other parts of the economy. Since regulated industries produce about 10 percent of national output, we all have a big stake in understanding how they operate and whether they should be regulated and if so, how. This is another aspect of the same general problem of how industries should be organized.

THE ELIMINATION OF POVERTY

As pointed out by Philip Wicksteed, a prominent twentieth-century British economist, "A man can be neither a saint, nor a lover, nor a poet, unless he has comparatively recently had something to eat." Although relatively few

Table 1.1

MARKET SHARE OF FOUR LARGEST FIRMS, SELECTED MANUFACTURING PRODUCT MARKETS, UNITED STATES, 1977

Industry	Market share of four largest firms (percent)
Automobiles	93
Photographic equipment	72
Soap	59
Tires	70
Aircraft	59
Construction machinery	47
Blast furnaces and steel plants	45

Source: Statistical Abstract of the United States.

Table 1.2

PERCENTAGE DISTRIBUTION OF PEOPLE, BY HOUSEHOLD MONTHLY CASH INCOME, UNITED STATES, 1983

Money income (dollars)	Percent of all people
Under 300	4.7
300– 599	7.8
600– 899	8.0
900–1,199	8.2
1,200–1,599	11.4
1,600–1,999	10.7
2,000–2,999	22.1
3,000–3,999	13.1
4,000 and over	14.1
Total	100ᵃ

ᵃ Because of rounding errors, the figures do not sum to total.

Source: U.S. Bureau of the Census. The data pertain to the third quarter of the year.

people in the United States lack food desperately, about 35 million American people, approximately 15 percent of the population of the United States, live in what is officially designated as *poverty.* These people have frequently been called invisible in a nation where the average yearly income per family is over $25,000; but the poor are invisible only to those who shut their eyes, since they exist in ghettos in the wealthiest American cities like New York, Chicago, and Los Angeles, as well as near Main Street in thousands of small towns. They can also be found in areas where industry has come and gone, as in the former coal-mining towns of Pennsylvania and West Virginia, and in areas where decades of farming have depleted the soil.

Table 1.2 shows the distribution of income in the United States in 1983. Clearly, there are very substantial differences among families in income level. You as a citizen and a human being need to understand the social mechanisms underlying the distribution of income, both in the United States and in other countries, and how reasonable and just they are. Our fourth economic problem is: *Why does poverty exist in the world today, and what can be done to abolish it?* To help the poor effectively, we must understand the causes of poverty.

Since poverty is intimately bound up with our racial problems and the decay of our cities, the success or failure of measures designed to eradicate poverty may also help us determine whether we can achieve a society where equality of opportunity is more than a slogan and where people do not have to escape to the suburbs to enjoy green space and fresh air. Nor does the economist's concern with poverty stop at our shoreline. One of the biggest problems of the world today is the plight of the poor countries of Asia, Africa, and Latin America—the so-called less developed countries. The industrialized countries of the world, like the United States, Western Europe, Japan, and the Soviet Union, are really just rich little islands surrounded by seas of poverty. Over half of the world's population lives in countries where per capita income is less than $3,000 per year. These countries lack equipment, technology, and education; sometimes (but by no means always) they also suffer from overpopulation. Economists have devoted considerable attention to the problems of the less developed countries, and to developing techniques to assist them.

Economics is divided into two parts: macroeconomics and microeconomics. *Macroeconomics* deals with the behavior of economic agregates like national output, the price level, and the level of unemployment, while *microeconomics* deals with the economic behavior of individual units like consumers, firms, and resource owners. This volume is concerned primarily with macroeconomics, but since one must know some microeconomics to understand macroeconomics, we include some microeconomics as well. However, some aspects of the economic problems cited in this and the previous section are too purely microeconomic in nature to be taken up in detail here. For a more intensive discussion of these sorts of problems, see the companion volume to this one, *Principles of Microeconomics.*

What Is Economics?

HUMAN WANTS AND RESOURCES

Now that we have looked at a number of specific economic problems, we must provide a definition of economics, as well as a description of the

Land

Labor

basic questions regarding any economic system that are of particular interest to economists. According to one standard definition, *economics is concerned with the way resources are allocated among alternative uses to satisfy human wants.* This definition is fine, but it does not mean much unless we define what is meant by *human wants* and by *resources.* What do these terms mean?

Human wants are the things, services, goods, and circumstances that people desire. Wants vary greatly among individuals and over time for the same individual. Some people like sports, others like books; some want to travel, others want to putter in the yard. An individual's desire for a particular good during a particular period of time is not infinite, but, in the aggregate, human wants seem to be insatiable. Besides the basic desires for food, shelter, and clothing, which must be fulfilled to some extent if the human organism is to maintain its existence, wants stem from cultural factors. For example, society, often helped along by advertising and other devices to modify tastes, promotes certain images of "the good life," which frequently entails owning an expensive car and living in a $150,000 split-level house in the suburbs.

Resources are the things or services used to produce goods which then can be used to satisfy wants. *Economic resources* are scarce, while *free resources,* such as air, are so abundant that they can be obtained without charge. The test of whether a resource is an economic resource or a free resource is price: economic resources command a nonzero price, but free resources do not. The number of free resources is actually quite limited. For instance, although the earth contains a huge amount of water, it is not a free resource to the typical urban or suburban home owner, who must pay a local water authority for providing and maintaining his or her water supply. In a world where all resources were free, there would be no economic problem, since all wants could be satisfied.

Economic resources can be classified into three categories, each of which is described below:

1. Land. A shorthand expression for natural resources, land includes minerals as well as plots of ground. Clearly, land is an important and valuable resource in both agriculture and industry. Think of the fertile soil of Iowa or Kansas, from which are obtained such abundant crops. Or consider Manhattan island, which supports the skyscrapers, shops, and theaters in the heart of New York. In addition, land is an important part of our environment, and it provides enjoyment above and beyond its contribution to agricultual and industrial output.

2. Labor. Human efforts, both physical and mental, are included in the category of labor. Thus, when you study for a final examination or make out an income tax return, this is as much labor as if you were to dig a ditch. In 1985, over 100 million people were employed (or looking for work) in the United States. This vast labor supply is, of course, an extremely important resource, without which our nation could not maintain its current output level.

3. Capital. Buildings, equipment, inventories, and other nonhuman producible resources that contribute to the production, marketing, and distribution of goods and services all fall within the economist's definition of capital. Examples are machine tools and warehouses; but not all types of capital are big or bulky: for example, a hand calculator, or a pencil for that matter, is a type of capital. American workers have an enormous

Capital

amount of capital to work with. Think of the oil refineries in New Jersey and Philadelphia, the blast furnaces and open hearths in Pittsburgh and Cleveland, the aircraft plants in California and Georgia, and the host of additional types of capital we have and use in this country. Without this capital, the nation's output level would be a great deal less than it is.

TECHNOLOGY AND CHOICE

As pointed out above, economics is concerned with the way resources are allocated among alternative uses to satisfy human wants. An important determinant of the extent to which human wants can be satisfied from the amount of resources at hand is technology. ***Technology*** is society's pool of knowledge concerning the industrial arts. It includes the knowledge of engineers, scientists, craftsmen, managers, and others concerning how goods and services can be produced. For example, it includes the best existing knowledge regarding the ways in which an automobile plant or a synthetic rubber plant should be designed and operated. The level of technology sets limits on the amount and types of goods and services that can be derived from a given amount of resources.

To see this, suppose that engineers and craftsmen do not know how an automobile can be produced with less than 500 hours of labor being used in its manufacture. Clearly, this sets limits on the number of automobiles that can be produced with the available labor force. Or suppose that scientists and engineers do not know how to produce a ton of synthetic rubber with less than a certain amount of capital being used in its manufacture. This sets limits on the amount of synthetic rubber that can be produced with the available quantity of capital.

Given the existing technology, the fact that resources are scarce means that only a limited amount of goods and services can be produced from them. In other words, the capacity to produce goods and services is limited — *far more limited than human wants.* Thus there arises the necessity for ***choice.*** Somehow or other, a choice must be made as to how the available resources will be used (or if they will be used at all). And somehow or other a choice must be made as to how the output produced from these resources will be distributed among the population.

Economics is concerned with how such choices are made. Economists have spent a great deal of time, energy, and talent trying to determine how such choices *are* made in various circumstances, and how they *should* be made. Indeed, as we shall see in the next section, the basic questions that economics deals with are problems of choice of this sort. Note that these problems of choice go beyond the problems of particular individuals in choosing how to allocate their resources; they are problems of social choice.

CENTRAL QUESTIONS IN ECONOMICS

Economists are particularly concerned with four basic questions regarding the working of any economic system—ours or any other. These questions are: (1) What determines what (and how much) is produced? (2) What determines how it is produced? (3) What determines how the society's output is distributed among the members? (4) What determines the rate at which the society's per capita income will grow? These questions lie at the core of economics, because they are directed at the most fundamental characteristics of economic systems. And as stressed in the previous section, they are problems of choice.

To illustrate the nature and basic importance of these questions, suppose that, because of war or natural catastrophe, your town is isolated from the adjoining territory. No longer is it possible for the town's inhabitants to leave, or for people or goods to enter. (Lest you regard this as fanciful, it is perhaps worthwhile to note that Leningrad was under siege in World War II for over two years.) In this situation, you and your fellow townspeople must somehow resolve each of these questions. You must decide what goods and services will be produced, how each will be produced, who will receive what, and how much provision there will be for increased output in the future.

In a situation of this sort, your very survival will depend on how effectively you answer these questions. If a decision is made to produce too much clothing and too little food, some of the townspeople may starve. If a decision is made to produce wheat from soil that is inappropriate for wheat, but excellent for potatoes, much the same result may occur. If a decision is made to allot practically all of the town's output to friends and political cronies of the mayor, those who oppose him may have a very rough time. And if a decision is made to eat, drink, and be merry today, and not to worry about tomorrow, life may be very meager in the days ahead.

Because we are considering a relatively small and isolated population, the importance of these questions may seem more obvious than in a huge country like the United States, which is constantly communicating, trading, and interacting with the rest of the world. But the truth is that these questions are every bit as important to the United States as to the isolated town. And, for this reason, it is important that we understand how these decisions are made, and whether they are being made effectively. Just as in the hypothetical case of the isolated town, your survival depends on these decisions—but in the United States the situation isn't hypothetical!

Test Yourself

1. Explain why each of the following resources is or is not capital: (a) iron ore in Minnesota that is still in the ground; (b) a Boeing 747 airplane operated by TWA Airlines; (c) a Chrysler dealer's inventory of unsold cars; (d) a telephone used by the University of Oklahoma.

2. Alfred Marshall, the great British economist, defined economics as follows: "Economics is a study of men as they live and move and think in the ordinary business of life. But it concerns itself chiefly with those motives which affect, most powerfully and most steadily, man's conduct *in the business part of life.* . . . [The] steadiest motive to ordinary business work is the desire for the pay which is the material reward of work."* Does this definition encompass all of the examples of economic analysis and problems contained so far in this chapter?

* A. Marshall, *Principles of Economics,* London: Macmillan, 1920.

3. C. J. Blank and E. Rosinski of Mobil Research and Development Corporation invented a new type of catalyst which enables oil refiners to save an estimated 200 million barrels of crude oil per year. Has this invention altered the technology of the oil refining industry? Has it changed the amount of goods and services that can be derived from a given amount of resources? Were resources used to obtain this invention? If so, what types of resources were used?

4. We described four basic questions that any economic system must answer. Which of these questions is involved in each of the following specific problems: (a) Should the United States use natural gas to produce ammonia? (b) Should taxes on the poor be lower? (c) Should American consumers save more? (d) Should more of our nation's industry be used to produce food?

Opportunity Cost: A Fundamental Concept

In previous sections, we have emphasized that economics is concerned with the way resources are allocated among alternative uses to satisfy human wants. To help determine how resources should be allocated, economists often use the concept of **opportunity cost.** We turn now to an introductory discussion of this concept, which should help to acquaint you with how it is used.

Since a specific case is more interesting than abstract discussion, let's return to the case of the town that is isolated from the adjoining territory, because of a war or natural catastrophe. Suppose that you are a member of the town council that is organized to determine how the town's resources should be utilized. To keep things simple, suppose that only two goods—food and clothing—can be produced. (This is an innocuous assumption that allows us to strip the problem to its essentials.) You must somehow figure out how much of each good should be produced. How can you go about solving this problem?

Clearly, the first step toward a solution is to list the various resources contained within the town. Using the technology available to the townspeople, each of these resources can be used to produce either food or clothing. Some of these resources are much more effective at producing one good than the other. For example, a tailor probably is better able to produce clothing than to produce food. But nonetheless most resources can be adapted to produce either good. For example, the tailor can be put to work on a farm, even though he may not be very good at farming.

After listing the various available resources and having determined how effective each is at producing food or clothing, the next step is to see how much food the town could produce per year, if it produced nothing but food, and how much clothing it could produce per year, if it produced nothing but clothing. Also, you should determine, if various amounts of food are produced per year, the maximum amount of clothing that the town can produce per year. For example, if the town produces 100 tons of food per year, what is the maximum amount of clothing it can produce per year? If the town produces 200 tons of food per year, what is the maximum amount of clothing it can produce per year? And so on.

Having carried out this step, suppose that the results are as shown in Table 1.3. According to this table, the town can produce (at most) 200 tons of clothing per year if it produces nothing but clothing (possibility *A*). Or it can produce (at most) 400 tons of food per year if it produces nothing but food (possibility *E*). Other possible combinations (labeled *B, C,* and *D*) of food output and clothing output are specified in Table 1.3.

The data in Table 1.3 put in bold relief the basic problem of choice facing you and the other members of the town council. Because the town's resources are limited, the town can only produce limited amounts of each good. There is no way, for example, that the town can produce 200 tons of clothing per year and 200 tons of food per year. This is beyond the capacity of the town's resources. If the town wants to produce 200 tons of clothing, it can produce no food—which is hardly a pleasant prospect. And if the town wants to produce 200 tons of food, it can produce 150 (not 200) tons of clothing per year. Table 1.3 shows what combinations of food and clothing outputs are attainable.

Table 1.3

COMBINATIONS OF OUTPUT OF FOOD AND CLOTHING THAT THE TOWN CAN PRODUCE PER YEAR

Possibility	Amount of food produced per year (tons)	Amount of clothing produced per year (tons)
A	0	200
B	100	180
C	200	150
D	300	100
E	400	0

*Basic Idea #2: The cost of using
resources in a particular way is the value
of what these resources could have
produced if they had been used in the
best alternative way. Thus the cost of
producing a particular commodity is the
value of what could have been produced
instead. In other words, it is the value of
what had to be given up to produce this
commodity.*

MORE FOOD MEANS LESS CLOTHING

A very important fact illustrated by Table 1.3 is that, whenever the town increases its production of one good, it must cut back its production of the other good. For example, if the town increases its production of food from 100 to 200 tons per year, it must cut back its production of clothing from 180 to 150 tons per year. Thus *the cost to the town of increasing its food output from 100 to 200 tons per year is that it must reduce its clothing output from 180 to 150 tons per year.*

Economists refer to this cost as **opportunity cost** (or **alternative cost**); it is one of the most fundamental concepts in economics. *The opportunity cost of using resources in a certain way is the value of what these resources could have produced if they had been used in the best alternative way.* In this case, the opportunity cost of the extra 100 tons of food per year is the 30 tons of clothing per year that must be forgone. This is what the town must give up in order to get the extra 100 tons of food.

Why is opportunity cost so important? Because for you and the other members of the town council to determine which combination of food and clothing is best, you should compare the value of increases in food output with the opportunity costs of such increases. For example, suppose that the town council is considering whether or not to increase food output from 100 to 200 tons per year. To decide this question, the council should compare the value of the extra 100 tons of food with the opportunity cost of the extra food (which is the 30 tons of clothing that must be given up). If the town council feels that the extra 100 tons of food are worth more to the town's welfare than the 30 tons of clothing that are given up, the extra food should be produced. Otherwise it should not be produced.

Parks and Opportunity Costs. As we have just seen, the concept of opportunity cost can be used to help solve the hypothetical problem of the town council described above. Used in a similar way, the concept of opportunity cost can throw significant light on many important real problems as well. For example, suppose that a bill is presented to Congress to set aside certain wilderness areas as national parks. At first glance, it may appear that such a step entails no cost to society, since the land is not being utilized and the resources required to designate the areas as national parks are trivial. But using the concept of opportunity cost, it is clear that this step may have very substantial costs to society. For instance, if these lands are made part of the national parks system, the minerals, timber, and other natural resources contained within the areas cannot be extracted nor can the lands be used as sites for factories or processing plants. As pointed out above, the opportunity cost of using resources in one way is the value of what these resources could have produced had they been used in the best alternative way. Suppose that if these lands are not turned into national parks, their most valuable alternative use is for development of copper mines which would produce benefits amounting to $25 million per year to the society. Then the actual cost to society of using these lands as parks is $25 million per year, since this is the amount that society is giving up when it uses them in this way (rather than selecting the most valuable alternative). Thus, whether these lands should be used as parks depends on whether the society believes that it is worth $25 million or more to do so.

The concept of opportunity cost is very important in analyzing personal, managerial, and judicial issues, as well as questions involving government policy. Example 1.1 shows how this concept can be applied to determine the true costs to a student of going to college. Example 1.2 indicates how this concept was used in a legal case to assess damages. Like the examples in subsequent chapters, they should be studied carefully.

The Impact of Economics on Society

In previous sections, we described some of the questions that concern economists. Now we must consider how much influence economics has had. The answer is that economics has influenced generations of states-men, philosophers, and ordinary citizens, and has played a significant role in shaping our society today.

Example 1.1   How Much Does It Cost to Go to College?

According to the College Board, the average college student incurred the following annual costs in 1984:

	Private College (dollars)	Public College
Tuition and fees	5,016	1,126
Meals, room, books, travel, and other expenses	4,006	3,755
Total	9,022	4,881

(a) Is $9,022 the total cost to the student of a year at a private college? (*Hint:* Are there opportunity costs?) (b) John Martin is a 40-year-old executive; James Miller is an 18-year-old with no job experience. They are both full-time students. Although both must pay the same costs (given above), the true cost to Martin is more than the true cost to Miller. Why? (c) Is $1,126 the total cost to the typical public college of a student's going there for a year? (d) Is $9,022 the total cost to society of a student's going to a private college for a year?

SOLUTION

(a) No, the true cost of going to college is considerably in excess of the out-of-pocket expenses because one can obtain wages by working rather than attending classes and studying. In other words, the time spent in school has opportunity costs, since it could be devoted to a job rather than to education. For example, if the student could earn $8,000 during a school year if he or she worked rather than going to college, the true total annual cost of a college education is $9,022 + $8,000 = $17,022. (b) Martin can earn much more than Miller if, rather than going to school, he were to work. Thus the opportunity cost of his time spent in school is greater than for Miller. (c) No. Tuition and fees cover only part of the public college's costs; the rest are covered by government support, alumni contributions, and other payments. (d) No. The cost to society equals the value to society of the resources used to teach, house, feed, and maintain the student, as well as the opportunity cost to society of his or her time. Although it is not easy to pin down all of the social costs, they clearly do not equal $9,022.

ADAM SMITH, FATHER OF MODERN ECONOMICS

To illustrate the importance of economic ideas, let's consider some of the precepts of Adam Smith (1723–90), the man who is often called the father of modern economics. Much of his masterpiece *The Wealth of Nations*[1] seems trite today, because it has been absorbed so thoroughly into modern thought, but it was not trite when it was written. On the contrary, Smith's ideas were revolutionary. *He was among the first to describe how a free, competitive economy can function—without central planning or government interference—to allocate resources efficiently. He recognized the virtues of the "invisible hand" that leads the private interest of firms and individuals toward socially desirable ends, and he was properly suspicious of firms that are sheltered from competition, since he recognized the potentially undesirable effects on resource allocation.*

In addition, Smith—with the dire poverty of his times staring him in the face—was interested in the forces that determined the evolution of the economy—that is, the forces determining the rate of growth of average income per person. Although Smith did not approve of avarice, he felt that saving was good because it enabled society to invest in machinery and other forms of capital. Accumulating more and more capital would, according to Smith, allow output to grow. In addition, he emphasized the importance of increased specialization and division of labor in bringing about economic progress. By specializing, people can concentrate on the tasks they do best, with the result that society's total output is raised.

All in all, Smith's views were relatively optimistic, in keeping with the intellectual climate of his time—the era of Voltaire, Diderot, Franklin, and Jefferson, the age of the Enlightenment, when men believed so strongly in rationality. Leave markets alone, said Smith, and beware of firms with too much economic power and government meddling. If this is done, there is no reason why considerable economic progress cannot be achieved. Smith's work has been modified and extended in a variety of ways in the past 200 years. Some of his ideas have been challenged and, in some cases, discarded. But his influence on modern society has been enormous.

THE INFLUENCE OF ECONOMICS TODAY

Turning from Adam Smith's day to the present, economics continues to have an enormous influence over the shape of our society. Economics, and economists, play an extremely important part in the formulation of public policy. Skim through the articles in a daily newspaper. Chances are that you will find a report of an economist testifying before Congress, perhaps on the costs and benefits of a program to reduce unemployment among black teenagers in the Bedford-Stuyvesant area of New York City, or on the steps to be taken to make American goods more competitive with those of Japan or West Germany. Still another economist may crop up on the editorial page, discussing the pros and cons of various proposed ways to reduce the federal deficit.

Economics and economists play a key role at the highest levels of our government. The president, whether a Democrat or a Republican, relies

---

[1] Adam Smith, *The Wealth of Nations,* New York: Modern Library, 1937. Originally published in 1776.

Adam Smith (1723–90) lived during the Industrial Revolution and was one of the first scholars to understand many of the central mechanisms of a free, or unplanned, economy. Much of his life was spent as professor of moral philosophy at the University of Glasgow in Scotland. In 1759, he published *The Theory of Moral Sentiments,* which established him as one of Britain's foremost philosophers, but this was not the book for which he is famous today. His masterpiece, published in 1776 (while the American colonists were brewing rebellion), was *The Wealth of Nations,* a long encyclopedic book 12 years in the writing. It was not an instant success, but the laurels it eventually won undoubtedly compensated for its early neglect.

One of Smith's central contentions was that firms and individuals, by pursuing their own objectives, often will promote the general welfare. In a famous passage, he stated that:

"It is only for the sake of profit that any man employs [his] capital in the support of industry, and he will always, therefore, endeavor to employ it in the support of that industry of which the produce is likely to be of greatest value, or to exchange the greatest quantity either of money or of other goods. But the annual revenue of every society is always precisely equal to the exchangeable value of the whole annual produce of its industry, or rather is precisely the same thing with that exchangeable value. As every individual, therefore, endeavors as much as he can both to employ his capital in the support of domestic industry, and so to direct that industry that its produce may be of the greatest value, every individual necessarily labors to render the annual revenue of the society as great as he can: He generally, indeed, neither intends to promote the public interest, nor knows how much he is promoting it. . . . He intends only his own security; and by directing that industry in such a manner as its produce may be of the greatest value, he intends only his own gain, and *he is in this, as in many other cases, led by an invisible hand to promote an end which was no part of his intention.* Nor is it always the worse for the society that it was no part of it. *By pursuing his own interest he frequently promotes that of the society more effectually than when he really intends to promote it.* I have never known much good done by those who affected to trade for the public good. It is an affectation, indeed, not very common among merchants, and very few words need be employed in dissuading them from it. . . ."

Adam Smith, *The Wealth of Nations,* London: George Routledge, 1900, p. 345. Originally published in 1776. (Italics added.)

heavily on his economic advisers in making the decisions that help to shape the future of the country. In Congress, too, economics plays a major role. Economists are frequent witnesses before congressional committees, staff members for the committees, and advisers to individual congressmen and senators. Many congressional committees focus largely on economic matters. For example, in 1985, many congressmen spent large chunks of their time wrestling with budgetary and tax questions.

Perhaps the most dramatic evidence of the importance of economics in the formulation of public policy is provided during presidential elections, when each candidate—with his or her own cadre of economic advisers supplying ideas and reports—stakes out a position on the major economic issues of the day. This position can be of crucial importance in determining victory or defeat, and you, the citizen, must know some economics to understand whether a candidate is talking sense or nonsense (or merely evading an issue). For example, if a candidate promises to increase government expenditures, lower taxes, and reduce the federal deficit, you can be pretty certain that he is talking through his hat. This may not be obvious to you now, but it should be later on.

Also, economics and economists play an extremely important role in private decision making. Their role in the decision-making process in business firms is particularly great, since many of the nation's larger corporations hire professional economists to forecast their sales, reduce their costs, increase their efficiency, negotiate with labor and government, and carry out a host of other tasks. Judging from the fancy salaries business economists are paid, the firms seem to think they can deliver the goods; and in fact, the available evidence seems to indicate that they do provide important guidance to firms in many areas of their operations.

POSITIVE ECONOMICS VERSUS NORMATIVE ECONOMICS

Before concluding this chapter, it is essential that we recognize the distinction between positive economics and normative economics. ***Positive economics*** *contains descriptive statements, propositions, and predictions about the world.* For instance, an economic theory may predict that the price of copper will increase by $.01 a pound if income per person in the United States rises by 10 percent; this is positive economics. Positive economics tells us only what will happen under certain circumstances. It says nothing about whether the results are good or bad—or about what we should do. ***Normative economics,*** *on the other hand, makes statements about what ought to be, or about what a person, organization, or nation ought to do.* For instance, a theory might say that Chile should introduce new technology more quickly in many of its copper mines; this is normative economics.

Clearly, positive economics and normative economics must be treated differently. Positive economics is science in the ordinary sense of the word. Propositions in positive economics can be tested by an appeal to the facts. In a nonexperimental science like economics, it is sometimes difficult to get the facts you need to test particular propositions. For example, if income per person in the United States does not rise by 10 percent, it may be difficult to tell what the effect of such an increase would be on the price of copper. Moreover, even if per capita income does increase by this amount, it may be difficult to separate the effect of the increase in income per person on the price of copper from the effect of other factors. But nonetheless, we can, in principle, test propositions in positive economics by an appeal to the facts.

In normative economics, however, this is not the case. *In normative economics, the results you get depend on your values or preferences.* For example, if you believe that reducing unemployment is more important than maintaining the purchasing power of the dollar, you will get one answer to certain questions; whereas if you believe that maintaining the purchasing power of the dollar is more important than reducing unem-

---

Example 1.2   The Assessment of Damages

In a well-known legal case, the United States was sued by O'Brien Bros., Inc., the owner of a Brooklyn-bound barge that was sunk by a U.S. Navy tug that collided with the barge. O'Brien Bros. received damages stemming from the collision. The calculation of the damages was turned over to a commissioner, who found them to be as follows:

	dollars
Costs of raising the wreck	7,732.21
Repairs	43,245.22
Compensation for loss of earnings from the barge during the time it was unavailable for work	6,620.25
Miscellaneous costs	3,423.91
Total	61,021.59

(a) Why should O'Brien Bros. be compensated for the loss of earnings? It did not pay out $6,620.25 to anyone. Why should it receive this amount in damages? (b) The United States appealed the decision. Government attorneys introduced evidence that a similar barge could have been built new for $33,000. Does this mean that the damages should have been $33,000? (c) Suppose that O'Brien Bros. could have bought a similar barge for $25,000 and that its forgone earnings during the time elapsing from the sinking of the old barge to the availability of the new barge was $5,000. If the sunk barge would cause no problems either to O'Brien Bros. or anyone else, should it have been raised and repaired? (d) Suppose that O'Brien Bros. could have obtained $8,500 for the wreck (for scrap metal, salvageable parts, and so forth) if it was raised? Should it have been raised?

SOLUTION

(a) If the barge had not been sunk, O'Brien Bros. would have earned this amount. It is the opportunity cost of the barge's being sunk. (b) No. The barge that was sunk may have been worth less than $33,000, since it was not new. On the other hand, the figure of $33,000 takes no account of lost earnings in the time interval until the barge was replaced. (c) No. The cost of raising and repairing it exceeded the cost of buying a similar barge. (d) Yes, because the amount that could be obtained for the wreck would exceed the cost of raising it.*

*For further description of this case, see "O'Brien Bros., Inc. v. The Helen B. Moran et al." in R. Byrns and G. Stone, Jr., *An Economics Casebook: Applications from the Law,* Santa Monica: Goodyear, 1980.

ployment, you are likely to get a different answer to the same questions. This is not at all strange. After all, if people desire different things (which is another way of saying that they have different values), they may well make different decisions and advocate different policies. It would be strange if they did not.

This book will spend a lot of time on the principles of positive economics—the principles and propositions concerning the workings of the economic system about which practically all economists tend to agree. Normative economics will also be treated, since we must discuss questions of policy—and all policy discussions involve individual preferences, not solely hard facts. In these discussions, we shall try to indicate how the conclusions depend on one's values. Then you can let your own values be your guide. The purpose of this book is not to convert you to a particular set of values. It is to teach you how to obtain better solutions to economic problems, whatever set of values you may have.

Test Yourself

1. In a famous passage from *The Wealth of Nations,* Adam Smith said that: "It is the maxim of every prudent master of a family, never to make at home what it will cost him more to make than to buy." Suppose that Mrs. Harris spends an hour preparing a meal. She is a psychologist in private practice and can obtain $25 per hour for her services. What is the cost to the Harris family of her preparing this meal? Explain.

2. "Resources are scarce and once a decision is made to use them for one purpose, they are no longer available for another. One opportunity cost of reading [an] ... article, for example, is not simultaneously being able to read [another article]."* Explain, and relate to the question of how a student should allocate his time among various course assignments.

3. Suppose that it costs a college student $1,000 per year more for room and board than if he or she works (and lives at home). If this assumption is correct, why is this amount, rather than the full cost of room and board, the proper amount to use in Example 1.1?

4. On the basis of positive economics alone, which of the following statements can be determined to be true or false? (a) The tax cut of 1975 reduced unemployment in the United States by 1 percent. (b) The tax cut was timed improperly. (c) The tax cut was a less equitable way of reducing unemployment than a program whereby the unemployed were hired by the government to perform important social functions.

* D. Eastburn, "Economic Man in Conflict with His Economic Self," *New York Times Magazine,* July 26, 1970.

Summary

1. According to one standard definition, economics is concerned with the way resources are allocated among alternative uses to satisfy human wants. A resource is a thing or service used to produce goods (or services) which can satisfy wants. Not all resources are scarce. Free resources, such as air, are so abundant that they can be obtained without charge.

2. Those resources that are scarce are called economic resources. The test of whether a resource is an economic resource or a free resource is price: economic resources command a nonzero price but free resources do not. Economists often classify economic resources into three categories: land, labor, and capital.

3. Since economic resources are scarce, only a limited amount of goods and services can be produced from them, and there arises the necessity for choice. For example, if an isolated town has a certain amount of resources, it must choose how much of each good it will produce from these resources. If it increases the amount produced of one good, it must reduce the amount produced of another good.

4. The opportunity cost (or alternative cost) of using a resource to increase the production of one good is the value of what the resource could have produced had it been used in the best alternative way. To illustrate the use of the concept of opportunity cost, which is one of the most important in economics, we discussed the cases of public parks and a college education.

5. Economists are particularly concerned with four basic questions regarding the working of any economic system, ours or any other. These questions are (1) What determines what (and how much) is produced? (2) What determines how it is produced? (3) What determines how the society's output is distributed among the members? (4) What determines the rate at which the society's per capita income will grow?

6. Economists often distinguish between positive economics and normative economics. Positive economics contains descriptive statements, propositions, and predictions about the world; whereas normative economics contains statements about what ought to be, or about what a person, organization, or nation ought to do.

7. In normative economics, the results you get depend on your basic values and preferences; in positive economics, the results are testable, at least in principle, by an appeal to the facts.

Concepts for Review

Unemployment	Resources	Technology
Inflation	Economic resources	Choice
Labor productivity	Free resources	Opportunity cost
Government regulation	Land	Alternative cost
Poverty	Labor	Positive economics
Economics	Capital	Normative economics
Human wants		

CHAPTER 2

Economic Models and Capitalism, American-Style

The United States, like all other nations, is beset by many economic problems. As pointed out in Chapter 1, the 1970s and early 1980s were a period of bewildering inflation and excessive unemployment. We have also been confronted by serious productivity and environmental problems. Yet, despite these problems, the American economy is among the most prosperous in the world. The average American family has plenty of food, clothing, housing, appliances, and luxuries of many kinds, and the average American worker is well educated and well trained. The tremendous strength and vitality of the American economy should be recognized, as well as its shortcomings. Nothing is gained by overlooking either the successes or the faults of our system.

As a first step toward understanding why we are so well-off in some respects and so lacking in others, we need to understand how our economy works. Of course, this is a big task. Indeed, you could say that this whole book is devoted to discussing this subject. So we will not try to present a detailed picture of the operation of the American economy at this point. All we will do now is give a preliminary sketch, a basic blueprint of what an economic system must do and how our mixed capitalistic system works.

First, however, we must provide a brief description of the role of model building in economics, since this will introduce you to the methods used by economists. Without such an introduction to economic methodology, it would be difficult, if not impossible, for you to understand fully much of the material that follows in this and succeeding chapters. Only after these preliminary matters are covered will we be able to turn to a discussion of the tasks of an economic system and the way our economy functions.

The Methodology of Economics

MODEL BUILDING IN ECONOMICS

Like other types of scientific analysis, economics is based on the formulation of *models. A model is a theory. It is composed of a number of assumptions from which conclusions—or predictions—are deduced.* An astronomer who wants to formulate a model of the solar system might represent each planet by a point in space and assume that each would change position in accord with certain mathematical equations. Based on this model, the astronomer might predict when an eclipse would occur, or estimate the probability of a planetary collision. The economist proceeds along similar lines when he sets forth a model of economic behavior.

There are several important points to be noted concerning models:

1. To be useful, a model must simplify the real situation. The assumptions made by a model need not be exact replicas of reality. If they were, the model would be too complicated to use. The basic reason for using a model is that the real world is so complex that masses of detail often obscure underlying patterns. The economist faces the familiar problem of seeing the forest as distinct from just the trees. Other scientists must do the same; physicists work with simplified models of atoms, just as economists work with simplified models of markets. However, this does not mean that *all* models are good or useful. A model may be so oversimplified and distorted that it is utterly useless. The trick is to construct a model so that irrelevant and unimportant considerations and variables are neglected, but the major factors—those that seriously affect the phenomena the model is designed to predict—are included.

2. The purpose of a model is to make predictions about the real world; and in many respects the most important test of a model is how well it predicts. In this sense, a model that predicts the price of copper within plus or minus $.01 a pound is better than a model that predicts it within plus or minus $.02 a pound. Of course, this does not mean that a model is useless if it cannot predict very accurately. We do not always need a very accurate prediction. For example, a road map is a model that can be used to make predictions about the route a driver should take to get to a particular destination. Sometimes, a very crude map is good enough to get you where you want to go, but such a map would not, for instance, serve the hiker who needs to know the characteristics of the terrain through which he plans to walk. How detailed a map you need depends on where you are going and how you want to get there.

3. A person who wants to predict the outcome of a particular event will be forced to use the model that predicts best, even if this model does not predict very well. The choice is not between a model and no model; it is between one model and another. After all, a person who must make a forecast will use the most accurate device available—and any such device is a model of some sort. Consequently, when economists make simplifying assumptions and derive conclusions that are only approximately true, it is somewhat beside the point to complain that the assumptions are simpler than reality or that the predictions are not always accurate. This may be true, but if the predictions based on the economists' model are better than those obtained on the basis of other models, their model must, and will, be used until something better comes along. Thus, if a model can predict the price of

Figure 2.1

Relationship between Annual Clothing Expenditures and Annual Household Income *Each family is represented by a dot. The line shows the average relationship. The line does not fit all families exactly, since all the points do not fall on it. The line does, however, show average clothing expenditure for each income level.*

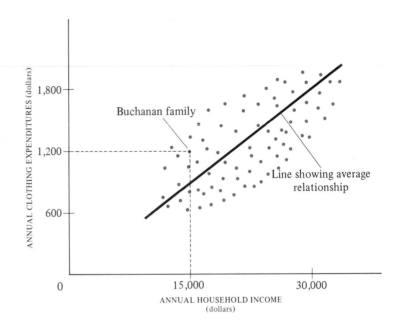

copper to within plus or minus $.01 per pound, and no other model can do better, this model will be used even if those interested in the predictions bewail the model's limitations and wish it could be improved.

ECONOMIC MEASUREMENT

To utilize and test their models, economists need facts of many sorts. For example, suppose that an economist constructs a model which predicts that a household's annual clothing expenditure tends to increase by $60 when its income increases by $1,000. To see whether this model is correct, he must gather data concerning the incomes and clothing expenditures of a large number of households and study the relationship between them. Suppose that the relationship he finds is as shown in Figure 2.1. The line represents an average relationship between household income and household consumption expenditure. Judging by Figure 2.1, his model is reasonably accurate, at least for households with incomes between $15,000 and $30,000 per year.[1]

Measurements like those in Figure 2.1 enable economists to *quantify* their models; in other words, they enable them to construct models that predict *how much* effect one variable has on another. If economists did not quantify their models, they (and their models) would be much less useful. For example, the economist in the previous paragraph might have been content with a model that predicts that higher household income results in higher household clothing expenditures; but this model would not have been interesting or useful, since you do not need an economist to tell you that. A more valuable model is one that is quantitative, that predicts how much clothing expenditure will increase if household income rises by a certain amount. This is the sort of model that economists usually try to construct.

[1] It is worth noting that, although it is useful to see how well a model would have fit the historical facts, this is no substitute for seeing how well it will predict the future. As a distinguished mentor of mine once observed, "It's a darned poor person who can't predict the past."

Graphs and Relationships

To conclude our brief discussion of economic methodology, we must describe the construction and interpretation of graphs, such as Figure 2.1, which economists use to present data and relationships. Such graphs are used repeatedly throughout this book, and it is essential that the following three points be understood:

1. A graph has a horizontal axis and a vertical axis, each of which has a scale of numerical values. For example, in Figure 2.1, the horizontal axis shows a household's annual income, and the vertical axis shows the annual amount spent by the household on clothing. The intersection of the two axes is called the origin and is the point where both the variable measured along the horizontal axis and the variable measured along the vertical axis are zero. In Figure 2.1, the origin is at the lower lefthand corner of the figure, labeled "0."

2. To show the relationship between two variables, one can plot the value of one variable against the value of the other variable. Thus, in Figure 2.1, each family is represented by a dot. For example, the dot for the Buchanan family is in the position shown in Figure 2.1 because its income was $15,000 and its clothing expenditure was $1,200. Clearly, the line showing the average relationship does not fit all the families exactly, since all the points do not fall on the line. This line does, however, give the average clothing expenditure for each level of income: it is an average relationship.

3. The relationship between two variables is *direct* if, as in Figure 2.1, the line of average relationship is upward sloping. In other words, if the variable measured along the vertical axis tends to increase (decrease) in response to increases (decreases) in the variable measured along the horizontal axis, the relationship is direct. On the other hand, if the line of average relationship is downward sloping, as in Figure 2.2, the relationship is *inverse.* In other words, if the variable measured along the vertical axis tends to decrease (increase) in response to increases (decreases) in the variable measured along the horizontal axis, the relationship is inverse.

To illustrate how one can graph a relationship between two variables,

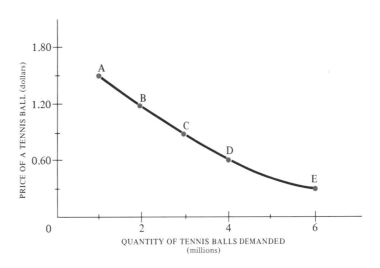

Figure 2.2

Relationship between Quantity Demanded and Price of Tennis Balls (as shown in Table 2.1)

consider. Table 2.1, which shows the amount of tennis balls demanded in a particular market at various prices. Putting price on the vertical axis and quantity demanded on the horizontal axis, one can plot each combination of price and quantity in this table as a point on a graph; and that is precisely what has been done in Figure 2.2 (points *A* to *E*).

Table 2.1

QUANTITY OF TENNIS BALLS DEMANDED IN A PARTICULAR MARKET AT VARIOUS PRICES

Price of a tennis ball (dollars)	Quantity of tennis balls demanded (millions)
1.50	1
1.20	2
0.90	3
0.60	4
0.30	6

The Tasks of an Economic System

Having discussed the nature and quantification of economic models, we now can turn to the primary purpose of this chapter, which is to provide a preliminary sketch of what an economic system must do and how our mixed capitalistic system works. In this section, we describe what an economic system—*ours or any other*—must do. Basically, as we saw in Chapter 1, there are four tasks that any economic system must perform:

1. An economic system must determine the level and composition of society's output. That is, it must answer questions like: To what extent should society's resources be used to produce new aircraft carriers and missiles? To what extent should they be used to produce sewage plants to reduce water pollution? To what extent should they be used to produce swimming pools for the rich? To what extent should they be used to produce low-cost housing for the poor? Pause for a moment to think about how important—and how vast—this function is. Most people simply take for granted that somehow it is decided what we as a society are going to produce, and far too few people really think about the social mechanisms that determine the answers to such questions.

2. An economic system must determine how each good and service is to be produced. Given existing technology, a society's resources can be used in various ways. Should the skilled labor in Birmingham, Alabama, be used to produce cotton or steel? Should a particular machine tool be used to produce aircraft or automobiles? The way questions of this sort are answered will determine the way each good and service is produced. In other words, it will determine which resources are used to produce which goods and services. If this function is performed badly, society's resources are put to the wrong uses, resulting in less output than if this function is performed well.

3. An economic system must determine how the goods and services that are produced are to be distributed among the members of society. In other words, how much of each type of good and service should each person receive? Should there be a considerable amount of income inequality, the rich receiving much more than the poor? Or should incomes be relatively equal? Take your own case. Somehow or other, the economic system determines how much income you will receive. In our economic system, your income depends on your skills, the property you own, how hard you work, and prevailing prices, as we shall see in succeeding chapters. But in other economic systems, your income might depend on quite different factors. This function of the economic system has generated, and will continue to generate, heated controversy. Some people favor a relatively egalitarian society where the amount received by one family varies little from that received by another family of the same size. Other people favor a society where the amount a family or person receives can vary a great deal. Few people favor a thoroughly egalitarian society, if for no other reason than that some differences in income are required to stimulate workers to do certain types of work.

4. An economic system must determine the rate of growth of per capita income. An adequate growth rate has come to be regarded as an important economic goal, particularly in the less developed countries of Africa, Asia, and Latin America. There is very strong pressure in these countries for changes in technology, the adoption of superior techniques, increases in the stock of capital resources, and better and more extensive education and training of the labor force. These are viewed as some of the major ways to promote the growth of per capita income.

Test Yourself

1. Suppose that the quantity of corn demanded annually by American consumers at each price of corn is as follows:

Price (dollars per bushel)	Quantity of corn (millions of bushels)
1	2.0
2	1.0
3	0.5
4	0.4

How much will farmers receive for their corn crop if it is 2 million bushels? If it is 1 million bushels? If you owned all of the farms producing corn, would you produce 2 million bushels? Why or why not?

2. Plot the relationship between price and quantity demanded in Question 1 in a graph. Is the relationship direct or inverse? Based on your graph, estimate how much corn is likely to be demanded if the price is (a) $1.50, (b) $2.50, and (c) $3.50.

3. Suppose that Americans begin to take up tennis in much larger numbers. Will the curve in Figure 2.2 shift? If so, will it shift to the right or to the left? Explain.

4. Suppose that you wanted to construct a model to explain and predict the breakfast food that your neighbor will choose tomorrow. What factors would you include? How well do you think you could predict?

The Economic System: A Simple Introductory Model

THE PRODUCTION POSSIBILITIES CURVE AND THE DETERMINATION OF WHAT IS PRODUCED

In a previous section, we said that economists use models to throw light on economic problems. At this point, let's try our hand at constructing a simple model to illuminate the basic functions any economic system, ours included, must perform. To keep things simple, suppose that society produces only two goods, food and tractors. This, of course, is unrealistic, but, as we stressed in a previous section, a model does not have to be realistic to be useful. Here, by assuming that there are only two goods, we eliminate a lot of unnecessary complexity and lay bare the essentials. In addition, we suppose that society has at its disposal a certain amount of resources, and that this amount is fixed for the duration of the period in question. This assumption is quite realistic. So long as the period is relatively short, the amount of a society's resources is relatively fixed (except, of course, under unusual circumstances, such as if a country annexes ad-

Table 2.2

ALTERNATIVE COMBINATIONS OF
OUTPUTS OF FOOD AND TRACTORS THAT
CAN BE PRODUCED

Possibility	Food (millions of tons)	Tractors (millions)
A	0	15
B	2	14
C	4	12
D	6	10
E	8	7
F	10	4
G	12	0

ditional land). Finally, we suppose as well that society's technology is fixed. So long as the period is relatively short, this assumption too is realistic.

Under these circumstances, it is possible to figure out the various amounts of food and tractors that society can produce. Specifically, we can proceed as in Chapter 1, where we determined the amounts of food and clothing that an isolated town could produce. Let's begin with how many tractors society can produce if all resources are devoted to tractor production. According to Table 2.2, the answer is 15 million tractors. Next, let's consider the opposite extreme, where society devotes all its resources to food production. According to Table 2.2, it can produce 12 million tons of food in this case. Next, let's consider cases where both products are being produced. Such cases are represented by possibilities B to F in the table. As emphasized in Chapter 1, the more of one good that is produced, the less of the other good that can be produced. Why? Because to produce more of one good, resources must be taken away from the production of the other good, lessening the amount of the other good produced.

Figure 2.3 shows how we can use a graph to show the various production possibilities society can attain. It is merely a different way of presenting the data in Table 2.2; the output of food is plotted on the horizontal axis and the output of tractors on the vertical axis. The curve in Figure 2.3, which shows the various combinations of output of food and tractors that society can produce, is called a ***production possibilities curve.***

The production possibilities curve sheds considerable light on the economic tasks facing any society. It shows the various production possibilities open to society. In Figure 2.3, society can choose to produce 4 million tons of food and 12 million tractors (point *C*), or 6 million tons of food and 10 million tractors (point *D*), but it cannot choose to produce 6 million tons of food and 12 million tractors (point *H*). Point *H* is inaccessible with this society's resources and technology. Perhaps it will become accessible if the society's resources increase or if its technology improves, but for the present, point *H* is out of reach.

Figure 2.3
Production Possibilities Curve *This curve shows the various combinations of tractors and food that can be produced efficiently with given resources and technology. Point* H *is unattainable.*

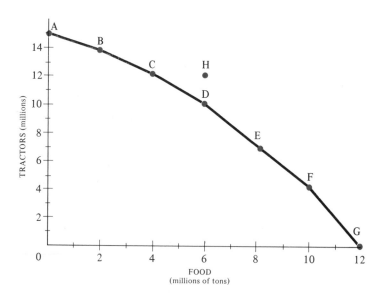

Example 2.1 Hay and Grain in Iowa

According to studies carried out at Iowa State University,* the following combinations of grain and hay could be produced in the 1940s from 100 acres of land in a particular part of Iowa:

Number of acres devoted to each use		Total production (pounds)	
Hay	Grain	Grain	Hay
0	100	224,000	0
25	75	212,920	89,600
33	67	166,194	96,400

That is, if all 100 acres were devoted to grain, 224,000 pounds of grain could be produced; if 75 of the 100 acres were devoted to grain, 212,920 pounds of grain and 89,600 pounds of hay could be produced; and so on.

(a) If a 100-acre farm in this part of Iowa was producing 212,920 pounds of grain and 89,600 pounds of hay, what was the approximate cost of increasing its production of grain by 1 pound? (b) Suppose that the profit to be made from a pound of grain was five times the profit to be made from a pound of hay, and that the owner of this farm claimed that, because this was the case, he should produce no hay. Would he be correct? (c) Suppose that, if hay production was increased from zero to about 100,000 pounds, the production of grain *increased*, not *decreased* (because hay contributed elements to the soil needed in the production of grain). Under these circumstances, would the slope of the production possibilities curve be negative at all points? Would it be rational for a farmer to produce no hay? (d) Would the production possibilities curve for a farm of this sort be the same now as in the 1940s?

SOLUTION

(a) If it increased its grain output by 11,080 pounds (from 212,920 to 224,000 pounds), it had to reduce its hay output by 89,600 pounds. Thus an extra pound of grain output cost the farm about 89,600 ÷ 11,080, or 8.09 pounds of hay. (b) No. If he produced 212,920 pounds of grain and 89,600 pounds of hay, his profits would be larger than if he produced no hay, because the profit from the extra 89,600 pounds of hay was greater than the profit from the 11,080 pounds of grain forgone. (c) No. No, because by producing up to 100,000 pounds of hay, the farmer increased the output of grain too. (d) No, because of changes in technology.

* E. Heady, *Economics of Agricultural Production and Resource Use,* New York: Prentice-Hall, 1952.

If resources are fully and efficiently utilized, *the first function of any economic system—to determine the level and composition of society's output—is really a problem of determining at what point along the production possibilities curve society should be.* Should society choose point *A, B, C, D, E, F,* or *G?* In making this choice, one thing is obvious from the production possibilities curve: *you cannot get more of one good without giving up some of the other good.* In other words, you cannot escape the problem of choice. So long as resources are limited and technology is less than magic, you must reckon with the fact (emphasized in Chapter 1) that more of one thing means less of another. The old saw that you don't "get something for nothing" is hackneyed but true, so long as resources are fully and efficiently utilized.

THE LAW OF INCREASING COST

In the previous section, we stressed that an increased output of one good (say, food) means a decreased output of the other good (say, tractors). This amounts to saying (in the language of Chapter 1) that the opportunity cost of producing more food is the output of tractors that must be forgone. In this section, we go a step further; we point out that, *as more and more of a good is produced, the production of yet another unit of this good is likely to entail a larger and larger opportunity cost* and we explain why this is true.

This so-called law of increasing cost can be demonstrated in Figure 2.3. As more and more food is produced, the cost of increasing food output by 2 million tons increases. To see this, note that the *first* 2 million tons of food cost 1 million tractors (because this is the amount that tractor output must be reduced if food output increases from 0 to 2 million tons). The *second* 2 million tons of food cost 2 million tractors (because this is the amount that tractor output must be reduced if food output increases from 2 to 4 million tons). Skipping to the *sixth* 2 million tons of food, the cost of this additional food output is 4 million tractors (because this is the amount that tractor output must be reduced if food output increases from 10 to 12 million tons). Clearly, the more food that is already being produced, the greater the cost of producing an additional 2 million tons.

Why is this the case? Basically, it is because resources are not as effective in producing one good as in producing the other. When society only produces a small amount of food, it can use in food production those resources that are well suited to producing food and not so well suited to producing tractors. But as society produces more and more food, it tends to run out of such resources, and must absorb into food production those resources that are less suited to producing food and better suited to producing tractors. To increase food output by 2 million tons with the latter type of resources, a greater reduction must occur in tractor output than when the 2-million-ton increase in food output occurred with the resources that were well suited to food production (and not so well suited to producing tractors). Thus the cost of producing an additional 2 million tons of food tends to increase as more food is already being produced.

This law of increasing cost explains why a production possibilities curve has the shape shown in Figure 2.3. That is, it explains why the production possibilities curve has the "bowed out" shape (rather than the "bowed in" shape) indicated in Figure 2.4. Because the cost of increasing food output

"Bowed out" shape

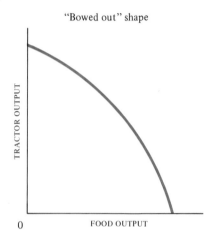

TRACTOR OUTPUT

0   FOOD OUTPUT

"Bowed in" shape

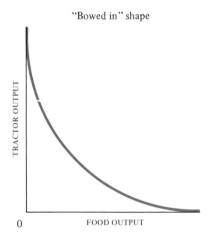

TRACTOR OUTPUT

0   FOOD OUTPUT

Figure 2.4
**Shape of the Production Possibilities
Curve** *So long as the law of increasing
cost holds true, the production possibilities curve will have the shape at the top
("bowed out"),* not *the shape at the
bottom ("bowed in").*

by a certain amount increases as more of it is already produced, the production possibilities curve tends to fall more steeply as one moves from left to right along the horizontal axis—which explains why the production possibilities curve has the "bowed out" shape.

THE PRODUCTION POSSIBILITIES CURVE AND THE DETERMINATION OF HOW GOODS ARE PRODUCED

Let's turn now to the second basic function of any economic system: to determine how each good and service should be produced. In Table 2.2, we assumed implicitly that society's resources would be fully utilized and that the available technology would be applied in a way that would get the most out of the available resources. In other words, we assumed that the firms making food and tractors were as efficient as possible and that there was no unemployment of resources. But if there is widespread unemployment of people and machines, will society still be able to choose a point on the production possibilities curve? Clearly, the answer is no. Since society is not using all of its resources, it will not be able to produce as much as if it used them all. Thus, *if there is less than full employment of resources, society will have to settle for points inside the production possibilities curve.* For example, the best society may be able to do under these circumstances is to attain point *K* in Figure 2.5. *K* is a less desirable point than *C* or *D*—but that is the price of unemployment.

Suppose, on the other hand, that there is full employment of resources but that firms are inefficient. Perhaps they promote relatives of the boss, regardless of their ability; perhaps the managers are lazy or not much interested in efficiency; or perhaps the workers like to take long coffee breaks and are unwilling to work hard. Whatever the reason, will society still be able to choose a point on the production possibilities curve? Again, the answer is no. Since society is not getting as much as it could out of its resources, it will not be able to produce as much as it would if its resources were used efficiently. Thus, *if resources are used inefficiently, society will*

Basic Idea #3: If there is unemployment of resources or inefficiency, society may be able to increase its output of one good (say guns) without producing less of another good (say butter). In the absence of unemployment or inefficiency, this cannot be done (so long as the quantity of resources and technology are fixed). As pointed out below, this is why the United States, but not the Soviet Union, could increase the output of guns without cutting the output of butter at the outset of World War II.

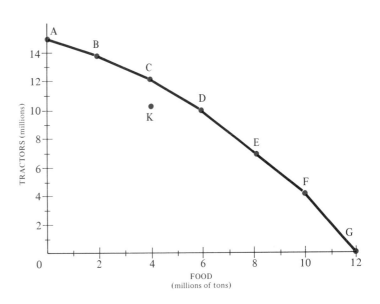

Figure 2.5
Production Possibilities Curve *This curve, like Figure 2.3, shows the various combinations of tractors and food that can be produced efficiently with given resources and technology. Point K is less desirable than points C or D, because less output is produced at this point. But because of unemployment or inefficiency, society may wind up at point K.*

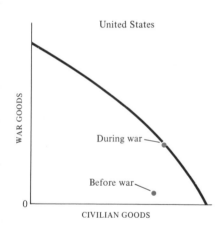

Figure 2.6

Effect of Increased Production of War Goods at the Beginning of World War II *Because the United States was at a point inside its production possibilities curve, we could increase our production of war goods without reducing production of civilian goods. Because the Russians were on their production possibilities curve, they could increase their output of war goods only by reducing output of civilian goods.*

have to settle for points inside the production possibilities curve. Perhaps in these circumstances, too, the best society can do may be point *K* in Figure 2.5. This less desirable position is the price of inefficiency.

At this point, it should be obvious that our model at least partially answers the question of how each good and service should be produced. The answer is to *produce each good and service in such a way that you wind up on the production possibilities curve, not on a point inside it.* Of course, this is easier said than done, but at least our model indicates a couple of villains to watch out for: unemployment of resources and inefficiency. When these villains are present, we can be sure that society is not on the production possibilities curve. Also, the old saw is wrong, and it is possible to "get something for nothing" when society is inside the production possibilities curve. That is, society can increase the output of one good without reducing the output of another good in such a situation. Society need not give up anything—in the way of production of other goods—to increase the production of this good under these circumstances.

The U.S. and the USSR in World War II. This simple model helps illuminate the sequence of events in various countries at the beginning of World War II. In certain countries, like the Soviet Union, the war effort meant a substantial decrease in the standard of living on the home front. Resources had to be diverted from the production of civilian goods to the production of military goods, and the war struck a severe blow at the living standards of the civilian population. In other countries, like the United States, it was possible to increase the production of military goods without making such a dent in the living standards of the civilian population. This happened because the United States at the beginning of World War II was still struggling to emerge from the Great Depression, and several million people were still unemployed. The same was not true in the Soviet Union. Thus we could increase the production of both guns and butter, whereas they could not.

Suppose that we divide all goods into two classes: war goods and civilian goods. Then, as shown in Figure 2.6, *we were inside our production possibilities curve at the beginning of the war, while the Russians were not.* Consequently, for the reasons discussed above, we could increase our production of war goods without reducing our production of civilian goods, while the Russians could not. (Note that in Figure 2.6 the two goods are war goods and civilian goods, not food and tractors.)

THE PRODUCTION POSSIBILITIES CURVE, INCOME DISTRIBUTION, AND GROWTH

Let's return now to the case where our economy produces food and tractors. The third basic function of any economic system is to distribute the goods and services that are produced among the members of society. Each point on the production possibilities curve in Figure 2.5 represents society's total pie, but to deal with the third function, we must know how the pie is divided up among society's members. Since the production possibilities curve does not tell us this, it cannot shed light on this third function.

Fortunately, the production possibilities curve is of more use in analyzing the fourth basic function of any economic system: to determine the society's rate of growth of per capita income. Suppose that the society in

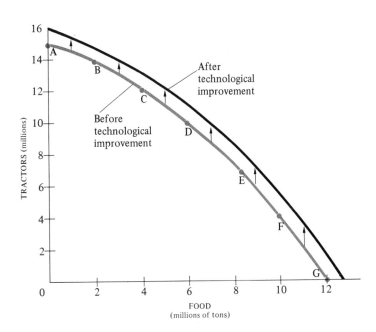

Figure 2.7

**Effect of Improvement in Technology on
Production Possibilities Curve** *An
improvement in technology results in an
outward shift of the production possibilities curve.*

Figure 2.5 invests a considerable amount of its resources in developing
improved processes and products. It might establish agricultural experiment stations to improve farming techniques and industrial research laboratories to improve tractor designs. As shown in Figure 2.7, the
production possibilities curve will be pushed outward. This will be the
result of improved technology, enabling more food and/or more tractors
to be produced from the same amount of resources. Thus one way for an
economy to increase its output—and its per capita income—may be to
invest in research and development.

Another way is by devoting more of its resources to the production of
capital goods rather than consumers' goods. **Capital goods** consist of plant
and equipment that are used to make other goods; **consumers' goods** are
items that consumers purchase like clothing, food, and drink. Since capital
goods are themselves resources, a society that chooses to produce lots of
capital goods and few consumers' goods will push out its production possibilities curve much farther than a society that chooses to produce lots of
consumers' goods and few capital goods.

To illustrate this point, consider our simple society that produces food
and tractors. The more tractors (and the less food) this society produces,
the more tractors it will have in the next period; and the more tractors it
has in the next period, the more of both goods—food and tractors—it will
be able to produce then. Thus the more tractors (and the less food) this
society produces, the farther out it will push its production possibilities
curve—and the greater the increase in output (and per capita income) that
it will achieve in the next period. If this society chooses point *F* (shown in
Figures 2.7, 2.5, or 2.3), the effect will be entirely different than if it
chooses point *C*. If it chooses point *F*, it produces 4 million tractors, which
we assume to be the number of tractors worn out each year. Thus, if it
chooses point *F*, it adds nothing to its stock of tractors: it merely replaces
those that wear out. Since it has no more tractors in the next period than

29

One of the most remarkable developments in human history was the Industrial Revolution. Until the middle of the eighteenth century, industry (as distinct from agriculture or commerce) played a small role in the economies of Europe or America. But during the late eighteenth and early nineteenth centuries a host of important technological innovations, such as James Watt's steam engine and Richard Arkwright's spinning jenny, made possible a very rapid growth in the output of industrial goods (like textiles and pig iron). And accompanying this growth of industrial output was the advent of the factory—a social and economic institution that is taken for granted today, but which was largely unknown prior to the Industrial Revolution.

The Industrial Revolution was characterized by major improvements in technology and by large increases in the amount of capital resources available to society. Both the improvements in technology and the additional capital resulted in an outward shift in the production possibilities curve in England, where the Industrial Revolution first took hold. (See Figures 2.7 and 2.8.) Due to this shift, the standard of living in England, as measured by per capita income (total income divided by population), grew at an unprecedented rate. As the Industrial Revolution spread, this rise in living standards occurred too on the European continent and in the United States; it remained one of the lasting effects of industrialization.

As stressed above, the Industrial Revolution was characterized by considerable increases in capital. How did England (and other countries) bring about this increase in capital? By saving and investing. In other words, the English people had to set aside some of their resources, and to say in effect, "These resources will *not* be used to satisfy the current needs of our population for food, clothing, and other forms of consumption. Instead, they will be used to produce capital—factories, machines, equipment, railroads, and canals—which will increase our future productive capacity." Much more will be said about this saving process in subsequent chapters. For now, the essential point is that this saving process was one of the necessary conditions that made possible the Industrial Revolution.

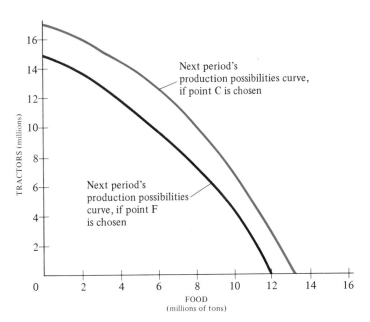

Figure 2.8

Effect of Increase in Capital Goods on Production Possibilities Curve *An increase in the amount of capital goods results in an outward shift of the production possibilities curve. The choice of point C means the production of more capital goods than the choice of point F.*

in the current period, the production possibilities curve does not shift out at all if point *F* is chosen. On the other hand, if point *C* is chosen, the society produces 12 million tractors, which means that it has 8 million additional tractors at the beginning of the next period. Thus, as shown in Figure 2.8, the production possibilities curve is pushed outward. By producing more capital goods (and less consumers' goods) our society has increased its production possibilities and its per capita income.

Capitalism: An Economic System

WHAT IS CAPITALISM?

In previous sections we have discussed the basic tasks that any economic system must perform. Now we must look at how our own economic system performs these tasks. The particular kind of economic system adopted by the United States is **capitalism.** Capitalism is one of those terms that is frequently used but seldom defined, and even less frequently understood. Its operation is complex, but its principal characteristics can be lumped into four major categories.

 1. Private Ownership of Capital. Under capitalism you or I can buy the tools of production. We can own factories, equipment, inventories, and other forms of capital. In a capitalistic system, somebody owns each piece of capital—and receives the income from it. Each piece of equipment has some sort of legal instrument indicating to whom it belongs. (If it belongs to a corporation, its owners basically are the stockholders who own the corporation.) Moreover, each piece of capital has a market value. This system is in marked contrast to a Communist or socialist state where the government owns the capital. In these states, the government decides how much and what kinds of capital goods will be produced; it owns the capital goods; and it receives and distributes the income they produce. In the Soviet Union or China, no one can buy or put up a new steel plant; it simply isn't allowed.

The United States is basically a capitalistic system, but there are certain areas where the government, not individuals, owns capital, and where individual property rights are limited in various ways by the government. The government owns much of the tooling used in the defense industries; it owns dams and the Tennessee Valley Authority; and it owns research laboratories in such diverse fields as atomic energy, space exploration, and health. Further, the government determines how much of a deceased person's assets can go to his or her heirs. (The rest goes to the government in the form of estate and inheritance taxes.) Also, the government can make a person sell his or her property to allow a road or other public project to be built. There are many such limitations on property rights. Ours is basically a capitalistic system, but it must be recognized that the government's role is important. More will be said about this in subsequent sections.

2. Freedom of Choice and Enterprise. Another important characteristic of capitalism is freedom of choice and freedom of enterprise. **Freedom of choice** means that consumers are free to buy what they please and reject what they please; that laborers are free to work where, when, and if they please; and that investors are free to invest in whatever property they please. By **freedom of enterprise,** we mean that firms are free to enter whatever markets they please, obtain resources in whatever ways they can, and organize their affairs as best they can. Needless to say, this does not mean that firms can run roughshod over consumers and workers. Even the strongest champions of capitalism are quick to admit that the government must set "rules of the game" to prevent firms from engaging in sharp or unfair practices. But granting such limitations, the name of the game under capitalism is economic freedom.

Freedom to do what? Under capitalism, individuals and firms are free to pursue their own self-interest. Put in today's idiom, each individual or firm can do his, her, or its own thing. However, it is important to note that this freedom is circumscribed by one's financial resources. Consumers in a capitalistic system can buy practically anything they like—if they have the money to pay for it. Similarly, workers can work wherever or whenever they please—if they don't mind the wages. And a firm can run its business as it likes—if it remains solvent. Thus an important regulator of economic activity under capitalism is the pattern of income and prices that emerges in the market place.

3. Competition. Still another important characteristic of capitalism is **competition.** Firms compete with one another for sales. Under perfect competition, there are a large number of firms producing each product; indeed, there are so many that no firm controls the product's price. Because of this competition, firms are forced to jump to the tune of the consumer. If a firm doesn't produce what consumers want—at a price at least as low as other firms are charging—it will lose sales to other firms. Eventually, unless it mends its ways, such a firm will go out of business. Of course, in real-life American markets, the number of producers is not always so large that no firm has any control over price. (Much more will be said about this below.) But in the purest form of capitalism, such imperfections do not exist. Also, lest you think that competition under capitalism is confined to producers, it must be remembered that owners of resources also compete. They are expected to offer their resources—including labor—to the buyer who gives them the best deal, and buyers of resources and products are supposed to compete openly and freely.

4. Reliance upon Markets. Finally, another very important characteristic of capitalism is its reliance upon markets. *Under pure capitalism, the market—the free market—plays a central role.* Firms and individuals buy and sell products and resources in competitive markets. Some firms and individuals make money and prosper; others lose money and fail. Each firm or individual is allowed freedom to pursue its or his or her interests in the market place, while the government guards against shady and dishonest dealings. Such is the nature of the economic system under pure capitalism.

HOW DOES CAPITALISM PERFORM THE FOUR BASIC ECONOMIC TASKS?

The **price system** lies at the heart of any capitalist economy. In a purely capitalist economy, it is used to carry out the four basic economic functions discussed above. The price system is a way to organize an economy. Under such a system, every commodity and every service, including labor, has a price. We all receive money for what we sell, including labor, and we use this money to buy the goods and services we want. If more is wanted of a certain good, the price of this good tends to rise; if less is wanted, the price of the good tends to fall. Producers base their production decisions on the prices of commodities and inputs. Thus increases in a commodity's price generally tend to increase the amount of it produced, and decreases generally tend to decrease the amount produced. In this way, firms' output decisions are brought into balance with consumers' desires.

The very important question of how the price system performs the basic economic functions we discussed above will be answered in some detail in the next chapter. All we can do here is provide a preliminary sketch of the way the price system carries out each of these four tasks.

1. How does the price system determine what society will produce? In a substantially capitalistic economy, such as ours, consumers choose the amount of each good that they want, and producers act in accord with these decisions. The importance consumers attach to a good is indicated by the price they are willing to pay for it. Of course, the principle of **consumer sovereignty**—producers dancing to the tune of consumers' tastes—should not be viewed as always and completely true, since producers do attempt to manipulate the tastes of consumers through advertising and other devices, but it is certainly a reasonable first approximation.

2. How does the price system determine how each good and service will be produced? Prices indicate the desires of workers and the relative value of various types of materials and equipment as well as the desires of consumers. For example, if plumbers are scarce relative to the demand for them, their price in the labor market—their wage—will be bid up, and they will tend to be used only in the places where they are productive enough so that their employers can afford to pay them the higher wages. The forces that push firms toward actually carrying out the proper decisions are profits and losses. Profits are the carrot and losses are the stick used to eliminate the less efficient and less alert firms and to increase the more efficient and the more alert.

3. How does the price system determine how much in the way of goods and services each member of the society is to receive? In general, an individual's income depends largely on the quantities of resources of various kinds that he or she owns and the prices he or she gets for them. For example, if a man both works and rents out farm land he owns, his income is the number of hours he works per year times his hourly wage rate plus the number of acres of land he owns times the annual rental per acre. Thus the distribution of income depends on the way resource ownership—including talent, intelligence, training, work habits, and, yes, even character—is distributed among the population. Also, to be candid, it depends on just plain luck.

4. How does the price system determine the nation's rate of growth of per capita income? A nation's rate of growth of per capita income depends on the rate of growth of its resources and the rate of increase of the efficiency with which they are used. In our economy, the rate at which labor and capital resources are increased is motivated, at least in part, through the price system. Higher wages for more skilled work are an incentive for an individual to undergo further education and training. Capital accumulation occurs in response to the expectation of profit. Increases in efficiency, due in considerable measure to the advance of technology, are also stimulated by the price system.

Our Mixed Capitalist System

Since the days of Adam Smith, economists have been fascinated by the features of a purely capitalistic economic system—an economy that relies entirely on the price system. Smith, and many generations of economists since, have gone to great pains to explain that in such an economic system, *the price system, although it is not controlled by any person or small group, results in economic order, not chaos.* The basic economic tasks any economy must perform can, as we have said, be carried out in such an economic system by the price system. It is an effective means of coordinating economic activity through decentralized decision making based on information disseminated through prices and related data.

But does this mean that the American economy is purely capitalistic? As we have noted repeatedly in previous sections, the answer is no. A purely capitalistic system is a useful model of reality, not a description of our economy as it exists now or existed in the past. It is useful because a purely capitalistic economy is, for some purposes, a reasonably close fit to our own. However, this does not mean that such a model is useful for all purposes. Many American markets are not perfectly competitive and never will be; they are dominated by a few producers or buyers who can influence price and thus distort the workings of the price system. Moreover, *the American economy is a mixed capitalistic economy, an economy where both government and private decisions are important.* The role of the government in American economic activity is very large indeed. Although it is essential

Basic Idea #4: The price system is a surprisingly effective way to organize an economy. Even though there is no small group of people directing the workings of the economy (as in the Soviet Union and other planned economies), the result is not chaos, as you might expect. Instead, prices provide the information needed for decentralized decision making.

to understand the workings of a purely capitalistic system, any model that omits the government entirely cannot purport to be adequate for the analysis of many major present-day economic issues.

To create a more balanced picture of the workings of the American economy, we must recognize that, although the price system plays an extremely important role, it is not permitted to solve all of the basic economic problems of our society. Consumer sovereignty does not extend—and cannot realistically be extended—to all areas of society. For example, certain public services cannot be left to private enterprise. The provision of fire protection, the operation of schools, and the development of weapons systems are examples of areas where we rely on political decision making, not the price system alone. Moreover, with regard to the consumption of commodities like drugs, society imposes limits on the decisions of individuals.

In addition, certain consequences of the price system are, by general agreement, unacceptable. Reliance on the price system alone does not assure a just or equitable or optimal distribution of income. It is possible, for example, that one person will have money to burn while another person will live in degrading poverty. Consequently, society empowers the government to modify the distribution of income by imposing taxes that take more from the rich than the poor, and by welfare programs that try to keep the poor from reaching the point where they lack decent food, adequate clothing, or shelter. Besides providing public services and maintaining certain minimum income standards, the government also carries out a variety of regulatory functions. Industries do not police the actions of their constituent firms, so it falls to the government to establish laws that impose limits on the economic behavior of firms. For example, these laws say that firms must not misrepresent their products, that child labor must not be employed, and that firms must not collude and form monopolies to interfere with the proper functioning of the price system. In this way, the government tries, with varying degrees of effectiveness, to establish the "rules of the game"—the limits within which the economic behavior of firms (and consumers) should lie.

Test Yourself

1. Suppose that a society's production possibilities curve is as follows:

	Output (per year)	
Possibility	Food (millions of tons)	Tractors (millions)
A	0	30
B	4	28
C	8	24
D	12	20
E	16	14
F	20	8
G	24	0

(a) Is it possible for the society to produce 30 million tons of food per year? (b) Can it produce 30 million tractors per year? (c) Suppose this society produces 20 million tons of food and 6 million tractors per year. Is it operating on the production possibilities curve? If not, what factors might account for this?

2. Plot the production possibilities curve in Question 1 in a graph. At what point along the horizontal axis does the curve cut the axis? At what point along the vertical axis does the curve cut the axis?

3. Suppose that, because of important technological improvements, the society in Question 1 can double its production of tractors at each level of food production. If so, is this society on its new production possibilities curve if it produces 20 million tons of food

and 16 million tractors? Plot the new production possibilities curve. At what point along the horizontal axis does the new curve cut the axis? At what point along the vertical axis does it cut the axis?

4. "[Some people] . . . fail to realize that the price system is, and ought to be, a method of coercion. . . . The very term 'rationing by the purse' illustrates the point. Economists defend such forms of rationing, but they have to do so primarily in terms of its efficiency and its fairness."* Comment.

5. "The great advantage of the [price system] . . . is that it permits wide diversity. It is, in political terms, a system of proportional representation. Each man can vote, as it were, for the color of tie he wants and get it; he does not have to see what color the majority wants and then, if he is in the minority, submit."** Comment.

* P. Samuelson, "The Economic Role of Private Activity," *A Dialogue on the Proper Economic Role of the State,* Chicago: University of Chicago Press, 1963.
** M. Friedman, *Capitalism and Freedom,* Chicago: University of Chicago Press, 1962, p. 15.

Summary

1. The methodology used by economists is much the same as that used in any other kind of scientific analysis. The basic procedure is the formulation and testing of models. A model must in general simplify and abstract from the real world. Its purpose is to make predictions, and in many respects the most important test of a model is how well it predicts. To test and quantify their models, economists gather data and utilize various statistical techniques.

2. The production possibilities curve, which shows the various production possibilities a society can attain, is useful in indicating the nature of the economic tasks any society faces. The task of determining the level and composition of society's output is really a problem of determining at what point along the production possibilities curve society should be.

3. Society has to recognize that it cannot get more of one good without giving up some of another good, if resources are fully and efficiently used. However, if they are not fully and efficiently used, society will have to settle for points inside the production possibilities curve—and it will be possible to obtain more of one good without giving up some of another good.

4. The task of determining how each good and service should be produced is, to a considerable extent, a problem of keeping society on its production possibilities curve, rather than at points inside the curve. The production possibilities curve does not tell us anything about the distribution of income, but it does indicate various ways that a society can promote growth in per capita income. By doing research and development, or by producing capital goods (rather than consumers' goods), society may push its production possibilities curve outward, thus increasing per capita income.

5. The American economy is a capitalistic economy, an economic system in which there is private ownership of capital, freedom of choice, freedom of enterprise, competition, and reliance upon markets.

6. Under pure capitalism, the price system is used to perform the four basic economic tasks. Although it is not controlled by any person or small group, the price system results in order, not chaos.

7. A purely capitalistic system is a useful model of reality, not a description of our economy as it exists now or in the past. The American economy is a mixed capitalistic economy, in which both government and private decisions are important.

8. Many public services (like defense and environmental protection) cannot be left to private enterprise, and society has said that certain consequences of the price system (like the existence of abject poverty) are unacceptable. For these reasons and others, the government carries out a long and impressive array of functions, many of which are discussed in subsequent chapters.

Concepts for Review

Model	**Consumers' goods**	**Competition**
Production possibilities curve	**Capitalism**	**Price system**
Capital goods	**Freedom of choice**	**Consumer sovereignty**
	Freedom of enterprise	

PART TWO

The Private Sector and the Public Sector: An Overview

CHAPTER 3

The Price System

Capitalist economies use the price system to perform the four basic tasks any economic system must carry out. Of course, as we pointed out in the previous chapter, the American economy is a mixed capitalist system, not a pure one. But this does not mean that the price system is unimportant. On the contrary, the price system plays a vital role in the American economy, and to obtain even a minimal grasp of the workings of our economic system, one must understand how the price system operates. This chapter takes up the nature and functions of the price system, as well as some applications of our theoretical results to real-life problems. For example, we show how the price system determines the quantity produced of a commodity like wheat, and how the pricing policies of the Broadway theater have hurt show business in a variety of ways. These applications should help illustrate the basic theory and indicate its usefulness.

Consumers, Firms, and Markets

We begin by describing and discussing consumers and firms, the basic building blocks that make up the private, or nongovernmental, sector of the economy.

Consumers. Sometimes—for example, when a person buys a beer on a warm day—the consumer is an individual. In other cases—for example, when a family buys a new car—the consumer may be an entire household. **Consumers** purchase the goods and services that are the ultimate end products of the economic system. When a man buys tickets to a ball game, he is a consumer; when he buys himself a Coke at the game, he is a consumer; and when he buys his wife a book on baseball for their twentieth wedding anniversary, he is a consumer.

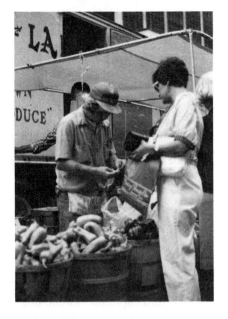

Firms. There are about 16 million firms in the United States. About nine-tenths of the goods and services produced in this country are produced by firms. (The rest are provided by government and not-for-profit institutions like universities and hospitals.) A **firm** is an organization that produces a good or service for sale. In contrast to not-for-profit organizations, firms attempt to make a profit. It is obvious that our economy is centered around the activities of firms.

Markets. Consumers and firms come together in a market. The concept of a market is not quite as straightforward as it may seem, since most markets are not well defined geographically or physically. For example, the New York Stock Exchange is an atypical market because it is located principally in a particular building. For present purposes, a **market** can be defined as a group of firms and individuals that are in touch with each other in order to buy or sell some good. Of course, not every person in a market has to be in contact with every other person in the market. A person or firm is part of a market even if it is in contact with only a subset of the other persons or firms in the market.

Markets vary enormously in their size and procedures. For some goods like toothpaste, most people who have their own teeth (and are interested in keeping them) are members of the same market; while for other goods like Picasso paintings, only a few dealers, collectors, and museums in certain parts of the world may be members of the market. And for still other goods, like lemonade sold by neighborhood children for a nickel a glass at a sidewalk stand, only people who walk by the stand—and are brave enough to drink the stuff—are members of the market. Basically, however, all markets consist primarily of buyers and sellers, although third parties like brokers and agents may be present as well.

Markets also vary in the extent to which they are dominated by a few large buyers or sellers. For example, in the United States, there was for many years only one producer of aluminum. This firm, the Aluminum Corporation of America, had great power in the market for aluminum. In contrast, the number of buyers and sellers in some other markets is so large that no single buyer or seller has any power over the price of the product. This is true in various agricultural markets, for example. When a market for a product contains so many buyers and sellers that none of them can influence the price, economists call the market **perfectly competitive.** In these introductory chapters, we make the simplifying assumption that markets are perfectly competitive. We will relax that assumption later.

The Demand Side of a Market

Every market has a demand side and a supply side. The **demand** side can be represented by a **market demand curve,** which shows the amount of the commodity buyers would like to purchase at various prices. Consider Figure 3.1, which shows the demand curve for wheat in the American market during the mid-1980s.[1] The figure shows that about 2.7 billion bushels of wheat

---

[1] I am indebted to officials of the U.S. Department of Agriculture for providing me with this information. Of course, these estimates are only rough approximations, but they are good enough for present purposes.

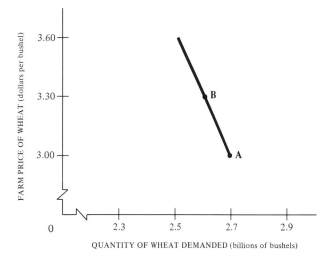

Figure 3.1

***Market Demand Curve for Wheat,
Mid-1980s*** *The curve shows the amount
of wheat buyers would demand at
various prices. At $3.00 per bushel, about
8 percent more wheat can be sold than at
$3.60 per bushel.*

Figure 3.2

***Effect of Increased Preference for Wheat
on Market Demand Curve*** *An increased
preference for wheat would shift the
demand curve to the right.*

will be demanded annually if the farm price is $3.00 per bushel, about 2.6
billion bushels will be demanded annually if the farm price is $3.30 per
bushel, and about 2.5 billion bushels will be demanded annually if the farm
price is $3.60 per bushel. The total demand for wheat is of several types: to
produce bread and other food products for domestic use, as well as for feed
use, for export purposes, and for industrial uses. The demand curve in Figure 3.1 shows the total demand—including all these components—at each
price. Any demand curve pertains to a particular period of time, and its
shape and position depend on the length of this period.

Take a good look at the demand curve for wheat in Figure 3.1. This
simple, innocent-looking curve influences a great many people's lives.
After all, wheat is the principal grain used for direct human consumption
in the United States. To states like Kansas, North Dakota, Oklahoma,
Montana, Washington, Nebraska, Texas, Illinois, Indiana, and Ohio,
wheat is a mighty important cash crop. Note that the demand curve for
wheat slopes downward to the right. In other words, the quantity of wheat
demanded increases as the price falls. This is true of the demand curve for
most commodities: they almost always slope downward to the right. This
makes sense; one would expect increases in a good's price to result in a
smaller quantity demanded.

Any demand curve is based on the assumption that the tastes, incomes,
and number of consumers, as well as the prices of other commodities, are
held constant. Changes in any of these factors are likely to shift the position of a commodity's demand curve, as indicated below.

Consumer Tastes. If consumers show an increasing preference for a
product, the demand curve will shift to the right; that is, at each price,
consumers will desire to buy more than previously. On the other hand, if
consumers show a decreasing preference for a product, the demand curve
will shift to the left, since, at each price, consumers will desire to buy less
than previously. Take wheat. If consumers become convinced that foods
containing wheat prolong life and promote happiness, the demand curve
may shift, as shown in Figure 3.2; and the greater the shift in preferences,
the larger the shift in the demand curve.

Figure 3.3

Effect of Increase in Income on Market Demand Curve for Wheat *An increase in income would shift the demand curve for wheat to the right, but only slightly.*

Income Level of Consumers. For some types of products, the demand curve shifts to the right if per capita income increases; whereas for other types of commodities, the demand curve shifts to the left if per capita income rises. Economists can explain why some goods fall into one category and other goods fall into the other, but, at present, this need not concern us. All that is important here is that changes in per capita income affect the demand curve, the size and direction of this effect varying from product to product. In the case of wheat, a 10 percent increase in per capita income would probably have a relatively small effect on the demand curve, as shown in Figure 3.3.

Number of Consumers in the Market. Compare Austria's demand for wheat with the United States'. Austria is a small country with a population of less than 8 million; the United States is a huge country with a population of over 200 million. Clearly, at a given price of wheat, the quantity demanded by American consumers will greatly exceed the quantity demanded by Austrian consumers, as shown in Figure 3.4. Even if consumer tastes, income, and other factors were held constant, this would still be true simply because the United States has so many more consumers in the relevant market.[2]

Level of Other Prices. A commodity's demand curve can be shifted by a change in the price of other commodities. Whether an increase in the price of good B will shift the demand curve for good A to the right or the left depends on the relationship between the two goods. If they are substitutes, such an increase will shift the demand curve for good A to the right. Consider the case of corn and wheat. If the price of corn goes up, more wheat will be demanded since it will be profitable to substitute wheat for corn. If the price of corn drops, less wheat will be demanded since it will be profitable to substitute corn for wheat. Thus, as shown in Figure 3.5, increases in the price of corn will shift the demand curve for wheat to the right, and decreases in the price of corn will shift it to the left.[3]

THE DISTINCTION BETWEEN CHANGES IN DEMAND AND CHANGES IN THE QUANTITY DEMANDED

It is essential to distinguish between a *shift in a commodity's demand curve* and a change in the *quantity demanded of the commodity.* A shift in a commodity's demand curve is a change in the *relationship* between price and quantity demanded. Figures 3.2, 3.3, and 3.5 show cases where such a change occurs. A change in the quantity demanded of a commodity may occur even if *no* shift occurs in the commodity's demand curve. For example, in Figure 3.1, if the price of wheat increases from $3.00 to $3.30 per bushel, the quantity demanded falls from 2.7 to 2.6 billion bushels. This change in the quantity demanded is due to a *movement along* the demand

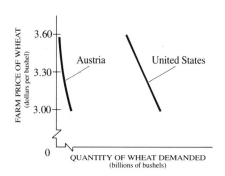

Figure 3.4

Market Demand Curve for Wheat, Austria and the United States *Since the United States has far more consumers than Austria, the demand curve in the United States is far to the right of Austria's.*

[2] Note that no figures are given along the horizontal axis in Figure 3.4. This is because we do not have reasonably precise estimates of the demand curve in Austria. Nonetheless, the hypothetical demand curves in Figure 3.4 are close enough to the mark for present purposes.

[3] If goods A and B are complements, an increase in the price of good B will shift the demand curve for good A to the left. Thus an increase in the price of gin is likely to shift the demand curve for tonic to the left. Why? Because gin and tonic tend to be used together. The increase in gin's price will reduce the quantity of gin demanded, which in turn will reduce the amount of tonic that will be demanded at each price of tonic.

Figure 3.5

Effect of Price of Corn on Market Demand Curve for Wheat *Price increases for corn will shift the demand curve for wheat to the right.*

Figure 3.6

Market Supply Curve for Wheat, Mid-1980s *The curve shows the amount of wheat sellers would supply at various prices. At $3.60 per bushel, about 17 percent more wheat would be supplied than at $3.00 per bushel.*

curve (from point *A* to point *B* in Figure 3.1), not to a *shift* in the demand curve.

When economists refer to an *increase in demand,* they mean a *rightward shift* in the demand curve. Thus Figures 3.2, 3.3, and 3.5 show increases in demand for wheat. When economists refer to a *decrease in demand,* they mean a *leftward shift* in the demand curve. An increase in demand for a commodity is not the same as an increase in the quantity demanded of the commodity. In Figure 3.1, the quantity demanded of wheat *increases* if the price falls from $3.30 to $3.00 per bushel, but this is not due to an increase in demand, since there is no rightward shift of the demand curve. Similarly, a decrease in demand for a commodity is not the same as a decrease in the quantity demanded of the commodity. In Figure 3.1, the quantity demanded of wheat *decreases* if the price rises from $3.00 to $3.30 per bushel, but this is not due to a decrease in demand, since there is no leftward shift of the demand curve.

The Supply Side of a Market

So much for our first look at demand. What about the other side of the market: supply? *The **supply** side of a market can be represented by a **market supply curve** that shows the amount of the commodity sellers would offer at various prices.* Let's continue with the case of wheat. Figure 3.6 shows the supply curve for wheat in the United States in the mid-1980s, based on estimates made informally by government experts.[4] According to the figure, about 2.4 billion bushels of wheat would be supplied if the farm price were $3.00 per bushel, about 2.6 billion bushels if the farm price were $3.30 per bushel, and about 2.8 billion bushels if the farm price were $3.60 per bushel.

Look carefully at the supply curve shown in Figure 3.6. Although it looks innocuous enough, it summarizes the potential behavior of thousands of American wheat farmers—and their behavior plays an important role in determining the prosperity of many states and communities. Note that the supply curve for wheat slopes upward to the right. In other words, the quantity of wheat supplied increases as the price increases. This seems plausible, since increases in price give a greater incentive for farms to produce wheat and offer it for sale. Empirical studies indicate that the supply curves for a great many commodities share this characteristic of sloping upward to the right.

Any supply curve is based on the assumption that technology and input prices are held constant. Changes in these factors are likely to shift the position of a commodity's supply curve, as indicated below.

Technology. Recall that technology was defined in Chapter 1 as society's pool of knowledge concerning the industrial arts. As technology progresses, it becomes possible to produce commodities more cheaply, so that firms often are willing to supply a given amount at a lower price than formerly. Thus technological change often causes the supply curve to shift

---

[4] Officials of the U.S. Department of Agriculture provided me with these estimates. Although rough approximations, they are good enough for present purposes.

Figure 3.7

Effect of Technological Change on Market Supply Curve for Wheat *Improvements in technology often shift the supply curve to the right.*

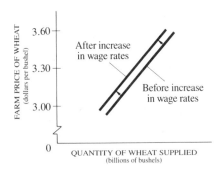

Figure 3.8

Effect of Increase in Farm Wage Rates on Market Supply Curve for Wheat *An increase in the wage rate might shift the supply curve to the left.*

to the right. This certainly has occurred in the case of wheat, as shown in Figure 3.7. There have been many important technological changes in wheat production, ranging from advances in tractors to the development of improved varieties, like semi-dwarf wheats.

Input Prices. The supply curve for a commodity is affected by the prices of the resources (labor, capital, and land) used to produce it. Decreases in the price of these inputs make it possible to produce commodities more cheaply, so that firms may be willing to supply a given amount at a lower price than they formerly would. Thus decreases in the price of inputs may cause the supply curve to shift to the right. On the other hand, increases in the price of inputs may cause it to shift to the left. For example, if the wage rates of farm labor increase, the supply curve for wheat may shift to the left, as shown in Figure 3.8.

An *increase in supply* is defined to be a *rightward shift* in the supply curve; a *decrease in supply* is defined to be a *leftward shift* in the supply curve. A change in supply should be distinguished from a change in the quantity supplied. In Figure 3.6, the quantity supplied of wheat will increase from 2.4 to 2.6 billion bushels if the price increases from $3.00 to $3.30 per bushel, but this is not due to an increase in supply, since there is no rightward shift of the supply curve in Figure 3.6.

Equilibrium Price

The two sides of a market, demand and supply, interact to determine the price of a commodity. Recall from the previous chapter that prices in a capitalistic system are important determinants of what is produced, how it is produced, who receives it, and how rapidly per capita income grows. It behooves us, therefore, to look carefully at how prices themselves are determined in a capitalist system. As a first step toward describing this process, we must define the equilibrium price of a product. At various points in this book, you will encounter the concept of an equilibrium, which is very important in economics, as in many other scientific fields.

Put briefly, an **equilibrium** is a situation where there is no tendency for change; in other words, it is a situation that can persist. Thus an **equilibrium price** is a price that can be maintained. Any price that is not an equilibrium price cannot be maintained for long, since there are basic forces at work to stimulate a change in price. The best way to understand what we mean by an equilibrium price is to take a particular case, such as the wheat market. Let's put both the demand curve for wheat (in Figure 3.1) and the supply curve for wheat (in Figure 3.6) together in the same diagram. The result, shown in Figure 3.9, will help us determine the equilibrium price of wheat.

We begin by seeing what would happen if various prices were established in the market. For example, if the price were $3.60 per bushel, the demand curve indicates that 2.5 billion bushels of wheat would be demanded, while the supply curve indicates that 2.8 billion bushels would be supplied. Thus, if the price were $3.60 a bushel, there would be a mismatch between the quantity supplied and the quantity demanded per year, since the rate at which wheat is supplied would be greater than the rate at which it is demanded. Specifically, as shown in Figure 3.9, there would be an *excess sup-*

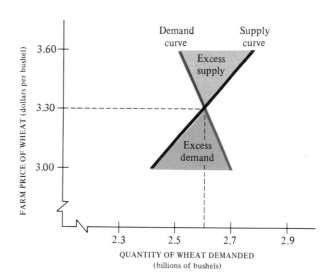

Figure 3.9

Determination of the Equilibrium Price of Wheat, Mid-1980s *The equilibrium price is $3.30 per bushel, and the equilibrium quantity is 2.6 billion bushels. At a price of $3.60 per bushel, there would be an excess supply of 300 million bushels. At a price of $3.00 per bushel, there would be an excess demand of 300 million bushels.*

ply of 300 million bushels. Under these circumstances, some of the wheat supplied by farmers could not be sold, and, as inventories of wheat built up, suppliers would tend to cut their prices in order to get rid of unwanted inventories. Thus a price of $3.60 per bushel would not be maintained for long—and for this reason, $3.60 per bushel is not an equilibrium price.

If the price were $3.00 per bushel, on the other hand, the demand curve indicates that 2.7 billion bushels would be demanded, while the supply curve indicates that 2.4 billion bushels would be supplied. Again we find a mismatch between the quantity supplied and the quantity demanded per year, since the rate at which wheat is supplied would be less than the rate at which it is demanded. Specifically, as shown in Figure 3.9, there would be an *excess demand* of 300 million bushels. Under these circumstances, some of the consumers who want wheat at this price would have to be turned away empty-handed. There would be a shortage. And given this shortage, suppliers would find it profitable to increase the price, and competition among buyers would bid the price up. Thus a price of $3.00 per bushel could not be maintained for long—so $3.00 per bushel is not an equilibrium price.

Under these circumstances, the equilibrium price must be the price where the quantity demanded equals the quantity supplied. Obviously, this is the only price at which there is no mismatch between the quantity demanded and the quantity supplied; and consequently the only price that can be maintained for long. In Figure 3.9, the price at which the quantity supplied equals the quantity demanded is $3.30 per bushel, the price where the demand curve intersects the supply curve. Thus $3.30 per bushel is the equilibrium price of wheat under the circumstances visualized in Figure 3.9, and 2.6 billion bushels is the equilibrium quantity.

Actual Price

The price that counts in the real world, however, is the **actual price,** not the equilibrium price, and it is the actual price that we set out to explain. In

45

Example 3.1   It's Not Just for Breakfast Anymore

In recent years, many oranges grown in California and Arizona have been provided to cattle for feed or given away to juicing plants. An 11-member committee of farmers and shippers establishes the number and size of oranges that can be sold. Anyone selling oranges without the committee's permission can face civil and criminal prosecution by the Department of Justice. Although some industry spokesmen claim that the oranges held off the market are too small to be sold, it is reported that the industry's figures show that some of these oranges are as large as those sent to market.*

(a) In the absence of government intervention, suppose that the demand and supply curves for oranges would be as shown below:

What would be the equilibrium price under these circumstances? (b) If the committee says that the quantity of oranges that can be sold must be 25 percent less than what would be sold in a free market, what will be the equilibrium price? (c) Under the committee's edict, will the growers receive more or less for their crop than under the free market? How much more or less? (d) How are consumers affected by the committee's edict?

SOLUTION

(a) 10 cents per orange. (b) In a free market, 100 billion oranges would be sold. If this quantity is reduced by 25 percent, only 75 billion oranges can be sold. Based on the demand curve, this amount can be sold for 15 cents per orange. Thus this will be the price. (c) Under the committee's edict, growers will sell 75 billion oranges at 15 cents each, so they will receive $11.25 billion. Under the free market, they will sell 100 billion oranges at 10 cents each, so they will receive $10 billion. Thus they will receive $1.25 billion more under the committee's edict than under the free market. (d) They consume fewer oranges and pay more for those they do consume.

*"Growers Bar Oranges from Market as Prices Dip," *New York Times,* February 15, 1981.

general, economists simply assume that the actual price will approximate the equilibrium price, which seems reasonable enough, since the basic forces at work tend to push the actual price toward the equilibrium price. Thus, if conditions remain fairly stable for a time, the actual price should move toward the equilibrium price.

To see that this is the case, consider the market for wheat, as described in Figure 3.9. What if the price somehow is set at $3.60 per bushel? As we saw in the previous section, there is downward pressure on the price of wheat under these conditions. Suppose the price, responding to this pressure, falls to $3.50. Comparing the quantity demanded with the quantity supplied at $3.50, we find that there is still downward pressure on price, since the quantity supplied exceeds the quantity demanded at $3.50. The price, responding to this pressure, may fall to $3.40, but comparing the quantity demanded with the quantity supplied at this price, we find that there is still a downward pressure on price, since the quantity supplied exceeds the quantity demanded at $3.40.

So long as the actual price exceeds the equilibrium price, there will be a downward pressure on price. Similarly, so long as the actual price is less than the equilibrium price, there will be an upward pressure on price. Thus there is always a tendency for the actual price to move toward the equilibrium price. But it should not be assumed that this movement is always rapid. Sometimes it takes a long time for the actual price to get close to the equilibrium price. Sometimes the actual price never gets to the equilibrium price because by the time it gets close, the equilibrium price changes (because of shifts in either the demand curve or the supply curve or both). All that safely can be said is that the actual price will move toward the equilibrium price. But of course this information is of great value, both theoretically and practically. For many purposes, all that is needed is a correct prediction of the direction in which the price will move.

Test Yourself

1. Assume that the market for electric toasters is competitive and that the quantity supplied per year depends as follows on the price of a toaster:

Price of a toaster (dollars)	Number of toasters supplied (millions)
6	4.0
8	5.0
10	5.5
12	6.0
14	6.3

Plot the supply curve for toasters. Is this a direct or inverse relationship? Are supply curves generally direct or inverse relationships?

2. Suppose that the quantity of toasters demanded per year depends as follows on the price of a toaster:

Price of a toaster (dollars)	Number of toasters demanded (millions)
6	7.0
8	6.5
10	6.2
12	6.0
14	5.8

Plot the demand curve for toasters. If the price is $8, will there be an excess demand of toasters? If the price is $14, will there be an excess demand? What is the equilibrium price of a toaster? What is the equilibrium quantity? (Use the data in Question 1.)

3. Suppose that the government imposes a price ceiling on toasters. In particular, suppose that it decrees that a toaster cannot sell for more than $8. Will the quantity supplied equal the quantity demanded? What sorts of devices may come into being to allocate the available supply of toasters to consumers? What problems will the government encounter in keeping the price at $8? What social purposes, if any, might such a price ceiling serve? (Use the data in Questions 1 and 2.)

4. Suppose that the government imposes a price floor on toasters. In particular, suppose that it decrees that a toaster cannot sell for less than $14. Will the quantity supplied equal the quantity demanded? How will the resulting supply of toasters be taken off the market? What problems will the government encounter in keeping the price at $14? What social purposes, if any, might such a price floor serve? (Use the data above.)

5. If the demand curve for butter is $Q_D = 20 - 4P$ (where Q_D is the quantity demanded and P is the price of butter) and the supply curve for butter is $Q_S = 2P$ (where Q_S is the quantity supplied), what is the equilibrium price? What is the equilibrium quantity? (Both Q_D and Q_S are measured in millions of pounds, and price is measured in dollars per pound.)

The Effects of Shifts in the Demand Curve

Heraclitus, the ancient Greek philosopher, said you cannot step in the same stream twice: everything changes, sooner or later. One need not be a disciple of Heraclitus to recognize that demand curves shift. Indeed, we have already seen that demand curves shift in response to changes in tastes, income, population, and prices of other products, and that supply curves shift in response to changes in technology and input prices. Any supply-and-demand diagram like Figure 3.9 is essentially a snapshot of the situation during a particular period of time. The results in Figure 3.9 are limited to a particular period because the demand and supply curves in the figure, like any demand and supply curves, pertain only to a certain period.

What happens to the equilibrium price of a product when its demand curve changes? This is an important question because it sheds a good deal of light on how the price system works. Suppose that consumer tastes shift in favor of foods containing wheat, causing the demand curve for wheat to shift *to the right,* as shown in Figure 3.10. It is not hard to see the effect on the equilibrium price of wheat. Before the shift, the equilibrium price is *OP.* But when the demand curve shifts to the right, a shortage develops at this price: that is, the quantity demanded exceeds the quantity supplied at this price.[5] Consequently, suppliers raise their prices. After some testing of market reactions and trial-and-error adjustments, the price will tend to settle at OP_1, the new equilibrium price, and quantity will tend to settle at OQ_1.

On the other hand, suppose that consumer demand for wheat products falls off, perhaps because of a great drop in the price of corn products. The demand for wheat now shifts *to the left,* as shown in Figure 3.11. What will be the effect on the equilibrium price of wheat? Clearly, the equilibrium price falls to OP_2, where the new demand curve intersects the supply curve.

In general, *a shift to the right in the demand curve results in an increase in the equilibrium price, and a shift to the left in the demand curve results in a*

[5] This shortage is equal to $OQ_1' - OQ$ in Figure 3.10.

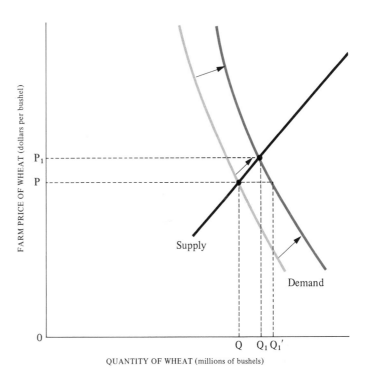

Figure 3.10

**Effect on the Equilibrium Price of a
Shift to the Right of the Market
Demand Curve** *This shift of the demand
curve to the right results in an increase
in the equilibrium price from* OP *to* OP_1
*and an increase in the equilibrium
quantity from* OQ *to* OQ_1.

Figure 3.11

**Effect on the Equilibrium Price of a
Shift to the Left of the Market Demand
Curve** *This shift of the demand curve to
the left results in a decrease in the
equilibrium price from* OP *to* OP_2 *and a
decrease in the equilibrium quantity from*
OQ *to* OQ_2.

decrease in the equilibrium price. This is the lesson of Figures 3.10 and 3.11. Of course, this conclusion depends on the assumption that the supply curve slopes upward to the right, but, as we noted in a previous section, this assumption is generally true.

At this point, since all of this is theory, you may be wondering how well this theory works in practice. In 1972 and 1973, there was a vivid demonstration of the accuracy of this model in various agricultural markets, including wheat. Because of poor harvests abroad and greatly increased foreign demand for American wheat, the demand curve for wheat shifted markedly to the right. What happened to the price of wheat? In accord with our model, the price increased spectacularly, from about $1.35 a bushel in the early summer of 1972 to over $4.00 a year later. Anyone who witnessed this phenomenon could not help but be impressed by the usefulness of this model.

The Effects of Shifts in the Supply Curve

What happens to the equilibrium price of a product when its supply curve changes? For example, suppose that, because of technological advances in wheat production, wheat farmers are willing and able to supply more wheat at a given price than they used to, with the result that the supply curve shifts *to the right,* as shown in Figure 3.12. What will be the effect on the equilibrium price? Clearly, it will fall from *OP* (where the original supply curve intersects the demand curve) to *OP₃* (where the new supply curve intersects the demand curve).

On the other hand, suppose that the weather is poor, with the result that the supply curve shifts *to the left,* as shown in Figure 3.12. What will be the

49

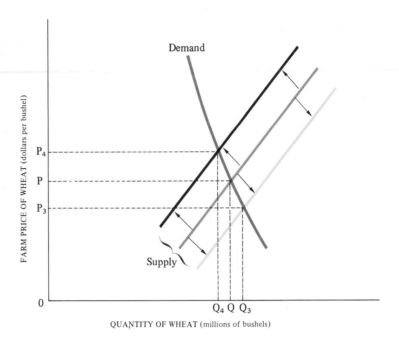

Figure 3.12

Effects on the Equilibrium Price of Shifts in the Market Supply Curve *The shift of the supply curve to the right results in a decrease in the equilibrium price from OP to OP₃. The shift of the supply curve to the left increases the equilibrium price from OP to OP₄.*

effect? The equilibrium price will increase from *OP* (where the original supply curve intersects the demand curve) to *OP₄* (where the new supply curve intersects the demand curve).

In 1984, law enforcement officers concerned with narcotics consumption in the United States were shown vividly what a shift to the right in the supply curve of a commodity will do. Because of a massive increase in the amount of coca production in South America, the supply curve for cocaine shifted dramatically to the right. The result was just what our theory would predict: a big drop in the price of cocaine. In some parts of the United States, cocaine sold in 1984 for one-half to one-third the price of a year before. According to one federal official, "At no time in the modern history of international drug control has the price of a drug dropped by half so quickly."

In general, a shift to the right in the supply curve results in a decrease in the equilibrium price, and a shift to the left in the supply curve results in an increase in the equilibrium price. Of course, this conclusion depends on the assumption that the demand curve slopes downward to the right, but, as we noted in a previous section, this assumption is generally true.

The Price System and the Determination of What Is Produced

Having described how prices are determined in free markets, we can now describe somewhat more fully how the price system goes about performing the four basic tasks that face any economic system. Let's begin by considering the determination of what society will produce: How does the price system carry out this task? Consumers indicate what goods and services they want in the market place, and producers try to meet these wants. More specifically, the demand curve for a product shows how much of that product consumers want at various prices. If consumers don't want much of it at a certain price, its demand curve will indicate that fact by being positioned close to the vertical axis at that price. In other words, the demand curve will show that, at this price for the product, the amount consumers will buy is small. On the other hand, if consumers want lots of the product at this price, its demand curve will be far from the vertical axis.

A product's demand curve is an important determinant of how much firms will produce of the product, since it indicates the amount of the product that will be demanded at each price. From the point of view of the producers, the demand curve indicates the amount they can sell at each price. In a capitalist economy, firms are in business to make money. Thus the manufacturers of any product will turn it out only if the amount of money they receive from consumers exceeds the cost of putting the product on the market. Acting in accord with the profit motive, firms are led to produce what the consumers desire. We saw in a previous section that if consumers' tastes shift in favor of foods containing wheat, the demand curve for wheat will shift to the right, which will result in an increase in the price of wheat. This increase will stimulate farmers to produce more wheat. For example, when the demand curve shifts to the right in Figure 3.10, the equilibrium quantity produced increases from OQ to OQ_1. Given the shift in the demand curve, it is profitable for firms to step up their production. Acting in their own self-interest, they are led to make production decisions geared to the wants of the consumers.

Thus the price system uses the self-interest of the producers to get them to produce what consumers want. Consumers register what they want in the market place by their purchasing decisions—shown by their demand curves. Producers can make more money by responding to consumer wants than by ignoring them. Consequently, they are led to produce what consumers want—and are willing to pay enough for to cover the producers' costs. Note that costs as well as demand determine what will be produced, and that producers are not forced by anyone to do anything. They can produce air conditioners for Eskimos if they like—and if they are prepared to absorb the losses. The price system uses prices to communicate the relevant signals to producers, and metes out the penalties and rewards in the form of losses or profits.

The Price System and the Determination of How Goods Are Produced

Next, consider how society determines how each good and service is produced. How does the price system carry out this task? The price of each resource gives producers an indication of how scarce this resource is, and how valuable it is in other uses. Clearly, firms should produce goods and services at minimum cost. Suppose that there are two ways of producing tables: Technique A and Technique B. Technique A requires 4 man-hours of labor and $10 worth of wood per table, whereas Technique B requires 5 man-hours of labor and $8 worth of wood. If the price of a man-hour of labor is $4, Technique A should be used since a table costs $26 with this

Example 3.2   Tennis Anyone?

In the early 1970s, the American public turned to tennis in droves, and many indoor tennis courts were built. In the late 1970s and early 1980s, the tennis fad began to fade. One indication: sales of tennis rackets fell by 20 percent in 1980. Also, during the late 1970s and early 1980s, the costs of operating an indoor tennis court increased markedly because of ballooning prices of electricity needed to light, heat, and air-condition the courts. For example, a 12-court facility near Philadelphia paid $8,600 a month for electricity in early 1981.*

(a) What sort of shift occurred during the late 1970s and early 1980s in the demand curve for playing time at indoor tennis courts? (b) Taken by itself, what effect did this shift in the demand curve have on the price per hour of playing time at indoor tennis courts? (c) Did the shift in the supply curve for playing time offset or reinforce this effect on price? (d) Based on the above facts, would you expect that the total amount of playing time sold by indoor tennis courts increased or decreased during the early 1980s? Why?

SOLUTION

(a) The demand curve shifted to the left because consumers demanded fewer hours of playing time at a given price. (b) Holding the supply curve constant, the leftward shift in the demand curve tended to reduce the price. (c) The supply curve shifted upward and to the left because of the increased price of electricity, a major input. Taken by itself, this shift in the supply curve tended to increase the price. Thus its effect was to offset the effect of the shift in the demand curve. (d) A leftward shift in both the demand curve and the supply curve would result in a decrease in the total amount of playing time sold (from $0Q$ to $0Q'$), as shown below:

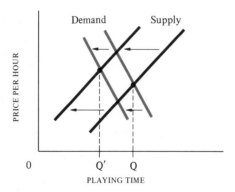

* See "As Racquet Fads Fade, Clubs Are Scrambling," *Philadelphia Inquirer,* May 4, 1981.

technique, as opposed to $28 with Technique B.[6] In other words, Technique A uses fewer resources per table.

The price system nudges producers to opt for Technique A rather than Technique B through profits and losses. If each table commands a price of $35, then by using Technique A, producers make a profit of $35 − $26 = $9 per table. If they use Technique B, they make a profit of $35 − $28 = $7 per table. Thus producers, if they maximize profit, will be led to adopt Technique A. Their desire for profit leads them to adopt the techniques that will enable society to get the most out of its resources. No one commands firms to use particular techniques. Washington officials do not order steel plants to substitute the basic oxygen process for open hearths, or petroleum refineries to substitute catalytic cracking for thermal cracking. It is all done through the impersonal market place.

You should not, however, get the idea that the price system operates with kid gloves. Suppose all firms producing tables used Technique B until this past year, when Technique A was developed: in other words, Technique A is based on a new technology. Given this technological change, the supply curve for tables will shift to the right, as we saw in a previous section, and the price of a table will fall. Suppose it drops to $27. If some firm insists on sticking with Technique B, it will lose money at the rate of $1 a table; and as these losses mount, the firm's owners will become increasingly uncomfortable. The firm will either switch to Technique A or go bankrupt. The price system leans awfully hard on producers who try to ignore its signals.

The Price System and the Determination of Who Gets What

Let's turn now to how society's output will be distributed among the people: How does the price system carry out this task? How much people receive in goods and services depends on their money income, which in turn is determined under the price system by the amount of various resources that they own and by the price of each resource. Thus, under the price system, each person's income is determined in the market place: the person comes to the market place with certain resources to sell, and his or her income depends on how much he or she can get for them.

The question of who gets what is solved at two levels by the price system. Consider an individual product—for example, the tables discussed in the previous section. For the individual product, the question of who gets what is solved by the equality of quantity demanded and quantity supplied. If the price of these tables is at its equilibrium level, the quantity demanded will equal the quantity supplied. Consumers who are willing and able to pay the equilibrium price (or more) get the tables, while those who are unwilling or unable to pay it do not get them. It is just as simple—and as impersonal—as that. It doesn't matter whether you are a nice guy or a scoundrel, or whether you are a connoisseur of tables or someone who doesn't know good workmanship from poor: all that matters is whether you are able and willing to pay the equilibrium price.

---

[6] To obtain these figures, note that the cost with Technique A is 4 man-hours times $4 plus $10, or $26, while the cost with Technique B is 5 man-hours times $4 plus $8, or $28.

Next, consider the question of who gets what at a somewhat more fundamental level. After all, whether a consumer is able and willing to pay the equilibrium price for a good depends on his money income. Thus the super-rich can pay the equilibrium price for an astonishing variety of things, whereas those in abject poverty can scrape up the equilibrium price for very little. As we have already seen, a consumer's money income depends on the amount of resources of various kinds that he or she owns and the price that he or she can get for them. Some people have lots of resources: they are endowed with skill and intelligence and industry, or they have lots of capital or land. Other people have little in the way of resources. Moreover, some people have resources that command a high price, while others have resources that are of little monetary value. The result is that, under the price system, some consumers get a lot more of society's output than do other consumers.

The Price System and Economic Growth

Let's turn now to the task of determining a society's rate of growth of per capita income. How does the price system do this? As pointed out in the previous chapter, a nation's rate of increase of per capita income depends on the rate of growth of its resources and the rate of increase of the efficiency with which they are used. First, consider the rate of growth of society's resources. The price system controls the amount of new capital goods produced much as it controls the amount of consumer goods produced. Similarly, the price system influences the amount society invests in educating, training, and upgrading its labor resources. To a considerable extent, the amount invested in such resource-augmenting activities is determined by the profitability of such investments, which is determined in turn by the pattern of prices.

Next, consider the rate of increase of the efficiency with which a society's resources are used. Clearly, this factor depends heavily on the rate of technological change. If technology is advancing at a rapid rate, it should be possible to get more and more out of a society's resources. But if technology is advancing rather slowly, it is likely to be difficult to get much more out of them. The price system affects the rate of technological change in a variety of ways: it influences the profitability of investing in research and development, the profitability of introducing new processes and products into commercial practice, and the profitability of accepting technological change—as well as the losses involved in spurning it.

The price system establishes strong incentives for firms to introduce new technology. Any firm that can find a cheaper way to produce an existing product, or a way to produce a better product, will have a profitable jump on its competitors. Until its competitors can do the same thing, this firm can reap higher profits than it otherwise could. Of course, these higher profits will eventually be competed away, as other firms begin to imitate this firm's innovation. But lots of money can be made in the period during which this firm has a lead over its competitors. These profits are an important incentive for the introduction of new technology.

Two Case Studies

THE PRICE SYSTEM IN ACTION BEHIND ENEMY LINES

Just as general discussions of tennis will take a neophyte only so far, after which he or she must watch and participate in a few matches, so a general discussion of the price system will take a student only so far. Then he or she should look at real-life examples of the price system at work. Our first illustration of the price system in operation is a prisoner-of-war camp in World War II. This case is not chosen because of its inherent importance, but because of its simplicity. Just as certain elementary forms of life illustrate important biological principles in a simple way, so the economic organization of a prisoner-of-war camp is an elementary form of economic system that illustrates certain important economic principles simply and well.

The prisoner-of-war camp was so elementary because no goods were produced there. All commodities were provided by the country running the camp, by the Red Cross, and by other outside donors. Each prisoner received an equal amount of food and supplies—canned milk, jam, butter, cookies, cigarettes, and so on. In addition, private parcels of clothing, cigarettes, and other supplies were received, with different prisoners, of course, receiving different quantities. Because no goods were produced in the prisoner-of-war camp, the first two tasks of an economic system (What will be produced? How will it be produced?) were not relevant; neither was the fourth task (What provision is to be made for growth?).

All that did matter in this elementary economic system was the third task: to determine who would consume the various available goods. At first blush, the answer may seem obvious: each prisoner would consume the goods he received from the detaining country, the Red Cross, and private packages. But this assumes that prisoners would not trade goods back and forth ("I'll swap you a cigarette for some milk"), which is clearly unrealistic. After all, some prisoners smoked cigarettes, others did not; some liked jam and didn't like canned beef, others liked canned beef and didn't like jam. Thus there was bound to be exchange of this sort, and the real question is in what way and on what terms such exchange took place.

How did the prisoners go about exchanging goods? According to one observer, the process developed as follows:

> Starting with simple direct barter, such as a nonsmoker giving a smoker friend his cigarette issue in exchange for a chocolate ration, more complex exchanges soon became an accepted custom. . . . Within a week or two, as the volume of trade grew, rough scales of exchange values came into existence. [Some prisoners], who had at first exchanged tinned beef for practically any other foodstuff, began to insist on jam and margarine. It was realized that a tin of jam was worth one-half pound of margarine plus something else, that a cigarette issue was worth several chocolate issues, and a tin of diced carrots was worth practically nothing. . . . By the end of the month, there was a lively trade in all commodities and their relative values were well known, and expressed not in terms of one another—one didn't quote [jam] in terms of sugar—but in terms of cigarettes. The cigarette became the standard of value.[7]

[7] R. A. Radford, "The Economic Organization of a P.O.W. Camp," reprinted in E. Mansfield, *Principles of Microeconomics: Readings, Issues, and Cases,* 4th ed., New York: Norton, 1983.

Figure 3.13

Determinants of Equilibrium Price of a Tin of Jam (in terms of cigarettes) in a P.O.W. Camp *The market supply for jam is fixed at OS tins. Thus the equilibrium price of a tin of jam is OP cigarettes. If the price were OP₁, OQ₁ tins would be demanded; if the price were OP₂, OQ₂ tins would be demanded.*

Thus the prisoners used the price system to solve the problem of allocating the available supply of goods among consumers. A market developed for each good. This market had, of course, both a demand and a supply side. Each good had its price—but this price was quoted in cigarettes, not dollars and cents. These markets were not started in a self-conscious, deliberate way. No one said, "Let's adopt the price system to allocate available supplies," or "Let's vote on whether or not to adopt the price system." Instead, the system just evolved ... and it worked.

To see how the supply of a particular good—jam, say—was allocated, look at Figure 3.13, which shows the market supply curve for jam. In the short run, this supply was fixed, so this supply curve is a vertical line. Figure 3.13 also provides the market demand curve for jam, which shows the amount of jam the prisoners wanted to consume at various prices of jam—expressed in terms of cigarettes. For example, the prisoners wanted OQ_1 tins of jam when a tin of jam cost OP_1 cigarettes, and OQ_2 tins of jam when a tin of jam cost OP_2 cigarettes. For the quantity demanded to equal the available supply, the price of a tin of jam had to be OP cigarettes; one tin of jam had to exchange for OP cigarettes. At this price, the available supply of jam was rationed, without resort to fights among prisoners or intervention by the prison authorities. Those prisoners who could and would pay the price had the jam—and there were just enough such consumers to exhaust the available supply. Moreover, this held true for each of the other goods (including cigarettes) as well.

THE PRICE SYSTEM IN ACTION ON THE GREAT WHITE WAY

It is a long way from a prisoner-of-war camp to the Broadway theater, but economics, like any good tool of analysis, applies to a very wide variety of problems. In this section, we discuss the theater's pricing problems—and the role of the price system in helping to solve these problems. Prices for tickets to Broadway shows are established at levels that are much the same whether the show is a success or a flop. An orchestra ticket to *Kelly* (which managed to hold out for one performance before closing) cost about as much as an orchestra ticket to such hits as *Fiddler on the Roof* or *Cats.* And once a play opens, the price of a ticket remains much the same whether the play is greeted with universal praise or with discontented critics and customers.

Because of these pricing methods, the Broadway theater has been beset for many years by serious problems. Here they are described by two veteran observers of the Broadway stage:

> For centuries the sale of theater tickets has brought on corruption and confusion. When there are more buyers than sellers, a black market results. The so-called "retail" price, the price printed on the ticket, becomes meaningless. Speculation doubles, triples, or quadruples the "real" as opposed to the "legal" asking price. A smash hit on Broadway means "ice"—the difference between the real and legal prices—a well-hidden but substantial cash flow that is divided among shadowy middlemen. Ticket scandals break out in New York as regularly as the flu. The scenario is familiar. A play opens and becomes a superhit. Tickets become difficult, then impossible, to obtain. There are letters to the newspapers.... Shocking corruption is discovered. Someone ... is convicted of overcharging and accepting illegal gratuities. Someone may even go to jail. The black market, valiantly scotched, *never stops for a single moment.*[8]

Besides enriching crooked box-office men and managers, as well as other shadowy elements of society, the black market for theater tickets has the additional undesirable effect of excluding the authors, composers, directors, and stars of the play from participation in the premium revenue. Almost all of these people receive a percentage of the play's revenues; and if the revenues at the box office are less than what customers pay for their seats (because of "ice"), these people receive less than they would if no black market existed. The amount of "ice" can be substantial. For example, Rodgers and Hammerstein estimated that, at one performance of their play, *South Pacific,* the public probably paid about $25,000 for tickets with a face value of $7,000, the amount turned in at the box office.

To focus on the problem here, let's look at the market for tickets to a particular performance of *A Chorus Line* (one of Broadway's all-time big hits) when it was at the height of its popularity. Since the supply of tickets to a given performance of this play is fixed, the market supply curve, shown in Figure 3.14, is a vertical line at the quantity of tickets corresponding to the capacity of the theater. The price set officially on a ticket was about $20. But because the show was enormously popular, the market demand curve was *D* in Figure 3.14, and the equilibrium price for a ticket was $50.[9]

Figure 3.14 makes the nature of the problem apparent: at the official price of $20, the quantity of tickets demanded is much greater than the quantity supplied. Supply and demand don't match. Obviously, there is an incentive for people to buy the tickets from the box office at $20 and sell

---

[8] S. Little and A. Cantor, *The Playmakers,* New York: Norton, 1970, p. 220.
[9] This figure is only a rough estimate, but it is good enough for present purposes.

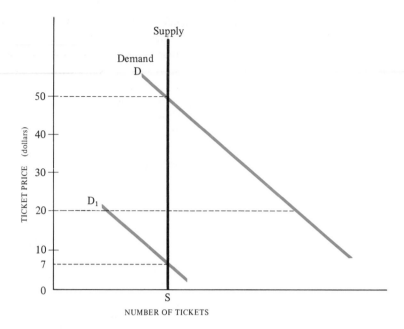

Figure 3.14

Equilibrium Price for Tickets to A Chorus Line *The market supply for tickets is fixed at OS per performance. If the demand curve is D, the equilibrium price of a ticket is $50. (If the demand curve is D_1, the equilibrium price is $7.) If the demand curve is D and the price of a ticket is $20, the quantity of tickets demanded will far exceed the quantity supplied.*

them at the higher prices customers are willing to pay. There is also an incentive for box-office men to sell them surreptitiously at higher prices and turn in only $20. The price system cannot play the role it did in the prisoner-of-war camp for jam and other goods. It cannot act as an effective rationing device because, to do so, the price of tickets would have to increase to its equilibrium level, $50.

Many theater experts believe that the solution to Broadway's pricing problems lies in allowing the price system to work more effectively by permitting ticket prices to vary depending on a show's popularity. For example, the official ticket price would be allowed to rise to $50 for *A Chorus Line*. On the other hand, if *A Chorus Line* had been much less popular and its market demand curve had been D_1 in Figure 3.14, its official ticket price would have been allowed to fall to $7. In this way, the black market for tickets would be eliminated, since the equilibrium price—which equates supply and demand—would be the official price. "Ice" would also be eliminated, since there would be no difference between the official and the actual price paid, and the people responsible for the show would receive its full receipts, not share them with crooked box-office men and illegal operators.[10]

Price Ceilings and Price Supports

During national emergencies, the government sometimes puts a lid on prices, not allowing them to reach their equilibrium levels. For example,

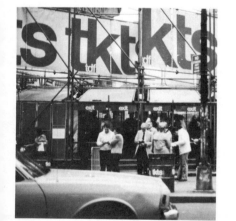

[10] Steps have been taken toward somewhat greater price flexibility for Broadway shows. For example, in the mid-1970s, a booth was established in Times Square where tickets to some shows were on sale at (approximately) half of the official ticket price. In this way, a show was enabled to cut its price, if it was unable to fill the theater at the official ticket price. Apparently, this innovation has worked quite well, both for the producers of the shows and the theatergoing public.

Basic Idea #6: Governments frequently establish price ceilings or price floors in an attempt to help particular parts of the population. Such intervention prevents the price system from doing the job expected of it. Price ceilings tend to result in shortages, and price floors tend to result in surpluses. Both can cause serious social waste.

during World War II, the government did not allow the prices of various foodstuffs to rise to their equilibrium levels, because it felt that this would have been inequitable (and highly unpopular). Under such circumstances, the quantity demanded of a product exceeds the quantity supplied. In other words, the situation is like that in Figure 3.14, where the quantity of tickets demanded for *A Chorus Line* exceeds the quantity supplied at a price of $20. There is a shortage.

Since the price system is not allowed to perform its rationing function, some formal system of rationing or allocating the available supply of the product may be required. Thus, in World War II, families were issued ration coupons which determined how much they could buy of various commodities. And in 1979, when the Organization of Petroleum Exporting Countries cut back oil production and reduced exports of oil to the United States, there was serious talk that gasoline and oil might be rationed in a similar way. Such rationing schemes may be justified in emergencies (of reasonably short duration), but they can result eventually in serious distortions, since prices are not allowed to do the job normally expected of them.

To illustrate the sorts of problems that can arise when price ceilings are imposed, consider the rent ceilings that exist on some apartments in New York City. Originally imposed to prevent dwelling costs from soaring during World War II, these ceilings have been defended on the ground that they help the poor, at least in the short run. Although this may be so, they have also resulted in a shortage of housing in New York City. Because they have pushed the price of housing below the equilibrium price, less housing has been supplied than has been demanded. The depressed price of housing has discouraged investors from building new housing, and has made it unprofitable for some owners of existing housing to maintain their buildings. Thus, although it would be socially desirable to channel more resources into New York housing, the rent ceilings have prevented this from occurring.

Government authorities may also impose price floors—or price supports, as they often are called. These floors are generally defended on the ground that they enable the producers of the good in question to make a better living. For example, the federal government has imposed price supports on a wide range of agricultural commodities, the purpose being to increase farm incomes. Just as in the case in Figure 3.14 where the demand curve is D_1 and where a price floor of $20 exists, the result is that the quantity supplied exceeds the quantity demanded at the support price. Thus there is a surplus of the commodity—and, in the case of agricultural commodities, the government has to buy up and store these surpluses. As in the case of a price ceiling, the result is that the price system is not allowed to do the job expected of it.

Whether price ceilings or floors are socially desirable depends on whether the loss in social efficiency resulting from them is exceeded by the gain in equity they achieve. As indicated above, their purpose is to help or protect particular parts of the population which would be treated inequitably by the unfettered price system. Since one person's view of what is equitable differ from another person's, this is an area of considerable controversy. More will be said about both price ceilings and floors in subsequent chapters, particularly Chapter 4.

The Circular Flows of Money and Products

So far we have been concerned largely with the workings of a single market—the market for wheat or tables or jam or tickets to *A Chorus Line.* But how do all of the various markets fit together? This is a very important question. Perhaps the best way to begin answering it is to distinguish between product markets and resource markets. As their names indicate, *product markets are markets where products are bought and sold; and resource markets are markets where resources are bought and sold.* Let's first consider product markets. As shown in Figure 3.15, firms provide products to consumers in product markets, and receive money in return. The money the firms receive is their receipts; to consumers, on the other hand, it represents their expenditures.

Next, let's consider resource markets. Figure 3.15 shows that consumers provide resources—including labor—to firms in resource markets, and they receive money in return. The money the consumers receive is their income; to firms, on the other hand, it represents their costs. Note that the flow of resources and products in Figure 3.15 is counterclockwise: that is, *consumers provide resources to firms which in turn provide goods and services to consumers.* On the other hand, the flow of money in Figure 3.15 is clockwise: that is, *firms pay money for resources to consumers who in turn use the money to buy goods and services from the firms.* Both flows—that of resources and products, and that of money—go on simultaneously and repeatedly.

So long as consumers spend all their income, the flow of money income from firms to consumers is exactly equal to the flow of expenditure from consumers to firms. Thus these circular flows, like Ole' Man River, just keep rolling along. As a first approximation, this is a perfectly good model. But as we pointed out in Chapter 1, capitalist economies have experienced periods of widespread unemployment and severe inflation that this model cannot explain. Also, note that our simple economy in Figure 3.15 has no

Figure 3.15

The Circular Flows of Money and Products *In product markets, consumers exchange money for products and firms exchange products for money. In resource markets, consumers exchange resources for money and firms exchange money for resources.*

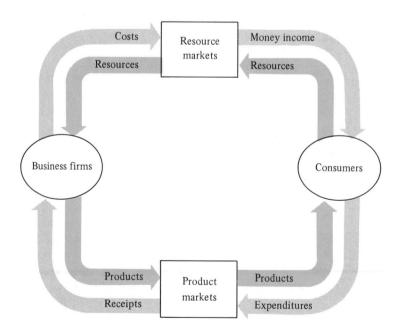

government sector. In the following chapter, we shall bring the government into the picture. Under pure capitalism, the government would play a limited role in the economic system, but in the mixed capitalistic system we have in the United States, the government plays an important role indeed.

Test Yourself

1. Will each of the following tend to shift the demand curve for toasters to the right, to the left, or not at all? (a) Consumer incomes rise by 20 percent. (b) The price of bread falls by 10 percent. (c) The price of electricity increases by 5 percent. (d) Medical reports indicate that toast prevents heart attacks. (e) The cost of producing a toaster increases by 10 percent.

2. Will each of the following tend to shift the supply curve for toasters to the right, to the left, or not at all? (a) The wage of workers producing toasters increases by 5 percent. (b) The price of the metal used to make toasters falls by 10 percent. (c) The price of bread falls by 10 percent. (d) Consumer incomes rise by 20 percent. (e) New technology makes toaster production much more efficient.

3. If both the demand and supply curve for a product shift to the right, can one predict whether the product's equilibrium price will increase or decrease? Can one predict whether its equilibrium quantity will increase or decrease?

4. In most years, New Jersey blueberry farmers can get up to 80 cents a pint. In the summer of 1984, prices were pushed to as low as 30 cents a pint. (a) Why do you think this happened? (b) New Jersey farmers complained that they couldn't make money at the 30-cent price. Should the government establish a price floor for blueberries? Explain.

5. Suppose that the American public becomes convinced that beets are more desirable than they have been, and string beans are less so. Describe the shifts that will occur in the demand and supply curves in the relevant markets, and the mechanisms that will signal and trigger a redeployment of resources.

Summary

1. There are two sides of every market: the demand side and the supply side. The demand side can be represented by the market demand curve, which almost always slopes downward to the right and whose location depends on consumer tastes, the number and income of consumers, and the prices of other commodities.

2. The supply side of the market can be represented by the market supply curve, which generally slopes upward to the right and whose location depends on technology and resource prices.

3. The equilibrium price and equilibrium quantity of the commodity are given by the intersection of the market demand and supply curves. If conditions remain reasonably stable for a time, the actual price and quantity should move close to the equilibrium price and quantity.

4. Changes in the position and shape of the demand curve—in response to changes in consumer tastes, income, population, and prices of other commodities—result in changes in the equilibrium price and equilibrium output of a product. Similarly, changes in the position and shape of the supply curve—in response to changes in technology and resource prices, among other things—also result in changes in the equilibrium price and equilibrium output of a product.

5. To determine what goods and services society will produce, the price system sets up incentives for firms to produce what consumers want. To the extent that they produce what consumers want and are willing to pay for, firms reap profits; to the extent that they don't, they experience losses.

6. The price system sets up strong incentives for firms to produce goods at minimum cost. These incentives take the form of profits for firms that minimize costs and losses for firms that operate with relatively high costs.

7. To determine who gets what, the price system results in each person's receiving an income that depends on the quantity of resources he or she owns and the prices that they command.

8. The price system establishes incentives for activities that result in increases in a society's per capita income. For example, it influences the amount of new capital goods produced, as well as the amount society spends on educating its labor force and improving its technology.

9. There are circular flows of money and products in a capitalist economy. In product markets, firms provide products to consumers and receive money in return. In resource markets, consumers provide resources to firms, and receive money in return.

Concepts for Review

Consumers	Market demand curve	Equilibrium price
Firms	Supply	Actual price
Markets	Market supply curve	Product market
Perfect competition	Equilibrium	Resource market
Demand		

CHAPTER 4

The Economic Role of the Government

To state that the United States is a mixed capitalist system, in which both government decisions and the price system play important roles, is hardly to provoke a controversy. But going a step beyond takes us into areas where viewpoints often diverge. The proper functions of government and the desirable size and nature of government expenditures and taxes are not matters on which all agree. Indeed, the question of how big government should be, and what its proper functions are, is hotly debated by conservatives and liberals throughout the land. This is only a preliminary airing of many of these issues. As the base of economic analysis is broadened in subsequent chapters, much more will be said on these matters, and you will be in a far better position to judge them for yourself.

Limitations of the Price System

Despite its many advantages, the price system suffers from limitations. Because these limitations are both prominent and well known, no one believes that the price system, left to its own devices, can be trusted to solve all society's basic economic problems. To a considerable extent, the government's role in the economy has developed in response to the limitations of the price system, which are described below.

Distribution of Income. There is *no* reason to believe that the distribution of income generated by the price system is *fair* or, in some sense, *best*. Most people feel that the distribution of income generated by the price system should be altered to suit humanitarian needs; in particular, that help should be given to the poor. Both liberals and conservatives tend to agree on this score, although there are arguments over the extent to which the poor

Basic Idea #7: *If the price system alone were used to organize an economy, there is no reason to believe that the resulting distribution of income would be equitable or that public goods would be produced in the right amount. Also, external economies and diseconomies might result in too little or too much production of some goods and services. In part, the government's role in the economy has developed in response to these perceived limitations of the price system.*

should be helped and the conditions under which they should be eligible for help. But the general principle that the government should step in to redistribute income in favor of the poor is generally accepted in the United States today.[1]

Public Goods. Some goods and services *cannot be provided through the price system because there is no way to exclude citizens from consuming the goods whether they pay for them or not.* For example, there is no way to prevent citizens from benefiting from national expenditures on defense, whether they pay money toward defense or not. Consequently, the price system cannot be used to provide such goods; no one will pay for them since they will receive them whether they pay or not. Further, some goods, like the quality of the environment and national defense (and others cited below), *can be enjoyed by one person without depriving others of the same enjoyment.* Such goods are called **public goods.** The government provides many public goods. Such goods are consumed collectively, or jointly, and it is inefficient to try to price them in a market. They tend to be indivisible; thus they frequently cannot be split into pieces and be bought and sold in a market.

External Economies and Diseconomies. In cases where *the production or consumption of a good by one firm or consumer has adverse or beneficial uncompensated effects on other firms or consumers, the price system will not operate effectively.* An **external economy** is said to occur when consumption or production by one person or firm results in uncompensated benefits to another person or firm. A good example of an external economy exists where fundamental research carried out by one firm is used by another firm. (To cite one such case, there were external economies from the Bell Telephone Laboratories' invention of the transistor. Many electronics firms, such as Texas Instruments and Fairchild, benefited considerably from Bell's research.) Where external economies exist, it is generally agreed that the price system will produce too little of the good in question and that the government should supplement the amount produced by private enterprise. This is the basic rationale for much of the government's huge investment in basic science. An **external diseconomy** is said to occur when consumption or production by one person or firm results in uncompensated costs to another person or firm. A good example of an external diseconomy occurs when a firm dumps pollutants into a stream and makes the water unfit for use by firms and people downstream. Where activities result in external diseconomies, it is generally agreed that the price system will tolerate too much of the activity and that the government should curb it. For example, as we shall see in Chapter 20, the government, in keeping with this doctrine, has involved itself in environmental protection and the reduction of air and water pollution.[2]

---

[1] Also, because the wealthy have more "dollar votes" than the poor, the sorts of goods and services that society produces will reflect this fact. Thus luxuries for the rich may be produced in larger amounts and necessities for the poor may be produced in smaller amounts than some critics regard as sensible and equitable. This is another frequently encountered criticism of the price system.

[2] The effects of external economies and diseconomies can also be taken care of by legal arrangements that assign liabilities for damages and compensate for benefits. However, such arrangements often are impractical or too costly to be used.

What Functions Should the Government Perform?

There are wide differences of opinion on the proper role of government in economic affairs. Although it is generally agreed that the government should redistribute income in favor of the poor, provide public goods, and offset the effects of external economies and diseconomies, there is considerable disagreement over how far the government should go in these areas, and what additional areas the government should be responsible for. Some people feel that "big government" is already a problem; that government is doing too much. Others believe that the public sector of the economy is being undernourished and that government should be allowed to do more. This is a fundamental question, and one that involves a great deal more than economics.

Conservative View. On the one hand, conservatives, such as Stanford University's Nobel laureate, Milton Friedman, believe that the government's role should be limited severely. They feel that economic and political freedom is likely to be undermined by excessive reliance on the state. Moreover, they tend to be skeptical about the government's ability to solve the social and economic problems at hand. They feel that the prevailing faith in the government's power to make a substantial dent in these problems is unreasonable, and they call for more and better information concerning the sorts of tasks government can reasonably be expected to do—and do well. They point to the slowness of the government bureaucracy, the difficulty in controlling huge government organizations, the inefficiencies political considerations can breed, and the difficulties in telling whether government programs are successful or not. On the basis of these considerations, they argue that the government's role should be carefully circumscribed.

Liberal View. To such arguments, liberals like Nobel laureate Paul Samuelson of the Massachusetts Institute of Technology respond with telling salvos of their own. Just as conservatives tend to be skeptical of the government's ability to solve important social and economic problems, so liberals tend to be skeptical about the price system's ability to solve these problems. They point to the limitations of the price system, discussed above, and they assert that the government can do a great deal to overcome these limitations, by regulating private activity and by subsidizing and providing goods and services that the private sector produces too little of. Liberals tend to be less concerned than conservatives about the effects on personal freedom of greater governmental intervention in the economy. They point out that the price system also involves coercion, since the fact that the price system awards the available goods and services to those who can pay their equilibrium price can be viewed as a form of coercion. In their view, people who are awarded only a pittance by the price system are coerced into discomfort and malnutrition.[3]

[3] See P. Samuelson, "The Economic Role of Private Activity," and G. Stigler, "The Government of the Economy," *A Dialogue on the Proper Economic Role of the State,* University of Chicago, Graduate School of Business, Selected Paper no. 7, in E. Mansfield, *Principles of Microeconomics: Readings, Issues, and Cases,* 4th ed.

Establishing "Rules of the Game"

Although there is considerable disagreement over the proper role of the government, both conservatives and liberals agree that it must do certain things. The first of these is to establish the "rules of the game"—that is, a legal, social, and competitive framework enabling the price system to function as it should. Specifically, *the government must see to it that contracts are enforced, that private ownership is protected, and that fraud is prevented.* Clearly, these matters must be tended to if the price system is to work properly. Also, *the government must maintain order (through the establishment of police and other forces), establish a monetary system (so that money can be used to facilitate trade and exchange), and provide standards for the weight and quality of products.*

As an example of this sort of government intervention, consider the Pure Food and Drug Act. This act, originally passed in 1906 and subsequently amended in various ways, protects the consumer against improper and fraudulent activities on the part of producers of foods and drugs. It prohibits the merchandising of impure or falsely labeled food or drugs, and it forces producers to specify the quantity and quality of the contents on labels. These requirements strengthen the price system. Without them, the typical consumer would be unable to tell whether food or drugs are pure or properly labeled. Unless consumers can be sure that they are getting what they pay for, the basic logic underlying the price system breaks down. Similar regulation and legislation have been instituted in fields other than food and drugs—and for similar reasons.

FDA inspectors

MAINTAINING A COMPETITIVE FRAMEWORK

Besides establishing a legal and social framework that will enable the price system to do its job, *the government must also see to it that markets remain reasonably competitive.* Only if they are will prices reflect consumer desires properly. If, on the other hand, markets are dominated by a few sellers (or a few buyers), prices may be "rigged" by these sellers (or buyers) to promote their own interests. For example, if a single firm is the sole producer of aluminum, it is a safe bet that this firm will establish a higher price than if there were many aluminum producers competing among themselves. The unfortunate thing about prices determined in noncompetitive markets—rigged prices, if you will—is that they give incorrect signals concerning what consumers want and how scarce resources and commodities are. Producers, responding to these incorrect signals, do not produce the right things in the right quantities. Consumers respond to these incorrect signals by not supplying the right resources in the right amounts, and by not consuming the proper amounts of the goods that are produced. Thus the price system is not permitted to solve the four basic economic problems properly in the absence of reasonable competition.

To try to encourage and preserve competition, the Congress has enacted a series of **antitrust laws,** such as the Sherman Antitrust Act and the Clayton Act, and it has established the Federal Trade Commission. The antitrust laws make it illegal for firms to collude or to attempt to monopolize the sale of a product. Both conservative and liberal economists, with some notable exceptions, tend to favor the intent and operation of the antitrust laws.

Redistribution of Income

We have already noted at several points the general agreement that the government should redistribute income in favor of the poor. In other words, *it is usually felt that help should be given to people who are ill, handicapped, old and infirm, disabled, and unable for other reasons to provide for themselves.* To some extent, the nation has decided that income—or at least a certain minimum income—should be divorced from productive services. Of course, this doesn't mean that people who are too lazy to work should be given a handout. It does mean that people who cannot provide for themselves should be helped. To implement this principle, various payments are made by the government to needy people—including the aged, the handicapped, the unemployed, and pensioners.

These **welfare payments** are to some extent a "depression baby," for they grew substantially during the Great Depression of the 1930s, when relief payments became a necessity. But they also represent a feeling shared by a large segment of the population that human beings should be assured that, however the wheel of fortune spins and whatever number comes up, they will not starve and their children will not be deprived of a healthy environment and basic schooling. Of course, someone has to pay for this. Welfare payments allow the poor to take more from the nation's output than they produce. In general, the more affluent members of society contribute some of their claims on output to pay for these programs, their contributions being in the form of taxes. By using its expenditures to help certain groups and by taxing other groups to pay for these programs, the government accomplishes each year, without revolt and without bayonets, a substantial redistribution of income. This is a crucial aspect of the government's role in our economy.

Stabilizing the Economy

It is also generally agreed that *the government should promote the maintenance of reasonably full employment with reasonably stable prices.* Capitalist economies have tended to alternate between booms and depressions in the past. The Great Depression of the 1930s hit the American economy—and the world economy—a particularly devastating blow, putting millions of people out of work and in desperate shape. When World War II ended, the American people vowed that they would not let a depression of this sort occur again. Congress passed the Employment Act of 1946, which stated that it was the responsibility of the federal government to maintain full employment in the United States. In particular, the federal government was not supposed to tolerate unemployment of the sort that materialized during severe depressions in the past.

Besides trying to maintain full employment, the government must also try to maintain a reasonably stable price level. No economy can function well if prices are gyrating wildly. Through its control of the money supply and its decisions regarding expenditures and taxation, the government has considerable impact on the price level, as well as on the level of employment. Unfortunately, during the 1970s in particular, the government was not very successful in maintaining price stability. According to many economists, the government's own policies (described in Chapters 12 and 16) contributed to this inflation.

Providing Public Goods

As we have indicated, the government provides many public goods. Let's consider the nature of public goods in more detail.

What Is a Public Good? One hallmark of a public good is that it can be consumed by one person without diminishing the amount that other people consume of it. Public goods tend to be relatively indivisible; they often come in such large units that they cannot be broken into pieces that can be bought or sold in ordinary markets. *Once such goods are produced, there often is no way to bar certain citizens from consuming them.* Whether or not citizens contribute toward their cost, they benefit from them. As pointed out in a previous section, this means that the price system cannot be used to handle effectively the production and distribution of such goods.

National Defense: A Public Good. National defense is a public good. The benefits of expenditure on national defense extend to the entire nation. Extension of the benefits of national defense to an additional citizen does not mean that any other citizen gets less of these benefits. Also, there is no way of preventing citizens from benefiting from them, whether they contribute to their cost or not. Thus there is no way to use the price system to provide for national defense. Since it is a public good, national defense, if it is to reach an adequate level, must be provided by the government. Similarly with flood control, environmental protection, and a host of other such services.

Decision Making Regarding Public Goods. Essentially, deciding how much to produce of a public good is a political decision. The citizens of the United States elect senators and congressmen who decide how much should be spent on national defense, and how it should be spent. These elected representatives are responsive to special-interest groups, as well as to the people as a whole. Many special-interest groups lobby hard for the production of certain public goods. For example, an alliance of military and industrial groups presses for increased defense expenditures, and other interested groups promote expenditures on other functions.

The tax system is used to pay for the production of public goods. In effect, the government says to each citizen, "Fork over a certain amount of money to pay for the expenses incurred by the government." The amount a particular citizen is assessed may depend on his or her income (as in the income tax), the value of all or specific types of his or her property (as in the property tax), the amount he or she spends on certain types of goods and services (as in the sales tax), or on still other criteria. In the 1980s, the tax system has often been the object of enormous controversy. Much more will be said about the tax system, and the controversies swirling around it, in a later section of this chapter and in the next chapter.

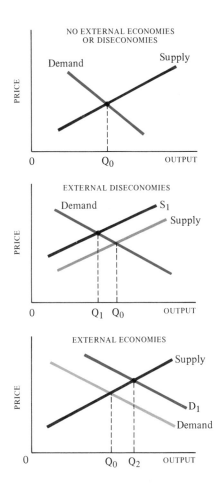

Figure 4.1
Effect of External Economies and Diseconomies on the Optimal Output of a Competitive Industry *The optimal output is* OQ$_0$ *if neither external economies nor diseconomies are present. If there are external diseconomies, curve* S$_1$ *reflects the true social costs of producing the product, and* OQ$_1$ *is the optimal output. If there are external economies, curve* D$_1$ *reflects the true social benefits of producing the product, and* OQ$_2$ *is the optimal output.*

Externalities

It is generally agreed that *the government should encourage the production of goods and services that entail external economies and discourage the production of those that entail external diseconomies.* Take the pollution of air and water. When a firm or individual dumps wastes into the water or air, other firms or individuals often must pay all or part of the cost of putting the water or air back into a usable condition. Thus the disposal of these wastes entails external diseconomies. Unless the government prohibits certain kinds of pollution, or enforces air and water quality standards, or charges polluters in accord with the amount of waste they dump into the environment, there will be socially undesirable levels of pollution.

Effects of External Diseconomies. To see how such externalities affect the social desirability of the output of a competitive industry, consider Figure 4.1, where the industry's demand and supply curves are contained in the top panel. As shown there, the equilibrium output of the industry is OQ_0. If the industry results in no external economies or diseconomies, this is likely to be the socially optimal output. But what if the industry results in external diseconomies, such as the pollution described above? Then the industry's supply curve does not fully reflect the true social costs of producing the product. The supply curve that reflects these social costs is S_1, which, as shown in the middle panel of Figure 4.1, lies to the left of the industry's supply curve. The optimal output of the good is OQ_1, which is less than the competitive output, OQ_0.

What can the government do to correct the situation? There are a variety of ways that it can intervene to reduce the industry's output from OQ_0 to OQ_1. For example, it can impose taxes on the industry, as we shall see in Chapter 5. If these taxes are of the right type and amount, they will result in the desired reduction of output.

Effects of External Economies. What if the industry results in external economies? For example, what if the manufacture of one industrial product makes it cheaper to produce other products? Then the industry's demand curve underestimates the true social benefits of producing the product. The demand curve that reflects these social benefits correctly is D_1, which, as shown in the bottom panel of Figure 4.1, lies to the right of the industry's demand curve. The optimal output of the good is OQ_2, which is greater than the competitive output, OQ_0.

As in the case where the industry results in external diseconomies, the government can intervene in various ways to change the industry's output. But in this case, the object is to increase, not decrease, its output. To accomplish this, the government can, among other things, grant subsidies to the industry. If they are of the right type and amount, they can be used to increase the industry's output from OQ_0 to OQ_2.

Size and Nature of Government Activities

HOW BIG IS THE GOVERNMENT?

Up to this point, we have been concerned primarily with the reasons why the government must intervene in our economy—and the types of role it

Example 4.1   The Economics of Urban Blight

During the past 30 years, the federal government has promoted and encouraged the redevelopment of the inner core of our major cities. Consider two adjacent urban properties. Suppose that the two owners, Mr. Lombardi and Mr. Moore, are each trying to determine whether to invest $100,000 to redevelop their properties. If they do not invest the $100,000 in redevelopment, each can get a 10 percent return from other forms of investment. The rate of return on the $100,000 investment by each owner (which depends on whether the other owner redevelops his property as well) is shown below:

	Other Owner Redevelops	Other Owner Does Not Redevelop
	(percent)	
Redevelop	12	5
Do not redevelop	15	10

(a) If Mr. Lombardi redevelops his property, is Mr. Moore better off by redeveloping his property as well? (b) If Mr. Lombardi does not redevelop his property, is Mr. Moore better off by redeveloping his property? (c) Will either owner redevelop his property? (d) In a situation of this sort, can social gains be achieved by government intervention?

SOLUTION

(a) No, because the rate of return Mr. Moore receives if he redevelops is 12 percent, whereas the rate of return he receives if he does not redevelop is 15 percent (because his property benefits from Mr. Lombardi's investment in redevelopment even though he pays nothing). (b) No, because the rate of return Mr. Moore receives if he redevelops is only 5 percent (because little is accomplished so long as Mr. Lombardi does not redevelop too), whereas the rate of return he receives if he does not redevelop is 10 percent (which is what he can obtain from other investments). (c) No. Consider Mr. Moore. As pointed out in (a) and (b), whether or not Mr. Lombardi redevelops, Mr. Moore receives a higher return if he does not redevelop than if he does. Thus he will not redevelop. Neither will Mr. Lombardi, for the same reasons. (d) Yes. From society's point of view, or from the point of view of the two owners acting together as a unit, redevelopment may be desirable. If carried out properly, government intervention may bring this about.

should play—but we have made little or no attempt to describe its role in quantitative terms. It is time now to turn to some of the relevant facts. One useful measure of the extent of the government's role in the American economy is the size of government expenditures, both in absolute terms and as a percent of our nation's total output.

The sum total of government expenditures—federal, state, and local—was about $1.2 trillion in 1983. Since the nation's total output was about $3.3 trillion, this means that government expenditures were about one-third of our total output. The ratio of government expenditures to total output in

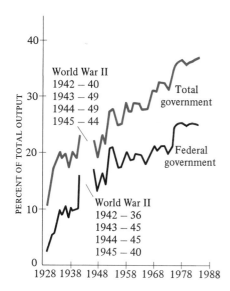

Figure 4.2

Government Spending as a Percent of Total Output, United States *Government expenditures—federal, state, and local—totaled about $1.2 trillion in 1983. These expenditures, which include transfer payments, have grown more rapidly than total output in this period.*

the United States has not always been this large, as Figure 4.2 shows. In 1929, the ratio was about 10 percent, as contrasted with over 30 percent in 1983. (Of course, the ratio of government spending to total output is smaller now than during World War II, but in a wartime economy, one would expect this ratio to be abnormally high.)

There are many reasons why government expenditures have grown so much faster than total output. Three of these are particularly important. First, *the United States did not maintain anything like the kind of military force in pre-World War II days that it does now.* In earlier days, when weapons were relatively simple and cheap, and when we viewed our military and political responsibilities much more narrowly than we do now, our military budget was relatively small. The cost of being a superpower in the days of nuclear weaponry is high by any standards. Second, *there has been a long-term increase in the demand for the services provided by government,* like more and better schooling, more extensive highways, more complete police and fire protection, and so forth. As incomes rise, people want more of these services. Third, **government transfer payments**—*payments in return for no products or services—have grown substantially.* For example, various types of welfare payments have increased markedly. (Another transfer payment, social security, increased from about $20 billion in 1965 to about $180 billion in 1984.) Since transfer payments do not entail any reallocation of resources from private to public goods, but a transfer of income from one private citizen or group to another, Figure 4.2 is, in some respects, an overstatement of the role of the public sector.

WHAT THE FEDERAL, STATE, AND LOCAL GOVERNMENTS SPEND MONEY ON

There are three levels of government in the United States—federal, state, and local. The state governments spend the least, while the federal government spends the most. This was not always the case. Before World War I, the local governments spent more than the federal government. In those days, the federal government did not maintain the large military establishment it does now, nor did it engage in the many programs in health, education, welfare, and other areas that it currently does. Figure 4.2 shows that federal spending is now a much larger percentage of the total than it was 40 years ago. Table 4.1 shows how the federal government spends its money. *About one-third of the federal expenditures goes for the defense and other items connected with international relations and national security. About one-half goes for social security, welfare (and other income security) programs, health, and education. The rest goes to support farm, transportation, housing, and other such programs, as well as to run Congress, the courts, and the executive branch of the federal government.*

What about the local and state governments? On what do they spend their money? Table 4.2 shows that *the biggest expenditure of the state and local governments is on schools.* After the end of World War II, these expenditures increased greatly because of the baby boom—the increase in number of school-age children. Traditionally, schools in the United States have been a responsibility of local governments—cities and towns. *State governments spend most of their money on education; welfare, old age, and unemployment benefits; and highways.* (Besides supporting education directly, they help localities to cover the costs of schooling.) In addition, the

Table 4.2

EXPENDITURES OF STATE AND LOCAL
GOVERNMENTS, UNITED STATES, 1983

Type of expenditure	Amount (billions of dollars)	Percent of total
Education	164	35
Highways	37	8
Public welfare	60	13
Other	205	44
Total	466	100

Source: Economic Report of the President,
1985.

Table 4.1

FEDERAL EXPENDITURES, FISCAL 1986

Purpose	Amount (billions of dollars)	Percent of total	Purpose	Amount (billions of dollars)	Percent of total
National defense	286	29	Transportation	26	3
International affairs	18	2	Community and regional development	7	1
Energy	5	1			
Veterans' benefits	27	3	Interest	143	15
General science, space, and technology	9	1	General government	5	1
			Income security	116	12
Agriculture	13	1	Administration of justice	5	1
Education, training, employment, and social services	29	3	General purpose fiscal assistance	3	b
Health	35	4	Social security and medicare	269	28
Natural resources and environment	12	1	Offsetting receipts	−37	−4
Commerce and housing credit	2	b	Total[a]	974	100

[a] Because of rounding errors, the figures may not sum to totals.
[b] Less than ½ of 1 percent.

Source: Economic Report of the President, 1985. These are estimates made in 1985.

local and state governments support hospitals, redevelopment programs, courts, and police and fire departments.

Changes in View of Government Responsibilities

We have already seen that government expenditures in the United States have grown considerably, both in absolute amount and as a percentage of our total output. This growth in government expenditures was part of a general trend in the United States toward a more extensive role of government in the economy. Two hundred years ago, there was considerable suspicion of government interference and meddling, freedom was the watchword, and governments were viewed as potential tyrants. In the nineteenth century, the United States prospered mightily under this *laissez-faire* system, but gradually—and not without considerable protest—the nation began to interpret the role of the government differently.

INCREASES IN GOVERNMENT ROLE

Responding to the dangers of noncompetitive markets, states were given the power to regulate public utilities and railroads. The Interstate Commerce Commission was established in 1887 to regulate railroads operating across state lines; and the Sherman Antitrust Act was passed in 1890 to curb monopoly and promote competition. To help control recurring business fluctuations and financial panics, banking and finance were regulated. In 1913, the Federal Reserve System was established as a central bank controlling the

About 29 percent of the federal budget goes for defense. Decisions concerning how much to spend on what kinds of weapons systems are enormously complex and involve a mixture of military, political, and economic considerations. To illustrate some of these considerations, take the case of the B-1 bomber. As early as 1954, the Air Force began to think about a replacement for the B-52 bomber, but both Presidents Kennedy and Johnson were not impressed with the need for it, since they felt that strategic missiles would be more efficient and accurate than a new manned bomber.

Nonetheless, the Air Force and its contractors did not give up on the idea of the new bomber, and even after President Carter blocked the production of such a bomber in 1977, they continued to push for it. Moreover, the Armed Services Committee of the House of Representatives approved more than $300 million for research and development on this airplane between 1977 and 1980. Within the Pentagon, a group of Air Force officers, led by General Kelly Burke, worked hard to make the bomber a reality. When the Reagan administration was elected in 1980, the political climate was much more favorable, and in January 1982 Congress voted approval of the B-1 program.

To help build political support for the B-1 program, Rockwell, the builder of the B-1, farmed out the airplane's production among thousands of subcontractors. For example, the prototype engines were built in Lynn, Massachusetts; the actuators were built in Kalamazoo, Michigan; and so on. Nearly every member of Congress had a firm in his or her district that had a stake in the B-1 program.

The B-1 program is likely to cost at least $20 billion. But the costs of weapons systems are often underestimated, since this makes it easier to sell them to Congress. For a long time, the B-1 systems program office at Wright-Patterson Air Force Base made two different cost estimates, according to one report. "One [estimate] showed what we'd said the B-1 would cost. The other showed what we really thought it would cost."*

Whether the B-1 will be an effective weapons system has been the subject of great controversy. Some argue that it will be slow, sluggish, and limited in range. Like the B-52, the B-1 would need mid-air refueling both going to and returning from the Soviet Union. According to some experts, it makes more sense to modernize the existing B-52 bombers until Stealth (a new bomber that is claimed to be more effective in avoiding enemy defenses than the B-1) comes along. In 1984, the first Stealth was tentatively scheduled to appear in 1991–92.

The amount of resources devoted to military programs of this sort is nothing less than mammoth. (In the case of the B-1, at least $20 billion will be spent for 100 airplanes!) Few people would question the need for a strong and effective national defense, but there is a widespread feeling that the weapons acquisition process is not as efficient as it might be. In August 1984, one of the first B-1 bombers crashed in the Mojave Desert, thus provoking more controversy concerning this already controversial military procurement program.

* "Is the B-1 a Plane Whose Time Has Come?" *Philadelphia Inquirer,* March 18, 1984.

member commercial banks. In 1933, the Federal Deposit Insurance Corporation was established to insure bank deposits. And in 1934, the Securities and Exchange Commission was established to watch over the financial markets.

In addition, the government's role in the fields of labor and welfare expanded considerably. For example, in the 1930s minimum-wage laws were enacted, old-age pensions and unemployment insurance were established, and the government became an important force in collective bargaining and labor relations. Furthermore, the power of government was used increasingly to ensure that citizens did not fall below a certain economic level. Food-stamp programs and programs to provide aid to dependent children were established. *In general, the broad trend in the United States in the century up to about 1975 or 1980 was for the government to be used to a greater and greater extent to achieve social objectives.*

RECENT CHANGES IN ATTITUDE

However, during the 1970s and early 1980s there was a pronounced change in the public's attitude toward the government. People seemed more inclined to question the government's capacity to solve the difficult social problems that confront our nation. In part, this seemed to be due to the apparent failure of large and expensive government programs initiated to solve a variety of social ills, such as poverty. In part, it seemed to reflect a general cynicism concerning government and politicians. One public-opinion poll after another showed that the public was irritated by the payment of what it regarded as excessively high taxes.

In 1978, California's voters supported Proposition 13 by nearly a 2-to-1 margin. Proposition 13 called for a 57 percent cut in the property tax and decreed that no local tax may increase by more than 2 percent per year. Californians were angry at the rapid increase in their property taxes during the 1970s. One Los Angeles family bought a house for $64,000 in 1968 and its property tax then was $1,800. By 1976, it had increased to $3,500, and without Proposition 13, it soon would have gone to $7,000. Californians supported Proposition 13 as a way to offset past increases and limit future increases in the property tax.

In the 1980 elections, Ronald Reagan won the presidency in part by promising to get government "off the backs" of citizens. In his first years in office, he cut back the rate of growth of federal expenditure and reduced many government programs. In 1984, he ran again on a platform that emphasized the reduction of government's role (but an increase in defense expenditure). Again he won. Certainly, the prevailing attitude was different than in the 1960s. How long this change in attitude will persist is hard to say, but while it lasts, conservatives tend to be happy and liberals tend to be concerned.

What the Federal, State, and Local Governments Receive in Taxes

To get the money to cover most of the expenditures discussed in previous sections, governments collect taxes from individuals and firms. As Table 4.3

Table 4.3

FEDERAL RECEIPTS BY TAX, FISCAL 1986

Type of tax	Amount (billions of dollars)	Percent of total
Personal income tax	359	45
Corporation income tax	74	9
Employment taxes	289	36
Excise taxes	35	4
Estate and gift taxes	5	1
Other revenues	31	4
Total[a]	794	100

[a] Because of rounding errors, the figures may not sum to totals.

Source: Economic Report of the President, 1985. These are estimates made in 1985.

FEDERAL, STATE, LOCAL GOV'T TAX
RECEIPTS

Table 4.4

STATE AND LOCAL TAX REVENUES, BY
SOURCE, 1983

Source	Revenues (billions of dollars)	Percent of total
General sales tax	100	25
Property tax	89	22
Personal income tax	55	14
Corporate income tax	14	4
Other taxes	138	35
Total[a]	396	100

[a] Because of rounding errors, the figures may not sum to the totals.

Source: Economic Report of the President, 1985.

shows, *at the federal level the* **personal income tax** *is the biggest single money raiser.* It brings in almost one-half of the tax revenue collected by the federal government. The next most important taxes at the federal level are the Social Security, payroll, and employment taxes. Other noteworthy taxes are the corporation income tax, excise taxes (levied on the sale of tobacco, liquor, imports, and certain other items), and death and gift taxes. (Even when the Grim Reaper shows up, the Tax Man is not far behind.)

At the local level, on the other hand, the most important form of taxation and source of revenue is the **property tax.** This is a tax levied primarily on real estate. Other important local taxes—although dwarfed in importance by the property tax—are local sales taxes and local income taxes. Many cities—for example, New York City—levy a sales tax, equal to a certain percent—4 percent in New York City—of the value of each retail sale. The tax is simply added on to the amount charged the customer. Also, many cities—for example, Philadelphia and Pittsburgh—levy an income (or wage) tax on their residents and even on people who work in the city but live outside it. *At the state level,* **sales (and excise) taxes** *are the biggest money raisers,* followed by income taxes and highway-user taxes. The latter include taxes on gasoline and license fees for vehicles and drivers. Often they exceed the amount spent on roads, and the balance is used for a variety of non-highway uses. (See Table 4.4.)

Although some people claim that taxes in the United States are higher than in most other industrialized countries, this really is not true. When we compare taxes in the United States (relative to total output) with those in other countries, we learn that the governments of Sweden, France, West Germany, and the United Kingdom tax more—as a percent of total output—than we do. In part, of course, this is because of the extensive welfare programs in Sweden and the United Kingdom. It is interesting, however, that, despite our huge military programs, our government does not tax and spend more (relative to total output) than these countries.

Test Yourself

1. "I believe the government should do only that which private citizens cannot do for themselves, or which they cannot do so well for themselves." Interpret and comment. Indicate how one might determine in practice what the legitimate functions of government are, according to this proposition.

2. "The ideal public policy, from the viewpoint of the state, is one with identifiable beneficiaries, each of whom is helped appreciably, at the cost of many unidentifiable persons, none of whom is hurt much."* Interpret and comment. Indicate how this proposition might be used to help predict government behavior.

3. Explain why national defense is a public good but a rifle is not a public good.

4. "I cannot get the amount of national defense I want and you, a different amount."** Explain. Is this true of all public goods?

5. According to the 1985 *Economic Report of the President,* the federal government will spend about $8.7 billion on general science, space, and technology in fiscal 1985. Why should the government support each of these activities?

* G. Stigler, "The Government of the Economy," in E. Mansfield, *Principles of Macroeconomics: Readings, Issues, and Cases.*

** M. Friedman, *Capitalism and Freedom.*

The Role of Government in American Agriculture

Thus far, we have been discussing the government's role in the American economy in rather general terms. Now we need to consider in some detail a particular example of the economic programs carried out by our government. The government's farm programs are a logical choice, because they illustrate the usefulness of the supply-and-demand analysis presented in the previous chapter. It is important to recognize at the outset that these farm programs are not being held up as a representative sample of what the government does. There are a host of other government economic programs—poverty programs, urban programs, defense programs, research programs, education programs, transportation programs, fiscal programs, monetary programs, and many more. Most of these programs will be discussed at some point in this book.

Agriculture is an enormously important sector of the American economy. Even though its size has been decreasing steadily—and this contraction has been going on for many decades—agriculture still employs about 3 million Americans. Its importance, moreover, cannot be measured entirely by its size. You need only think about how difficult it would be to get along without food to see the strategic role agriculture plays in our economic life. Also, when it comes to technological change, agriculture is one of the most progressive parts of the American economy. The efficiency of American agriculture is admired throughout the world.

The Farm Problem

Nonetheless, it is widely acknowledged that American agriculture has had serious problems. Perhaps the clearest indication of these problems is shown by a comparison of per capita income of American farmers with per capita income among the rest of the population. Until the past ten years, it is clear that farm incomes have tended to be much lower than nonfarm incomes. In 1970, per capita income on the farms was about 20 percent below that for the nonfarm population. Moreover, a large proportion of the rural population is poor. Thus the National Advisory Commission on Rural Poverty found that "rural poverty is so widespread, and so acute, as to be a national disgrace."[4] Of course, this does not mean that all farmers are poor: on the contrary, many do very well indeed. But a large percentage of the nation's farmers are poor by any standard.

This farm problem is nothing new. During the first two decades of the twentieth century, farmers enjoyed relatively high prices and relatively high incomes. But in 1920, the country experienced a sharp depression that jolted agriculture as well as the rest of the economy. Whereas the Roaring Twenties saw a recovery and boom in the nonfarm sector of the economy, agriculture did not recover as completely, and the 1930s were dreadful years; the Great Depression resulted in a sickening decline in farm prices and farm incomes. World War II brought prosperity to agriculture, but in

[4] National Advisory Committee on Rural Poverty, *The People Left Behind*, Washington, D.C., 1967.

the postwar period, farm incomes continually have been well below non-farm incomes. In 1973 to 1975, prosperity returned to the farms, but the late 1970s and 1980s saw renewed complaints by farmers about prices and incomes. All in all, agriculture has had difficulties for several decades.

CAUSES OF THE FARM PROBLEM

In Chapter 1, we claimed that relatively simple economic models are of considerable use in understanding important public and private problems. To back up this claim, we will apply the simple models of market behavior presented in the previous chapter—the models involving market demand curves and market supply curves—to explain the basic causes of the problems that have tended to besiege agriculture.

Characteristics of Demand and Supply. Let's start with the market demand curve for farm products. If you think about it for a moment, you will agree that this market demand curve must have two important characteristics. First, *its shape must reflect the fact that food is a necessity and that the quantity demanded will not vary much with the price of food.* Second, *the market demand curve for food is unlikely to shift to the right very much as per capita income rises,* because consumption of food per capita faces natural biological and other limitations.

Next, consider the market supply curve for farm products. Again, you should be aware of two important characteristics of this market supply curve. First, *the quantity of farm products supplied tends to be relatively insensitive to price,* because the farmers have only limited control over their output. (Weather, floods, insects, and other such factors are very important.) Second, because of the rapid technological change emphasized in a previous section, *the market supply curve has been shifting markedly and rapidly to the right.*

Decline in Relative Food Prices. If you understand these simple characteristics of the market demand curve and market supply curve for farm products, it is no trick at all to understand why we have had the sort of farm problem just described. Figure 4.3 shows the market demand and market supply curves for farm products at various points in time. As you would expect, the market demand curve for farm products shifts rather slowly to the right as incomes (and population) grow over time. Specifically, the market demand curve shifted from D in the first period to D_1 in the second period to D_2 in the third period. On the other hand, the market supply curve for farm products shifted rapidly to the right as technology improved over time. Specifically, it shifted from S in the first period to S_1 in the second period to S_2 in the third period.

What was the consequence of these shifts in the market demand and supply curves for food products? Clearly, *the equilibrium price of food products fell (relative to other products).* Specifically, the equilibrium price fell from OP to OP_1 to OP_2 in Figure 4.3. This price decrease was, of course, a large part of the farm problem. If we correct for changes in the general level of prices (which have tended to rise over time), there was, in general, a declining trend in farm prices. That is, agricultural prices generally fell, relative to other prices, in the last 60 years. Moreover, *given this fall in farm prices, farm incomes tended to fall, because, although lower prices were as-*

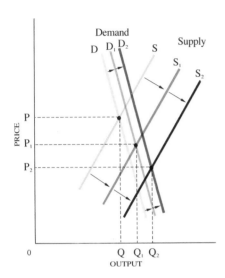

Figure 4.3

**Shifts over Time in Market Demand and
Supply Curves for Farm Products** *The
market demand curve has shifted rather
slowly to the right (from D to D₁ to D₂),
whereas the market supply curve has
shifted rapidly to the right (from S to S₁
to S₂), with the result that the equilibrium
price has declined (from OP to OP₁ to
OP₂).*

sociated with greater amounts sold, the reduction was much greater
than the increase in quantity sold, as shown in Figure 4.3.[5]

Thus the simple model of market behavior described in the previous
chapter makes it possible to explain the fact that, in real terms, farm prices
and farm incomes have tended to fall in the United States. Certainly there is
nothing mysterious about these trends. Given the nature and characteristics
of the market demand curve and market supply curve for farm products,
our simple model shows that these trends are as much to be expected as
parades on the Fourth of July.

SLOW EXIT OF RESOURCES

However, one additional fact must be noted to understand the farm problem: *people and nonhuman resources have been relatively slow to move out
of agriculture in response to these trends.* Recall from the previous chapter
that the price system uses such trends—lower prices and lower incomes—to
signal producers that they should use their resources elsewhere. Farmers
have been loath to move out of agriculture (even though they often could
make more money elsewhere)—and this has been a primary cause of the
farm problem that has existed over most of the past 40 years. If more people and resources had left farming, agricultural prices and incomes would
have risen, and ultimately farm incomes would have come closer to nonfarm incomes. (Poor education and color were, of course, significant barriers to migration.)

Nonetheless, even though farmers have been slow to move out of agriculture, they have left the farm in the long run. In 1930 the farm population
was about 30 million, or 25 percent of the total population; in 1950, it was
about 23 million, or 15 percent of the total population; and in 1983, it was
about 6 million, or 3 percent of the total population. Thus the price system
has had its way. Resources have been moving out of agriculture in response
to the signals and pressures of the price system. This movement of people
and nonhuman resources unquestionably has contributed to greater efficiency and production for the nation as a whole. But during most of the
past 40 years, we have continued to have a "surplus" of farmers—and this
has been the root of the farm problem.

Government Aid to Agriculture

Traditionally, farmers have had a disproportionately large influence in
Congress; and faced with declining economic fortunes, they appealed to
the government for help. They extolled the virtues of rural life, emphasized that agriculture is a competitive industry, and claimed that it was
unfair for their prices to fall relative to the prices they have had to pay. In
addition, they pointed out that the movement of resources out of agriculture has entailed large human costs, since this movement, although bene-

---

[5] The amount farmers receive is the amount they sell times the price. Thus, in Figure 4.3, the
amount farmers receive in income is $OP \times OQ$ in the first period, $OP_1 \times OQ_1$ in the second
period, and $OP_2 \times OQ_2$ in the third period. Clearly, since the price is decreasing much more
rapidly than the quantity is increasing, farm incomes are falling.

ficial to the nation as a whole, has been traumatic for the farm population. For reasons of this sort, they argued that the government should help farmers; and in particular, that the government should act to bolster farm prices and farm incomes.

THE CONCEPT OF PARITY

Their voices were heard. In the Agricultural Adjustment Act of 1933, the Congress announced the concept of parity as the major objective of American farm policy. This concept acquired great importance—and must be clearly understood. Put in its simplest terms, the concept of *parity* says that a farmer should be able to exchange a given quantity of his output for as much in the way of nonfarm goods and services as he could at some time in the past. For example, if a farmer could take a bushel of wheat to market in 1912 and get enough money to buy a pair of gloves, today he should be able to get enough money for a bushel of wheat to buy a pair of gloves.

To see what the concept of parity implies for farm prices, suppose that the price of gloves triples. Obviously, if parity is to be maintained, the price of wheat must triple too. Thus the concept of parity implies that farm prices must increase at the same rate as the prices of the goods and services farmers buy. Of course, farmers buy lots of things besides gloves, so in actual practice the parity price of wheat or other farm products is determined by the changes over time in the average price of all the goods and services farmers buy.

Two major points should be noted about parity. First, to use this concept, one must agree on some base period, such as 1912 in the example above, during which the relationship of farm to nonfarm prices is regarded as equitable. Obviously, the higher farm prices were relative to nonfarm prices in the base period, the higher farm prices will be in subsequent periods if parity is maintained. It is interesting to note that 1910-14 was used for many years as the base period. Since this was a period of relatively high farm prices and of agricultural prosperity, the farm bloc must have wielded considerable political clout on this issue. Second, note that the concept of parity is an ethical, not a scientific proposition. It states what the relative economic position of a bushel of wheat ought to be—or more precisely, it states one particular view of what the relative economic position of a bushel of wheat should be. Based on purely scientific considerations, there is no way to prove (or disprove) this proposition, since it is based on one's values and political preferences. Using the terminology of Chapter 1, it is a proposition in normative, not positive economics.

Price Supports and Surplus Controls

During the four decades up to 1973, the concept of parity was the cornerstone of a system of government price supports. In many cases, the government did not support farm prices at the full 100 percent of parity. For example, Congress may have enacted a bill saying that the secretary of agriculture could establish a price of wheat, corn, cotton, or some other

Figure 4.4

Effects of Farm Price-Support Program
The support price, OP′, *is above the equilibrium price,* OP, *so the public buys* OQ₂, *farmers supply* OQ₁ *units of output, and the government buys the difference* (OQ₁ − OQ₂).

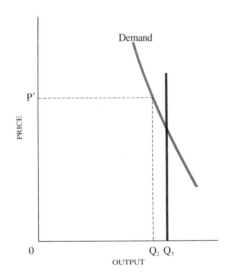

Figure 4.5

Effects of Price Supports and Output Restrictions *The government restricts output to* OQ₃, *with the result that it buys* (OQ₃ − OQ₂) *units of output.*

product that is between 65 and 90 percent of parity. But whatever the exact level of the price supports, the idea behind them was perfectly simple: it was to maintain farm prices above the level that would result in a free market.

Using the simple supply-and-demand model developed in the previous chapter, we can see more clearly the effects of these price supports. The situation is shown in Figure 4.4. A support price, OP', was set by the government. Since this support price was above the equilibrium price, OP, the public bought *less* of farm products (OQ_2 rather than OQ) and paid a *higher* price for them. Farmers gained from the price supports, since the amount they received for their crop under the price support was equal to $OP' \times OQ_1$, a greater amount than what they would have received in a free market, which was $OP \times OQ$.

Note, however, that since the support price exceeded the equilibrium price, the quantity supplied of the farm product, OQ_1, exceeded the quantity demanded, OQ_2. That is, *there was a surplus of the farm product in question,* which the government had to purchase, since no one else would. These surpluses were an embarrassment, both economically and politically. They showed that society's scarce resources were being utilized to produce products consumers simply did not want at existing prices. Moreover the cost of storing these surpluses was very large indeed: in some years, these storage costs alone hit the $1-billion mark.

POLICIES TO CUT SURPLUSES

To help reduce these surpluses, the government followed two basic strategies. First, *it tried to restrict output of farm products.* In particular, the government established an acreage allotment program, which said that farmers had to limit the number of acres they planted in order to get price supports on their crops. The Department of Agriculture estimated how much of each product would be demanded by buyers (other than the government) at the support price, and tried to cut back the total acreage planted with this crop to the point where the quantity supplied equaled the quantity demanded. These output restrictions did not eliminate the surpluses, because farmers managed to increase the yields from acreage they were allowed to plant, but undoubtedly they reduced the surpluses. With these restrictions, the situation was as shown in Figure 4.5, where OQ_3 was the total output that could be grown on the acreage that could be planted with the crop. Because of the imposition of this output control, the surplus—which the government had to purchase—was reduced from $(OQ_1 - OQ_2)$ to $(OQ_3 - OQ_2)$. Farmers continued to benefit from price supports because the amount they received for their crop—$OP' \times OQ_3$—was still greater than they would have received in a free market, because the amount demanded of farm products was not very sensitive to their price.

Second, *the government tried to shift the demand curve for farm products to the right.* An effort was made to find new uses for various farm products. Also, various antipoverty programs, such as the food-stamp program, used our farm surpluses to help the poor. In addition, the government tried to expand the export markets for American farm products. Western Europe

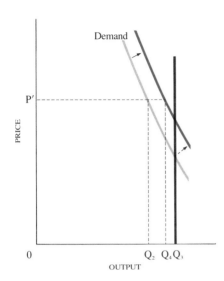

Figure 4.6

Effects of Price Supports, Output Restrictions, and a Shift to the Right in the Demand Curve for Farm Products

By shifting the demand curve to the right, the government reduces the surplus from (OQ₃ − OQ₂) to (OQ₃ − OQ₄) units of output.

and Japan increased their demand for food, and the Communist countries purchased our farm products to offset their own agricultural deficiencies. Moreover, the less developed countries were permitted by Public Law 480 to buy our farm products with their own currencies, rather than dollars. The result was a reduction in farm surpluses, as shown in Figure 4.6. Since the market demand curve for farm products shifted to the right, the surplus was reduced from *(OQ₃ − OQ₂)* to *(OQ₃ − OQ₄)*. Because of these demand-augmenting and output-restricting measures, surpluses during the late 1960s and early 1970s were considerably smaller than they were during the late 1950s and early 1960s.

The 1973 Farm Bill and More Recent Developments

In 1973, farm prices increased markedly, due partly to very great increases in foreign demand for American agricultural products. This increase in foreign demand was due partly to poor harvests in the Soviet Union, Australia, Argentina, and elsewhere, as well as to devaluations of the dollar. (In 1972–73, the Soviet Union alone bought over $1 billion of grain—on terms that provoked considerable controversy in the United States.) As a result, farm incomes reached very high levels, farm surpluses disappeared, and for the first time in 30 years the government was trying to stimulate farm production rather than restrict it.

THE 1973 BILL

Taking advantage of this new climate, Congress passed a new farm bill which ended price supports. This bill, the Agriculture and Consumer Protection Act of 1973, aimed at reducing government involvement in agriculture and at a return to freer markets. Specifically, agricultural prices were allowed to fluctuate freely in accord with supply and demand. However, the government made cash payments to farmers if prices fell below certain "target" levels established by the law. These target levels were above the prices that generally prevailed in the past, but they were below the high levels of prices prevailing in 1973.

Besides establishing these new forms of subsidies, the 1973 farm bill limited total subsidy payments to any individual farmer to $20,000 per year. This provision was meant to deal more effectively than did the prior law with the problem of very large subsidies being paid to wealthy farmers. Also, the 1973 law stated that whether or not land is taken out of production is at the discretion of the secretary of agriculture. In 1974, Secretary Earl Butz said that none should be taken out of production, and encouraged farmers to produce as much as they wanted. Nonetheless, in 1974, American crop production as a whole suffered its biggest setback in almost 40 years, due primarily to bad weather. Coupled with continued strong foreign demand for farm products, as well as domestic demand, the result was another year of high farm prices.

CHANGES IN GOVERNMENT INVOLVEMENT

By 1975 it appeared to many knowledgeable observers that the farm sector no longer was suffering from overcapacity, and that, in this respect at least, an equilibrium had been achieved. However, this attitude did not last long. During 1976 and 1977 U.S. farmers harvested bumper crops, with the result that prices fell considerably. The price of wheat, which had been about $3.50 per bushel in 1975, fell to about $2.30 per bushel in 1977. Farmers protested, and exerted political pressure for increased government price and income supports.

In 1977 Congress passed the Food and Agricultural Act, which contained flexible price-support levels and income supports. And in the late 1970s Secretary of Agriculture Bob Bergland said that a substantial amount of farmland had to be taken out of production. No longer was there much talk about a return to freer markets. Instead, the emphasis seemed to be on more support for farm prices and incomes.

In 1983 the Reagan administration adopted the $9 billion payment-in-kind program (PIK) in response to large grain harvests—the idea being to pay farmers for idling acreage by giving them crops stored by the government. Although this program was supposed to hold down government cash payments, expenditures soared to about $19 billion. Faced with huge government deficits, the Reagan administration announced in 1985 that it would try to persuade Congress to slash farm subsidy programs. However, many congressmen and senators (particularly from farm states) were skeptical about the chances that such a dramatic policy shift would be adopted.

Indeed, in late 1985, the trend seemed to be in the other direction. A substantial number of farmers were reported to be unable to pay their debts, and farm groups (and banks) were pressing for government help. Congress passed a bill calling for about $169 billion in spending over five years.

Evaluation of Government Farm Programs

It is obviously hard to evaluate the success of the government's farm programs. Farmers will certainly take a different view of price supports and other measures than their city cousins. Nonetheless, from the point of view of the nation as a whole, these farm programs have received considerable criticism. To understand these criticisms, we must hark back to our discussion earlier in this chapter of the proper functions of government, and ask what justification there is for the government's intervening in this way in agriculture. Perhaps the most convincing justification is that the government ought to help the rural poor. As we saw in previous sections, most people agree that the government should redistribute income in this way.

Have the Poor Been Helped? Unfortunately, however, *our farm programs have done little for the farmers most in need of help,* because the amount of money a farmer has gotten from these programs has depended on how much he produced. Thus the big farmers have gotten the lion's share of the subsidies—and they, of course, needed help least. On the other hand, the small farmers, the farmers who are mired mostly deeply in poverty, have received little from these programs. Recognizing this fact, many observers have pointed out that, if these programs are really aimed at helping the rural poor, it would be more sensible to channel the money to them through direct subsidies, than to finance programs where much of the benefits goes to prosperous commercial farmers.

Has the Farm Problem Been Solved? It must also be recognized that *our farm programs have not dealt with the basic causes of the farm problem.* In the past at least, we have had too many people and resources in agriculture. This, as we stressed in previous sections, is why farmers' incomes have tended to be low. Yet the government's farm programs have been directed more toward supporting farm prices and incomes (and stabilizing a sector of the economy that historically has been unstable), rather than toward promoting the needed movement of people and resources out of agriculture. Indeed, some people would say that the government's farm programs have made it more difficult for the necessary adjustments to take place.

Given these defects, many proposals have been made to alter our farm programs. In the view of many observers, agriculture should return to something more closely approximating free markets, and the price system should be allowed to work more freely. The changes that occurred in 1973 were in that direction, but it is important to note that the government is still intervening heavily in agriculture.

A BASIC MORAL

Basic Idea #8: Just because the price system has well-known limitations, it does not follow that the task of organizing the nation's economic activities should be turned over to the government. As illustrated by our agricultural policies, the government has limitations of its own. Neither the price system nor the government is a panacea.

Finally, before closing this chapter, we must point out a fundamental moral of our farm programs:

The government, like the price system, can bungle the job of organizing a nation's economic activities. We began this chapter by stressing the fact that the price system breaks down under some circumstances, and that the government must intervene. It is also worth stressing that the government sometimes intervenes when it shouldn't—and that even when it should intervene, it sometimes does so in a way that wastes resources. This, of course, doesn't mean that the government should play no part in the American economy. On the contrary, the government must—and does—play an important role. What it does mean is that, just as the price system is no all-purpose cure-all, neither is the government.

Test Yourself

1. Suppose that the demand and supply curves for paper are as shown on the right. If paper production results in serious pollution of rivers and streams, is the socially optimal output of paper less than, greater than, or equal to *OQ*? Does the supply curve reflecting the true social costs of producing paper lie to the right or to the left of the supply curve shown on the right? Why?

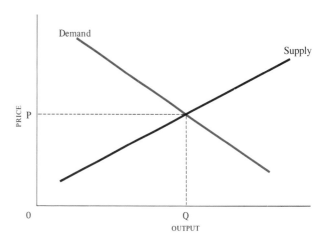

2. Suppose that paper production results in some important uncompensated benefits to other industries. If there are major external economies of this sort (and if paper production no longer results in any pollution), is the socially optimal output of paper less than, greater than, or equal to OQ in Question 1? Does the demand curve reflecting the true social benefits from paper output lie to the right or to the left of the demand curve shown in Question 1? Why?

3. Explain the nature of America's farm problem. To what extent have government policies solved the problem?

4. Suppose that the demand curve for corn is as follows:

Price (dollars per bushel)	Quantity demanded per year (millions of bushels)
1	70
2	65
3	60
4	55
5	50
6	45

If the government supports the price of corn at $4 per bushel, and if it restricts output to 60 million bushels per year, how much corn will the government have to buy each year? If the government stopped supporting the price of corn, what would its price be?

5. On August 8, 1982, David Stockman, director of President Reagan's Office of Management and Budget, wrote that, "There is ... [an] asymmetry between powerful and persuasive interest groups on the one hand and the general taxpayer on the other. For example, dairy subsidies are $7,000 per dairy producer but the individual taxpayer pays only about $18 a year for dairy subsidies." Explain how such an asymmetry can result in high levels of government spending.

6. "The sharp increases in the price of wheat during the mid-1970s were due primarily to shifts in the supply curve for wheat." Comment.

Summary

1. The price system, despite its many virtues, suffers from serious limitations. There is no reason to believe that the distribution of income generated by the price system is equitable or optimal. Also, there is no way for the price system to handle public goods properly, and because of external economies or diseconomies, the price system may result in too little or too much of certain goods being produced.

2. To a considerable extent, the government's role in the economy has developed in response to these limitations of the price system. There is considerable agreement that the government should redistribute income in favor of the poor, provide public goods, and offset the effects of external economies and diseconomies. Also, it is generally felt that the government should establish a proper legal, social and competitive framework for the price system, and that it should promote the maintenance of relatively full employment with reasonably stable prices.

3. Beyond this, however, there are wide differences of opinion on the proper role of government in economic affairs. Conservatives tend to be suspicious of "big government" while liberals are inclined to believe that the government should do more.

4. In the past 50 years, government spending has increased considerably, both in absolute terms and as a percent of total output. (It is now about one-third of our total output.) To a large extent, this increase has been due to our greater military responsibilities, as well as to the fact that, as their incomes have risen, our citizens have demanded more schools, highways, and other goods and services provided by government. Also, government transfer payments have grown substantially.

5. To get the money to cover most of these expenditures, governments collect taxes from individuals and firms. At the federal level, the most important form of taxation is the personal income tax; at the local level, the property tax is very important; and at the state level, sales (and excise) taxes are the biggest money raisers.

6. One example of the role of government in the American economy is the farm program. American agriculture has been plagued by relatively low incomes. In general, the demand for farm products grew slowly, while rapid technological change meant that the people and resources currently in agriculture could supply more and more farm products. Because people and resources did not move out of agriculture as rapidly as the price system dictated, farm incomes tended to be relatively low.

7. In response to political pressures from the farm blocs, the government set in motion a series of programs to aid farmers. A cornerstone of these programs was the concept of parity, which said that the prices farmers receive should increase at the same rate as the prices of the goods and services farmers buy. The government instituted price supports to keep farm prices above their equilibrium level. But since the support prices exceeded the equilibrium prices, there was a surplus of the commodities that the government had to purchase and store. To help reduce these surpluses, the government tried to restrict the output of farm products and expand the demand for them.

8. These farm programs received considerable criticism. From the point of view of income redistribution, they suffered from the fact that they did little for the farmers most in need of help. As tools of resource allocation, they suffered because they dealt more with the symptoms of the farm problem than with its basic causes. In 1973, price supports were ended, but the government pledged to make cash payments to farmers if farm prices fall below certain target levels. During the late 1970s and 1980s, the government continued to intervene heavily in agriculture.

9. The government's farm programs illustrate the fact that government intervention, like the price system, has plenty of limitations. Neither the price system nor government intervention is an all-purpose cure-all.

Concepts for Review

Public goods	**Welfare payments**	**Property tax**
External economy	**Transfer payments**	**Sales tax**
External diseconomy	**Personal income tax**	**Parity**
Antitrust laws		

CHAPTER 5

Government Expenditures, Taxation, and the Public Debt

The government plays an extremely important role in the American economy. It is obvious that it influences our economic lives and fortunes in countless ways. At this point, we must look in detail at how decisions are made concerning the level and distribution of government expenditures. Also, we must describe the theory of public choice. These topics are of central importance in understanding the public sector of our economy.

In addition, we must discuss the principles of taxation, as well as the characteristics of the major taxes used to support government activities in the United States. Further, we must describe in some detail the nature, size, and burden of the public debt, a subject that has been surrounded by as many myths as any in economics.

Government Expenditures

Determining how much the federal government should spend is a mammoth undertaking, involving literally thousands of people and hundreds of thousands of man-hours. Decisions on expenditures are part of the budgetary process. The **budget** is a statement of the government's anticipated expenditures and revenues. The federal budget is for a fiscal year, from October 1 to September 30. About 15 months before the beginning of a particular fiscal year, the various agencies of the federal government begin to prepare their program proposals for that year. Then they make detailed budget requests which the president, with his Office of Management and Budget, goes over. Since the agencies generally want more than the president wants to spend, he usually cuts down their requests.

In January (preceding the beginning of the fiscal year), the president submits his budget to Congress, which then spends several months in intensive deliberation and negotiation. Congressional committees concerned with particular areas like defense or education recommend changes in the president's budget. The Congressional Budget Office, headed in 1985 by Rudolph Penner (formerly an economist at the American Enterprise Institute), makes various types of economic analyses to help senators and representatives evaluate alternative programs. By mid-May, Congress is supposed to pass a resolution setting tentative targets for overall spending and revenues; this resolution is based on the joint recommendations by the House and Senate Budget Committees. The targets in the resolution are to be kept in mind by the various congressional committees dealing with specific spending or tax actions. If these actions add up to bigger totals than the resolution called for, the budget committees and Congress are supposed to decide how the discrepancies are to be reconciled: by changes in expenditures, taxes, or initial targets. Before late September, Congress is supposed to adopt a second resolution, setting final ceilings for overall expenditure and a floor on revenues.

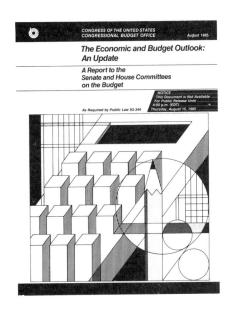

CONGRESS OF THE UNITED STATES
CONGRESSIONAL BUDGET OFFICE   August 1985

**The Economic and Budget Outlook:
An Update**

A Report to the
Senate and House Committees
on the Budget

As Required by Public Law 93-344

NOTICE
This Document is Not Available
For Public Release Until
4:00 p.m. (EDT)
Thursday, August 15, 1985

Benefit-Cost Analysis

How much should the government spend on various activities and services? Basically, the answer must be provided by the nation's political processes. For example, with regard to the provision of public goods

> voting by ballot must be resorted to in place of dollar voting. . . . Decision making by voting becomes a substitute for preference revelation through the market. The results will not please everybody, but they will approximate—more or less perfectly, depending on the efficiency of the voting process and the homogeneity of preferences—the community's preferences.[1]

Basic Idea #9: A particular government program is worthwhile if the benefits from the program exceed its costs. To see whether the program should be expanded or contracted, compare the extra benefit from the change in the program's scope to the extra cost. Although it may be difficult to obtain precise measures of benefit and cost, an analysis of this sort frequently is illuminating.

Under certain circumstances, particular types of economic analysis can prove helpful to the policy makers and citizens who must determine how much the government should spend on various programs. Let's begin by supposing that we can measure the benefits and costs of each such program. What is the optimal amount to spend on each one? The answer, clearly enough, is that *spending on the program should be pushed to the point where the extra benefit from an extra dollar spent is at least equal to the dollar of cost.* This would ensure that the amount spent on each government program yields a benefit at least as great as the value of output forgone in the private sector. This would also make sure that one government program is not being expanded at the expense of other programs that would yield greater benefits if they were expanded instead.

The principle that extra benefit should be compared with extra cost is valuable—and, as we shall see in the next section, widely applicable—but it can solve only a small part of the problem of allocating resources in the public sector. Why? Because it is impossible to measure the benefits from

---

[1] Richard and Peggy Musgrave, *Public Finance in Theory and Practice,* New York: McGraw-Hill, 1973, p. 8.

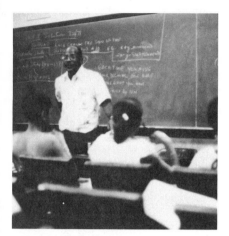

*"Project Double Discovery" class
sponsored through Upward Bound*

Table 5.1

BENEFIT-COST ANALYSIS FOR
CONSTRUCTING A DAM

Alternative policies	Annual cost (dollars)	Annual benefit (dollars)
Build a low dam	600,000	650,000
Build a high dam	750,000	850,000

defense or police protection or the courts in dollars and cents. Only in certain cases can benefits be quantified at all precisely. And it is not only a question of the amount of the benefits and costs; it is also a question of who benefits and who pays. Nonetheless, it is difficult to see how rational choices can be made without paying attention to costs and benefits—even if they are measured imprecisely, and are by no means the whole story.

UPWARD BOUND: A CASE STUDY[2]

Despite the difficulties involved, in recent years more and more benefit-cost analyses have been carried out to help guide public policy. For example, consider the following study, by the Greenleigh Associates, of Upward Bound, a U.S. Office of Economic Opportunity program begun in the 1960s to select and give underprivileged young people a special college preparatory education. The study surveyed over 7,000 people who entered the Upward Bound program in 1966 to 1968. It tried to estimate the costs and benefits from the program.

On the average, the cost per person in the program was determined to be about $3,400. To estimate the benefits, each person in the program was compared with his or her older sibling with respect to earnings in the years subsequent to the program. In other words, the older siblings were viewed as a "control" group that could be used to indicate how much a person would have made if he or she had not taken part in the program. Based on such a comparison, it appeared that the benefits to society were about $7,000 per person in the program. That is, the extra earnings of such a person—used as an estimate of the value of the extra output he or she produced due to the program—was estimated to be about $7,000.

Since the benefits exceeded the costs, it appeared that the program was worthwhile. Of course, there are many difficulties in this and other such analyses, and they should be viewed with caution. Nonetheless, this study is an interesting example of a benefit-cost analysis.

OTHER EXAMPLES

Benefit-cost analyses have proved useful in many areas of government. In particular, they have been used for many years in the Department of Defense. Decisions to develop one weapons system rather than another, or to procure a certain amount of a given weapon, have been based in part on such studies. Other areas where benefit-cost analyses have been used extensively are water projects (irrigation, flood control, hydroelectric, and other projects), transportation projects, and urban renewal, recreation, and health projects. For example, in water projects, benefit-cost analysis has frequently been used by the Corps of Engineers and others to determine whether it is worthwhile to spend additional money on flood control, and if so, how much extra expenditure is justified.

A highly simplified example of a benefit-cost analysis of the construction of a dam is shown in Table 5.1. The alternative policies are to build a low dam or a high dam. Table 5.1 shows the annual costs and benefits associated with each of these policies. Clearly, the high dam should be

[2] This section is based on E. Gramlich, *Benefit-Cost Analysis of Government Programs,* Englewood Cliffs, N.J.: Prentice-Hall, 1981, pp. 162–65. The figures pertain to white males.

built because the extra cost involved ($150,000 more than for the low dam) is more than outweighed by the extra benefits received ($200,000 more than for the low dam). Note, however, that this is a very simple case. In general, data on costs and benefits are not laid out so straightforwardly. Instead, there are very wide bands of uncertainty about the relevant costs and benefits.

Scope and Efficiency of Government Activities

It is not easy to decide how large government expenditures should be. As we saw in Chapter 4, opinions differ widely on the proper role of government in economic affairs, and it is often impossible to measure the costs and benefits of government programs with dependable accuracy. Thus economists differ considerably in their opinions concerning the optimal size of government expenditures. Some, like Harvard's John Kenneth Galbraith, believe that the public sector of the economy has been deprived of needed resources, whereas the private sector has catered to relatively unimportant wants. Others, like Stanford's Milton Friedman, believe that government spending is far too large, and that it should be trimmed greatly.

To a considerable extent, this argument is over the proper *scope* of government. To see what we mean, assume that we can divide all goods into publicly provided goods and privately provided goods, and that Figure 5.1 shows the society's production possibilities curve. In other words, as you recall from Chapter 2, Figure 5.1 shows the maximum amount of publicly provided goods that can be produced, given each quantity produced of privately provided goods. What Galbraith and Friedman (among others) disagree about is the point that society should choose on the production possibilities curve. Should society choose point *A* (where more publicly provided goods and less privately provided goods are produced) or point *B* (where less publicly provided goods and more privately provided goods are produced)? Galbraith would be likely to choose point *A;* Friedman would be likely to choose point *B*.

But there is another important question: How can we attain a point *on* the production possibilities curve, rather than one (like point *C*) that is *inside* it? As we know from Chapter 2, inefficiency will result in society's being on a point inside the production possibilities curve. Thus, to attain a point on the production possibilities curve, government officials (and others) must do their best to eliminate inefficiency. By doing so, society can get more from the available resources. For example, it can attain points *A* or *B* rather than point *C*. Whether society wants to use its added efficiency to attain point *A* or point *B* is then a political question. However, regardless of how this question is decided, society is better off to eliminate inefficiency.

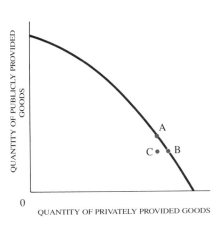

Figure 5.1

Production Possibilities Curve, Publicly Provided and Privately Provided Goods

At point B, *society produces less publicly provided goods and more privately provided goods than at point* A. *Thus a movement from point* A *to point* B *reduces government expenditures by reducing the* scope *of government services. At point* C, *society is producing inefficiently, and a movement from point* C *to point* B *or point* A *can be attained by increasing the* efficiency *of government (and/or private) operations.*

The Theory of Public Choice

According to many economists interested in the theory of public choice, there are a variety of factors that induce the government to make decisions that are not efficient from an economic point of view. Thus, just as the price system suffers from the limitations cited in Chapter 4, so the government has shortcomings as a mechanism for promoting economic welfare. These factors, discussed below, often result in expanded government expenditures.

SPECIAL-INTEREST GROUPS

It is no secret that politicians try to stay in office. In some cases, they must decide whether or not to adopt a policy which benefits a small number of people each of whom will gain a great deal at the expense of a very large number of people each of whom will lose very little. The small group of gainers (the special-interest group) is likely to be well organized, well financed, and vocal. The large group of losers is likely to be unaware of its losses and indifferent to the outcome of this decision, since each member of this group has little at stake. In a case of this sort, a politician will be inclined to adopt the policy favoring the special-interest group. Why? Because the politician, if he or she does not adopt this policy, will lose the support of this group. On the other hand, by adopting this policy, the politician is unlikely to lose the support of the large group of people that are hurt by it because they are much more interested in other issues where they have more at stake.

There are many cases where politicians have adopted policies favoring special-interest groups, even though the total gains to the special-interest group are less than the total losses to other segments of society. Whereas such policies are unsound economics, they have been regarded as good politics. One example is the enactment of tariffs and quotas that reduce domestic competition and result in consumers' paying higher prices. According to many observers, another example is the farm programs described in Chapter 4. Government services that benefit special-interest groups often are expanded, to the detriment of society at large.

BUREAUCRATIC INEFFICIENCY

Many observers contend that government agencies are less efficient than private firms. As we have seen in previous chapters, the price system establishes strong incentives for firms to minimize their costs. If firms can lower their costs, they can increase their profits, at least temporarily. Government officials, on the other hand, often have less incentive to reduce costs. Indeed, it is sometimes claimed that there is an incentive to increase costs since an agency's power and influence is directly related to the size of its budget. Unfortunately, we do not have a great deal of evidence concerning whatever differences exist between the efficiency of government agencies and of private firms, due largely to the difficulties in measuring the efficiency or inefficiency of government agencies. For example, how efficient is the Environmental Protection Agency? Because it is so difficult to measure EPA's output, and because it is so difficult to find a standard against which to measure its performance, this question is exceedingly difficult to answer.

One area where there has been evidence of inefficiency has been the development and production of new weapons by the Department of Defense and its contractors. There have been spectacular overruns in development and production costs. For example, the cost of the Lockheed C5A transport plane increased from the $3.4 billion estimated in 1965 to $5.3 billion in 1968. To some extent, such cost increases reflect the fact that new weapons systems tend to push the state of the art, so that unexpected problems must be expected. But, in addition, the firms that develop and produce these weapons systems often submit unrealistically low bids to get a contract, knowing that they are likely to get approval for cost increases later on. According to some observers, like Merton J. Peck of Yale University and F. M. Scherer of Swarthmore College, these cost overruns have also been due to "inadequate attention to the efficient utilization of technical, production, and administrative manpower—areas in which major cost reductions are possible."[3]

NONSELECTIVITY

Another point made by public choice theorists is that, when citizens vote for their elected officials, they vote for a "bundle" of political programs. For example, in a particular election, the two candidates may be John Brown, who favors increased defense spending, reduced capital gains taxes, and the development of nuclear power, and Jane Smith, who opposes all of these things. If you favor increased defense spending and the development of nuclear power, but oppose reduced capital gains taxes, there is no way that you can elect a candidate that mirrors your preferences. All that you can do is vote for the candidate whose bundle of programs is closest to your preferences.

In contrast, citizens, when making choices in the market place, are better able to pick a set of goods and services that is in accord with their preferences, since they do not have to buy items that they do not want. If you want a green shirt and a purple tie (for formal occasions, of course), you can buy them without having to buy a pair of socks as well. Since citizens cannot be so selective with regard to goods and services in the public sector, public-choice theorists hold that the provision of such goods and services tends to be inefficient.

To conclude this brief section on the theory of public choice, it is important to recognize that no one is accusing government officials of being stupid, lazy, or corrupt. Some undoubtedly are, but this is true of business executives (and college professors) as well. The point is that the incentives faced by government officials and the nature of the political process result in decision making that can be suboptimal from an economic point of view. This helps to explain why the government, like the price system, can bungle the job of organizing the nation's economic activities. Neither is a panacea.

Taxation and Government Revenues

THE FEDERAL TAX LEGISLATIVE PROCESS

It is one thing for the federal government to decide how much to spend and on what; it is another to raise the money to underwrite these programs. This

[3] M. J. Peck and F. M. Scherer, *The Weapons Acquisition Process,* Cambridge, Mass.: Harvard University Press, 1962, p. 594.

section describes how the federal government decides how much to tax. Of course, this problem is not solved from scratch every year. Instead, the government takes the existing tax structure as given and changes it from time to time as seems desirable. Frequently the major initiative leading to a change in the tax laws comes from the president, who requests tax changes in his State of the Union message, his budget message, or a special tax message. (For example, in January 1985 President Reagan announced a proposal for tax simplification.) Much of the spadework underlying his proposals will have been carried out by the Treasury Department, particularly the Treasury's Office of Tax Analysis, Office of the Tax Legislative Counsel, and Internal Revenue Service.

Example 5.1   Brown-Lung Disease and Benefit-Cost Analysis

Byssinosis, commonly known as "brown-lung disease," is a major hazard for textile workers. In 1978, the Occupational Safety and Health Administration (OSHA) issued standards for levels of cotton dust in textile plants, because it felt that cotton dust was a significant cause of byssinosis and other diseases. The following table shows estimates by Robert Crandall of the Brookings Institution of the cost of avoiding an additional case of byssinosis:

Concentration of dust (milligrams per cubic foot of air)	Cost per case avoided (dollars)
0.5	31,000
0.2	572,000
0.1	1,431,000

As you can see, as the level of cotton dust decreases (from 0.5 to 0.2 to 0.1 milligrams per cubic foot), the cost per case avoided goes up.

(a) Suppose that OSHA were to say that the concentration of dust should be no higher than 0.1 milligrams per cubic foot of air. What is OSHA's estimate (explicit or implicit) of the social benefit (in dollars) of avoiding an extra case of byssinosis? (b) Is this estimate correct? (c) What are the difficulties in using benefit-cost analysis to determine how stringent OSHA's standards should be?

SOLUTION

(a) By setting this standard, OSHA is saying (implicitly) that the avoidance of an extra case is worth at least $1,431,000. If it were worth less than this, a less stringent standard should be adopted. (b) Since it is so difficult to set a dollar value on human life or health, there is no simple way to answer this question. However, it should be noted that society implicitly puts a dollar value on human life by spending no more than particular amounts to protect life. (c) As pointed out in (b), it is extremely difficult to estimate and evaluate (in dollars and cents) the social benefits from reductions of various amounts in the incidence of byssinosis. Thus it is hard to know at what point further reductions are no longer worth their cost.

The proposal of a major tax change generally brings about considerable public debate. Representatives of labor, industry, agriculture, and other economic and social groups present their opinions. Newspaper articles, radio shows, and television commentators analyze the issues. By the time the Congress begins to look seriously at the proposal, the battle lines between those who favor the change and those who oppose it are generally pretty clearly drawn. The tax bill incorporating the change is first considered by the Ways and Means Committee of the House of Representatives, a very powerful committee composed of members drawn from both political parties. After public hearings, the committee goes into executive session and reviews each proposed change with its staff and with the Treasury staff. After careful study, the committee arrives at a bill it recommends—though this bill may or may not conform to what the president asked for. Then the bill is referred to the entire House of Representatives for approval. Only rarely is a major tax bill recommended by the committee turned down by the House.

Next, the bill is sent to the Senate. There it is referred to the Finance Committee, which is organized like the House Ways and Means Committee. The Finance Committee also holds hearings, discusses the bill at length, makes changes in it, and sends its version of the bill to the entire Senate, where there frequently is considerable debate. Ultimately, it is brought to a vote. If it does not pass, that ends the process. If it does pass (and if it differs from the House version of the bill, which is generally the case), then a conference committee must be formed to iron out the differences between the House and Senate versions. Finally, when this compromise is worked out, the result must be passed by both houses and sent to the president. The president rarely vetoes a tax bill, although it has occasionally been done.[4]

Principles of Taxation

According to the English political philosopher, Edmund Burke, "To tax and to please, no more than to love and to be wise, is not given to men." What constitutes a rational tax system? Are there any generally accepted principles to guide the nation in determining who should pay how much? The answer is that there are some principles most people accept, but they are so broad and general that they leave plenty of room for argument and compromise. Specifically, two general principles of taxation command widespread agreement.

Benefit Principle. The first principle is that *people who receive more from a certain government service should pay more in taxes to support it.* Certainly few people would argue with this idea. However, it is frequently difficult, if not impossible, to apply. For example, there is no good way to measure the amount of the benefits received by a particular taxpayer from many public services, such as police protection.

Ability-to-Pay Principle. The second principle is that *people should be*

[4] For an excellent discussion of the federal tax legislative process, see J. Pechman, *Federal Tax Policy,* 3rd ed., Washington, D.C.: Brookings Institution, 1977, part of which is reprinted in E. Mansfield, *Principles of Macroeconomics: Readings, Issues, and Cases,* 4th ed., New York: Norton, 1983.

taxed so as to result in a socially desirable redistribution of income. In practice, this has ordinarily meant that the wealthy have been asked to pay more than the poor. This idea, too, has generally commanded widespread assent—although this, of course, has not prevented the wealthy from trying to avoid its application to them.

APPLICATIONS OF THESE PRINCIPLES

It follows from these principles that if two people are in essentially the same circumstances (their income, purchases, utilization of public services are the same), then they should pay the same taxes. This is an important rule, innocuous though it may seem. It says that equals should be treated equally—*whether one is a Republican and the other is a Democrat, or whether one is a friend of the president and the other is his enemy, or whether one has purely salary income and the other has property income, they should be treated equally.* Certainly, this is a basic characteristic of an equitable tax system.

It is easy to relate most of the taxes in our tax structure to these principles. For example, the first principle—the benefit principle—is the basic rationale behind taxes on gasoline and license fees for vehicles and drivers. Those who use the roads are asked to pay for their construction and upkeep. Also, the property tax, levied primarily on real estate, is often supported on these grounds. It is argued that property owners receive important benefits—fire and police protection, for example—and that the extent of the benefits is related to the extent of their property.

The personal income tax is based squarely on the second principle: ability to pay. A person with a large income pays a higher proportion of income in personal income taxes than does a person with a smaller income. In 1984, if a couple's income (after deductions and exemptions) were $16,000, their federal income tax would be $1,741, whereas if their income were $60,000, their federal income tax would be $15,168. Also, estate and inheritance taxes hit the rich much harder than the poor.

The principles cited above are useful and important, but they do not take us very far toward establishing a rational tax structure. They are too vague and leave too many questions unanswered. If I use about the same amount of public services as you do, but my income is twice yours, how much more should I pay in taxes? Twice as much? Three times as much? Fifty percent more? These principles throw no real light on many of the detailed questions that must be answered by a real-life tax code.

The Personal Income Tax

The federal **personal income tax** brings in over $350 billion a year. Yet many people are perhaps unaware of just how much they are contributing because it is deducted from their wages each month or each week, so that they owe little extra when April 15 rolls around. (Indeed, they may even be due a refund.) This pay-as-you-go scheme reduces the pain but, of course, it does not eliminate it; taxes are never painless.

The Tax Schedule. Obviously, how much a family has to pay in personal income taxes depends on the family's income. The tax schedule (as of 1984) is as shown in Table 5.2. The second column shows how much a couple would have to pay if their income was the amount shown in the first column. At an income of $29,900, their income tax would be $4,790; at an income of $109,400, their income tax would be $36,630. Clearly, the percentage of income owed in income tax increases as income increases, but this percentage does not increase indefinitely. The percentage of income going for personal income taxes never exceeds 50 percent, no matter how much money the couple makes.

The Marginal Tax Rate. It is instructive to look further at how the "tax bite" increases with income. In particular, let's ask ourselves what proportion of an *extra* dollar of income the couple will have to pay in personal income taxes. In other words, what is the **marginal tax rate:** the tax on an extra dollar of income? The fourth column of Table 5.2 shows that the

Table 5.2

FEDERAL PERSONAL INCOME TAX, COUPLE WITHOUT CHILDREN, 1984

Income—after deductions and personal exemptions (dollars)	Personal income tax (dollars)	Average tax rate (percent)	Marginal tax rate (percent)
5,500	231	4.2	12
16,000	1,741	10.9	18
29,900	4,790	16.0	28
60,000	15,168	25.3	42
109,400	36,630	33.5	49
1,000,000	481,400	48.1	50

marginal tax rate is 12 percent if the couple's income is $5,500, 18 percent if their income is $16,000, 42 percent if their income is $60,000, and 50 percent if their income is $1 million. Thus, the greater the couple's income, the greater the proportion of an extra dollar that goes for personal income taxes.

Effect on Income Inequality. Clearly, the personal income tax tends to reduce the inequality of after-tax income, since the rich are taxed more heavily than the poor. However, the personal income tax does not bear down as heavily on the rich as one might surmise from Table 5.2. This is because there are a variety of perfectly legal ways for people to avoid paying taxes on their incomes. Current tax laws are favorable to homeowners, who can deduct the payment of local real estate taxes and the interest on their mortgage from their income to get the adjusted level of income on which they pay income taxes. Also, money a person makes on the stock market or from some other situation where his assets go up in value, known as a **capital gain,** is subject to lower personal income tax rates than other income. Interest paid by state and local governments on their bonds is not taxable at all by the federal government. In addition, of course, there is some illegal tax evasion, such as underreporting of income, fake expenses, and imaginary dependents. But evasion is much less important than legal tax avoidance, despite Will Rogers's quip that the income tax has made more liars among the American public than golf.

Lawyers and accountants like to distinguish between *tax avoidance* and *tax evasion.* Tax avoidance occurs when taxpayers take legal steps to minimize their tax bill. Tax evasion occurs when taxpayers misreport their income or take other illegal steps to cut down on what they actually pay Uncle Sam.

Tax avoidance is a particularly profitable pastime of the well-to-do. With the help of a good lawyer or accountant, one frequently can cut one's income taxes considerably. To

illustrate, consider the actual case of a wealthy socialite who took a job as an editor. Because of this job, she may be able to deduct many expenses that she would have incurred anyhow. For example, if she takes a trip to Europe, many of her expenses may be deductible, if she can argue (convincingly) that the trip is somehow related to the development of a book. A deduction is an item that is subtracted from one's income to obtain the net income figure on which the amount of income tax is figured. If you can deduct an expense that otherwise would not be deductible, this reduces your income tax by an amount equal to your marginal income tax rate times the expense. Thus, in the case of the socialite, if she spends $5,000 on a trip to Europe, and if her marginal tax rate is 50 percent, she will save $2,500 in income taxes (that is, .50 × $5,000) if she can convince the Internal Revenue Service that the trip pertained to her business interests.

Many economists feel that the tax system would be more equitable if the tax code were simplified and if many of these ways to avoid income taxes were eliminated. In December 1984, the U.S. Treasury proposed a major revision of the tax laws which would call for only three tax rates, the highest being 35 percent. No deductions would be allowed for state and local income taxes, charitable contributions would be deductible only under certain circumstances, and deductions for interest on second-home mortgages, auto loans, and personal loans would be limited. The Treasury hailed this proposal as a major attempt to simplify the tax code and to make it more equitable.

Other proposals have been put forth as well. In 1983, Congressman Jack Kemp (NY) and Senator Robert Kasten (WIS) introduced a bill for a *"flat tax"* whereby the tax rate would be a flat 25 percent for families with incomes exceeding $3,500. Congressman Richard Gephardt (MO) and Senator William Bradley (NJ) introduced a rival bill that would simplify the tax code but keep somewhat lower tax rates for lower-income families. According to the 1985 annual report of President Reagan's Council of Economic Advisers, "Broadening the tax base would eliminate many sources of misallocation. In addition, because it also allows lower marginal tax rates for the same revenue raised, it would further reduce the inefficiencies arising from the tax system by reducing the differential between the return to taxed activities and the return to activities that are untaxed even under base-broadening."*

* Council of Economic Advisers, *Annual Report,* Washington, D.C.: Government Printing Office, 1985, p. 83.

The Corporate Income Tax

The federal government imposes a tax on the incomes of corporations as well as of people. If a corporation's profits exceed $100,000, the corporate income tax equals $25,750 plus 46 percent of the amount by which the corporation profits exceed $100,000. A corporation with annual profits of $150,000 would pay $48,750 in *corporate income tax*—$25,750 plus $23,000 (46 percent of $50,000).[5] The corporate income tax involves double taxation. The federal government taxes a corporation's earnings both through the corporate income tax (when the corporation earns the profits) and through the personal income tax (when the corporation's earnings are distributed to the stockholders as dividends).

It is generally agreed that the personal income tax is paid by the person whose income is taxed; he or she cannot shift this tax to someone else. But the incidence of the corporate income tax is not so clear. To some extent, corporations may pass along some of their income tax bill to customers in the form of higher prices or to workers in the form of lower wages. Some economists feel that a corporation shifts much of the tax burden in this way; others disagree. This is a controversial issue that has proved very difficult to resolve.

[5] If a corporation's profits are less than $100,000, the corporate income tax equals 15 percent of the first $25,000 of annual profits, 18 percent of the second $25,000 of annual profits, 30 percent of the third $25,000 of annual profits, and 40 percent of the fourth $25,000 of annual profits.

Test Yourself

1. Suppose that the government is trying to determine whether it should build a road from A to B, or whether it should build one that goes from B to C as well. The annual costs and benefits from the two alternative projects are as follows:

	Road from A to B	Road from A to B to C
Annual cost (millions of dollars)	10	15
Annual benefit (millions of dollars)	20	22

Which project, if any, should the government accept? Why?

2. Can you be sent to jail for tax avoidance? Why do people often prefer to receive capital gains rather than ordinary forms of income? If a person's marginal income tax rate is 25 percent and he receives $100 in tax-free income, how much does this equal in before-tax income?

3. Suppose that if it produces the indicated amount of private goods, the maximum amount of public goods that a society can produce is as follows:

Quantity of private goods	Quantity of public goods
0	12
1	11
5	6
8	1
10	0

If this society produces 5 units of private goods and 5 units of public goods, is it being as efficient as it could be? If not, can we tell whether the inefficiency occurs in the public or private sector? And if so, how?

4. In 1985, there was considerable discussion of the pros and cons of a "flat rate" income tax, whereby everyone would pay the same proportion of income in income taxes. Would such a tax simplify the tax code? Would it be in accord with the benefit principle? The ability-to-pay principle?

The Property Tax and the Sales Tax

The **property tax** is the fiscal bulwark of our local governments. The way it works is simple enough. Most towns and cities estimate the amount they will spend in the next year or two, and then determine a property tax based on the assessed property values in the town or city. If there is $500 million in assessed property values in the town and the town needs to raise $5 million, the tax rate will be 1 percent of assessed property value. In other words, each property owner will have to pay 1 percent of the assessed value of his property. There are well-known problems in the administration of the property tax. First, assessed values of property often depart significantly from actual market values; the former are typically much lower than the latter. And the ratio of assessed to actual value is often lower among higher-priced pieces of property; thus wealthier people tend to get off easier. Second, there is widespread evasion of taxes on **personal property**—securities, bank accounts, and so on. Many people simply do not pay up. Third, the property tax is not very flexible: assessments and rates tend to change rather slowly.

The **sales tax,** of course, is a bulwark of state taxation. It provides a high yield with relatively low collection costs. Most of the states have some form of general sales tax, the rate being usually between 3 and 6 percent. For example, New York has a 4 percent sales tax, and California has a 4¾ percent sales tax. Retailers add to the price of goods sold to consumers an amount equal to 3 to 6 percent of the consumer's bill. This extra amount is submitted to the state as the general sales tax. Some states exempt food purchases from this tax, and a few exempt medical supplies. Where they exist, these exemptions help reduce the impact of the sales tax on the poor; but in general the sales tax imposes a greater burden relative to income on the poor than on the rich, for the simple reason that the rich save a larger percentage of their income. Practically all of a poor family's income may be subject to sales taxes; a great deal of a rich family's income may not be, because it is not spent on consumer goods, but is saved.

Who really pays the property tax or the sales tax? To what extent can these taxes be shifted to other people? The answer is not as straightforward as one might expect. For the property tax, the owner of unrented residential property swallows the tax, since there is no one else to shift it to. But the owner of rented property may attempt to pass along some of the tax to the tenant. In the case of a general sales tax, it is generally concluded that the consumer pays the tax. But if the tax is imposed on only a single commodity, the extent to which it can be shifted to the consumer depends on the demand and supply curves for the taxed commodity. The following section explains in some detail why this is the case.

Basic Idea #10: Do not assume that a tax on a particular commodity is paid by the producers of this commodity. Taxes frequently can be shifted to other people. For example, if a price increase will not reduce appreciably the quantity demanded of the good, consumers may wind up paying most of the tax.

Tax Incidence

Suppose that a sales or excise tax is imposed on a particular good, say beer. In Figure 5.2, we show the demand and supply curves for beer before the imposition of the tax. With no tax, the equilibrium price of a case of beer is $6, and the equilibrium quantity is 100 million cases. If a

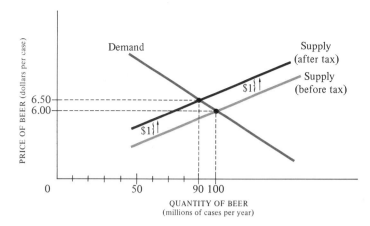

Figure 5.2

Effect of a $1.00 Tax on a Case of Beer
The tax shifts the supply curve upward by $1.00. Since the demand curve is unaffected, the equilibrium price of beer increases from $6.00 to $6.50 per case.

A

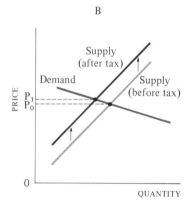

B

Figure 5.3

Effect on Tax Incidence of the Sensitivity of the Quantity Demanded to Price *The supply curve is the same in panel A as in panel B. The quantity demanded is more sensitive to price in panel B than in panel A. Before the tax the equilibrium price is OP$_0$ in both panels. After the tax the equilibrium price is OP$_2$ in panel A and OP$_1$ in panel B. The increase in price to the consumer is greater if the quantity demanded is less sensitive to price (panel A) than if it is more sensitive (panel B).*

tax of $1 is imposed on each case produced, what is the effect on the price of each case? Or to see it from the beer guzzler's perspective, how much of the tax is passed on to the consumer in the form of a higher price?

Since the tax is collected from the sellers, *the supply curve is shifted upward by the amount of tax*, as shown in Figure 5.2. For example, if the pretax price had to be $5 a case to induce sellers to supply 80 million cases of beer, the posttax price would have to be $1 higher—or $6 a case—to induce the same supply. Similarly, if the pretax price had to be $6 a case to induce sellers to supply 100 million cases of beer, the posttax price would have to be $1 higher—or $7 a case—to induce the same supply. The reason why the sellers require $1 more per case to supply the pretax amount is that they must pay the tax of $1 per case to the government. Thus, to wind up with the same amount as before (after paying the tax), they require the extra $1 per case.

Who Pays the Tax? Figure 5.2 shows that, after the tax is imposed, the equilibrium price of beer is $6.50, an increase of $.50 over its pretax level. Consequently, in this case, half of the tax is passed on to consumers, who pay $.50 per case more for beer. And half of the tax is swallowed by the sellers, who receive (after they pay the tax) $.50 per case less for beer. But it is not always true that sellers pass half of the tax on to consumers and absorb the rest themselves. On the contrary, in some cases, consumers may bear almost all of the tax (and sellers may bear practically none of it), while in other cases consumers may bear almost none of the tax (and sellers may bear practically all of it). The result will depend on how sensitive the quantity demanded and the quantity supplied are to the price of the good.

Sensitivity of Demand to Price. In particular, holding the supply curve constant, *the less sensitive the quantity demanded is to the price of the good, the bigger the portion of the tax that is shifted to consumers.* To illustrate this, consider Figure 5.3, which shows the effect of a $1 per case tax on beer in two markets, one (panel B) where the quantity demanded is much more sensitive to price than in the other case (panel A). As is evident, the price increase to consumers resulting from the tax is much greater in the latter case than in the former. And the amount of the tax that is absorbed by producers is much less in the latter case (panel A) than in the former (panel B).

Sensitivity of Supply to Price. It can also be shown that, holding the demand curve constant, *the less sensitive the quantity supplied is to the price of the good, the bigger the portion of the tax that is absorbed by producers.*

A

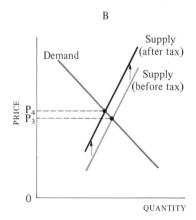

B

Figure 5.4

Effect on Tax Incidence of the Sensitivity of the Quantity Supplied to Price *The demand curve is the same in panel A as in panel B. The quantity supplied is more sensitive to price in panel A than in panel B. Before the tax the equilibrium price is OP_3 in both panels. After the tax the equilibrium price is OP_5 in panel A and OP_4 in panel B. The increase in price to the consumer is greater if the quantity supplied is more sensitive to price (panel A) than if it is less sensitive (panel B).*

To illustrate this, consider Figure 5.4, which shows the effect of a $1-per-case tax on beer in two markets, one (panel A) where the quantity supplied is much more sensitive to price than in the other (panel B). As is evident, the price increase to consumers resulting from the tax is much greater in the former case than in the latter. And the amount of the tax that is absorbed by producers is much less in the former case (panel A) than in the latter case (panel B).

Effect of Tax on Quantity. Finally, note that the tax reduces the equilibrium quantity of the good that is taxed—beer in this case. One reason why governments impose taxes on goods like cigarettes and liquor is that they are regarded (in some circles at least) as socially undesirable. Clearly, the more sensitive the quantity demanded and quantity supplied are to price, the larger the reduction in the equilibrium quantity. Thus, if the government imposes a tax of this sort to reduce the quantity consumed of the good, the effect will be greater if both the quantity demanded and the quantity supplied are relatively sensitive to price.

Supply-Side Economics

In the late 1970s and 1980s, some economists advocated tax reductions in order to stimulate national output. Their views came to be known as ***"supply-side economics,"*** and received considerable attention when some of them received high-level posts in the Reagan administration. They played an important role in formulating and helping to push through the very large tax cut passed in August 1981.

Tax Reductions on Labor Income. The supply-siders advocated cuts in taxes on labor income on the grounds that people will work longer and harder. Many economists are skeptical of this proposition. The available evidence seems to indicate that the hours worked by prime-age males would not be affected much by tax changes. But the amount of work done by married women seems more responsive to changes in tax rates. (If the marginal tax rate is high, some women feel that it is not worthwhile to take a job outside their home.)

Tax Reductions on Capital Income. Supply-siders also advocated reductions in taxes on capital income. For example, they called for cuts in taxes on dividends, interest income, and capital gains. In their view, such cuts would encourage additional saving. Although economists agree that saving and investment tend to promote the growth of an economy, there is considerable controversy over the extent to which saving is influenced by tax cuts. Early studies of consumption and saving found saving behavior to be relatively insensitive to changes in the rate of return that savers receive. (That is, if people can obtain a 15 percent annual return from their savings in banks and elsewhere, they may not save much more than if they can obtain only 10 percent.) Recent studies, particularly by Stanford's Michael Boskin, challenge this conclusion, but critics respond that the 1981 tax cut has not increased the percent of total income devoted to saving.

The Laffer Curve. According to some supply-siders, the tax burden is currently so high that further increases in the marginal tax rate would result in lower, not higher, total tax revenue. To explain why they believe this to be true, they use the *Laffer curve*, which relates the amount of income tax revenue collected by the government to the marginal tax rate. According to the University of Southern California's Arthur Laffer (after whom the curve was named), tax revenues will be zero if the tax rate is zero. This is indisputable. Also, he points out that tax revenues will be zero if the marginal tax rate is 100 percent. Why? Because if the government takes all the income in taxes, an individual has no incentive to earn taxable income.

According to the Laffer curve, the maximum tax revenue is reached when the tax rate is at some intermediate level between zero and 100 percent. In

---

Example 5.2   Should Income or Consumption Be Taxed?

Some economists have suggested that the income tax might be replaced by a tax on consumption expenditure. For example, a family's taxes might depend in the following way on the total amount it spends on consumption of food, clothing, and other such items:

Consumption expenditure (dollars)	Tax (dollars)
5,000	1,000
10,000	2,500
20,000	5,000
50,000	15,000
100,000	40,000

(a) Suppose that the Jones family and the Moran family both earn $20,000 a year, but that the Joneses save 10 percent of their income, whereas the Morans save nothing. Will they pay the same tax? (b) According to proponents of a consumption tax, it will encourage people to save. Do you agree? Why or why not? (c) Why should the United States be interested in increasing the amount that people save? (d) What objections can you see to the replacement of the income tax by a consumption tax? *

SOLUTION

(a) No. The Morans will pay a larger tax than the Joneses because they spend more on consumption than the Joneses. (b) It seems likely that it would encourage saving because the future consumption that can be obtained for a given sacrifice of present consumption will be greater than under an income tax. (c) As pointed out in Chapter 1, saving enables society to invest in new plant and equipment, which will promote more rapid productivity increase. In recent years, the U.S. rate of productivity increase has been relatively low. (d) There are a plethora of difficulties in making such a fundamental change in the tax system. To take but one example, consider retired people who have paid income taxes all their working lives. It would not be equitable to subject them to a consumption tax.

* For further discussion, see J. Pechman. ed., *Options for Tax Reform,* Washington, D.C.: Brookings, 1984.

Figure 5.5

The Laffer Curve *Beyond point* a,
*further increases in the marginal tax rate
result in less revenue collected. According
to some economists like Arthur Laffer,
U.S. tax rates currently are at this point.
Other economists disagree. There is
considerable controversy over the shape
and usefulness of the Laffer curve.*

Figure 5.5, this level is *Oa.* According to Laffer, U.S. tax rates already have
reached or exceeded this level. Many other economists deny this. Although
they admit that a reduction in tax rates could reduce the incentive to cheat
on taxes and to find tax loopholes (as well as to encourage people to work
harder and save more), they feel that Laffer's evidence is too weak to support his conclusions.

Some supply-siders asserted that the 1981 tax cut would result in such
large increases in output and income that tax receipts would surge despite
the reduction in tax rates. Thus they felt that federal revenues would not fall
short of federal expenditures. In fact, however, federal revenues were about
$200 billion less than federal expenditures in fiscal 1985.

It seems fair to say that there is considerable uncertainty about the shape
of the Laffer curve and where the United States is located on it. Even the
existence and usefulness of such a curve is a matter of dispute.

Government Debt

THE NATIONAL DEBT: SIZE AND GROWTH

No subject in economics has more confused the public than the national
debt. When the federal government spends more than it receives in taxes, it
borrows money to cover the difference. The **national debt**—composed of
bonds, notes, and other government IOUs of various kinds—is the result of
such borrowing. These IOUs are held by individuals, firms, banks, and
public agencies. There is a large and very important market for government
securities, which are relatively riskless and highly liquid. If you look at the
New York Times or *Wall Street Journal,* for example, you can find each day
the prices at which each of a large number of issues of these bonds, notes,
and bills are quoted.

How large is the national debt? In 1984, as shown in Figure 5.6, it was
about $1.6 trillion. This certainly seems to be a large amount, but it is im-
portant to relate the size of the national debt to the size of our national
output. After all, a $1.6-trillion debt means one thing if our annual output
is $2 trillion, and another thing if our annual output is $200 billion. As a
percent of output, the national debt is smaller now than in 1939, and no
larger now than shortly after the Civil War. In 1984, the debt was about 40
percent of output; in 1939, it was about 50 percent of output; and in 1868,
it was about 40 percent of output. The debt—expressed as a percentage of
output—is shown in Figure 5.7. Surely the figures do not seem to provide
any cause for immediate alarm.[6] (However, many economists have warned
that there are problems in incurring the large deficits that were responsible
for the rapid rate of increase in the debt during the 1980s. Much more will
be said on this score in Chapter 12.)

A Burden on Future Generations? Although a discussion of many aspects
of the national debt must be postponed to later chapters, it is essential that
we look more closely at why the public has been so agitated about the debt's
size. One important reason has been that they have felt that the debt was a
burden that was being thrust on future generations. To evaluate this idea it
is important to recognize that a public debt is not like your debt or mine,

---

[6] Note too that much of the public debt is in the hands of government agencies, not held by
the public. For example, in 1984 only about $1 trillion was held by private investors.

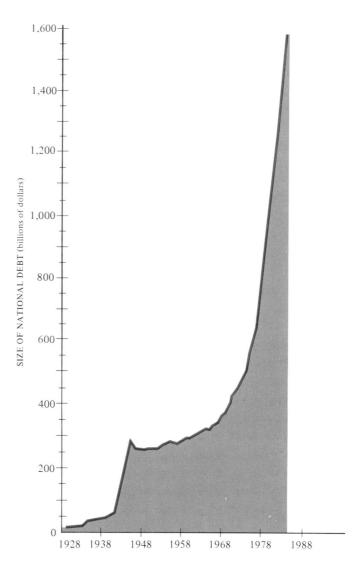

Figure 5.6

Size of the National Debt, United States, 1929–84 *The national debt, about $1.6 trillion in 1984, has been growing at a rapid rate due to huge government deficits.*

which must be paid off at a certain time in the future. In practice, new government debt is issued by the government to pay off maturing public debt. There never comes a time when we must collectively reach into our pockets

Figure 5.7

National Debt as a Percent of National Output, United States, 1929–84 *As a percent of national output, the national debt declined steadily from World War II to about 1980. During the 1980s, it increased, but not very greatly.*

to pay off the debt. And even if we did pay it off, the same generation would collect as the one that paid.

Effects of Externally Held Debt. Of course, this does not mean that the debt is of no economic consequence. On the contrary, to the extent that the debt is held by foreigners, we must send goods and services overseas to pay the interest on it. This means that less goods and services are available for our citizens. Thus, if we finance a particular government activity by borrowing from foreigners, the costs may be transferred to future generations, since they must pay the interest. But from the point of view of the world as a whole, the current generation sacrifices goods and services, since the lending country forgoes current goods and services. Also, it must be recognized that, if the debt is incurred to purchase capital goods, they may produce enough extra output to cover the interest payments.

Effects of Internally Held Debt. Even if the debt is internally held, it may have some undesirable effects. Taxes must be collected from the public at large to pay interest to the holders of government bonds, notes, and other obligations. To the extent that the bondholders receiving the interest are wealthier than the public as a whole, there is some redistribution of income from the poor to the rich. To the extent that the taxes needed to obtain the money to pay interest on the debt reduce incentives, the result also may be a smaller national output.

A final word should be added about the idea that the national debt imposes a burden on future generations. *The principal way in which one generation can impose such a burden on another is by using up some of the country's productive capacity or by failing to add a normal increment to this capacity.* This, of course, is quite different from incurring debt. For example, World War II would have imposed a burden on subsequent generations whether or not the national debt was increased. However it was financed, the war would have meant that our resources had to be used for tanks and war planes rather than for keeping up and expanding our productive capacity during 1941–45. And this imposed a burden, a real burden, on Americans living after 1945—as well, of course, as on those living during the war.

Alternative Ways of Financing Government Expenditures—and Their Effects

To complete the present discussion of public finance, it is important to recognize that there are three ways that the federal government can finance any expenditure. The first way is to *raise taxes* to cover the expenditure. The effect of this method of financing the expenditure is straightforward: purchasing power is transferred from the people paying the extra taxes to the government. Thus the costs are borne by the taxpayer. The second way is to *borrow the money* from willing lenders. In this case, too, the effect is straightforward: purchasing power is transferred from the lenders to the government. The current costs of the government programs are borne by the lenders, who receive interest subsequently in return.

The third way the federal government can finance any expenditure is to

Average U.S. citizens have very little direct contact with the Department of the Treasury. If they work for the federal government, they receive a bimonthly check; if they are so fortunate as to have overpaid their income tax, they may receive a lovely green refund check. In fact, the processing of checks is (at least, to the nonrecipient economist) much less important than many other functions of the Treasury. Should the Congress or the president wish technical advice on the effect of a new tax measure, the Treasury Department will supply the analysis. In addition, it represents American interests in negotiations over international monetary arrangements with other countries; and, through the Internal Revenue Service and the Customs Service, it collects most federal taxes.*

But from an economist's point of view, one of the most interesting tasks the Treasury performs may be the management of the national debt. Imagine yourself with a debt of about $1 trillion (held by private investors), with a few billion coming due each week. Obviously, much of the Treasury's time must be spent scratching for new Peters in order to pay old Pauls. This may not sound like an easy task; and, in fact, it isn't. Over the years the Treasury has developed a bewildering array of devices—refinancing Series E bonds, U.S. savings bonds, short-term bills, long-term bonds—for coaxing new lenders to release their cash, or persuading old lenders to defer collection. One of the most important of these instruments is U.S. Treasury bills, which in 1984 amounted to over $350 billion. (Should you ever have a spare $10,000, the smallest denomination in which Treasury bills are sold, their current prices can be found in the financial pages of any major newspaper.)

Almost every month the undersecretary of the Treasury for monetary affairs must decide in what form the portion of the debt coming due should be refinanced. Are interest rates going up? If so, he might refinance by selling long-term bonds, locking up money at the present low rate. Will interest rates fall? If so, he might prefer the 90-day bill. Before an issue is floated, he gets a reading of market conditions from committees of the American Bankers Association and the Investment Bankers Association. But cost is not his only problem. He must also worry about the effect of Treasury operations on financial markets and must have developed future refunding policies. In any case, an elaborate financial network of banks, big insurance companies, pension funds, and investment houses is always waiting to respond to the Treasury's next offering.

E.A.

---

* Moreover, faithful television fans may realize that, through its Bureau of Customs, the Treasury is responsible for controlling the importation of narcotics.

create new money. In other words, it can print extra currency (or create new money in other ways that will be described in Chapters 14–16). If the economy is already at full employment, this procedure is likely to cause inflation. The increase in the price level will mean that households and firms will have to buy less than would otherwise have been the case. At the same time, the government will use the new money to finance the expenditure (and obtain the resources it wants). Thus purchasing power is transferred from the consumers and firms whose incomes and receipts do not keep pace with inflation to the government. One disadvantage of this means of finance is that these consumers and firms are often the weakest and least able to bear this burden.

If the economy is not at full employment, the opportunity costs of government programs may be much less than if the economy is at full employment. Recall from Chapter 1 that the opportunity cost of using resources in a particular way is the value of the output that could have been obtained if these resources had been used in some other way. Clearly, if the resources used in a particular government program would have been unemployed if this program had not been started, society is giving up very little by using these resources in this program. Why? Because they would have been idle otherwise. On the other hand, if there is full employment, these resources would not have been idle, and the opportunity costs of the program would be the value of what they could produce elsewhere.

Test Yourself

1. Suppose that the supply curve for gin is as follows:

Price of gin (dollars per quart)	Quantity supplied (millions of quarts)
4	5
5	6
6	7
7	8
8	9
9	10

Plot the supply curve on graph paper. Suppose that the government imposes a tax of $2 per quart on gin, and that the tax is collected from the sellers. Plot the posttax supply curve on graph paper.

2. Under the circumstances described in Question 1, suppose that the quantity of gin demanded is 7 million quarts, regardless of the price (so long as it is between $4 and $9 per quart). What will be the equilibrium price of gin before the tax, and after it? How much of the tax is passed on to the consumer?

3. Under the circumstances described in Question 1, suppose that the demand curve for gin is a horizontal line at $6 per quart. If this is the case, what will be the equilibrium price of gin before the tax, and after it? How much of the tax is passed on to the consumer?

4. "The national debt is of little or no economic consequence because we owe it to ourselves." Comment and evaluate.

Summary

1. The spending decisions of the federal government take place in the context of the budgetary process. The president submits his budget, which is a statement of anticipated expenditures and revenues, to Congress, which votes appropriations. The Ways and Means Committee of the House of Representatives and the

Senate Finance Committee play important roles in the federal tax legislative process.

2. Basically, the amount that the government spends on various activities and services must be decided through the nation's political processes. Voting by ballots must be substituted for dollar voting. In making such decisions, it is important to distinguish between changes in government expenditure that alter the scope of government and changes in government expenditures due to changes in efficiency.

3. Spending on each government program should be pushed to the point where the extra benefit from an extra dollar spent is at least equal to the dollar of cost. In some areas, benefit-cost analyses have proved useful in determining which of a variety of projects can accomplish a particular goal most economically, and whether any of them is worth carrying out. However, accurate measurement of the relevant benefits and costs is frequently difficult.

4. Just as the price system suffers from limitations, so does the government. Special-interest groups sometimes gain at the expense of society as a whole. Government agencies sometimes have little incentive to increase efficiency. Citizens find it difficult to be selective in their choice of goods and services in the public sector. In recent years, economists seem to have put more emphasis on these (and other) limitations of the public sector.

5. It is generally agreed that people who receive more in benefits from a certain government service should pay more in taxes to support it. It is also generally agreed that people should be taxed so that the result is a socially desirable redistribution of income, and that equals should be treated equally. But these general principles, although useful, cannot throw light on many of the detailed questions a real-life tax code must answer.

6. The personal and corporate income taxes are very important sources of federal revenues, the sales tax is an important source of state revenues, and the property tax is an important source of local revenues.

7. When the government spends more than it receives in revenues, the government borrows money to cover the difference. It could simply print money for this purpose, but it has chosen to borrow a considerable proportion of what has been needed. The resulting debt is often called the national debt.

8. Despite much public worry about the size of the national debt, as a percentage of national output it is smaller now than in 1939. There are important differences between government debt and private debt. Although the size of the debt is certainly of consequence, it is not true that it somehow may lead to bankruptcy.

Concepts for Review

Budget	Corporate income	Sales tax
Benefit-cost analysis	tax	Tax incidence
Benefit principle	Tax avoidance	Supply-side
Ability-to-pay principle	Tax evasion	economics
Personal income tax	Flat tax	Laffer curve
Marginal tax rate	Property tax	National debt
Capital gain		

CHAPTER 6

The Business Firm: Organization, Motivation, and Technology

It is hard to overstate the importance of business firms in the American economy. They produce the bulk of our goods and services, hire most of the nation's workers, and issue stocks and bonds that represent a large percentage of the nation's wealth. Judged by any yardstick—even less complimentary ones like the responsibility for environmental pollution—business firms are an extremely important part of the American economy. In this chapter, we discuss the various types of business firms, such as proprietorships and corporations. Then we describe the various types of securities—common stock, bonds, and so forth—issued by firms, and discuss the workings of the stock market. Next, we take up the motivation and structure of firms, as well as their technology. Finally, we provide some essential elements of accounting. This material is a necessary introduction to the workings of the business enterprise, absolutely essential to anyone who works for, manages, or invests in a firm.

The IBM Corporation: A Case Study

To begin with, let's look in some detail at one of America's biggest firms: the IBM Corporation. A description of its history and vicissitudes should give you a better feel for what firms do and the sorts of problems they face.

ELECTRONIC COMPUTERS: COMING FROM BEHIND

The IBM Corporation operated under the strong leadership of Thomas Watson, Sr., until his death in 1956. Watson joined the Computing-Tabulating-Recording Corporation in 1914, and renamed it International Business Machines in 1924. The firm became a very successful and fast-growing office-equipment company. In the late 1940s and early 1950s, the first electronic computers were developed, but IBM did not then appreciate the commercial potential of such equipment. According to Watson's son:

> During these really earth-shaking developments in the accounting machine industry, IBM slept soundly. We had put the first electronically-operated punched card calculator on the market in 1947. We clearly knew that electronic computing even in those days was so fast that the machine waited 9/10 of every card cycle for the mechanical portions of the machine to feed the next card. In spite of this, we didn't jump to the obvious conclusion that if we could feed data more rapidly, we could increase speeds by 900 percent. Remington Rand and Univac drew this conclusion and were off to the races.
>
> Finally we awoke and began to act. We took one of our most competent operating executives with a reputation for fearlessness and competence and put him in charge of all phases of the development of an IBM large-scale electronic computer. He and we were successful.
>
> How did we come from behind? First, we had enough cash to carry loads of engineering, research, and production, which were heavy. Second, we had a sales force which enabled us to tailor our machine very closely to the market. Finally, and most important, we had good company morale. All concerned realized that this was a mutual challenge to us as an industry leader. We had to respond with all that we had to win, and we did.[1]

SNOW WHITE AND THE SEVEN DWARFS

Although IBM was a slow starter, it soon became the dominant producer of electronic computers. By 1956, it had over 80 percent of the market. According to many observers, its success was due particularly to its marketing skills. In the 1960s, it became known as Snow White, while its rivals—Burroughs, Univac, NCR, Control Data, Honeywell, GE, and RCA—were referred to as the Seven Dwarfs. In the 1970s, after GE and RCA left the computer industry, only five dwarfs remained.

On January 17, 1969, the federal government brought a massive antitrust case against IBM, accusing it of monopolistic practices. The case went on for thirteen years. According to IBM's former chairman, Frank Cary, "The suit was a tremendous cloud that was over the company.... It couldn't help influencing us in a whole variety of ways. Ending it lifted a huge burden from management's shoulders." In January 1982, the Justice Department dropped the case, saying that it was "without merit."

Since the settlement of the case, IBM has been selling aggressively and entering new markets. Some observers are worried that it is becoming too big and powerful; others feel that it has plenty of competition from the Japanese, among others. In 1983, its net income of $5.5 billion made IBM the

[1] T. Belden and M. Belden, *The Lengthening Shadow: The Life of Thomas J. Watson,* Boston: Little, Brown, 1962.

world's most profitable industrial corporation, although sales of $40.2 billion made it only the world's seventh largest. In 1984, its profits were over $6.5 billion.

THE IBM PERSONAL COMPUTER

One of IBM's most dramatic recent moves was its entrance into the personal computer market in 1981. The job of overseeing the development of IBM's personal computer (PC) was entrusted to a twelve-member group, which worked for about a year on the project. The group broke with tradition by making the PC's technical specifications available to other firms, thus allowing outsiders to write software and make peripheral equipment for the PC that would extend its appeal. Within a few months after its introduction, the IBM PC was setting the standard for the industry. By 1983, IBM had garnered about 28 percent of the market for personal computers.

According to some observers, IBM will eventually gain a much larger share of the personal computer market, thus cutting into the sales of Apple Computer and others. Only time will tell whether this is true. But without question IBM's very successful entrance into the personal computer market during the early 1980s has transformed the computer industry.

Characteristics of American Firms: Some Salient Facts

IBM world headquarters

IBM is an economic colossus—a huge organization with over 300,000 employees. Of course it is not typical of American business firms. If we broaden our focus to take in the entire population of business firms in the United States, the first thing we note is their tremendous number; according to government statistics, there are about 16 million. The vast majority of these firms, as one would expect, is very small. There are lots of grocery stores, gas stations, auto dealers, drugstores, clothing shops, restaurants, and so on. You see hundreds of them as you walk along practically any downtown city street. But these small firms, although numerous, do not control the bulk of the nation's productive capacity. The several hundred largest firms have great economic power, measured by their sales, assets, employment, or other such indices. The small firms tend to be weak and short-lived. Although some prosper, many small firms go out of business after only a few years of existence.

The next thing to note is that *most of the nation's business firms are engaged in agriculture, services, and retail trade.* Table 6.1 shows that about three-quarters of the firms in the United States are in these industries, an understandable figure since these industries tend to have lots and lots of small businesses. *Although manufacturing firms constitute only about 3 percent of all American firms, they account for more than one-third of all business receipts.* On the other hand, agriculture (including forestry and fisheries) includes about 25 percent of the nation's business firms, but accounts for only 3 percent of the total receipts. Clearly, this is because manufacturing firms tend to be much bigger, in terms of receipts, employment, and assets, than agricultural firms. Think, for example, of the steel plants in Pittsburgh or Cleveland, or of the aircraft plants in California or

Table 6.1

NUMBER AND RECEIPTS OF BUSINESS FIRMS, BY INDUSTRY, UNITED STATES[a]

Industry	Number of firms (millions)	Receipts of firms (billions of dollars)
Agriculture, forestry, and fisheries	4.0	170
Mining	0.1	143
Construction	1.4	318
Manufacturing	0.5	2,099
Transportation, communication[b]	0.5	456
Wholesale and retail trade	3.4	1,968
Financial	2.1	353
Services	4.5	368
Total	16.2	5,877

[a] Figures may not sum to total due to rounding.
[b] Includes electric and gas.
Source: Statistical Abstract of the United States.

Georgia. They dwarf the typical farm—and they are only parts of a manufacturing firm.

Finally, note that *most of the nation's business firms are proprietorships;* indeed, almost four-fifths fall into this category, while about 14 percent are corporations, and about 8 percent are partnerships. You often hear the terms *proprietorship, partnership, corporation.* What do these terms mean?

Proprietorships

A proprietorship is a legal form of business organization—the most common form, as we saw in the previous section, and also the simplest. Specifically, a **proprietorship** is a firm owned by a single individual. A great many of the nation's small businesses are proprietorships. For example, the corner drugstore may well be one. If so, it has a single owner. He hires the people he needs to wait on customers, deliver orders, do the bookkeeping, and so forth. He borrows, if he can, whatever money he feels he needs. He reaps the profits, or incurs the losses. All his personal assets—his house, his furniture, his car—can be taken by creditors to meet the drugstore's bills; that is, he has unlimited liability for the debts of the business.

Pros. What Lincoln said about the common man applies as well to proprietorships: God must love them, or He wouldn't have created so many of them. If proprietorships didn't have advantages over other legal forms of business organization under many sorts of circumstances, there wouldn't be so many of them. What are these advantages? First, *owners of proprietorships have complete control over their businesses.* They don't have to negotiate with partners or other co-owners. They are the boss—and the only boss. Anyone who has been in a position of complete authority knows the joy it can bring. Many proprietors treasure this feeling of independence. Second, *a proprietorship is easy and inexpensive to establish:* all you have to do is hang out your shingle and announce you are in business. This too is a great advantage.

Cons. But proprietorships have important disadvantages as well—and for this reason, they are seldom found in many important industries. One disadvantage is that *it is difficult for a proprietor to put together enough financial resources to enter industries like automobiles, steel, or computers.* No one in the world has enough money to establish, by himself or herself, a firm of IBM's present size. Another disadvantage is that *proprietors are liable for all of the debts of the firm.* If their business fails, their personal assets can be taken by their creditors, and they can be completely wiped out.

Partnerships

A *partnership* is somewhat more complicated than a proprietorship. As its name implies, it is a form of business organization where two or more people agree to own and conduct a business. Each partner agrees to contribute some proportion of the capital and labor used by the business, and to receive some proportion of the profits or losses. There are a variety of types of partnerships. In some cases, one or more of the partners may be "silent partners," who put up some of the money, but have little or nothing to do with the operations of the firm. The partnership is a common form of business organization in some industries and professions, like the law. But as we saw in a previous section, partnerships are found less frequently than proprietorships or corporations in the United States.

Pros. A partnership has certain advantages. Like a proprietorship, *it can be established without great expense or legal red tape.* (However, if you ever go into a partnership with someone, you would be well advised to have a good lawyer draw up a written agreement establishing such things as the salaries of each partner and how profits are to be shared.) In addition, a partnership can avoid some of the problems involved in a proprietorship. *It can usually put together more financial resources and specialized know-how than a proprietorship*—and this can be an important advantage.

Cons. But the partnership also has certain drawbacks. First, *each partner is liable without limit for the bills of the firm.* For example, even if one partner of a law firm has only a 30 percent share of the firm, he or she may be called upon to pay all the firm's debts if the other partners cannot do so. Second, *there is some red tape in keeping a partnership in existence.* Whenever a partner dies or withdraws, or whenever a new partner is admitted, a new partnership must be established. Third, like the proprietorship, *the partnership is not a very effective way to obtain the large amounts of capital required for some modern industries.* A modern automobile plant may cost $500 million, and not many partnerships could assemble that much capital. For these reasons, as well as others discussed in the next section, the corporation has become the dominant form of business organization.

Corporations

A far more complicated form of business organization than either the proprietorship or partnership, the **corporation** is a fictitious legal person, separate and distinct from its owners. A corporation is formed by having lawyers draw up the necessary papers stating (in general terms) what sorts of activities the owners of the corporation intended to engage in. The owners of the corporation are the stockholders. **Stock,** pieces of paper signifying ownership of the corporation, is issued to the owners, generally in exchange for their cash. Ordinarily, each **share** of stock gives its owner one vote. The corporation's **board of directors,** which is responsible for setting overall policy for the firm, is elected by the stockholders. The firm's owners can, if they are dissatisfied with the company's policies or think they have better opportunities elsewhere, sell their stock to someone else, assuming, of course, that they can find a buyer.

Pros. The corporation has many advantages over the partnership or proprietorship. In particular, *each of the corporation's owners has limited, not unlimited, liability.* If I decide to become one of the owners of IBM and if a share of IBM stock sells for $125 a share, I can buy ten shares of IBM stock for $1,250. And I can be sure that, if IBM falls on hard times, I cannot lose more than $1,250 I paid for the stock. There is no way that I can be assessed beyond this. Moreover, *the corporation, unlike the partnership or proprietorship, has unlimited life.* If several stockholders want to withdraw from the firm, they simply sell their stock. The corporation goes on, although the identity of the owners changes. For these reasons, *the corporation is clearly a better device for raising large sums of money than the partnership or proprietorship.* This is an enormous advantage of the corporation, particularly in industries like automobiles and steel, which could not otherwise finance their operations.

Cons. Without question, the corporation is a very important social invention. It permits people to assemble the large quantities of capital required for efficient production in many industries. Without limited liability and the other advantages of the corporation, it is doubtful that the opportunities and benefits of large-scale production could have been reaped. However, this does not mean that the corporate form will work for all firms. In many cases, a firm requires only a modest amount of capital, and there is no reason to go to the extra trouble and expense of establishing a corporation. Moreover, one disadvantage of the corporation is **double taxation of income,** since, as you will recall from Chapter 5, corporations pay income taxes—and the tax rate is often almost one-half of every extra dollar earned. Thus every dollar earned by a corporation and distributed to stockholders is taxed twice by the federal government—once when it is counted as income by the corporation, and once when the remainder is counted as income by the stockholders.

Corporate Securities

The corporation raises money by issuing various kinds of securities; of these, three kinds—common stock, preferred stock, and bonds—are particularly significant. Each of these types of securities is important to the workings of the corporation and to people's investment decisions.

Common Stock. **Common Stock** is the ordinary certificate of ownership of the corporation. Holders of common stock are owners of the firm. They share in the firm's profits—if there are any profits. At frequent intervals, the board of directors of the firm may declare a dividend of so much per share for the common stockholders. For example, the common stockholders of IBM received dividends of $4.40 per share in 1984. **Dividends** are thus the income the owners of common stock receive. (In addition, of course, common stockholders may make money by selling their stock for more than they paid for it; as noted in the previous chapter, such income is called **capital gains.**) Common stock is generally regarded as more risky than preferred stock or bonds, for reasons that will be explained.

Preferred Stock. **Preferred stock** is a special kind of certificate of ownership that pays at most a stated dividend. For example, consider the General Motors Corporation, the huge auto maker. Owners of one type of General Motors preferred stock receive $5 a share per year, as long as the firm makes enough to pay this dividend. To protect the owners of preferred stock, it is stipulated that no dividends can be paid on the common stock unless the dividends on the preferred stock are paid in full. Since the common stockholders cannot receive their dividends unless the preferred stock's dividends have been paid, common stock is obviously more risky than preferred stock. But by the same token, the amount preferred stockholders have to gain if the company prospers is less than the amount common stockholders have to gain, since however high its profits may be, the firm will pay only the stated dividend—for example, $5 per share per year in the case of General Motors—to the owners of preferred stock.

Bonds. Bonds are quite different from both common and preferred stocks. **Bonds** are debts of the firm; in other words, they are IOUs issued by the firm. In contrast to stockholders, the bondholders are not owners of a firm: they are its creditors, and receive interest, not dividends. Specifically, a bond is a certificate bearing the firm's promise to pay the interest every six months until the bond matures, at which time the firm also promises to pay the bondholders the principal (the amount they lent the firm) as well. Often bonds are sold in $1,000 denominations. For example, one type of bond issued by IBM is a 9⅜ percent bond, due in 2004. The owner of each such bond receives $93.75 per year in interest, and IBM promises to pay him or her the principal of $1,000 when the bond falls due in 2004. A firm must pay the interest on the bonds and the principal when it is due, or it can be declared bankrupt. In other words, the bondholders are legally entitled to receive what is due them before the stockholders can get anything.

Thus, from the point of view of the investor, bonds are generally considered less risky than preferred stock, and preferred stocks are considered less risky than common stock. But we have ignored another fact: inflation. The tendency for the price level in the United States to increase over time has meant that bondholders have been paid off with dollars that were worth less than those they lent. For this reason, together with the fact that owners of common stocks reaped substantial capital gains during the 1960s and early 1970s, many investors tended to favor common stocks. Indeed, during the 1960s, a "cult of equities" developed; these were the years when it appeared that stock prices were headed only one way—even higher. It became very fashionable to buy common stock. But in the middle 1970s, the public's infatuation with common stocks seemed to fade, as stock prices fell; and the 1980s have seen considerable variation in stock prices. To understand why the value of stocks can gyrate so considerably, it is necessary to look briefly at the workings of the stock market.

The Stock Market

In general, large corporations do not sell stock directly to the investor. Instead, the investor buys stock on the stock market. Two major stock exchanges in the United States are the New York Stock Exchange and the American Stock Exchange, both in New York City. On these and similar exchanges in other cities, the common stocks of thousands of corporations are bought and sold.

Price Fluctuations. The price of each common stock fluctuates from day to day, indeed from minute to minute. Basically, the factors responsible for these price fluctuations are the shifts in the demand curve and supply curve for each kind of common stock. For example, if a strike breaks out at a General Motors plant, this may cause the demand curve for General Motors stock to shift downward to the left, since the strike is liable to mean lower profits for General Motors. Because of this downward, or leftward, shift in the demand curve, the price of General Motors common stock will tend to fall, as in fact happened during a United Auto Workers strike in 1974.

The Great Crash. Occasionally, the stock market gets a case of the jitters over economic conditions, stock prices tumble, and old investors think back to the Great Crash of 1929. The 1920s witnessed a feverish interest in investing in the stock market. Along with raccoon coats, Stutz Bearcats, and the Charleston, common stocks were the rage. Both the professionals on Wall Street and the neophytes on Main Street bought common stocks and more common stocks. Naturally, as the demand curves for common stocks shifted upward to the right, their prices rose, thus whetting the appetites of investors for still more common stocks. This upward spiral continued until 1929, when the bubble burst. Suddenly the prices of common stocks fell precipitously—and continued to drop during the early 1930s. The most famous average of industrial stock prices, the Dow-Jones average, fell from 381 in 1929 to 41 in 1933. Many investors, large and small, were wiped out.

Stocks Come Back. The Great Crash made investors wary of common stocks for many years. But by the 1960s confidence in them was fully restored, and there certainly was no tendency for investors to shy away from them. In the 1970s and 1980s, although many small investors (and some large ones) lost their shirts, the stock market remained a major outlet for savings. Judging from historical experience, the public's taste for common stocks seems to be justified. Studies show that, during the course of a lifetime, the typical investor would have done better to invest in common stocks than in the best-quality bonds, because stock prices have tended to rise. This tended to apply in a great many cases, even for investors who lived through the Great Crash. And it has certainly been borne out over the past 40 or 50 years. Thus, although common stocks are riskier in some respects than bonds or preferred stocks, they seem to have performed better, on the average, at least in recent times.

MAKING MONEY ON STOCKS

During periods when the average of stock prices is going up, such as the 1920s and much of the 1950s and 1960s (as well as in more recent bull markets), it is relatively easy to be a financial wizard, whether by luck or calculation. A much more exacting test of your financial acumen is how

115

Over 30 million Americans own common stocks, which indicates that you don't have to be wealthy to be an investor. Suppose that you are interested in buying IBM stock. To determine its current price, you need only look at the financial pages of any major newspaper. For example, on April 1, 1985, the *Wall Street Journal* showed the following information concerning IBM common stock:

52-week				Sales				Net
High	Low	Stock	Div	100s	High	Low	Last	Change
138¼	99	IBM	4.40	6950	127⅛	125⅝	127	+⅜

Reading from left to right, $138.25 and $99 are the highest and lowest prices of IBM stock in the previous year, and $4.40 is the level of IBM's dividends in the previous year. The last five figures show the number of shares sold (695,000), the highest price (127.12½), the lowest price (125.62½), and the final price ($127) of a share on the previous day, as well as the change in the price from the day before (up $.37½ per share).

To determine whether IBM common stock is a good buy, you would be well advised to look at IBM's recent earnings record and to obtain as much information as you can concerning the firm's earnings prospects. This is because, as a firm's earnings (per share of common stock) go up, the price of its stock tends to go up too. Some economists and business analysts have gone so far as to publish formulas by which one can determine, on the basis of forecasts of what a firm's earnings will be, how much the stock is worth. They believe that one should buy if the current price of the stock is below this measure of the stock's intrinsic value and sell if the price is above it.

In contrast, other economists believe that the movement of stock prices has more to do with psychology than with financial valuation of this sort. As John Maynard Keynes put it, "[Most persons] are concerned, not with what an investment is really worth to a man who buys it 'for keeps,' but with what the market will value it at, under the influence of mass psychology, three months or a year hence. . . . For it is not sensible to pay 25 for an investment of which you believe the prospective yields to justify a value of 30, if you also believe that the market will value it at 20 three months hence." As Yale's Burton Malkiel observes, "This theory might . . . be called the 'greater-fool theory.' It's perfectly all right to pay three times what a stock is worth as long as later on you can find some innocent to pay five times what it's worth."*

There is no simple, foolproof way to determine whether IBM common stock is a good buy. Since even the most astute traders on Wall Street frequently do no better than one could do by buying the Dow-Jones average, you would do well to approach the stock market with caution. More than one economic savant has lost his or her shirt.

* B. Malkiel, *A Random Walk down Wall Street,* 4th ed., New.York: Norton, 1985.

well you can pick which stocks will outperform the averages. If you can predict that increases will occur in a certain firm's profits, and if other people don't predict the same thing, you may be able to pass this test. However, the sobering truth is that "playing the stock market" is much more an art than a science. The stock market is affected by psychological as well as economic considerations. Moreover, when you try to spot stocks that will increase in price, you are pitting your knowledge and experience against those of skilled professionals with big research staffs and with friends and acquaintances working for the companies in question. And even these professionals can do surprisingly poorly at times.

Do economists have a nose for good investments? John Maynard Keynes was an extremely successful speculator who made millions of dollars. Other economists have been far less successful. Certainly, a knowledge of basic economics is not sufficient to enable you to make money on the stock market, but insofar as the market reflects economic realities, a knowledge of basic economics should be helpful.

The Giant Corporation

Much of the trading on the stock market centers around the relatively small number of giant corporations that control a very substantial percentage of the total assets and employment in the American economy. And well it might, for the largest 100 manufacturing corporations control about half of this country's manufacturing assets. These firms have tremendous economic and political power. They include the giant automobile manufacturers (General Motors, Ford), the big oil firms (Exxon, Standard Oil of Indiana, Mobil, Standard Oil of California, Texaco, Atlantic-Richfield), the big steel firms (U.S. Steel, Bethlehem, Armco), the big computer and office machinery producers (IBM and Xerox), the leading tobacco firms (American Brands, R. J. Reynolds, Philip Morris), the electrical equipment producers (General Electric, Westinghouse), and many others.

MANAGEMENT

Usually, the president is the chief operations officer in the firm, although sometimes the chairman of the board of directors fills this role. As for the board of directors, some members are chosen for their reputations and contacts, while others are chosen for their knowledge of the firm, the industry, or some profession or specialty.

The board generally contains at least one representative of the financial community, and a university president or former government official is often included to show that the firm is responsive to broad social issues. Members of IBM's board include Harold Brown, a former Secretary of Defense; Patricia Harris, a professor at George Washington University; and Richard Lyman, president of the Rockefeller Foundation.

The board of directors is concerned with overall policy. Since it meets only a few times a year, it seldom becomes involved in day-to-day decisions; and it usually goes along with management's policies, so long as management retains the board's confidence.

SEPARATION OF OWNERSHIP FROM CONTROL

An interesting and important feature of the large corporation is the fact that it is owned by many people, practically all of whom have little or no detailed information about the firm's operations. The owners of IBM number over 700,000, but most of them know relatively little about what is going on in the firm. Moreover, because of the wide diffusion of ownership, working control of a large corporation can often be maintained by a group with only one-fifth or less of all the voting stock. The result is a *separation of ownership from control.* In other words, the owners control the firm in only a limited and somewhat sporadic sense.

So long as a firm's management is not obviously incompetent or corrupt, it is difficult for insurgent stockholders to remove the management from office. Most stockholders do not go to the annual meetings to vote for members of the firm's board of directors. Instead, they receive *proxies,* which, if returned, permit the management to exercise their votes. Usually enough shareholders mail in their proxies to give management the votes it needs to elect a friendly board of directors. In recent years, the Securities and Exchange Commission, which oversees and regulates the financial markets, has attempted to make the giant corporations more democratic by enabling insurgent groups to gain access to mailing lists of stockholders and so forth. But there is still a noteworthy and widespread separation of ownership from control.

Test Yourself

1. In its 1979 annual report, the Exxon Corporation reported that it was building a new olefins plant (costing $500 million) in Baytown, Texas. Is this plant a firm? Why or why not? Do you think that a proprietorship would be likely to build and own such a plant? Why or why not?

2. Assume that a partnership wanted to enter the automobile industry. What problems would such a legal form of organization impose upon the potential entrants? Are any of the Big Three in the U.S automobile industry (General Motors, Ford, and Chrysler) partnerships?

3. Explain why each of the following statements is true or false. (a) The University of Texas is a firm. (b) Massachusetts General Hospital is a firm. (c) A firm must be owned by more than one person. (d) The owner of a firm must participate in its management.

4. On February 19, 1985, the common stock of Exxon Corporation closed at $47.25 per share. What effect would each of the following have on its price? (a) A marked increase in the demand for gasoline. (b) A prolonged strike at a major Exxon refinery. (c) Price ceilings on gas and oil.

5. Explain why bondholders do not vote for a corporation's board of directors and why common stockholders are not guaranteed a particular dividend rate.

Motivation of the Firm

What determines the behavior of the business firm? As a first approximation, *economists generally assume that firms attempt to maximize* **profits,** which are defined as the difference between the firm's revenue and its costs.

Basic Idea #11: Economists frequently assume that firms maximize profit. Although this is an oversimplification, models based on this assumption have proved very useful, both in explaining why firms and markets behave as they do and in indicating rules of business behavior for firms that want to try to maximize profit.

In other words, economists generally assume that firms try to make as much money as possible. This assumption certainly does not seem unreasonable; most businessmen appear to be interested in making money. Nonetheless, the assumption of profit maximization oversimplifies the situation. Although businessmen certainly want profits, they are interested in other things as well. Some firms claim that they want to promote better cultural activities or better racial relations in their community. At a less lofty level, other firms say that their aim is to increase their share of the market. Whether or not one takes these self-proclaimed goals very seriously, it is clear that firms are not interested *only* in making money—often for the same reason that Dr. Johnson gave for not becoming a philosopher: "because cheerfulness keeps breaking in."[2]

Intrafirm Politics. In a large corporation, there are some fairly obvious reasons why firms may not maximize profits. Various groups within such firms develop their own party lines, and intrafirm politics is an important part of the process determining firm behavior. Whereas in a small firm it may be fairly accurate to regard the goals of the firm as being the goals of the proprietor, in the large corporation the decision on the goals of the firm is a matter of politics, with various groups within the organization struggling for power. In addition, because of the separation of ownership from control, top management usually has a great deal of freedom as long as it seems to be performing reasonably well. Under these circumstances, the behavior of the firm may be dictated in part by the interests of the management group, resulting in higher salaries, more perquisites, and a bigger staff for their own benefit than would otherwise be the case.

Risk and Uncertainty. Also, in a world full of risk and uncertainty, it is difficult to know exactly what profit maximization means, since the firm cannot be sure that a certain level of profit will result from a certain action. Instead, the best the firm can do is to estimate that a certain probability distribution of profit levels will result from a certain action. Under these circumstances, the firm may choose less risky actions, even though they have a lower expectation of profit than other actions. In a world where ruin is ruinous, this may be perfectly rational policy.

PROFIT MAXIMIZATION IS THE STANDARD ASSUMPTION

Nonetheless, profit maximization remains the standard assumption in economics. As we agreed in our discussion of model building in Chapter 2, to be useful models need not be exact replicas of reality. Economic models based on profit maximization have been very useful indeed. For one thing, they help to show how the price system functions. For another, in the real world, they suggest how a firm should operate if it wants to make as much money as possible. Even if a firm does not want to maximize profit, these theories can be utilized. For example, they can show how much profit the firm is forgoing by taking certain courses of action. In recent years, the theory of the profit-maximizing firm has been studied more and more for the sake of determining profit-maximizing rules of business behavior.

[2] This quote is taken from R. Solow, "The New Industrial State, or Son of Affluence," *The Public Interest,* Fall 1967. Since footnotes are so often used to cite dreary material, it seems worthwhile to use them occasionally to cite humor as well.

Technology, Inputs, and the Production Function

The decisions a firm should make in order to maximize its profits are determined by the current state of technology. Technology, it will be recalled from Chapter 1, is the sum total of society's knowledge concerning the industrial arts. Just as consumers are limited by their income, firms are limited by the current state of technology. If the current state of technology is such that we do not know how to produce more than 40 bushels of corn per year from an acre of land and 2 man-years of labor, then this is as much as the firm can produce from this combination of land and labor. In making its decisions, the firm must take this into account.

INPUTS

In constructing a model of the profit-maximizing firm, economists must somehow represent the state of technology and include it in their model. As a first step toward this end, we must define an *input*. Perhaps the simplest definition of an input is that it is anything the firm uses in its production process. Some of the inputs of a farm producing corn might be seed, land, labor, water, fertilizer, various types of machinery, as well as the time of the people managing the farm.

PRODUCTION FUNCTION

Having defined an input, we can now describe how economists represent the state of technology. The basic concept economists use for this purpose is the production function.

For any commodity, *the **production function** is the relationship between the quantities of various inputs used per period of time and the maximum quantity of the commodity that can be produced per period of time.* More specifically, the production function is a table, a graph, or an equation showing the maximum output rate that can be achieved from any specified set of usage rates of inputs. The production function summarizes the characteristics of existing technology at a given point in time. It reflects the technological constraints the firm must reckon with.

To see more clearly what we mean by a production function, consider the Milwaukee Machine Company, a hypothetical machine shop that produces a simple metal part. Suppose that we are dealing with a period of time that is so short that the firm's basic plant and equipment cannot be altered. For simplicity, suppose that the only input whose quantity can be altered in this period is the amount of labor used by the machine shop. Suppose that the firm collects data showing the relationship between the quantity of its output and the quantity of labor it uses. This relationship, given in Table 6.2, is the firm's production function. It shows that, when 1 worker is employed, 100 parts are produced per month; when 2 workers are employed, 210 parts are produced per month; and so on. Information concerning a firm's production function is often obtained from the firm's engineers, as well as its craftsmen and technicians. Much more will be said about production functions in later chapters. All that we want to do here is to introduce the concept of the production function.

Table 6.2

PRODUCTION FUNCTION, MILWAUKEE MACHINE COMPANY

Quantity of labor used per month (number of men employed)	Output per month (number of parts)
0	0
1	100
2	210
3	315
4	415
5	500

Elements of Accounting: The Firm's Balance Sheet

Having touched on the firm's technology, we must return to the motivation of the firm. In a previous section, we stated that economists generally assume that firms attempt to maximize profits. Viewed as a first approximation, this assumption does not seem too hard to swallow, but exactly what do we mean by profit? This is an important question, of interest to businessmen and investors as well as to economists. The accounting profession provides the basic figures that are reported in the newspapers and in a firm's annual reports to its stockholders. If IBM reports that it made $5.5 billion last year, this figure is provided by IBM's accountants. How do the accountants obtain this figure? What are its limitations?

Basically, accounting concepts are built around two very important statements: the balance sheet and the income statement. A *firm's balance sheet* shows the nature of its assets, tangible and intangible, at a certain point in time.

LEFT-HAND SIDE OF THE BALANCE SHEET

Let us return to the Milwaukee Machine Company. Its balance sheet might be as shown in Table 6.3. The left-hand side of the balance sheet shows the assets of the firm as of December 31, 1985. *Current assets* are assets that will be converted into cash relatively quickly (generally within a year), whereas *fixed assets* generally will not be liquidated quickly. The firm has $20,000 in cash, $120,000 in inventory, $160,000 in equipment, and $180,000 in buildings. At first glance, these figures may seem more accurate than they are likely to be. It is very difficult to know how to value various assets. For example, should they be valued at what the firm paid for them, or at what it would cost to replace them? More will be said about these problems below.

RIGHT-HAND SIDE OF THE BALANCE SHEET

The right-hand side of the firm's balance sheet shows the claims by creditors on the firm's assets and the value of the firm's ownership. In Table 6.3,

Table 6.3

BALANCE SHEET, MILWAUKEE MACHINE COMPANY, AS OF DECEMBER 31, 1985

Assets (dollars)		Liabilities and net worth (dollars)	
Current assets		Current liabilities	
Cash	20,000	Accounts payable	20,000
Inventory	120,000	Notes payable	40,000
Fixed assets		Long-term liabilities	
Equipment	160,000	Bonds	160,000
Buildings	180,000		
		Net worth	
		Preferred stock	100,000
		Common stock	100,000
		Retained earnings	60,000
Total	480,000	Total	480,000

the Milwaukee Machine Company has total liabilities—or debts—of $220,000. There is $60,000 in **current liabilities,** which come due in less than a year; and $160,000 in **long-term liabilities,** which come due in a year or more. Specifically, there is $20,000 in **accounts payable,** which are bills owed for goods and services that the firm bought; $40,000 in **notes payable,** short-term notes owed to banks, finance companies, or other creditors; and $160,000 in **bonds payable,** or bonds outstanding.

LEFT-HAND SIDE = RIGHT-HAND SIDE

The difference between the value of a firm's assets and the value of its liabilities is its **net worth,** which is the value of the firm's owners' claims against the firm's assets. In other words, the value of the firm to its owners is the total value of its assets less the value of the debts owed by the firm. Since

total value of assets − total liabilities = net worth,

it follows that

total value of assets = total liabilities + net worth.

That is, *the sum of the items on the left-hand side of the balance sheet must equal the sum of the items on the right-hand side.* This, of course, must be true because of the way we define net worth.

In the case of the Milwaukee Machine Company, the firm's net worth—the difference between its assets and its liabilities—is $260,000. Specifically, there is $100,000 worth of preferred stock and $100,000 worth of common stock; there is also $60,000 in retained earnings. **Retained earnings** is the total amount of profit that the stockholders have reinvested in the business. In other words, the stockholders of the Milwaukee Machine Company have reinvested $60,000 of their profits in the business. Rather than withdrawing this sum as dividends, they have kept it invested in the firm.

The Firm's Income Statement

A firm's **income statement** *shows its sales during a particular period, its costs incurred in connection with these sales, and its profits during this period.* Table 6.4 shows the Milwaukee Machine Company's income statement during the period January 1, 1986 to December 31, 1986. Sales during this period were $240,000. The cost of manufacturing the items made during this period was $110,000, which includes $30,000 for materials, $40,000 for labor, $34,000 for depreciation (discussed below), and $6,000 for miscellaneous operating expenses.

However, because the firm has reduced its inventory from $120,000 to $110,000 during the period, the cost of manufacturing the items *made* during the period does not equal the cost of manufacturing the items *sold* during the period. To find the *cost of goods sold*—which is the amount that logically should be deducted from sales to get the profits made from the sale of these goods—we must add the decrease in the value of inventory to

Table 6.4

INCOME STATEMENT, MILWAUKEE MACHINE COMPANY, JANUARY 1, 1986, TO DECEMBER 31, 1986 (DOLLARS)

Net Sales		240,000
Manufacturing cost of goods sold		120,000
Materials	30,000	
Labor	40,000	
Depreciation	34,000	
Miscellaneous operating cost	6,000	
Total	110,000	
Plus beginning inventory	120,000	
Less closing inventory	−110,000	
Adjusted total	120,000	
Selling and administrative costs		20,000
Fixed interest charges and state and local taxes		10,000
Net earnings before income taxes		90,000
Corporation income taxes		40,000
Net earnings after taxes		50,000
Dividends on preferred stock		4,000
Net profits of common stockholders		46,000
Dividends paid on common stock		20,000
Addition to retained earnings		26,000

the total manufacturing cost. (Why? Because the firm sold more items than it produced during this period. Thus the cost of the items it sold equals the cost of the items it produced during this period plus the cost of the items it sold from its inventory. Since the cost of the items it sold from its inventory equals the decrease in the value of its inventory, the cost of the items it sold equals the cost of the items it produced during this period plus the decrease in inventory.) Putting it another way, we must add the beginning inventory and subtract the closing inventory, as shown in Table 6.4. The resulting figure for cost of goods sold is $120,000.

But manufacturing costs are not the only costs the firm incurs. To estimate the firm's profits, we must also deduct from sales its selling and administrative expenses, its interest charges, and its state and local taxes, as well as its federal income taxes. Table 6.4 shows that the Milwaukee Machine Company's after tax earnings during 1986 were $50,000. This is the amount left for the owners of the business. The income statement also shows what the owners do with what is left. Table 6.4 shows that the Milwaukee Machine Company used $4,000 to pay dividends to holders of preferred stock. When this was done, the holders of common stock were free to distribute some of the profits to themselves. According to Table 6.4, they distributed $20,000 to themselves in dividends on the common stock, and plowed the rest—$26,000—back into the business as retained earnings.

DEPRECIATION

Before leaving the income statement, we should explain one element of manufacturing cost—*depreciation.* While the other elements of manufacturing cost are self-explanatory, this one is not. The idea behind depreciation is that the buildings and equipment will not last forever; eventually

Cross-Chapter Case/Part Two

SHOULD AMERICA ADOPT AN INDUSTRIAL POLICY?

In Chapters 3–6, we have been concerned primarily with the role of the price system and of firms and the government in the American economy. In the mid-1980s, one of the leading questions in this area has been: Should the United States adopt an industrial policy? It is difficult to define an "industrial policy" with precision, since economists do not all use the same definition. But all industrial policies involve some form of government action designed to stimulate and revitalize a nation's industry. In particular, according to many advocates of an industrial policy, the government should encourage new high-technology industries and help older, declining industries to adjust to lower output and employment levels.

In the United States, those favoring the adoption of an industrial policy have proposed a variety of ways in which the government's role in directing the allocation of resources might be expanded. For example, there might be a central agency to formulate the government's industrial policy. Councils including representatives of business, labor, and government might obtain data on particular industries and construct a consensus strategy. A government development bank might invest money in sectors and industries that are regarded as receiving too little capital from private financial sources. Declining industries (so-called "sunset" industries) might get protection from imports and other government help to ease the adjustment to new economic realities.

Advocates of an industrial policy argue that the United States already has an industrial policy of sorts, but that it is largely uncoordinated. For example, the U.S. government spends large amounts on research, sets import quotas, and subsidizes many kinds of firms, just as other countries do. Moreover, this is nothing new. In 1643, Massachusetts granted a fledgling firm exclusive iron-making privileges for 21 years in order to encourage the industry. More recently, the federal government provided a loan guarantee to the Chrysler Corporation to help keep the auto maker in business. Since the U.S. government is already engaged in many of the activities encompassed under the broad heading of "industrial policy," the real question, according to the proponents of an industrial policy, is whether these activities should be better coordinated. In their view, councils of business, labor, and government could do a better job than is now being done of coordinating these far-flung activities of the government, many of which conflict with one another.

Many proponents of an industrial policy also argue that a government-financed industrial development bank should provide industrial firms with money for high-risk, long-term projects. One reason why such a bank is needed, in their opinion, is that private investors tend to be averse to risk and too inclined to want quick pay-backs. Consequently, they invest too little in risky ventures extending for 5 or 10 years or more. Moreover, according to Felix Rohatyn, chairman of New York City's Municipal Assistance Corporation, such a federal bank "could make sure that the aid would be conditional on management and labor concessions needed to make the business viable." In other words, it could force firms to make tough decisions.

Many advocates of an industrial policy feel that the government should act to slow the decline in "basic" industries like steel. Besides providing loans and special tax benefits, the government would sponsor plans to spread adjustment burdens among labor, management, stockholders, creditors, and suppliers. If the industry faces competition from imports, industry commitments to restructure would be the price of protection from imports. Retraining and compensation programs would be employed to help workers whose jobs are lost.

Whereas some economists are strong advocates of an industrial policy for the United States, others feel that it would be a mistaken, and even dangerous, step to take. To begin with, they feel that councils of business, labor, and government experts would be no more effective in improving coordination of various policies of the government than the existing coordinating mechanisms. In particular, they point out that other countries with industrial policies continue to have coordination problems of this sort.

As for the creation of a government-supported industrial bank, many economists react negatively to this proposal, because they feel that political considerations would inevitably enter into the allocation of funds and that money would be wasted on "targeted growth" industries with no commercial future. According to President Reagan's Council of Economic Advisers:

> The proposal to target emerging industries suggests that government can obtain better information than the private sector. It is difficult to understand how government officials, together with private business and labor leaders, will be able to gather more accurate information and use the information more wisely than the private sector. The United States has numerous investors willing to finance new ventures through equity or bank loans. Private investment analysts spend a great deal of time and effort evaluating new technologies and advising private investors on the most promising firms. Information on emerging industries is also exchanged by job shifting among scientists and engineers who are close to the development of new technologies. Ties between industry and the academic community also contribute to the spread of new ideas. In the United States the private sector already has information at least as good as the proposed government councils and banks could expect to gather.
>
> In any event, a government agency is more likely to be short-sighted and risk averse than private investors. Since politicians face frequent elections, they often have very short time horizons. A government agency is also more likely to make decisions based on the shared expectations that are the conventional wisdom of the time; these processes tend to neglect or reject the idiosyncratic information that is the basis for decisions by the most successful private entrepreneurs.
>
> Finally, government officials will often make investments based on politics rather than economics. One country tries to develop a computer industry before it has sufficient technical workers. Other countries invest in highly visible but wasteful energy projects that private firms think are likely to fail.[1]

[1] Council of Economic Advisers, *1984 Annual Report,* Washington, D.C.: Government Printing Office, 1984.

they will have to be replaced. Clearly, it would be foolish to charge the entire cost of replacing them to the year when they are replaced. Instead, a better picture of the firm's true profitability will be drawn if the cost of replacing them is spread gradually over the life of buildings and equipment, thus recognizing that each year's output has a hand in wearing them out. One frequently used technique is so-called *straight-line depreciation,* which spreads the cost of buildings and equipment (less their scrap value) evenly over their life. Thus, if the Milwaukee Machine Company buys a piece of equipment for $20,000 and if it is expected to last ten years (its scrap value being zero), it would charge depreciation of $2,000 per year

---

Example 6.1   How to Depreciate a Baseball Club

Suppose that you decide to buy the Philadelphia Phillies for $30 million. There are some important tax advantages you should understand. According to Bill Veeck, former owner of the Chicago White Sox, "It is almost impossible not to make money on a baseball club when you are buying it new, because, unless you are inordinately successful, you pay no income tax."* In particular, half of the purchase price of the team can be regarded as the cost of the players, which are depreciable assets like machinery or breeding cattle. Suppose that you regard 5 years as being the "useful life" of the players, and that you use straight-line depreciation.

(a) How much depreciation (of the players) can you deduct from the Phillies' receipts each year to figure your profits? (b) Suppose that you pay $3 million in cash and borrow the remaining $27 million to pay for the Phillies. If you pay 15 percent interest, how much interest expense do you deduct from the Phillies' receipts each year to figure your profits? (c) Suppose that this year the Phillies' receipts equal $35 million and their operating expenses (excluding depreciation of the players and the interest on your loan) equal $28 million. Must you pay any income tax? (Assume that you have no income from sources other than the Phillies.)

SOLUTION

(a) Since the cost of the players can be regarded as one-half of the purchase price of the team, it equals one-half of $30 million, or $15 million. Since the life of the players is 5 years, annual depreciation equals $15 million divided by 5, or $3 million. (b) $27 million times 15 percent, or $4.05 million. (c) Your income from the Phillies is as follows:

Earnings (before depreciation and interest)	$7 million
Less depreciation	−3 million
Less interest	−4.05 million
	−$.05 million

Since you incurred a loss (because of the depreciation of the players), you pay no income tax.

* *Philadelphia Inquirer,* March 15, 1981.

for this machine (for ten years after its purchase). The $34,000 charge for depreciation in Table 6.4 is the sum of such charges. Clearly, this is only a rough way to estimate the true depreciation charges, but it is good enough for many purposes.

Economic versus Accounting Profits

The previous section described the nature of profit, as defined by accountants. This is the concept on which practically all published figures in business reports are based. But economists define profits somewhat differently. In particular, economists do not assume that the firm attempts to maximize the current, short-run profits measured by the accountant. Instead they assume that the firm will attempt to maximize the sum of profits over a long period of time.[3] Also, when economists speak of profit, they mean profit after taking account of the capital and labor provided by the owners. Thus, suppose that the owners of the Milwaukee Machine Company, who receive profits but no salary or wages, put in long hours for which they could receive $30,000 in 1986 if they worked for someone else. Also suppose that if they invested their capital somewhere other than in this firm, they could obtain a return of $22,000 on it in 1986. Under these circumstances, economists would say that the firm's after-tax profits in 1986 were $50,000 − $30,000 − 22,000, or −$2,000, rather than the $50,000 shown in Table 6.4. In other words, the economists' concept of profit includes only what the owners make above and beyond what their labor and capital employed in the business could have earned elsewhere. In this case, that amount is negative.

To a considerable extent, the differences between the concepts used by the accountant and the economist reflect the difference in their functions. The accountant is concerned with controlling the firm's day-to-day operations, detecting fraud or embezzlement, satisfying tax and other laws, and producing records for various interested groups. On the other hand, the economist is concerned primarily with decision making and rational choice among prospective alternatives. Although the figures published on profits almost always conform to the accountant's, not the economist's, concept, the economist's concept is the more relevant one for many kinds of decisions. (And this, of course, is recognized by sophisticated accountants.) For example, suppose the owners of the Milwaukee Machine Company are trying to decide whether they should continue in business. If they are interested in making as much money as possible, the answer depends on the firm's profits as measured by the economist, not the accountant. If the firm's economic profits are greater than (or equal to) zero, the firm should continue in existence; otherwise, it should not. Thus the Milwaukee Machine Company should not stay in existence if 1986 is a good indicator of its future profitability.

Basic Idea #12: To economists, profit is the amount that a firm's owners receive over and above what they could make from the capital and labor they provide, if this capital and labor were used outside the firm. Only if profit in this sense is non-negative should the firm stay in existence. (Note that this is closely related to Basic Idea #2 on p. 10.)

---

[3] The profits earned at various points in time should be *discounted* before being added together, but, for simplicity's sake, we neglect this point here.

Test Yourself

1. Which of the following are inputs in the steel industry? (a) coke, (b) iron ore, (c) labor, (d) land, (e) capital, (f) water, (g) oxygen, (h) food eaten by U.S. Steel's workers.

2. The 1981 tax law allowed firms to depreciate assets more quickly. For example, they could depreciate some types of assets over 3 years, rather than 5 years. If a firm depreciates an asset more quickly, will its accounting profits in the first year after it buys the asset be increased or decreased?

3. Suppose that a firm's balance sheet is as follows:

Assets (dollars)		Liabilities and net worth (dollars)	
Current assets		Current liabilities	
Cash	200,000	Accounts payable	100,000
Inventory	300,000	Notes payable	_____
Fixed assets		Long-term liabilities	
Equipment	_____	Bonds	400,000
Buildings	800,000		
		Net worth	400,000
Total	2,000,000	Total	_____

Fill in the three blanks. What is the total amount that the firm owes? How much have the owners contributed? What is the difference between current assets and fixed assets?

4. Suppose that a firm's accounting profits for 1986 are $20,000. The firm is a proprietorship, and the owner worked 500 hours managing the business during 1986, for which she received no compensation other than the profits. If she could have gotten $10 an hour working for someone else, how much were her economic profits during 1986? Suppose that she also contributed $50,000 in capital to the firm, and that she could have obtained 6 percent interest on this capital if she had invested it elsewhere. In this case, how much were her economic profits?

Summary

1. There are three principal types of business firms: proprietorships, partnerships, and corporations. The corporation has many advantages over the other two—limited liability, unlimited life, and greater ability to raise large sums of money. Nonetheless, because the corporation also has disadvantages, many firms are not corporations.

2. The corporation raises money by issuing various kinds of securities, of which three kinds—common stock, preferred stock, and bonds—are particularly important.

3. A relatively small number of giant corporations control a very substantial proportion of the total assets and employment in the American economy. In the large corporation, ownership and control tend to be separated.

4. As a first approximation, economists generally assume that firms attempt to maximize profits. In large part, this is because it is a close enough approximation to reality for many of the most important purposes of economics. Also, economists are interested in the theory of the profit-maximizing firm because it provides rules of behavior for firms that do want to maximize profits.

5. To summarize the characteristics of existing technology at a given point in time, the economist uses the concept of the production function, which shows the maximum output rate of a given commodity that can be achieved from any specified set of usage rates of inputs.

6. Accounting concepts are built around two very important statements: the balance sheet and the income statement. The balance sheet shows the nature of the firm's assets and liabilities at a given point in time. The difference between its assets and its liabilities is its net worth, which is the value of the firm's owners' claims against its assets.

7. A firm's income statement shows its sales during a particular period, its costs incurred in connection with these sales, and its profits during the period.

8. Economists define profits somewhat differently than accountants do. In defining profit, economists deduct the amount the owners could receive from the capital and labor they provide, if this capital and labor were used outside the firm. Also, economists are interested in longer periods than those to which accounting statements apply. Although the profit figures that are published almost always conform to the accountant's concept, the economist's concept is the more relevant one for many kinds of decisions.

Concepts for Review

Proprietorship	**Dividends**	**Balance sheet**
Partnership	**Preferred stock**	**Current assets**
Corporation	**Bonds**	**Fixed assets**
Board of directors	**Profits**	**Net worth**
Double taxation of income	**Input**	**Income statement**
Common stock	**Production function**	**Depreciation**

PART THREE

National Output, Income, and Employment

CHAPTER 7

National Income and Product

America's **gross national product**—or GNP, as it is often called—was $3,663 billion in 1984, as compared with $3,305 billion in 1983. Put in the simplest terms, GNP is the value of the total amount of final goods and services produced by our economy during a particular period of time. This measure is important for its own sake, and because it helps us to understand both inflation and unemployment. The federal government and the business community watch GNP figures avidly. Government officials, from the president down, are interested because these figures indicate how prosperous we are, and because they are useful in forecasting the future health of the economy. Business executives are also extremely interested in GNP figures because the sales of their firms are related to the level of GNP, and so the figures are useful in forecasting the future health of their businesses. All in all, it is no exaggeration to say that the gross national product is one of the most closely watched numbers in existence.

In this chapter, we discuss the measurement, uses, and limitations of the gross national product, as well as a variety of other commonly-used measures of national income and output. At the outset, it is worth noting that measures of national income and national product are of comparatively recent vintage. The Department of Commerce first made such estimates in 1932, after experiments at various universities and at the National Bureau of Economic Research. A leading pioneer in this field was the late Nobel laureate Simon Kuznets, then at the University of Pennsylvania. The concepts that Kuznets and others developed are often called the **national income accounts,** and the Bureau of Economic Analysis of the U.S. Department of Commerce compiles these figures on a continuing basis. Just as the accounts of a firm are used to describe and analyze its financial health, so the national income accounts are used to describe and analyze the economic health of the nation as a whole.

Gross National Product

As noted above, gross national product is a measure of how much the economy produces in a particular period of time. But the American economy produces millions of types of goods and services. How can we add together everything from lemon meringue pies to helicopters, from books to houses? The only feasible answer is to use money as a common denominator and to make the price of a good or service—the amount the buyer is willing to pay—the measure of value. In other words, we add up the value in money terms of the total output of goods and services in the economy during a certain period, normally a year, and the result is the gross national product during that period.

Although the measurement of gross national product may seem straightforward ("just add up the value in money terms of the total output of the economy"), this is by no means the case. Some of the more important pitfalls that must be avoided and problems that must be confronted are the following:

Avoidance of Double Counting. Gross national product does not include the value of *all* goods and services produced: it includes only the value of *final* goods and services produced. **Final goods and services** are goods and services destined for the ultimate user. For example, flour purchased for family consumption is a final good, but flour to be used in manufacturing bread is an **intermediate good,** not a final good. We would be double counting if we counted both the bread and the flour used to make the bread as output. Thus the output of intermediate goods—goods that are not destined for the ultimate user, but are used as inputs in producing final goods and services—must not be included in gross national product.

Steel used in the production of automobiles and cotton used in the production of blue jeans must not be included. They will be counted when we count the automobiles and jeans, which are final goods. The value of the steel will be included in the price of the automobiles, and the value of the cotton will be included in the price of the jeans. To avoid double counting, we include only the value of final goods and services in gross national product.

Valuation at Cost. Some final goods and services that must be included in gross national product are not bought and sold in the market place, so they are valued at what they cost. Consider the services performed by government—police protection, fire protection, the use of the courts, defense, and so forth. Such services are not bought and sold in any market (despite the old saw about the New Jersey judge who was "the best that money could buy"). Yet they are an important part of our economy's final output. Economists and statisticians have decided to value them at what they cost the taxpayers. This is by no means ideal, but it is the best practical solution advanced to date.

Nonmarket Transactions. It is necessary for practical reasons to omit certain types of final output from gross national product. In particular, some nonmarketed goods and services, such as the services performed by housewives, are excluded from the gross national product. This is not because economists fail to appreciate these services, but because it would be extremely difficult to get reasonably reliable estimates of the money value of a housewife's services. At first glance, this may seem to be a very important weakness in our measure of total output, but so long as the value of these services does not change much (in relation to total output), the variation in gross national product will provide a reasonably accurate picture of the variation in total output—and, for many purposes, this is all that is required.

Nonproductive Transactions. Purely financial transactions are excluded from gross national product because they do not reflect current production. Such financial transactions include government transfer payments, private transfer payments, and the sale and purchase of securities. **Government transfer payments** are payments made by the government to individuals who do not contribute to production in exchange for them. Payments to welfare recipients are a good example of government transfer payments. Since these payments are not for production, it would be incorrect to include them in GNP. **Private transfer payments** are gifts or other transfers of wealth from one person or private organization to another. Again these are not payments for production, so there is no reason to include them in GNP. The sale and purchase of securities are not payments for production, as you will recall from our discussion in Chapter 6, so they too are excluded from GNP.

Secondhand Goods. Sales of secondhand goods are also excluded from gross national product. The reason for this is clear. When a good is produced, its value is included in GNP. If its value is also included when it is sold on the secondhand market, it will be counted twice, thus leading to an overstatement of the true GNP. Suppose that you buy a new bicycle and resell it a year later. The value of the new bicycle is included in GNP when the bicycle is produced. But the resale value of the bicycle is not included in GNP; to do so would be double counting.

Adjusting GNP for Price Changes

CURRENT DOLLARS VERSUS CONSTANT DOLLARS

In Chapter 1, we stressed that the general price level has changed over time. (Recall the rapid inflation of the 1970s and early 1980s.) Since gross national product values all goods and services at their current prices, it is bound to be affected by changes in the price level as well as by changes in total output. If all prices doubled tomorrow, this would produce a doubling of gross national product. Clearly, if gross national product is to be a reliable measure of changes in total output, we must correct it somehow to eliminate the effects of such changes in the price level.

To make such a correction, economists choose some **base year** and express the value of all goods and services in terms of their prices during the base year. If 1983 is taken as the base year and if the price of beef was $2 per pound in 1983, beef is valued at $2 per pound in all other years. Thus, if 100 million pounds of beef were produced in 1986, this total output is valued at $200 million even though the price of beef in 1986 was actually higher than $2 per pound. In this way, distortions caused by changes in the price level are eliminated.

Gross national product is expressed either in current dollars or in constant dollars. Figures expressed in **current dollars** are actual dollar amounts, whereas those expressed in **constant dollars** are corrected for changes in the price level. Expressed in current dollars, gross national product is affected by changes in the price level. Expressed in constant dollars, gross national product is not affected by the price level because the prices of all goods are maintained at their base-year level. GNP, after being corrected for changes in the price level, is called **real GNP.**

Figure 7.1 shows the behavior of both real GNP and GNP expressed in current dollars. GNP expressed in current dollars has increased more rapidly (due to inflation) than GNP in constant dollars.

PRICE INDEXES

It is often useful to have some measure of how much prices have changed over a certain period of time. One way to obtain such a measure is to divide the value of a set of goods and services expressed in current dollars by the value of the same set of goods and services expressed in constant (or base year) dollars. Suppose that a set of goods and services costs $100 when valued at 1986 prices, but $70 when valued at 1983 prices. Apparently, prices have risen an average of 43 percent for this set of goods between 1983 and 1986. How do we get 43 percent? The ratio of the cost in 1986 prices to the cost in 1983 prices is $100 \div 70 = 1.43$; thus prices must have risen on the average by 43 percent for this set of goods.

The ratio of the value of a set of goods and services in current dollars to the value of the same set of goods and services in constant (base year) dollars is a **price index.** Thus 1.43 is a price index in the example above. An important function of a price index is to convert values expressed in current dollars into values expressed in constant dollars. This conversion, known as **deflating,** can be achieved simply by dividing values expressed in current dollars by the price index. In the illustration above, values expressed in 1986 dollars can be converted into constant (i.e., 1983) dollars by dividing by 1.43. This procedure is an important one, with applications in many fields other than the measurement of gross national product. For example, firms use it to compare their output in various years. To correct for price changes, they deflate their sales by a price index for their products.

In many cases, price indexes are multiplied by 100; that is, they are expressed as percentage changes. Thus, in the case described in the previous paragraph, the price index might be expressed as 1.43×100, or 143, which would indicate that 1986 prices on the average were 143 percent of their 1983 level. In the next chapter, we shall say more about price indexes that are expressed in this way. For now, we assume that the price index is not multiplied by 100.

APPLICATIONS OF PRICE INDEXES

To illustrate how a price index can be used to deflate some figures, suppose that we want to measure how much the output of bread rose *in real terms* —that is, in constant dollars—between 1983 and 1987. Let us suppose that the value of output of bread in current dollars during each year was as shown in the first column of Table 7.1, and that the price of bread during each year was as shown in the second column. To determine the value of output of bread in 1983 dollars, we form a price index with 1983 as the base

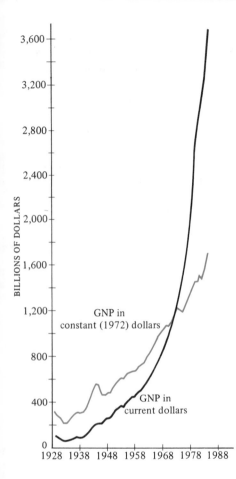

Figure 7.1

Gross National Product, Expressed in Current Dollars and 1972 Dollars, United States, 1929–84 *Because of inflation, GNP expressed in current dollars has increased more rapidly in recent years than GNP in constant (1972) dollars. This was particularly true in the 1970s and early 1980s, reflecting the price surge then.*

Table 7.1

USE OF PRICE INDEX TO CONVERT FROM CURRENT TO CONSTANT DOLLARS

Year	(1) Output of bread in current dollars	(2) Price of bread (dollars)	(3) Price index (price ÷ 1983 price)	(4) Output of bread in 1983 dollars[a]
1983	1,600 million	0.50	1.00	1,600 million
1984	1,768 million	0.52	1.04	1,700 million
1985	1,980 million	0.55	1.10	1,800 million
1986	2,090 million	0.55	1.10	1,900 million
1987	2,204 million	0.58	1.16	1,900 million

[a] This column was derived by dividing column 1 by column 3.

Basic Idea #13: Output measures expressed in current dollars can be misleading because they reflect changes in prices as well as output. To correct for price changes, such an output measure should be divided by a price index, the result being an output measure expressed in constant dollars.

year, as shown in the third column. Then dividing the figures in the first column by this price index, we get the value of output of bread during each year in 1983 dollars, shown in the fourth column. Thus the fourth column shows how much the output of bread has grown in real terms. The real output of bread has risen by 19 percent—$(1,900 - 1,600) \div 1,600$—between 1983 and 1987.

Next, let's take up an actual case. The first column of Table 7.2 shows the gross national product in selected years during the 1970s. The second column shows the relevant price index for GNP for each of these years. (The base year is 1972.) What was real GNP in 1981? To answer this question, we must divide GNP in current dollars in 1981 by the price index for 1981. Thus the answer is $2,938 billion divided by 1.9358, or $1,518 billion. In other words, when expressed in constant 1972 dollars, GNP in 1981 was $1,518 billion. What was real GNP in 1978? Applying the same principles, the answer is $2,156 billion divided by 1.5005, or $1,437 billion. In other words, when expressed in constant 1972 dollars, GNP in 1978 was $1,437 billion. To test your understanding, see if you can figure out the value of real GNP in 1975. (To check your answer, consult footnote 1.)[1]

Table 7.2

CALCULATION OF REAL GROSS NATIONAL PRODUCT

Year	GNP in billions of current dollars	Price index (1972 = 1.0000)	Real GNP (billions of 1972 dollars)
1972	1,171	1.0000	1,171 (= 1,171 ÷ 1.0000)
1975	1,529	1.2718	
1978	2,156	1.5005	1,437 (= 2,156 ÷ 1.5005)
1981	2,938	1.9358	1,518 (= 2,938 ÷ 1.9358)

Using Value-Added to Calculate GNP

We have pointed out that gross national product includes the value of only the final goods and services produced. Obviously, however, the output of

[1] The real GNP in 1975 equaled $1,529 billion divided by 1.2718, or 1,202 billion of 1972 dollars.

Table 7.3

VALUE-ADDED BY VARIOUS INDUSTRIES, UNITED STATES, 1984

Industry	Value-added (billions of dollars)
Agriculture, forestry and fisheries	91
Mining	118
Construction	148
Manufacturing	776
Transportation	130
Communication	103
Electricity, gas, and sanitation	110
Wholesale and retail trade	602
Finance, insurance, and real estate	598
Other services	529
Government[a]	422
Rest of the world	44
Gross national product	3,663[b]

[a] Equals wages and salaries of government workers.
[b] Because of rounding errors and a statistical discrepancy, figures do not sum to total.
Source: U.S. Department of Commerce.

final goods and services is not due solely to the efforts of the producers of the final goods and services. The total value of an automobile when it leaves the plant, for example, represents the work of many industries besides the automobile manufacturers. The steel, tires, glass, and many other components of the automobile were not produced by the automobile manufacturers. In reality, the automobile manufacturers only added a certain amount of value to the value of the intermediate goods—steel, tires, glass, and so forth—they purchased. This point is basic to an understanding of how the gross national product is calculated.

To measure the contribution of a firm or industry to final output, we use the concept of value-added. **Value-added** means just what it says: *the amount of value added by a firm or industry to the total worth of the product.* It is a measure in money terms of the extent of production taking place in a particular firm or industry. Suppose that $160 million of bread was produced in the United States in 1986. To produce it, farmers harvested $50 million of wheat, which was used as an intermediate product by flour mills, which turned out $80 million of flour. This flour was used as an intermediate product by the bakers who produced the $160 million of bread. What is the value-added at each stage of the process? For simplicity, assume that the farmers did not have to purchase any materials from other firms in order to produce the wheat. Then the value-added by the wheat farmers is $50 million; the value-added by the flour mills is $30 million ($80 million − $50 million); and the value-added by the bakers is $80 million ($160 million − $80 million). The total of the value-added at all stages of the process ($50 million + $30 million + $80 million) must equal the value of the output of final product ($160 million), because each stage's value-added is its contribution to this value.

Table 7.3 shows the value-added by various industrial groups in the United States in 1984. Since the total of the value-added by all industries must equal the value of all final goods and services, which, of course, is gross national product, it follows that 3,663 billion—the total of the figures in Table 7.3—must have been equal to gross national product in 1984. It is interesting to note that most of the value-added in the American economy in 1984 was not contributed by manufacturing, mining, construction, transportation, communication, or electricity or gas. Instead, most of it came from services—wholesale and retail trade, finance, insurance, real estate, government services, and other services. This is a sign of a basic change taking place in the American economy, which is turning more and more toward producing services, rather than goods.

Net National Product

One major drawback of GNP as a measure of national output must now be faced: it does not take into account the fact that plant and equipment wear out with use, and that a certain amount of each year's national output must be devoted to replacing the capital goods worn out in producing the year's output. Economists have therefore developed another important measure, net national product (NNP), that recognizes what every accountant knows—the relevance of depreciation. (Recall the discussion in Chapter 6.)

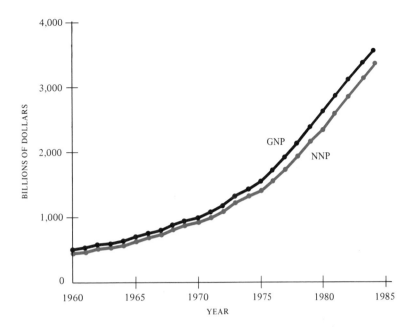

Figure 7.2

Gross National Product and Net National Product, United States, 1960–84 *It is evident that GNP and NNP move together quite closely. Thus, for many practical purposes, which one you use doesn't matter much.*

Specifically, **net national product** *equals gross national product minus depreciation.* To obtain net national product, government statisticians estimate the amount of depreciation—the amount of the nation's plant, equipment, and structures that are worn out during the period—and deduct it from gross national product. Net national product is a more accurate measure of the economy's output than gross national product because it takes depreciation into account, but estimates of net national product contain whatever errors are made in estimating depreciation (which is not easy to measure).

As we shall see in succeeding chapters, data on gross national product are more often used, even if net national product may be a somewhat better measure. Actually, since GNP and NNP move together quite closely, which one you use doesn't matter much for most practical purposes. (See Figure 7.2.)

The Limitations of GNP and NNP

It is essential that the limitations of both gross national product and net national product be understood. Although they are very useful, these figures are by no means ideal measures of economic well-being. At least five limitations of these measures must always be borne in mind.

Population. GNP and NNP are not very meaningful unless one knows the size of the population of the country in question. For example, the fact that a particular nation's GNP equals $50 billion means one thing if the nation has 10 million inhabitants, and quite another thing if it has 500 million inhabitants. To correct for the size of the population, GNP per capita—GNP divided by the population—is often used as a rough measure of output per person in a particular country.

Leisure. GNP and NNP do not take into account one of mankind's most

137

prized activities, leisure. During the past century, the average work week in the United States has decreased substantially. It has gone from almost 70 hours in 1850 to about 40 hours today. As people have become more affluent, they have chosen to substitute leisure for increased production. Yet this increase in leisure time, which surely contributes to our well-being, does not show up in GNP or NNP. Neither does the personal satisfaction (or displeasure and alienation) people get from their jobs.

Quality Changes. GNP and NNP do not take adequate account of changes in the quality of goods. An improvement in a product is not reflected accurately in GNP and NNP unless its price reflects the improvement. For example, if a new type of drug is put on the market at the same price as an old drug, and if the output and cost of the new drug are the same as the old drug, GNP will not increase, even though the new drug is twice as effective as the old one. Because GNP and NNP do not reflect such increases in product quality, it is sometimes argued that the commonly used price indices overestimate the amount of inflation, since although prices may have gone up, quality may have gone up too.

Value and Distribution. GNP and NNP say nothing about the social desirability of the composition and distribution of the nation's output. Each good and service produced is valued at its price. If the price of a Bible is $10 and the price of a pornographic novel is $10, both are valued at $10, whatever you or I may think about their respective worth. Moreover, GNP and NNP measure only the total quantity of goods and services produced. They tell us nothing about how this output is distributed among the people. If a nation's GNP is $500 billion, this is its GNP whether 90 percent of the output is consumed by a relatively few rich families or whether the output is distributed relatively equally among the citizens.

Social Costs. GNP and NNP do not reflect some of the social costs arising from the production of goods and services. In particular, they do not reflect the environmental damage resulting from the operation of our nation's factories, offices, and farms. It is common knowledge that the atmosphere and water supplies are being polluted in various ways by firms, consumers, and governments. Yet these costs are not deducted from GNP or NNP, even though the failure to do so results in an overestimate of our true economic welfare.

Economists are beginning to correct the GNP figures to eliminate some of these problems. For example, William Nordhaus and James Tobin, both of whom have served on the Council of Economic Advisers, have tried to correct the GNP figures to take proper account of the value of leisure, the value of housewives' services, and the environmental costs of production, among other things.[2] (See Example 7.1.) Unquestionably, more work along this line is needed, and will be done. However, it is also worth noting that many of these adjustments and corrections are necessarily quite rough, since there is no accurate way to measure the relevant values and costs.

---

[2] W. Nordhaus and J. Tobin, "Is Growth Obsolete?" *Fiftieth Anniversary Colloquium,* New York: National Bureau of Economic Research, 1972.

Example 7.1   Measured Economic Welfare and National Defense

William Nordhaus and Nobel laureate James Tobin of Yale University have attempted to adjust the net national product to obtain a better measure of economic welfare in the United States. Simplifying somewhat, they add to net national product the value of leisure and nonmarketed services, and they deduct the cost of various disamenities such as pollution. Their result, called *measured economic welfare,* is shown below:

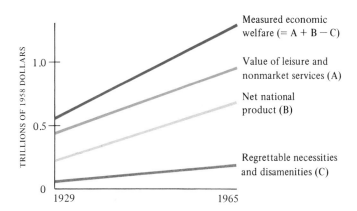

(a) Did NNP grow more or less rapidly during 1929–65 than measured economic welfare? (b) Does this mean that NNP exaggerated the percentage rate of increase of economic welfare during this period? (c) Nordhaus and Tobin include defense expenditures as "regrettable necessities," and deduct them from NNP to calculate measured economic welfare. (According to Nordhaus and Tobin, regrettable necessities are expenditures that "yield no direct satisfaction.") What do you think their reasons are for treating defense expenditures in this way? (d) What is the argument against this treatment of defense expenditures?

SOLUTION

(a) NNP increased by 206 percent (from $184 billion to $563 billion in 1958 dollars). Measured economic welfare increased by 128 percent (from $544 billion to $1,241 billion in 1958 dollars). Thus, in percentage terms, NNP grew more rapidly than measured economic welfare. (b) Yes, based on the above figures. (c) They argue that "we see no direct effect of defense expenditures on household economic welfare. No reasonable country (or household) buys 'national defense' for its own sake. If there were no war or risk of war, there would be no need for defense expenditures and no one would be the worse without them." (d) According to economists like Wilfred Beckerman, "the same sort of reasoning [used by Tobin and Nordhaus in (c)] applies to almost any component of GNP. Nobody would want hospital accident wards, or even home first aid kits, for their own sake."*

*See Nordhaus and Tobin, *op. cit.,* and W. Beckerman, *Two Cheers for the Affluent Society,* New York: St. Martin's Press, 1974.

Test Yourself

1. The following table shows the value of GNP in the nation of Puritania. The figures shown are in millions of 1960 dollars and current dollars. Fill in the blanks.

Year	GNP in millions of 1960 dollars	GNP in millions of current dollars	Price index $\left(\dfrac{current\ price\ level}{1960\ price\ level}\right)$
1974	1,000	____	1.00
1976	____	1,440	1.20
1978	1,300	____	1.40
1980	1,500	____	1.60
1986	____	2,720	1.70

2. If Ronald Reagan wins $100,000 from Walter Mondale in a poker game, will this increase, decrease, or have no effect on GNP? Explain.

3. If a paper mill produces $1 million worth of paper this year, but adds considerably to the pollutants in a nearby river, are the social costs arising from this pollution reflected in the gross national product? If so, how? Should these costs be reflected in the GNP? If so, why?

4. A (small) country contains only ten firms. William Moran, the country's top statistician, calculates the country's GNP by totaling the sales of these ten firms. Do you agree with this procedure? Why, or why not?

Two Approaches to GNP

Suppose that we want to measure the market value of an automobile. One way to do this is to look at how much the consumer pays for the automobile. Although this is the most straightforward way to measure the automobile's market value, it is not the only way it can be done. Another, equally valid way is to add up all of the wage, interest, rental, and profit incomes generated in the production of the automobile. As pointed out in the circular flow model in Chapter 3 (Figure 3.15), the amount that the automobile producer receives for this car is equal to its profit (or loss) on the car plus the amount it pays the workers and other resource owners who contributed their resources to its production. Thus, if we add up all of the wage, interest, rental, and profit incomes resulting from the production of the automobile, the result is the same as if we determine how much the consumer pays for the automobile.

By the same token, there are two ways to measure the market value of the output of the economy as a whole. Or, put differently, there are two ways of looking at GNP. One is the *expenditures approach,* which regards GNP as the sum of all the expenditures on the final goods and services produced this year. The other is the *income approach,* which regards GNP as the sum of incomes derived from the production of this year's total output.

Since both of these approaches are valid, it follows that GNP can be viewed as either the total expenditure on this year's total output or as the total income stemming from the production of this year's total output. In other words,

The total expenditure on this year's total output = GNP = The total income stemming from the production of this year's total output.

Basic Idea #14: Gross national product, since it equals the value of all final goods and services produced, can be viewed as either the total expenditure on this year's total output or as the total income stemming from the production of this year's total output. (For the flow of output, income, and expenditure in the national economy, see Figure 7.3.)

This is an identity; the left-hand side of this equation must equal the right-hand side. (More precisely, the right-hand side should also include depreciation and indirect business taxes, as we shall see below. But this refinement can be ignored at this point.)

It is important to understand both the income and the expenditures approaches to GNP. In the following sections, we describe both approaches in more detail, and provide a more formal proof that they do in fact provide the same result.

The Expenditures Approach to GNP

To use the **expenditures approach** to determine GNP, one must add up all the spending on final goods and services. Economists distinguish among four broad categories of spending, each of which is taken up below.

PERSONAL CONSUMPTION EXPENDITURES

Personal consumption expenditures include the spending by households on durable goods, nondurable goods, and services. This category of spending includes your expenditures on items like food and drink, which are nondurable goods. It also includes your family's expenditures on a car or on an electric washer or dryer, which are durable goods. Further, it includes your payments to a dentist, who is providing a service (painful though it sometimes may be). Table 7.4 shows that in 1984 personal consumption accounted for about 64 percent of the total amount spent on final goods and services in the United States. Expenditures on consumer durable goods are clearly much less than on consumer nondurable goods, whereas expenditures on services are now larger than expenditures on either durable or nondurable goods.

GROSS PRIVATE DOMESTIC INVESTMENT

Gross private domestic investment consists of all investment spending by U.S. firms. As shown in Table 7.4, three broad types of expenditures are included in this category. First, all *final purchases of tools, equipment, and machinery* are included. Second, all *construction expenditures,* including expenditures on residential housing, are included. (One reason why houses are treated as investment goods is that they can be rented out.) Third, the *change in total inventories* is included. An increase in inventories is a positive investment; a decrease in inventories is a negative investment. The change in inventories must be included, because GNP measures the value of all final goods and services produced, *even if they are not sold this year.* Thus GNP must include the value of any increases in inventories that occur during the year. On the other hand, if a decrease occurs during the year in the value of inventories, the value of this decrease in inventories must be subtracted in calculating GNP because these goods and services were produced prior to the beginning of this year. In other words, a decline in inventories means that society has purchased more than it has produced during the year.

Table 7.4

EXPENDITURES ON FINAL GOODS AND SERVICES, UNITED STATES, 1984

Type of expenditure		Amount (billions of dollars)
Personal consumption		2,342
Durable goods	319	
Nondurable goods	857	
Services	1,166	
Gross private domestic investment		638
Expenditures on plant and equipment	426	
Residential structures	154	
Increase in inventories	58	
Net exports		−64
Exports	364	
Imports	428	
Government purchases of goods and services		747
Federal	295	
State and local	452	
Gross national product		3,663

Source: U.S. Department of Commerce.

Gross private domestic investment is "gross" in the sense that it includes all additions to the nation's stock of investment goods, whether or not they are replacements for equipment or plant that are used up in producing the current year's output. *Net private domestic investment* includes only the addition to the nation's stock of investment goods after allowing for the replacement of used-up plant and equipment. To illustrate the distinction between gross and net private domestic investment, consider the situation in 1984. In that year, the nation produced $638 billion worth of investment goods; thus gross private domestic investment equaled $638 billion. But in producing the 1984 GNP, $403 billion worth of investment goods were used up. Thus net private domestic investment equaled $638 billion minus $403 billion, or $235 billion. This was the net addition to the nation's stock of investment goods.

Net private domestic investment indicates the change in the nation's stock of capital goods. If it is positive, the nation's productive capacity, as gauged by its capital stock, is growing. If it is negative, the nation's productive capacity, as gauged by its capital stock, is declining. As pointed out in Chapter 1, the amount of goods and services that the nation can produce is influenced by the size of its stock of capital goods. (Why? Because these capital goods are one important type of resource.) Thus this year's net private domestic investment is a determinant of how much the nation can produce in the future.

GOVERNMENT PURCHASES OF GOODS AND SERVICES

This category of spending includes the expenditures of the federal, state, and local governments for the multitude of functions they perform: defense, education, police protection, and so forth. It does not include transfer payments, since they are not payments for current production. Table 7.4 shows that government spending in 1984 accounted for about 20 percent of the total amount spent on final goods and services in the United States. State and local expenditures are bigger than federal expenditures. As you recall from Chapter 4, many of the expenditures of the federal government are on items like national defense, health, and education, while at the state and local levels the biggest expenditure is for items like education and highways.

NET EXPORTS

Net exports equal the amount spent by other nations on our goods and services less the amount we spent on other nations' goods and services. This factor must be included since some of our national output is destined for foreign markets, and since we import some of the goods and services we consume. There is no reason why this component of spending cannot be negative, since imports can exceed exports. The quantity of net exports tends to be quite small. Table 7.4 shows that net exports in 1984 were equal (in absolute terms) to about 2 percent of the total amount spent on final goods and services in the United States. Because net exports are so small, we shall ignore them until Chapters 21 and 22, where we shall focus attention exclusively on international trade and finance.

PUTTING TOGETHER THE SPENDING COMPONENTS

Finally, because the four categories of expenditure described above include all possible types of spending on final goods and services, their sum equals the gross national product. In other words,

GNP = personal consumption expenditures +
 gross private domestic investment +
 government purchases of goods and
 services +
 net exports.

As shown in Table 7.4, the gross national product in 1984 equaled 2,342 + 638 + 747 − 64, or $3,663 billion.

The Income Approach to GNP

To use the *income approach* to determine GNP, one must add up all of the income stemming from the production of this year's output. This income is of various types: compensation of employees, rents, interest, proprietors' income, and corporate profits. In addition, for reasons described in detail in a later section, we must also include a capital consumption allowance and indirect business taxes. Each of these items is defined and discussed below.

COMPENSATION OF EMPLOYEES

This is the largest of the income categories. It includes the wages and salaries that are paid by firms and government agencies to suppliers of labor. In addition, it contains a variety of supplementary payments by employers for the benefit of their employees, such as payments into public and private pension and welfare funds. These supplementary payments are part of the employers' costs and are included in the total compensation of employees.

RENTS

In the present context, *rent* is defined as a payment to households for the supply of property resources. For example, it includes house rents received by landlords. Quite different definitions of rent are used by economists in other contexts.

INTEREST

Interest includes payments of money by private businesses to suppliers of money capital. If you buy a bond issued by General Motors, the interest payments you receive are included. Interest payments made by the government on Treasury bills, savings bonds, and other securities are excluded on the grounds that they are not payments for current goods and services. They are regarded as transfer payments.

PROPRIETORS' INCOME

What we have referred to as profits are split into two parts in the national income accounts: proprietors' income and corporate profits. ***Proprietors' income*** consists of the net income of unincorporated businesses. In other words, it consists of the net income of proprietorships and partnerships (as well as cooperatives).

CORPORATE PROFITS

Corporate profits consist of the net income of corporations. This item contains three parts: (1) dividends received by the stockholders, (2) retained earnings, and (3) the amount paid by corporations as income taxes. In other words, this item is equal to corporate profits before the payment of corporate income taxes.

DEPRECIATION

All of the items discussed above—compensation of employees, rents, interest, proprietors' income, and corporate profits—are forms of income. In addition, there are two nonincome items, depreciation and indirect business taxes, that must be added to the sum of the income items to obtain GNP. As we know from an earlier section, ***depreciation*** is the value of the nation's plant, equipment, and structures that are worn out this year. In the national income accounts, depreciation is often called a *capital consumption allowance,* because it measures the value of the capital consumed during the year. The reason why depreciation must be added to the sum of the income items to obtain GNP is given in a subsequent section.

INDIRECT BUSINESS TAXES

The government imposes certain taxes, such as general sales taxes, excise taxes, and customs duties, which firms treat as costs of production. These taxes are called ***indirect business taxes*** because they are not imposed directly on the business itself, but on its products or services instead. A good example of an indirect business tax is the tax on cigarettes; another is the general sales tax. Before a firm can pay out incomes to its workers, suppliers, or stockholders, it must pay these indirect business taxes to the government. As shown in the next section, these indirect business taxes, like depreciation, must be added to the total of the income items to get GNP.

PUTTING TOGETHER THE INCOME COMPONENTS (PLUS DEPRECIATION AND INDIRECT BUSINESS TAXES)

As we have stated repeatedly, the sum of the five types of income described above (plus depreciation and indirect business taxes) equals gross national product. In other words,

GNP = compensation of employees + rent + interest + proprietors' income + corporate profits + depreciation + indirect business taxes.

A proof that this is true is contained in the next section.

GNP Equals the Total Claims on Output: A Proof

In the previous section, we said that GNP exactly equals the total claims on output—the sum total of the wages of the workers who participated in the productive efforts, the interest paid to the investors who lent money to the firms that produced the output, the profits of the owners of the firms which produced the output, and the rents paid the owners of land or buildings used to produce the output, as well as indirect business taxes and depreciation. However, until now we have not proved that GNP equals the sum of these total claims on output.

To provide such a proof, let's start with a single firm, the General Electric Corporation, a huge producer of electrical equipment, appliances, and other products. By the simple rules of accounting discussed in Chapter 6,

$$\text{profit} = \text{sales} - \text{costs}. \tag{7.1}$$

Thus it follows that

$$\text{sales} = \text{costs} + \text{profit}. \tag{7.2}$$

Suppose we put the value of General Electric's output (i.e., its sales) on the left-hand side of Table 7.5 and its costs and profits on the right-hand side. Clearly, by Equation (7.2), the total of the right-hand side must equal the total of the left-hand side.

Now, suppose that we deduct one element of costs, "Intermediate products bought from other firms," from both sides of Table 7.5, and present the results in Table 7.6. Since the left-hand total equals the right-hand total in Table 7.5, the same must hold in Table 7.6. The total of the left-hand side of Table 7.6 equals value-added, since General Electric's value-added equals its sales minus its expenditures on intermediate goods bought from other firms. The total of the right-hand side of Table 7.6 equals the total claims against General Electric's output, which is the total income paid out (or owed) by the firm—wages, interest, rent, profits—plus

Table 7.5
SALES, COSTS, AND PROFIT, GENERAL ELECTRIC COMPANY, 1984

Sales (millions of dollars)		Costs and profit (millions of dollars)	
Sales	27,947	Employee compensation	10,939
		Interest and rent	22
		Depreciation	1,100
		Indirect business taxes	264
		Intermediate products bought from other firms	13,311
		Total costs	25,636
		Profits	2,311
Total	27,947	Total	27,947

Source: 1984 Annual Report, General Electric Company. To simplify the results, we have compressed and altered the data somewhat. Although they are adequate for present purposes, these figures are only approximate and should not be used in other contexts.

145

Table 7.6

VALUE-ADDED AND CLAIMS AGAINST OUTPUT, GENERAL ELECTRIC COMPANY, 1984

Value-added (millions of dollars)		Claims against output	
Sales	27,947	Employee compensation	10,939
		Interest and rent	22
Subtract: Intermediate products bought		Profits	2,311
from other firms:	13,311	Depreciation	1,100
		Indirect business taxes	264
Value-added	14,636	Total	14,636

Table 7.7

CLAIMS ON OUTPUT, UNITED STATES, 1984

Type of claim on output	Amount of claim (billions of dollars)
Employee compensation	2,173
Rental income	62
Interest	284
Income of proprietors and professionals	154
Corporate profits	286
Indirect business taxes	304
Depreciation	403
Statistical discrepancy[a]	−3
Gross national product	3,663

[a] This also includes some minor items that need not be of concern here. See the source.
Source: U.S. Department of Commerce.

indirect business taxes and depreciation. And, as pointed out above, the total of the left-hand side must equal the total of the right-hand side of Table 7.6.

Next, imagine constructing a table like Table 7.6 for each employer in the economy, putting sales less intermediate products bought from other firms on the left and costs plus profits less intermediate products bought from other firms on the right. For every employer, the total of the left side must equal the total of the right side. Thus, if we add up the total of the left-hand sides for all employers in the economy, the result must equal the total of the right-hand sides for all employers in the economy. But what is the total of the left-hand sides for all employers in the economy? It is the sum of value-added for all employers, which, as we saw in a previous section, equals gross national product. And the total of the right-hand sides for all employers in the economy is the total of all income paid out (or owed) in the economy—wages, interest, rent, profits—plus indirect business taxes and depreciation. Consequently, gross national product must equal the total of all income paid out (or owed) in the economy plus indirect business taxes and depreciation.

Table 7.7 shows the total amounts of various types of income paid out (or owed) in the American economy during 1984. It also shows depreciation and indirect business taxes. You can see for yourself that the total of these items equals gross national product. Besides helping to prove the point stated at the beginning of this section, this table is an interesting description of the relative importance of various types of income. For example, it shows the great importance of wages and salaries in the total income stream in the United States. In 1984, roughly 60 percent of gross national product was paid out in employee compensation.

Finally, to see how these income flows are related to the flows of output and expenditure, look carefully at Figure 7.3, which shows diagrammatically the relationships among them. Beginning at the top left-hand side of the figure, we see that the total claims on output equal GNP. Then moving to the right, we see that part of the income goes to firms, part goes to the government, and the rest goes to households. These receipts are then used by households, firms, and the government to buy the gross national product, as shown on the left-hand side of the figure. (For simplicity, this figure assumes that net exports are zero and that the government has a balanced budget.)

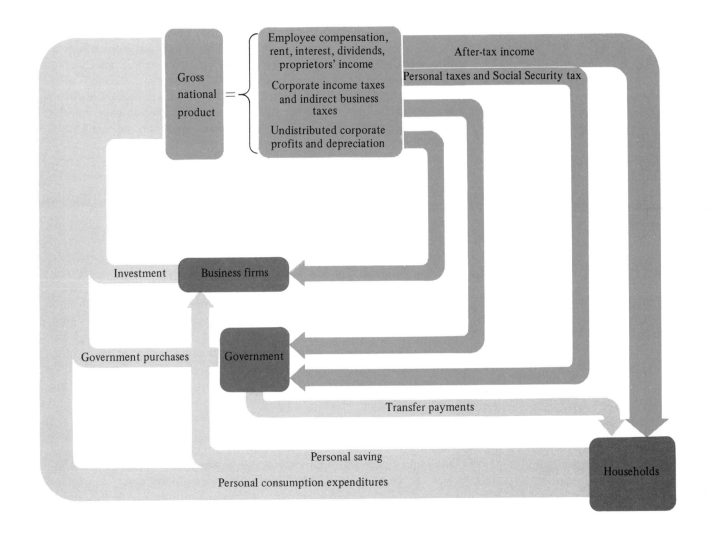

National Income, Personal Income, and Disposable Income

Besides gross national product and net national product, there are several other national accounting concepts that are of importance—namely, national income, personal income, and disposable income. In this section, we describe each of these concepts.

National Income. We are sometimes interested only in the total amount of income paid out (or owed) by employers, an amount called **national income.** Clearly, it is easy to derive national income if you know gross national product. All you have to do is subtract indirect business taxes and depreciation from gross national product. Or putting it another way, all you have to do is subtract indirect business taxes from net national product, since gross national product minus depreciation equals net national product.[3] Table 7.8 shows the result for 1984.

---

[3] Two other small items must also be taken into account. As shown in Table 7.8, we must subtract *business transfer payments*—pensions and other payments made by firms that are transfer payments—and add *subsidies less surpluses of government enterprises,* which corrects

(continued)

Table 7.8

GROSS NATIONAL PRODUCT, NET
NATIONAL PRODUCT, NATIONAL INCOME,
PERSONAL INCOME, AND DISPOSABLE
INCOME, UNITED STATES, 1984

Measure	Amount (billions of dollars)
Gross national product	3,663
Subtract: Depreciation	403
Net national product	3,260
Subtract: Indirect business taxes	304
Business transfers	17
Statistical discrepancy	−7
Add: Subsidies less surpluses of government enterprises	14
National income	2,960
Subtract: Corporate profits	286
Contributions for social insurance	306
Add: Government transfers to persons	399
Dividends	78
Business transfers	17
Other items	150
Personal income	3,012
Subtract: Personal taxes	435
Disposable income	2,577

Source: U.S. Department of Commerce.

Personal Income. For some purposes, we may need to know how much the people of a nation receive in income. This is **personal income,** and it differs from national income in two ways. First, some people who have a claim on income do not actually receive it. For example, although all a firm's profits belong to the owners, not all of its profits are paid out to them. As we saw in Chapter 6, part of the profits are plowed back into the business, and part go to the government for corporate income taxes. Also, wage earners do not actually receive the amounts they and their employers pay currently for Social Security. Second, some people receive income that is not obtained in exchange for services rendered. You will recall from an earlier section that government transfer payments are made to welfare recipients, people receiving unemployment compensation or Social Security, and so forth. Also, there are business transfer payments—pensions and other payments made by firms that are not in exchange for current productive services.

If you know national income, it is easy to derive personal income. You begin by subtracting corporate profits from national income and adding dividends to the result. This will correct for the fact that profits not distributed as dividends do not actually enter people's hands. Then you must deduct contributions for social insurance, and add government and business transfer payments. (Note once again that interest paid by governments on their debt is regarded as a transfer payment, on the grounds that it is not a payment for current goods and services.) These calculations are shown in detail in Table 7.8.

Disposable Income. It is also useful for many purposes to know how much of their personal income people get to keep after personal taxes. This is **disposable income.** If you know what personal income is, you can obtain disposable income by deducting personal taxes from personal income, as shown in Table 7.8. Disposable income plays a very important role in subsequent chapters because it has a major influence on how much consumers spend. According to Table 7.8, disposable income equaled about 70 percent of gross national product in 1984.

for the fact that some government agencies pay out more to income recipients than they produce in value-added. In addition, of course, there is a statistical discrepancy that must be recognized. It is purely a statistical matter.

Test Yourself

1. Given the following data (in millions of dollars) concerning the Puritanian economy in 1986, compute its gross national product and net national product.

Gross private domestic investment	400
Personal consumption expenditure	1,000
Exports	300
Imports	100
Government purchases	300
Increase in inventories	50
Depreciation	100

2. An economic historian, after careful research, makes the following estimates (in millions of dollars) concerning the Puritanian economy in 1910.

Disposable income	400
Business transfer payments	0
Statistical discrepancy	0
Subsidies less surpluses of government enterprises	0
Net national product	600
National income	550
Personal income	460

How much were personal taxes and indirect business taxes in Puritania in 1910?

3. Based on the following data (in millions of dollars), use the income approach to determine GNP.

Compensation of employees	50
Interest	10
Rents	5
Indirect business taxes	8
Corporate profits	10
Transfer payments	22
Proprietors' income	6
Depreciation	4

4. What is the difference between gross private domestic investment and net private domestic investment? Can the former be less than the latter? If the latter is negative, does this mean that the nation's capital stock is increasing or decreasing? Explain.

5. In 1977, there was an $11.6-billion increase in business inventories. Why should this be regarded as a form of investment? Explain why GNP would be calculated incorrectly if this increase in inventories were ignored.

6. Which of the following are included in calculating GNP this year? (a) Interest on a government bond; (b) Payment by the government to a person on welfare; (c) Payment by the government to a naval officer; (d) Wages paid by the University of Michigan to a professor; (e) Payment for a secondhand car by a Florida student; (f) The amount a husband would be willing to pay for his wife's housekeeping services; (g) The amount John Jones pays for 30 shares of IBM stock; (h) The allowances a father gives his 12-year-old son.

Summary

1. One of the key indicators of the health of any nation's economy is the gross national product, which measures the total value of the final goods and services the nation produces in a particular period. Since gross national product is affected by the price level, it must be deflated by a price index to correct for price-level changes. When deflated in this way, GNP is called real GNP, or GNP in constant dollars.

2. There are many pitfalls in calculating the gross national product. One must avoid counting the same output more than once. Purely financial transactions that do not reflect current production must be excluded. Also, some final goods and services that must be included in GNP are not bought and sold in the market place, so they are valued at what they cost.

3. GNP is not an ideal measure of total economic output, let alone a satisfactory measure of economic well-being. It takes no account of a nation's population, the amount of leisure time, or the distribution of income. It does not reflect many changes in the quality of goods and many social costs like pollution. Economists are beginning to correct the GNP figures to eliminate some of these problems.

4. One approach to GNP is the expenditures approach, which regards GNP as the sum of all the expenditures that are involved in taking the total output of final goods and services off the market. To determine GNP in this way, one must add up all the spending on final goods and services. Economists distinguish among four broad categories of spending: personal consumption expenditures, gross private domestic investment, government purchases, and net exports. GNP equals the sum of these four items.

5. Another approach to GNP is the income approach, which regards GNP as the sum of incomes derived from the production of this year's output (plus depreciation and indirect business taxes). To determine GNP in this way, one must add up all the income stemming from the production of this year's total output (plus depreciation and indirect business taxes). Economists identify five broad categories of income: compensation of employees, rents, interest, proprietors' income, and corporate profits. GNP equals the sum of these five items (plus depreciation and indirect business taxes).

6. Net national product is gross national product minus depreciation. It indicates the value of net output when account is taken of capital used up. National income is the total amount of income paid out (or owed) by employers; personal income is the total amount people actually receive in income; and disposable income is the total amount they get to keep after taxes.

Concepts for Review

Gross national product	Value-added	Compensation of
National income accounts	Net national product	employees
Final goods and services	Expenditures approach	Rent
Intermediate good	to GNP	Interest
Transfer payments	Personal consumption	Proprietors' income
Base year	expenditures	Corporate profits
Current dollars	Gross private domestic	Depreciation
Constant dollars	investment	Indirect business
Real gross national	Government purchases	taxes
product	Net exports	National income
Price index	Income approach to	Personal income
Deflating	GNP	Disposable income

CHAPTER 8

Unemployment and Inflation

Two of the most important indicators of the health of any nation's economy are its unemployment rate and its rate of inflation. In late 1985, about 7 percent of the labor force in the United States was unemployed, and the annual rate of inflation was about 3 percent. Neither the unemployment rate nor the inflation rate were as low as many government officials and private citizens desired, but, relative to some previous years, both were a marked improvement. Every government, including our own, watches these two indicators with great interest. And most societies today are committed to policies designed to keep each of them at a reasonably low level. These goals certainly seem sensible, since high rates of unemployment cause enormous economic waste and social hardship, and serious inflation causes an inequitable redistribution of income and major economic inefficiencies.

In this chapter, we begin to study unemployment and inflation. Our first objective is to discuss the nature and costs of unemployment. Then we take up the nature and costs of inflation and how the rate of inflation may be related to the rate of unemployment.

Unemployment

Almost a century ago, Pope Leo XIII said, "Among the purposes of a society should be to arrange for a continuous supply of work at all times and seasons."[1] The word **unemployment** is one of the most frightening in the English language—and for good reason. Unemployed people become de-

[1] Pope Leo XIII, "Encyclical Letter on the Conditions of Labor," May 15, 1891.

moralized, suffer loss of prestige and status, and their families tend to break apart. Sometimes they are pushed toward crime and drugs; often they feel terrible despair. Their children are innocent victims too. Indeed, perhaps the most devastating effects of unemployment are on children, whose education, health, and security may be ruined. After a few minutes' thought, most people would agree that in this or any other country, every citizen who is able and willing to work should be able to get a job.

We are not saying that all unemployment, whatever its cause or nature, should be eliminated. (For example, some unemployment may be voluntary.) According to the U.S. government, any person 16 years old or more who does not have a job and is looking for one is unemployed. Since this definition is necessarily quite broad, it is important that we distinguish among several different kinds of unemployment.

FRICTIONAL UNEMPLOYMENT

Some people quit their jobs and look for something better. They may get angry at their bosses, or they may feel that they can get more money elsewhere. Others, particularly ex-students, are looking for their first job. Still others are temporarily laid off because their work is seasonal, as in the construction industry. Unemployment of this sort is called *frictional unemployment.* Frictional unemployment is inevitable, since people find it desirable to change jobs, and such job changes often involve a period of temporary unemployment.

John Caruso may quit his job after the boss calls him a fathead. It may take him a month to find another job, perhaps because he is unaware of job opportunities or perhaps because the boss was right. During this month, he is numbered among the unemployed. We don't necessarily think that unemployment of this sort is a good thing, but it would not make much sense to try to eliminate it entirely. On the contrary, a free labor market could not function without a certain amount of frictional unemployment.

STRUCTURAL UNEMPLOYMENT

Changes continually occur in the nature of consumer demand and in technology. For example, consumers grow tired of one good and become infatuated with another. And new technologies supplant old ones. Thus some workers are thrown out of work, and because the new goods and the new technologies call for different skills than the old ones did, they cannot use their skills elsewhere. Unemployment of this sort is called *structural unemployment.* It exists when jobs are available for qualified workers, but the unemployed do not have the necessary qualifications. This sort of unemployment results from a mismatch between job requirements and the skills of the unemployed.

Consider the case of Mary Jones, a 58-year-old bookkeeper who was thrown out of work by the introduction of a new technology and who lacks the skills needed to get a job in another field. Ms. Jones is one of the structurally unemployed. To some extent, structural unemployment can be reduced by monetary and fiscal policies of the sort described in the following chapters. But in many cases, the principal way to attack it is by retraining (for jobs in other occupations, industries, or areas) workers whose skills are no longer in demand.

CYCLICAL UNEMPLOYMENT

Cyclical unemployment occurs when, because of an insufficiency of aggregate demand, there are more workers looking for work than there are jobs. Cyclical unemployment is associated with business fluctuations, or the so-called business cycle. Industrialized capitalistic economies have been subject to fluctuations, with booms often succeeding busts and vice versa. (More will be said about the nature and recent history of business fluctuations in the following chapter.) One feature of these fluctuations has been that the American economy has periodically gone through depressions, during which unemployment has been high. The Great Depression of the 1930s was particularly long and severe, and when World War II ended, the American people resolved that the gigantic social costs of the enormous unemployment of the 1930s must not be repeated in the postwar period. To avoid this, Congress passed the Employment Act of 1946, which says,

> It is the continuing policy and responsibility of the Federal Government to use all practicable means . . . [to create and maintain] conditions under which there will be afforded useful employment opportunities, including self-employment, for those able, willing, and seeking to work and to promote maximum employment, production, and purchasing power.

The Employment Act of 1946 was an extremely important piece of legislation, for it committed the federal government to combat cyclical unemployment.[2]

The Measurement and Incidence of Unemployment

Having discussed various types of unemployment, we must look next at the way in which the unemployment rate is measured in the United States and at the characteristics of the unemployed.

THE UNEMPLOYMENT RATE

Each month, the federal government conducts a scientific survey of the American people, asking a carefully selected sample of the population whether they have a job, and, if not, whether they are looking for one. According to most expert opinion, the resulting figures are quite reliable but subject to a number of qualifications. One of these is that the figures do not indicate the extent to which people are underemployed. Some

---

[2] This commitment was extended by the Humphrey-Hawkins Act of 1978, which set specific goals for the unemployment rate and the inflation rate. Although it has not been possible to meet these specific goals (for reasons discussed in subsequent chapters), the enactment of these goals was a noteworthy reaffirmation of the public commitment to fight cyclical unemployment.

people work only part-time, or at jobs well below their level of education or skill, but the government figures count them as fully employed. Also, some people have given up looking for a job and are no longer listed among the unemployed, even though they would be glad to get work if any was offered. To be counted as unemployed in the government figures, one must be actively seeking employment.

To obtain the unemployment rate, the Bureau of Labor Statistics (the government agency responsible for producing the unemployment data) divides the estimated number of people who are unemployed by the estimated number of people in the *labor force*. To be in the labor force, a person must either be employed or unemployed. Note that the unemployment rate can rise either because people who formerly were employed are thrown out of work or because people who formerly were not in the labor force decide to look for jobs. For example, an increasing number of married women who decide to enter the labor force may tend to raise the unemployment rate.

Some critics of the official unemployment statistics would use a definition of unemployment that focuses attention on "serious" cases of joblessness. They would exclude unemployed people with a working spouse, unemployed teenagers living with a parent with a job, and unemployed people who have been out of work less than a month. Also, they would have the government try harder to find out whether those who say they are unemployed are making a serious effort to find work. Officials of the Bureau of Labor Statistics reply that such a change in definition would convert the statistics into a measure of hardship rather than of unemployment.

In interpreting the unemployment statistics, do not jump to the conclusion that unemployment means starvation. For one thing, as we shall see in later chapters, unemployed workers receive unemployment compensation. In the case of some auto workers who were laid off in 1974, unemployment benefits were almost equal to what they made when they were working. But this is the exception, not the rule. In the United States, unemployment compensation typically replaces a third to a half of an unemployed worker's previous before-tax wages. But it replaces a great deal more of his or her after-tax income, because jobless benefits are exempt from taxes.

According to Martin Feldstein of Harvard University, unemployment insurance increases unemployment, since it encourages (or at least enables) the jobless to remain unemployed longer than they otherwise would. Many economists agree with Feldstein, but there is considerable argument over the extent of this effect. Stephen Marston of the Brookings Institution has estimated that unemployment insurance increases the unemployment rate by about 0.25 percentage points, while Feldstein has estimated the increase at about 1.25 percentage points.

HOW MUCH UNEMPLOYMENT IS THERE?

To get some idea of the extent of unemployment, we can consult Figure 8.1, which shows the percent of the labor force unemployed during each year from 1929 to 1984. Note the wide fluctuations in the unemployment rate, and the very high unemployment rates during the 1930s. Fortunately,

Figure 8.1

***Unemployment Rates, United States,
1929–84*** *The unemployment rate has
varied substantially. Fortunately, since
World War II it has not approached the
very high levels of the Great Depression of
the 1930s. But the recession of 1981
showed that the nation is not immune to
severe bouts of unemployment.*

Table 8.1

UNEMPLOYMENT RATE, SELECTED
SEGMENTS OF THE POPULATION, UNITED
STATES, 1984

Population segment	Unemployment rate
Whites	
Males	
16–19 years	16.8
20 years and over	5.7
Females	
16–19 years	15.2
20 years and over	5.8
Nonwhites	
Males	
16–19 years	42.7
20 years and over	14.3
Females	
16–19 years	42.6
20 years and over	13.5
Experienced wage and salary workers	7.1
Women who maintain families	10.3
Married men, spouse present	4.6

*Source: Economic Report of the President,
1985.*

unemployment since World War II has never approached the tragically high
levels of the Great Depression of the 1930s. Between 1958 and 1964, it
averaged about 6 percent, and then declined steadily until it fell below 4
percent in 1966–69. In 1970–74, it bounced back up to 5 or 6 percent, and
then rose to 8½ percent in 1975, after which it receded to 5.8 percent in
1979. In 1981 and 1982, it rose to about 9.5 percent, after which it fell to
about 7.0 percent in 1985. Although many of these variations in the unemployment rate may seem small, they are important. With a labor force of
over 100 million in the United States, a 1 percentage point increase in the
unemployment rate means that over 1 million more people are unemployed. Any administration, Democratic or Republican, watches these figures closely and tries to avoid significant increases in unemployment.

WHO ARE THE UNEMPLOYED?

The overall unemployment rate indicates what percentage of the labor force
is out of work, but it doesn't tell us whether the unemployed are young or
old, white or nonwhite. Since it is important to know the characteristics of
the unemployed, this is the next topic to be considered.

Teenagers. The unemployment rate tends to be higher among younger
than older segments of the labor force. As shown in Table 8.1, the unemployment rate among teenagers is extremely high. In 1984, it was 17 percent
for white males, 15 percent for white females, 43 percent for nonwhite
males, and 43 percent for nonwhite females. To some extent, this is because
many teenagers are new entrants to the labor force. They must spend some
time searching for a job. Also, minimum-wage laws make it difficult for employers to hire teenagers because, in some cases, an employer would find it
worthwhile to hire teenagers only if they could be paid less than the minimum wage.

155

Nonwhites. The unemployment rate tends to be much higher among nonwhites than among whites. Among males 20 years old or more, the unemployment rate in 1984 was 14 percent among nonwhites and 6 percent among whites (Table 8.1). To a considerable extent, this difference can probably be explained by discrimination, now and in the past. Nonwhites have a more difficult time finding a job because of present discriminatory practices, such as unfair hiring practices, and previous discriminatory practices, such as inferior schooling.

The Costs of Unemployment

Basic Idea #15: Unemployment results in less goods and services being produced by society, and in obvious social and personal hardships. Government policies can help to reduce unemployment, as we will see in subsequent chapters, but these policies may have undesirable effects on inflation, at least in the short run.

As stressed at the beginning of this chapter, high levels of unemployment impose great costs on society. In this section, we describe these costs, which are both economic and noneconomic, in more detail.

ECONOMIC COSTS

The economic costs of unemployment include the goods and services that could have been produced by the unemployed. Because these people were unemployed, society had to forgo the production of the goods and services they might have produced, with the result that human wants were less effectively fulfilled than would otherwise have been the case. To determine how much society loses in this way by tolerating an unemployment rate above the minimum level resulting from frictional (and some structural) unemployment, economists estimate the *potential GNP,* which is the level of gross national product that could be achieved if there had been full employment. Thus, if full employment is defined as a 5 percent unemployment rate, potential GNP can be estimated by multiplying 95 percent of the labor force times the normal hours of work per year times the average output per man-hour at the relevant time.

The gap between actual and potential GNP is a measure of what society loses by tolerating less than full employment. Figure 8.2 shows the estimated size of this gap from 1952 to 1985. (Note that both actual and potential GNP are expressed in 1972 prices.) Clearly, the economic costs of unemployment have been very substantial. Consider 1975, a recession year when unemployment was about 8½ percent. As shown in Figure 8.2, society lost about $100 billion in that year alone. Although this estimate is very rough, it is accurate enough to suggest the social waste that accompanies large-scale unemployment.

One important problem in estimating this gap stems from the difficulty of defining "full employment." For many years, a common definition of *full employment* was a 4 percent unemployment rate, since it was felt that frictional and structural unemployment could not be reduced below this level. During the seventies, there was criticism of this definition on the grounds that an unemployment rate of about 5 percent was a more realistic measure of full employment than 4 percent because there were more young people, women, and minority workers in the labor force. All of these groups find it relatively difficult to find jobs. In 1979, the Council of Economic

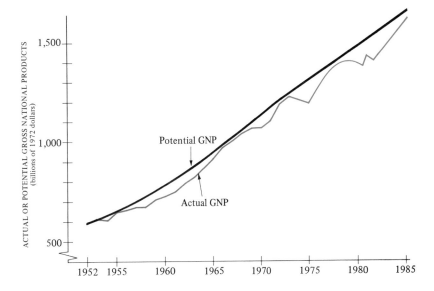

Figure 8.2

Actual and Potential GNP, United States, 1952–85 *The gap between actual and potential GNP is a measure of what society loses because there is less than full employment. In Figure 9.11, we show the size of this gap in earlier years.*

Advisers used a figure of 5.1 percent. Since this debate is unresolved, we shall not try to give a precise numerical definition of full employment.[3]

NONECONOMIC COSTS

Unemployment strikes at the social fabric of families and societies; it is not merely an economic phenomenon. Since general descriptions of the plight of the unemployed often have relatively little impact, a real-life case study may give you a better feel for what unemployment is like. Consider Joseph Torrio, a New Haven factory worker who was laid off after 18 years on the job. He describes in his own words how he spent several mornings:

> Up at seven, cup of coffee, and off to Sargent's. Like to be there when the gang comes to work, the lucky devils. Employment manager not in. Waited in his outer office.... Three others waiting, two reporting for compensation. Other one laid off two weeks ago and said he called at office every day. He inquired what I was doing and when I said "looking for work" he laughed. "You never work here? No? What chance you think you got when 400 like me who belong here out?" Employment manager showed up at 9:30. I had waited two hours. My time has no value. A pleasant fellow; told me in a kind but snappy way business was very bad. What about the future, would he take my name? Said he referred only to the present. Nothing more for me to say, so left. Two more had drifted into office. Suppose they got the same story. Must be a lot of men in New Haven that have heard it by now.
>
> [On May 21], interview with sales manager of the Real Silk Hosiery Mills. Had seen their ads for salesmen in the paper. Sales manager approached me with his hand sticking out, the first one who had offered to shake hands with

[3] Note that Figure 8.2 is based on a definition of full employment that sometimes exceeded 4 percent. For example, in 1977, it was 4.8 percent. For the definitions used, see *Economic Report of the President*, 1978, p. 84. Also see *Economic Report of the President*, 1979, 1981, and 1982.

me. I told him my name and inquired about the position. He took me into his private office, well furnished, and asked me if I had had any selling experience. I told him that I hadn't any but I thought I could do the work.... Asked me to report at 9 A.M. the next morning for further instructions.... [On May 22], I kept my appointment with the sales manager. Spent the morning learning about different kinds of stockings. Made another appointment for the afternoon which I did not keep because he wanted me to bring along $6 as security on a bag and some stock. I did not have the $6.[4]

No single case study can give you an adequate picture of the impact on people of being without a job. There are a wide variety of responses to unemployment. Some people weather it pretty well, others sink into despair; some people have substantial savings they can draw on, others are hard pressed; some people manage to shield their families from the blow, others allow their misfortunes to spread to the rest of the family. But despite these variations, being without work deals a heavy blow to a person's feeling of worth. It hits hard at a person's self-image, indicating that he or she is not needed, cannot support a family, is not really a full and valuable member of society. The impact of widespread and persistent unemployment is most clearly visible at present among the blacks and other racial minorities, where unemployment rates are much higher than among the white population. Unquestionably, the prevalence of unemployment among blacks greatly influences how the blacks view themselves, as well as the way they interact with the rest of the community.

Theories of Unemployment

THE CLASSICAL VIEW OF UNEMPLOYMENT

Until the 1930s, most economists were convinced that the price system, left to its own devices, would hold unemployment to a reasonable minimum. Thus most of the great names of economics in the nineteenth and early twentieth centuries—including John Stuart Mill, Alfred Marshall, and A. C. Pigou—felt that there was no need for government intervention to promote a high level of employment. To be sure, they recognized that unemployment was sometimes large, but they regarded these lapses from high employment as temporary aberrations that the price system would cure automatically. We begin by taking an initial, brief look at why the classical economists felt this was true. (More will be said below and in later chapters about their theories.)

The classical economists recognized the fact that the level of total spending determines the unemployment rate. They believed that total spending was unlikely to be too small to purchase the full-employment level of output, because of *Say's Law* (named after the nineteenth-century French economist, J. B. Say). According to this law, the production of a certain amount of goods and services results in the generation of an amount of income which, if spent, is precisely sufficient to buy that output. (Recall the circular flow discussed in Chapters 3 and 7.) In other words,

The ideas of John Stuart Mill (1806–73) and his arguments in support of individual freedom are particularly famous. He was one of the great philosophers of the nineteenth century. He was also a great economist; his Principles of Political Economy *(1848) is his best-known work. He advocated many social reforms, including shorter working hours and tax reform.*

[4] E. W. Bakke, *The Unemployed Worker,* Hamden, Conn.: Archon, 1969, pp. 168, 169, 174, and 175.

Example 8.1 Should We Look at Employment, not Unemployment?

Some economists believe that the rate of employment is a better measure of job availability than the rate of unemployment. The civilian rate of employment is the number of persons employed (over 16 years of age) in the civilian labor force divided by the number of persons (over 16) in the noninstitutional population (which excludes people in penal, mental, and nursing institutions and the very young). Changes over time in the rate of employment and the rate of unemployment are shown below:

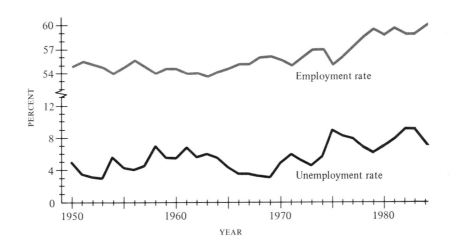

(a) What advantages are there in using the rate of employment? (b) Does it make any real difference as to which of these measures we use? (c) According to some economists, the gradual increase in the labor force participation of women has increased the rate of employment. Do you think that it has also influenced the unemployment rate? (d) Should we forget about the unemployment rate and focus attention only on the employment rate?

SOLUTION

(a) One advantage is that it does not depend on the judgment as to whether a person really is "available for work" or "actively seeking employment." Some economists feel that some people say they are looking for work, but really aren't. Other people who want work may be discouraged and give up looking for it. (b) Yes. For example, in the late 1970s, the rate of employment was high and growing, indicating that the economy was providing lots of job opportunities. At the same time, however, the unemployment rate also was high. (c) Yes. Female workers tend to move in and out of the labor force more than men. Also, men with working wives are under less pressure to stay at their present jobs or to minimize the length of time they are unemployed. (d) No. A high unemployment rate indicates that the labor market is not functioning efficiently. Both the employment rate and the unemployment rate should be considered.

supply creates its own demand, since the total amount paid out by the producers of the goods and services to resource owners must equal the value of the goods and services. Thus, if this amount is spent, it must be sufficient to purchase all of the goods and services that are produced.

But what if resource owners do not spend all of their income, but save some of it instead? How, then, will the necessary spending arise to take all of the output off the market? The answer the classical economists offered is that each dollar saved will be invested. Therefore, investment (made largely by business firms) will restore to the spending stream what resource owners take out through the saving process. Recall that the economist's definition of investment is different from the one often used in common parlance. To the economist, investment means expenditure on plant, equipment, and other productive assets. The classical economists believed that the amount invested would automatically equal the amount saved because the interest rate—the price paid for borrowing money—would fluctuate in such a way as to maintain equality between them. In other words, there is a market for loanable funds, and the interest rate will vary so that the quantity of funds supplied equals the quantity demanded. Thus, since funds are demanded to be used—that is, invested—the amount saved will be invested.

Further, the classical economists said that the amount of goods and services firms can sell depends upon the prices they charge, as well as on total spending. For example, $1 million in spending will take 100 cars off the market if the price is $10,000 per car, and 200 cars off the market if the price is $5,000 per car. Recognizing this, the classical economists argued that firms would cut prices to sell their output. Competition among firms would prod them to reduce their prices in this way, with the result that the high-employment level of output would be taken off the market.

Looking at this process more closely, it is obvious that the prices of resources must also be reduced under such circumstances. Otherwise firms would incur losses because they would be getting less for their product, but paying no less for resources. The classical economists believed that it was realistic to expect the prices of resources to decline in such a situation. Indeed they were quite willing to assume that the wage rate—the price of labor—would be flexible in this way. They expected this flexibility because of competition among laborers. Through the processes of competition, they felt that wage rates would be bid down to the level where everyone who really wanted to work could get a job.

THE VIEWS OF KARL MARX

Quite a different view of unemployment was held by Karl Marx (1818–83), the intellectual father of communism. A man of unquestioned genius, he became an object of quasi-religious devotion to a large part of the world and a hated (and sometimes feared) revolutionary figure to another large part of the world. Because Marx the revolutionary has had such an enormous effect on modern history, it is difficult to discuss Marx the economist. But he was a very profound and influential economist. A meticulous German scholar who spent much of his life in poverty-ridden circumstances in Britain, he wrote a huge, four-volume work on econom-

1860s factory workers in Great Britain

ics, *Das Kapital.*[5] Eighteen years in the making, it remains one of the most influential books ever written.

To understand Marx, we need to know something about the times in which he lived. The period was characterized by revolutionary pressures against the ruling classes. In most of the countries of Europe, there was little democracy, as we know it. The masses participated little, if at all, in the world of political affairs, and very fully in the world of drudgery. For example, at one factory in Manchester, England, in 1862, people worked an average of about 80 hours per week. For these long hours of toil, the workers generally received small wages. They often could do little more than feed and clothe themselves. Given these circumstances, it is little wonder that revolutionary pressures were manifest.

Marx, viewing the economic system of his day, believed that capitalism was doomed to collapse. He believed that the workers were exploited by the capitalists—the owners of factories, mines, and other types of capital. And he believed that the capitalists, by introducing new labor-saving technology, would throw more and more workers into unemployment. This army of unemployed workers, by competing for jobs, would keep wages at a subsistence level. As machinery was substituted for labor, Marx felt that profits would fall. Unemployment would become more severe. Big firms would absorb small ones. Eventually the capitalistic system was bound to collapse.

To get the flavor of his reasoning and emotions, consider the following famous passage from *Das Kapital,* describing his vision of the death knell of the capitalist system:

> Along with the constantly diminishing number of the magnates of capital, who usurp and monopolize all advantages of this process of transformation, grows the mass of misery, oppression, slavery, degradation, exploitation; but with this too grows the revolt of the working-class, a class always increasing in numbers, and disciplined, united, organized by the very mechanism of the process of capitalist production itself.... Centralization of the means of production and socialization of labor at last reach a point where they become incompatible with their capitalist integument. This integument bursts asunder. The knell of capitalist private property sounds. The expropriators are expropriated.[6]

According to Marx, the inevitable successor to capitalism would be socialism, an economic system with no private property. Instead, property would be owned by society as a whole. Socialism, constituting a "dictatorship of the proletariat," would be only a transitional step to the promised land of communism. Marx did not spell out the characteristics of communism in detail. He was sure that it would be a classless society where everyone worked and no one owned capital, and he was sure that the state would "wither away," but he did not attempt to go much beyond this in his blueprint for communism. Marx's doctrines had plenty of limitations. The important point here is that, although the classical view (discussed in the previous section) was the dominant one, it did not go unchallenged, even in the nineteenth century.

[5] Karl Marx, *Das Kapital,* New York: Modern Library, 1906.
[6] Marx, pp. 836–837.

Crowd outside employment office, 1931

JOHN MAYNARD KEYNES AND THE GREAT DEPRESSION

Son of a British economist who was famous in his own right, John Maynard Keynes (1883–1946) was enormously successful in a variety of fields. He published a brilliant book on the theory of probability while still a relatively young man. Working for a half-hour in bed each morning, he made millions of dollars as a stock market speculator. He was a distinguished patron of the arts and a member of the Bloomsbury set, a group of London intellectuals who were the intellectual pacesetters for British society. He was a faculty member at Cambridge University, and a key figure at the British Treasury. In short, he was an extraordinarily gifted and accomplished man.

Keynes lived and worked almost a century after Marx. His world was quite different from Marx's world; and Keynes himself—polished, successful, a member of the elite—was quite different from the poverty-stricken, revolutionary Marx. But the two great economists were linked in at least one important respect. Both were preoccupied with unemployment and the future of the capitalistic system. As we saw in the previous section, Marx predicted that unemployment would get worse and worse, until at last the capitalist system would collapse. In the 1930s, when Keynes was at the height of his influence, the Great Depression seemed to many people to be proving Marx right.

In 1936, while the world was still in the throes of this economic disaster, Keynes published his *General Theory of Employment, Interest, and Money.*[7] His purpose in this book was to explain how the capitalist economic system could get stalled in the sort of depressed state of equilibrium that existed in the 1930s. He also tried to indicate how governments might help to solve the problem. Contrary to the classical economists, Keynes concluded that no automatic mechanism in a capitalistic society would generate a high level of employment—or, at least, would generate it quickly enough to be relied on in practice. Instead, the equilibrium level of national output might for a long time be below the level required to achieve high employment. His reasons for believing that this could be the case are discussed in detail in this and subsequent chapters.

To push the economy toward a higher level of employment, Keynes advocated the conscious, forceful use of the government's power to spend and tax. As we shall see in Chapter 12, many years passed before these powers became accepted tools of national economic policy, but it was Keynes who provided much of the intellectual stimulus. According to many economists, Keynes made a major contribution to saving the capitalist system.

KEYNES'S CRITICISMS OF THE CLASSICAL VIEW

There were at least two basic flaws in the classical model, as Keynes and his followers saw it. First, in their view, *there is no assurance that intended saving will equal intended investment at a level insuring high employment.* The people and firms who save are often not the same as the people and

---

[7] John Maynard Keynes, *The General Theory of Employment, Interest, and Money,* New York: Harcourt, Brace, 1936.

firms who invest, and they often have quite different motivations. In particular, a considerable amount of saving is done by families who want to put something aside for a rainy day or for a car or appliance. On the other hand, a considerable amount of investment is done by firms that are interested in increasing their profits by expanding their plants or by installing new equipment. According to Keynes, one cannot be sure that changes in the interest rate will bring about the equality of saving and investment visualized by the classical economists. In his view, intended saving may not equal intended investment at a level insuring high employment. Instead, they may be equal at a level corresponding to considerable unemployment (or to considerable inflation). Thus a purely capitalist economic system, in the absence of appropriate government policies, has no dependable rudder to keep it clear of the shoals of serious unemployment or of serious inflation.

Second, *Keynes and his followers pointed out the unreality of the classical economists' assumption that prices and wages are flexible.* Contrary to the classical economists' argument, the modern economy contains many departures from perfect competition that are barriers to downward flexibility of prices and wages. In particular, many important industries are dominated by a few producers who try hard to avoid cutting price. Even in the face of a considerable drop in demand, such industries have sometimes maintained extraordinarily stable prices. Moreover, the labor unions fight hard to avoid wage cuts. In view of these facts of life, the classical assumption of wage and price flexibility seems rather unrealistic. And to many economists, it seems unlikely that price and wage reductions can be depended on to maintain full employment.

POST-KEYNESIAN DEVELOPMENTS

Forty years have elapsed since Keynes's death, and the nature of our economic problems has changed considerably. The Great Depression of the 1930s is a distant memory, while double-digit inflation is fresh in the minds of practically everyone. The unemployment problem is still of concern to our people (particularly during 1982, when the unemployment rate reached over 9 percent), but the electorate has learned to fear inflation as well as unemployment.

The past 40 years have also witnessed considerable changes and improvements in our understanding of unemployment and its relation to inflation. While Keynes is still regarded as a very great economist (even by those who criticize the policies he espoused), the theory of unemployment has come a long way since his day, as we shall see in subsequent chapters.

John Maynard Keynes

Test Yourself

1. "Unemployed workers make about as much as when they were employed because of unemployment insurance, so the nation need not worry about the unemployed." Specify at least two fundamental errors in this statement.

2. The unemployment rate shows the percentage of the labor force out of work, but not how long they have been out of work. Does the average duration of unemployment matter too? Do you think that the average duration of unemployment is directly or inversely related to the unemployment rate? Explain.

3. Explain the differences among frictional unemployment, structural unemployment, and cyclical unemployment. Should the government attempt to reduce all types of unemployment to zero? Why or why not?

4. The data on the right came from the 1985 *Economic Report of the President*. Fill in the blanks.

	1983	1984
Percent of civilian labor force unemployed	9.6	7.5
Percent of civilian labor force employed	——	——
Civilian labor force	111.6 million	113.5 million
Total employment	——	——
Total unemployment	——	——

Inflation

It is hard to find anyone these days who does not know the meaning of inflation firsthand. Try to think of commodities you regularly purchase that cost less now than they did several years ago. Chances are that you can come up with precious few. *Inflation* is a general upward movement of prices. In other words, inflation means that goods and services that currently cost $10 may soon be priced at $11 or even $12, and wages and other input prices increase as well. It is essential to distinguish between the movements of individual prices and the movement of the entire price level. As we saw in Chapter 3, the price of an individual commodity can move up or down with the shifts in the commodity's demand or supply curve. If the price of a particular good—corn, say—goes up, this need not be inflation, since the prices of other goods may be going down at the same time, so that the overall price level—the general average level of prices—remains much the same. Inflation occurs only if most prices for goods and services in the society move upward—that is, if the average level of prices increases.

In periods of inflation, the value of money is reduced. A dollar is worth what it will buy, and what it will buy is determined by the price level. Thus a dollar was more valuable in 1940, when a Hershey chocolate bar was 5 cents, than in 1985, when it was about 40 cents. But it is important to recognize that inflations may vary in severity. *Runaway inflations* wipe out the value of money quickly and thoroughly, while *creeping inflations* erode its value gradually and slowly. There is a lot of difference between runaway inflation and a creeping inflation, as the following examples indicate.

RUNAWAY INFLATION

The case of Germany after World War I is a good example of runaway inflation. Germany was required to pay large reparations to the victorious Allies after the war. Rather than attempting to tax its people to pay these amounts, the German government merely printed additional quantities of paper money. This new money increased total spending in Germany, and the increased spending resulted in higher prices because the war-devastated economy could not increase output substantially. As more and more money was printed, prices rose higher and higher, reaching utterly fantastic levels. By 1923, it took a *trillion* marks (the unit of German currency) to buy what one mark would buy before the war.

The effect of this runaway inflation was to disrupt the economy. Prices had to be adjusted from day to day. People rushed to the stores to spend the money they received as soon as possible, since very soon it would buy much less. Speculation was rampant. This inflation was a terrible blow to Germany. The middle class was wiped out; its savings became completely worthless. It is no wonder that Germany has in recent years been more sensitive than many other countries to the evils of inflation.

CREEPING INFLATION

For the past 50 years, the price level in the United States has tended to go one way only—up. In practically all years during this period, prices have risen. Since 1955, there hasn't been a single year when the price level has fallen. Certainly, this has not been a runaway inflation, but it has resulted in a very substantial erosion in the value of the dollar. Like a beach slowly worn away by the ocean, the dollar has gradually lost a considerable portion of its value. Specifically, prices now tend to be about 6 times what they were 40 years ago. Thus the dollar now is worth about a sixth of what it was worth then. Although a creeping inflation of this sort is much less harmful than a runaway inflation, it has a number of unfortunate social consequences, which are described in detail in subsequent sections of this chapter.

The Measurement of Inflation

The most widely quoted measure of inflation in the United States is the Consumer Price Index, published monthly by the Bureau of Labor Statistics. Until 1978, the purpose of this index was to measure changes in prices of goods and services purchased by urban wage earners and clerical workers and their families. In 1978, the index was expanded to include all urban consumers (although the narrower index was not discontinued). The first step in calculating the index is to find out how much it costs in a particular month to buy a market basket of goods and services that is representative of the buying patterns of these consumers. Then this amount is expressed as a ratio of what it would have cost to buy the same market basket of goods and services in the base period (1967 at present), and this ratio is multiplied by 100. In contrast to the price indices in the previous chapter, this (like most commonly used indices) shows the *percentage,* not the proportional, change in the price level. For example, the Consumer Price Index equaled 324.5 in September 1985, which meant that it cost 224.5 percent more to buy this market basket in September 1985 than in 1967. To obtain results based on the previous chapter's definition of a price index, all we have to do is divide this index by 100.

The market basket of goods and services that is included in the Consumer Price Index is chosen with great care and is the result of an extensive survey of people's buying patterns. Among the items that are included are food, automobiles, clothing, homes, furniture, home supplies, drugs, fuel, doctors' fees, legal fees, rent, repairs, transportation fares, recreational goods, and so forth. Prices, as defined in the index, include sales and excise taxes. Also, real estate taxes, but not income or personal property taxes, are included in the index. Besides the overall index, a separate price

165

index is computed for various types of goods or services, such as food, rent, new cars, medical services, and a variety of other items. Also, a separate index is computed for each of 28 metropolitan areas, as well as for the entire urban population.

The Consumer Price Index is widely used by industry and government. Labor agreements often stipulate that, to offset inflation, wages must increase in accord with changes in the index. Similarly, pensions, welfare payments, royalties, and even alimony payments are sometimes related to the index. However, this does not mean that it is an ideal, all-purpose measure of inflation. For one thing, it does not include the prices of industrial machinery or raw materials. For another thing, it is not confined to currently produced goods and services. For some purposes, it is less appropriate than other indices, such as the GNP deflator or the Wholesale Price Index (now the Producer Price Index).

Figure 8.3 shows the behavior of the Consumer Price Index since 1929. As pointed out in the previous section, the price level has increased considerably in the United States in the past 40 years. Substantial inflation followed World War II; the price level increased by about 34 percent between 1945 and 1948. Bursts of inflation recurred during the Korean War and then during the Vietnam War. The 1970s were a period of particularly high inflation; between 1969 and 1979 the price level doubled. The 1980s began with more double-digit inflation, but there was a reduction in the inflation rate in 1982–85. How long this respite will continue is by no means certain.

Figure 8.3
Consumer Price Index, 1929–84
Inflation has been a continual problem in the United States, particularly in the late 1970s and early 1980s. During 1979 and 1980, the Consumer Price Index rose at a double-digit annual rate.

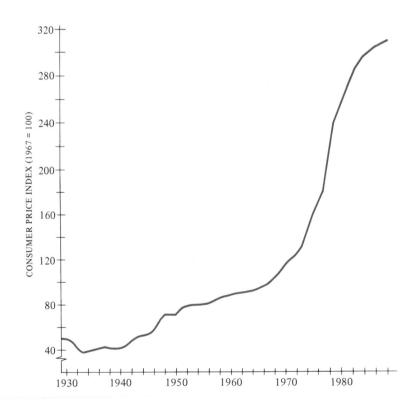

166

Impact of Inflation

Citizens and policy makers generally agree that inflation, like unemployment, should be minimized. Indeed, in 1981, the Council of Economic Advisers identified inflation as the chief economic problem confronting the United States. Even during 1985, when inflation had subsided substantially, there was widespread fear that it would increase again. Why is inflation so widely feared? What are its impacts? Inflation affects the distribution of income and wealth, as well as the level of output, as indicated below.

REDISTRIBUTIVE EFFECTS

Basic Idea #16: Because all incomes do not go up at the same rate as prices, inflation results in an arbitrary redistribution of income. People with relatively fixed incomes, lenders, and savers tend to be hurt by it, and major inflations tend to cripple total output as well. Government policies can help to reduce inflation, as we will see in subsequent chapters, but they may have an undesirable effect on unemployment, at least in the short run.

Perhaps the most important impact of inflation is on the distribution of income and wealth. To understand the redistributive effects of inflation, it is necessary to distinguish between ***money income*** and ***real income.*** A family's money income is its income measured in current dollars, whereas its real income is adjusted for changes in the price level. Suppose that the Murphy family earns $22,000 this year and $20,000 last year, and that the price level is 10 percent higher this year than last year. Under these circumstances, the Murphy family's money income has increased by $2,000, but its real income has not increased at all (because its money income has risen by the same percentage as the price level). The distinction between money income and real income plays an important role in understanding the effects of inflation on people with relatively fixed incomes, lenders, and savers, three groups that tend to be hit hard by inflation.

Fixed Money Incomes. Inflation may seem no more than a petty annoyance; after all, most people care about relative, not absolute, prices. For example, if the Murphy family's money income increases at the same rate as the price level, the Murphy family may be no better or worse off under inflation than if its money income remained constant and no inflation occurred. But not all people are as fortunate as the Murphys. Some people cannot increase their wages to compensate for price increases because they work under long-term contracts, among other reasons. These people take a considerable beating from inflation.

One group that tends to be particularly hard-hit by inflation is the elderly. Old people often must live on pensions and other relatively fixed forms of income. According to a study carried out by Joseph Minarik of the Brookings Institution, the effect of a 2 percent increase in the rate of inflation is to reduce the real income of elderly households (with incomes over $10,000) by about 10 percent.[8] This is a substantial, inequitable, and unwelcome impact of inflation on our older citizens.

Lenders. Inflation hurts lenders and benefits borrowers, since it results in the depreciation of money. A dollar is worth what it will buy, and what it will buy is determined by the price level. If the price level increases, a dollar is worth less than it was before. Consequently, if you lend Bill Dvorak $100 in 1985 and he pays you $100 in 1995—when a dollar will buy much less than in 1985—you are losing on the deal. In terms of what the money will buy, he is paying you less than what he borrowed. Of course, if you antici-

[8] J. Minarik, "Who Wins, Who Loses from Inflation," *The Brookings Bulletin*, Summer 1978.

Example 8.2   Money Wages and Real Wages in Manufacturing

In many situations, ranging from the formation of government economic policy to a particular labor negotiation between management and a union, it is important to distinguish between *money* and *real* wages. Money wages are wages expressed in current dollars, whereas real wages are adjusted for changes in the price level. The average weekly earnings in U.S. manufacturing are shown below for 1947–84, together with the Consumer Price Index for the same years.

Year	Average Weekly Earnings (current dollars)	Consumer Price Index (1967 = 100)
1947	49.13	66.9
1957	81.59	84.3
1967	114.49	100.0
1977	228.50	181.5
1984	373.22	311.1

(a) Convert the above money wages into real wages expressed in 1967 dollars. (b) In percentage terms, did real money wages in U.S. manufacturing increase as much during 1967–77 as during 1947–57? (c) John Murphy, a vegetarian who spends the bulk of his income on spinach, cauliflower, and books, received the above wages during 1947–84. Are you confident that the changes in real wages you calculated in (a) are a good indication of the changes in Mr. Murphy's standard of living during this period? (d) If the Consumer Price Index had been calculated so that 1977 = 100, would the value of this index for 1967 have been higher or lower than that shown above?

SOLUTION

(a) 1947: $49.13 ÷ .669 = $73.44
     1957: $81.59 ÷ .843 = $96.79
     1967: $114.49 ÷ 1.000 = $114 49
     1977: $228.50 ÷ 1.815 = $125.90
     1984: $373.22 ÷ 3.111 = $119.97

(b) During 1967–77, real wages increased by 10.0 percent (from $114.49 to $125.90). During 1947–57, they increased by 31.8 percent (from $73.44 to $96.79). Thus, percentagewise, they rose less during 1967–77 than during 1947–57. (c) No, because the prices of the goods on which he spends most of his income may have behaved quite differently from the Consumer Price Index (since the goods he buys are quite different from the market basket of goods and services bought by all urban consumers). Also, his standard of living may depend on the extent of his assets as well as the size of his earnings. (d) It would have been lower. If the 1977 price level were set equal to 100, the 1967 price level would have to be less than 100.

pate considerable inflation, you may be able to recoup by charging him a high enough interest rate to offset the depreciation of the dollar, but it is not so easy to forecast the rate of inflation and protect yourself.

Savers. Inflation can have a devastating and inequitable effect on savers. The family that works hard and saves for retirement (and a rainy day) finds that its savings are worth far less, when it finally spends them, than the amount it saved. Consider the well-meaning souls who invested $1,000 of their savings in United States savings bonds in 1939. By 1949, these bonds were worth only about 800 1939 dollars, including the interest received in the 10-year period. Thus these people had $200 taken away from them, in just as real a sense as if someone picked their pockets.[9]

EFFECTS OF ANTICIPATED AND UNANTICIPATED INFLATION

Economists are fond of pointing out that the effects of anticipated inflation tend to be less severe than those of unanticipated inflation. To see why this is the case, suppose that everyone anticipates (correctly) that the price level will be 6 percent higher next year than this year. In such a situation, everyone will build this amount of inflation into his or her decisions. Workers will realize that their money wage rates must be 6 percent higher next year just to avoid a cut in their real wage rates. The Murphy family, which earns $22,000 this year, will realize that it must earn 1.06 × $22,000, or $23,320, next year if it is to avoid a reduction in its real earnings. And people who are thinking of lending money for a year will recognize that they must charge 6 percent interest just to break even. Why? Because when the money is repaid next year, $1.06 will be worth no more in real terms than $1.00 is now.

Because people build the anticipated rate of inflation into their calculations, the effects of anticipated inflation are likely to be less pronounced than those of unanticipated inflation. However, in the real world in which we all live, this frequently is of small comfort, since it is very difficult to anticipate the rate of inflation correctly. Even the most sophisticated econometric models have not had a very distinguished record in forecasting the rate of inflation. Thus it seems foolish to believe that the typical citizen (like those who invested in United States savings bonds in 1939) can anticipate inflation well enough to protect himself or herself against its consequences.

AN ARBITRARY "TAX"

While inflation hurts some people, it benefits others. Those who are lucky enough to invest in goods, land, equipment, and other items that experience particularly rapid increases in price may make a killing. For this reason, speculation tends to be rampant during severe inflations. However, it is important to recognize that the rewards and penalties resulting from inflation are meted out with little or no regard for society's values or goals. As the late Arthur Okun, a former chairman of the Council of Economic

---

[9] However, it is important to recognize that the form of the savings matters. If one can put his or her savings in a form where its monetary value increases as rapidly as the price level, the saver is not harmed by inflation. But this isn't always easy to do.

169

Advisers, put it, " 'sharpies' . . . make sophisticated choices and often reap gains on inflation which do not seem to reflect any real contribution to economic growth. On the other hand, the unsophisticated saver who is merely preparing for the proverbial rainy day becomes a sucker."[10] This is one of the most undesirable features of inflation, and it helps to account for inflation's sometimes being called an arbitrary "tax."

EFFECTS ON OUTPUT

Creeping inflation, unlike unemployment, does not seem to reduce national output; in the short run, output may increase, for reasons taken up in a later section. But, although a mild upward creep of prices at the rate of a few percent per year is not likely to reduce output, a major inflation can have adverse effects on production. For one thing, it encourages speculation rather than productive use of savings. People find it more profitable to invest in gold, diamonds, real estate, and art (all of which tend to rise in monetary value during inflations) than in many kinds of productive activity. Also, businessmen tend to be discouraged from carrying out long-range projects because of the difficulty of forecasting what future prices will be. If the rate of inflation reaches the catastrophic heights that prevailed in Germany after World War I, the monetary system may break down. People may be unwilling to accept money. They may insist on trading goods or services directly for other goods and services. The result is likely to be considerable inefficiency and substantially reduced output.

Is Indexation the Answer to Inflation?

In the mid-1970s, when inflation in the United States was excessive in the eyes of practically all observers, some economists, like Milton Friedman (then at the University of Chicago), proposed a device called *indexation* to ameliorate the effects of inflation. Indexation is another word for the use of price-escalator clauses in private and public contracts. For example, in many industries, wages now rise automatically in accord with increases in the price level. And many government pensions now have similar provisions. What these economists were proposing was that such provisions be extended throughout the economy, or at least throughout much of it. For example, a person's income tax liability would be geared to the value of his or her income, after correcting for the effects of price-level changes. And interest rates would rise automatically with the rate of inflation.

Without question, indexation would help to reduce some of the harmful effects of inflation. If the U.S. Treasury were to issue bonds where the principal and interest were adjusted to compensate for rises in the price level, it would be possible for small savers to put aside some money for the future, without being victimized by inflation. To see how such bonds might work, suppose that you invested $1,000 in them, and that you cashed them in two years after you bought them. If the price level then was 20 percent higher than when you bought them, you would receive

[10] Arthur Okun, "The Costs of Inflation," in *The Battle against Unemployment,* rev. ed., New York: Norton, 1972.

$1,200 in principal. (Why $1,200? Because, since the price level was 20 percent higher, $1,200 at the time you cashed in the bonds would be the same as $1,000 at the time when you invested in them.) In addition, the interest you would receive on the bond would also be indexed.

Indexation really is not a new idea. Such great names of economics as Alfred Marshall of Cambridge and Irving Fisher of Yale were interested in the idea earlier in this century. And it has been tried on a limited scale in Canada and Israel, and to a greater extent in Brazil. But it has not received widespread support in the United States (although the 1981 tax bill introduced some indexing of people's income tax liabilities). Undoubtedly, one reason is that many people feel that indexation represents a surrender in the fight against inflation. In their view, it is better to quell inflation than to try to live with it.

Further, some observers believe that indexation of a comprehensive sort simply is not feasible. As the Council of Economic Advisers has pointed out, "A major obstacle is that many current dollar payment obligations have been incurred in past periods. Furthermore, individuals can hardly be forced to index their future contrasts if . . . they wish to make other allowances for the price movements they expect."[11] As inflation abated somewhat, talk of indexation died down. But that did not mean that the idea was abandoned. During the late 1970s and early 1980s, when the nation suffered another bout of double-digit inflation, it again received considerable attention.

The Relationship between Inflation and Unemployment

Inflation has a bad name, both among economists and with the general public. The novelist Ernest Hemingway, overstating his case more than a bit, wrote, "The first panacea for a mismanaged nation is inflation of currency: the second is war. . . . Both are the refuge of political and economic opportunists."[12] Yet according to some economists, full employment sometimes can be achieved only if a moderate amount of inflation is tolerated. In this section, we explain their reasons for believing this.

Both the unemployment rate and the inflation rate are determined by the total level of spending on the goods and services produced by the economy. Consumers, firms, and governments all spend money on the goods and services the nation produces. The level of output in our economy depends on how much money they spend. If their expenditures are very low, this means that the economy will operate in Range A in Figure 8.4, where national output is far below its maximum. Because the low level of expenditure means a low level of demand for the nation's goods and services, firms cannot sell enough goods and services to make it profitable to hire many of the workers who want to work. Thus employment is low, and the unemployment rate is high. As for the inflation rate, it is low, since there are plenty of excess capacity and unemployed resources. It is no time to raise prices.

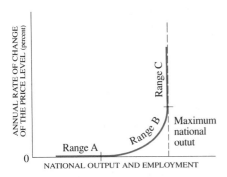

Figure 8.4

Output, Employment, and the Rate of Inflation *Chapter 2 pointed out that any economy can only produce so much, given its resources and the existing technology. The maximum output level, if all the economy's resources are fully and efficiently employed, is shown by the broken vertical line. In Range A, where national output is far below this maximum, the rate of inflation is very low but the unemployment rate is very high. In Range B, the unemployment rate is substantially less than in Range A, but the price level begins to rise. In Range C, national output is at its maximum, and increases in total spending result only in inflation.*

[11] Council of Economic Advisers, *Annual Report,* 1975, p. 141.

[12] Ernest Hemingway, "Notes on the Next War," *Esquire,* September 1935.

Economic problems, like smugglers, have no respect for international boundaries. In the 1980s, unemployment and inflation afflicted most of the industrialized world, as shown in the accompanying table.

Compared with previous experience since World War II, recent unemployment rates have been high. For example, in 1969, West Germany's unemployment rate was only 0.9 percent, as compared with 7.4 percent in 1984.

A comparison of the U.S. unemployment rate with that in other countries shows that our 1984 unemployment rate was lower

than that in Canada, France, and Great Britain, and higher than that in Germany, Italy, and Japan. To some extent, these international differences in unemployment rates are due to the fact that unemployment is defined differently in one country than in another. In some countries, to be counted as unemployed, you must register with government unemployment exchanges. Another reason for the international differences in unemployment rates is that institutional and cultural arrangements differ from country to country. In Japan many large firms commit themselves to a policy of lifetime employment for workers. This is one reason for Japan's relatively low unemployment rates.

As for the rate of inflation, the accompanying table shows that the price level increased at a rapid rate during 1978 and 1984 in most of these countries—the exceptions being Germany and Japan. U.S. performance seemed better than in a number of the other countries. While France and Italy experienced increases in consumer prices of over 7 percent per year during 1984, we managed to keep the rate of inflation down to about 4 percent per year during that period. But a 4 percent annual rate of inflation is high, relative to 25 years ago. Many economists, and citizens as well, would be glad to return to the days when the price level seldom rose at more than a couple of percentage points per year—and unemployment rarely exceeded 4 or 5 percent.

UNEMPLOYMENT AND INFLATION RATES IN THE UNITED STATES AND SIX OTHER COUNTRIES

Country	Unemployment rate[a]		Inflation rate[b]	
	1978	1984	1978	1984
United States	6.0	7.5	7.6	4.3
Canada	8.4	11.3	9.0	4.4
France	5.5	10.2	9.2	7.4
Germany	3.4	7.4	2.7	1.8
Italy	3.5	5.6	12.2	10.3
Japan	2.3	2.8	3.9	2.3
Great Britain	6.1	13.5	8.3	4.7

[a] For France and Japan, the 1984 figure pertains to the last quarter for which data are available.

[b] Estimates in *Economic Report of the President,* 1979 and 1985. The figures for 1984 are rough estimates but sufficiently reliable for present purposes. The data are not comparable with those given in other tables.

Under these circumstances, suppose that an increase occurs in the total level of spending. National output and employment will rise, and the unemployment rate will fall, but there will be little or no increase in the price level since output can be increased without bidding up the prices of labor and other inputs. When the level of expenditure increases to the point where output and employment are in Range B, the unemployment rate will be substantially lower than in Range A, but the price level will begin to rise. Why? Because bottlenecks occur in some parts of the economy, and labor pushes harder for wage increases (and firms are more willing to agree to such increases).

Finally, if the level of spending increases to the point where output and employment are in Range C, there will be no further decreases in the unemployment rate, since national output, which has reached its maximum, can grow no longer. In this range, the rate of inflation is very high, since total spending far exceeds the value of national output at initial prices. There are "too many dollars chasing too few goods."

Under the circumstances shown in Figure 8.4, the inflation rate is likely to increase as output and employment increase—which means that it is likely to increase as unemployment decreases. Thus some economists maintain that there is likely to be an inverse relationship between the unemployment rate and the inflation rate, at least in the short run. In their view, it sometimes is necessary to accept some inflation to reduce unemployment. But in recent years, this view has become increasingly controversial. More and more economists seem to have become persuaded that the reductions in unemployment due to increased inflation are only transitory and that increases in inflation bring little in the way of reduced unemployment in the long run. Much more will be said on this score in Chapter 18.

Test Yourself

1. "The Employment Act of 1946 should be amended to include the goal of stabilizing the purchasing power of the dollar as well as the goal of maintaining high-level employment." Comment and evaluate.

2. "Inflation is a necessary cost of economic progress." Comment and evaluate.

3. Suppose that a family's money income remains constant at $20,000, and that the price level increases 10 percent per year. How many years will it take for the family's real income to be cut in half?

4. If you believe that the United States is about to suffer severe inflation, would you be better off to invest money in land or in government bonds? Explain your answer.

5. According to a 1976 statement by the Research and Policy Committee of the Committee for Economic Development, "The inflation rate has receded substantially from its double-digit levels of 1974, but it still remains unacceptably high, particularly for a period in which the economy is operating far below its potential."* Why do they say this is particularly true for a period when output is far less than its potential? Explain.

* Committee for Economic Development, *Fighting Inflation and Promoting Growth,* Washington, D.C., 1976, p. 12.

Summary

1. Unemployment is of various types: frictional, structural, and cyclical. The Employment Act of 1946 committed the federal government to combat cyclical unemployment. The overall unemployment rate conceals considerable differences among types of people. The unemployment rate tends to be higher for teenagers than for older people, for nonwhites than for whites, and for females than for males. The Bureau of Labor Statistics publishes monthly data concerning unemployment rates for various segments of the population.

2. High levels of unemployment impose great costs on society. The economic costs of unemployment include the goods and services that could have been produced (but weren't) by the unemployed. The potential GNP is the level of GNP that could have been achieved if full employment had been reached. For many years, a common definition of full employment was a 4 percent unemployment rate, but many economists now believe that a figure of 5 percent or more is more realistic. The gap between actual and potential GNP is a measure of the economic costs of high unemployment.

3. Until the 1930s, most economists were convinced that the price system, left to its own devices, would ensure the maintenance of full employment. They thought it unlikely that total spending would be too small to purchase the full-employment level of output, and argued that prices would be cut if any problem of this sort developed. A notable exception was Karl Marx, who felt that the capitalistic system would suffer from worse and worse unemployment, leading to the system's eventual collapse.

4. John Maynard Keynes, in the 1930s, developed a theory to explain how the capitalist economic system remained mired in the Great Depression, with its tragically high levels of unemployment. Contrary to the classical economists, he concluded that there was no automatic mechanism in a capitalistic system to generate and maintain full employment—or, at least, to generate it quickly enough to be relied on in practice.

5. Inflation is a general upward movement of prices. Runaway inflation occurs when the price level increases very rapidly, as in Germany after World War I. Creeping inflation occurs when the price level rises a few percent per year, as in the United States during the 1950s and 1960s. The Consumer Price Index, published monthly by the Bureau of Labor Statistics, is a key measure of the rate of inflation.

6. High rates of inflation produce considerable redistribution of income and wealth. People with relatively fixed incomes, such as the elderly, tend to take a beating from inflation. Inflation hurts lenders and benefits borrowers, since it results in the depreciation of money. Inflation can also have a devastating effect on savers. The penalties (and rewards) resulting from inflation are meted out arbitrarily, with no regard for society's values or goals. Substantial rates of inflation may also reduce efficiency and total output.

Concepts for Review

Unemployment	**Potential GNP**	**Runaway inflation**
Frictional unemployment	**Full employment**	**Creeping inflation**
Structural unemployment	**Say's Law**	**Money income**
Cyclical unemployment	**Inflation**	**Real income**

CHAPTER 9

Aggregate Demand, Aggregate Supply, and Business Fluctuations

1984 was a year of rising output. Gross national product (in constant dollars) was about 7 percent higher in 1984 than in 1983. In contrast, in late 1981, the output of the American economy was not increasing. Total output, as measured by the GNP (in constant dollars), fell by over one percent in 1981's last quarter. Why the pronounced difference between these two periods? To help answer this question, as well as to understand the causes of severe unemployment and inflation, we must begin to study the nature of, and reasons for, business fluctuations.

Since aggregate demand and supply curves are useful tools in understanding why changes occur in national output and in the price level, this chapter begins by describing these demand and supply curves. Then we provide a brief introduction to business fluctuations (or "business cycles," as they are often called). Since unemployment and inflation are intimately related to business fluctuations, it is essential to have some grasp of the nature of business fluctuations in order to understand the behavior of unemployment and inflation. Only a preliminary description of business fluctuations can be presented here; much more will be said on this score in subsequent chapters.

Aggregate Supply and Demand

In Chapter 3, we described the demand and supply curves for an individual commodity like wheat. Using these demand and supply curves, we analyzed the forces determining the price and output of a commodity in a competitive market. For example, we saw that a shift to the right in the demand curve for wheat tends to increase both the price and output of wheat.

In this chapter, we will analyze the changes in the price level and output of the entire economy. That is, we are going to determine why the price level increases in some periods, but not in others, and why the gross national product soars in some periods and plummets in others. To understand the factors underlying inflation and unemployment, we must know why changes occur in the price level and in national output.

Can we use demand and supply curves for the entire economy in much the same way as we did in individual markets? Are there demand and supply curves for the whole economy that are analogous to the demand and supply curves for individual products like wheat? The answer to both questions is *yes*. And in the next few sections of this chapter, we shall indicate the nature and usefulness of these aggregate demand and supply curves.

The Aggregate Demand Curve

To begin with, consider the **aggregate demand curve**. *The aggregate demand curve shows the level of real national output that will be demanded at each price level.* (Recall from Chapter 7 that real national output is measured by real gross national product or by real net national product. Thus real national output is composed of the output of food, automobiles, machine tools, ships, and the host of other final goods and services that are produced.) As can be seen in Figure 9.1, the aggregate demand curve slopes downward and to the right. In other words, when other things are held equal, the higher the price level, the smaller the total output demanded will be; and the lower the price level, the higher the total output demanded will be. This might be expected, since the demand curve for an

Figure 9.1

Aggregate Demand Curve The aggregate demand curve shows the level of total real output that will be demanded at each price level. If the price level is 100, a total real output of $220 billion will be demanded. If the price level is 103, a total real output of $200 billion will be demanded.

individual product also slopes downward and to the right, as we saw in Chapter 3.

There are two fundamental reasons why the demand curve for an individual commodity like wheat slopes downward and to the right. (1) As the price of the commodity falls, consumers buy more of it because it is less expensive relative to other commodities. (2) As its price falls, each consumer's money income (which is held constant) will buy a larger total amount of goods and services, so it is likely that more will be bought of this commodity.

Neither of these reasons can be used to explain the shape of the aggregate demand curve, which relates the economy's total real output to the price level. When the price level falls, the average price of *all* goods and services falls.[1] Unlike the demand curve for an individual commodity, there is not just a single price that falls, with the result that consumers find the relevant commodity relatively cheap and buy more of it. The aggregate demand curve is concerned with the effects of the price level on the economy's *total* real output, not the effects of the price of a single commodity on its output alone. Since the aggregate demand curve is concerned with the economy's price level and total real output, not the price and output of a single commodity, the reasons for the downward slope of a demand curve for an individual commodity are not applicable to the aggregate demand curve.

REASONS FOR THE AGGREGATE DEMAND CURVE'S SHAPE

Why then does the aggregate demand curve slope downward and to the right? The basic reasoning is described in the following two steps. In Chapters 14–17, we will fill in many of the details regarding the demand for money and the effects of the supply of money on interest rates and of interest rates on total spending. For present purposes, only a rough sketch is needed.

Step 1: Increases in the price level will push up interest rates. In constructing the aggregate demand curve, it is assumed that the quantity of money in the economy is fixed. An increase in the price level increases the average *money* cost of each transaction because the price of each good tends to be higher. Thus, if the price level increases considerably, people will have to hold more money in their wallets and checking accounts to pay for the items they want to buy, since prices will be so much higher. Since the quantity of money is fixed, and the demand for money increases, there will be a shortage of money. In an attempt to increase their money holdings, people will borrow or will sell government securities and other financial assets. As this happens, interest rates will be bid up.

Step 2: Increases in interest rates will reduce total output. When the interest rate goes up, firms that borrow money to invest in plant and equipment and consumers that borrow money to buy automobiles or houses tend to cut down on their spending on these items. Due to the higher interest rates, the cost of borrowing money is greater, and hence some of these investment projects and purchases no longer seem profitable

---

[1] Of course, this does not mean that the price of each good and service falls when the price level falls. Only the *average* falls.

or worthwhile. Because of the reduced spending on these items, the nation's total real output declines.[2]

The Aggregate Supply Curve

Just as the aggregate demand curve is analogous to the demand curve for an individual product, so the **aggregate supply curve** is analogous to the supply curve for an individual product. *The aggregate supply curve shows the level of real national output that will be supplied at each price level.* As can be seen in Figure 9.2, the aggregate supply curve slopes upward and to the right. In other words, when other things are held equal, the higher the price level, the larger the total output supplied will be; and the lower the price level, the smaller the total output supplied will be. This might be expected since the supply curve for an individual product also slopes upward and to the right, as we saw in Chapter 3.

But just as we could not derive the aggregate demand curve simply by adding up the demand curves for all the individual commodities in the economy, so we cannot derive the aggregate supply curve by adding up the supply curves for all the individual commodities. If we did this, we would commit a grave error because the factors held constant in constructing an individual supply curve are not held constant in constructing an aggregate supply curve. In particular, in constructing an individual supply curve, the price of only one commodity is allowed to vary, whereas in constructing an aggregate supply curve, the price level (and thus every price) is allowed to vary.

Figure 9.2

Aggregate Supply Curve *The aggregate supply curve shows the level of total real output that will be supplied at each price level. If the price level is 100, a total real output of $190 billion will be supplied. If the price level is 103, a total real output of $200 billion will be supplied.*

TOTAL REAL OUTPUT
(billions of dollars)

[2] There are other reasons for the shape of the aggregate demand curve. For one thing, an increase in the price level reduces the real value of the currency and government bonds held by the public. This reduction in their real wealth causes a decrease in consumption expenditure. For another thing, a rise in the U.S. price level encourages imports from abroad and discourages our exports, thus reducing the demand for American output.

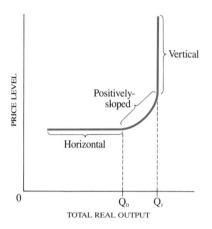

Figure 9.3
Three Ranges of the Aggregate Supply Curve *The aggregate supply curve contains three ranges: (1) a horizontal range, (2) a positively-sloped range, and (3) a vertical range.*

REASONS FOR THE AGGREGATE SUPPLY CURVE'S SHAPE

As indicated in Figure 9.3, the aggregate supply curve can be divided into three ranges: (1) a horizontal range (for output levels up to OQ_0), (2) a vertical range (when output reaches OQ_1), and (3) a positively sloped range (for output levels between OQ_0 and OQ_1). To understand the overall shape of the aggregate supply curve, we must know why each of these ranges exist.

Horizontal Range. In this range, national output can be increased without increasing the price level. This is sometimes called the *Keynesian range* because it corresponds to a situation of substantial unemployment, which is the situation (during the Great Depression) that concerned John Maynard Keynes, the great British economist (who was introduced in the previous chapter). Basically, the horizontal shape of the aggregate supply curve in this range is due to the fact that there is *no upward pressure* on prices as output increases because there are plenty of unemployed workers, equipment, and other resources. Since these resources can be used to produce additional output at about the same cost per unit of output as the existing volume of output, firms do not have to receive higher prices for their products to be willing to expand production. And since wages and the prices of other resources are relatively fixed, there is little or no downward pressure on prices as output decreases. Of course, the horizontal shape of the curve is a simplification, not an exact description of the behavior of the economy. But it seems to be a useful approximation to reality.

Vertical Range. In this range, output cannot be expanded, no matter how much the price level increases. Thus, in Figure 9.3, OQ_1 is the maximum amount that the economy can produce. This is sometimes called the *classical range* because it represents the situation that concerned the so-called classical economists (cited in Chapter 8 and discussed further in subsequent chapters). It is a situation where the economy's resources are fully employed. In contrast to the Keynesian range, there are no unemployed resources in the classical range.

Of course, this range, like the horizontal range, is a simplification. In fact, it is always possible to get a bit more output from any economic system. People can work longer hours. Equipment can be used around the clock. Children and old people can be brought into the labor force. But under normal conditions there does seem to be a point beyond which further increases in the price level result in little or no increases in output. And this is the reality that this range of the aggregate supply curve approximates.

Positively-Sloped Range. In this range, as output increases, shortages of some products begin to develop. Thus the prices of some commodities are pushed up, and the price level (which is the average of all prices of goods and services) rises. For this reason, there is a direct relationship between total real output and the price level.

This is an *intermediate* range between the horizontal range, where there is considerable unemployment of resources, and the vertical range where there is full employment. As output rises from the depressed levels in the horizontal range, some sectors of the economy reach relatively full employment before others do. Prices begin to be bid up in some markets, but not in others. As output continues to increase, more and more sectors of the economy reach their capacities, and find it increasingly difficult and

179

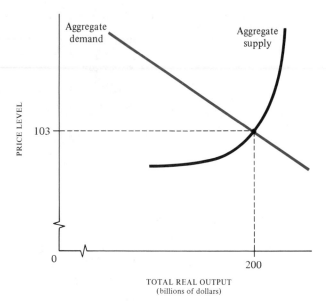

Figure 9.4
Equilibrium Price Level and Total Real
Output *The equilibrium level of total*
real output and the equilibrium price level
are given by the intersection of the
aggregate demand and supply curves.
Here the equilibrium price level is 103
and the equilibrium level of total real
output is $200 billion.

costly to increase their output further. Thus the aggregate supply curve becomes steeper as output rises—and eventually it enters the vertical range.

National Output and the Price Level

The equilibrium level of real national output and the equilibrium price level are given by the intersection of the aggregate demand curve and the aggregate supply curve. In Figure 9.4, the equilibrium level of real national output is $200 billion and the equilibrium price level is 103. The reasoning here is essentially the same as in Chapter 3, where we showed that the equilibrium price and output of a commodity are given by the intersection of the commodity's demand and supply curves. In the present case, an equilibrium can occur only at a price level and level of real national output where aggregate demand equals aggregate supply.

Shifts in the Aggregate Demand Curve

In Chapter 3, we saw that shifts in the demand curve for an individual commodity result in changes in the price and output of this commodity. We now see that shifts in the aggregate demand curve result in changes in the price level and total real output.

EFFECT OF A RIGHTWARD SHIFT

Suppose that consumers or investors decide to *increase* their spending, perhaps because of a change in their expectations. (That is, they anticipate

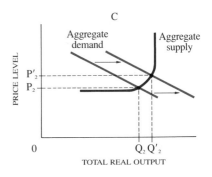

Figure 9.5

Effect of a Shift to the Right in the Aggregate Demand Curve *Panel A shows that, in the* horizontal *range of the aggregate supply curve, a rightward shift of the aggregate demand curve increases output, but not the price level. Panel B shows that, in the* vertical *range of the aggregate supply curve, a rightward shift of the aggregate demand curve increases the price level, but not output. Panel C shows that, in the* positively-sloped *range of the aggregate supply curve, a rightward shift of the aggregate demand curve increases both output and the price level.*

a marked improvement in economic conditions.) Since the level of total real output demanded at each price level increases, the aggregate demand curve shifts outward and to the right, as shown in Figure 9.5. What is the effect on the price level and on total output? The answer depends on where the aggregate demand curve intersected the aggregate supply curve before the shift in the aggregate demand curve.

Horizontal Range of the Aggregate Supply Curve. If the intersection occurred in the horizontal range of the aggregate supply curve, the rightward shift of the aggregate demand curve will increase total real output, but have no effect on the price level. (See panel A of Figure 9.5.) As pointed out above, this is because there is considerable unemployment of resources. More output does not entail increased prices.

Vertical Range of the Aggregate Supply Curve. If the intersection occurred in the vertical range of the aggregate supply curve, the rightward shift of the aggregate demand curve will increase the price level but have no impact on total real output. (See panel B of Figure 9.5.) As pointed out above, this is because there is full employment of resources. More spending bids up prices, but cannot augment total real output, which is at its maximum level.

Positively-Sloped Range of the Aggregate Supply Curve. If the intersection occurred in the positively-sloped range of the aggregate supply curve, the rightward shift of the aggregate demand curve will increase both the price level and total real output. (See panel C of Figure 9.5.) This is because increases in output can be attained in this range only if the price level increases, as we saw in a previous section.

EFFECT OF A LEFTWARD SHIFT

In contrast to the previous situation, suppose that consumers or investors decide to *reduce* their spending. Since the level of total real output demanded at each price level falls, the aggregate demand curve shifts inward and to the left, as shown in Figure 9.6. The effect of this shift depends on where the aggregate demand curve intersected the aggregate supply curve before the shift occurred.

If the intersection occurred in the horizontal range of the aggregate supply curve, the leftward shift of the aggregate demand curve will reduce total real output, but have no effect on the price level (panel A of Figure

181

Figure 9.6

Effect of a Shift to the Left in the Aggregate Demand Curve Panel A shows that, in the horizontal *range of the aggregate supply curve, a leftward shift of the aggregate demand curve reduces output, but not the price level. Panel B shows that, in the* vertical *range of the aggregate supply curve, a leftward shift of the aggregate demand curve reduces the price level, but not output. Panel C shows that, in the* positively-sloped *range of the aggregate supply curve, a leftward shift of the aggregate demand curve reduces both output and the price level.*

Basic Idea #17: *To reduce unemployment, the government may shift the aggregate demand curve to the right. To do so, it must encourage and augment spending. If inflation is the principal problem, the government may shift the aggregate demand curve to the left by cutting back spending.*

9.6). If the intersection occurred in the vertical range of the aggregate supply curve, this shift will reduce the price level, but have no effect on total real output (panel B of Figure 9.6). If the intersection occurred in the positively-sloped range of the aggregate supply curve, this shift will reduce both the price level and total real output.

According to many economists, leftward shifts of the aggregate demand curve generally have much more effect on total real output than on the price level, which (as pointed out below) seldom tends to decline. If this is the case, panel A (or perhaps panel C) in Figure 9.6 is a closer approximation to reality than panel B.

GOVERNMENT STABILIZATION POLICIES

Consumers and firms are not the only actors on the economic stage that can influence the amount of spending, and thus shift the aggregate demand curve. The government can do the same thing. Through its monetary and fiscal policies, the federal government can shift the aggregate demand curve to either the right or the left. By encouraging and augmenting spending, the government can shift the aggregate demand curve to the right. By discouraging and cutting back spending, the government can shift the aggregate demand curve to the left.

Anti-Unemployment Policy. Suppose that the unemployment rate is very high, and that the nation's most important economic problem is to get its citizens back to work. This was the case in the Great Depression of the Thirties, as well as in subsequent serious recessions (which will be cited later in this chapter). Clearly, under these circumstances, the sensible strategy is for the government to shift the aggregate demand curve to the right. This situation is shown in Figure 9.7. A rightward shift of the aggregate demand curve will increase total real output and have little or no effect on the price level since the economy is in the horizontal range of the aggregate supply curve (because there is substantial unemployment). The increase in total real output will reduce unemployment because more workers and other resources will have to be employed to produce the extra output.

In fact, this is the sort of strategy that both Democratic and Republican administrations have adopted on many occasions to try to reduce unemployment. For example, in the early 1960s, President John Kennedy's (and

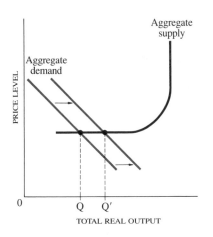

President Lyndon Johnson's) tax (and monetary) policies resulted in a rightward shift in the aggregate demand curve, thus reducing unemployment from about 5.7 percent in 1963 to 4.5 percent in 1965. And in the mid-1970s, President Gerald Ford's economic policies pushed the aggregate demand curve to the right, with the result that unemployment fell from 8.7 percent in March 1975 to 7.5 percent in March 1976.

Anti-Inflationary Policy. In the late 1970s and early 1980s, many American people felt that inflation, not unemployment, was the number one problem. Since the price level was increasing at over 10 percent per year during early 1980, this concern over inflation was not hard to understand. If the government anticipates that the price level is going to rise either because of a rightward shift of the aggregate demand curve or a leftward shift of the aggregate supply curve, it can reduce the prospective increase in the price level by using monetary or fiscal policy to shift the aggregate demand curve to the left. This situation is shown in Figure 9.8. If the government does not intervene, the equilibrium will be at point *A,* and the price level will be *OP,* which presumably is much higher than it is at present. To avoid reaching point *A,* the government shifts the aggregate demand curve to the left, with the result that the equilibrium will be at point *B,* and the price level will be *OP′,* which is considerably lower than *OP.* Although this results in less real output (*OQ′* versus *OQ*), less inflation occurs than would otherwise be the case.

Both Democratic and Republican administrations have used this sort of anti-inflationary strategy. For example, prior to its 1975 policies to reduce unemployment (described above), the Ford administration adopted policies resulting in a leftward shift in the aggregate demand curve. By discouraging and cutting back spending, inflation was reduced in 1974. In subsequent chapters, we shall describe in detail how fiscal and monetary policies can be established to do this, and the pros and cons of such policies. All that we want to establish at present is the fact that this is the way in which governments often attempt to curb inflation.

Figure 9.7

Anti-Unemployment Policy *If there is considerable unemployment, the economy is likely to be operating in the horizontal range of the aggregate supply curve. By pushing the aggregate demand curve to the right, the government can increase output and employment without pushing up the price level.*

Figure 9.8

Anti-Inflation Policy *In the absence of government action, the equilibrium would be at point A, and the price level would equal OP. Since this represents an unacceptably high rate of inflation, the government pushes the aggregate demand curve to the left, so the equilibrium is at point B. The price level is lower (OP′ rather than OP). Output is also somewhat lower (OQ′ rather than OQ).*

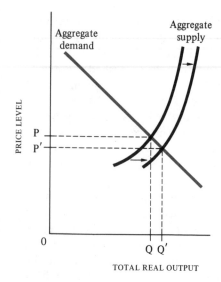

Figure 9.9
Effect of a Shift to the Right in the Aggregate Supply Curve *If the aggregate supply curve shifts to the right, the result will be increased real output (OQ' rather than OQ) and a lower price level (OP' rather than OP). In the 1980s, the Reagan administration emphasized "supply-side" policies to promote such a shift in the aggregate supply curve.*

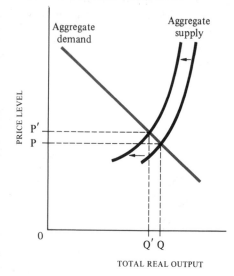

Figure 9.10
Effect of a Shift to the Left in the Aggregate Supply Curve *If the aggregate supply curve shifts to the left, the result will be reduced real output (OQ' rather than OQ) and a higher price level (OP' rather than OP).*

Shifts in the Aggregate Supply Curve

Shifts in the aggregate supply curve, like those in the aggregate demand curve, result in changes in the price level and total real output, as indicated below.

EFFECT OF A RIGHTWARD SHIFT

Suppose that, because of increases in productive capacity or changes in technology, firms are willing and able to supply *more* goods and services (at any given price level) than in the past. Under these circumstances, the aggregate supply curve shifts outward and to the right, as shown in Figure 9.9. What is the effect on the price level and on total output? If prior to this shift the aggregate demand curve intersected the aggregate supply curve at a point where the latter was positively sloped (or vertical), the result will be an increase in total real output and a reduction in the price level, as shown in Figure 9.9.

EFFECT OF A LEFTWARD SHIFT

On the other hand, suppose that firms are willing and able to supply *less* goods and services (at any given price level) than in the past. For example, suppose that there is a world wide shortage of important raw materials like oil or iron ore which results in increases in their prices. Given that this is the case, a given level of total real output can be produced only at a higher price level than was previously the case. That is, the aggregate supply curve shifts upward and to the left, as shown in Figure 9.10. The effect will be a reduction in total real output and an increase in the price level, as shown in Figure 9.10.

"Supply-Side" Government Policies

From the previous discussion, it is clear that rightward shifts of the aggregate supply curve are likely to result in more output and a quelling of inflationary pressures. (See Figure 9.9.) Since these are desirable goals, it is not surprising that government policies have begun to emphasize measures designed to push the aggregate supply curve outward and to the right. This emphasis on the aggregate supply curve is not new; for example, in 1776, Adam Smith recognized the importance of such shifts in the aggregate supply curve, although he did not couch his discussion in precisely these terms. But in the late 1970s and 1980s, much more talk was heard about "the supply side"—that is, shifts in the aggregate supply curve—than in previous decades.

When the Reagan administration took office, it pushed through Congress a number of measures that it felt would help to shift the aggregate supply curve to the right. In particular, the 25 percent cut in the personal income tax and the accelerated depreciation of plant and equipment (both included in the 1981 tax bill) were supposed to further this aim. According to the administration, the important thing was to encourage people and firms to work, invest, and take prudent risks. There has been considerable controversy inside and outside the economic profession as to the effectiveness and side-effects of some of these proposals, which have been described in Chapter 5 and which will be discussed in more detail in Chapter 17 (and elsewhere). All that we want to emphasize here is that the Reagan administration emphasized measures to shift the aggregate supply curve.

Example 9.1   A Ratchet Effect on Aggregate Supply

Suppose that prices are rigid downward; that is, they can be increased but not decreased. The aggregate supply curve (which is assumed here to have only a horizontal and a vertical range) is P_1BS, as shown below. The government adopts monetary and fiscal policies that shift the aggregate demand curve to the right (from D to D').

(a) Will the movement of the aggregate demand curve from D to D' affect the aggregate supply curve? If so, how and why? (b) If the aggregate demand curve were to return to its original position (at D), would the aggregate supply curve return to its original position? Why or why not?

SOLUTION

(a) Yes. The movement of the aggregate demand curve from D to D' results in an increase in the price level from OP_1 to OP_2. Since the price level rises in this way, firms will be unwilling to supply the old amounts at the old prices. To supply the same amount of output as they formerly supplied when prices were OP_1, they now insist on prices of OP_2. Thus the aggregate supply curve will shift from P_1BS to P_2CS. (b) No. Because prices are rigid downward, the aggregate supply curve will remain at P_2CS (at least for a considerable period of time). Thus there is a "ratchet effect" whereby rightward shifts in the aggregate demand curve push the aggregate supply curve upward, but leftward shifts in the aggregate demand curve do not push it back to its original position.*

* A ratchet is a device that permits a wheel to turn one way but not the other.

Test Yourself

1. What sort of shifts in either the aggregate demand curve or the aggregate supply curve (or both) would result in an increase in the price level but constant real output?

2. "One of the principal reasons why the aggregate supply curve slopes upward to the right is that, as total real output increases, the quantity of money must increase as well, which means that the price level must rise, at least beyond some point." Do you agree? Why or why not?

3. Suppose that the aggregate demand curve is $P = 120 - Q$, where P is the price level and Q is real output (in billions of dollars). If the aggregate supply curve (which is a horizontal line in the relevant range) shifts upward from $P = 102$ to $P = 104$, what will happen to real output?

4. The aggregate demand curve in Country X shifts to the right, with the result that the price level rises. Do you think that this will affect Country X's aggregate supply curve? Why or why not?

5. Suppose that the Organization of Petroleum Exporting Countries raises oil prices by 50 percent in 1987. What effect will this have on the U.S. aggregate demand curve? On the U.S. aggregate supply curve?

Business Fluctuations

One of the principal reasons for presenting aggregate demand and supply curves is that they help us to understand business fluctuations—the ups and downs of the economy. Business executives, government officials, and practically everyone else is interested in business fluctuations because they influence our welfare. Business fluctuations are intimately related to the twin economic evils of unemployment and inflation, discussed in the previous chapter.

To illustrate what we mean by business fluctuations—or the business cycle—let's look at how national output has grown in the United States since World War I. Figure 9.11 shows the behavior of real GNP (in constant dollars) in the United States since 1919. It is clear that output has grown considerably during this period. Indeed, GNP is more than 5 times what it was 50 years ago. It is also clear that this growth has not been

Figure 9.11

Gross National Product (in 1958 dollars), United States 1919–84, Excluding World War II *Real GNP has not grown steadily. Instead, it has tended to approach its potential level (that is, its full-employment level), then to falter and fall below this level, then to rise once more, and so on. This movement of national output is sometimes called the business cycle. (Note that GNP is expressed in 1958—not 1972—dollars here.)*

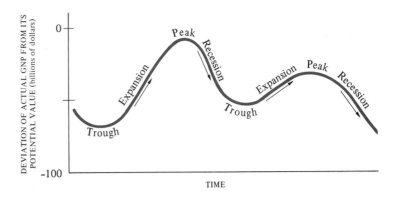

Figure 9.12
Four Phases of Business Cycle *Each cycle can be divided into four phases: trough, expansion, peak, and recession.*

steady. On the contrary, although the long-term trend has been upward, there have been periods—like 1919–21, 1929–33, 1937–38, 1944–46, 1948–49, 1953–54, 1957–58, 1969–70, 1973–75, January–July 1980, and 1981–82—when national output has declined.

Recall that the potential GNP is the total amount of goods and services that could have been produced if there had been full employment. Figure 9.11 shows that national output tends to rise and approach its potential level (that is, its full-employment level) for a while, then falter and fall below this level, then rise to approach it once more, then fall below it again, and so on. For example, output remained close to its potential level in the prosperous mid-1920s, fell far below this level in the depressed 1930s, and rose again to this level once we entered World War II. This movement of national output is sometimes called the **business cycle,** but it must be recognized that these cycles are far from regular or consistent. On the contrary, they are very irregular.

Each cycle can be divided into four phases, as shown in Figure 9.12. The **trough** is the point where national output is lowest relative to its potential level (that is, its full-employment level). **Expansion** is the subsequent phase during which national output rises. The **peak** occurs when national output is highest relative to its potential level. Finally, **recession** is the subsequent phase during which national output falls.[3]

Two other terms are frequently used to describe stages of the business cycle. A **depression** is a period when national output is well below its potential level; it is a severe recession. Depressions are, of course, periods of excessive unemployment. **Prosperity** is a period when national output is close to its potential level. Prosperity, if total spending is too high relative to potential output, can be a time of inflation. (Of course, in some business cycles, the peak may not be a period of prosperity because output may be below its potential level, or the trough may not be a period of depression because output may not be far below its potential level.)

Since World War II, peaks have occurred in 1948, 1953, 1957, 1960, 1969, 1973, 1980 (January), and 1981, while troughs have occurred in 1949, 1954, 1958, 1961, 1970, 1975, 1980 (July), and 1982 (November). None of these recessions has been very long or very deep (although the

[3] More precisely, the peak and trough are generally defined in terms of deviations from the long-term trend of national output, rather than in terms of deviations from the potential (that is, the full-employment) level of national output. But the latter definition tends to be easier for beginners to grasp.

187

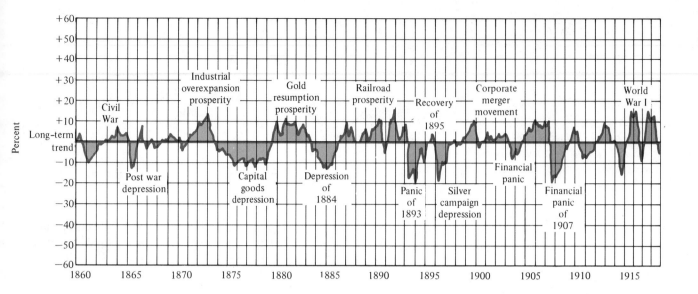

Figure 9.13

Business Fluctuations in the United States, 1860-1980 *To construct this chart, a single index of economic activity was used. After fitting a trend line to it, the deviations of this index from its trend value were plotted. The results show the fluctuations in economic activity in the U.S.*

1974–75 and 1981–82 recessions resulted in substantial unemployment). We have done better since the war at avoiding and cushioning recessions, partly because of improvements in economic knowledge of the causes and cures of business cycles.

Although business cycles have certain things in common, they are highly individualistic. (See Figure 9.13.) For certain classes of phenomena, it may be true that "if you've seen one, you've seen them all," but not for business cycles. They vary too much in length and nature. Moreover, the basic set of factors responsible for the recession and the expansion differs from cycle to cycle.[4] This means that any theory designed to explain them must be broad enough to accommodate their idiosyncracies. In subsequent chapters, much will be said about the causes of business fluctuations.

Business Fluctuations During 1929–85: A Brief Overview

In the previous section, we described the general nature of business fluctuations. Now we turn to a description of the actual fluctuations that have occurred in the United States in recent decades. Our treatment is necessarily sketchy, since this is only a brief introductory discussion, but it should help to provide a useful background for subsequent chapters.

[4] For example, there is some evidence that every so often, a business boom, or peak, takes place at about the same time as a boom in building construction; thus such a peak is buoyed further by this favorable conjuncture—and every so often, a trough is lowered by it. These long swings in building (and other phenomena), lasting 15 to 25 years, are called Kuznets cycles after Harvard's late Nobel laureate, Simon Kuznets, who devoted considerable study to them.

Source: Ameri Trust Company. Adapted with changes.

Figure 9.14
Shift of the Aggregate Demand Curve,
1929–33 *A marked shift to the left in the*
aggregate demand curve was the
principal reason for the onset of the
Great Depression. (For simplicity, we
assume here that the aggregate supply
curve remained fixed.) Output fell
drastically (from OQ₁ to OQ₂); the price
level fell too (from OP₁ to OP₂).

THE GREAT CRASH

Let's begin with the late 1920s. During 1928 and 1929, the American economy was in the midst of a prosperity. As shown in Figure 9.11, gross national product was approximately equal to its potential value. Unemployment was low. Among the reasons for this prosperity was a relatively strong demand for machinery and equipment to produce new products (like the automobile, radio, telephone, and electric power) and to replace old machinery and equipment that had been worn out or outmoded during World War I and its aftermath.

The picture changed dramatically in 1929. After the stock market plummeted in October of that year, the economy headed down at a staggering pace. Real GNP fell by almost one-third between 1929 and 1933. Unemployment rose to an enormous 25 percent of the labor force by 1933. One important reason for this debacle was the severe contraction of gross private domestic investment. (Recall from Chapter 7 that gross private domestic investment is spending on tools, equipment, machinery, construction, and additional inventories.) Whereas gross private domestic investment was about $16 billion in 1929, it fell to about $1 billion in 1933. (The reasons for this decrease will be discussed in later chapters.) Another important factor was the decrease in the supply of money between 1929 and 1933. The money supply shrank from $26 billion in 1929 to $20 billion in 1933. This too tended to depress spending and output.

Put in terms of the aggregate demand and supply curves discussed earlier in this chapter, the situation was as shown in Figure 9.14. For the reasons given in the previous paragraph, the aggregate demand curve shifted markedly to the left; and as would be expected on the basis of Figure 9.14, total real output and the price level fell between 1929 and 1933.

Figure 9.15
Shifts of the Aggregate Demand Curve in World War II *When we entered World War II, the aggregate demand curve shifted to the right as military expenditures mushroomed. Output increased (from OQ_0 to OQ_1 to OQ_2), and inflationary pressures mounted. (For simplicity, we assume that the aggregate supply curve remained fixed.) Much the same thing occurred during the Vietnam War.*

WORLD WAR II

The United States remained mired in the Great Depression until World War II (and the mobilization period that preceded the war). To carry out the war effort, the government expanded the money supply and spent huge amounts on military personnel and equipment. One result of this increase in spending was a substantial increase in real GNP, which rose by about 75 percent between 1939 and 1945. Another result was a marked reduction in unemployment, as the armed forces expanded and as jobs opened up in defense plants (and elsewhere). Still another result was the appearance of serious inflationary pressures. As the aggregate demand curve marched to the right, there was severe upward pressure on the price level as increases in spending pushed national output to its maximum. (See Figure 9.15.) To counter this pressure, the government instituted price controls and other measures that kept a temporary lid on prices; but when these controls were lifted after the termination of the war, the price level increased dramatically. Between 1945 and 1948, the Consumer Price Index rose by about 34 percent.

THE POSTWAR YEARS

In 1948, the U.S. economy reached a peak, after which the unemployment rate increased to about 6 percent in 1949. But this recession was short-lived. The Korean conflict began in 1950, and, once again, the federal government increased its spending on armaments, resulting in substantial increases in real GNP, as well as lower unemployment and a higher rate of inflation. In 1953, another recession began, but it was relatively mild. After the trough was reached in 1954, GNP rose substantially during the next several years, only to fall back once more in the recession of 1957–58. The fifties were characterized by relatively slow growth of real GNP and by a rising unemployment rate, both of which were the cause of considerable concern.

THE PROSPEROUS SIXTIES

As previous paragraphs have shown, the American economy experienced recurring fluctuations prior to 1960. During the 1960s, this pattern seemed to change, as the United States entered a period of expansion which was uninterrupted until 1969. There were a variety of reasons for this extremely long expansion, including the tax cut of 1964, which increased after-tax income and stimulated consumer spending and investment. The increases in the money supply during this period are also given credit for this long expansion. Another important factor was the Vietnam War. Like World War II and the Korean conflict, the Vietnam War resulted in substantial increases in military spending (and a reduction in unemployment due to the draft). Due in part to Vietnam, the unemployment rate fell below 4 percent during 1966–69.

While unemployment was being squeezed to minimal levels, inflation was heating up. This is precisely what would be expected, based on our discussion of Figure 9.15. The government's spending on Vietnam was added to an already high level of expenditure on other goods and services, the result being that national output was at its maximum level in the late

1960s. Indeed, spending was so great that prices were pushed up at an increasingly alarming rate. And as prices rose, there was pressure for corresponding wage increases, which in turn pushed up firms' costs, and which were reflected in further price increases. By the end of the 1960s, inflation seemed to be the nation's foremost economic problem.

THE TURBULENT SEVENTIES

In 1969, the government adopted policies to restrict aggregate demand. Although this helped to restrain inflation, it had the undesirable effect of increasing unemployment, which rose to about 6 percent in 1971. Further, although inflation probably was reduced by these policies, it was not reduced greatly. During the first half of 1971, prices rose at an annual rate of about 4½ percent. In August 1971, the government established controls on prices, wages, and rents. This was the first time such controls had been adopted by an American government in peacetime. Although these controls seemed to hold down prices for a while, the government regarded them as increasingly unworkable, and they were phased out in 1973 and 1974.

During most of 1973, the economy was in a boom. In early 1974, the price of oil was quadrupled by the OPEC countries. This, together with a hike in farm prices, spearheaded a severe inflationary spurt. (The Consumer Price Index rose by 12 percent during 1974.) At the same time, the nation's real output fell, as the economy experienced the most serious recession since World War II. By March 1975, the unemployment rate was almost 9 percent. In mid-1975, the economy began to revive, and the unemployment rate fell gradually through 1976, 1977, and 1978. By the beginning of 1979, it was about 5.9 percent. Inflation, which had receded somewhat during 1975–77, began to reach alarming levels once again. In early 1979, the annual rate of price increase once again reached double-digit levels.

The middle and late 1970s were characterized by **stagflation,** a combination of high unemployment and high inflation. (The term stagflation was coined by putting together *stag*nation and in*flation*.) What caused this turn of events? According to many economists, it was because the aggregate supply curve shifted upward and to the left. In their view, the situation was like that in Figure 9.16. This shift in the aggregate supply curve both reduced national output and increased the price level. Since a reduction in national output means high unemployment and an increase in the price level means inflation, it is easy to see that such a shift in the aggregate supply curve might result in stagflation.

But why did the aggregate supply curve shift upward and to the left during the 1970s? The following reasons are among those frequently cited: (1) Food prices shot up, beginning in late 1972, because of bad crops around the world (and the disappearance of Peruvian anchovies, which caused a drop in the fish catch off the South American coast). (2) Many other raw material prices increased rapidly, due to worldwide shortages. (3) As pointed out above, the price of crude oil increased greatly in 1974, 1979, and other years, due to the actions of Arab and other oil-producing countries. Because of these factors, a given level of NNP could be produced only at a higher price level than was previously the case. That is, the aggregate supply curve shifted upward and to the left.

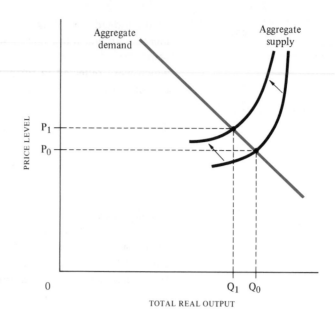

Figure 9.16

Shift of the Aggregate Supply Curve in the Seventies and Early Eighties

According to many economists, the stagflation of the late 1970s was due in considerable part to a shift of the aggregate supply curve upward and to the left due to marked shortages and price increases for oil, food, and other materials. Assuming for simplicity that the aggregate demand curve remained fixed, output fell from OQ_0 to OQ_1, and the price level rose from OP_0 to OP_1.

THE UNFOLDING EIGHTIES

In 1980, inflation continued to soar. By November 1980, the Consumer Price Index was about 13 percent above its level a year earlier. At the same time, the unemployment rate rose from about 5.8 percent in 1979 to 7.1 percent in 1980, as a very brief recession occurred early in 1980. During 1981, there seemed to be some decrease in the rate of inflation, although it was still very high by historical standards. Between December 1980 and December 1981, the price level increased by about 9 percent.

In the latter part of 1981, the economy slumped into another recession, and the unemployment rate increased considerably. By the middle of 1982, it was over 9 percent, and unemployment, not inflation, seemed to be the nation's biggest economic problem. But this did not mean that inflation was quelled. The price level continued to rise, but at a less alarming rate.

November 1982 saw the trough of the recession. During 1983, real GNP grew by about 3.4 percent. Moreover, inflation continued to fall, the increase in the Consumer Price Index during 1983 being 3.2 percent. In 1984, the economy continued to show considerable strength, with real GNP growing at about 6.8 percent and inflation being held to about 4.3 percent. Although unemployment was still about 7.0 percent, most observers seemed to regard the economy as being reasonably healthy in 1985.

Test Yourself

1. "Most depressions are caused by massive shifts to the left of the aggregate supply curve." Do you agree? Why or why not?

2. There is a seasonal cycle in many industries. For example, soft drink manufacturers have higher sales in the summer than in the winter. Is this the same as the business cycle? Why or why not?

3. In many industries, there is a long-term upward trend in

sales due to growing population and living standards. Is this the same as the business cycle? Why or why not?

4. Describe the four phases of the business cycle. In early 1985, was the U.S. economy in an expansion? A recession?

5. What policies might the United States adopt to push the aggregate supply curve to the right? If a policy has this effect, can we be sure it is desirable? Why or why not?

Summary

1. The aggregate demand curve shows the level of real national output that will be demanded at each price level. It slopes downward and to the right because (a) increases in the price level push up interest rates, and (b) increases in interest rates reduce real national output.

2. The aggregate supply curve shows the level of real national output that will be supplied at each price level. It can be divided into three ranges: (a) the horizontal or Keynesian range where there is considerable unemployment and where output can be increased without increasing the price level, (b) an intermediate range where shortages begin to develop and where increases in output require increases in the price level, and (c) a vertical or classical range where output is at its maximum and where increases in the price level have no effect on output.

3. The equilibrium level of real national output and the equilibrium price level are given by the intersection of the aggregate demand and supply curves.

4. If the equilibrium occurs in the horizontal range of the aggregate supply curve, a rightward shift of the aggregate demand curve will increase output (and thus decrease unemployment) but have no effect on the price level. This corresponds to a depression where a considerable amount of resources are unemployed. Governments frequently try to push the aggregate demand curve to the right under these circumstances.

5. If it appears likely that there will be a substantial increase in the price level, the government is likely to try to induce a leftward shift of the aggregate demand curve, thus causing the price level to be lower than it otherwise would be.

6. In recent years, there has been considerable attention given to "supply-side" economics, which focuses on shifting the aggregate supply curve to the right. If this can be done, real output will increase and inflationary forces will be quelled.

7. National output tends to rise and approach its potential (that is, its full-employment) level for a while, then falter and fall below this level, then rise to approach it once more, and so on. These ups and downs are called business fluctuations, or business cycles.

8. Each cycle can be divided into four phases: trough, expansion, peak, recession. These cycles are very irregular and highly variable in length and amplitude. Unemployment tends to be higher at the trough than at the peak; inflation tends to be higher at the peak than at the trough.

9. Our most severe recession occurred in 1929–33. Not until World War II did we really get out of the Great Depression. The war brought major inflationary pressures which subsided when it ended. Since World War II, we have had recurring recessions, and the problem of inflation has gotten worse.

10. During the late 1970s and the early 1980s, we suffered from stagflation, the combination of high unemployment and high inflation. According to many economists, this was attributable in part to a shift upward and to the left of the aggregate supply curve due to the increase in oil prices and the shortage of other raw materials. During the mid-1980s, inflation eased substantially, but the unemployment rate remained about 7 percent.

Concepts for Review

Aggregate demand curve	**Expansion**	**Depression**
Aggregate supply curve	**Peak**	**Prosperity**
Business cycle	**Recession**	**Stagflation**
Trough		

CHAPTER 10

The Determination of National Output

In the previous chapter, we presented an introductory sketch of business fluctuations and indicated how aggregate demand and supply curves can be used to analyze these fluctuations. In this chapter, we go a step further. Rather than simply taking the position of the aggregate demand curve as given, we are concerned with why the equilibrium level of national output is what it is. That is, why is the aggregate demand positioned so as to intersect the aggregate supply curve at this (rather than some other) output?

National output is defined as net national product in this chapter, since it is the best measure of how much the economy is producing when depreciation is taken into account. But since net national product and gross national product move up and down together, this theory will also enable us to explain movements in gross national product, and to help forecast them.

SIMPLIFYING ASSUMPTIONS

In this chapter, we shall make three major simplifying assumptions:

1. We assume that there are no government expenditures and that the economy is closed (no exports or imports). Thus *total spending on final output—that is, on net national product—in this simple case equals consumption expenditure plus net investment.*[1] (Why? Because the other two components of total spending—government expenditures and net exports—are zero.)

---

[1] Since personal consumption expenditure and net private domestic investment are cumbersome terms, we shall generally use consumption expenditure and net investment instead in this and subsequent chapters.

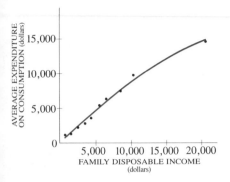

Figure 10.1

Relation between Family Expenditures on Consumption and Family Disposable Income, United States *Families with higher incomes spend more on consumption than families with lower incomes.*

Figure 10.2

Relationship between Personal Consumption Expenditure and Disposable Income, United States, 1929–84 (excluding World War II) *There is a very close relationship between personal consumption expenditure and disposable income in the United States. In this figure a dot is given for each year. The dot's horizontal distance from the origin measures the disposable income that year, and its vertical distance from the origin measures the consumption expenditure that year. As you can see, the dots generally are very close to the line.*

2. We assume that there are no taxes, no transfer payments, and no undistributed corporate profits. Thus *NNP equals disposable income in this simple case,* because the items in Table 7.8 that are taken from, or added to, NNP to get disposable income total zero. Later chapters relax this and the first assumption.

3. We shall assume that the total amount of intended investment is *independent* of the level of net national product. This, of course, is only a rough simplification, since, as we noted in the previous chapter, the amount firms invest will be affected by the level of national output. But this simplification is very convenient and, as we shall show in the next chapter, it is relatively easy to extend the model to eliminate this assumption.

The Consumption Function

An important part of our theory of the determination of national output is the **consumption function**, *which is the relationship between consumption spending and disposable income.* It seems clear that *consumption expenditures—whether those of a single household or the total consumption expenditures in the entire economy—are influenced heavily by income.* For individual households, Figure 10.1 shows that families with higher incomes spend more on consumption than families with lower incomes. Of course, individual families vary a good deal in their behavior; some spend more than others even if their incomes are the same. But, on the average, a family's consumption expenditure is tied very closely to its income.

What is true for individual families also holds for the entire economy: total personal consumption expenditures are closely related to disposable income. This fact is shown in Figure 10.2, where personal consumption expenditure in each year (from 1929 to 1984) is plotted against disposable income in the same year (from 1929 to 1984). The points fall very near the straight line drawn in Figure 10.2, but not right on it. For most practical purposes, however, we can regard the line drawn in Figure 10.2 as representing the relationship between personal consumption expenditures and disposable income. In other words, we can regard this line as the consumption function.

The consumption function is at the heart of the modern theory of the determination of national output. It is a working tool that is used widely and often by economists to analyze and forecast the behavior of the economy. There have been many statistical studies of the consumption function. Some of these studies have been based on cross-section data—comparisons of the amount spent on consumption by families at various income levels. (Figure 10.1 is based on cross-section data.) Others have been based on time-series data—comparisons of the total amount spent on consumption in the economy with total income over various periods of time. (Figure 10.2 is based on time-series data.)

THE MARGINAL PROPENSITY TO CONSUME

Suppose that we know what the consumption function for a given society looks like at a particular period in time. For example, suppose that it is

Table 10.1
THE CONSUMPTION FUNCTION

Disposable income (billions of dollars)	Personal consumption expenditure (billions of dollars)	Marginal propensity to consume	Average propensity to consume
1,000	950		.95
		$\frac{30}{50} = .60$	
1,050	980		.93
		$\frac{30}{50} = .60$	
1,100	1,010		.92
		$\frac{30}{50} = .60$	
1,150	1,040		.90
		$\frac{30}{50} = .60$	
1,200	1,070		.89
		$\frac{30}{50} = .60$	
1,250	1,100		.88
		$\frac{30}{50} = .60$	
1,300	1,130		.87

Figure 10.3

The Marginal Propensity to Consume Equals the Slope of the Consumption Function *The slope of the consumption function between points A and B equals the vertical change (which is the change in personal consumption expenditure) divided by the horizontal change (which is the change in disposable income). Since the marginal propensity to consume equals the change in personal consumption expenditure divided by the change in disposable income, it follows that the slope equals the marginal propensity to consume.*

given by the figures for disposable income and personal consumption expenditure in the first two columns of Table 10.1. Based on our knowledge of the consumption function, we can determine the *extra* amount families will spend on consumption if they receive an *extra* dollar of disposable income. *This amount—the fraction of an extra dollar of income that is spent on consumption—is called the* **marginal propensity to consume.** For reasons discussed in the next chapter, the marginal propensity to consume, shown in column 3 of Table 10.1, plays a major role in the theory of national output determination.

To make sure that you understand exactly what the marginal propensity to consume is, consult Table 10.1. What is the marginal propensity to consume when disposable income is between $1,000 billion and $1,050 billion? The second column shows that, when income rises from $1,000 billion to $1,050 billion, consumption expenditure rises from $950 billion to $980 billion. Consequently, the fraction of the extra $50 billion of income that is consumed is $30 billion ÷ $50 billion, or 0.60. Thus the marginal propensity to consume is 0.60.[2] Based on similar calculations, the marginal propensity to consume when disposable income is between $1,050 billion and $1,100 billion is 0.60; the marginal propensity to consume when disposable income is between $1,100 billion and $1,150 billion is 0.60; and so forth.

The marginal propensity to consume can be interpreted geometrically as the slope of the consumption function. The slope of any line is, of course, the ratio of the vertical change to the horizontal change when a small movement occurs along the line. As shown in Figure 10.3, the vertical change is the change in personal consumption expenditure, and the horizontal change is the change in disposable income. Thus the ratio of the vertical change to the horizontal change must equal the marginal propensity to consume.

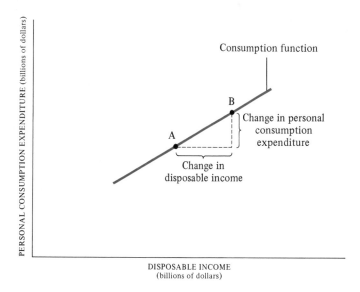

PERSONAL CONSUMPTION EXPENDITURE (billions of dollars)

Consumption function

B

A

Change in personal consumption expenditure

Change in disposable income

DISPOSABLE INCOME
(billions of dollars)

[2] Students with some knowledge of mathematics will recognize that this is an approximation since $50 billion is a substantial change in income, whereas the marginal propensity to consume pertains to a small change in income. But this is an innocuous simplification. Similar simplifications are made below.

In general, the marginal propensity to consume can differ, depending on the level of disposable income. For example, the marginal propensity to consume may be higher at lower levels than at higher levels of disposable income. Only if the consumption function is a straight line, as in Figure 10.2 and Table 10.1, will the marginal propensity to consume be the same at all levels of income. For simplicity, we assume in much of the subsequent analysis that the consumption function is a straight line, but this assumption can easily be relaxed without affecting the essential aspects of our conclusions.

THE AVERAGE PROPENSITY TO CONSUME

It is important to distinguish between the marginal propensity to consume and the *average propensity to consume.* The average propensity to consume equals the proportion of disposable income that is consumed. In other words, it equals

$$\frac{\text{personal consumption expenditure}}{\text{disposable income}}.$$

Clearly, this will not in general equal the marginal propensity to consume, which is

$$\frac{\text{change in personal consumption expenditure}}{\text{change in disposable income}}.$$

The point is that the marginal propensity to consume is the proportion of *extra* income consumed, and this proportion generally is quite different from the proportion of *total* income consumed. For example, in Table 10.1, the average propensity to consume when disposable income is $1,100 billion is 0.92; but the marginal propensity to consume when disposable income is between $1,050 billion and $1,100 billion is 0.60.

The Saving Function

If people don't devote their disposable income to personal consumption expenditure, what else can they do with it? Of course, they can save it. When families refrain from spending their income on consumption goods and services—that is, when they forgo present consumption to provide for larger consumption in the future—they save. Thus we can derive from the consumption function the total amount people will save at each level of disposable income. All we have to do is subtract the total personal consumption expenditure at each level of disposable income from disposable income. The difference is the total amount of saving at each level of disposable income. This difference is shown in the next to last column of Table 10.2. We can plot the total amount of saving against disposable income, as in Figure 10.4. The resulting relationship between total saving and disposable income is the *saving function.* Like the consumption function, it plays a major role in the theory of national output determination.

Table 10.2
THE SAVING FUNCTION

Disposable income (billions of dollars)	Personal consumption expenditure (billions of dollars)	Saving (billions of dollars)	Marginal propensity to save
1,000	950	50	
			$\frac{20}{50} = .40$
1,050	980	70	
			$\frac{20}{50} = .40$
1,100	1,010	90	
			$\frac{20}{50} = .40$
1,150	1,040	110	
			$\frac{20}{50} = .40$
1,200	1,070	130	
			$\frac{20}{50} = .40$
1,250	1,100	150	
			$\frac{20}{50} = .40$
1,300	1,130	170	

THE MARGINAL PROPENSITY TO SAVE

If we know the saving function, we can calculate the marginal propensity to save at any level of disposable income. The *marginal propensity to save is the proportion of an extra dollar of disposable income that is saved.* To see how to calculate it, consult Table 10.2 again. The third column shows that, when income rises from $1,000 billion to $1,050 billion, saving rises from $50 billion to $70 billion. Consequently, the fraction of the extra $50 billion of income that is saved is $20 billion ÷ $50 billion, or 0.40. Thus the marginal propensity to save is 0.40. Similar calculations show that the

Figure 10.4
The Saving Function *The saving function describes the total amount of saving at each level of disposable income. The slope of the saving function equals the change in saving divided by the change in disposable income. Thus the slope of the saving function equals the marginal propensity to save.*

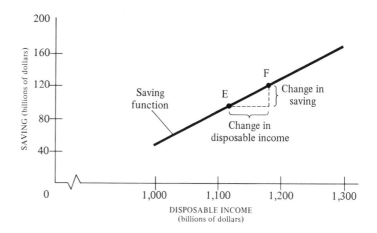

199

marginal propensity to save when disposable income is between $1,050 billion and $1,100 billion is 0.40; the marginal propensity to save when disposable income is between $1,100 billion and $1,150 billion is 0.40; and so forth.

Note that, *at any particular level of disposable income, the marginal propensity to save plus the marginal propensity to consume must equal one.* By definition, the marginal propensity to save equals the proportion of an extra dollar of disposable income that is saved, and the marginal propensity to consume equals the proportion of an extra dollar of income that is consumed. The sum of these two proportions must equal one, for, as stated above, the only things that people can do with an extra dollar of disposable income are consume it or save it. Table 10.2 shows this fact quite clearly.

Finally, it is worth noting that the marginal propensity to save equals the slope of the saving function—just as the marginal propensity to consume equals the slope of the consumption function. As pointed out above, the slope of a line equals the vertical distance between any two points on the line divided by the horizontal distance between them. Since (as shown in Figure 10.4) the vertical distance is the change in saving and the horizontal distance is the change in disposable income, the slope of the saving function must equal the marginal propensity to save.

The Permanent-Income and Life-Cycle Hypotheses

The consumption function, as described in previous sections, is a relationship between *current* consumption expenditure and *current* disposable income. In Figures 10.1 and 10.2, for example, it is presumed that current consumption expenditure in a given period, whether for a family or a nation, depends upon disposable income in that same period. Some economists, led by Milton Friedman of Stanford University, Franco Modigliani of the Massachusetts Institute of Technology, and Albert Ando of the University of Pennsylvania, have challenged this presumption. In their view, a household's current personal consumption expenditure does not depend on current disposable income; instead, it depends on the household's expected stream of disposable income over a long period of time (as well as the household's wealth). Thus two households that have the same current disposable income may spend quite different amounts on consumption goods, if their expected income streams over the long term are quite different.

To illustrate what these economists mean, consider two hypothetical families: the Rosenbergs and the Goulds. Although both Mr. Rosenberg and Ms. Gould will earn $12,000 this year, their long-run income prospects are quite different. Mr. Rosenberg is a businessman who ordinarily makes $50,000 per year, but whose income is much lower this year because of a foolish decision by one of his employees that caused a sizable one-time loss to Rosenberg's firm. Based on all available evidence, Rosenberg's annual income will return to about $50,000 in the future. Ms. Gould, on the other hand, has been unemployed for many years, and there is no prospect that she will return to work. Her $12,000 income this year was due to her having won a lottery. What Friedman, Modigliani, and Ando are saying is that one would expect each family to spend an amount on consumption goods this year that is commensurate with its long-term income, not just its income this year. Thus one would expect the Rosenbergs to spend a lot more on consumption goods than the Goulds, even though their current incomes are the same.

Although Friedman's theory (often called the permanent-income hypothesis) differs in many respects from the Modigliani-Ando theory (often called the life-cycle hypothesis), the differences need not concern us here. What is important for present purposes is that both of these theories predict that a transitory change in income may not have much impact on a household's consumption expenditure, if the household's long-run income prospects remain relatively unaffected. In contrast, the basic consumption function discussed earlier in this chapter assumes that consumption expenditure is dependent on current disposable income. To keep the analysis as simple as possible, we generally shall use the basic consumption function in subsequent chapters; but the fact that it is a simplification should be recognized. (In discussing the effects of temporary tax changes in Chapter 12, we shall put the Friedman and Modigliani-Ando theories to good use.)

Basic Idea #19: Personal consumption expenditure is closely related to disposable income. As disposable income goes up, so does personal consumption expenditure. However, personal consumption expenditure is more closely related to long-run income than to current income.

Determinants of Investment

In Chapter 7, we stressed that investment consists largely of the amount firms spend on new buildings and factories, new equipment, and increases in inventory. Investment plays a central role in the modern theory of output and employment. To understand this theory, it is essential that you understand the factors determining the level of net private domestic investment (which is gross private domestic investment less depreciation). Basically, there are two broad determinants of the level of net private domestic investment—the expected rate of return from capital, and the interest rate.

RATE OF RETURN

The *expected rate of return from capital* is the perceived rate of return that businessmen believe they can obtain if they put up new buildings or factories, add new equipment, or increase their inventories. Each of these forms of investment requires the expenditure of money. The rate of return measures the profitability of such an expenditure; it shows the annual profits to be obtained per dollar invested. Thus a rate of return of 10 percent means that, for every dollar invested, an annual profit of 10 cents is obtained. Clearly, the higher the expected rate of return from a particular investment, the more profitable the investment is expected to be.

INTEREST RATE

The *interest rate* is the cost of borrowing money. More specifically, it is the annual amount that a borrower must pay for the use of a dollar for a year. Thus, if the interest rate is 8 percent, a borrower must pay 8 cents per year for the use of a dollar. And if the interest rate is 12 percent, a borrower must pay 12 cents per year for the use of a dollar. Anyone with a savings account knows what it is to earn interest; anyone who has borrowed money from a bank knows what it is to pay interest.

The Investment Decision

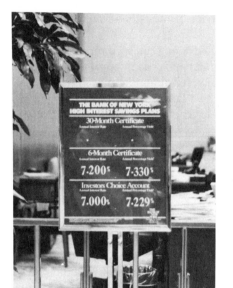

To determine whether to invest in a particular project (a new building, piece of equipment, or other form of investment), a firm must compare the expected rate of return from the project with the interest rate. If the expected rate of return is less than the interest rate, the firm will lose money if it borrows money to carry out the project. For example, if the firm invests in a project with a 10 percent rate of return and borrows the money to finance the project at 12 percent interest, it will receive profits of 10 cents per dollar invested and pay out interest of 12 cents per dollar invested. So it will lose 2 cents (12 cents minus 10 cents) per dollar invested.

Even if the firm does not borrow money to finance the project, it will be unlikely to invest in a project where the expected rate of return is less than the interest rate. Why? Because, if the firm can lend money to others at the prevailing interest rate, it can obtain a greater return from its money by doing this than by investing in the project. Thus, if the interest rate is 12 percent and an investment project has an expected rate of return of 10 percent, a firm will do better, if it has a certain amount of money, to lend it out at 12 percent than to earn 10 percent from the investment project.

Since firms are likely to invest only in projects where the expected rate of return exceeds the interest rate, it is obvious that *the level of both gross and net private domestic investment depends on the total volume of investment projects where the expected rate of return exceeds the interest rate.* For example, if the interest rate is 10 percent, the level of (gross and net) investment depends on the total volume of investment projects where the expected rate of return exceeds 10 percent. The more such projects there are, the higher will be the level of (gross and net) investment. The fewer such projects there are, the lower will be the level of (gross and net) investment. In the following sections, we discuss a number of factors that influence how many such projects there are.

TECHNOLOGICAL CHANGE

The rate of technological change can have an important influence on the volume of investment projects where the rate of return exceeds the interest rate. New technology frequently opens up profitable investment opportunities. For example, Du Pont, after successfully developing nylon in 1938, found it profitable to invest millions of dollars in new plant and equipment to produce this new synthetic fiber. In other words, the invention of nylon resulted in an additional number of investment projects where the rate of return was high enough to induce firms to invest. Another case of this sort was the continuous wide strip mill, one of the most important developments in steel technology in this century. After the invention of the continuous wide strip mill by Armco in the 1920s, American steel producers invested huge sums in new rolling mills to replace the old hand mills.

In general, *a more rapid rate of technological change is likely to result in a greater dollar amount of investment projects where the rate of return exceeds the interest rate. Thus a more rapid rate of technological change is likely to increase the level of investment.*

EXISTING STOCK OF CAPITAL

Another factor that influences the volume of investment projects where the rate of return exceeds the interest rate is the size of the existing stock of capital (relative to the level of sales). As a firm's sales go up, its need for plant, equipment, and inventories clearly goes up as well. Beyond some point, increases in sales result in pressure on the capacity of existing plant and equipment, so that the firm finds it profitable to invest in additional plant and equipment. The crucial relationship is between a firm's sales and its stock of capital goods—that is, its stock of plant, equipment, and inventories. If its sales are well below the amount it can produce with its stock of capital goods, there is little pressure on the firm to invest in additional capital goods. But if its sales are at the upper limit of what can be produced with its capital goods, the firm is likely to view the purchase of additional capital goods as yielding a high rate of return.

In general, *the smaller the existing stock of capital goods—relative to present and prospective sales levels—the greater the dollar amount of investment projects where the expected rate of return exceeds the interest rate.* Conversely, *the bigger the existing stock of capital goods—relative to present and prospective sales levels—the smaller the dollar amount of investment projects where the expected rate of return exceeds the interest rate.*

BUSINESS EXPECTATIONS

Still another factor that influences the volume of investment projects where the expected rate of return exceeds the interest rate is the state of business expectations. Sometimes business executives are optimistic; sometimes they are pessimistic. If they believe that their sales are about to drop dramatically, they will be unlikely to invest much in additional capital goods. On the other hand, if they believe that their sales are about to increase greatly, they may be led to invest heavily in capital goods. Firms must make investment decisions on the basis of forecasts. There is no way any firm can tell exactly what the future will bring, and the investment decisions it makes will be influenced by how optimistic or pessimistic its forecasts are. This, in turn, will depend on existing business conditions, as well as on many other factors. Sometimes government actions and political developments have an important impact on business expectations. Sometimes unexpected changes in the fortune of one industry have a major effect on expectations in other industries.

In general, *the more optimistic business expectations are, the larger the dollar amount of investment projects where the expected rate of return exceeds the interest rate. Conversely, the more pessimistic business expectations are, the smaller the dollar amount of investment projects where the expected rate of return exceeds the interest rate.*

Table 10.3

EXPECTED RATES OF RETURN FROM
INVESTMENT PROJECTS CONSIDERED BY
A FIRM

Project	Expected rate of return (percent)
A	12
B	14
C	8
D	11
E	7
F	10

Finally, the volume of investment projects where the expected rate of return exceeds the interest rate clearly depends on the level of the interest rate. The higher the interest rate, the smaller the volume of projects that have expected rates of return exceeding the interest rate. The lower the interest rate, the larger the volume of projects that have expected rates of return exceeding the interest rate. Suppose that a firm is considering the six investment projects shown in Table 10.3. If the interest rate is 6 percent, all of them have expected rates of return exceeding the interest rate. If the interest rate is 10 percent, only three of them (projects A, B, and D) have expected rates of return exceeding the interest rate. And if the interest rate is 15 percent, none of them has an expected rate of return exceeding the interest rate.

In general, *increases in the interest rate tend to reduce investment, while decreases in the interest rate tend to increase investment.* In 1982, this fact was reiterated frequently by both President Reagan and his critics. There was a general feeling that increases in interest rates had cut back on investment which would have been helpful in getting the economy out of its recession. In 1985, reductions in interest rates were expected to increase investment.

Test Yourself

1. Suppose that only three families inhabit a nation and that (regardless of the level of its income) each family spends 90 percent of its income on consumption goods. For the nation as a whole, what is the marginal propensity to save? How much difference is there between the marginal propensity to consume and the average propensity to consume? To what extent does the nation's marginal propensity to consume depend on the distribution of income? Is this realistic?

2. Assume that the consumption function is as follows:

Disposable income (billions of dollars)	Personal consumption expenditure (billions of dollars)
900	750
1,000	800
1,100	850
1,200	900
1,300	950
1,400	1,000

(a) How much will be saved if disposable income is $1,000 billion? (b) What is the average propensity to consume if disposable income is $1,000 billion? (c) What is the marginal propensity to consume if disposable income is between $1,000 billion and $1,100 billion? (d) What is the marginal propensity to save if disposable income is between $1,000 billion and $1,100 billion?

3. Suppose that the relationship between personal consumption expenditure and disposable income in the United States were as follows:

Consumption (billions of dollars)	Disposable income (billions of dollars)
750	700
830	800
910	900
970	1,000
1,030	1,100
1,100	1,200

Draw the consumption function on a graph. On another graph, draw the saving function. Is the marginal propensity to consume constant, or does it vary with the level of disposable income? Does the average propensity to consume rise or fall as disposable income rises?

4. "Unless firms make profits, they cannot invest in plant and equipment. Profits set an upper limit on how much they can invest." Comment and evaluate.

5. What effect would each of the following have on the amount of investment? That is, would each increase it, decrease it, or have no effect on it? (a) Expectations of greater likelihood of impending recession by firms; (b) a decrease in interest rates; (c) increased rate of invention of important new synthetic materials; (d) a marked reduction in the percent of existing plant that is utilized; (e) an increase in the perceived profitability of building up inventories.

The Equilibrium Level of Net National Product

As stressed in Chapter 3, an equilibrium is a situation where there is no tendency for change; in other words, it is a situation that can persist. In Chapter 3, we studied the equilibrium value of a product's price. Here we are interested in the equilibrium value of net national product. In Chapter 3, we saw that price is at its equilibrium value when the quantity demanded equals the quantity supplied. Here we shall see that NNP is at its equilibrium value when the flow of income (generated by this value of NNP) results in a level of spending that is just sufficient (not too high, not too low) to take this level of output off the market. To understand this equilibrium condition, it is essential to keep three points in mind:

1. The production of goods and services results in a flow of income to the workers, resource owners, and managers that help to produce them. Each level of NNP results in a certain flow of income. More specifically, under the assumptions made here, NNP equals disposable income. Thus whatever the level of NNP may be, we can be sure that the level of disposable income will be equivalent to it.

2. The level of spending on final goods and services is dependent on the level of disposable income. As we saw earlier in this chapter, consumption expenditure depends on the level of disposable income. (For the moment, we assume that investment is independent of the level of output in the economy.) Thus, if we know the level of disposable income, we can predict what level of spending will be forthcoming.

3. The level of production is dependent mainly on the level of spending. If producers find that they are selling goods faster than they are producing them, their inventories will decline. If they find that they are selling goods slower than they are producing them, their inventories will rise. *If NNP is at its equilibrium value, the intended level of spending must be just equal to NNP.* Why? Because otherwise there will be an unintended increase or decrease in producers' inventories—a situation which cannot persist. Much more will be said on this score in the sections that follow.

Aggregate Flows of Income and Expenditure

OUTPUT DETERMINES INCOME

Let's look in more detail at the process whereby national output (that is, NNP) determines the level of income, which in turn determines the level of spending. Suppose that the first column of Table 10.4 shows the various possible output levels—that is, the various possible values of NNP—that the economy might produce this year. This column shows the various output levels that might be produced, *if producers expect that there will be enough spending to take this much output off the market at the existing price level.* And, as stressed above, disposable income equals NNP.

INCOME DETERMINES SPENDING

Since disposable income equals NNP (under our current assumptions), the first column of Table 10.4 also shows the level of disposable income cor-

Table 10.4

DETERMINATION OF EQUILIBRIUM LEVEL OF NET NATIONAL PRODUCT (BILLIONS OF DOLLARS)

(1) Net national product (= disposable income)	(2) Intended consumption expenditure	(3) Intended saving	(4) Intended investment	(5) Total intended spending (2) + (4)	(6) Tendency of national output
1,000	950	50	90	1,040	Upward
1,050	980	70	90	1,070	Upward
1,100	1,010	90	90	1,100	No change
1,150	1,040	110	90	1,130	Downward
1,200	1,070	130	90	1,160	Downward
1,250	1,100	150	90	1,190	Downward

responding to each possible level of NNP. From this, it should be possible to determine the level of spending corresponding to each level of NNP. Specifically, suppose that the consumption function is as shown in Table 10.1 (page 197). In this case, intended consumption expenditure at each level of NNP will be shown in column 2 of Table 10.4. For example, if NNP equals $1,000 billion, intended consumption expenditure equals $950 billion.

But consumption expenditure is not the only type of spending. What about investment? Suppose that firms want to invest $90 billion (net of depreciation) regardless of the level of NNP. Under these circumstances, total spending at each level of NNP will be as shown in column 5 of Table 10.4. (Since total intended spending equals intended consumption expenditure plus intended investment, column 5 equals column 2 plus column 4.)

OUTPUT MUST EQUAL SPENDING

Column 5 of Table 10.4 shows the level of total *intended spending* at each level of national output (and income). *If NNP is at its equilibrium value, total intended spending must equal total output.* In other words, *if NNP is at its equilibrium value, total intended spending must equal NNP.* The easiest way to show this is to show that, if intended spending is not equal to NNP, NNP is *not* at its equilibrium value. The following discussion provides such a proof. First we show that, if intended spending is greater than NNP, NNP is not at its equilibrium level. Then we show that, if intended spending is less than NNP, NNP is not at its equilibrium level.

If intended spending is *greater* than NNP, what will happen? Since the total amount that will be spent on final goods and services exceeds the total amount of final goods and services produced (the latter being, by definition, NNP), firms' inventories will be reduced. Consequently, firms will increase their output rate to avoid continued depletion of their inventories and to bring their output into balance with the rate of aggregate demand. Since an increase in the output rate means an increase in NNP, it follows that NNP will tend to increase if intended spending is greater than NNP. NNP therefore is not at its equilibrium level.

On the other hand, what will happen if intended spending is *less* than NNP? Since the total amount that will be spent on final goods and services

Basic Idea #20: For NNP to be at its equilibrium value, total intended spending on final goods and services must equal NNP. If this spending exceeds NNP, NNP will tend to rise (as firms increase their output to avoid continued depletion of their inventories). If it is less than NNP, NNP will tend to fall (as firms cut back their output in response to increased inventories).

falls short of the total amount of final goods and services produced (the latter being, by definition, NNP), firms' inventories will increase. As inventories pile up unexpectedly, firms will cut back their output to bring it into better balance with aggregate demand. Since a reduction in output means a reduction in NNP, it follows that NNP will tend to fall if intended spending is less than NNP. Once again, NNP is not at its equilibrium level.

Since NNP is not at its equilibrium value when it exceeds or falls short of intended spending, it must be at its equilibrium value only when it equals intended spending.

Why NNP Must Equal Intended Spending: Three Cases

To get a better idea of why NNP will be at its equilibrium value only if it equals intended spending, consider three possible values of NNP—$1,050 billion, $1,100 billion, and $1,150 billion—and see what would happen in our simple economy (in Table 10.4) if these values of NNP prevailed.

CASE 1: NNP = $1,050 BILLION

What would happen if firms were to produce $1,050 billion of final goods and services? Given our assumptions, disposable income would also equal $1,050 billion (since disposable income equals NNP), so that consumers would spend $980 billion on consumption goods and services. (This follows from the nature of the consumption function: see column 2 of Table 10.4.) Since firms want to invest $90 billion, total intended spending would be $1,070 billion ($980 billion + $90 billion, as shown in column 5). But the total amount spent on final goods and services under these circumstances would exceed the total value of final goods and services produced by $20 billion ($1,070 billion − $1,050 billion), so that firms' inventories would be drawn down by $20 billion. Clearly, this situation could not persist very long. As firms become aware that their inventories are becoming depleted, they would step up their production rates, so that the value of output of final goods and services—NNP—would increase.

CASE 2: NNP = $1,150 BILLION

What would happen if firms were to produce $1,150 billion of final goods and services? Given our assumptions, disposable income would also equal $1,150 billion (since disposable income equals NNP), with the result that consumers would spend $1,040 billion on consumption goods and services. (Again, this follows from the consumption function: see column 2 of Table 10.4.) Since firms want to invest $90 billion, total spending would be $1,130 billion ($1,040 billion + $90 billion, as shown in column 5). But the total amount spent on final goods and services under these circumstances would fall short of the total value of final goods and services produced by $20 billion ($1,150 billion − $1,130 billion), so that firms' inventories would increase by $20 billion. Clearly, this situation, like the previous one, could not continue very long. When firms see that their inventories are increasing, they reduce their production rates, causing the value of output of final goods and services—NNP—to decrease.

CASE 3: NNP = $1,100 BILLION

What would happen if firms were to produce $1,100 billion of final goods and services? Disposable income would also equal $1,100 billion (since disposable income equals NNP), so that consumers would spend $1,010 billion on consumption goods and services. (Once again, this follows from the consumption function: see column 2 of Table 10.4.) Since firms want to invest $90 billion, total spending would be $1,100 billion ($1,010 billion + $90 billion, as shown in column 5). Thus the total amount spent on final goods and services under these circumstances would exactly equal the total value of final goods and services produced. Consequently, there would be no reason for firms to alter their production rates. Thus this would be an equilibrium situation—a set of circumstances where there is no tendency for NNP to change—and the equilibrium level of NNP in this situation would be $1,100 billion.

These three cases illustrate the process that pushes NNP toward its equilibrium value (and maintains it there). So long as NNP is below its equilibrium value, the situation is like that described in our first case. So long as NNP is above its equilibrium value, the situation is like that described in our second case. Whether NNP is below or above its equilibrium value, there is a tendency for production rates to be altered so that NNP moves toward its equilibrium value. Eventually, NNP will reach its equilibrium value, and the situation will be like that described in our third case. The important aspect of the third case—the equilibrium situation—is that for it to occur, intended spending must equal NNP.

USING A GRAPH TO DETERMINE EQUILIBRIUM NNP

For the sake of absolute clarity, we can represent the same argument in a diagrammatic, rather than tabular, analysis. Let's show again that the equilibrium level of NNP is at the point where intended spending equals NNP, but now using a graph. Since disposable income equals net national product in this simple case, we can plot consumption expenditure (on the vertical axis) versus net national product (on the horizontal axis), as shown in Figure 10.5. This is the consumption function. Also, we can plot the sum of consumption expenditure *(C)* and investment expenditure *(I)* against NNP, as shown in Figure 10.5. This relationship, shown by the *C + I* line, indicates the level of total intended spending on final goods and services for various amounts of NNP. Finally, we can plot a **45-degree line,** as shown in Figure 10.5. This line contains all points where the amount on the horizontal axis equals the amount on the vertical axis. Thus, since NNP is on the horizontal axis and intended spending is on the vertical axis, it contains all points where total intended spending equals net national product.

The equilibrium level of net national product will be at the point where total intended spending equals NNP. Consequently, the *equilibrium level of NNP will be at the point on the horizontal axis where the C + I line intersects the 45-degree line.* In Figure 10.5, this occurs at $1,100 billion. Under the conditions assumed here, no other level of NNP can be maintained for any considerable period of time.

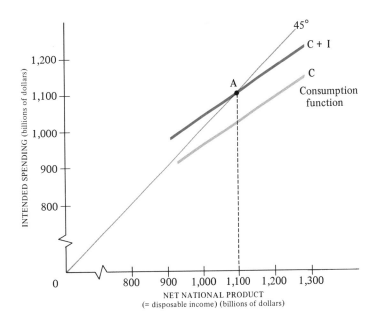

Figure 10.5

Determination of Equilibrium Value of Net National Product *The consumption function is* C, *and the sum of consumption and investment expenditure is* C + I. *The equilibrium value of NNP is at the point where the* C + I *line intersects the 45-degree line, here $1,100 billion.*

Why can we be sure that the point where the *C + I* line intersects the 45-degree line is the point where intended spending equals NNP? Because a 45-degree line is, by construction, a line that includes all points where the amount on the horizontal axis equals the amount on the vertical axis. In this case, as noted above, intended spending is on the vertical axis and NNP is on the horizontal axis. Thus at point *A*, the point where the *C + I* line intersects the 45-degree line, intended spending must equal NNP, because point *A* is on the 45-degree line.

Reconciling Aggregate Demand and Supply Curves with Income-Expenditure Analysis

At this point, we must reconcile and integrate the income-expenditure analysis presented here with the aggregate demand-aggregate supply analysis presented in Chapter 9. According to the *income-expenditure analysis,* the equilibrium level of NNP occurs at the point where the *C + I* line intersects the 45-degree line, as shown in the top panel of Figure 10.6. This analysis assumes that firms set their output levels in accord with the level of demand at current prices. If intended spending increases, firms increase their output levels; if intended spending falls, firms cut their output levels.

The income-expenditure analysis assumes that firms will produce whatever is demanded at the going price level. In other words, it assumes that the economy is situated on the horizontal range of its aggregate supply curve. As shown in the bottom panel of Figure 10.6, the aggregate demand curve intersects the aggregate supply curve in this range. Put differently, the income-expenditure analysis assumes that the equilibrium level of output is demand determined and that supply adjusts passively to demand.

209

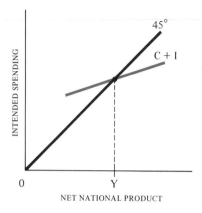

A

Income Expenditure Analysis

INTENDED SPENDING

45°

C + I

0   Y

NET NATIONAL PRODUCT

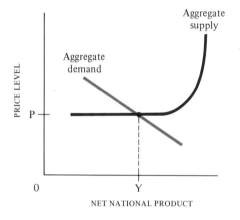

B

Aggregate Demand–Aggregate Supply Analysis

PRICE LEVEL

Aggregate
supply

Aggregate
demand

P

0   Y

NET NATIONAL PRODUCT

Figure 10.6

Relationship between Income-Expenditure Analysis and Aggregate Demand-Aggregate Supply Analysis *Income-expenditure analysis uses the intersection of the C + I line and the 45-degree line to find the equilibrium level of NNP. Aggregate demand-aggregate supply analysis uses the intersection of the aggregate demand and supply curves to find the equilibrium level of NNP. Income-expenditure analysis assumes that the economy is operating on the horizontal range of the aggregate supply curve. Both types of analysis yield the same result—namely, that the equilibrium value of NNP is OY.*

If the economy is experiencing considerable unemployment, and the horizontal range of the aggregate supply curve is the relevant one, the income-expenditure analysis tends to be a more revealing way of looking at the determinants of national output than the aggregate demand-aggregate supply analysis. It shows the nature of the changes in spending, which are the prime movers in the model.

But if the economy is operating at a point where the aggregate supply curve is vertical (or close to it), the aggregate demand-aggregate supply analysis is more relevant than the income-expenditure analysis because it focuses on changes in the price level, which are not included or shown in the income-expenditure analysis.

In subsequent chapters, both of these types of analysis will be used. They both are important parts of the economist's tool kit.

Leakages and Injections: Another Approach

In studying any topic, it helps to look at it from more than one angle. Another approach to income-expenditure analysis is the so-called *leakage-injection approach.* The basic idea underlying this approach is that, under our assumptions, the production of a particular level of output (that is, NNP) results in a level of disposable income that is equivalent to this level of NNP. But, as we know from our previous discussions, not all of this disposable income is spent by households; some of it is saved. This saving is a *leakage* from the spending stream, because it withdraws spending from the flow of income and expenditure. Such a leakage tends to reduce the equilibrium value of NNP because, unless it is offset, it results in total spending being too small to take the entire output (that is, NNP) off the market.

But firms do not sell their whole output to consumers. As we know from previous chapters, some of NNP (including items like blast furnaces and oil refineries) is sold to firms, this spending being called investment. Investment is an *injection* into the spending stream, because it adds spending to the flow of income and expenditure. That is, it is a supplement to consumption expenditure. Such an injection tends to increase the equilibrium value of NNP because it offsets the leakage of saving. If intended investment is less than intended saving, it is only a partial offset of this leakage. If intended investment is greater than intended saving, it more than offsets this leakage.

The equilibrium value of NNP is the one where the leakages equal the injections. Why? Because intended spending will equal NNP only if the intended amount of income not spent on output (leakages) equals the intended spending on output that is a supplement to consumer expenditure (injections). If leakages are greater than injections, NNP is above its equilibrium value, since intended spending will be too small to take the existing NNP off the market. If leakages are less than injections, NNP is below its equilibrium value, since intended spending will be more than sufficient to take the existing NNP off the market.

Example 10.1   Asking "What If" Questions

Economists find it useful to ask "what if" questions. For example, what if NNP in a particular country assumed various alternative values? What would be the results? Suppose that you know three things about the country in question. First, in this country, personal consumption expenditure = $100 million + 0.75$D$, where D is disposable income. Second, intended investment in this country equals $150 million. Third, this country has a primitive economy with neither a government nor foreign trade.

(a) Suppose that NNP in this country assumes the alternative values shown below. What are the corresponding values of intended consumption expenditure, intended investment, and total intended spending? Fill in the blanks below.

Net national product	Intended consumption expenditure	Intended investment	Total intended spending
		(millions of dollars)	
800	_____	_____	_____
900	_____	_____	_____
1,000	_____	_____	_____
1,100	_____	_____	_____

(b) What is the equilibrium level of net national product? (c) If NNP equals $900 million, what is the intended value of saving? (d) At what value of NNP does intended saving equal intended investment?

SOLUTION

(a) The complete table is:

Net national product	Intended consumption expenditure	Intended investment	Total intended spending
		(millions of dollars)	
800	700	150	850
900	775	150	925
1,000	850	150	1,000
1,100	925	150	1,075

(b) $1,000 million, since at this level of NNP total intended spending equals NNP. (c) $900 million minus $775 million, or $125 million. (d) When NNP equals $1,000 million, both intended saving and intended investment equal $150 million.

Table 10.5

THE LEAKAGE-INJECTION APPROACH TO THE DETERMINATION OF NET NATIONAL
PRODUCT (BILLIONS OF DOLLARS)

(1) Net national product (= disposable income)	(2) Intended consumption expenditure	(3) Leakages (intended saving)	(4) Injections (intended investment)	(5) Tendency of national output
1,000	950	50	90	Upward
1,050	980	70	90	Upward
1,100	1,010	90	90	No change
1,150	1,040	110	90	Downward
1,200	1,070	130	90	Downward
1,250	1,100	150	90	Downward

A Numerical Example

To illustrate the use of the leakage-injection approach, consider Table 10.5, which is based on the same data as Table 10.4. Column 3 shows **intended saving** at each level of NNP. Saving is, as we have seen, a leakage. Thus the total leakages at each level of NNP are given in column 3. Column 4 shows **intended investment** at each level of NNP. Investment is, as we have seen, an injection. Thus the total injections at each level of NNP are given in column 4.

WHAT IF NNP IS LESS THAN $1,100 BILLION?

If NNP is *less* than $1,100, Table 10.5 indicates that the total leakages are less than the total injections. The intended amount withdrawn from the expenditure stream via saving is less than the intended amount added via investment. Thus total intended spending is greater than NNP, and, as we saw in previous sections, this will result in an increase in NNP. For example, suppose that NNP equals $1,050 billion. At this level of NNP, intended saving is $70 billion, whereas intended investment is $90 billion. Consumers withdraw $70 billion from the expenditure stream via saving, while firms want to add $90 billion to it via investment. Consequently, total intended spending exceeds NNP by $90 billion minus $70 billion, or $20 billion. Since firms' inventories are drawn down by $20 billion, there is a tendency for NNP to increase, as we saw in a previous section.

WHAT IF NNP IS GREATER THAN $1,100 BILLION?

If NNP is *greater* than $1,100 billion, Table 10.5 indicates that the total leakages are more than the total injections. The intended amount withdrawn from the expenditure stream via saving is more than the intended amount added via investment. Thus total intended spending is less than NNP, and, as we saw in previous sections, this will result in a decrease in NNP. For example, suppose that NNP equals $1,150 billion. At this level of NNP, intended saving is $110 billion, whereas intended investment is $90 billion. Consumers want to withdraw $110 billion from the expenditure stream via saving, while firms want to add $90 billion to it via investment. Consequently, total intended spending falls short of NNP by $110 billion minus $90 billion, or $20 billion. Since firms' inventories increase by $20 billion, there is a tendency for NNP to fall, as we saw in a previous section.

WHAT IF NNP EQUALS $1,100 BILLION?

Only when NNP *equals* $1,100 billion will there be no tendency for NNP to rise or fall. As shown in Table 10.5, this is the value of NNP where the total leakages equal the total injections. (Specifically, both intended saving and intended investment equal $90 billion at this level of NNP). Thus, as pointed out above, the equilibrium value of NNP is the one where the total leakages equal the total injections.

Note that the equilibrium value of NNP, as determined by the leakage-injection approach, is the same as the one determined by the approach used in previous sections. Using either approach, we get the same answer—an equilibrium NNP of $1,100 billion. This will always be true. To see why, recall that according to the approach used in previous sections, NNP is at its equilibrium value when total intended spending on output equals NNP. This condition will be met if and only if the total leakages (intended saving) equal the total injections (intended investment). Since

$$\text{total intended spending} = \text{intended consumption}$$
$$\text{expenditure} + \text{intended investment,}$$

and

$$\text{disposable income} = \text{intended consumption}$$
$$\text{expenditure} + \text{intended saving,}$$

it follows that, because NNP equals disposable income here, total intended spending will equal NNP if and only if intended saving equals intended investment. Thus, if we use one approach, we will get the same answer as if we use the other approach.

Leakages and Injections: A Graphical View

Graphs can be used to determine the equilibrium value of NNP when the leakage-injection approach is used. To do so, we plot the saving function and the investment function on the same graph. (The **investment function** is the relationship between NNP and intended investment.) The equilibrium value of NNP is the value of NNP at which these two functions intersect. Why? Because at the value of NNP at which they intersect, the total leakages (represented by the saving function) equal the total injections (represented by the investment function).

Based on the data in Table 10.5, the saving function and investment function are as shown in Figure 10.7. Thus the equilibrium value of NNP must be $1,100 billion, since this is the point where the two functions intersect. For the reasons given in the previous section, the equilibrium value of NNP, as determined by a graph of this sort, must be the same as the one determined by Figure 10.5. And in accord with this fact, both Figures 10.5 and 10.7 yield the same answer—namely, that the equilibrium value of NNP is $1,100 billion.

Figure 10.7

Determination of Equilibrium Value of Net National Product *The equilibrium value of NNP is at the point where the saving function intersects the investment function, which here is $1,100 billion. At this point, the total leakages equal the total injections, since the saving function represents the leakages and the investment function represents the injections.*

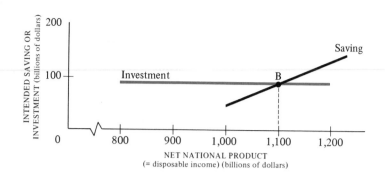

Actual Saving Equals Actual Investment

In the previous sections, we stressed that intended saving need not equal intended investment. This is an important fact, which must be understood. At the same time, however, it must be recognized that, whether or not intended saving equals intended investment, ***actual saving** must always equal **actual investment.*** In other words, although the amount people *set out to save* during a particular year may not equal the amount firms *set out to invest,* the *actual amount saved* will always equal the *actual amount invested.* This must be true because, as pointed out in a previous section, NNP has to equal consumption expenditure plus net investment.[3] At the same time, since it equals disposable income here, NNP must also equal consumption expenditure plus saving. Subtracting consumption expenditure from each of these expressions for NNP, saving must equal investment.

TWO ILLUSTRATIONS

Consider the case (in Table 10.4) where NNP is $1,050 billion. In this case, intended saving is $70 billion but intended investment is $90 billion. How does it turn out that actual saving equals actual investment? As pointed out in a previous section, there is an unintended ***disinvestment*** (i.e., negative investment) of −$20 billion in inventories if NNP is $1,050 billion. (Recall from Chapter 7 that a build-up of inventories is a form of investment, so a $1 billion increase in inventories equals $1 billion of investment.) Thus the actual investment is $90 billion (in intended investment) minus $20 billion (in unintended disinvestment), or $70 billion.[4] Actual saving equals intended saving, or $70 billion. Thus actual saving equals actual investment.

As a further illustration, consider the case where NNP is $1,150 billion. In this case, intended saving is $110 billion but intended investment is $90

[3] Recall from Chapter 7 that net national product equals consumption expenditure plus government expenditure plus net exports plus net investment. Since government expenditure and net exports are assumed to be zero, it follows that net national product equals consumption expenditure plus net investment.

[4] To make this case more concrete, suppose that the intended investment of $90 billion consists of $80 billion of expenditures on plant and equipment and a $10 billion increase in inventories. Because of the unintended disinvestment in inventories of −$20 billion, inventories will decline by $10 billion, and actual investment will equal $70 billion ($80 billion of expenditures on plant and equipment plus the −$10 billion change in inventories).

billion. How does it turn out that actual saving equals actual investment? As pointed out in a previous section, there is an unintended investment in inventories of $20 billion (because total spending falls short of NNP by this amount). Thus actual investment turns out to equal the intended investment of $90 billion plus the unintended investment of $20 billion, or $110 billion in all. Since actual saving also equals $110 billion, actual saving equals actual investment.[5]

In general, actual saving always must equal actual investment, even though intended saving does not always equal intended investment.

Usefulness of the Leakage-Injection Approach

Why bother to look at the determination of NNP in terms of the leakage-injection approach? After all, as we have stated repeatedly, we can get the same answer by comparing total intended spending on final goods and services with NNP. One important reason for looking at the determination of NNP in terms of intended saving (leakage) and intended investment (injection) is that it helps to lay bare the reasons why equilibrium NNP may be different from the level of NNP that would result in reasonably full employment at reasonably stable prices. As we pointed out in our discussion in Chapter 8 of criticisms of the classical view of unemployment, these reasons revolve about the fact that intended saving and intended investment are carried out by different parts of society and for different reasons. Households do much of the saving. They abstain from consuming now in order to provide for retirement, college educations for their children, emergencies, and other ways of consuming later. Firms, on the other hand, do most of the investing. They build plants and equipment and expand their inventories in response to profit opportunities. Because of this cleavage between the savers and the investors, *there is no assurance that intended saving will equal intended investment at a level of NNP that results in reasonably full employment at reasonably stable prices.*[6]

[5] Note that we assume here that actual saving will equal intended saving and that unintended changes in inventories will make actual investment conform to actual and intended saving. There are other ways for adjustments to take place. The important thing is that, one way or another, actual saving will equal actual investment.

[6] Note that, under the simplifying assumptions made in this chapter, there is only one leakage (saving) and one injection (investment). In subsequent chapters, we shall be concerned with models where other leakages (taxes and imports) and injections (government expenditures and exports) are involved.

Test Yourself

1. Suppose that the consumption function in a particular economy is given by the table on the right:

Disposable income (billions of dollars)	Consumption expenditure (billions of dollars)
400	300
500	360
600	410
700	440
800	470

If firms want to invest $140 billion, what is the equilibrium value of NNP? Can we be sure that this is the full-employment value of NNP? Why or why not? (The full-employment value of NNP is defined as the value of NNP that can be produced if there is full employment.)

2. Using the data in Question 1, plot the consumption function and the $C + I$ line on a graph, and derive the equilibrium value of NNP graphically. Is the consumption function a straight line? If the consumption function is not a straight line, does this affect the validity of the analysis in any way?

3. Using the data in Question 1, plot the saving function and the investment function, and show how they can be used to determine the equilibrium value of NNP. Does intended saving equal intended investment if NNP equals $800 billion? If NNP were $800 billion, show how actual saving would turn out to equal actual investment.

4. Suppose that the consumption function in a certain economy is $C = 100 + 0.8D$, where C is consumption expenditure and D is disposable income. If intended investment equals 10, what is the equilibrium value of NNP?

5. (Advanced) In a certain economy, the average propensity to consume is always equal to the marginal propensity to consume. If the equilibrium level of NNP equals $300 billion and if intended investment equals $100 billion, what is the equation for the consumption function in this economy?

Summary

1. The consumption function—the relation between personal consumption expenditure and disposable income—is at the heart of the modern theory of the determination of national output. There have been many studies of the consumption function, some based on cross-section data, some based on time-series data. From the consumption function, one can determine the marginal propensity to consume, which is the proportion of an extra dollar of income that is spent on consumption, as well as the saving function (the relationship between total saving and disposable income) and the marginal propensity to save (the proportion of an extra dollar of income that is saved).

2. Current consumption expenditure does not depend solely on disposable income in the current period. Instead, as stressed by the permanent-income and life-cycle hypotheses, it depends on the expected stream of disposable income over a long period of time.

3. The level of both gross and net private domestic investment is determined by the expected rate of return from capital and the interest rate. The expected rate of return from capital is the perceived rate of return that businesses expect to obtain if new buildings are put up, new equipment is added, or inventories are increased. The interest rate is the cost of borrowing money. The level of investment is directly related to the expected rate of return from capital, and inversely related to the interest rate.

4. The expected rate of return from capital is itself dependent upon the rate of technological change, the size of the existing stock of capital goods (relative to present and prospective sales levels), and the optimism or pessimism of business executives' expectations.

5. The equilibrium level of net national product will be at the point where intended spending on final goods and services equals NNP. If intended spending exceeds NNP, NNP will tend to increase. If intended spending falls short of NNP, NNP will tend to fall.

6. Another way to describe this equilibrium condition is to say that NNP is at its equilibrium level if intended saving equals intended investment. This is the so-called leakage-injection approach.

7. If NNP is below its equilibrium level, the total amount spent on goods and services will exceed the total amount produced, so that firms' inventories will be reduced. Firms will step up their output rates, thus increasing NNP.

8. If NNP is above its equilibrium value, the total amount spent on goods and services will fall short of the total amount produced, so that firms' inventories will rise. Firms will cut their output rates, thus reducing NNP.

9. Because of the cleavage between savers and investors, there is no assurance that intended saving will equal intended investment at a level of NNP that results in reasonably full employment at stable prices. But actual saving and actual investment always must turn out to be equal.

Concepts for Review

Consumption function	**Permanent-income**	**Leakage-injection**
Marginal propensity to	**hypothesis**	**approach**
consume	**Expected rate of return**	**Intended saving**
Average propensity to	**Interest rate**	**Intended investment**
consume	**Intended spending**	**Investment function**
Saving function	**45-degree line**	**Actual saving**
Marginal propensity to	**Income-expenditure**	**Actual investment**
save	**analysis**	**Disinvestment**

CHAPTER 11

Multiplier Analysis and Changes in Output

If you look at the business section of the morning newspaper, or if you switch on a television program dealing with the economy, there is a pretty good chance that you will find a forecast of the change in GNP or NNP in the next year or the next quarter. If so, more than one forecast may be given, for economic analysts do not always agree, particularly in detail. There is good reason why both economists and the general public are so interested in prospective changes in NNP. Besides being intrinsically important, they are related to changes in the unemployment rate and the inflation rate. In the previous chapter, we were concerned entirely with the factors determining the *level* of national output in a particular period. Now we must focus attention on the factors determining *changes* in national output.

Since changes in investment spending can result in important changes in output, we begin by describing the volatility of investment spending and the way in which changes in such spending have an amplified effect on output. Then we show that shifts in the consumption function have similar effects on national output. Finally, we discuss induced investment and the so-called paradox of thrift.

The Volatility of Investment

As shown in Figure 11.1, investment expenditure tends to be relatively unstable. That is, it varies from year to year by greater percentages than does consumption expenditure. Based on our discussion in the previous chapter, it is easy to see why this is the case.

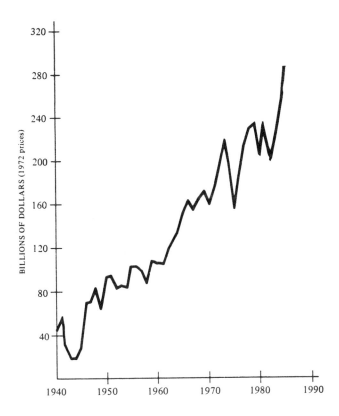

Figure 11.1

Gross Private Domestic Investment, United States, 1940–84 *Gross investment varies considerably from year to year. So does net investment.*

Irregularity of Innovation Rate. Technological innovation occurs irregularly—that is, in fits and starts—not at a constant rate. Thus investment (which, as we have seen, is dependent on the rate of technological change) also tends to occur irregularly. Investment booms seem to have occurred in response to major innovations like the railroad and the automobile. According to some forecasts, important innovations are likely to occur during the 1980s and 1990s in microelectronics and biotechnology. If so, they may be major stimuli to investment.

Durability of Capital Goods. Because capital goods tend to be quite durable, firms frequently can postpone investment decisions. For example, they can postpone the replacement of a piece of equipment by using it even though it is not as reliable as it once was. Or they can postpone the construction of a new building by tolerating crowded conditions in their existing buildings. Since many investment decisions are postponable, the exact time when projects are accepted may depend on the state of business expectations and the level of firms' profits, both of which are highly variable. Also, since the optimism or pessimism of business expectations tends to be contagious, firms often tend to invest at the same time.

Capacity Utilization. There are great differences from one year to the next in the extent to which existing productive capacity is being utilized. In some years, sales are so great that firms are working their plants at full capacity. In other years, sales are so slack that firms have plenty of excess capacity. In periods when the existing stock of capital goods is more than sufficient to meet current sales, the level of investment will tend to be lower than in periods when the existing stock of capital goods is only

219

barely sufficient to meet current sales. Because of the year-to-year variation in the extent to which sales levels press against productive capacity, there is considerable variation in the level of investment.

Effects of Changes in Intended Investment

Looking at the highly simplified model we constructed in the previous chapter to explain the level of national output, what is the effect of a change in the amount of intended investment? Specifically, if firms increase their intended investment by $1 billion, what effect will this increase have on the equilibrium value of net national product?

This is a very important question, the answer to which sheds considerable light on the reasons for changes in national output. The following sections are devoted to answering this question. We assume that the change in investment is autonomous, not induced. An *autonomous* change in spending is one that *is not* due to a change in income or NNP. An *induced* change in spending is one that *is* due to a change in income or NNP. We shall discuss induced investment near the end of this chapter.

THE SPENDING CHAIN: ONE STAGE AFTER ANOTHER

If there is a $1 billion increase in intended investment, the effects can be divided into a number of stages. In the first stage, firms spend an additional $1 billion on plant, equipment, or inventories. This extra $1 billion is received by workers and suppliers as extra income, which results in a second stage of extra spending on final goods and services. How much of their extra $1 billion in income will the workers and suppliers spend? If the marginal propensity to consume is 0.6, they will spend 0.6 times $1 billion, or $.6 billion. This extra expenditure of $.6 billion is received by firms and disbursed to workers, suppliers, and owners as extra income, bringing about a third stage of extra spending on final goods and services. How much of this extra income of $.6 billion will be spent? Since the marginal propensity to consume is 0.6, they will spend 60 percent of this $.6 billion, or $.36 billion. This extra expenditure of $.36 billion is received by firms and disbursed to workers, suppliers, and owners as extra income, which results in a fourth stage of spending, then a fifth stage, a sixth stage, and so on.

TOTALING UP THE STAGES

Table 11.1 shows the total increase in expenditure on final goods and services arising from the original $1 billion increase in intended investment. The total increase in expenditures is the increase in the first stage, plus the increase in the second stage, plus the increase in the third stage, and so on. Since there is an endless chain of stages, we cannot list all the increases. But because the successive increases in spending get smaller and smaller, we can determine their sum, which in this case is $2.5 billion. Thus the $1 billion increase in intended investment results—after all stages of the spending and responding process have worked themselves out—in a

Table 11.1

THE MULTIPLIER PROCESS

Stage	Amount of extra spending (billions of dollars)
1	1.00
2	.60
3	.36
4	.22
5	.13
6	.08
7	.05
8	.03
9 and beyond	.03
Total	2.50

$2.5 billion increase in total expenditures on final goods and services. In other words, it results in a $2.5 billion increase in NNP.

WHY $2.5 BILLION?

Why does the $1 billion increase in intended investment result in a $2.5 billion increase in NNP? To see why, recall from the previous chapter that intended saving must equal intended investment, if NNP is at its equilibrium value. Thus, if intended investment increases by $1 billion, intended saving must increase by the same amount. But if intended saving must increase by $1 billion, disposable income must increase by $2.5 billion because the marginal propensity to save equals 0.4 (since it equals one minus the marginal propensity to consume, which is 0.6 in this case). In other words, *since each extra dollar of disposable income results in 40 cents of additional intended saving, and since NNP equals disposable income (under the conditions assumed here), it will take an extra $2.5 billion of NNP to result in an extra $1 billion of intended saving.*

ANOTHER WAY TO DERIVE $2.5 BILLION

An alternative way of proving that a $1 billion increase in intended investment results in a $2.5 billion increase in NNP is the following. Because 0.6 is the marginal propensity to consume, a $1 billion increase in intended investment will result in increased total spending of $(1 + .6 + .6^2 + .6^3 + \dots)$ billions of dollars. This is evident from Table 11.1, which shows that the increased spending in the first stage is $1 billion, the increased spending in the second stage is $.6 billion, the increased spending in the third stage is $.6^2$ billion, and so on. But it can be shown that $(1 + .6 + .6^2 + .6^3 + \dots) = \dfrac{1}{1 - .6}$. (See footnote 1.)[1] Consequently, since $1/(1-.6) = 2.5$, the total increase in NNP must be $2.5 billion.

Since the marginal propensity to save equals $(1 - .6)$, another way of stating the findings of the previous paragraph is to say that *a $1 billion increase in intended investment results in an increase in equilibrium NNP of $(1/MPS)$ billions of dollars, where MPS is the marginal propensity to save.* This is a very important conclusion. To understand more clearly what it means, let's consider a couple of numerical examples involving values of

---

[1] To see this, let's divide 1 by $(1 - m)$, where m is less than 1. Using the time-honored rules of long division, we find that

$$
\begin{array}{r}
1 + m + m^2 + m^3 + \dots \\
1 - m \,\overline{)\,1} \\
\underline{1 - m} \\
m \\
\underline{m - m^2} \\
m^2 \\
\underline{m^2 - m^3} \\
m^3 \\
\underline{m^3 - m^4} \\
m^4
\end{array}
$$

Thus letting $m = 0.6$, it follows that 1 divided by $(1 - .6)$ equals $1 + .6 + .6^2 + .6^3 + \dots$

the marginal propensity to save other than 0.4. For instance, if the marginal propensity to save is ⅓, a $1 billion increase in intended investment will increase equilibrium NNP by 1 ÷ ⅓ billion dollars; that is, by $3 billion. Or take a case where the marginal propensity to consume equals ¾. What is the effect of a $1 billion increase in intended investment? Since the marginal propensity to save must equal 1 − ¾, or ¼, the answer must be 1 ÷ ¼ billion dollars. That is, equilibrium NNP will increase by $4 billion.

Example 11.1   Investment and a Great Crash

Between 1929 and 1933, annual investment spending in the United States fell by about $50 billion (1972 dollars). To get some idea of how a Great Crash, such as occurred then, can take place, let's consider a simple economy with no government or foreign trade. Suppose that intended investment in this economy falls from $52 billion to $2 billion. Assume that the saving function is as shown below:

(a) What is the marginal propensity to save? (b) What is the multiplier? (c) What is the equilibrium value of NNP before the fall in investment? (c) What is the equilibrium value of NNP after the fall in investment?

SOLUTION

(a) According to the graph, intended saving equals $2 billion when NNP is $100 billion, and it equals $52 billion when NNP is $300 billion. Thus, since NNP equals disposable income under the assumed (highly simplified) conditions, the marginal propensity to save equals (52 − 2) ÷ (300 − 100) = 0.25. (b) The multiplier equals the reciprocal of the marginal propensity to save, or 1/0.25 = 4 in this highly simplified case. (c) $300 billion, since at this value of NNP intended investment ($52 billion) equals intended saving. (d) $100 billion, since at this value of NNP intended investment ($2 billion) equals intended saving.

The Multiplier

Since a dollar of extra intended investment results in (1/MPS) dollars of extra NNP, (1/MPS) is called the **multiplier.** If you want to estimate the effect of a given increase in intended investment on NNP, multiply the increase in intended investment by (1/MPS). The result will be the increase in NNP. Moreover, it is easy to show that the same multiplier holds for decreases in intended investment as well as for increases. That is, a dollar less of intended investment results in (1/MPS) dollars less of NNP. Consequently, if you want to estimate the effect of a given change in intended investment (positive or negative) on NNP, multiply the change in intended investment by (1/MPS).

It is important to note that, since MPS is less than one, *the multiplier must be greater than one.* In other words, an increase in intended investment of $1 will result in an increase in NNP of more than $1. This means that NNP is relatively sensitive to changes in intended investment. Moreover, since the multiplier is the reciprocal of the marginal propensity to save, the smaller the marginal propensity to save, the higher the multiplier—and the more sensitive is NNP to changes in intended investment. As we shall see, this result has important implications for public policy. For example, because our system of taxes and transfer payments tends to increase the marginal propensity to save out of NNP, the destabilizing effect of a sharp change in investment expenditures frequently is reduced.

USING A GRAPH TO DERIVE THE SIZE OF THE MULTIPLIER

The sort of graphical analysis we used in Figure 10.7 can be used to show the effect of an increase in intended investment on equilibrium NNP. Since such a geometric formulation provides further confirmation of our results in the previous section, it seems worthwhile presenting it at this point.

Let's begin by noting once again that, if NNP is at its equilibrium level, intended saving must equal intended investment. If the saving function in our simplified economy is as shown in Figure 11.2 and intended investment is $100 billion, what will be the effect of a $1 billion increase in intended investment on equilibrium NNP? Before the increase in intended investment, equilibrium NNP was equal to $1,000 billion. (See Figure 11.2.) The increase of $1 billion in intended investment will shift the investment function up by $1 billion, to the new position, shown in Figure 11.2. This shift in the investment function will increase the equilibrium level of NNP, but by how much?

The resulting increase in equilibrium NNP, ΔY, can be derived by the following geometrical reasoning. First, the slope of the saving function times the change in equilibrium NNP must equal the increase in intended investment, $1 billion. This follows from the definition of the slope of a line. The slope equals the vertical distance between any two points on the line divided by the horizontal difference between them. The vertical distance between points *A* and *B* in Figure 11.2 is the increase in intended investment ($1 billion), and the horizontal distance between points *A* and

Basic Idea #21: A $1 billion increase in intended investment results in a more than $1 billion increase in NNP. In the simple model considered here, it results in an increase in equilibrium NNP of (1/MPS) billions of dollars. Since the marginal propensity to save (MPS) is less than one, the increase in equilibrium NNP must exceed $1 billion.

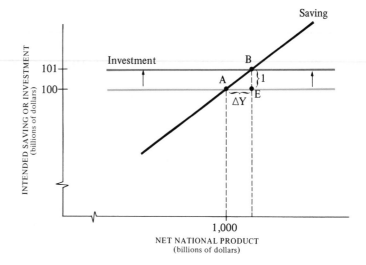

Figure 11.2

The Multiplier *If investment increases by $1 billion, the equilibrium value of NNP increases by ΔY. The slope of the saving function equals the vertical distance from A to B (which equals $1 billion) divided by the horizontal distance from A to B (which equals ΔY). Since this slope equals the marginal propensity to save (MPS), 1/ΔY = MPS. Thus ΔY = 1/MPS.*

B is the change in equilibrium NNP (Δ Y). Consequently, the change in equilibrium NNP must equal the increase in intended investment divided by the slope of the saving function.

Since the slope of the saving function is the marginal propensity to save—as pointed out in the previous chapter—it follows that the *change in equilibrium NNP equals the increase in intended investment divided by the marginal propensity to save. Thus a $1 billion increase in intended investment will result in an increase in equilibrium NNP of (1/MPS) billions of dollars,* which is precisely what we concluded in the previous sections.

Test Yourself

1. Suppose that the consumption function in a particular economy is given by the following table:

Disposable income (billions of dollars)	Consumption expenditure (billions of dollars)
400	300
500	360
600	410
700	440
800	470

Suppose that intended investment increases from $140 billion to $141 billion. Using a graph showing the old and new C + I line, indicate what effect this will have on the equilibrium value of NNP.

2. In question 1, plot the old and new investment functions on the same graph as the saving function. Show that you get the same answer as in question 1.

3. Suppose that the consumption function in a particular economy is C = 100 + 0.8D, where C is consumption expenditure and D is disposable income. What is the value of the multiplier?

4. Intended investment increases by $1000 in an economy where the marginal propensity to save is .2. What is the amount of extra spending in the *first* stage of the spending and responding process?

5. If the marginal propensity to consume is three times the marginal propensity to save, what is the multiplier? Why?

Determinants of Consumption: Nonincome Factors

In previous sections of this chapter, we were concerned with the effects on NNP of changes in investment spending. Now we must consider the effects of changes in consumption expenditure. It is important to recognize that many other factors besides disposable income have an effect on personal consumption expenditure. Holding disposable income constant, personal consumption expenditure is likely to vary with the amount of wealth in the hands of the public, the ease and cheapness with which consumers can borrow money, the expectations of the public, the amount of durable goods on hand, the income distribution, and the size of the population. In this section, we discuss the effects of these nonincome factors on consumption expenditure.

Amount of Wealth. Holding disposable income constant, it is clear that personal consumption expenditure will be higher if the public has a large amount of wealth—stocks, bonds, savings accounts, and so on—than if it has a small amount. Why? Because people are more willing to spend out of current income when they have large assets to tide them over if their incomes fall. Thus, if the Merriwether family has $100,000 in stocks and bonds, it is more likely to spend a large percentage of its income than if it has little or nothing in wealth.

Ease and Cheapness of Borrowing. Holding disposable income constant, it is clear that personal consumption expenditure will be higher if the public can borrow money easily and cheaply. This is particularly important for expenditures on consumer durables like automobiles and appliances. If required down payments are increased, and interest rates go up, some potential buyers will be persuaded (or forced) to postpone purchases of such items. For example, the Merriwethers may want a new car, and they may be quite willing to borrow the money to pay for it at 10 percent per year. But if the interest rate is raised to 15 percent per year, they may decide to stick with their old car until it is run into the ground.

Expectations. Holding disposable income constant, personal consumption expenditure may be higher if the public feels that price increases are in the wind or that goods will become harder to get. Why? Because the public may want to stock up on goods before their prices rise and while they are still available. (In the late 1970s, the expectation of price rises with regard to such items as autos and sugar seems to have had such an effect.) But this may not always occur. The expectation of price increases may have the opposite effect if the public is alarmed by inflation, and wants to build up its savings to cushion it against hard times ahead.

Amount of Durable Goods on Hand. Holding disposable income constant, personal consumption expenditure may be higher if the public has few durable goods on hand. For example, during World War II, very few automobiles were produced for ordinary civilian purposes. When such goods became available once again immediately after the war, there was an increase in the proportion of disposable income spent on durable goods, particularly since the public came out of the war with considerable savings and liquid assets. More will be said about this later on in this chapter.

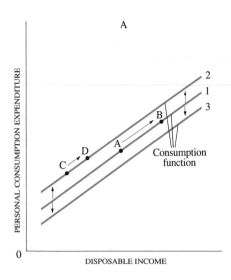

A Shift versus a Movement in the Consumption Function *If the consumption function moves from position 1 to position 2 (or position 3), this is a* shift *in the consumption function. A movement from* A *to* B *(or from* C *to* D*) is a* movement along *a given consumption function.*

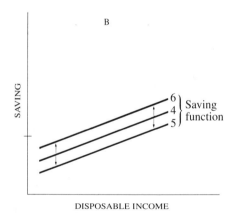

Effects of Shifts in Consumption Function on Saving Function *An* upward *shift in the consumption function (as from position 1 to position 2 in panel* A*) is accompanied by a* downward *shift in the saving function (from position 4 to position 5 in panel* B*). A* downward *shift in the consumption function (as from position 1 to position 3 in panel* A*) is accompanied by an* upward *shift in the saving function (from position 4 to position 6 in panel* B*).*

Distribution of Income. Holding disposable income constant, personal consumption expenditure would be expected to increase as a nation's income becomes more nearly equally distributed. Why? Because one would expect that the marginal propensity to consume would be higher (and the marginal propensity to save would be lower) among poor families than among rich ones. Thus, if a dollar of income is transferred from a rich family to a poor one, the poor family would be expected to save a smaller proportion of this extra dollar than the rich family from whom it was taken. Consequently, total consumption expenditure would be expected to increase as a result of transfers of income of this sort.

Size of Population. Holding disposable income constant, personal consumption expenditure would be expected to increase as a nation's population increases. As there are more and more mouths to feed, bodies to clothe, and families to house, one would expect that more would be spent on consumption goods, and less saved.

Shifts in the Consumption and Saving Functions

Suppose that a change occurs in one of the factors discussed in the previous section. For example, suppose that there is a marked increase in the amount of wealth in the hands of the public. What effect will this have on the consumption function? Obviously, it will shift the consumption function upward, as from position 1 to position 2 in Figure 11.3A. Or suppose that it becomes more difficult and expensive for consumers to borrow money. What effect will this have on the consumption function? Obviously, it will shift the consumption function downward, as from position 1 to position 3 in Figure 11.3A.

SHIFTS IN FUNCTIONS VERSUS MOVEMENTS ALONG THEM

It is important to distinguish between a *shift* in the consumption function and a *movement along* a given consumption function. A ***shift in the consumption function*** means that the public wants to spend a different amount on consumption goods out of a given amount of disposable income than in the past. Thus, if the consumption function shifts to position 2 in Figure 11.3A, this means that the public wants to spend more on consumption goods out of a given amount of disposable income than when the consumption function was at position 1. And if the consumption function shifts to position 3 in Figure 11.3A, this means that the public wants to spend less on consumption goods out of a given amount of disposable income than when the consumption function was at position 1.

In contrast, a movement along a given consumption function is a change in personal consumption expenditure induced by a change in disposable income, with no change in the relationship between personal consumption expenditure and disposable income. For example, the movement from Point *A* to point *B* is a movement along a consumption function (in position 1). Similarly, the movement from point *C* to point *D* is a movement along a consumption function (in position 2).

Figure 11.4

Shift in the Consumption Function *If the consumption function shifts from C_1 to C_2, this means that, at each level of disposable income, consumers intend to spend $1 billion more on consumption goods and services. Such a shift results in an increase of $\left(\dfrac{1}{MPS}\right)$ billions of dollars in equilibrium NNP, as shown in Figure 11.5.*

Figure 11.5

Effect of a Downward Shift of the Saving Function *A $1 billion upward shift in the consumption function results in a $1 billion downward shift in the saving function. Thus, if the consumption function shifts from C_1 to C_2 in Figure 11.4, the saving function shifts downward from S_1 to S_2, as shown here. The point where the saving function intersects the investment function shifts from A to E, and the equilibrium value of NNP increases by ΔY, which is the same amount that it increases when intended investment increases by $1 billion. (See Figure 11.2.)*

HOW SHIFTS IN THE CONSUMPTION FUNCTION ARE RELATED TO SHIFTS IN THE SAVING FUNCTION

Note that an *upward* shift in the consumption function must be accompanied by a *downward* shift in the saving function. If the public wants to spend *more* on consumption goods out of a given amount of disposable income, it must want to save *less* out of that amount of disposable income. (Why? Because personal consumption expenditure plus saving equals disposable income). Thus, if the consumption function shifts upward from position 1 to position 2 in Figure 11.3A, the saving function must shift downward from position 4 to position 5 in Figure 11.3B.

Also, a *downward* shift in the consumption function must be accompanied by an *upward* shift in the saving function. If the public wants to spend *less* on consumption goods out of a given amount of disposable income, it must want to save *more* out of that amount of disposable income. (Why? Because personal consumption expenditure plus saving equals disposable income.) Thus, if the consumption function shifts downward from position 1 to position 3 in Figure 11.3A, the saving function must shift upward from position 4 to position 6 in Figure 11.3B.

Effects of Shifts in the Consumption Function

Earlier in this chapter, we showed that changes in intended investment have an amplified effect on NNP, with the extent of the amplification measured by the multiplier. But it is important to note at this point that a shift in the consumption function will also have such an amplified effect on NNP. For example, in Figure 11.4, if the consumption function shifts from C_1 to C_2, this means that at each level of disposable income, consumers intend to spend $1 billion more on consumption goods and services. *This $1 billion upward shift in the consumption function will have precisely the same effect on equilibrium NNP as a $1 billion increase in intended investment.*

To see that this is the case, recall from the previous section that an upward shift in the consumption function results in a downward shift in the saving function. Specifically, a $1 billion upward shift in the consumption function means that the saving function shifts downward by $1 billion (because, if consumers desire to spend $1 billion *more* out of each level of disposable income than before, they must desire to save $1 billion *less* out of each level of disposable income than before). As shown in Figure 11.5, a $1 billion downward shift in the saving function results in an increase in the equilibrium value of NNP. And this increase is the same as when intended investment increases by $1 billion, the situation we observed in Figure 11.2. In either case, the increase equals $\left(\dfrac{1}{MPS}\right)$ billions of dollars.[2]

Moreover, *a $1 billion downward shift in the consumption function will have precisely the same effect on equilibrium NNP as a $1 billion decrease in*

---

[2] For an algebraic demonstration that this is true, see the Appendix to this chapter.

intended investment. Thus both upward and downward shifts in the consumption function—due to changes in tastes, assets, prices, population, and other things—will have a magnified effect on NNP. In other words, NNP is sensitive to shifts in the consumption function in the same way that it is sensitive to changes in intended investment. This is an important point. Finally, to prevent misunderstanding, recall from the previous sections that a *shift* in the consumption function is quite different from a *movement along* a given consumption function. (An example of the latter would be the movement from point *G* to point *H* in Figure 11.4.) We are concerned here with shifts in the consumption function, not movements along a given consumption function.

The Accuracy of Postwar Forecasts: A Case Study

Now that we have discussed some elements of the basic theory of the determination of NNP in the abstract, it is time to look at a specific application of this theory. Consider a famous incident that occurred at the end of World War II. Economists, using the best models then available, had been able to forecast the pace of the economy reasonably well during the war. When the war was coming to an end, they were charged with forecasting the level of national product in 1946, the year immediately after the war. This was an important task, since the government was worried that the economy might suffer severe postwar unemployment. The Great Depression of the 1930s was a recent—and still bitter—memory.

HOW THE GOVERNMENT FORECAST WAS MADE

Basic Idea #22: A $1 billion shift upward (or downward) in the consumption function results in the same increase (or decrease) in equilibrium NNP as a $1 billion increase (or decrease) in intended investment. In either case, the result is an increase (or decrease) in equilibrium NNP of (1/MPS) billions of dollars.

A group of economists in Washington was given the responsibility for this forecast. They made it in terms of gross national product, not net national product, but they used essentially the same theory as that discussed in previous sections. To forecast gross national product in 1946, these Washington economists began by using prewar data to estimate the consumption function. Then they estimated the amount of investment that would take place in 1946. To obtain their forecast of the change in GNP, they computed the multiplier $\left(\dfrac{1}{\text{MPS}}\right)$ and multiplied it by their estimate of the prospective change in intended investment. Then since their model—unlike ours—included government spending and taxes, other calculations, which will be discussed in Chapter 12, had to be made as well. The result was a forecast of a gross national product in 1946 of about $170 billion. This forecast received considerable attention and publicity inside and outside the government.

Before discussing the accuracy of this forecast, an important empirical question must be considered: in real-world studies like this, what is the estimated value of the multiplier? Judging from our findings in the previous sections, we would guess a figure of at least 2½, since the marginal propensity to consume should be at least 0.6. But these results are based on the assumption of no taxation. For reasons discussed in Chapter 12, the multiplier will be lower if there is taxation. Including the effects of taxation (and other factors like imports) most estimates of the multiplier seem to center around a value of 2. But these estimates can vary considerably, depending, of course, on the shape of the consumption function and other factors.

The government forecasters' estimate of a GNP of about $170 billion caused a severe chill in many parts of the government, as well as among business executives and consumers. A GNP of only about $170 billion would have meant a great deal of unemployment in 1946. Indeed, according to some predictions, about 8 million people would have been unemployed in the first quarter of 1946. Unfortunately for the forecasters—but fortunately for the nation—the GNP in 1946 turned out to be not $170 billion, but about $190 billion. And unemployment was only about a third of the forecasted amount. These are very large errors in practically anyone's book—so big that they continue to embarrass the economics profession 40 years later. Of course, our knowledge of the economy has expanded considerably over the past 40 years, and an error of this magnitude is much less likely now. Moreover, even at the end of World War II, some economists forecasted GNP in 1946 pretty well. Not everyone, by any means, agreed with the forecast of $170 billion. But it is worth bearing this notable mistake in mind when considering economic forecasts of this sort. Economics is not as exact a science as physics or chemistry—and mischief can result if one assumes otherwise.

WHY THE FORECAST WENT AWRY

What went wrong in the Washington economists' forecast? To a considerable extent, the answer lies in a topic of a previous section—a shift in the consumption function. When World War II ended, households had a great deal of liquid assets on hand. They had saved money during the war. There had been rationing of many kinds of goods, and other goods—like automobiles or refrigerators—could not be obtained at all. When the war ended and these goods flowed back on the market, consumers spent more of their income on consumption goods than in the previous years. In other words, there was a pronounced upward shift of the consumption function.

To see why this shift in the consumption function caused the forecasters to underestimate GNP in 1946, recall from the previous sections that an upward shift of $1 billion in the consumption function will result in an increase of $\left(\dfrac{1}{\text{MPS}} \right)$ billions of dollars in national product. Bearing this in mind, suppose the forecasters assumed that the consumption function remained fixed, when in fact there was an $8 billion shift upward. Then if the multiplier— $\left(\dfrac{1}{\text{MPS}} \right)$ —was 2½, national product would turn out to be $20 billion higher than the forecasters expected. (Since $\left(\dfrac{1}{\text{MPS}} \right)$ is assumed to be 2½, national product will increase $2.5 billion for every $1 billion shift in the consumption function, so an $8 billion shift in the consumption function will result in a $20 billion increase in national product.) Of course, these figures—a multiplier of 2½ and an $8 billion shift in the consumption function—are only illustrative, not precise estimates of the actual situation. For one thing, as noted above, the multiplier is wrong because it assumes no taxation. But they indicate the sort of thing that occurred, and they show dramatically the effects of a shift in the consumption function.

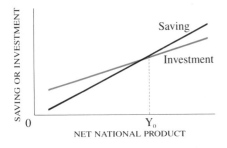

Figure 11.6

Determination of Equilibrium Value of Net National Product, with Induced Investment *If the level of investment depends on NNP, the investment function is positively sloped, and the equilibrium level of NNP is at the point where the investment function intersects the saving function.*

Induced Investment

In previous sections, we have assumed that intended net investment is a certain amount, regardless of the level of NNP. This assumption has been reflected in the fact that the investment function—for example, in Figures 11.2 and 11.5—is horizontal. Although this assumption may be a useful first approximation, it neglects the fact that firms are much more likely to invest in plant and equipment when NNP is high than when it is low. After all, NNP measures output; and the greater the output of the economy, the greater the pressure on the capacity of existing plant and equipment—and the greater the pressure to expand this capacity by investing in additional plant and equipment.

Our theory can be extended to take account of the fact that, to some extent, increases in NNP may *induce* increases in intended investment. (In other words, not all changes in investment are autonomous.) Rather than portraying the investment function as a horizontal line, we need only assume that it is positively sloped, as in Figure 11.6. Then, as before, the equilibrium level of NNP is at the point where the saving function intersects the investment function—that is, at point Y_0, the point where intended saving equals intended investment. (Much more will be said about the relationship between investment and changes in NNP in Chapter 13.)

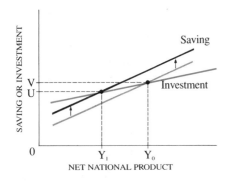

Figure 11.7

The Paradox of Thrift *If the saving function shifts upward (as shown here), the equilibrium value of NNP falls from Y_0 to Y_1—and despite its attempt to save more, the public saves less (U rather than V).*

The Paradox of Thrift

Despite all of the praise heaped upon it by moral philosophers, thrift (as spendthrifts have long suspected) can be a dangerous thing. If society as a whole desires to save more, the result may well be a decrease in national output and no increase in saving. To see why this is so, consider Figure 11.7, which shows a situation where the saving function shifts upward. Since the investment function remains constant, the equilibrium level of NNP falls from Y_0 to Y_1. And despite the public's attempt to save more, saving falls from V to U, as shown in Figure 11.7.

Of course, the fact that an upward shift in the saving function is likely to cause a decrease in the equilibrium value of NNP is really no news. As we pointed out earlier in this chapter, an upward shift in the saving function is accompanied by a downward shift in the consumption function. (Recall Figure 11.3B.) And as we also saw in earlier parts of this chapter, a downward shift in the consumption function will result in a decrease in the equilibrium value of NNP.

The important point here is that, *although thrift may be a private virtue, it can be a problem from the viewpoint of society as a whole.* Suppose, for example, that a recession occurs, with the result that NNP falls and unemployment rises. Under such circumstances, the public may well be inclined to cut back on its spending. That is, faced with economic storm signals, the public may try to save more. But what will be the unintended result? As indicated in Figure 11.7, the equilibrium value of NNP will be reduced, thus aggravating the recession. And to add insult to injury, the public may not be able to accomplish its goal of increasing saving. Thus all that will be achieved is an undesirable reduction in national output (and employment).

Example 11.2   Shifting Both the Saving and Investment Functions

Suppose that a nation adopts economic policies to encourage both saving and investment. To get some idea of the possible effects, consider a simple economy (with zero government spending, zero taxes, and no foreign trade) which adopts such policies. Suppose that the saving and investment functions before the adoption of these policies are S and I below, and that these policies shift them to S' and I'.

(a) Will these policies result in an increase in the equilibrium value of NNP? (b) Will these policies result in an increase in saving? (c) Will these policies result in an increase in investment? (d) How can we determine whether these policies will result in an increase in consumption expenditure? (e) Will a simultaneous upward shift in the saving and investment functions always result in an increase in the equilibrium value of NNP?

SOLUTION

(a) Yes. The intersection of the S' and I' lines lies to the right of the intersection of the S and I lines. (b) Yes. The intersection of the S' and I' lines lies above the intersection of the S and I lines. (c) The answer is the same as in (b), since saving equals investment. (d) Consider the point where the S line intersects the I line and the point where the S' line intersects the I' line. The horizontal difference between these two points equals the increase in NNP. The vertical difference between these two points equals the increase in saving. Under these highly simplified circumstances, NNP equals consumption expenditure plus saving. Thus the change in consumption expenditure equals the horizontal difference minus the vertical difference between these two points. (e) No, whether NNP will rise or fall depends on the extent of the shift of each function.

However, if a society increases *both* its saving and its investment, this may well promote a more rapid rate of growth of NNP. To see that this is the case, consult Example 11.2. Thus the effect of increased saving depends on the behavior of investment. Much more will be said on this score in Chapter 19.

Test Yourself

1. What effect would each of the following have on the position of the consumption function? That is, would each raise it, lower it, or have no effect on it? (a) An increase in interest rates; (b) expectations of greater inflation; (c) a catastrophe that wiped out half the nation's assets; (d) a marked increase in liquid assets held by people; (e) a rumor that major shortages of goods are about to occur.

2. Suppose that the consumption function in a particular economy is as follows:

Disposable income (billions of dollars)	Consumption expenditure (billions of dollars)
400	300
500	360
600	410
700	440
800	470

Suppose that consumers want to spend $50 billion more at each level of disposable income than is shown above. Using the $C + I$ line, show what effect this will have on the equilibrium value of NNP. (Assume that investment expenditure equals $140 billion.)

3. In Question 2, what effect will the indicated change in consumers' spending desires have on the saving function?

4. In Question 2, use the change in the saving function to show what change will occur in the equilibrium value of NNP.

5. If a $5 billion downward shift in the consumption function results in a $15 billion reduction in the equilibrium value of NNP, what is the marginal propensity to consume?

Summary

1. Investment expenditure tends to vary from year to year by greater percentages than does consumption expenditure. This is due in part to the irregularity of innovation, the durability of capital goods, and the differences from year to year in the extent to which existing productive capacity is utilized.

2. A $1 billion change in intended investment will result in a change in equilibrium NNP of $\left(\dfrac{1}{\text{MPS}}\right)$ billions of dollars, where MPS is the marginal propensity to save. In other words, the multiplier is $\left(\dfrac{1}{\text{MPS}}\right)$. The multiplier can be interpreted in terms of—and derived from—the successive stages of the spending process. An example of the use of the multiplier was the formulation at the end of World War II of GNP forecasts for 1946.

3. Holding disposable income constant, personal consumption expenditure is likely to depend on the amount of wealth in the hands of the public, the ease and cheapness with which consumers can borrow money, the expectations of the public, the amount of durable goods on hand, the income distribution, and the size of the population. Changes in these factors are likely to cause shifts in the consumption function.

4. A shift in the consumption function will also have an amplified effect on NNP, a $1 billion shift in the consumption function resulting in a change of $\left(\dfrac{1}{\text{MPS}}\right)$ billions of dollars in NNP. To a considerable extent, the large error in government forecasts of GNP in 1946 was due to an unanticipated shift in the consumption function. Responding to large accumulated wartime savings and pent-up wartime demands, consumers spent more of their income on consumption goods than in previous years.

5. Our theory can be extended to take account of the fact that, to some extent, increases in NNP may induce increases in intended investment. All we need to do is assume that the investment function is positively sloped, not horizontal.

6. If society as a whole desires to save more, and if there is no shift in the investment function, the result may well be a decrease in national output and no increase in saving. This is the so-called paradox of thrift.

Concepts for Review

Multiplier   **Induced investment**
Shifts in the consumption function   **Paradox of thrift**

Appendix: Using Basic Algebra to Derive the Multiplier

Equations speak more clearly to some than words, and so for those with a taste for (elementary) algebra, we will show how some of the principal results of this chapter can be derived algebraically. We begin by recalling that the equilibrium value of NNP is attained at the point where NNP equals total intended spending on output. This condition can be expressed in the following equation:

$$\text{NNP} = C + I, \tag{11.1}$$

which says that NNP must equal intended expenditure on consumption goods (C) plus intended investment (I). Since intended consumption expenditures plus intended investment equals total intended spending, it follows that this equation states that NNP must equal total intended spending.

Next, let's introduce a friend from this and the previous chapter, the consumption function. The consumption function in the first two columns of Table 10.4 can be represented by the following equation:

$$C = 350 + 0.6D, \tag{11.2}$$

which says that desired consumption equals $350 billion plus 0.6 times disposable income (D). Figure 11.8 shows the consumption function. As you can see, $350 billion is the intercept on the vertical axis, while 0.6 is the slope of the consumption function. Since—as we noted in the previous chapter—the slope of the consumption function equals the marginal propensity to consume, 0.6 equals the marginal propensity to consume.

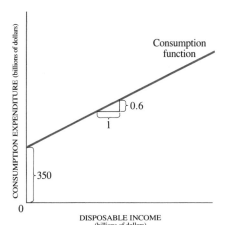

Figure 11.8

Consumption Function *The consumption function is derived from the data in Table 10.4. The marginal propensity to consume is 0.6, so the slope is 0.6.*

The next step is to substitute the right-hand side of Equation (11.2) for C in Equation (11.1). The result is:

$$NNP = 350 + 0.6D + I. \tag{11.3}$$

But recall that disposable income is equal to NNP in our simplified economy. Consequently, we can substitute NNP for D in this equation to get

$$NNP = 350 + 0.6NNP + I. \tag{11.4}$$

And going a step further, we can subtract 0.6 times NNP from both sides of Equation (11.4), which gives

$$NNP - 0.6NNP = 350 + I, \tag{11.5}$$

or, collecting terms,

$$0.4NNP = 350 + I. \tag{11.6}$$

Finally, dividing both sides by 0.4, we have

$$NNP = \frac{350}{0.4} + \frac{I}{0.4}. \tag{11.7}$$

Now we can see what happens to NNP if there is a \$1 billion increase in I. In other words, suppose that I is increased from some amount, \$$X$ billion, to \$$(X + 1)$ billion. How much will this increase NNP? From Equation (11.7), it is clear that NNP will equal

$$\frac{350}{0.4} + \frac{X}{0.4}$$

if intended investment equals \$$X$ billion. It is also clear from Equation (11.7) that NNP will equal

$$\frac{350}{0.4} + \frac{(X + 1)}{0.4}$$

if intended investment is equal to \$$(X + 1)$ billion. Consequently the increase in NNP due to the \$1 billion increase in intended investment is equal to

$$\left[\frac{350}{0.4} + \frac{(X + 1)}{0.4} \right] - \left[\frac{350}{0.4} + \frac{X}{0.4} \right]$$

$$= \frac{X + 1}{0.4} - \frac{X}{0.4} = \frac{X}{0.4} + \frac{1}{0.4} - \frac{X}{0.4} = \frac{1}{0.4}.$$

That is, a \$1 billion increase in intended investment will result in an increase of $\frac{1}{0.4}$ billion dollars in NNP. Recalling that 0.6 is the marginal propensity to consume and that the sum of the marginal propensity to consume and the marginal propensity to save equals one—it follows that *a*

$1 billion increase in intended investment will result in an increase of $\left(\dfrac{1}{MPS}\right)$ *billions of dollars in NNP, where MPS is the marginal propensity to save—0.4 in this case.*

This is precisely the same conclusion we arrived at in the text of the chapter. Thus we have derived the value of the multiplier by an algebraic route rather than the other routes used before.

In addition, Equation (11.7) can be used to determine the effects of a shift in the consumption function. A $1 billion shift upward in the consumption function causes the intercept to increase from its former amount, $350 billion, to $351 billion. What is the effect of this increase in the intercept on the equilibrium value of NNP? If the intercept is $350 billion, the equilibrium value of NNP will equal

$$\frac{350}{0.4} + \frac{I}{0.4}.$$

If the intercept is $351 billion, the equilibrium value of NNP will equal

$$\frac{351}{0.4} + \frac{I}{0.4}.$$

Consequently, the increase in NNP from the $1 billion upward shift in the consumption function is

$$\left[\frac{351}{0.4} + \frac{I}{0.4}\right] - \left[\frac{350}{0.4} + \frac{I}{0.4}\right] = \frac{351}{0.4} - \frac{350}{0.4} = \frac{1}{0.4}.$$

That is, a $1 billion upward shift in the consumption function results in an increase of $\dfrac{1}{0.4}$ billions of dollars in NNP. Recalling that 0.4 = MPS, it follows that *a $1 billion upward shift in the consumption function will result in an increase of* $\left(\dfrac{1}{MPS}\right)$ *billions of dollars in NNP.* This is precisely what we said on this score in the chapter.

CHAPTER 12

Fiscal Policy and National Output

In the period since World War II, the idea that the government's power to spend and tax should be used to stabilize the economy—that is, to reduce unemployment and fight inflation—has gained acceptance throughout the world. Most economists believe that this idea is essentially correct. However, time has also revealed that fiscal policy is far from a panacea. Witness the severe inflationary pressures and the high unemployment rates that plagued the American economy in the late 1970s and early 1980s. Both the power and the limitations of fiscal policy must be recognized.

This chapter presents a first look at fiscal policy, in the context of the simplest Keynesian model. In effect, we assume here that the money supply is fixed, and that the interest rate is not affected by changes in total intended spending (or that, if it is affected, it has little effect on total intended spending). In Chapter 17 (and in the Appendix to this book), a more sophisticated analysis of fiscal policy is presented, with money and financial assets included in the model.

Government Expenditure and Net National Product

In the previous chapters, we showed how the equilibrium level of net national product was determined in a simplified economy without government spending or taxation. We must now extend this theory to include both government spending and taxation. As we shall see, the results form the basis for some of our nation's past and present economic policy. In this section, we incorporate government spending into the theory of the determination of net national product. In so doing, we assume that government spending will not affect the consumption function or the level of intended investment. In other words, we assume that government spending does not reduce or increase private desires to spend out of each level of income. (Government includes here federal, state, and local.)

Suppose that the government purchases $50 billion worth of goods and services and that it will purchase this amount whatever the level of NNP. (As pointed out in Chapter 7, only government purchases, not transfer payments, are included here.) Clearly, adding this public expenditure to the private expenditures on consumption and investment results in a higher total level of intended spending. In an economy with government spending (but no net exports), total intended spending on output equals consumption expenditure plus intended investment expenditure plus intended government expenditure. Thus, since an increase in government expenditure (like increases in consumption or investment expenditure) results in an increase in total intended spending, and since the equilibrium value of net national product is at the point where total intended spending equals NNP, it follows that an increase in government expenditure, as well as the induced increase in private spending, brings about an increase in the equilibrium value of NNP.

To see the effects of government expenditure on the equilibrium value of NNP, we can use a simple graph similar to those introduced in Chapter 10. We begin by plotting the consumption function, which shows intended consumption expenditure at each level of NNP (since NNP equals disposable income under our assumptions): the result is line C in Figure 12.1. Then we can plot the sum of intended consumption expenditure and investment expenditure at each level of NNP. The result is line C + I. Next, we plot the sum of intended consumption expenditure, investment expenditure, and government expenditure at each level of NNP, to get line C + I + G. Since the **C + I + G line** shows total intended spending, and since, as we stressed in Chapter 10, the equilibrium value of NNP is at the point where total intended spending equals NNP, it follows that the equilib-

Figure 12.1
Determination of Net National Product, Including Government Expenditure *The consumption function is* C, *the sum of consumption and investment expenditures is* C + I, *and the sum of consumption, investment, and government expenditures is* C + I + G. *The equilibrium value of NNP is at the point where the* C + I + G *line intersects the 45-degree line, which here is $1,225 billion.*

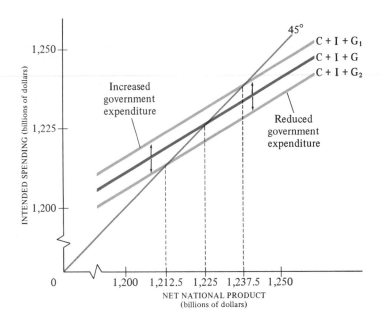

Figure 12.2

Effects on Equilibrium Net National Product of a $5 Billion Increase and Decrease in Government Expenditure *A $5 billion increase raises the equilibrium value of NNP from $1,225 billion to $1,237.5 billion. A $5 billion decrease reduces the equilibrium value of NNP from $1,225 billion to $1,212.5 billion.*

rium value of NNP is at the point where the $C + I + G$ line intersects the 45-degree line. This is at an output of $1,225 billion.

EFFECT OF INCREASED GOVERNMENT EXPENDITURE

What happens to the equilibrium level of NNP if government expenditure increases? Figure 12.2 shows the results of a $5 billion increase in government spending. The increased government expenditure (G_1) will raise the $C + I + G$ line by $5 billion, as the figure shows. Since the $C + I + G_1$ line must intersect the 45-degree line at a higher level of NNP, increases in government expenditure result in increases in the equilibrium level of NNP. In Figure 12.2, the $5 billion increase in government expenditure raises the equilibrium value of NNP from $1,225 billion to $1,237.5 billion.

EFFECT OF DECREASED GOVERNMENT EXPENDITURE

Figure 12.2 also shows what happens when government spending goes down by $5 billion (to G_2). The new $C + I + G_2$ line is $5 billion lower than the old $C + I + G$ line. Since the new $C + I + G_2$ line intersects the 45-degree line at a lower level of NNP, decreases in government expenditure result in decreases in the equilibrium level of NNP. In Figure 12.2, the $5 billion decrease in government expenditure reduces the equilibrium value of NNP from $1,225 billion to $1,212.5 billion.

WHAT IS THE MULTIPLIER EFFECT FOR GOVERNMENT EXPENDITURE?

How sensitive is the equilibrium level of NNP to changes in government spending? In the previous chapter, we found that a $1 billion change in intended investment—or a $1 billion shift in the consumption function—

results in a change in equilibrium NNP of $\left(\dfrac{1}{\text{MPS}}\right)$ billions of dollars, where MPS is the marginal propensity to save. The effect of a $1 billion change in government expenditure is exactly the same. In other words, *it will result in a change in equilibrium NNP of* $\left(\dfrac{1}{\text{MPS}}\right)$ *billion dollars.* Thus *a change in government expenditure has the same multiplier effect on NNP as a change in investment or a shift in the consumption function.* For example, if the marginal propensity to consume is 0.6, an extra $1 billion in government expenditure will increase equilibrium NNP by $2.5 billion.[1]

Taxation and Net National Product

The previous section added government expenditures to our theory, but it did not include taxes. (Here we assume taxes to be net of transfer payments.) For simplicity, it is assumed that all tax revenues stem from personal taxes. How do tax collections influence the equilibrium value of net national product? For example, if consumers pay 16⅔ percent of their income to the government in taxes, what effect does this have on NNP? Clearly, the imposition of this tax means that, for each level of NNP, people have less disposable income than they would with no taxes. In particular, disposable income now equals 83⅓ percent of NNP, whereas without taxes it equaled NNP. Thus *the relationship between consumption expenditure and NNP is altered by the imposition of the tax.* Before the tax was levied, the relationship was given by line C_0 in Figure 12.3; after the imposition of the tax, it is given by line C_1.

The relationship between consumption expenditure and national output changes in this way because consumption expenditure is determined by the level of disposable income. For instance, in the case in Figure 12.3, consumption expenditure equals $350 billion plus 60 percent of disposable income. Thus, since the tax reduces the amount of disposable income at each level of NNP, it also reduces the amount of consumption expenditure at each level of NNP. In other words, since people have less after-tax income to spend at each level of NNP, they spend less on consumption goods and services at each level of NNP. This seems eminently reasonable. It is illustrated in Figure 12.3, where, at each level of NNP, consumption expenditure after tax (given by line C_1) is less than before the tax (given by line C_0).

Because the imposition of the tax influences the relationship between consumption expenditure and NNP, it also influences the equilibrium value of NNP. As we have stressed repeatedly, the equilibrium value of NNP is at the point where intended spending on output equals NNP. Lines C_0 and C_1 in Figure 12.3 show intended consumption expenditure at each level of NNP, before and after the tax. Adding intended investment and govern-

---

[1] For an algebraic proof that this is true (in the context of this simple model), see the Appendix to this chapter. A more complete model is provided in Chapter 17 and in the Appendix to this book. The conditions under which this proposition holds in this more complete model are given in footnote 1 of the Appendix to this book.

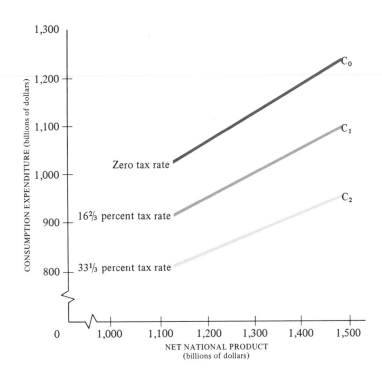

Figure 12.3

***Relationship between Consumption
Expenditure and Net National Product,
Given Three Tax Rates*** *If taxes are
zero, C_0 is the relationship between
consumption expenditure and NNP. If
consumers pay $16\frac{2}{3}$ percent of their
income in taxes, C_1 is the relationship;
and if consumers pay $33\frac{1}{3}$ percent of
their income in taxes, C_2 is the relationship. Clearly, the higher the tax rate, the
less consumers spend on consumption
from a given NNP.*

ment expenditure to each of these lines, we get the total intended spending
before and after the tax. The results are shown in Figure 12.4, under the
assumption that the sum of intended investment and government spending equals $140 billion. The $C_0 + I + G$ line shows intended spending
before the tax, while the $C_1 + I + G$ line shows intended spending after
the tax.

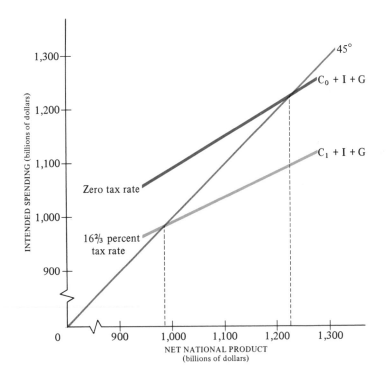

Figure 12.4

***Determination of Equilibrium Value of
Net National Product, with Zero and
$16\frac{2}{3}$ Percent Tax Rates*** *The tax rate influences the relationship between
consumption expenditure and NNP. (C_0
is this relationship with a zero tax rate,
while C_1 is the relationship with a $16\frac{2}{3}$
percent tax rate. See Figure 12.3.) The
$C_0 + I + G$ line shows total intended
spending at each level of NNP if the tax
rate is zero, and the $C_1 + I + G$ line
shows total intended spending at each
level of NNP if the tax rate is $16\frac{2}{3}$
percent. Consequently, the equilibrium
value of NNP is $1,225 billion if the tax
rate is zero, and $980 billion if it is $16\frac{2}{3}$
percent.*

EFFECT OF THE TAX

The equilibrium level of NNP is appreciably lower after the imposition of the tax than before. Specifically, as shown in Figure 12.4, it is $980 billion after the imposition of the tax and $1,225 billion before. The tax reduced the equilibrium level of NNP because it lowered the $C + I + G$ line from $C_0 + I + G$ to $C_1 + I + G$. It did this because, as pointed out above, it reduced the amount people wanted to spend on consumption goods at each level of NNP. People still wanted to spend the same amount *from each (after-tax) income level,* but because of the tax, their spending decisions had to be based on a *reduced (after-tax) income,* so that they spent less on consumption goods and services at each level of NNP.

EFFECT OF A TAX INCREASE

Going a step further, *the higher the tax rate, the lower the equilibrium value of NNP; and the lower the tax rate, the higher the equilibrium value of NNP.* This is a very important proposition, as we shall see in subsequent sections. To demonstrate it, let's see what will happen to the equilibrium value of NNP when the tax rate is increased from 16⅔ percent of NNP to 33⅓ percent of NNP. If the tax rate is 33⅓ percent, total intended spending at each level of NNP will be given by line $C_2 + I + G$ in Figure 12.5. Since the equilibrium value of NNP will be at the point where the $C_2 + I + G$ line intersects the 45-degree line, the equilibrium value of NNP will be $816⅔ billion, rather than $980 billion (which was the equilibrium value when the tax rate was 16⅔ percent). Thus the increase in the tax rate will reduce the equilibrium value of NNP. By reducing the amount people want to spend on consumption at each level of NNP, it will lower the $C + I + G$ line from $C_1 + I + G$ to $C_2 + I + G$.

Figure 12.5
Determination of Equilibrium Value of Net National Product, with 16⅔ Percent and 33⅓ Percent Tax Rates *The* $C_1 + I + G$ *line shows total intended spending at each level of NNP if the tax rate is 16⅔ percent, and the* $C_2 + I + G$ *line shows total intended spending at each level of NNP if the tax rate is 33⅓ percent. Consequently, the equilibrium value of NNP is $980 billion if the tax rate is 16⅔ percent and $816⅔ billion if it is 33⅓ percent.*

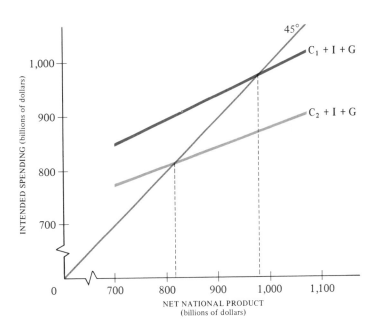

EFFECT OF A TAX CUT

On the other hand, suppose that the tax rate is lowered from 16⅔ percent of NNP to a lesser amount. What will happen to the equilibrium value of NNP? If the tax rate is less than 16⅔ percent, the intended spending on output at each level of NNP will be given by a $C + I + G$ line that lies between $C_0 + I + G$ and $C_1 + I + G$ in Figure 12.4. Since the equilibrium value of NNP will be at the point where this line intersects the 45-degree line, the equilibrium value of NNP will be greater than $980 billion. Thus the decrease in the tax rate will increase the equilibrium value of NNP. By increasing the amount people want to spend on consumption at each level of NNP, it will raise the $C + I + G$ line from $C_1 + I + G$ to a higher level.

How Government Expenditure and Taxes Affect NNP: A Tabular Illustration

To illustrate how one can determine the equilibrium level of NNP when both government expenditure and taxation are included in our model, consider the numerical example shown in Table 12.1. The numbers in this table are the same as in Table 10.4, except that we now assume that the government spends $50 billion per year on goods and services and that it receives $50 billion in taxes per year. (For simplicity, we assume in this table that the amounts of both government expenditure and taxes are independent of the level of NNP. This is in contrast to the previous section where we assumed that taxes were proportional to NNP.) Column 1 of the table shows various possible levels of NNP. To obtain the level of disposable income corresponding to each level of NNP, we must subtract taxes (in column 2) from NNP, the result being shown in column 3.

Since the consumption function is assumed to be the same as in Table 10.4 (and Table 10.1), the intended consumption expenditure at each level of disposable income is as shown in column 4. Note that disposable income no longer equals NNP, as it did in Table 10.4, because taxes have

Table 12.1

(1) Net national product	(2) Taxes	(3) Disposable income (1) − (2)	(4) Intended consumption expenditure	(5) Intended saving (3) − (4)	(6) Intended investment	(7) Government expenditure	(8) Total intended spending (4) + (6) + (7)	(9) Tendency of national output
1,000	50	950	920	30	90	50	1,060	Upward
1,050	50	1,000	950	50	90	50	1,090	Upward
1,100	50	1,050	980	70	90	50	1,120	Upward
1,150	50	1,100	1,010	90	90	50	1,150	No change
1,200	50	1,150	1,040	110	90	50	1,180	Downward
1,250	50	1,200	1,070	130	90	50	1,210	Downward
1,300	50	1,250	1,100	150	90	50	1,240	Downward

entered the picture; this means that the relationship between intended consumption expenditure and NNP is also different. But since the consumption function is unchanged, the relationship between intended consumption expenditure and disposable income is the same as in Table 10.4.

Columns 5 to 8 of the table seem self-evident. Since intended saving equals disposable income less intended consumption expenditure, column 5 equals column 3 minus column 4. Column 6 shows intended investment, which is $90 billion. Column 7 shows government expenditure, which is $50 billion. And column 8 shows total intended spending on output at each level of NNP. Since total intended spending equals consumption expenditure plus intended investment expenditure plus intended government expenditure, column 8 equals column 4 plus column 6 plus column 7.

WHAT IS EQUILIBRIUM NNP?

As emphasized in previous discussions (in this and the previous chapters), *national output will be at its equilibrium value only if total intended spending is equal (no more, no less) to NNP.* Thus, based on the data in Table 12.1, it is clear that the equilibrium value of NNP is $1,150 billion. Why? Because a comparison of columns 1 and 8 in Table 12.1 shows that this is the only value of NNP at which total intended spending (column 8) equals NNP (column 1).

If NNP is *less* than $1,150 billion, there will be a tendency for it to increase. Total spending will exceed the value of output produced, the result being that firms' inventories will be depleted. Firms will respond by raising their production rates, thus increasing NNP. If NNP is *greater* than $1,150 billion, there will be a tendency for it to decline. Total spending will fall short of the value of output produced, the result being that firms' inventories will mount. Firms will respond by lowering their production rates, thus decreasing NNP.

USING THE LEAKAGE-INJECTION APPROACH

Finally, the leakage-injection approach described in the previous chapters is an alternative way of determining the equilibrium level of NNP. To use this approach, two points must be understood. First, *taxes are a leakage because they withdraw spending from the flow of income and expenditure.* After all, money that goes for taxes cannot be spent on output. Second, *government expenditure is an injection since it adds spending to the flow of income and expenditure.* It is a supplement to consumption expenditure and investment.

Since taxes are a leakage, the total leakages in Table 12.1 are intended saving plus taxes, or column 5 plus column 2. And since government expenditure is an injection, the total injections in Table 12.1 are intended investment plus government expenditure, or column 6 plus column 7. According to our discussion in the previous chapters, *the equilibrium value of NNP must be the value of NNP at which total leakages equal total injections*—in other words, the value of NNP at which intended saving plus taxes (column 5 plus column 2) equals intended investment plus government expenditure (column 6 plus column 7). Table 12.1 shows that this

243

value of NNP is $1,150 billion. Of course, the answer obtained by the leakage-injection approach coincides, as it must, with that obtained by comparing the value of total intended spending (column 8) with the value of NNP (column 1).

The Balanced-Budget Multiplier

According to our previous conclusions, increases in government expenditures tend to increase NNP, while increases in tax receipts tend to reduce NNP. What will be the result when *both* government expenditures and tax receipts are increased *by the same amount?* Clearly, the increase in government expenditures will push NNP up, while the tax increase will push NNP down. But which force will prevail? According to an economic proposition called the ***balanced-budget multiplier,*** the result will be an *increase* in equilibrium NNP—and under the assumptions made in Table 12.1, *this increase equals the increase in both government expenditures and taxes.*

To see that this proposition is true, compare Table 10.4 with Table 12.1. The only difference between the situations represented by these two tables is that both government expenditures and taxes are $50 billion higher in Table 12.1 than in Table 10.4. (Specifically, both government expenditures and taxes equal $50 billion in Table 12.1, while both equal zero in Table 10.4.) What is the effect on NNP of this $50 billion increase in both government expenditures and taxes? In accord with the balanced-budget multiplier, the equilibrium level of NNP is $50 billion higher in Table 12.1 than in Table 10.4. (For a more general proof of the balanced-budget multiplier, see the Appendix to this chapter.)

On the other hand, suppose that both government expenditures and tax receipts are *decreased* by the same amount. What will be the effect on NNP? Clearly, the decrease in government expenditures will push NNP down, while the tax cut will push NNP up. But which force will prevail? According to the balanced-budget multiplier, the result will be a *decrease* in equilibrium NNP—and under the assumptions made in Table 12.1, *this decrease equals the decrease in both government expenditures and taxes.*

To illustrate the application of this proposition, consider a proposal made by President Ford in 1975 to cut both taxes and government expenditures by $28 billion. Assuming that both the expenditure and tax cuts went into effect at the same time, this would have reduced NNP, as we have just seen. (However, if the tax cut occurred before the expenditure cut, as some observers claimed it would, the proposal might not have had this effect at all. Recall that the balanced-budget multiplier is concerned with a *simultaneous* change in government receipts and tax revenues.)

Recessionary and Inflationary Gaps

In this and the previous chapters, we have shown how the equilibrium level of net national product is determined. But it is of central importance to

recognize that *this equilibrium level of NNP may not correspond to full
employment.* As pointed out in Chapter 10, a basic theme of modern economics is that there is no automatic tendency for NNP to equal its full-
employment level. For example, in Table 12.1, there is no assurance that
$1,150 billion is the level of NNP corresponding to full employment. It
may be below the full-employment level, in which case the unemployment
rate will be relatively high. Or it may be above the full-employment level,
in which case there will be considerable inflation.

COPING WITH A RECESSIONARY GAP

For simplicity, suppose that, so long as total spending does not exceed the
value (at initial prices) of the full-employment level of output, the price
level remains constant. (As pointed out in Chapter 9, this really is not true,
but it is a useful simplification to begin with.) Then if the equilibrium
NNP is *below* the full-employment level, the **recessionary gap** *is the increase in intended spending required to push the equilibrium NNP up to the
full-employment level.* For example, if the full-employment level of NNP is
$1,400 billion in Figure 12.6, the recessionary gap is $40 billion. Why?
Because this is the amount by which intended spending must be increased
if NNP is to rise from its current equilibrium level, $1,300 billion, to its
full-employment level of $1,400 billion. In other words, as shown in Fig-
ure 12.6, this is the amount by which the $C + I + G$ line must be raised in
order to increase the equilibrium level of NNP from $1,300 billion to
$1,400 billion. *To prevent excessive unemployment, such a recessionary gap
should be eliminated.*

COPING WITH AN INFLATIONARY GAP

On the other hand, if the equilibrium NNP is *above* the full-employment
level, the **inflationary gap** *is the reduction in intended spending required to
push the equilibrium NNP down to the full-employment level.* For example,
if the full-employment level of NNP is $1,400 billion in Figure 12.7, the
inflationary gap is $40 billion. Why? Because this is the amount by which
intended spending must be reduced if NNP is to fall from its current
equilibrium level, $1,500 billion, to its full-employment level of $1,400
billion. In other words, as shown in Figure 12.7, this is the amount by
which the $C + I + G$ line must fall in order to reduce the equilibrium
level of NNP from $1,500 billion to $1,400 billion. Assuming that $1,400
billion is the maximum value of real NNP (in initial prices) that can be
achieved, any increase of the money value of NNP above $1,400 billion is
due entirely to inflation. Thus, *to curb inflationary pressures, such an inflationary gap should be eliminated.*

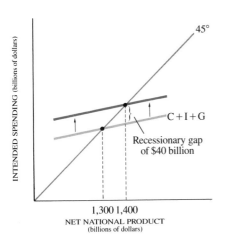

Figure 12.6

Recessionary Gap *The equilibrium level
of NNP, $1,300 billion, is too low to
result in full employment. The level of
NNP corresponding to full employment is
$1,400 billion. To raise the equilibrium
level of NNP from $1,300 billion to
$1,400 billion, intended spending must
be increased by $40 billion. In other
words, the* C + I + G *line must be raised
by $40 billion. This amount—the vertical
distance between the 45-degree line and
the* C + I + G *line at the full-employment
level of NNP—is called the recessionary
gap.*

The Nature and Objectives of Fiscal Policy

Our discussions in previous sections make it easy to understand the basic
ideas underlying modern fiscal policy. For example, suppose that the
economy is suffering from an undesirably high unemployment rate. What

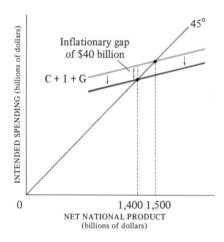

Figure 12.7
Inflationary Gap *For simplicity, assume that $1,400 billion, the full-employment level of NNP, is the maximum value of real NNP (in initial prices) that can be achieved. Thus any increase of the money value of NNP above $1,400 billion is due entirely to inflation. To reduce the equilibrium NNP from $1,500 billion (its current level) to $1,400 billion, intended spending must be reduced by $40 billion. In other words, the C + I + G line must be lowered by $40 billion. This amount—the vertical distance between the 45-degree line and the C + I + G line at the full employment level of NNP—is called the inflationary gap.*

should the government do? Since there is a recessionary gap, the economy needs increased spending. In other words, as shown in Figure 12.6, the economy needs an upward lift of the $C + I + G$ line, which by increasing NNP will increase employment as well. There are three ways that the government can try to bring this about. First, *it can reduce taxes,* which, as shown in a previous section, will shift the relation between consumption expenditure and NNP—and consequently the $C + I + G$ line—upward. Second, *it can increase government expenditures,* which will also shift the $C + I + G$ line upward. Third, *the government can encourage firms to invest more,* perhaps by enacting tax credits to make investment more profitable for them. The resulting increase in intended investment will shift the $C + I + G$ line upward too.

On the other hand, perhaps we are suffering from a high rate of inflation. What should the government do? Since there is an inflationary gap, the economy needs reduced spending. In other words, what is required is a downward shift of the $C + I + G$ line, as shown in Figure 12.7. The government has three ways to try to bring this about. First, *it can increase taxes.* This, as shown in a previous section, will shift the relation between consumption expenditure and NNP—and consequently the $C + I + G$ line—downward. Second, *it can cut government expenditures,* which will also shift the $C + I + G$ curve downward. Third, *it can change the tax laws and do other things to discourage firms from investing in plant and equipment or inventories.* The resulting decrease in intended investment will shift the $C + I + G$ line downward too.

Certainly, these ideas do not seem very hard to understand. Advocates of fiscal policy maintain that, *if there is too much unemployment, the government should promote, directly or indirectly, additional public and/or private spending, which will result in additional output and jobs.* On the other hand, *if there is too much inflation, the government should reduce, directly or indirectly, spending (public and/or private). This will curb the inflationary pressure on prices.* Most economists believe that these propositions are useful—although by themselves they cannot deal as effectively as one would like with times like the 1970s and early 1980s, when excessive unemployment and inflation occurred together. (We shall discuss such situations in detail in Chapter 18.)

How can fiscal policy be included in the aggregate demand-aggregate supply analysis presented in Chapter 9? Clearly, *an anti-unemployment fiscal policy* (where government spending is increased and/or taxes are reduced) *tends to push the aggregate demand curve to the right. An anti-inflationary fiscal policy* (where government spending is reduced and/or taxes are increased) *tends to push the aggregate demand curve to the left.* The effects of each type of fiscal policy are shown in Figures 9.7 and 9.8.

Makers of Fiscal Policy

When you go to a ball game, you generally get a program telling you who on each team is playing each position. To understand the formulation and implementation of fiscal policy in the United States we need the same kind of information. Who are the people who establish our fiscal policy?

Who decides that in view of the current and prospective economic situation, tax rates or government expenditures should be changed? This is not a simple question because lots of individuals and groups play important roles. In the Congress, the House and Senate Budget Committees—as well as the Congressional Budget Office—have been charged with important responsibilities in this area. Also, the Appropriations Committees, the House Ways and Means Committee, and the Senate Finance Committee have considerable influence. In addition, another congressional committee is of importance: the Joint Economic Committee of Congress. Established by the Employment Act of 1946, this committee goes over the annual Economic

Example 12.1   Fiscal Policy, Deficits, and Surpluses

The following table provides some information concerning a small Latin American country:

	(billions of dollars)
Net national product (this year)	16.0
Net national product (full-employment level)	20.0
Government expenditures on goods and services	1.8

According to experts on this country's economy, the government's tax receipts are equal to 10 percent of its NNP.

(a) Is the government of this country running a deficit or a surplus? (That is, are government expenditures greater than or less than tax receipts?) (b) If the country wants to achieve full employment, should it increase government spending? Why or why not? (c) Suppose that, when NNP is at its full-employment level of $20 billion, intended saving equals $1.8 billion and intended investment equals $1.5 billion. If tax rates cannot be changed, and if government expenditures are altered to push the economy to full employment, will there be a balanced budget? (That is, will government spending equal tax receipts?) (d) If not, how large will be the deficit or surplus?

SOLUTION

(a) Government expenditures equal $1.8 billion. Tax receipts equal 10 percent of NNP, or $1.6 billion. Thus there is a deficit of $0.2 billion. (That is, spending exceeds receipts by $0.2 billion.) (b) Net national product currently is $4 billion below its full-employment level. One way to increase NNP is to increase government spending. Another way is to reduce taxes. (c) In equilibrium, taxes plus saving equal government spending plus investment. Thus, if equilibrium NNP is at its full-employment value of $20 billion, government spending must equal $2 billion + $1.8 billion − $1.5 billion, or $2.3 billion. Why? Because $2 billion is the value of taxes if NNP is at its full-employment value. (Recall that taxes equal 10 percent of NNP.) Since government spending equals taxes plus saving minus investment, it follows that government spending equals $2.3 billion. And since taxes equal $2.0 billion, the budget is not balanced. (d) Government spending ($2.3 billion) exceeds taxes ($2.0 billion) by $0.3 billion, which is the size of the deficit.

Report of the President on the state of the economy and, through its hearings, provides a major forum for review of economic issues.

In the executive branch of government, the most important person in the establishment of fiscal policy is, of course, the president. Although he must operate in the context of the tax and expenditure laws passed by Congress, he and his advisers are the country's principal analysts of the need for fiscal expansion or restraint and its leading spokesmen for legislative changes to meet these needs. Needless to say, he doesn't pore over the latest economic data and make the decisions all by himself. The Office of Management and Budget, which is part of the Executive Office of the President, is a very powerful adviser to the president on expenditure policy, as is the Treasury Department on tax policy. In addition, there is the *Council of Economic Advisers*, which is part of the Executive Office of the President. Established by the Employment Act of 1946, its job is to help the president carry out the objectives of that act. During the past 30 years, the Council of Economic Advisers, headed by a series of distinguished economists who left academic and other posts to contribute to public policy, has become a very important actor on the national economic policy stage.

Automatic Stabilizers

Now that we have met some of the major players, we must point out that, in their efforts to fight off serious unemployment or inflation, they get help from some *automatic stabilizers:* structural features of our economy that tend to stabilize national output. Although these economic stabilizers cannot do all that is required to keep the economy on an even keel, they help a lot. As soon as the economy turns down and unemployment mounts, they give the economy a helpful shot in the arm. As soon as the economy gets overheated and inflation crops up, they tend to restrain it. These stabilizers are automatic because they come into play without the need for new legislation or administrative decisions.

TAX REVENUES

Changes in income tax revenues are an important automatic stabilizer. One of the major points emphasized in Chapter 4 was that our federal system relies heavily on the income tax. The amount of income tax collected by the federal government goes up with increases in NNP and goes down with decreases in NNP. Moreover, because the income tax is progressive, the average tax rate goes up with increases in NNP, and goes down with decreases in NNP. This, of course, is just what we want to occur. When output falls off and unemployment mounts, tax collections fall off too, so disposable income falls less than NNP. This means less of a fall in consumption expenditure, which tends to brake the fall in NNP. When output rises too fast and the economy begins to suffer from serious inflation, tax collections rise too—which tends to brake the increase in NNP. Of course, corporation income taxes, as well as personal income taxes, play a significant role here.

Before World War II, there was relatively little place in the government for economists. The Treasury had a small number, the antitrust division of the Justice Department a handful, but there was no place for economists who aspired to give advice on broad policy matters. The Employment Act of 1946 changed that situation by creating a council to "gather timely and authoritative information . . . to develop and recommend to the President national economic policies . . . and to make and furnish studies . . . as the President may request."

But as demonstrated by the first chairman, Edwin Nourse, the act was really a hunting license for a chairman to peddle his good counsel. Nourse, who believed that the Council's role was to "interpret literal facts . . . without becoming involved in any way in the advocacy of particular measures," found that such services were rarely required by the president. It is hard to find any trace of the Nourse era on the economic policies of the late forties.

Beryl Sprinkel

Even the election of John F. Kennedy, who was eager to increase the U.S. rate of economic growth, did not insure the Council's future. Kennedy was inclined to fiscal conservatism and less interested in domestic than in foreign affairs. It was Walter Heller, the new chairman under Kennedy, who made the CEA an integral part of the New Frontier. The tax cut of 1964, which Heller sold to a president committed to balanced budgets, is a tribute to his success in making a body without formal powers or legislative prerogatives an integral part of the policy-making process.

The Council's influence has risen and ebbed in recent years with both the state of the economy and with other pressures on the president. In 1966, as the Vietnam War intensified, the Council urged a tax increase; Lyndon Johnson, more attuned to the political considerations, did not take action on the proposal until 1967. The Council's position in the Nixon administration further exemplified this process. Led by Paul McCracken and Herbert Stein, the Council championed restraint in fiscal and monetary policies early in Nixon's first term. But faced with mounting inflationary pressures, the Council members reluctantly joined other administration economists in setting up wage and price controls.

In the Reagan administration, the CEA's position became precarious after Martin Feldstein, its chairman until 1984 (when he returned to Harvard), clashed openly with administration officials about the dangers inherent in large federal deficits. (See p. 258.) For a time, President Reagan appointed no one to succeed Feldstein, and there was talk in early 1985 that the Council might be abolished. However, in February 1985, the president named Beryl Sprinkel, former under secretary of the treasury, as CEA chairman.

UNEMPLOYMENT COMPENSATION AND WELFARE PAYMENTS

Unemployment compensation is paid to workers who are laid off, according to a system that has evolved over the past 50 years. When an unemployed worker goes back to work, he stops receiving unemployment compensation. Thus, when NNP falls off and unemployment mounts, the tax collections to finance unemployment compensation go down (because of lower employment), while the amount paid out to unemployed workers goes up. On the other hand, when NNP rises too fast and the economy begins to suffer from serious inflation, the tax collections to finance unemployment compensation go up, while the amount paid out goes down because there is much less unemployment. Again, this is just what we want to see happen. The fall in spending is moderated when unemployment is high, and the increase in spending is curbed when there are serious inflationary pressures. Various welfare programs have the same kind of automatic stabilizing effect on the economy.

CORPORATE DIVIDENDS, FAMILY SAVING, AND FARM PROGRAMS

Since corporations tend to maintain their dividends when their sales fall off, and moderate the increase in their dividends when their sales soar, their dividend policy tends to stabilize the economy. This is very important. Also, to the extent that consumers tend to be slow to raise or lower their spending in response to increases or decreases in their income, this too tends to stabilize the economy. Finally, there are the agricultural support programs, described in Chapter 4. The government has buttressed farm prices and incomes when business was bad and unemployment was high. When output was high and inflation occurred, the government distributed the commodities in its warehouses and received dollars. In both cases, these programs acted as stabilizers.

Having painted such a glowing picture of the economy's automatic stabilizers, we are in danger of suggesting that they can stabilize the economy all by themselves. It would be nice if this were true, but it isn't. All the automatic stabilizers do is *cut down* on variations in unemployment and inflation, not *eliminate* them. Discretionary tax and spending programs are needed to supplement the effects of these automatic stabilizers. Some economists wish strongly that it were possible to set well-defined rules for government action, rather than leave things to the discretion of policy makers. Indeed, Milton Friedman, among others, forcefully argues for greater reliance on such rules, but most economists feel that it is impossible to formulate a set of rules flexible and comprehensive enough to let us do away with the discretionary powers of policy makers. Instead their concern is with sharpening the tools available to government economic decision makers.

Test Yourself

1. Suppose that the consumption function in a particular economy is given by the following table:

Disposable income (billions of dollars)	Consumption expenditure (billions of dollars)
400	350
500	425
600	500
700	575
800	650

Assuming that no taxes are imposed, what is the equilibrium value of NNP if government expenditures are $50 billion and intended investment is $50 billion?

2. Based on the data in Question 1, plot the $C + I + G$ line in a graph. Using a graph of this sort, estimate the effect on the equilibrium level of NNP of a $10 billion increase in government spending.

3. Suppose that taxes are 20 percent of NNP. Using the data in Question 1, fill in the blanks below.

NNP (billions of dollars)	Consumption expenditure (billions of dollars)
—	350
—	425
—	500
—	575
—	650

4. Using the data in Question 3, what is the equilibrium value of NNP if government expenditures are $50 billion and intended investment is $50 billion? How does this result compare with that in Question 1? Explain the difference between these two results.

5. Using the data in Question 3, is the government's budget balanced at the equilibrium level of NNP if government expenditures are $50 billion and intended investment is $50 billion? If not, how big is the surplus or deficit?

The Tools of Discretionary Fiscal Policy

Suppose that the Council of Economic Advisers, on the basis of information concerning recent economic developments, believes that national output may decline soon, causing serious unemployment, and that other agencies, like the Treasury and the Federal Reserve System, agree. What specific measures can the Council recommend that the government take under such circumstances?

1. The government can vary its expenditure for public works and other programs. If increased unemployment seems to be in the wind, it can step up outlays on roads, urban reconstruction, and other public programs. Of course, these programs must be well thought out and socially productive. There is no sense in pushing through wasteful and foolish public works programs merely to make jobs. Or if, as in 1969, the economy is plagued by inflation, it can (as President Nixon ordered) stop new federal construction programs temporarily.

2. The government can vary welfare payments and other types of transfer payments. For example, a hike in Social Security benefits may provide a very healthy shot in the arm for an economy with too much unemployment. An increase in veterans' benefits or in aid to dependent children may do the same thing. The federal government has sometimes helped the states to extend the length of time that the unemployed can receive unemployment compensation; this too will have the desired effect. On the other hand, if there is full employment and inflation is a dangerous problem, it may be worthwhile to cut back on certain kinds of transfer payments. For example, if it is agreed that some veterans' benefits should be reduced, this reduction might be timed to occur during a period when inflationary pressures are evident.

3. The government can vary tax rates. For example, if there is considerable unemployment, the government may cut tax rates, as it did in 1975. Or if inflation is the problem, the government may increase taxes, as it did in 1968 when, after considerable political maneuvering and buckpassing, the Congress was finally persuaded to put through a 10 percent tax surcharge to try to moderate the inflation caused by the Vietnam War. However, temporary tax changes may have less effect than permanent ones, since, as pointed out in Chapter 10, consumption expenditure may be influenced less by transitory changes in income than by permanent changes.

PROS AND CONS OF VARIOUS FISCAL POLICY TOOLS

Of course there are advantages and disadvantages in each of these tools of fiscal policy. *One of the big disadvantages of public works and similar spending programs is that they take so long to get started.* Plans must be made, land must be acquired, and preliminary construction studies must be carried out. By the time the expenditures are finally made and have the desired effect, the dangers of excessive unemployment may have given way to dangers of inflation, so that the spending, coming too late, does more harm than good. To some extent, this problem may be ameliorated by having a backlog of productive projects ready to go at all times. In this way, at least a portion of the lag can be eliminated.

In recent years, there has been a widespread feeling that government expenditures should be set on the basis of their long-run desirability and productivity and not on the basis of short-term stabilization considerations. The optimal level of government expenditure is at the point where the value of the extra benefits to be derived from an extra dollar of government expenditure is at least equal to the dollar of cost. This optimal level is unlikely to change much in the short run, and it would be wasteful to spend more—or less—than this amount for stabilization purposes when tax changes could be used instead. Thus many economists believe that tax cuts or tax increases should be the primary fiscal weapons to fight unemployment or inflation.

However, *one of the big problems with tax changes is that it sometimes is difficult to get Congress to take speedy action.* There is often considerable debate over a tax bill, and sometimes it becomes a political football. Another difficulty with tax changes is that it generally is much easier to reduce taxes than it is to get them back up again. To politicians, lower taxes are attractive because they are popular, and higher taxes are dangerous because they may hurt a politician's chances of re-election. In discussing fiscal policy (or most other aspects of government operations, for that matter), to ignore politics is to risk losing touch with reality.

Fiscal Policy: Three Case Studies

THE TAX CUT OF 1964

With some knowledge of the players and the plays they can call, we can look now at three examples of fiscal policy in action. When the Kennedy administration took office in 1961, it was confronted with a relatively high unemployment rate—about 7 percent in mid-1961. By 1962, although unemployment was somewhat lower (about 6 percent), the president's advisers, led by Walter W. Heller, chairman of the Council of Economic Advisers, pushed for a tax cut to reduce unemployment further. The president, after considerable discussion of the effects of such a tax cut, announced in June 1962 that he would propose such a measure to the Congress; and in January 1963, the bill was finally sent to Congress.

The proposed tax bill was a victory for Heller and the CEA. Even though it would mean a deliberately large deficit, the president had been convinced to cut taxes to push the economy closer to full employment. But the Congress was not so easily convinced. Many congressmen labeled the proposal irresponsible and reckless. Others wanted to couple tax reform with tax reduction. It was not until 1964, after President Kennedy's death, that the tax bill was enacted. It took a year from the time the bill was sent to Congress for it to be passed, and during this interval, there was a continuous debate in the executive branch and the Congress. The secretary of the Treasury, Douglas Dillon, the chairman of the Federal Reserve Board, William M. Martin, and numerous congressmen—all powerful and all initially cool to the proposal—were eventually won over. The result was a tax reduction of about $10 billion per year.

The effects of the tax cut are by no means easy to measure, in part because the rate of growth of the money supply increased at the same time, which (as we shall see in Chapter 14) should also affect GNP. But in line with the theory presented in earlier sections, consumption expenditure did increase sharply during 1964. Moreover, the additional consumption expenditure undoubtedly induced additional investment. According to some estimates, the tax cut resulted in an increase in GNP of about $24 billion in 1965 and more in subsequent years.[3] The unemployment rate, which had been about 5½ to 6 percent during 1962 and 1963, fell to 5 percent during 1964 and to 4.7 percent in the spring of 1965. It is fair to say that most economists were extremely pleased with themselves in 1965. Fiscal policy based on their theories seemed to work very well indeed! Unfortunately, however, this pleasure did not last very long, there being another, and sadder, tale to tell.

THE TAX SURCHARGE OF 1968

In late July 1965, President Lyndon Johnson announced that the United States would send 50,000 more men to Vietnam. From fiscal 1965 to fiscal 1966, defense expenditures rose from $50 billion to $62 billion—a large increase in government expenditure, and one that took place at a time of

Walter Heller

---

[3] Arthur Okun, "Measuring the Impact of the 1964 Tax Reduction," in Walter W. Heller, *Perspectives on Economic Growth,* New York: Random House, 1968, p. 33.

relatively full employment. Such an increase in government expenditure would be expected to cause inflationary pressures. The Council of Economic Advisers recognized this danger, and recommended in late 1965 that the president urge Congress to increase taxes. Johnson was reluctant. The inflationary pressures mounted during 1966, and little was done by fiscal policy makers to quell them.

Even in 1967, the Congress was unwilling to raise taxes. The case for fiscal restraint was, it felt, not clear enough. As for the president, he said, "It is not a popular thing for a President to do . . . to ask for a penny out of a dollar to pay for a war that is not popular either."[4] Finally, in mid-1968, a 10 percent surcharge on income taxes, together with some restraint in government spending, was enacted. This increase in taxes was obviously the right medicine, but it was at least two years too late, and its effects were delayed and insufficient.

THE TAX CUT OF 1975

In late 1974, the unemployment rate began to mount. Whereas it was 5.5 percent in August, it reached 7.2 percent in December. Although economists were rather slow to recognize that the economy was slumping into a severe recession, by early 1975 it was clear that some stimulus was needed. Inflation, which President Ford had labeled "Public Enemy Number One" in the fall of 1974, continued to be a problem, but most policy makers felt that unemployment rates were reaching intolerable levels. By March 1975, the unemployment rate was 8.7 percent, the highest level in over 30 years, and something clearly had to be done to lower it.

In early 1975, President Ford proposed a $16 billion tax cut. As his Council of Economic Advisers stated, its purpose was "to halt the decline in production and employment so that growth of output can resume and unemployment can be reduced."[5] In March 1975, Congress passed a $23 billion tax cut, which provided rebates (of $100 to $200) on 1974 personal income taxes as well as reductions in 1975 income taxes. Both personal and corporate income taxes were cut. Personal tax liabilities were reduced through a $30 credit for each taxpayer and each dependent, as well as through increased standard deductions and low-income allowances. Corporate tax liabilities were reduced through a liberalization of the investment tax credit, as well as changes in tax rates.

The evidence seems to indicate that the tax cut was the right kind of medicine. In accord with our theories, national output did, in fact, increase in the latter half of 1975, and unemployment eased somewhat. By the end of 1975, the recovery was well under way—due in part, according to most economists, to the tax cut. However, the tax cut had less impact than some economists predicted because consumers did not spend, but instead saved, much of the tax reduction. This behavior by consumers is what the permanent-income hypothesis (in Chapter 10) would predict. Because the tax reduction was temporary, it had less effect on consumers' permanent income —and thus less effect on consumption expenditure—than if it was permanent.

[4] Arthur Okun, *The Political Economy of Prosperity,* New York: Norton, 1970, p. 88.
[5] Council of Economic Advisers, *1975 Annual Report,* Washington, D.C.: Government Printing Office, 1975.

IMPLICATIONS OF THE CASE STUDIES—AND THE REAGAN TAX CUT OF 1981

Based on the histories of all three of these tax changes (1964, 1968, and 1975), it is clear that, although we know a great deal more than we used to about how fiscal policy should be employed to avoid inflation or considerable unemployment, there is no guarantee that it will be used in this way. In the early 1960s and in 1974–75, policy makers seemed to make reasonably correct choices. In 1965–68, they did not. Without question, mistakes will continue to be made. All that we can do is try to learn from past mistakes.

In this connection, it is interesting to note that President Reagan, when he argued for a large tax reduction in 1981, frequently cited the beneficial effects of the tax cut of 1964. His critics pointed out that economic conditions in 1981 were different from those in 1964. Nonetheless, a huge tax cut was passed in 1981. Since much of this tax cut went into effect in 1982 and later, it was hoped in 1982 that it would help lift the economy out of the recession that afflicted the United States then. But some observers, in Wall Street and elsewhere, were worried that it might rekindle inflation, which was relatively low in early 1982.

In fact, the economy began to expand in late 1982, and 1983 was a year of vigorous cyclical recovery. (Real GNP rose by about 6 percent, and the unemployment rate fell by 2.5 percentage points in 1983.) Moreover, the expansion, which did not increase inflation substantially, continued throughout 1984—and helped to re-elect President Reagan. Although the 1981 tax cut was only one of the relevant factors, it certainly helped to bring about the desired expansion.

President Reagan signing the 1981 tax cut bill

Deficit and Surplus Financing

Now that you have studied the basic elements of fiscal policy, let's see how well you would fare with some of the problems that confront our nation's top policy makers.

CASE 1: AN IMMINENT RECESSION

Suppose that, through some inexplicable malfunctioning of the democratic process, you are elected president of the United States. Your Council of Economic Advisers reports to you that, on the basis of various forecasts, national output is likely to drop next year, and unemployment is likely to be much higher. Naturally, you are concerned; and having absorbed the ideas presented in this chapter, you ask your advisers—the Council of Economic Advisers, the Treasury, and the Office of Management and Budget —what sort of fiscal policy should be adopted to head off this undesirable turn of events. On the basis of their advice, you suggest to Congress that taxes should be cut and government expenditures should be increased.

When they receive your message, a number of key congressmen point out that if the government cuts taxes and raises expenditures it will operate in the red. In other words, government revenue will fall short of government spending—there will be a *deficit.* They warn that such fiscal behavior is irresponsible, since it violates the fundamental tenet of public finance that the budget should be balanced. Income should cover outgo. For further clarification on this point, you call in your advisers, who deny that the budget should be balanced each year. They point out that if a deficit is run in a particular year, the government can borrow the difference; and they claim that the national debt is in no sense dangerously large in the United States at present. Whose advice would you follow—that of your economic advisers or that of the congressmen?

CASE 2: INFLATIONARY SIGNALS

Suppose your advisers tell you that inflation is a growing problem and that you should cut back government spending and raise taxes. Since this advice seems sensible, based on the principles set forth in this chapter, you propose this course of action to Congress. Some prominent newspapers point out that by raising taxes and cutting expenditures, the government will take in more than it spends. In other words, there will be a *surplus.* They say that there is no reason for the government to take more money from the people than it needs to pay for the services it performs, and argue that taxes should not be increased because the government can cover its expenditures without such an increase. Whose advice would you follow— that of your economic advisers or that of the newspapers?

WHAT SHOULD YOU DO?

You would be wise to go along with your economic advisers in both cases. Why? Because, for reasons discussed in more detail in the next section, it is not essential or necessarily desirable for the budget to be balanced each year. Although it may well be prudent for individuals and families not to spend more than they earn, this does not carry over to the federal government. When we need to stimulate the economy and raise national output, it is perfectly legitimate and desirable for the federal government to run a deficit, provided it gets its full money's worth for what it spent. Thus, in the first case, you should not have been worried by the fact that a deficit would result. And in the second case, while it is true that the government could support its expenditures with lower taxes, this would defeat your purpose. What you want to do is to cut total spending, public and private, and raising taxes will cut private spending.

SHOULD THE BUDGET BE BALANCED ANNUALLY?

At least three policies concerning the government budget are worthy of detailed examination. The first policy says that *the government's budget should be balanced each and every year.* This is the philosophy that generally prevailed, here and abroad, until a few decades ago. Superficially, it seems reasonable. After all, won't a family or firm go bankrupt if it continues to spend more than it takes in? Why should the government be any different? However, the truth is that the government has economic capabilities, powers, and responsibilities that are entirely different from those of any family or firm, and it is misleading—sometimes even pernicious—to assume that what is sensible for a family or firm is also sensible for the government.

99TH CONGRESS
1ST SESSION   **S. 1712**

To provide an extension of certain excise tax rates.

IN THE SENATE OF THE UNITED STATES

SEPTEMBER 26 (legislative day, SEPTEMBER 23), 1985

Mr. DOLE (for himself, Mr. HELMS, Mr. FORD, and Mr. MITCHELL) introduced the following bill; which was read twice, considered, read the third time, and passed

A BILL

To provide an extension of certain excise tax rates.

1   *Be it enacted by the Senate and House of Representa-*

2   *tives of the United States of America in Congress assembled,*

3   That section 283(c) of the Tax Equity and Fiscal Responsi-

4   bility Act of 1982 is amended by striking out "October 1,

5   1985" and inserting in lieu thereof "November 15, 1985."

Passed the Senate September 26 (legislative day, September 23), 1985.

Attest: JO-ANNE L. COE,
                                            Secretary.

Budget
of the
United States
Government

Fiscal Year 1986

EXECUTIVE OFFICE OF THE PRESIDENT
OFFICE OF MANAGEMENT AND BUDGET

If this policy of balancing the budget is accepted, the government cannot use fiscal policy as a tool to stabilize the economy. Indeed, if the government attempts to balance its budget each year, it is likely to make unemployment or inflation worse rather than better. For example, suppose that severe unemployment occurs because of a drop in national output. Since incomes drop, tax receipts drop as well. Thus, if the government attempts to balance its budget, it must cut its spending and/or increase tax rates, both of which will tend to lower, not raise, national output. On the other hand, suppose that inflation occurs because spending increases too rapidly. Since incomes increase, tax receipts increase too. Thus, for the government to balance its budget, it must increase its spending and/or decrease tax rates, both of which will tend to raise, not lower, spending.

Despite these considerations, there has been a considerable amount of political support for a constitutional amendment to mandate a balanced federal budget. In large part, this seems to be a reaction to persistent, large deficits which are widely regarded as having been inflationary. No doubt, the federal government, through inappropriate fiscal or monetary policies, has frequently been responsible for excessive inflation. Some economists go so far as to say that the real problem is how to prevent the government from creating disturbances, rather than how to use the government budget (and monetary policy) to offset disturbances arising from the private sector. But for the reasons discussed above, most economists would not go so far as to conclude that the government should balance its budget each year.

SHOULD THE BUDGET BE BALANCED OVER THE BUSINESS CYCLE?

A second budgetary philosophy says that *the government's budget should be balanced over the course of each "business cycle."* As we have seen in previous chapters, the rate of growth of national output tends to behave cyclically. It tends to increase for a while, then drop, increase, then drop. Unemployment also tends to ebb and flow in a similar cyclical fashion. According to this second budgetary policy, the government is not expected to balance its budget each year, but is expected to run a big enough surplus during periods of high employment to offset the deficit it runs during the ensuing period of excessive unemployment. This policy seems to give the government enough flexibility to run the deficits or surpluses needed to stabilize the economy, while at the same time allaying any public fear of a chronically unbalanced budget. It certainly seems to be a neat way to reconcile the government's use of fiscal policy to promote noninflationary full employment with the public's uneasiness over chronically unbalanced budgets.

Unfortunately, however, it does contain one fundamental flaw. There is no reason to believe that the size of the deficits required to eliminate excessive unemployment will equal the size of the surpluses required to moderate the subsequent inflation. Suppose that national output falls sharply, causing severe and prolonged unemployment; then regains its full-employment level only briefly; then falls again. In such a case, the deficits incurred to get the economy back to full employment are likely to exceed by far the surpluses run during the brief period of full employment. Thus there would be no way to stabilize the economy without run-

257

In early 1984, unemployment was receding, while sales and profits were rising substantially, and inflation remained at moderate levels. Yet President Reagan's economic advisers were engaged in a public debate that reached the front pages of the nation's newspapers and magazines. What was the fracas about? The huge and growing federal deficit.

Martin Feldstein   *Donald Regan*

The projected 1984 deficit was estimated to be about $200 billion; and by the Reagan administration's own projections, the cumulative deficits from 1984 through 1989 were expected to total a whopping $1 trillion. According to Martin Feldstein, chairman of President Reagan's Council of Economic Advisers, these deficits were very dangerous to the long-term health of the American economy. If they were allowed to occur, they would push up interest rates and result in a crowding out of private investment on plant and equipment. Also, U.S. exports would be hurt because high U.S. interest rates would push up the value of the dollar relative to other currencies, thus making our exports more expensive to foreign purchasers. For these and other reasons, Feldstein (and many other economists) were extremely worried about the deficit.

In contrast, Donald Regan, who in 1984 was secretary of the Treasury, played down the importance of the deficit. In his view, deficits do not push up interest rates and they did not result in an overvaluation of the dollar relative to other currencies. In part, his arguments seemed to be based on studies carried out by some supply-side economists, including members of the Treasury staff. But most economists did not buy these arguments. If the government increases its demands for credit because of the very large deficits, the interest rate (which is the price of borrowing money) will rise.

The contrast between the two combatants, as well as the acidity of the squabble, fascinated news commentators as well as the general public. Feldstein, the whistle blower, was a highly respected economics professor on leave from Harvard University, a winner of the John Bates Clark medal (given every two years to the most distinguished economist under 40 years of age), and a former president of the National Bureau of Economic Research. Regan, the defender of the president's program, was the former head of Merrill Lynch, the huge brokerage firm, and one of the leading lights on Wall Street. *Time Magazine* called Feldstein "a combination of gadfly, maverick, and doomsayer . . . an adviser who insists on proferring unwanted advice," and labeled Regan as "the President's chief economic cheerleader."

The clash between them was almost certainly one of the most visible and highly publicized feuds among major presidential economic advisers in the recent history of the United States. Many observers were surprised that the president allowed it to continue so openly for so long. Finally, in the summer of 1984, Feldstein resigned his post and returned to Harvard. Regan remained in the second Reagan administration and in 1985 was given the key job as White House chief of staff.

ning an unbalanced budget over the course of this business cycle. If this policy were adopted, and if the government attempted to balance the budget over the course of each business cycle, this would interfere with an effective fiscal policy designed to promote full employment with stable prices.

SHOULD WE WORRY ABOUT BALANCING THE BUDGET?

Finally, a third budgetary policy says that *the government's budget should be set so as to promote whatever attainable combination of unemployment and inflation seems socially optimal,* even if this means that the budget is unbalanced over considerable periods of time. This policy is sometimes called *functional finance.*[6] Proponents of functional finance point out that, although this policy may mean a continual growth in the public debt, the problems caused by a moderate growth in the public debt are small when compared with the social costs of unemployment and inflation.

CHANGES IN PUBLIC ATTITUDES

Certainly, the history of the past 40 years has been characterized by enormous changes in the nation's attitude toward the government budget. Forty years ago, the prevailing attitude was that the government's budget should be balanced. The emergence of the Keynesian theory of the determination of national output and employment shook this attitude, at least to the point where it became respectable to advocate a balanced budget over the business cycle, rather than in each year. In many circles, functional finance was advocated.

In the late 1970s and early 1980s, there was some movement back toward earlier views favoring balanced budgets. Conservatives emphasized the usefulness of the balanced budget as a device to limit government spending, which they regarded as excessive. The public tended to blame very high rates of inflation on large deficits. Although neither political party was prepared (even remotely) to renounce deficits, considerable lip service was paid to the desirability of a balanced budget. For example, in August 1982, the Senate approved a constitutional amendment requiring a balanced budget, while at the same time the government was running a deficit of over $100 billion!

The Full-Employment Budget

Some of the misconceptions about budget deficits and surpluses can be avoided by the use of the *full-employment budget,* which shows the difference between tax revenues and government expenditures that would result if we had full employment. For example, in 1958, the Eisenhower administration ran a deficit of over $10 billion—a reasonably large deficit by historical standards. Basically, the reason for this deficit was that, with the unemployment rate at about 7 percent, there was a substantial gap

---

[6] See Abba Lerner, *Economics of Control,* New York: Macmillan, 1944.

between actual and potential output. Net national product fell from 1957 to 1958, and, as a result, incomes and federal tax collections fell, and the government ran a deficit. But this $10 billion deficit was entirely due to the high level of unemployment the country was experiencing.

Had we been at full employment, there would have been a surplus of about $5 billion in 1958. NNP, incomes, and federal tax receipts would all have been higher. Government spending and the tax rates in 1958 were not such as to produce a deficit if full employment had been attained. On the contrary, the full-employment budget shows that, if full employment had prevailed, tax receipts would have increased so that federal revenues would have exceeded expenditure by about $5 billion. It is important to distinguish between the full-employment budget and the actual budget. When, as in 1958, the actual budget shows a deficit but the full-employment budget does not, most economists feel that fiscal policy is not too expansionary, since at full employment the federal government would be running a surplus.

Recognizing these considerations, recent administrations have officially adopted the full-employment budget as their measure of the stabilization impact of the budget. As you can see in Figure 12.8, President Nixon ran a full-employment surplus during his first term in office to combat inflation.

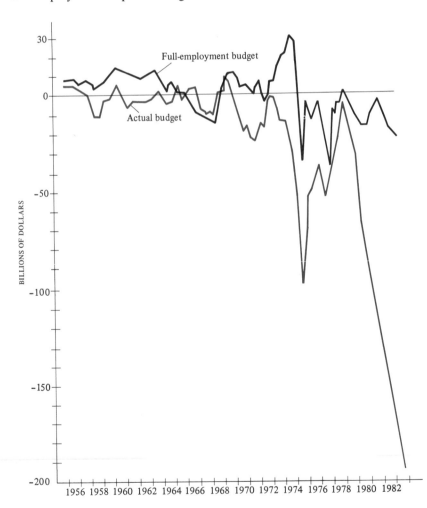

Figure 12.8
Full-Employment and Actual Budget Deficits and Surpluses, 1956–83 *The full-employment budget shows the difference between tax revenues and government expenditures that would result if there was full employment.*

In 1972, there was a full-employment deficit, but in 1973, and to a greater extent 1974, there were full-employment surpluses. This is in contrast to the actual budget, which was in deficit for most of these years. President Ford ran a large full-employment deficit in 1975 to promote recovery from the recession. In subsequent years, Presidents Carter and Reagan incurred full-employment deficits too.

As you can see in Figure 12.8, the full-employment budget can differ substantially from the actual budget. To understand whether fiscal policy is restrictive or stimulative, you must understand the difference.

Effects of How a Deficit Is Financed, or How a Surplus Is Used

Before leaving the topic of budget deficits and surpluses, it is important to note that the effect of a deficit may depend on how it is financed, as well as on its size. One way for the government to finance a deficit is *to borrow from consumers and business firms.* (Such borrowing results in increases in the national debt, discussed in Chapter 5.) When the government borrows from consumers and business firms, it takes funds from them that might otherwise be spent on consumption or investment goods. Thus some of the expansionary effect of a budget deficit may be offset by reduced private spending, if a deficit is financed by borrowing from the public.[7]

A second way for the government to finance a budget deficit is *to create new money.* For example, the government can simply print additional money to meet the deficit. (As will become clearer in Chapter 16, a similar result may be obtained if the government borrows from the central bank—the Federal Reserve in the United States.) When the government spends newly created money, it does not use funds that might otherwise be spent by the private sector. Consequently, *the expansionary effects of a deficit may be greater if it is financed by the creation of new money than if it is financed by borrowing from the public.*

Similarly, the effect of a surplus may depend on how it is used, as well as on its size. One way that the government can use a surplus is *to buy back some of its bonds from the public.* (Such purchases reduce the national debt.) When the government buys back some of its bonds, it provides the sellers of the bonds (consumers and firms) with additional spendable funds. Thus some of the anti-inflationary effects of a surplus may be offset by additional private spending.

Another way that the government can use a surplus is to *impound the funds,* that is, keep the funds idle. Since this latter use of the surplus does not provide the private sector with additional spendable funds, there is no such offset to the surplus's anti-inflationary effect. Consequently, *the anti-inflationary effects of a surplus may be greater if the surplus is impounded than if it is used to reduce the national debt.*

Basic Idea #24: If the government spends more than it receives in revenue, it will not go bankrupt. Instead, it will borrow (or create) the money to finance the deficit. If new debt is created, an intolerable burden will not be imposed on future generations (as some people claim), but this does not mean that government deficits do not have undesirable effects. For example, we must send goods and services overseas to pay interest on our foreign-held public debt, and deficit financing under the wrong circumstances can be inflationary.

[7] In Chapter 17 and in the Appendix, we shall see that a deficit financed by borrowing from the public tends to increase interest rates, which is likely to shift the investment function and possibly the consumption function downward. This will reduce the net increase in spending due to the increase in government expenditures. In other words, the increase in interest rates will reduce private spending. In the highly simplified model presented at the beginning of this chapter, we ignored this effect, which is discussed in Chapter 17 and in the Appendix.

Example 12.2   Interpreting Federal Budget Deficits

The actual deficits of the U.S. government in selected years are shown below:

Year	Billions of dollars
1954	1.2
1961	3.4
1967	8.7
1968	25.2
1975	45.2
1980	59.6

(a) Are all of these deficits the result of spendthrift government spending? (b) In 1954, 1961, 1975, and 1980, there were drops in NNP which helped to cause tax revenue to fall below government expenditure. From the above figures alone can one determine the extent to which a particular government deficit is due to high government spending or a weak economy? (c) Were the deficits in 1967 and 1968 the result of a weak economy? What information would you obtain to answer this question?

SOLUTION

(a) No. In some years, like 1954, 1961, 1975, and 1980, at least part of the reason for the deficit was a weak economy due to recession. (b) No. What one needs to know is the full-employment deficit or surplus in each year. (c) No. The unemployment rate is of use in indicating whether the economy was weak. Since the unemployment rate was less than 4 percent in 1967 and 1968, the economy certainly was not weak in these years. The full-employment deficit or surplus would help to answer this question. See Figure 12.8.

Recent American Experience with Fiscal Policy

It should be evident by now that much more is known today about the impact of fiscal policy than at the time when the economy was staggered by the Great Depression. But this does not mean that economists have all (or nearly all) the answers. Enough is known to keep the economy from careening off a bumpy road; avoiding the potholes (some of which are very large) is another matter.

THE FORD YEARS

The hard choices faced by economists in the top councils of government can be demonstrated by a close inspection of the recent attempts to give the economy a smoother side. Let's begin with the situation in the mid-1970s. In early 1974 the price of foreign oil was increased very substantially by the

OPEC countries. This price increase, as well as considerable increases in farm prices (recall Chapter 4), spearheaded a bewildering inflationary spurt. During 1974 consumer prices rose by about 12 percent! From the point of view of inflation, this was the worst year in decades. At the same time, the nation's real output fell, as the economy dropped into the most serious recession since World War II. The result was a marked increase in unemployment. By March 1975 the unemployment rate was 8.7 percent, as compared with 4.9 percent in December 1973.

Faced with a combination of excessive unemployment and excessive inflation, President Ford proposed a $16 billion tax cut, and, as we saw above, Congress passed a $23 billion tax cut in March 1975. As we have seen before, the economy began to revive in mid-1975, and unemployment fell from 8.7 percent in March 1975 to 7.5 percent in March 1976. However, stagflation (the combination of a high unemployment rate and a high rate of inflation) was by no means vanquished. On the contrary, both unemployment and inflation continued to be excessive.

THE CARTER YEARS

In 1977 the federal government ran a deficit of about $50 billion; the full-employment deficit was about $20 billion. And in January 1978 President Carter proposed personal tax reductions of $24 billion. But during 1978 the rate of inflation increased sharply, and approached double-digit levels. Since the inflation rate was higher than expected, the Carter administration scaled back its proposed tax cut to $20 billion, and Congress actually passed a $19 billion tax cut. (About $14 billion of this tax cut went to individuals, the rest to corporations.)

In the face of heightened inflation, fiscal policy did not attempt to rein in the economy very much. The deficit in 1978 was about $30 billion; the full-employment deficit was over $10 billion. There was a continuing debate within the administration over whether the inflation rate could be reduced substantially without a recession—and whether a recession was the proper medicine. In 1980, there was a very brief recession, but it did little to cool off inflation. As in previous years, the federal government ran a full-employment deficit.

THE REAGAN YEARS

When the Reagan administration took office in 1981, it was committed to cut both government expenditures and taxes. In August 1981 the administration pushed through Congress a huge tax cut for both individuals and businesses. At the same time, it reduced federal expenditures (relative to the level that former president Carter had proposed). However, the tax cuts were far in excess of the spending cuts, particularly since reductions in GNP in late 1981 also tended to reduce tax receipts. Thus the administration was faced with record deficits of over $100 billion in fiscal 1982 and about $200 billion in fiscal 1983. In early 1982 President Reagan said he would try to cut spending further in an attempt to soak up some of the red ink. But the economy was in a recession (with an unemployment rate of 9 percent) and there was little sympathy on Capitol Hill for further spending cuts. Since inflation had fallen to well under double-digits, unemployment once again seemed to be Public Enemy Number One.

263

In November 1982 the economy pulled out of the recession, and the expansion began. Economists of all schools, but particularly supply-side economists (recall Chapter 5), gave the 1981 tax cut considerable credit for increasing real NNP and reducing unemployment. During 1983 and 1984, both years of healthy expansion, the federal government ran huge deficits of about $200 billion. President Reagan vowed that he would not raise taxes, and proposed cuts in nonmilitary government expenditures; whereas his critics asked for tax increases and reductions in military spending. In December 1985, a bill mandating that the budget be balanced in annual steps over the next five years was passed, but there were doubts about its effectiveness and constitutionality.

Clearly, judging from our recent history, fiscal policy is no panacea. Policy makers are continually confronted with difficult choices, and the tools of fiscal policy, at least as they are currently understood and used, are not sufficient to solve or dispel many of the problems at hand. However, it is important to recognize that fiscal policy is not the only available means by which policy makers attempt to stabilize the economy. There is also monetary policy, which we shall discuss in detail in Chapter 16. A sensible fiscal policy can be formulated only in conjunction with monetary policy, and although it is convenient to discuss them separately, in real life they must be coordinated. Also, lest you become overly pessimistic, you should note that, despite the problems that remain unsolved, our improved understanding of fiscal and monetary policy has enabled us to steer a better and more stable course than in the days before World War II.

Test Yourself

1. Describe the balanced-budget multiplier. If both government expenditures and taxes rise by the same amount, what is the effect, according to the balanced-budget multiplier?

2. "An important advantage of public works as a tool of fiscal policy is that they can be started quickly. An important advantage of tax rate changes is that they almost never get embroiled in partisan politics." Comment and evaluate.

3. "The full-employment budget is just a lot of hocum to persuade the public that big deficits are smaller and less inflationary than they really are." Comment and evaluate.

4. According to Joseph Pechman of the Brookings Institution, "Among taxes, the federal individual income tax is the leading [automatic] stabilizer." Explain why, and discuss the significance of this fact. He also says that "on the expenditure side, the major built-in stabilizer is unemployment compensation." Again, explain why, and discuss the significance of this fact.

Summary

1. The equilibrium level of net national product is the level where intended consumption plus intended investment plus intended government spending equal net national product. A $1 billion change in government purchases will result in a change in equilibrium NNP of the same amount as a $1 billion change in intended investment or a $1 billion shift in the relation between consumption expenditures and NNP. In any of these cases, there is a multiplier effect.

2. An increase in the tax rate shifts the relationship between consumption expenditure and NNP downward, thus reducing the equilibrium value of NNP. A decrease in the tax rate shifts the relationship upward, thus increasing the equilibrium value of NNP.

3. The equilibrium level of NNP may not be the level corresponding to full employment. A recessionary gap is the increase in intended spending required to push the equilibrium NNP up to the full-employment level. An inflationary gap is the decrease in intended spending required to push the equilibrium NNP down to its full-employment level (at initial prices).

4. Policy makers receive a lot of help in stabilizing the economy from our automatic stabilizers—automatic changes in tax revenues, unemployment compensation and welfare payments, corporate dividends, family saving, and farm aid. However, the automatic stabilizers can only cut down on variations in unemployment and inflation, not eliminate them.

5. Discretionary programs are needed to supplement the effects of these automatic stabilizers. Such discretionary actions include changing government expenditure on public works and other programs, changing welfare payments and other such transfers, and changing tax rates. An important problem with some of these tools of fiscal policy is the lag in time before they can be brought into play.

6. At least three policies concerning the government budget have received considerable attention. First, the budget can be balanced each and every year. Second, the budget can be balanced over the course of the business cycle. Third, the budget can be set in a way that will promote full employment with stable prices whether or not this means that the budget is unbalanced over considerable periods of time.

7. The history of the past 40 years has seen enormous changes in the public's attitude toward the government budget. Forty years ago, the prevailing doctrine was that the budget should be balanced each year. Now (although a balanced budget has more support than a few years ago) the attitude seems to be that the budget should be used as a tool to reduce unemployment and inflation.

8. Some of the popular misconceptions concerning budget deficits and budget surpluses can be avoided by the use of the full-employment budget, which shows the difference between tax revenue and government expenditure that would result if we had full employment. When the actual budget shows a deficit but the full-employment budget does not, most economists feel that fiscal policy is not too expansionary.

Concepts for Review

$C + I + G$ line	Council of Economic	Balanced budget
Balanced-budget	Advisers	Functional finance
multiplier	Automatic stabilizers	Full-employment
Recessionary gap	Deficit	budget
Inflationary gap	Surplus	

Appendix: The Effect of a Change in Government Expenditure and the Balanced-Budget Multiplier (an Algebraic Treatment)

The first purpose of this Appendix is to prove that a $1 billion change in government expenditure will result in a change in equilibrium NNP of $\left(\dfrac{1}{\text{MPS}} \right)$ billions of dollars. To prove this proposition, recall that the equilibrium value of NNP is where intended spending—$C + I + G$—equals NNP. Thus

$$NNP = C + I + G. \tag{12.1}$$

Assuming that the consumption function is as given in Table 10.1 (and Table 12.1), it follows that

$$C = 350 + 0.6\,NNP \tag{12.2}$$

where 0.6 is the marginal propensity to consume. (Note that NNP equals disposable income. This is because there are no taxes, no transfer payments, and no undistributed corporate profits. Taxes are brought into the picture later in this appendix.) Substituting the right-hand side of Equation (12.2) for C in Equation (12.1), we have

$$NNP = 350 + 0.6\,NNP + I + G. \tag{12.3}$$

Thus

$$(1 - 0.6)\,NNP = 350 + I + G$$
$$NNP = \frac{350}{0.4} + \frac{I}{0.4} + \frac{G}{0.4}. \tag{12.4}$$

What happens to NNP when G increases from X billion to $(X + 1)$ billion? How much will this increase the equilibrium value of NNP? From Equation (12.4), it is clear that equilibrium NNP will be

$$\frac{350}{0.4} + \frac{I}{0.4} + \frac{X}{0.4}$$

if government expenditure equals X billion. And it is equally clear from Equation (12.4) that NNP will equal

$$\frac{350}{0.4} + \frac{I}{0.4} + \frac{(X + 1)}{0.4}$$

if government expenditure is $(X + 1)$ billion. Consequently the increase in NNP due to the $1 billion increase in government spending is

$$\left[\frac{350}{0.4} + \frac{I}{0.4} + \frac{(X + 1)}{0.4} \right] - \left[\frac{350}{0.4} + \frac{I}{0.4} + \frac{X}{0.4} \right],$$

which equals

$$\frac{X + 1}{0.4} - \frac{X}{0.4} = \frac{1}{0.4}.$$

That is, a \$1 billion increase in government expenditure will result in an increase of $\frac{1}{0.4}$ billion dollars of NNP—which is equal to $\left(\frac{1}{\text{MPS}}\right)$ billions of dollars of NNP, since $0.4 = \text{MPS}$. This is what we set out to prove.

The second purpose of this Appendix is to prove that, if both government expenditures and taxes are increased by \$1 billion, equilibrium NNP will be increased by \$1 billion. This is the balanced-budget multiplier. To prove this proposition, note that disposable income equals $NNP - T$, where T is the amount of taxes. Thus the consumption function is

$$C = 350 + 0.6\,(NNP - T). \tag{12.5}$$

Substituting the right-hand side of Equation (12.5) for C in Equation (12.1), we have

$$NNP = 350 + 0.6\,(NNP - T) + I + G.$$

Thus

$$(1 - 0.6)\,NNP = 350 - 0.6T + I + G$$

$$NNP = \frac{350}{0.4} - \frac{0.6T}{0.4} + \frac{I}{0.4} + \frac{G}{0.4}.$$

What happens if both G and T increase by \$1 billion? The effect of increasing T by \$1 billion is to reduce the equilibrium value of NNP by $0.6/0.4$ billions of dollars. The effect of increasing G by \$1 billion is to increase the equilibrium value of NNP by $1/0.4$ billions of dollars. Thus the effect of increasing both G and T by \$1 billion is to increase the equilibrium value of NNP by $1/0.4 - 0.6/0.4 = 0.4/0.4$, or 1 billion dollars. This is what we set out to prove.

CHAPTER 13

Business Fluctuations and Economic Forecasting

The American economy has not grown at a constant rate. Instead, as pointed out in Chapter 9, output has expanded rapidly in some periods; little, if at all, in others; and actually contracted in still others. The average citizen, as well as the government official or the business executive, needs to know why these business fluctuations occur and whether they can be avoided. This chapter investigates the causes of business fluctuations.

We also take up a related question of great practical importance. Can business fluctuations be forecasted? More and more, economic models are being used by government and industry to forecast changes in GNP and other economic variables. Economic forecasting has become a very important part of the economist's job. Although no reputable economist would claim that economic forecasting is very precise or reliable, the forecasts produced by economic models are watched closely by decision makers around the world. In the latter part of this chapter, we describe some of the more widely used forecasting techniques, and see how accurate they have proved in the past.

Business Fluctuations and Variation in Investment Spending

In Chapter 9, we described the anatomy of the business cycle. Each cycle can be divided into four phases: trough, expansion, peak, and recession. There is considerable variation in the length and severity of business fluctuations. Some recessions, like that in the early thirties, are very severe;

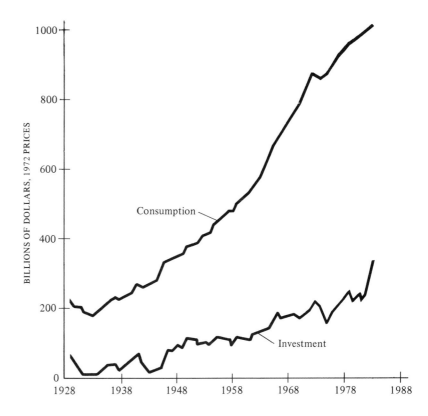

Figure 13.1

Consumption Expenditure and Gross Private Domestic Investment, United States, 1929–84 *Investment varies more from year to year than does consumption spending.*

others, like those in the fifties, are relatively mild. Some expansions, like that in the sixties, are relatively long-lived. Others, like that in the late fifties, are of relatively short duration. Moreover, the basic set of factors responsible for the recession and the expansion differs from cycle to cycle.

As we pointed out in Chapter 11, investment varies much more from year to year than does consumption expenditure. Figure 13.1 shows that investment goes up and down, while consumption climbs steadily with only slight bumps and dips.[1] *The volatility of investment is an important factor in explaining the changes in national output over time.* Why does investment in plant and equipment vary so much over the course of the business cycle? The acceleration principle throws important light on this question.

The Acceleration Principle

The acceleration principle is a theory that says that investment is related to the rate of change of output. When output is increasing beyond previous levels, investment is required to increase the capacity to produce output. When output is falling, it may be unnecessary even to replace old capital as it is scrapped, let alone to spend money on new capital.

[1] Net exports are excluded from Figure 13.1. They were almost always under $10 billion during this period. Government expenditures are considered in Figure 13.2.

Table 13.1

RELATIONSHIP BETWEEN SALES AND INVESTMENT, JOHNSON SHOE CORPORATION

Year	Sales	Needed stock of capital	Actual stock of capital	Replacement investment (millions of dollars)	Net investment	Gross investment
1977	10	20	20	1	0	1
1978	12	24	24	1	4	5
1979	14	28	28	1	4	5
1980	15	30	30	1	2	3
1981	16	32	32	1	2	3
1982	16	32	32	1	0	1
1983	15	30	31	0	−1	0
1984	15	30	30	0	−1	0
1985	15	30	30	1	0	1
1986	17	34	34	1	4	5

THE ACCELERATION PRINCIPLE IN ACTION: A NUMERICAL EXAMPLE

Suppose that the Johnson Shoe Corporation, a maker of women's shoes, requires 1 machine to make 50,000 pairs of shoes per year. Since each machine (and related plant and facilities) costs $2 million and each pair of shoes costs $20, it takes $2 worth of plant and equipment to produce $1 worth of output per year. In 1977, we suppose that the quantity of the firm's plant and equipment was exactly in balance with its output. In other words, the firm had no excess capacity; sales were $10 million and the actual stock of capital was $20 million. The firm's sales in subsequent years are shown in Table 13.1. For example, in 1978 its sales increased to $12 million; in 1979 they increased to $14 million; and so forth.

Table 13.1 also shows the amount the firm will have to invest each year in order to produce the amount it sells. Let's begin with 1978. To produce $12 million worth of product, the firm must have $24 million worth of capital. This means that it must increase its stock of capital from $20 million —the amount it has in 1977—to $24 million.[2] In other words, it must increase its stock of capital by $4 million, which means that its net investment in plant and equipment must equal $4 million. But this is not the same as its gross investment—the amount of plant and equipment the firm must buy—because the firm must also replace some plant and equipment that wears out. Suppose that $1 million of plant and equipment wear out each year. Then gross investment in 1978 must equal net investment ($4 million) plus $1 million, or $5 million.

Next, let's look at 1979. The firm's sales in that year are $14 million. To produce this much output, the firm must have $28 million of capital, which means that it must increase its stock of capital by $4 million—from $24 million to $28 million. In addition, there is $1 million of replacement investment to replace plant and equipment that wear out in 1979. In all, the firm's gross investment must be $5 million. In 1980, the firm's sales are $15

[2] Note that the firm's stock of capital is an entirely different concept than its common stock or preferred stock. See Chapter 6.

million. To produce this output, this firm must have $30 million of capital, which means that it must increase its stock of capital by $2 million—from $28 million to $30 million. In addition, there is $1 million of replacement investment. In all, the firm's gross investment must be $3 million. Table 13.1 shows the results for subsequent years.

MAGNIFIED PERCENTAGE CHANGES IN INVESTMENT

From Table 13.1, it is clear that *changes in sales can result in magnified percentage changes in investment.* For example, between 1977 and 1978 sales went up by 20 percent, whereas gross investment went up by 400 percent. Between 1985 and 1986, sales went up by about 13 percent, whereas gross investment went up by 400 percent. The effect of a decrease in sales is even more spectacular because it tends to drive net investment to zero (or to negative values, as in 1983). Indeed, even gross investment may be driven to zero, as in 1983, if the firm wants to reduce the value of its plant and equipment. To accomplish this, the firm simply does not replace the plant and equipment that wear out.

THE IMPORTANCE OF THE RATE OF CHANGE OF SALES

Table 13.1 shows that *the amount of gross investment depends on the amount by which sales increase.* In particular, for gross investment to remain constant year after year, the annual increase of sales must also remain constant. You can see this in 1978 and 1979. In each of these years, since sales increased from the previous year by the same amount ($2 million), gross investment remained constant at $5 million per year. It is very important to note that *gross investment will fall when sales begin to increase by decreasing amounts.* The fact that sales are increasing does not insure that gross investment will increase. On the contrary, if sales are increasing by decreasing amounts, gross investment will fall. This is a very important point.

This effect of changes in sales on gross investment is often called the ***acceleration principle,*** since changes in sales result in accelerated, or magnified, changes in investment, and since an increase in investment results from an increase in the annual growth (an ***acceleration***) of sales. The acceleration principle applies to kinds of investment other than plant and equipment. For example, it is easy to show that it applies to inventories and housing as well, since firms often try to maintain a certain amount of inventory for each dollar of sales—just as they often maintain a certain amount of plant and equipment for each dollar of sales.

The Interaction between the Acceleration Principle and the Multiplier

Economists—led by Nobel laureates Paul Samuelson and Sir John Hicks—*have shown that the acceleration principle combined with the multiplier may produce business cycles like those experienced in the real world.* Suppose that national output is increasing, and the economy is moving up

271

toward full employment. Sales are increasing at an increasing rate. Because of the acceleration principle, the increases in sales result in a high level of investment. And via the multiplier, the high level of investment promotes further increases in national output. Thus the accelerator and multiplier tend to reinforce one another, resulting in a strong upward movement of national output. The economy is in an expansion. It is a good time to be president of the United States, president of a major corporation, or an average citizen.

Example 13.1   Investment at the Howe Company

The Howe Company is a manufacturer of electrical equipment. It wants to maintain $3 worth of plant and equipment for every dollar of output per year. Each year $1 million worth of Howe Company's plant and equipment wears out. In 1983, the firm's actual value of plant and equipment is $150 million.
   (a) Fill in the blanks below (all figures are in millions of dollars).

Year	Output during year	Desired value of plant and equipment	Net investment	Gross investment
1983	50	_____	_____	_____
1984	60	_____	_____	_____
1985	70	_____	_____	_____
1986	80	_____	_____	_____
1987	100	_____	_____	_____
1988	105	_____	_____	_____

(b) Is the rate of gross investment in plant and equipment highest in the year when output is greatest? (c) Why does gross investment drop in 1988, even though output continues to increase?

SOLUTION

(a) The complete table is:

Year	Output during year	Desired value of plant and equipment	Net investment	Gross investment
1983	50	150	0	1
1984	60	180	30	31
1985	70	210	30	31
1986	80	240	30	31
1987	100	300	60	61
1988	105	315	15	16

(b) No. (c) Because 1988 output differed from 1987 output by a smaller amount than 1987 output differed from 1986 output.

WHY A PEAK?

Eventually, however, the economy nears full employment. And since we have only a certain amount of land, labor, and capital, it simply is impossible to increase national output at the rate experienced during the recovery. Sales, which cannot increase forever at the old rate, begin to increase more slowly. But as we saw in the previous section, the reduction in the rate of increase of sales is the kiss of death for investment. Even though sales continue to increase, the drop in their rate of increase means decreasing investment. And this reduction in investment sounds the death knell for the boom, since it reduces national output directly and via the multiplier. The reduction in national output means a reduction in sales, and the reduction in sales means a drastic reduction in investment, through the acceleration principle. The drastic reduction in investment means a further reduction in national output. The economy is in a recession. Everything is moving downward, with the notable exception of unemployment. People are getting nervous—including the president of the United States, the presidents of major corporations, and many average citizens.

WHY A TROUGH?

Basic Idea #25: The level of investment is related to the rate of change of output. Gross investment is likely to fall when sales begin to increase by decreasing amounts. This is one reason for a peak. Sales cannot increase forever at a non-decreasing rate because there is only a limited amount of resources in the economy. As sales begin to increase at a decreasing rate, investment falls, thus reducing NNP (via the multiplier).

Eventually, however, firms reduce their stock of capital to the point where it is in balance with their reduced sales. In other words, they go through the sort of process shown in Table 13.1 during 1983–84, when the Johnson Shoe Corporation reduced its stock of capital by refusing to replace wornout plant and equipment. At the end of this process, the stock of capital is in balance with sales. To keep this balance, firms must now replace worn-out equipment, which means an increase in gross investment. Via the multiplier, this increase in investment results in an increase in national product, which means an increase in sales. Via the acceleration principle, this increase in sales results in an increase in investment, which in turn increases national product. The economy is once again in the midst of a recovery. It is again a good time to be president of the United States, president of a major corporation, or an average citizen. As moviegoers put it, this is where we came in.

This theory, although highly simplified, provides a great many insights into the nature of business fluctuations. One aspect of the theory in particular should be noted. Business cycles are self-starting and self-terminating. Recession, trough, recovery, peak—each phase of the business cycle leads into the next. This theory shows that one need not look outside the economic system for causes of the upper and lower turning points—that is, the points where the economy begins to turn down after a recovery or begins to turn up after a recession. These turning points can occur for the reasons we have just indicated.

The Role of Expectations

Firms' expectations concerning their future sales and profits vary a great deal from one phase to another of the business cycle. For example, in the recession of 1974–75, businesses' expectations became decidedly more pessimistic. Capital spending was cut by over $15 billion and inventory investment by over $17 billion.

Firms' expectations play a significant role in amplifying business fluctuations. Decisions made at any point in time depend on expectations concerning the future. For example, when a firm builds a new warehouse, it has certain expectations concerning the extent of its sales in the future, the price it will have to pay for labor and transportation, and so on. In forming their expectations, business executives often tend to follow the leader. As more and more business executives and analysts predict a rosy future, others tend to jump on the bandwagon. This means that, as the economy advances from a trough, optimistic expectations concerning sales and profits tend to spread, slowly at first, then more and more rapidly. These expectations generate investment, which in turn increases national output. Thus the rosy expectations are self-fulfilling, at least up to a point. (In this area, even if "wishing won't make it so," expecting may turn the trick!) The result is that the expansion is fueled by self-fulfilling and self-augmenting expectations.

Eventually, however, these expectations are not fulfilled, perhaps because full-employment ceilings cause national output to grow at a slower rate, perhaps because the government cuts back its spending (as in 1953–54), perhaps for some other reason. Now the process goes into reverse. Pessimistic expectations appear; and as national output begins to decline, these expectations spread more and more rapidly. These expectations also tend to be self-fulfilling. Business executives, feeling that the outlook for sales and profits is unfavorable, cut back on their investing, which in turn reduces national output. Thus the recession is made more serious by the epidemic of gloom. In any theory of business fluctuations, it is necessary to recognize the importance of self-fulfilling expectations.

The Effect of Innovations and Random External Events

Let's turn now to a different sort of explanation of business fluctuations. The acceleration principle is only one factor influencing gross investment. Since a firm will invest in any project where the returns exceed the costs involved, many investment projects are not triggered by changes in sales. For example, a new product may be invented, and large investments may be required to produce, distribute, and market it. Consider the computer industry. It took big investments to launch the personal computers that are becoming so common in offices and homes.

TIMING OF INNOVATIONS

Major innovations do not occur every day. Neither do they occur at a constant rate. There are more in some years than in others, and sheer chance influences the number of innovations in a given year. Similarly, chance greatly influences the timing of many other types of events that bear on the level of output and investment. These include crop failures, hurricanes, and other such natural disasters, as well as man-made events, like strikes in major industries and financial panics, which also affect output and investment.

Let's suppose that these events—innovations and other occurrences that have a major effect on investment—occur more or less at random. Because so many factors influence the timing of each such event, we cannot predict how many will occur in a particular year. Instead, the number is subject to chance variation, like the number thrown in a dice game or the number of spades in a poker hand. In particular, suppose that the chance that one of these events occurs in one year is about the same as in another year.

EFFECTS OF RANDOM SHOCKS

If this is the case, economists—led by Norway's Nobel laureate, Ragnar Frisch—have shown that business cycles are likely to result. The basic idea is that the economy, because of its internal structure, is like a pendulum or rocking chair. *If it is subjected to random shocks—like pushing a rocking chair every now and then—it will move up and down.* These **random shocks** are the bursts of investment that arise as a consequence of a great new invention or of the development of a major new deposit of a vital resource like oil, or for some other such reason. These bursts play the role of the forces hitting the pendulum or the rocking chair. To a considerable extent, they may be due to nonecomomic events or forces, but whatever their cause, they bang into the economy and shove it in one direction or another.

Of course, the occurrence of these shocks is not the whole story. *Business fluctuations in this model do not occur only because of the random events that affect investment. In addition, the economy must respond to—and amplify—the effects of these stimuli.* The economy must be like a rocking chair, not a sofa. (If you whack a sofa every now and then, you are likely to hurt your hand, but not to move the sofa much.) Frisch showed that the economy is likely to respond to, and amplify, these shocks. This model explains the fact, stressed in a previous section, that although cycles bear some family resemblance, no two are really alike. Thus the model has the advantage of not explaining more than it should. It does not imply that business fluctuations are more uniform and predictable than they are.

This theory provides valuable insight into the nature of business fluctuations. Like the theory of the interaction of the acceleration principle and the multiplier, it contains important elements of truth, although it obviously is highly simplified. Each of these theories focuses on factors that may be partly responsible for business fluctuations. They complement one another, in the sense that both processes—the interaction of the multiplier and the acceleration principle, and the random external stimuli to investment—may be at work. There is no need to choose between these theories. Both help to explain business fluctuations, and both are far from the whole truth.

Ragnar Frisch

Inventory Cycles

The "minor" or "short" business cycle, lasting about two to four years, is sometimes called an *inventory cycle* because it is often due largely to variations in inventories. This cycle proceeds as follows. Firms, having let their inventories decline during a business slowdown, find that they are short of inventories. They increase their inventories, which means that they produce more than they sell. This investment in inventories has a stimulating effect on national output. So long as the rate of increase of their sales holds up, firms continue to increase their inventories at this rate.[3] Thus inventory investment continues to stimulate the economy. But when their sales begin to increase more slowly, firms begin to cut back on their inventory investment. This reduction in inventory investment has a depressing effect on national output. As their sales decrease, firms cut back again on their inventory investment, further damping national output. Then when inventories are cut to the bone, the process starts all over again.

As an illustration, consider the recession of 1974–75. During the fourth quarter of 1974, inventories were still increasing at an annual rate of about $10 billion. Then because of a drop in sales, firms found themselves with excess inventories. They cut back their orders from suppliers, which in turn had to reduce output and employment. Inventories were reduced at an annual rate of about $20 billion during early 1975. This inventory liquidation played a major role in the recession. Production plummeted. Fortunately, the reduction in inventories all but ceased in the second half of 1975, and production and employment picked up.

Variation in Government Spending

It should not be assumed that business fluctuations are solely or necessarily due to the behavior of the private sector. Particularly during and after wars, government spending has sometimes been a major destabilizing force. Figure 13.2 shows the great bulge in government spending during World War II and the lesser bulges during the Korean War and Vietnam War. These increases in spending produced strong inflationary pressures. The price level rose over 50 percent during 1940–46 (World War II), and major inflationary spurts also occurred during the wars in Korea and Vietnam.

Government spending has been a destabilizing force after, as well as during, wars. The recession in 1953–54 was caused primarily by the reduction in government expenditures when the Korean War came to a close. When hostilities terminated, government expenditures were reduced by more than $10 billion. Government spending sometimes has also had the same destabilizing effect in other than wartime or postwar situations. The recession in 1957–58 was aggravated by a drop in defense expenditures in late 1957. Faced with this drop, the defense contractors cut their inventories and expenditures for plant and equipment.

---

[3] As noted above, the acceleration effect discussed in previous sections applies to inventories as well as to plant and equipment, since firms often try to maintain inventories equal to a certain percentage of sales. Thus the amount by which sales increase will affect the rate of investment in inventories as well as plant and equipment.

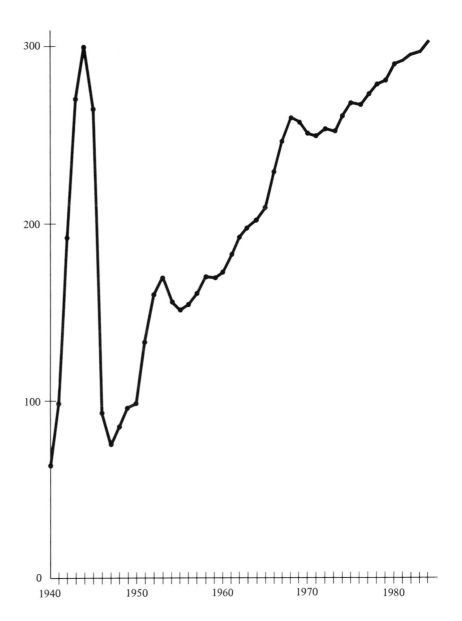

Figure 13.2
Government Purchases of Goods and Services, United States, 1940–84
Clearly, government expenditures have varied considerably from year to year. Note the big increase in spending during World War II and the smaller increases during the Korean and Vietnam conflicts.

The Political Business Cycle

Still another explanation of business fluctuations is based on the so-called political business cycle. According to a number of prominent economists, some business fluctuations, rather than being due to instability of spending by the private sector or to wartime or postwar changes in government expenditures, are caused by politicians' use of fiscal (and monetary) policy for their own political ends. As stressed in the previous chapter, economic policy in the United States is inextricably intertwined with politics, so it would not be surprising if politicians tried to use economic policy to further their own objectives.

277

According to economists who have studied these political business cycles, the scenario runs roughly as follows. To begin with, a year or two before the election, the incumbent president (and congressmen and senators whose eyes are fixed on the election) promotes an expansionary fiscal policy. Government expenditures are increased; taxes are cut. Also, the president may do his best to get the Federal Reserve to increase the money supply at a relatively rapid rate. Because of all this economic stimulus, the economy is in an expansion when the election comes around. The unemployment rate is relatively low—or at least, it is falling. People's money incomes are rising. The voters are put in a mood to return the incumbents to office.

After the election, the inflationary impact of the expansionary economic policy becomes evident. If the economy was reasonably close to full employment when it was stimulated in this way, much of the increase in spending is likely to result in inflation, not higher real output. But in the short run, the effect on production and employment is much greater than the effect on the price level. Thus the inflationary effects of the expansionary pre-election fiscal (and monetary) policies become evident only after the election.

Not too long after the election, the president and Congress, faced with public outcries about the accelerated rate of inflation, assume an anti-inflationary posture. They cut back on the rate of increase of government spending and, if necessary, increase taxes. Also, the Federal Reserve is likely to reduce the rate of growth of the money supply. The result is a recession—but the incumbents are likely to call it a "slowdown," a "pause," or a "readjustment." After the recession has reduced the inflationary pressures, the stage is set for the process to start all over again, since it is close to a year or two before the next presidential election.

This description of the political business cycle is clearly oversimplified. For one thing, it is not easy for the president (or anyone else) to predict the timing of the effects of an expansionary policy. Yet this simple model seems to contain a certain amount of truth, both in the United States and in other countries. During election years, the American economy has been much more likely to be expanding than slowing down. Moreover, the available evidence seems to indicate that this is true in a wide variety of other democracies around the world. It appears unlikely that this difference in economic conditions between election and nonelection years could be due to chance.

Monetary Factors

Finally, we must stress that *monetary factors are of great importance in causing business fluctuations.* By monetary factors we mean the rate at which the money supply grows, the rate of interest, and the availability of credit. As noted above, the Federal Reserve has major powers over these factors in the United States. In Chapter 16, we shall see that these factors figured significantly in slowing down the boom of the late 1960s and in reducing inflationary pressures during the mid-1970s and the early and mid-

1980s. These factors are so important that we shall devote the next several chapters entirely to them. In economics as in other aspects of life, money counts.

Can Business Fluctuations Be Avoided?

Now that we have looked at some theories designed to explain business fluctuations, we are led to ask whether these fluctuations can be avoided in the future. To some extent, a discussion of this question is premature, since we have not yet taken up monetary policy. But there is no reason to postpone answering it in general terms, waiting for subsequent chapters to provide more detailed discussions of various aspects of the answer.

On the basis of our increased knowledge of the reasons for business fluctuations and the growing acceptance of modern monetary and fiscal policy, some people have suggested that the business cycle can be licked. That is, they have felt that the government, if it makes proper use of monetary and fiscal policy, can head off a recession or a boom, and in this way offset the processes and events that destabilize the economy. This is a rather optimistic view, although the evidence does indicate that we have been able to reduce the severity and frequency of major recessions in recent years. Our record in this regard seems to have been better than in pre-World-War-II days, although the 1973–75 and 1981–82 recessions were rather severe.

Does this mean that a major depression—like that experienced in the 1930s—is impossible? The answer is no. Even though we now know how to prevent a depression, one could still occur through stupidity or some weird sequence of events. *But the probability of such a depression is very small,* given our automatic stabilizers and the fact that policy makers—and the electorate—know now that fiscal policy and monetary policy can be used to push the economy toward full employment.

There is every reason to expect, however, that the small recessions—the "dips" and "pauses"—will continue. There will be ups and downs in spending on plant and equipment, there will be fluctuations in inventories, there will be military build-ups and cutbacks, and changes in government spending and in tax rates. All these things can be destabilizing, and existing economic knowledge is not sufficiently precise to allow policy makers to iron out the resulting small deviations of national output from its long-term upward trend. *Although there has been a certain amount of optimistic talk about "fine-tuning" of the economy, the truth is that we lack the knowledge or the means to do it.*

Finally, the prospect for inflation is troublesome. The recent record of the United States has not been particularly encouraging. Serious inflationary pressures have arisen whenever the economy has gotten reasonably close to full employment. *To a considerable extent, federal policy makers have felt it necessary to engineer recessions (or "slowdowns," as they frequently are termed in Washington) to curb these pressures.* This is a very difficult problem, and an important one, which we shall discuss in much greater detail in Chapters 14, 16, 17, and 18.

1. Suppose that a firm requires $3 in capital for every $1 of its sales. Suppose that none of its capital ever wears out, and that it had $450,000 in capital at the end of 1980. Its sales in subsequent years were as follows:

Year	Sales (dollars)
1981	150,000
1982	180,000
1983	210,000
1984	220,000
1985	225,000
1986	220,000

How much did the firm invest each year?

2. Describe how the multiplier and acceleration principle can interact to result in business fluctuations. Be sure to explain why the amount of investment depends on the rate of change of sales.

3. In a recent recession, the Conference Board reported the results of its latest consumer survey, which indicated that consumers' expectations concerning the economic future turned considerably more optimistic. How might this change in expectations help to pull the economy out of the recession occurring then? (*Hint:* Intentions to buy autos and appliances moved higher.)

4. "The government itself is frequently the cause of business fluctuations." Comment and evaluate.

Can Business Fluctuations Be Forecasted?

How useful are modern economic theories in forecasting NNP? This is a perfectly reasonable question. After all, when you study solid state physics, you expect to come away with certain principles that will enable you to predict physical phenomena—for example, the effects of small but controlled amounts of impurities on the properties of metal. To the extent that economics is a science, you have a right to expect the same thing, since an acid test of any science is how well it predicts.

This question is also of great practical importance. Government officials are enormously interested in what NNP is likely to be in the next year or so, since they must try to anticipate whether excessive unemployment or serious inflationary pressures are developing. Business executives are equally interested, since their firms' sales, profits, and needs for equipment depend on NNP. For these reasons, forecasting is one of the principal jobs of economists in government and industry.

FORECASTING, NO EXACT SCIENCE

The first thing that must be said is that, *in forecasting as in most other areas, economics is not an exact science.* If economists tell you they can predict exactly what NNP will be next year, you can be pretty sure that they are talking through their hats. Of course, by luck, they may be able to predict correctly, but lucky guesses do not a science make. However, although economic forecasting is not perfectly accurate, economic forecasts are still useful. Since governments, firms, and private individuals must continually make decisions that hinge on what they expect will happen, there is no way that they can avoid making forecasts, explicit or implicit. The only question is how best to make them.

There is considerable evidence that, *even though forecasts based on economic models are sometimes not very good, they are better—on the average—than those made by noneconomists.* There is no substitute for economic analysis in accurate forecasting over the long haul. This really isn't very surprising. It would be strange if economists, whose profession it is to study and predict economic phenomena, were to do worse than those without this training—even if the others are tycoons or politicians. Further, it would be strange if government and industry were to hire platoons of economists at fancy prices—which they do—if they couldn't predict any better than anyone else.

Economists have no single method for forecasting NNP or GNP. They vary in their approaches just as physicians, for example, differ in theirs. But reputable economists tend to use one of a small number of forecasting techniques, each of which is described below. Of course, many economists do not restrict themselves to one technique, but rely on a combination of several, using one to check on another.

Leading Indicators

Perhaps the simplest way to forecast business fluctuations is to use **leading indicators,** which are certain economic series that typically go down or up before national output does. The National Bureau of Economic Research, founded by Wesley C. Mitchell (1874–1948), has carried out detailed and painstaking research to examine the behavior of various economic variables over a long period of time, in some cases as long as 100 years. The Bureau has attempted to find out whether each variable goes down before, at, or after the peak of the business cycle, and whether it turns up before, at, or after the trough. Variables that go down before the peak and up before the trough are called **leading series.** Variables that go down at the peak and up at the trough are called **coincident series.** And those that go down after the peak and up after the trough are called **lagging series.**

It is worthwhile examining the kinds of variables that fall into each of these three categories, since they give us important facts concerning the anatomy of the cycle. According to the Bureau, *some important leading series are business failures, new orders for durable goods, average work week, building contracts, stock prices, certain wholesale prices, and new incorporations.* These are the variables that tend to turn down before the peak and turn up before the trough.[4] Coincident series include employment, industrial production, corporate profits, and gross national product, among many others. Some typical lagging series are retail sales, manufacturers' inventories, and personal income.

HOW LEADING INDICATORS ARE USED, AND WITH WHAT SUCCESS

Economists sometimes use leading series as forecasting devices. There are good economic reasons why these series turn down before a peak or up

---

[4] Of course, business failures turn *up* before the peak and *down* before the trough.

before a trough. In some cases, they indicate changes in spending in strategic areas of the economy, while in others they indicate changes in business executives' and investors' expectations. Both to guide the government in determining its economic policies and to guide firms in their planning, it is important to try to spot turning points—peaks and troughs—in advance. This, of course, is the toughest part of economic forecasting. Economists sometimes use these leading indicators as evidence that a turning point is about to occur. *If a large number of leading indicators turn down, this is viewed as a sign of a coming peak. If a large number turn up, this is thought to signal an impending trough.* The Department of Commerce publishes a composite index that is a weighted average of twelve leading indicators, such as those listed in the previous paragraph. The behavior of this index is shown in Figure 13.3.

Unfortunately, the leading indicators are not very reliable. It is true that the economy has seldom turned down in recent years without a warning from these indicators. This is fine. But unfortunately these indicators have turned down on a number of occasions—1952 and 1962, for example—when the economy did not turn down subsequently. Thus they sometimes provide false signals. Also, in periods of expansion, they sometimes turn down too long before the real peak. And in periods of recession, they sometimes turn up only a very short while before the trough, so that they give us little notice of the impending turning point. Nonetheless, these indicators are not worthless. They are watched closely and used to supplement other, more sophisticated forecasting techniques.

Figure 13.3

Leading Indicators and Real GNP, United States, 1950–84 *Both GNP and the composite index of leading indicators are plotted against time, the scales of the two series being constructed so that they can readily be compared. As you can see, the leading indicators often give warnings of impending troughs or peaks. But sometimes they herald troughs or peaks that never occur.*

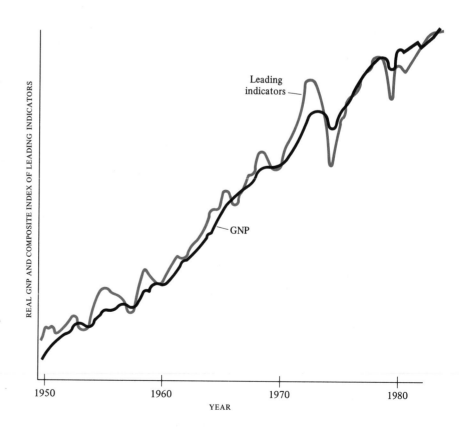

Simple Aggregate Models

Leading indicators are used primarily to spot turning points—peaks and troughs. They are of little or no use in predicting GNP (or NNP). To forecast GNP, we need a more sophisticated approach, one more firmly rooted in economic theory. (Leading indicators are largely the product of strictly empirical analysis.) To forecast GNP, it is worthwhile bringing into play the theory we described in Chapters 10–12. After all, if the theory is any good, it should help us to forecast GNP. This theory can be used in a variety of ways to help prepare such forecasts, and a first course in economics can provide no more than the most basic introduction to these methods.

A SIMPLE APPROACH

One simple way of trying to forecast GNP is to treat certain components of total spending as given and to use these components to forecast the total. This method is sometimes used by the president's Council of Economic Advisers, among others. For example, suppose that we decide to forecast investment spending and government expenditures as a first step, after which we will use these forecasts to predict GNP.[5] As we know from Chapter 7, investment spending is made up of three parts: expenditures on plant and equipment, residential construction, and changes in inventories. *To forecast expenditures on plant and equipment, the results of surveys of firms' expenditure plans for the next year are helpful.* The Department of Commerce and the Securities and Exchange Commission send out questionnaires (at the beginning of each year) to a large number of firms, asking them how much they plan to spend on plant and equipment during the year. The results, which appear in March in the *Survey of Current Business* (a Department of Commerce publication), are pretty accurate. For example, the average error in 1951–63 was only about 3 percent.

These surveys can help us forecast business expenditures on plant and equipment, but what about the other parts of investment spending—residential construction and changes in inventories? Lots of techniques are used to forecast them. *Some people use construction contracts and similar indicators as the basis for forecasts of residential construction. For inventory changes, some people watch surveys (like those that have been carried out by* Fortune *magazine and the Commerce Department) which ask companies about their inventory plans.*

Next, we need a forecast of government expenditures. At the federal level, it is possible to forecast government expenditures on the basis of the president's proposed budget or Congress's appropriations (although these forecasts can sometimes be quite wrong, as in the case of the Vietnam build-up when expenditures were higher than expected). At the state and local level, it is often possible to extrapolate spending levels reasonably well.

---

[5] We continue to ignore net exports in this part of the book because they are quite small. Chapters 21–22 will study them in some detail.

HOW CAN GNP BE FORECASTED?

Suppose that, having studied as many relevant factors as we can, we finally conclude that in our best estimate investment spending plus government expenditure will equal $600 billion next year. How do we go from this estimate to an estimate of GNP? Suppose that consumers in the past have devoted about 90 percent of their disposable income to consumption expenditure, and that disposable income has been about 70 percent of GNP. Assuming that this will also be true again next year, it follows that consumption expenditure will equal 63 percent (90 percent times 70 percent) of GNP. In other words,

$$C = .63Y, \tag{13.1}$$

where C is consumption expenditure and Y is GNP. Also, by definition,

$$Y = C + I + G,$$

where I is gross private investment and G is government expenditure. Since $I + G = 600$, it follows that

$$Y = C + 600. \tag{13.2}$$

Substituting the right-hand side of Equation (13.1) for C,

$$Y = .63Y + 600,$$

or

$$Y - .63Y = 600$$
$$.37Y = 600$$
$$Y = \frac{600}{.37}$$
$$= 1,622.$$

Thus our forecast for GNP next year is $1,622 billion.

At this point, our job may seem to be over. But it really isn't; we must check this forecast in various ways. For example, it implies that consumption expenditures next year will be $1,022 billion. (Since $C = .63Y$, according to Equation (13.1), and Y equals 1,622, C must equal 1,022.) Does this seem reasonable? For example, how does it compare with the latest results of the survey of consumer buying plans carried out at the Survey Research Center at the University of Michigan? Also, the forecasted level of GNP must be compared with the productive capacity of the economy. Do we have the physical capacity to produce this much at stable prices? To what extent will the general price level be pushed upward? Moreover, our assumptions concerning investment and government spending must be re-examined in the light of our forecast of GNP. If GNP is $1,622 billion, is it reasonable to assume that I will be the amount we initially forecasted? Or do we want to revise our forecast of investment? A great many steps must be carried out before we finally put forth a GNP forecast, if we are conscientious and professional in our approach. Moreover, even after the forecast is made, it is often updated as new information becomes available, so the process goes on more or less continuously.

Econometric Models

In recent years, more and more emphasis has been placed on econometric models. *Econometric models are systems of equations estimated from past data that are used to forecast economic variables.* Twenty years ago, econometric models were in their infancy. But now the president's Council of Economic Advisers, the Treasury, the Federal Reserve Board, and other parts of the federal government pay attention to the forecasts made by econometric models—and sometimes construct their own econometric models. Business firms too hire economists to construct econometric models for them, to forecast both GNP and their own sales.

There are many kinds of econometric models. For example, some are designed to forecast wage rates; others are designed to forecast the sales of a new product; and still others are designed to forecast a particular company's share of the market. We are concerned here only with econometric models designed to forecast GNP.

The essence of any econometric model is that it blends theory and measurement. It is not merely a general, nonquantitative theory. Useful as such a theory may be, it does not in general permit quantitative or numerical forecasts. Nor is an econometric model a purely empirical result based on little or no theoretical underpinning. Although such results may also be useful, they generally are untrustworthy once the basic structure of the economic situation changes. Most econometric models designed to forecast GNP are built, at least in part, on the theoretical foundations described in previous chapters. In other words, they contain a number of equations, one of which is designed to explain consumption expenditures, one to explain investment expenditures, and so forth.

LARGE ECONOMETRIC MODELS

Econometric models, like many of the good things in life, come in various sizes. Some are composed of lots of equations; some contain only a few. Bigger models are not necessarily to be preferred to smaller ones, or vice versa. The sort of model that is best for a particular purpose depends on which one predicts best and how costly it is to operate.

In recent years, there has been a remarkable amount of activity in the economics profession here and abroad, aimed at the construction of larger econometric models, which may be able to represent the behavior of the economy in richer and more complete detail. The leading figure in the development of such models has been Nobel Laureate Lawrence Klein of the University of Pennsylvania. The principal model that he has constructed—or helped to construct—is known as the Wharton model.

The original Wharton model, published in 1967, contained about 50 equations: 3 equations that explain various components of consumer spending (consumer nondurable goods, automobiles, and other consumer durable goods), 6 equations to explain various components of private investment (expenditure on plant and equipment, residential housing, and inventory changes), 4 explaining depreciation, 4 explaining tax receipts and transfer payments, 5 explaining the level of output in various sectors of the economy, 7 explaining price level changes in various sectors of the economy, and other equations explaining hours worked, wage rates, unemployment, interest rates, profits, and other variables. This model was used to make quarterly forecasts of GNP, unemployment, changes in the price level, and other variables a year or more ahead. It was also used to forecast the effects on the economy of alternate government policies—for example, to estimate the effects of changes in tax rates on GNP and unemployment. Its forecasts were watched closely and publicized widely in the business community and in government. In recent years, the Wharton model has been extended and refined in numerous ways. It currently contains hundreds of equations.

Other large econometric models have been built by Data Resources, Inc., Chase Econometrics, Evans Economics, the University of Michigan, UCLA, and the Bureau of Economic Analyses of the Department of Commerce, among others.

THE NUTS AND BOLTS OF A SMALL ECONOMETRIC MODEL (FOR THE MATHEMATICALLY INCLINED)

The best way to get a feel for the nature of an econometric model is to examine one. Let's consider a very simple model that might be used to forecast GNP. Although it is hypothetical and far smaller than most of the models in general use, it illustrates the nature of such models.[6] Our discussion in this section, while at an elementary level, requires familiarity with the idea of, and notation for, a set of equations. Readers who do not have this familiarity can skip this section without losing the thread of the argument.

There are four variables used in this model, and the symbol for each is as follows:

Y = gross national product
C = consumption expenditure
I = investment expenditure
G = government expenditure plus net exports.

All variables are measured in billions of dollars. Another symbol that must be explained is Δ, which means the change in a particular variable. For example, ΔY means "the change in Y," or, since Y is GNP, it means "the change in GNP." Still another symbol is the subscript $_{-1}$. Any variable with a subscript $_{-1}$ means the value of the variable in the preceding period. Thus a change with a subscript $_{-1}$ means a change occurring between the previous two periods. For example, ΔC_{-1} means the change in consumption expenditure between the last period and the period before. In this model, each period is six months.

Having disposed of the preliminaries, let's look at the model. The first equation explains ΔC, the change in consumption expenditure between this period and last period. According to this equation,

$$\Delta C = 2.18 + .37\Delta Y + .10\Delta C_{-1}. \qquad (13.3)$$

---

[6] This model is not completely hypothetical. It is based in part on Irwin Friend and Paul Taubman, "A Short-Term Forecasting Model," *Review of Economics and Statistics,* August 1964. However, it is presented solely as a simple pedagogical device (for students with some mathematical background). It is not meant to be realistic.

In other words, the change in consumption expenditures equals 2.18 billion dollars plus .37 times the change in GNP between this period and last period plus .10 times the change in consumption expenditures between last period and the period before. It is reasonable to expect that the change in consumption will be directly related to the change in GNP. This follows from our discussion of the consumption function in Chapter 10. It is also reasonable to expect that the change in consumption between this period and the last will depend on the change in consumption between the last period and the one before. Basically the reason for this is that there is likely to be a lag in adjustment (due in part to the permanent-income hypothesis discussed in Chapter 10). The numbers in Equation (13.3), like those in all the equations in the model, are assumed to have been estimated from past data.

The second equation explains ΔI, the change in gross private investment expenditure between this period and the last period. According to data concerning past experience, suppose that

$$\Delta I = 1.50 + .13 (\Delta Y - \Delta Y_{-1}). \tag{13.4}$$

In other words, the change in investment expenditure equals 1.50 billion dollars plus .13 times the change in the rate of change of GNP. From the acceleration principle, one would expect that investment expenditure would be directly related to the rate of change of GNP. Thus the change in investment expenditure would be expected to vary directly with the change in the rate of change of GNP.

Finally, the third equation merely states the obvious fact that the change in GNP must equal the change in consumption expenditures plus the change in gross private investment plus the change in government expenditures (plus net exports). In other words,

$$\Delta Y = \Delta C + \Delta I + \Delta G. \tag{13.5}$$

This must be true because Y = consumption expenditure + gross private domestic investment + government expenditures (plus net exports). In other words, $Y = C + I + G$. Thus the change in Y must equal the sum of the changes in C, I, and G.

Econometric models—even small ones like this—are fairly complicated. It is easy to get so engrossed in the details of each equation that we lose sight of the basic purpose of the model—to forecast GNP, in this case. How can we use this model to forecast GNP? As a first step, let's substitute the right-hand side of Equation (13.3) for ΔC in Equation (13.5). Also, let's substitute the right-hand side of Equation (13.4) for ΔI in Equation (13.5). These substitutions give us an expression for ΔY. In particular,

$$\Delta Y = 2.18 + .37\Delta Y + .10\Delta C_{-1} + 1.50 + .13\Delta Y - .13\Delta Y_{-1} + \Delta G.$$

Collecting terms,

$$\Delta Y = 7.36 + .20\Delta C_{-1} - .26\Delta Y_{-1} + 2.00\Delta G. \tag{13.6}$$

This equation can be used to forecast the changes in gross national product between the *next* period and the *present* period. To do so, one must insert the appropriate values of ΔC_{-1}, ΔY_{-1}, and ΔG into Equation (13.6). For example, if the change in consumption between this period and the last period was $1 billion, we would substitute 1 for ΔC_{-1} in Equation

(13.6). And if the change in gross national product between this period and the last period was \$2 billion, we would substitute 2 for ΔY_{-1}. When the value of each of the variables has been inserted in Equation (13.6), we are the proud possessor of a forecast of ΔY—the change in gross national product between the next period and the present period.

Econometric Forecasts: The Track Record

GOOD PERFORMANCE DURING THE SIXTIES

How well can econometric models forecast? Table 13.2 compares the success of the Wharton model, the Friend-Taubman model, and a model constructed at the University of Michigan's Research Seminar in Quantitative Economics in predicting GNP during 1959–67 with the forecasts of the Council of Economic Advisers and a composite forecast of GNP from about 50 economists which is tabulated each year by the Federal Reserve Bank of Philadelphia. With the exception of the Friend-Taubman model, these forecasts were made at the end of the previous year. The Friend-Taubman forecasts were made in mid-March.

In this period, the econometric models seemed to do better than the average forecast of general economists. While the general economists were off, on the average, by about \$8 billion during the period, the econometric models were off by an average of about \$5 billion. The performance of the Wharton model in this period was particularly impressive. Its average error was only about \$3 billion—or less than ½ of 1 percent. In this ball game, that is a very fancy batting average.

Basic Idea #26: Although economic forecasts should be viewed with considerable caution, they tend to be better over the long run than forecasts made by non-economists. Leading indicators, simple aggregate models, and econometric models are all useful. The important point is that economic forecasts are neither sufficiently accurate to dispel much of the fog covering the economic future, nor so inaccurate as to be completely useless.

Table 13.2

PREDICTIVE RECORD OF SOME LEADING ECONOMIC FORECASTING TECHNIQUES, 1959–67

Year	Actual GNP	Average general forecast (Federal Reserve Bank of Philadelphia)	Council of Economic Advisers	Michigan model	Friend-Taubman model	Wharton model
			Error (in billions of dollars)			
1959	484	−13	—	−19	—	
1960	504	4	—	−10	—	
1961	520	− 7	—	2	—	
1962	560	4	14	4	—	1
1963	591	−11	− 6	− 6	4	1
1964	632	− 7	− 4	− 4	5	1
1965	685	−10	− 6	−14	−3	−4
1966	748	− 7	−10	− 7	—	−4
1967	790	4	6	13	—	3
Average error (1963–67)		7.8	6.4	8.8	4.0	2.8

Source: Michael Evans, *Macroeconomic Activity.* New York: Harper & Row, 1969, p. 516.

MIXED RESULTS DURING THE SEVENTIES

Before you jump to the conclusion that the problem of economic forecasting is now solved, let's turn to the predictive performance of various models in more recent years. Table 13.3 shows how well five well-known models (including those of Chase Econometrics, Data Resources, Inc., General Electric, and Wharton) forecasted the annual rate of increase of GNP during the 1970s. Clearly, these forecasts were much poorer in the mid-1970s than in the early 1970s. In particular, the average one-year forecast of the percentage change in GNP (in money terms) was off by 4.1 percentage points for the year ending in the first quarter of 1975.

An important reason for this decline in performance was the difficulty in incorporating the effects of the Arab oil embargo, the drastic oil price increase, and the high inflation rate of 1973–74 into such models. The assumption underlying any econometric model is that the basic structure of the economy—the numbers in the equations of the model—will not change much. If this assumption does not hold, the model is in trouble. After all, any econometric model is powered by past data, not magic. Another reason why the models did better during 1959–67 was that this was a period of sustained prosperity. It is easier to forecast GNP during a period when it is steadily rising (or steadily falling) than at a turning point in the business cycle, such as 1970 or 1974. Unfortunately, the turning points are often of major significance to policy makers.

After 1975, economic forecasts became significantly more accurate than in 1974. As shown in Table 13.3, the average one-year forecast of the percentage change in GNP (in money terms) was off by 2.2 percentage points for the year ending in the first quarter of 1976, by 1.7 percentage points for the year ending in the first quarter of 1977, and so on. These errors are much smaller than those for the forecasts made in 1974.

In interpreting these results, note that any forecast made by an econometric model is based on assumptions concerning the future course of government policy. Indeed, one important purpose of such forecasts is to indicate what the effects of alternative policies would be. An econometric model

Table 13.3

ERROR (IN PERCENTAGE POINTS) OF AVERAGE FORECAST BY FIVE FORECASTERS OF RATE OF INCREASE OF GNP, 1971–79

Forecast pertaining to year ending in first quarter of:	*Rate of increase of GNP (in money terms)*	*Rate of increase of GNP (in real terms)*
1971	−1.0	0.5
1972	−0.5	0.6
1973	−2.3	−1.3
1974	−0.2	3.8
1975	4.1	7.0
1976	−2.2	−3.0
1977	1.7	1.0
1978	1.8	1.7
1979	−2.3	0.1

Source: Stephen McNees, "The Forecasting Record for the 1970s," *New England Economic Review,* September 1979.

THE ECONOMIC FORECASTS OF 1984

In most respects, 1983 was a good year for the American economy. In his economic report at the beginning of 1984, President Reagan stated that: "The economy's performance in 1983 was very gratifying. . . . The 3.2 percent rise in consumer prices between 1982 and 1983 was the lowest rate of inflation since 1967. The recovery produced a sharp drop in unemployment and a substantial increase in the income of American families. . . . The 6.1 percent rise in real gross national product last year means that real annual income per person in the United States rose $700."

In its annual report, the president's Council of Economic Advisers compared the composition of the expansion in real GNP during 1983 with what has generally occurred during the first year after a postwar trough of the business cycle. The results, shown in Table 1, were reported "in terms of percentage point contributions to the total change in GNP over the four quarters of 1983. For example, real personal consumption expenditures accounted for 3.6 percentage points of the total 6.1 percent growth in real GNP; by comparison, during the first four quarters of the typical postwar recovery, personal consumption accounted for 3.6 percentage points out of the total 6.8 percent increase in real GNP. The major conclusion to be drawn from Table 1 is that the magnitude and composition of the 1983 expansion was similar in most respects to the typical first four quarters of business expansion following a cyclical trough."[1]

Table 1

CONTRIBUTION OF GNP COMPONENTS TO TOTAL GNP GROWTH OVER THE FIRST YEAR OF BUSINESS CYCLE RECOVERIES

	1982 IV to 1983 IV	Typical postwar recovery
Real GNP [percentage point change]	6.1	6.8
Personal consumption expenditures	3.6	3.6
Durable goods	1.4	1.3
Nonresidential fixed investment	1.2	.5
Producers' durable equipment	1.3	.5
Structures	−.1	.0
Residential investment	1.0	1.0
Change in business inventories	2.0	1.8
Net exports of goods and services	−1.4	−.4
Exports	.3	.0
Imports (minus denotes increase)	−1.7	−.4
Government purchases of goods and services	−.4	.3
Federal	−.5	−.2
State and local	.1	.5
Final sales	4.0	5.0

[1] Council of Economic Advisers, *Annual Report,* 1984, Washington, D.C.: Government Printing Office, p. 176.

Table 2

COUNCIL OF ECONOMIC ADVISERS' FORECASTS FOR 1984

	1983	1984 forecast
Percent change (fourth quarter to fourth quarter):		
Real gross national product	6.1	4.5
Personal consumption expenditures	5.4	2.0
Nonresidential fixed investment	11.5	9.5
Residential investment	38.2	6.0
Federal purchases	−6.0	3.7
State and local purchases	.6	4.2
GNP implicit price deflator	4.1	5.0
Compensation per hour	4.6	5.5
Output per hour	3.2	2.1
Level in fourth quarter:		
Unemployment rate (percent)	8.4	7.6
Housing starts (millions of units, annual rate)	1.7	1.8

Having reviewed economic developments in 1983, the CEA proceeded to forecast what would occur in 1984. Its forecast of the economic outlook, shown in Table 2, called for the rate of growth of real GNP to fall to about 4.5 percent in 1984, for the unemployment rate to be about 7.6 percent in the fourth quarter of 1984, and for the inflation rate to rise slightly to about 5 percent.

Other private forecasts were not vastly different. Data Resources, Inc., predicted a 4.4 percent increase in real GNP, a 7.8 percent unemployment rate, and a 5 percent inflation rate. Chase Econometrics forecasted a 4 percent increase in real GNP, an 8.1 percent unemployment rate, and a 5 percent inflation rate. Wharton Econometrics came up with a 6.6 percent increase in real GNP, a 7.8 percent unemployment rate, and a 3.9 percent inflation rate.

What actually happened? In December 1984, the U.S. Department of Commerce reported that real GNP had increased by about 6.7 percent during 1984. According to the U.S. Department of Labor, the civilian unemployment rate in November 1984 was 7.2 percent, and the Consumer Price Index in November 1984 was 4 percent higher than in November 1983.

A number of magazines and newspapers ran articles criticizing economic forecasters for their performance. *Time* magazine pointed out that most forecasts had underestimated the rate of growth of real GNP and overestimated the rate of inflation. This was true for most forecasters, but not for all. Wharton's forecasts for the year as a whole seemed quite accurate.

The most important moral to be drawn from this brief case study is that it is unrealistic to expect economic forecasters to hit the target on the nose. No reputable economist would claim that he or she could do so. Moreover, to be useful, economic forecasts frequently do not have to be very accurate. For many purposes, all that is required is a rough estimate of what will occur, a partial dissipation of the fog that surrounds the economic future.

may be more accurate in forecasting the effects of such policies than in forecasting what actually occurs. Suppose that a forecast is based on the incorrect assumption that the government is going to cut taxes. Even though this incorrect assumption may result in a poor forecast, the model may forecast the effect of such a tax cut reasonably well. That is, it may be a good forecaster of the change in GNP due to the tax cut—and this may be what policy makers are most interested in.

THE EIGHTIES AND BEYOND

Economic forecasting remains a difficult and uncertain business, as illustrated by the forecasts (made at the end of 1983) of what would occur in 1984. Most economists underestimated the rate of increase of real GNP, and overestimated the inflation rate, in the first half of the year. The result was a good deal of criticism of economic forecasters in the newspapers and popular magazines. (See the cross-chapter case on pp. 290–91.)

Nonetheless, despite the rather large errors in some recent economic forecasts, neither government nor industry can swear off forecasting. For decades, economic forecasting has played an important role in the decision-making process, both in government and industry. In recent years, President Reagan has relied on economic forecasts prepared by the Council of Economic Advisers to help him formulate policies dealing with inflation, unemployment, and a host of other topics. Presidents Eisenhower, Kennedy, Johnson, Nixon, Ford, and Carter also paid close attention to economic forecasts. So do most corporate presidents. This isn't because these forecasts are always very good. It's because they are the best available. As Thomas Huxley put it, "If a little knowledge is dangerous, who is the man who has so much as to be out of danger?"

Test Yourself

1. "What goes up must come down. There is a cycle in economic activity just as in many other things, and one can use this cycle to forecast quite accurately." Comment and evaluate.

2. A leading business magazine reports that the leading indicators "are dead on center. This suggests that, although the downward trend of business has halted, there is still no clear upward thrust." Explain what this means.

3. Suppose that consumption expenditure was $100 billion in 1983 and $105 billion in 1984, and that GNP increased by $10 billion per year from 1984 to 1989. Based on Equation (13.3), what was the value of consumption expenditure from 1985 to 1989?

4. Suppose that investment spending plus government expenditure will equal $700 billion next year, and that consumption expenditure will equal 65 percent of GNP. Forecast next year's GNP.

5. In Question 4, suppose that your estimate of investment expenditure plus government expenditure is in error by $10 billion. If your other estimates are correct how big an error will occur in your forecast of GNP?

Summary

1. Changes in sales can result in magnified or accelerated changes in investment; the amount of gross investment depends on the rate of increase of sales. The fact that sales are increasing does not insure that gross investment will increase. On the contrary, if sales are increasing by decreasing amounts, gross investment is likely to fall. This effect of sales on investment is called the acceleration principle.

2. The interaction of the acceleration principle with the multiplier can cause business cycles. Thus turning points can be generated within the economic system. Investment is also determined by many events that occur more or less at random, like innovations, wars, and so on. The effects of these random shocks can also cause business fluctuations. Many short cycles are inventory cycles. The acceleration principle also applies to inventories.

3. The government's economic activities can help to cause business fluctuations. Particularly during and after wars, government spending has sometimes been a major destabilizing force. In addition, according to a number of prominent economists, some business fluctuations have been due to politicians' use of fiscal (and monetary) policy for their own political ends.

4. Although we are not in a position to erase the small dips and pauses in economic activity, it seems extremely unlikely that we will have another depression of the severity of the 1930s. The reason is that policy makers—and the electorate—know that monetary and fiscal policy can be used to push the economy back toward full employment. However, the prospect for price stability may not be so bright.

5. Although economics is by no means an exact science, economic forecasts are useful for many purposes. This does not mean that these forecasts are always very accurate. It means only that they are better than noneconomists' forecasts. Economists have a number of techniques for forecasting. One makes use of leading indicators—variables that historically have turned up or down before GNP.

6. Another technique is based on the use of simple models plus surveys and other data. Investment and government expenditures (and net exports) are sometimes estimated as a first step. Then, using the historical relationship between consumption and GNP, it is possible to forecast GNP.

7. Still another technique is based on econometric models, which are systems of equations estimated from past data. Econometric models blend theory and measurement. Econometric models may be big or small.

8. Econometric models have frequently done better than the average forecasts of general economists. However, it is important to recognize that econometric models —like any forecasting device in the social sciences—are quite fallible, as indicated by the large errors in the 1974 forecasts.

Concepts for Review

Acceleration principle	**Expectations**	**Lagging series**
Random shocks	**Leading series**	**Econometric models**
Inventory cycle	**Coincident series**	

PART FOUR

Money, Banking, and Stabilization Policy

CHAPTER 14

Money and the Economy

According to the maxim of an ancient Roman, "Money alone sets all the world in motion." Although a statement that leaves so little room for the laws of physics or astronomy may be a mite extravagant, no one would deny the importance of money in economic affairs. The quantity of money is a very significant factor in determining the health and prosperity of any economic system. Inadequate increases in the quantity of money may bring about excessive unemployment, while excessive increases in the quantity of money may result in serious inflation. To many economists, a discussion of business fluctuations and economic stabilization that ignores the money supply is like a performance of *Hamlet* that omits the prince.

In this chapter, we are concerned with the nature and value of money, as well as with the relationship between a nation's money supply and the extent of unemployment and inflation. In particular, we consider questions like: What is money? What determines its value? What factors influence the demand for money, and what factors influence its quantity? What is the relationship between the quantity of money and the price level? What is the relationship between the quantity of money and the level of net national product? To understand the workings of our economy and the nature of our government's economic policies, you must be able to answer these questions.

What Is Money?

We begin by defining money. At first blush, it may seem natural to define it by its physical characteristics. You may be inclined to say that money consists of bills of a certain size and color with certain words and symbols printed on them, as well as coins of a certain type. But this definition would be too restrictive, since money in other societies has consisted of whale teeth, wampum, and a variety of other things. Thus it seems better to define money by its functions than by its physical characteristics. Like beauty, money is as money does.

MEDIUM OF EXCHANGE

Money acts as a medium of exchange. People exchange their goods and services for something called money, and then use this money to buy the goods and services they want. To see how important money is as a medium of exchange, let's suppose that it did not exist. To exchange the goods and services they produce for the goods and services they want to consume, people would resort to *barter,* or direct exchange. If you were a wheat farmer, you would have to go to the people who produce the meat, clothes, and other goods and services you want, and swap some of your wheat for each of these goods and services. Of course this would be a very cumbersome procedure, since it would take lots of time and effort to locate and make individual bargains with each of these people. To get some idea of the extent to which money greases the process of exchange in any highly developed economy, consider all the purchases your family made last year—cheese from Wisconsin and France, automobiles from Detroit, oil from Texas and the Middle East, books from New York, and thousands of other items from all over the world. Imagine how few of these exchanges would have been feasible without money.

STANDARD OF VALUE, STORE OF VALUE

Money acts as a standard of value. It is the unit in which the prices of goods and services are measured. How do we express the price of coffee or tea or shirts or suits? In dollars and cents. Thus money prices tell us the rates at which goods and services can be exchanged. If the money price of a shirt is $30 and the money price of a tie is $10, a shirt will exchange for 3 ties. Put differently, a shirt will be "worth" 3 times as much as a tie.

Money acts as a store of value. A person can hold on to money and use it to buy things later. You often hear stories about people who hoard a lot of money under their mattresses or bury it in their back yards. These people have an overdeveloped appreciation of the role of money as a store of value. But even those of us who are less miserly use this function of money when we carry some money with us, and keep some in the bank to make future purchases.

Finally, it should be recognized that money is a social invention. It is easy to assume that money has always existed, but this is not the case. Someone had to get the idea, and people had to come to accept it. Nor has money always had the characteristics it has today. In ancient Greece and Rome, money consisted of gold and silver coins. By the end of the seventeenth century, paper money was established in England; but this paper currency, unlike today's currency, could be exchanged for a stipulated amount of gold. Only recently has the transition been made to money that is not convertible into a fixed amount of gold or silver. But regardless of its form or characteristics, anything that is a medium of exchange, a standard of value, and a store of value is money.

The Money Supply, Narrowly Defined

In practice, it is not easy to draw a hard-and-fast line between what is money and what is not money, for reasons discussed below. But everyone agrees that coins, currency, demand deposits, and other checkable deposits are money. And the sum total of coins, currency, demand deposits, and other checkable deposits is called the money supply, narrowly defined.[1]

COINS AND CURRENCY

Coins are a small proportion of the total quantity of money in the United States. This is mainly because coins come in such small denominations. It takes a small mountain of pennies, nickels, dimes, quarters, and half-dollars to make even a billion dollars. Of course, the metal in each of these coins is worth less than the face value of the coin; otherwise people would melt them down and make money by selling the metal. In the 1960s, when silver prices rose, the government stopped using silver in dimes and quarters to prevent coins from meeting this fate.

Currency—paper money like the $5 and $10 bills everyone likes to have on hand—constitutes a second and far larger share of the total money supply than coins. Together, currency and coins outstanding totaled about $159 billion in 1984, as shown in Table 14.1. The Federal Reserve System, described in the next chapter, issues practically all of our currency in the form of Federal Reserve notes. Before 1933, it was possible to exchange currency for a stipulated amount of gold, but this is no longer the case. (The price of gold on the free market varies; thus the amount of gold one can get for a dollar varies too.) All American currency (and coin) is presently "fiat" money. It is money because the government says so and because the people accept it. There is no metallic backing of the currency anymore. But this does not mean that we should be suspicious of the soundness of our currency, since gold backing is not what gives money its value. (In fact, to some extent, cause and effect work the other way. The use of gold to back currencies has in the past increased the value of gold.) Basically, the value of currency depends on its acceptability by people. And the government, to insure its acceptability, must limit its quantity.

DEMAND DEPOSITS AND OTHER CHECKABLE DEPOSITS

Demand deposits—bank deposits subject to payment on demand—are the third part of the narrowly defined money supply. They are much larger than the other two parts, as shown in Table 14.1. At first you may question whether these demand deposits—or checking accounts, as they are commonly called—are money at all. In everyday speech, they often are not considered money. But economists include demand deposits as part of the money supply, and for good reason. After all, you can pay for goods and

Table 14.1

MONEY SUPPLY, NOVEMBER 1984

	Amount (billions of dollars)
Demand deposits	248
Currency and coins[a]	159
Other checkable deposits[b]	142
Travelers checks[c]	5
Total[d]	553

[a] Only currency and coins outside bank vaults (and the Treasury and Federal Reserve) are included.
[b] Includes ATS and NOW balances at all institutions, credit union, share draft, and other minor items.
[c] See footnote 1.
[d] Because of rounding errors, figures do not sum to total.

[1] In addition, travelers checks are included in the money supply, narrowly defined, since one can pay for goods and services about as easily with travelers checks as with cash. As indicated in Table 14.1, travelers checks are only about 1 percent of the money supply, narrowly defined. Since they are so small a percentage of the money supply, we ignore them in the following discussion.

services just as easily by check as with cash. Indeed, the public pays for more things by check than with cash. This means that checking accounts are just as much a medium of exchange—and just as much a standard of value and a store of value—as cash. Thus, since they perform all of the functions of money, they should be included as money.

Other checkable deposits include negotiable order of withdrawal (NOW) accounts and other accounts that are very close to being demand deposits. A *NOW account* is essentially an interest-bearing checking account at banks, savings banks and other thrift institutions. First created in 1972 by a Massachusetts savings bank, such accounts became legal in more and more states, particularly in the northeast. In 1980, Congress passed a financial reform act that permitted federally chartered thrift institutions to have NOW accounts. Banking innovations like NOW accounts have blurred the distinction between checking and savings accounts. Since many savings and loan associations, mutual savings banks, and credit unions are now providing accounts against which checks can be drawn, it would make no sense to include as money only demand deposits in commercial banks. Instead, all such checkable deposits are included.

Figure 14.1 shows how the narrowly defined money supply—the sum total of coins, paper currency, demand deposits, and other checkable deposits—has behaved since World War II. You can see that the quantity of

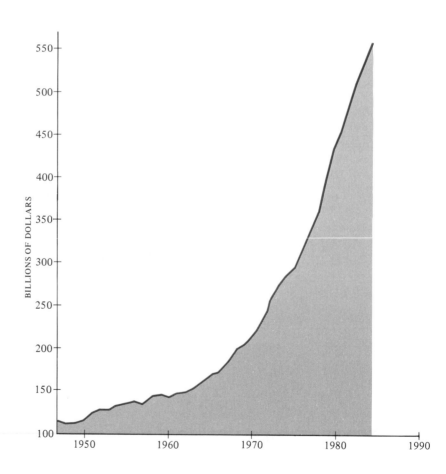

Figure 14.1
Behavior of Money Supply (Narrowly Defined), United States, 1947–84 *The money supply, about $550 billion in 1984, has generally increased from year to year, but the rate of increase has by no means been constant.*

money has generally increased from one year to the next, and that the increase has been at an average rate of about 4 or 5 percent per year. However, the rate of increase of the quantity of money has by no means been constant. In some years, like 1983, the quantity of money increased by about 9 percent; in others, like 1975, it increased by about 4 percent. A great deal will be said later about the importance and determinants of changes in the quantity of money.

The Money Supply, Broadly Defined

The narrowly defined money supply (which includes coins, currency, demand deposits, and other checkable deposits) is not the only definition of the money supply that is used by economists. There is also the money supply, broadly defined, which includes savings and small time deposits (deposits under $100,000 with a specific maturity, for example, one year) and money market mutual fund balances and money market deposit accounts, as well as coins, currency, demand deposits, and other checkable deposits. The money supply, narrowly defined, is often called *M*-1, while the money supply, broadly defined, is often called *M*-2.

The traditional reason for excluding time and saving deposits from the narrow definition of money has been that, in most instances, you could not pay for anything with them. For example, suppose that you had a savings account at a commercial bank. You could not draw a check against it, as you could with a demand deposit. And to withdraw your money from the account, you might have to give the bank a certain amount of notice (although in practice this right might be waived and the bank would ordinarily let you withdraw your money when you desired). Nonetheless, since this savings account could so readily be transformed into cash, it was almost like a checking account. Not quite, but almost.

Besides time and savings accounts, many other assets can also be transformed into cash without much difficulty—though not quite as easily as time and savings deposits. For example, it is not difficult to convert government bonds into cash. There is no way to draw a hard-and-fast dividing line between money and nonmoney, since many assets have some of the characteristics of money. Consequently, there are still other definitions of the money supply that are more inclusive than *M*-2. But most economists feel that, although assets like government bonds have some of the properties of money, it would be stretching things too far to include them in the money supply. (For one thing, their price varies as interest rates change.)

Economists call such assets *near-money,* and recognize that the amount of near-money in the economy has an important effect on spending habits. There is some disagreement among economists as to exactly what is and what isn't near-money, but this needn't concern us here. The major point we want to make is that any dividing line between money and nonmoney must be arbitrary.

In this book, we shall use the narrow definition, *M*-1, when we refer to the money supply. But it should be recognized that the choice is arbitrary.

Fortunately, our results will not depend in any very important way on this decision.

The Value of Money

Let's go back to one very important point that was mentioned briefly in a previous section. There is no gold backing for our money. In other words, there is no way that you can exchange a $10 bill for so many ounces of gold. (If you look at a $10 bill, you will see that it says nothing about what the government will give you in exchange for it.) Currency and demand (and other checkable) deposits are really just debts, or IOUs. Currency is the debt of the government, while demand deposits are the debts of the banks. Intrinsically, neither currency nor deposits have any real value. A $10 bill is merely a small piece of paper, and a deposit is merely an entry in a bank's accounts. And, as we have seen, even coins are worth far less as metal than their monetary value.

All this may make you feel a bit uncomfortable. After all, if our coins, currency, demand deposits, and other checkable deposits have little or no intrinsic value, doesn't this mean that they can easily become worthless? To answer this question, we must realize that basically, *money has value because people will accept it in payment for goods and services.* If your university will accept your check in payment for your tuition, and your grocer will accept a $20 bill in payment for your groceries, your demand deposit and your currency have value. You can exchange them for goods and services you want. And your university or your grocer accepts this money only because they have confidence that they can spend it for goods and services they want.

MONEY'S VALUE DEPENDS ON THE PRICE LEVEL

Thus money is valuable because it will buy things. But how valuable is it? For example, how valuable is $1? Clearly, *the value of a dollar is equivalent to what a dollar will buy. And what a dollar will buy depends on the price level.* If all prices doubled, the value of a dollar would be cut in half, because a dollar would be able to buy only half as many goods and services as it formerly could. On the other hand, if all prices were reduced by 50 percent, the value of a dollar would double, because a dollar would be able to buy twice as many goods and services as it formerly could. You often hear people say that today's dollar is worth only $.50. What they mean is that it will buy only half what a dollar could buy at some specified date in the past.

It is interesting and important to see how the value of the dollar, as measured by its purchasing power, has varied over time. Figure 14.2 shows how an index of the price level in the United States has changed since 1779. Over time, prices have fluctuated sharply, and the greatest fluctuations have resulted from wars. For example, the price level fell sharply after the Revolutionary War, and our next war—the War of 1812—sent prices skyrocketing, after which there was another postwar drop in prices. The period from about 1820 to about 1860 was marked by

Figure 14.2

Index of Wholesale Prices, United States, 1779-1984 (1910-14 = 100) *The price level has fluctuated considerably, sharp increases generally occurring during wars. Since World War II, the price level has tended to go only one way—up. In the past 20 years, the price level has more than tripled.*

relative price stability, but the Civil War resulted in an upward burst followed by a postwar drop in prices. After a period of relative price stability from 1875 to 1915, there was a doubling of prices during World War I and the usual postwar drop. World War II saw an increase of about 40 percent, but there was no postwar drop in prices. Instead there has been a very sharp inflation. During the past 20 years, the price level has more than tripled.

The value of money is inversely related to the price level. In inflationary times, the value of money decreases; the opposite is true when the price level falls (an infrequent phenomenon in the past three decades). Thus the wartime periods when the price level rose greatly were periods when the value of the dollar decreased greatly. The doubling of prices during World War I meant that the value of the dollar was chopped in half. Similarly, the postwar periods when the price level fell greatly were periods when the value of the dollar increased. The 50 percent decline in prices after the Civil War meant a doubling in the value of the dollar. Given the extent of the variation of the price level shown in Figure 14.2, it is clear that the value of the dollar has varied enormously during our history.

Inflation and the Quantity of Money

As we have pointed out repeatedly, the value of money is reduced in periods of inflation. In runaway inflation, its value can be largely wiped out, as in Germany after World War I. (Recall Chapter 8.) Our own country suffered from runaway inflations during the Revolutionary War and the Civil War. You may have heard the expression that something is "not worth a continental." It comes from the fact that the inflated dollars in use during the Revolutionary War were called continentals.

Generally, such severe inflations have occurred because the government increased the money supply at an enormously rapid rate. It is not hard to see why a tremendous increase in the quantity of money will result in a runaway inflation. Other things held constant, increases in the quantity of money will result in increases in total intended spending, and once full employment is achieved, such increases in intended spending will cause more and more inflation.

Eventually, when the inflation is severe enough, households and businesses may refuse to accept money for goods and services because they fear that it will depreciate significantly before they have a chance to spend it. Instead, they may insist on being paid in merchandise or services. Thus the economy will turn to barter, with the accompanying inconveniences and inefficiency.

To prevent such an economic catastrophe, the government must manage the money supply responsibly. As we have stressed in previous sections, the value of money depends basically on the public's willingness to accept it, and the public's willingness to accept it depends on money's being reasonably stable in value. If the government increases the quantity of money at a rapid rate, thus causing a severe inflation and an accompanying precipitous fall in the value of money, public confidence in money will be shaken, and the value of money will be destroyed. The moral is clear: *the government must restrict the quantity of money, and conduct its economic policies so as to maintain a reasonably stable value of money.*

Unemployment and the Quantity of Money

In the previous section, we were concerned primarily with what happens when the quantity of money grows too rapidly. As we have seen, the result is inflation. But this is only part of the story. The quantity of money can grow too slowly as well as too rapidly; and when this happens the result is increased unemployment. If the money supply grows very slowly, or decreases, there will be a tendency for total intended spending to grow very slowly or decrease. This in turn will cause national output to grow very slowly or decrease, thus causing unemployment to increase. The result will be the social waste and human misery associated with excessive unemployment.

According to many economists, the recession of 1974–75 was due partly to an inadequate growth of the money supply. The Federal Reserve, trying to stem the inflationary tide in 1974, cut back on the rate of increase of the money supply. Looking back over past business fluctuations, it appears that an inadequate rate of increase in the quantity of money was responsible, at least in part, for many recessions. According to Harvard's James Duesenberry, "Every major depression has been accompanied by a substantial decline in the money supply, and often by a complete collapse of the banking system. Among the many causes responsible for our major depressions, money and banking difficulties have always been prominent."[2] Recall that in our discussion of business fluctuations in the previous chapter, we stressed the importance of monetary factors. In this chapter, as well as Chapters 15 to 18, we will study these factors in detail.

Determinants of the Quantity of Money

Judging from our discussion thus far, it is clear that to avoid excessive unemployment or excessive inflation, the quantity of money must not grow too slowly or too fast. But what determines the quantity of money? When the United States was on the gold standard, the amount of money in circulation was determined by the amount of monetary gold in the country. When gold flowed into the country, the money supply increased; when it flowed out, the money supply decreased. This is no longer the case, since we are no longer on the gold standard—and neither is any other major nation.

If gold doesn't determine the amount of money in circulation in the U.S., what does? The answer is that the supply of money is determined to a considerable degree by the Federal Reserve, which, as we have noted before, is our nation's central bank. Within limits, the Federal Reserve can and does control the quantity of money. But to some extent the private sector of the

---

[2] J. Duesenberry, *Money and Credit: Impact and Control,* Englewood Cliffs, N.J.: Prentice-Hall, 1972, p. 3.

economy also determines the quantity of money. For example, the nation's commercial banks, through their lending (and other) decisions, can influence the money supply.[3] In the remainder of this chapter, we shall make the simplifying assumption that the money supply is governed solely by the Federal Reserve. In the following chapter, we shall see how the commercial banks also play an important role in this regard.

The Demand for Money

We have discussed in general terms how changes in the quantity of money affect the tempo of economic activity. Now let's look in detail at how changes in the quantity of money affect net national product. The first step in doing this is to discuss the demand for money. Why does a family or firm want to hold money? Certainly, a family can be wealthy without holding much money. We all know stories about very rich people who hold very little money, since virtually all of their wealth is tied up in factories, farms, and other nonmonetary assets. Unlike assets that yield profits or interest, money produces no direct return; so why do people and firms want to hold money, rather than other kinds of assets? Two of the most important reasons are the following.

1. Transactions Demand for Money. To carry out most transactions, money is required. Thus people and firms like to keep some money on their person and in their checking accounts to buy things. The higher a person's income—in dollars, not real terms—the more money he or she will want to hold for transaction purposes. For example, in 1985, when a doctor makes about $90,000 a year, the average physician will want to keep more money on hand for transactions purposes than in the days—many years ago— when a doctor made perhaps $10,000 a year. Because the quantity of money demanded by a household or firm increases with its income, it follows that the total quantity of money demanded for transactions purposes in the economy as a whole is directly related to net national product. That is, the higher (lower) the level of NNP, the greater (less) the quantity of money demanded for transactions purposes.

2. Precautionary Demand for Money. Besides the transactions motive, households and firms like to hold money because they are uncertain concerning the timing and size of future disbursements and receipts. Unpredictable events often require money. People get sick, and houses need repairs. Also, receipts frequently do not come in exactly when expected. To meet such contingencies, people and firms like to put a certain amount of their wealth into money and near-money. In the economy as a whole, the total quantity of money demanded for precautionary purposes (like the quantity demanded for transactions purposes) is likely to vary directly with NNP. If NNP goes up, households and firms will want to hold more money for pre-

---

[3] Of course, banks do not create money all by themselves. The public's preferences and actions, as well as bank behavior, influence the amount of demand deposits. Also, commercial banks may not be as unique in this respect as it appears at first sight. See James Tobin, "Commercial Banks as Creators of Money" in R. Teigen, ed., *Readings in Money, National Income, and Stabilization Policy,* 4th ed., Homewood, Ill.: Irwin, 1978.

cautionary purposes, because their incomes and sales will be higher than before the increase in NNP.[4]

THE INTEREST RATE AND THE DEMAND CURVE FOR MONEY

Up to this point, we have discussed why individuals and firms want to hold money. But we must recognize that there are disadvantages, as well

[4] Still another motive for holding money is the speculative motive. People like to hold some of their assets in a form in which they can be sure of its monetary value and can take advantage of future price reductions. The amount of money individuals and firms will keep on hand for speculative reasons will vary with their expectation concerning future price movements. In particular, if people feel that the prices of bonds and stocks are about to drop soon, they are likely to demand a great deal of money for speculative reasons. By holding money, they can obtain such securities at lower prices than at present.

Example 14.1   Empirical Evidence Regarding the Demand for Money

In 1973, Stephen Goldfeld of Princeton University made a study of the factors influencing the demand for money.* He found that a 1 percent increase in real GNP or a 1 percent increase in interest rates had the following effect on the real quantity of money demanded (that is, the quantity of money demanded divided by the price level):

	Effect of 1 percent increase in real GNP (percent)	Effect of 1 percent increase in interest rate (percent)
Short run	+0.19	−0.045
Long run	+0.68	−0.160

(a) The short-run effects are the effects after three months; the long-run effects are the effects after a few years. Why are the effects in the long run greater than in the short run? (b) If real GNP increases by 10 percent, what is the effect on the real quantity of money demanded in the long run? (c) If the interest rate increases from 8 percent to 10 percent, what is the effect on the real quantity of money demanded in the short run? (d) Goldfeld also found that the quantity of money demanded is proportional to the price level. Why do you think that this is the case?

SOLUTION

(a) Because it takes time for households and business firms to recognize and adapt to changing conditions. In the short run, they tend to be locked in to existing patterns of behavior, and it takes time to adjust. (b) The real quantity of money demanded will increase by about 6.8 percent. (c) Since the interest rate increases by 25 percent (from 8 to 10 percent), the real quantity of money demanded will fall by about 25 × .045, or 1.125 percent. (d) People demand money to pay for things. As the price level goes up, they require more money to pay for the same things. In other words, as the price level goes up, more money is demanded in order to have the same purchasing power as before.

* Stephen Goldfeld, "The Demand for Money Revisited," *Brookings Papers on Economic Activity,* 1973. For simplicity, only his results concerning the interest rate for time deposits are included. Also, see R. Dornbusch and S. Fisher, *Macroeconomics,* New York: McGraw-Hill, 1978.

---

as advantages, in holding money. One is that the real value of money will fall if inflation occurs. Another is that an important cost of holding money is the interest or profit one loses, since instead of holding money, one might have invested it in assets that would have yielded interest or profit. For example, the annual cost of holding $5,000 in money if one can obtain 6 percent on existing investments, is $300, the amount of interest or profit forgone.

With NNP constant, the amount of money demanded by individuals and firms is *inversely* related to the interest rate. *The higher the interest rate, the smaller the amount of money demanded. The lower the interest rate, the greater the amount of money demanded.* This is because the cost of holding money increases as the interest rate or yield on existing investments increases. For example, if the interest rate were 7 percent rather than 6 percent, the cost of holding $5,000 in money for one year would be $350 rather than $300. Thus, as the interest rate or profit rate increases, people try harder to minimize the amount of money they hold. So do firms. Big corporations like IBM or U.S. Steel are very conscious of the cost of holding cash balances.

Figure 14.3 summarizes two important conclusions of our discussion in this and the previous section. Panel A of Figure 14.3 shows that, *holding the interest rate constant, the quantity of money demanded is directly related to NNP.* As we explained in the previous section, the higher (lower) the level of NNP, the greater (less) the quantity of money demanded. Panel B of Figure 14.3 shows that, *with NNP constant, the quantity of money demanded is inversely related to the interest rate.*[5] This latter relationship, described in this section, is called the ***demand curve for money.***

Figure 14.3

The Demand for Money Holding the *interest rate constant, the quantity of money demanded is* directly *related to NNP, as shown in panel A. Holding NNP constant, the quantity of money demanded is* inversely *related to the interest rate, as shown in panel B. The latter relationship is known as the demand curve for money.*

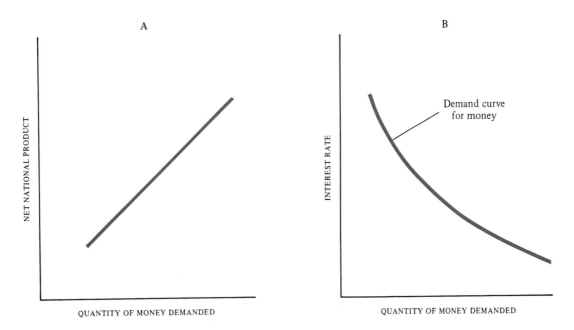

A

NET NATIONAL PRODUCT

QUANTITY OF MONEY DEMANDED

B

INTEREST RATE

Demand curve for money

QUANTITY OF MONEY DEMANDED

[5] However, this relationship between the quantity of money and the interest rate is only short-run. In the long run, increases in the money supply, if they result in increased inflation, may *raise* interest rates, because lenders will require a greater return to offset the greater rate of depreciation of the real value of the dollar. Still, however, the real rate of interest—the rate of interest adjusted for inflation—may decline.

Test Yourself

1. "Money, in and of itself, has no value whatsoever. It is valuable only because of what it can buy." Comment and evaluate.

2. Explain in detail why the following items are not money: (a) government bonds, (b) U.S. Steel stock, (c) gold, (d) uranium.

3. Give some reasons why savings accounts should be regarded as money. Give some reasons why they should not. Which side of the argument do you find more convincing?

4. Why is the interest rate regarded as the "price" of holding money? What factors will shift the demand curve for money to the right? To the left?

Changes in the Money Supply and National Output

EFFECTS OF AN INCREASE IN THE MONEY SUPPLY: THE KEYNESIAN MODEL

Now that we have investigated the demand for money, we are ready to show how changes in the quantity of money influence the value of NNP. Given the demand curve for money, it is a simple matter to show how the money supply can be inserted into the Keynesian model (in Chapters 10 to 12) aimed at explaining the level of NNP.

To begin with, let's trace the effects of an increase in the money supply from $200 billion to $250 billion. If the demand curve for money is as shown in panel A of Figure 14.4, the result will be a *decrease in the interest rate* from 8 percent to 6 percent. Why? Because, if the interest rate is 8 percent, people will demand only $200 billion of money, not the $250 billion that is supplied. Having more money on hand than they want, they will invest the excess in bonds, stocks, and other financial assets, with the result that the price of bonds, stocks, and other financial assets will rise.[6]

Such a rise in the price of bonds is equivalent to a fall in the rate of interest. (To see why, suppose that a very long-term bond pays interest of $300 per year. If the price of the bond is $3,000, the interest rate on the bond is 10 percent. If the price of the bond rises to $4,000, the interest rate on the bond falls to 7½ percent. Thus the increase in price amounts to a reduction in the interest rate.) When the interest rate has fallen to 6 percent, people will be willing to hold the $250 billion in money. At this interest rate, the quantity of money demanded will equal the quantity of money supplied.

The decrease in the interest rate from 8 percent to 6 percent affects the investment function.[7] Recall from Chapter 10 that the level of investment is inversely related to the interest rate. Because it is less costly to invest—and

---

[6] For simplicity, we assume that when people have excess money balances, they use the money to buy financial assets. (In the next section, we assume that when people have smaller money balances than they want, they sell financial assets to get more money.) A more complete analysis is provided in Chapter 17 and in the Appendix to this book. The results are essentially the same as those provided here.

[7] Changes in the money supply, interest rates, and credit availability affect the consumption function and government spending, as well as the investment function. For example, *increases (decreases) in interest rates shift the consumption function and the level of government spending*

A. Demand curve for money

INTEREST RATE (percent)

8
6

0

200 250

QUANTITY OF MONEY
(billions of dollars)

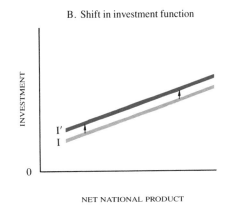

B. Shift in investment function

INVESTMENT

I'
I

0

NET NATIONAL PRODUCT

C. Change in net national product

INTENDED SPENDING

45°

C + I' + G
C + I + G

0

D E

NET NATIONAL PRODUCT

Figure 14.4

Effect of an Increase in the Money Supply *If the money supply increases from $200 billion to $250 billion, the interest rate drops from 8 percent to 6 percent (panel A). Because of the decrease in the interest rate, the investment function shifts upward (panel B), and the equilibrium level of NNP increases from D to E (panel C).*

because credit is more readily available[8]—*the investment function will shift upward,* as shown in panel B of Figure 14.4. This occurs because at each level of net national product, firms will want to invest more, since investment is more profitable (because of the cut in the interest rate) and funds are more readily available.[9]

This shift in the investment function then affects the equilibrium level of net national product. As shown in panel C of Figure 14.4, *the equilibrium level of net national product will increase* from *D* to *E,* in accord with the principles discussed in Chapter 12. (Recall that the equilibrium value of NNP is at the point where the *C + I + G* line intersects the 45-degree line.) Thus *the effect of the increase in the money supply is to increase net national product.*

This, in simplified fashion, is how an increase in the money supply affects NNP, according to the Keynesian model.[10] To summarize, *the increase in the money supply results in a reduction in the interest rate, which results in an increase in investment, which results in an increase in NNP.* Obviously, this theory is of great importance in helping us to understand more completely why our economy behaves the way it does. For example, we can now understand better why vast increases in the quantity of money will result in runaway inflation. NNP (in money terms) will be pushed upward at a very rapid rate, driving the price level out of sight.

downward (upward). These factors augment the effect of monetary policy described in the text. We focus attention on the investment function in Figures 14.4 and 14.5 merely because this simplifies the exposition.

[8] Note that it is not just a matter of interest rates. Availability of credit is also important. In times when money is tight, some potential borrowers may find that they cannot get a loan, regardless of what interest rate they are prepared to pay. In times when money is easy, people who otherwise might find it difficult to get a loan may be granted one by the banks. To repeat, both availability and interest rates are important.

[9] Many firms depend to a considerable extent on retained earnings to finance their investment projects. Thus, since they do not borrow externally, the effect on their investment plans of changes in interest rates and credit availability may be reduced. However, since changes in the interest rate reflect changes in the opportunity cost of using funds to finance investment projects, they still may have an appreciable effect on the investment function.

[10] The alert reader will recognize that the increase in NNP in panel C will shift the demand curve for money in panel A of Figure 14.4. For simplicity, we ignore this feedback. It is included in the more complete model presented in the Appendix.

307

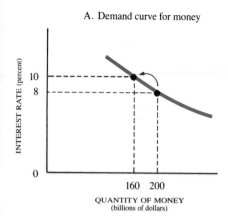

A. Demand curve for money

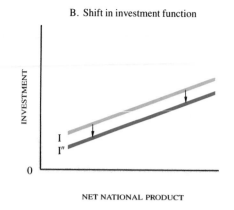

B. Shift in investment function

C. Change in net national product

Figure 14.5

Effect of a Decrease in the Money Supply *If the money supply decreases from $200 billion to $160 billion, the interest rate increases from 8 percent to 10 percent (panel A). Because of the increase in the interest rate, the investment function shifts downward (panel B) and the equilibrium level of NNP decreases from D to F (panel C).*

Basic Idea #27: *Increases in the quantity of money tend to increase NNP; decreases in the quantity of money tend to decrease NNP. According to the simple Keynesian model, changes in the quantity of money influence the interest rate which in turn affects investment which in turn affects NNP.*

EFFECTS OF A DECREASE IN THE MONEY SUPPLY: THE KEYNESIAN MODEL

Next, let's trace the effects of a decrease in the money supply from $200 billion to $160 billion. If the demand curve for money is as shown in panel A of Figure 14.5, the result will be an *increase in the interest rate* from 8 percent to 10 percent. Why? Because, if the interest rate is 8 percent, people will demand $200 billion in money, not the $160 billion that is supplied. Having less money on hand than they want, they will sell some of their bonds, stocks, and other financial assets to build up their money balances, with the result that the prices of bonds, stocks, and other financial assets will fall. *Such a fall in the price of bonds is equivalent to a rise in the rate of interest.* (To see why, suppose that a very long-term bond pays interest of $300 per year. If the price of the bond is $3,000, the interest rate on the bond is 10 percent. If the price of the bond falls to $2,400, the interest rate on the bond is 12½ percent. Thus the fall in price amounts to an increase in the interest rate). When the interest rate has increased to 10 percent, people will be willing to hold only the $160 billion in money. At this interest rate, the quantity of money demanded will equal the quantity of money supplied.

The increase in the interest rate from 8 percent to 10 percent affects the investment function. Because it is more costly for firms to invest—and more difficult to obtain credit—*the investment function will shift downward,* as shown in panel B of Figure 14.5. This shift occurs because, at every level of net national product, firms want to invest less. The reasons why an increase in the interest rate reduces investment were given in detail in Chapter 10.

This downward shift in the investment function has an effect in turn on the equilibrium level of net national product. As shown in panel C of Figure 14.5, *the equilibrium level of net national product will decrease from* D *to* F (since the equilibrium level of NNP is at the point where the C + I + G line intersects the 45-degree line). Thus *the effect of the decrease in the money supply is to decrease net national product.*

308

This, in simplified fashion, is how a decrease in the money supply affects NNP, according to the Keynesian model.[11] To summarize, *the decrease in the money supply results in an increase in the interest rate, which results in a decrease in investment, which results in a decrease in NNP.* This theory helps to explain, among other things, why an inadequate rate of growth of the money supply can lead to excessive unemployment. If the money supply is too small, NNP will not reach its potential level (that is, its full-employment level).[12]

The Monetarists

Some prominent economists, led by Milton Friedman of Stanford University's Hoover Institution, have expressed disagreement with the models in the previous section. They have formulated a different view of the way in which the quantity of money affects NNP. Since their criticisms of Keynesian economics have extended to many topics besides the way in which the quantity of money affects NNP, we must postpone a complete discussion of their controversies with the Keynesians to Chapter 17. All that we take up in this chapter is their view concerning the effects of the quantity of money on NNP.

These economists share a point of view called monetarism; hence they are called monetarists. It is not easy to summarize the differences between the monetarists and the Keynesians because all monetarists do not agree on all aspects of their theory, and neither do all Keynesians agree on all aspects of theirs. Consequently, not all monetarists disagree in the same way with all Keynesians. Equally important, the differences between the monetarists and the Keynesians have tended to change over time. As we shall see in Chapter 17, many of the points of disagreement during the 1950s and 1960s have become less important in the 1970s and 1980s, as one side or the other has changed its position or as economic conditions have changed. (Because of revisions in the Keynesian view, the Keynesians are often called neo-Keynesians.)

The differences between the monetarists and Keynesians lie in at least two areas. First, the monetarists couch their theory in a different set of concepts than the Keynesians. Rather than use the theory set forth in Chapters 10 and 12, they use the so-called quantity theory of money, which is described below. Although this theory employs different concepts than those used above, it is important to recognize at the outset that these concepts are not irreconcilable. One can translate a monetarist model into

Milton Friedman

[11] For simplicity, we ignore the fact that the decrease in NNP in panel c will shift the demand curve for money in panel A of Figure 14.5. Feedback of this sort is included in the more complete model presented in the Appendix.

[12] Harking back to Chapter 9, we are in a better position to understand now why the aggregate demand curve slopes downward and to the right. An increase in the price level increases the transactions demand for money because the average money cost of each transaction tends to go up. Thus the demand curve for money shifts to the right, with the result that the interest rate increases. As indicated in this section, the higher interest rate results in reduced spending on output. Thus there is an inverse relationship between the price level and aggregate demand.

Keynesian concepts or translate a Keynesian model into monetarist concepts. Second, the monetarists have hypothesized that certain central relationships, such as the demand curve for money, have a somewhat different shape than posited by the Keynesians. Differences of this sort are empirical matters, which can be adjudicated (at least in principle) by an appeal to facts.

Monetarists regard the rate of growth of the money supply as the principal determinant of nominal NNP. (**Nominal NNP** means NNP in money, not real terms. In other words, nominal NNP is NNP measured in current, not constant, dollars.) Some monetarists have gone so far as to say that fiscal policy, although it will alter the composition of net national product, may have little or no long-run effect on the size of nominal NNP unless it influences the money supply. This latter view, explained in more detail in Chapter 17, is not now accepted by most economists.

The monetarists have had a great impact on economic thought in the postwar period, even though theirs remains a minority view. Professor Friedman's most severe critics admit that his research in this area (which helped win him a Nobel prize) has been pathbreaking and extremely important. According to his findings,

> the rate of change of the money supply shows well-marked cycles that match closely those in economic activity in general and precede the latter by a long interval. On the average, the rate of change of the money supply has reached its peak nearly 16 months before the peak in general business and has reached its trough over 12 months before the trough in general business.[13]

Clearly, findings of this sort must be taken seriously. Moreover, research carried out at the Federal Reserve Bank of St. Louis showed a close relationship between short-run changes in the quantity of money and short-run changes in NNP. Based on this relationship, the St. Louis Bank has constructed some simple econometric models that have had some success in forecasting NNP. Although criticized on various grounds, these results have also strengthened the hand of the monetarists.

The Velocity of Money

As noted above, the monetarists have revived interest in the so-called quantity theory of money, which was developed many years ago by such titans of economics as Alfred Marshall of Cambridge and Irving Fisher at Yale. To understand this theory, it is useful to begin by defining a new term: the velocity of circulation of money. The **velocity of circulation of money** is the rate at which the money supply is used to make transactions for final goods and services. That is, it equals the average number of times per year that a dollar is used to buy the final goods and services produced

---

[13] Milton Friedman, testimony before the Joint Economic Committee, "The Relationship of Prices to Economic Stability and Growth," 85th Congress, 2d Session, 1958.

by the economy. In other words,

$$V = \frac{NNP}{M},$$ (14.1)

where V is velocity, NNP is the nominal net national product, and M is the money supply. For example, if our nominal net national product is $1 trillion and our money supply is $200 billion, the velocity of circulation of money is 5, which means that, on the average, each dollar of our money consummates $5 worth of purchases of net national product.

Nominal net national product can be expressed as the product of real net national product and the price level. In other words,

$$NNP = P \times Q,$$ (14.2)

where P is the price level—the average price at which final goods and services are sold—and Q is net national product in real terms. For example, suppose that national output in real terms consists of 200 tons of steel. If the price of a ton of steel is $100, then nominal NNP equals $P \times Q$, or 100×200, or $20,000.[14]

If we substitute $P \times Q$ for NNP in Equation (14.1), we have

$$V = \frac{P \times Q}{M}.$$ (14.3)

That is, velocity equals the price level *(P)* times the real NNP *(Q)* divided by the money supply *(M)*. This is another way to define the velocity of circulation of money—a way that will prove very useful.

Irving Fisher

The Equation of Exchange

Now that we have a definition of the velocity of circulation of money, our next step is to present the so-called equation of exchange. The ***equation of exchange*** is really nothing more than a restatement, in somewhat different form, of our definition of the velocity of circulation of money. To obtain the equation of exchange, all we have to do is multiply both sides of Equation (14.3) by M. The result is

$$MV = PQ.$$ (14.4)

To understand exactly what this equation means, let's look more closely at each side. *The right-hand side equals the amount received for final goods and services during the period,* because Q is the output of final goods and services during the period and P is their average price. Thus the product of P and Q must equal the total amount received for final goods and services during the period—or nominal NNP. For example, if national output in real terms equals 200 tons of steel, and if the price of a ton of steel is $100, then 100×200—that is, $P \times Q$—must equal the total amount received for final goods and services during the period.

---

[14] Since real NNP is measured here in physical units (tons), P is the price level. If real NNP has been measured in constant dollars, P would have been a price index. In either event, our conclusions would be basically the same.

The left-hand side of Equation (14.4) equals the total amount spent on final goods and services during the period. Why? Because the left-hand side equals the money supply—*M*— times the average number of times during the period that a dollar was spent on final goods and services—*V*. Consequently, *M × V* must equal the amount spent on final goods and services during the period. For example, if the money supply equals $10,000 and velocity equals 2, the total amount spent on final goods and services during the period must equal $10,000 × 2, or $20,000.

Thus, since the *amount received for* final goods and services during the period must equal the *amount spent on* final goods and services during the period, the left-hand side must equal the right-hand side.

The equation of exchange—Equation (14.4)—is what logicians call a tautology. It holds by definition. Yet it is not useless. On the contrary, economists regard the equation of exchange as very valuable, because it sets forth some of the fundamental factors that influence NNP and the price level. This equation has been used by economists for many years. It is the basis for the crude quantity theory of money used by the classical economists, as well as the recent theories put forth by the monetarists.

The Crude Quantity Theory of Money and Prices

The classical economists discussed in Chapter 8 assumed that both *V* and *Q* were constant. They believed that *V* was constant because it was determined by the population's stable habits of holding money, and they believed that *Q* would remain constant at its full employment value.[15] On the basis of these assumptions, they propounded the **crude quantity theory** of money and prices, a theory that received a great deal of attention and exerted considerable influence in its day.

If these assumptions hold, it follows from the equation of exchange—Equation (14.4)—that the price level *(P)* must be proportional to the money supply *(M)*, because *V* and *Q* have been assumed to be constant. (In the short run, the full-employment level of real net national product will not change much.) Thus we can rewrite Equation (14.4) as

$$P = \left(\frac{V}{Q}\right)M,$$

(14.5)

where *(V/Q)* is a constant. So *P* must be proportional to *M* if these assumptions hold.

The conclusion reached by the crude quantity theorists—namely, *that the price level will be proportional to the money supply*—is very important, if true. To see how they came to this conclusion, one must recognize that they stressed the transaction motive for holding money. Recall from an earlier section that, based on this motive, one would expect the quantity of money demanded to be directly related to the level of nominal NNP. Further, the demand for money was assumed to be stable, and little or no

---

[15] In some cases, they did not really assume continual full employment. Instead, they were concerned with the long-run changes in the economy and compared the peaks of the business cycle, where full employment frequently occurs.

attention was paid to the effect of the interest rate on the demand for money. Indeed, the crude quantity theorists went so far as to assume that the quantity of money demanded was *proportional* to the level of nominal NNP. This amounted to assuming that velocity was constant.

Suppose there is a 10 percent increase in the quantity of money. Why would the crude quantity theorists predict a 10 percent increase in the price level? To begin with, they would assert that, since the quantity of money has increased relative to the value of nominal NNP, households and firms now hold more money than they want to hold. Further, they would argue that households and firms will spend their excess money balances on commodities and services, and that the resulting increase in total intended spending will increase the nominal value, but not the real value of NNP (since full employment is assumed). In other words, the increase in aggregate demand will bid up prices. More specifically, they would argue that prices will continue to be bid up until they have increased by 10 percent, since only then will the nominal value of NNP be big enough so that households and firms will be content to hold the new quantity of money.

EVALUATION OF THE CRUDE QUANTITY THEORY

The crude quantity theory is true to its name: it is only a crude approximation to reality. One important weakness is its assumption that velocity is constant. Another is its assumption that the economy is always at full employment, which we know from previous chapters to be far from true. But despite its limitations, the crude quantity theory points to a very important truth. If the government finances its expenditures by an enormous increase in the money supply, the result will be drastic inflation. For example, if the money supply is increased tenfold, there will be a marked increase in the price level. If we take the crude quantity theory at face value, we would expect a tenfold increase in the price level; but that is a case of spurious accuracy. Perhaps the price level will go up only eightfold. Perhaps it will go up twelvefold. The important thing is that it will go up a lot.

Basic Idea #28: If the quantity of money increases by a very large percentage, the price level is likely to increase greatly as well. According to the crude quantity theory, the price level is expected to increase by the same percentage as the quantity of money, since real NNP and velocity are assumed to be constant. Whether or not this is true, the important point is that severe inflation is likely to occur under these circumstances.

There is a great deal of evidence to show that the crude quantity theory is a useful predictor during periods of runaway inflation, such as in Germany after World War I. The German inflation occurred because the German government printed and spent large bundles of additional money. You often hear people warn of the dangers in this country of the government's "resorting to the printing presses" and flooding the country with a vast increase in the money supply. It is a danger in any country. And one great value of the crude quantity theory is that it predicts correctly what will occur as a consequence—rapid inflation.

There is also considerable evidence that the crude quantity theory works reasonably well in predicting long-term trends in the price level. For example, during the sixteenth and seventeenth centuries, gold and silver were imported by the Spanish from the New World, resulting in a great increase in the money supply. The crude quantity theory would predict a great increase in the price level, and this is what occurred. Or consider the period during the nineteenth century, when the discovery of gold in the United States, South Africa, and Canada brought about a considerable increase in the money supply. As the crude quantity theory would lead us to expect, the price level rose considerably as a consequence.

A More Sophisticated Version of the Quantity Theory

The crude quantity theory was based on two simplifying assumptions, both of which are questionable. One assumption was that real net national product *(Q)* remains fixed at its full-employment level. The other was that the velocity of circulation of money *(V)* remains constant. A more sophisticated version of the quantity theory can be derived by relaxing the first assumption. This version of the quantity theory recognizes that the economy is often at less than full employment and consequently that real net national product *(Q)* may vary a good deal for this reason.

So long as velocity remains constant, the equation of exchange—Equation (14.4)—can be used to determine the relationship between net national product in current dollars and *M*, even if *Q* is allowed to vary. On the basis of the equation of exchange, it is obvious that $P \times Q$ should be proportional to *M*, if the velocity of circulation of money *(V)* remains constant. Since $P \times Q$ is the nominal net national product, it follows that, if this assumption holds, *the nominal net national product should be proportional to the money supply.* In other words,

$$NNP = aM, \tag{14.6}$$

where NNP is the nominal net national product and *V* is assumed to equal a constant—*a*. Thus, if the money supply increases by 10 percent, the nominal value of NNP should increase by 10 percent. If the money supply increases by 20 percent, the nominal value of NNP should increase by 20 percent. And so forth.

If velocity is constant, this version of the quantity theory should enable us to predict nominal net national product if we know the money supply. Also, if velocity is constant, this version of the quantity theory should enable us to control nominal net national product by controlling the money supply. Clearly, if velocity is constant, Equation (14.6) is an extremely important economic relationship—one that will go a long way toward accomplishing the goals of Chapters 10 to 13, which were to show how net national product could be forecasted and controlled. But is velocity constant? Since Equation (14.6) is based on this assumption, we must find out.

Figure 14.6 shows hows the velocity of circulation of money has behaved since 1920.[16] Obviously velocity has not been constant. But on the other hand, it has not varied enormously. Excluding the war years, it has generally been between 2.5 and 6.5 in the United States. It has changed rather slowly, although it has varied a good deal over the business cycle. Velocity tends to decrease during depressions and increase during booms. *All in all, one must conclude from Figure 14.6 that, although velocity has not varied*

---

[16] The velocity figures in Figure 14.6 are based on gross national product, not net national product. But for present purposes, this makes little real difference.

Figure 14.6
Velocity of Circulation of Money,
United States, 1920–84 *The velocity of*
circulation of money has generally been
between 2.5 and 6.5, except during
World War II.

*enormously, it is not so stable that Equation (14.6) alone can be used in any
precise way to forecast or control net national product.*[17]

However, this does not mean that Equation (14.6) is useless, or that the
more sophisticated quantity theory is without value. On the contrary, this
version of the quantity theory points out a very important truth, which is
that *the money supply has an important effect on net national product (in
money terms). Increases in the quantity of money are likely to increase
nominal NNP, while decreases in the quantity of money are likely to decrease nominal NNP.* Because velocity is not constant, the relationship
between the money supply and net national product is not as neat and
simple as that predicted by Equation (14.6), but there is a relationship—as
shown in Figure 14.7.

Going a step further, sophisticated monetarists often relax the assumption that V is constant, and assert that it is possible to predict V as a
function of other variables, like the frequency with which people are paid,
the level of business confidence, and the cost of holding money (the interest rate). According to some economists, one of Friedman's major con-

---

[17] It is important to note that the velocity figures in Figure 14.6 are based on the narrow
definition of the money supply, *M*-1. If *M*-2 is used instead, velocity is more nearly constant.
For example, between 1960 and 1976, velocity based on *M*-2 varied within a very narrow range.
See Robert Gordon, *Macroeconomics*, Boston: Little Brown, 1978.

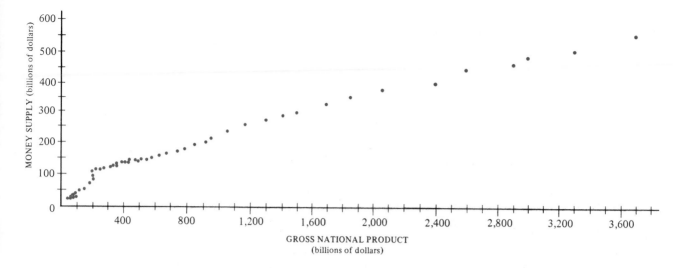

GROSS NATIONAL PRODUCT
(billions of dollars)

Figure 14.7

Relationship between Money Supply and National Product, United States, 1929–84 *There is a reasonably close relationship between the money supply and the money value of national product. As one goes up, the other tends to go up too.*

tributions was to replace the constancy of V with its predictability. Other economists feel that changes in V reflect, rather than cause, changes in NNP.

The Importance of Money

Whether one is a Keynesian using the model presented in Figures 14.4 and 14.5 or a monetarist using the more sophisticated form of quantity theory can make a considerable difference, as we shall see in Chapter 17. But it is important to underscore the fact that *the effect of the money supply on nominal NNP is qualitatively the same in both the Keynesian and monetarist models.* Whatever theory you look at, you get the same qualitative result.

Increases in the money supply would be expected to increase nominal NNP, and decreases in the money supply would be expected to decrease nominal NNP.

Furthermore, no matter which view is accepted, it would be expected that, as the economy approaches full employment, a bigger and bigger share of the increase in nominal NNP due to increases in the money supply will reflect price increases, not increases in real output. *If the economy is at considerably less than full employment, increases in the money supply would be expected to increase real NNP, while decreases in the money supply would be expected to reduce real NNP. However, once full employment is approached, increases in the money supply result more and more in increases in the price level, as distinct from increases in real NNP.*

These expectations are shared by economists of many types, which is fortunate since, as we shall see, they are important guides to the formulation of monetary policy, both here and abroad.

316

Test Yourself

1. If the value of NNP (in money terms) increases 10 percent and the money supply remains fixed, does velocity increase? Why or why not? What are some of the factors that might cause an increase in velocity?

2. "The history of the United States is an account of one inflation after another. The currency is being debased further and further. Soon we may experience a runaway inflation." Comment and evaluate.

3. Describe how the quantity of money influences nominal and real NNP according to (a) the Keynesian model, (b) the crude quantity theory, and (c) the more sophisticated quantity theory.

4. Suppose that a bond pays annual interest of $100 forever. What is the interest rate if its price is (a) $1,000, (b) $2,000, (c) $3,000?

Summary

1. Money performs several basic functions. It serves as a medium of exchange, a standard of value, and a store of value. The money supply, narrowly defined, is composed of coins, currency, demand deposits, and other checkable deposits. Economists include demand (and other checkable) deposits as part of the money supply because you can pay for goods and services about as easily by check as with cash.

2. Besides this narrow definition of money, broader definitions include savings and time deposits (and money market mutual fund shares). In addition, there are lots of other assets—for example, government bonds—that can be transformed without much difficulty into cash. It is not easy to draw a line between money and nonmoney, since many assets have some of the characteristics of money.

3. America's history has seen many sharp fluctuations in the price level. Generally, severe inflations have occurred because the government expanded the money supply far too rapidly. However, too small a rate of growth of the money supply can also be a mistake, resulting in excessive unemployment.

4. Most economists believe that the lower the interest rate, the greater the amount of money demanded. Thus increases in the quantity of money result in lower interest rates, which result in increased investment (and other types of spending), which results in a higher NNP. Conversely, decreases in the quantity of money result in higher interest rates, which result in decreased investment (and other types of spending), which results in a lower NNP. This is the Keynesian approach.

5. The equation of exchange is $MV = PQ$, where M is the money supply, V is velocity, P is the price level, and Q is net national product in real terms. The velocity of circulation of money is the rate at which the money supply is used to make transactions for final goods and services. Specifically, it equals NNP in money terms divided by the money supply.

6. If the velocity of circulation of money remains constant and if real net national product is fixed at its full employment level, it follows from the equation of exchange that the price level will be proportional to the money supply. This is the crude quantity theory, which is a reasonably good approximation during periods of runaway inflation, and works reasonably well in predicting long-term trends in the price level.

7. A more sophisticated version of the quantity theory recognizes that real net national product is often less than its full-employment value; consequently, Q is not fixed. Thus, if velocity remains constant, net national product in money terms should be proportional to the money supply. In fact, velocity has by no means remained stable over time. However, nominal NNP has been fairly closely related to the money supply, and the monetarists assert that velocity is predictable.

8. The monetarists, led by Milton Friedman, prefer the quantity theory over the Keynesian model. There have been many disagreements between the monetarists and the Keynesians, but both approaches agree that increases in the money supply will tend to increase nominal NNP while decreases in the money supply will tend to decrease nominal NNP.

Concepts for Review

Coins	*M*-2	**Nominal NNP**
Currency	**Near money**	**Velocity of circulation**
Demand deposits	**Time deposits**	**Equation of exchange**
Checkable deposits	**Demand curve for money**	**Crude quantity theory**
M-1		

CHAPTER 15

The Banking System and the Quantity of Money

Banking is often viewed as a colorless, dull profession whose practitioners are knee-deep in deposit slips and canceled checks. Also, when the time comes to reject a loan application, the bankers are often viewed as heartless skinflints—even if they advertise that "you have a friend at Chase Manhattan." Yet despite these notions, most people recognize the importance of the banks in our economy, perhaps because the banks deal in such an important and fascinating commodity—money.

In this chapter, we look in detail at how commercial banks operate. We begin by discussing the Federal Reserve System and the functions of commercial banks. Then we describe the nature of commercial banks' loans and investments, as well as the important concept of reserves. After looking into legal reserve requirements we go on to describe how commercial banks create money—a very important and commonly misunderstood process. Finally, we take up the effects of currency withdrawals and desired excess reserves on our results. The purpose of this chapter is to introduce you to the operations of the banking system, which is neither as colorless nor as mysterious as is sometimes assumed.

The Federal Reserve System

Any nation must exercise control over the quantity of money. In the United States, the Federal Reserve System is charged with this responsibility. The Federal Reserve System—or "Fed," as it is called by the *cognoscenti*—plays a central role in the economy as a whole. After a severe

Figure 15.1

Organization of the Federal Reserve System *The Federal Reserve System contains over 5,000 commercial banks, the 12 regional Federal Reserve Banks, and the Board of Governors, as well as the Federal Open Market Committee and various advisory councils and committees.*

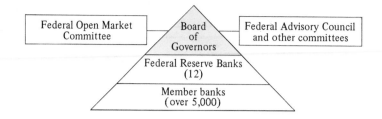

financial panic in 1907, when a great many banks failed, there was strong public pressure to do something to strengthen our banking system. At the same time, there was great fear of centralized domination of the nation's banks. The result—after six years of negotiation and discussion—was the establishment by Congress of the **Federal Reserve System** in 1913.

MEMBER BANKS

As shown in Figure 15.1, the organization of the Federal Reserve System can be viewed as a triangle. At the base are the commercial banks that belong to the system—the **member banks.** All **national banks** (so called because they receive their charters from the federal government) have to be members, and many of the larger **state banks** (chartered by the states) are members too. Member banks, which number over 5,000 out of the nation's almost 15,000 commercial banks, hold about 70 percent of the nation's demand deposits.

FEDERAL RESERVE BANKS

In the middle of the triangle in Figure 15.1 are the 12 Federal Reserve Banks, each located in a Federal Reserve district. The entire nation is divided into 12 Federal Reserve districts, with Federal Reserve Banks in New York, Chicago, Philadelphia, San Francisco, Boston, Cleveland, St. Louis, Kansas City, Atlanta, Richmond, Minneapolis, and Dallas. Each of these banks is a corporation owned by the member banks, but, despite this fact, the member banks do not in any sense act as owners of the Federal Reserve Bank in their district. Instead, each Federal Reserve Bank is a public agency. These Federal Reserve Banks act as "bankers' banks," performing much the same sorts of functions for commercial banks that commercial banks perform for the public. That is, they hold the deposits of member banks and make loans to them. In addition, as noted in previous chapters, the Federal Reserve Banks perform a function no commercial bank can perform: They issue Federal Reserve notes, which are the nation's currency.

THE BOARD OF GOVERNORS

At the top of the triangle in Figure 15.1 is the Board of Governors of the Federal Reserve System. Located in Washington, this board—generally called the Federal Reserve Board—has 7 members appointed by the president for 14-year terms. The board, which coordinates the activities of the Federal Reserve System, is supposed to be independent of partisan politics and to act to promote the nation's general economic welfare. It is responsible for supervising the operation of the money and banking system of the United States. The board is assisted in important ways by the Federal Open Market Committee, which establishes policy concerning the purchase and sale of government securities. The Federal Open Market Committee is composed of the board plus the presidents of five Federal Reserve Banks. The board is also assisted by the Federal Advisory Council, a group of 12 commercial bankers that advises the board on banking policy.

Functions of the Federal Reserve

The Federal Reserve Board, with the 12 Federal Reserve Banks, constitutes the central bank of the United States. Every major country has a central bank. England has the Bank of England, and France has the Bank of France. *Central banks* are very important organizations, whose most important function is to help control the quantity of money. One interesting feature of our central bank is that its principal allegiance is to Congress, not to the executive branch of the federal government. This came about because Congress wanted to protect the Fed from pressure by the president and the Treasury Department. Thus the Fed was supposed to be independent of the executive branch. In fact, although the Fed has sometimes locked horns with the president, it has generally cooperated with him and his administration, as we shall see in Chapter 16.

To repeat, a central bank's most important function is to control the money supply. But this is not its only function. A central bank also handles the government's own financial transactions, and coordinates and controls the country's commercial banks. Specifically, the Federal Reserve System is charged with the following responsibilities.

Member Bank Reserves. The Federal Reserve Banks hold deposits, or reserves, of the member banks. As we shall see, these reserves play an important role in the process whereby the Fed controls the quantity of money.

Check Collection. The Federal Reserve System provides facilities for check collection. In other words, it enables a bank to collect funds for checks drawn on other banks.

Currency. The Federal Reserve Banks supply the public with currency through the issuance of Federal Reserve notes.

Government Fiscal Agent. The Federal Reserve Banks act as fiscal agents for the federal government. They hold some of the checking accounts of the U.S. Treasury, and aid in the purchase and sale of government securities.

Bank Supervision. Federal Reserve Banks supervise the operation of the member commercial banks. More will be said about the nature of bank supervision and regulation later in the chapter, and much more will be said about the functions of the Federal Reserve in the next chapter.

Commercial Banks in the United States

In 1983, there were about 15,000 commercial banks in the United States. This testifies to the fact that, in contrast to countries like England, where a few banks with many branches dominate the banking scene, the United States has promoted the growth of a great many local banks. In part, this has stemmed from a traditional suspicion in this country of "big bankers." ("Eastern bankers" are a particularly suspect breed in some parts of the country.) Most of our banks are state, not national, banks. There are about 10,000 state banks, but only about 5,000 national banks.

Commercial banks have two primary functions. First, *banks hold demand deposits and permit checks to be drawn on these deposits.* This function is familiar to practically everyone. Most people have a checking account in some commercial bank, and draw checks on this account. Second, *banks lend money to industrialists, merchants, homeowners, and other individuals and firms.* At one time or another, you will probably apply for a loan to finance some project for your business or home. Indeed, it is quite possible that some of the costs of your college education are being covered by a loan to you or your parents from a commercial bank.

In addition, commercial banks perform a number of other functions, such as holding time and savings accounts. You will recall that these accounts bear interest and, although technically one must give a certain amount of notice before withdrawal, in practice they can usually be withdrawn whenever their owner likes. Commercial banks also sell money orders and traveler's checks, and handle estates and trusts. Because of their work with trusts, some banks—for example, the First Pennsylvania Bank and Trust Company, a large Philadelphia bank—include the word *trust* in their title. In addition, commercial banks rent safe-deposit boxes and provide a variety of services for customers.

Needless to say, commercial banks are not the only kind of financial institution. Mutual savings banks and savings and loan associations hold savings and time deposits and various forms of checkable deposits; "consumer finance" companies lend money to individuals; insurance companies lend money to firms and governments; "factors" provide firms with working capital; and investment bankers help firms sell their securities to the public. All these types of financial institutions play an important role in the American economy. In general, they all act as intermediaries between savers and investors; that is, they all turn over to investors money that they received from savers. As we saw in Chapter 11, this process of converting savings into investment is very important in determining net national product.[1]

THE BANK OF AMERICA: A CASE STUDY

We can learn something about banking in the United States from the history of a particular bank—the Bank of America, the nation's largest commercial bank. In 1904, Amadeo Peter Giannini, a 34-year-old son of

---

[1] The relationships among the various types of financial institutions are governed in part by law. In 1980, the Congress passed a financial reform act which changed some of these relationships. For example, federally-chartered thrift institutions were permitted to have NOW accounts, and federally chartered savings and loan associations were permitted to invest up to 20 percent of their assets in consumer loans, commercial paper, and corporate debt securities. Technological change also influences the relationships among various types of financial institutions. Many firms, such as Merrill Lynch, Sears Roebuck, and American Express, are involved in some aspects of "banking."

Amadeo Peter Giannini

an Italian immigrant, founded the Bank of Italy in the Italian district of San Francisco. Giannini was a man of enormous energy and drive. At the age of 12, he had gone to school by day, while working in his stepfather's produce firm for much of each night. At 19, he was a full-fledged member of the produce firm, and at 31 had become rich enough to retire from the produce business—and eventually to turn to banking.

Giannini showed the sort of entrepreneurial zeal in banking that would be expected from his previous track record. As an illustration, consider the following episode:

> In 1906, the city of San Francisco was rocked by earthquake and swept by fire. As the flames approached the little Bank of Italy, the young banker piled his cash and securities into a horsedrawn wagon and with a guard of two soldiers took them to his home at San Mateo, twenty miles from San Francisco, where he buried them in the garden; and then while the ruins of the city were still smoking he set up a desk in the open air down by the waterfront, put up a sign over the desk which read BANK OF ITALY, and began doing business again—the first San Francisco bank to resume.[2]

Clearly, Giannini was a banker who did not observe banker's hours.

Giannini's bank prospered and grew. By the time he was 50, it had over 25 branches. During the 1920s, he acquired more and more branches, until old-line California bankers began to realize that the Bank of Italy had become a factor to be reckoned with. They did their best to prevent its further expansion, but to no avail. A man who can turn an earthquake to his advantage is unlikely, after all, to submit to such pressures. Indeed, by 1929, Giannini had 453 banking offices in California alone, as well as a considerable number elsewhere. His was the fourth largest commercial bank in the country.

In 1930, Giannini's bank was renamed the Bank of America. The 1930s were not particularly kind to it, any more than they were to the rest of the

Table 15.1

THE TEN LARGEST COMMERCIAL BANKS IN THE UNITED STATES IN TERMS OF DEPOSITS, DECEMBER 31, 1983

Bank and location	Deposits (billions of dollars)
Bank of America, San Francisco	90
Citibank, New York	78
Chase Manhattan Bank, New York	60
Manufacturers Hanover Trust Company, New York	42
Morgan Guaranty Trust Company, New York	39
Chemical Bank, New York	33
Continental Illinois National Bank, Chicago	30
First National Bank, Chicago	28
Security Pacific National Bank, Los Angeles	28
Bankers Trust Company, New York	24

Source: Moody's.

[2] Frederick Lewis Allen, *The Lords of Creation,* New York: Harper and Bros., 1935, p. 320. Much of this section is based on Allen's account.

economy. But in the past 40 years, the Bank of America has grown and grown. In 1940, its loans (and discounts) totaled $778 million; in 1950, $3.3 billion; in 1960, $6.7 billion; and in 1970, $16 billion. Clearly, the Bank of America was on the move. By 1983, it had deposits of about $90 billion, and was the largest commercial bank in the United States. (The ten largest banks in the United States, in terms of deposits, are listed in Table 15.1.) It had come a long way since the days of the open-air desk on the waterfront.

How Banks Operate

The Bank of America, the biggest in the country, is hardly a typical commercial bank. It has had a remarkable history and a gifted founder. Many commercial banks are very small, as you would guess from the fact that there are about 15,000 of them in the United States. And there is a great deal of variation among banks in their operating procedures and styles. Some are principally for firms; they do little business with individuals. Others are heavily engaged in lending to consumers. Nonetheless, although it is difficult to generalize about the operations of commercial banks because they vary so much, certain principles and propositions generally hold.

1. Banks generally make loans to both firms and individuals, and invest in securities, particularly the bonds of state and local governments, as well as federal government bonds. The relationship between a business firm and its bank is often a close and continuing one. The firm keeps a reasonably large deposit with the bank for long periods of time, while the bank provides the firm with needed and prudent loans. The relationship between an individual and his or her bank is much more casual, but banks like consumer loans because they tend to be relatively profitable. In addition, besides lending to firms and individuals, banks buy large quantities of government bonds. For example, in the early 1970s, commercial banks held about $60 billion of state and local government bonds.

2. Banks, like other firms, are operated to make a profit. They don't do it by producing and selling a good, like automobiles or steel. Instead, they perform various services, including lending money, making investments, clearing checks, keeping records, and so on. They manage to make a profit from these activities by lending money and making investments that yield a higher rate of interest than they must pay their depositors. For example, the Bank of America may be able to get 15 percent interest on the loans it makes, while it must pay only 9 percent interest to its depositors. (Commercial banks pay interest on some, but not all, deposits. Also, they provide services at less than cost to holders of deposits.) If so, it receives the difference of 6 percent, which goes to meet its expenses—and to provide it with some profits.

3. Banks must constantly balance their desire for high returns from their loans and investments against the requirement that these loans and investments be safe and easily turned into cash. Since a bank's profits increase if it makes loans or investments that yield a high interest rate, it is clear why a bank favors high returns from its loans and investments. But those that yield a high interest rate often are relatively risky, which means that they may not be repaid in full. Because a bank lends out its depositors' money, it must be careful to limit the riskiness of the loans and investments it makes. Otherwise it may fail.

Until about 50 years ago, banks used to fail in large numbers during recessions, causing depositors to lose their money. Even during the prosperous 1920s, over 500 banks failed per year. It is no wonder that the public viewed the banks with less than complete confidence. Since the mid-1930s, bank failures have been rare, in part because of tighter standards of regulation by federal and state authorities. For example, bank examiners audit the books and practices of the banks. In addition, confidence in the banks was strengthened by the creation in 1934 of the Federal Deposit Insurance Corporation, which insures over 99 percent of all commercial bank depositors. At present, each deposit is insured up to $100,000.

The Balance Sheet of an Individual Bank

A good way to understand how a bank operates is to look at its balance sheet. Table 15.2 shows the Bank of America's balance sheet as of the end of 1983.

The Left-Hand Side. The left-hand side shows that the total assets of the Bank of America were $109.5 billion, and that these assets were made up as follows: $15.6 billion in cash, $8.4 billion in bonds and other securities, 73.0 billion in loans, and 12.5 billion in other assets. In particular, note that the loans included among the assets of the Bank of America are the loans it made to firms and individuals. As we have emphasized repeatedly, lending money is one of the major functions of a commercial bank.

The Right-Hand Side. The right-hand side of the balance sheet says that the total liabilities—or debts—of the Bank of America were $105.0 billion, and that these liabilities were made up of $89.9 billion in deposits (both demand and time), and $15.1 billion in other liabilities. Note that the deposits at the Bank of America are included among its liabilities, since the Bank of America owes the depositors the amount of money in their deposits. It will be recalled from the previous sections that maintaining these deposits is one of the major functions of a commercial bank. Returning to the balance sheet of the Bank of America, the difference between its total assets and its total liabilities—$4.5 billion—is, of course, its net worth.

Table 15.2

BALANCE SHEET, BANK OF AMERICA, DECEMBER 31, 1983 (BILLIONS OF DOLLARS)

Assets		Liabilities and net worth	
Cash	15.6	Deposits	89.9
Securities	8.4	Other liabilities	15.1
Loans	73.0	Net worth	4.5
Other assets	12.5		
Total	109.5	Total	109.5

Source: 1983 Annual Report, Bank of America.

CASH LESS THAN DEPOSITS

One noteworthy characteristic of any bank's balance sheet is the fact that *a very large percentage of its liabilities must be paid on demand.* For example, if all the depositors of the Bank of America tried to withdraw their demand deposits, a substantial proportion of its liabilities would be due on demand. Of course, the chance of everyone wanting to draw out his or her money at once is infinitesimally small. Instead, on a given day some depositors withdraw some money, while others make deposits, and most neither withdraw nor deposit money. Consequently, any bank can get along with an amount of cash to cover withdrawals that is much smaller than the total amount of its deposits. For example, the Bank of America's cash equaled about one-sixth of its total deposits. Note that "cash" here includes the bank's deposit with the Federal Reserve system and its deposits with other banks, as well as cash in its vault.

The Bank of America's practice of holding an amount of cash—including its deposits with the Federal Reserve and with other banks—much less than the amount it owes its depositors may strike you as dangerous. Indeed, if you have a deposit at the Bank of America, you may be tempted to go over and withdraw the money in your account and deposit it in some bank that does have cash equal to the amount it owes its depositors. But you won't be able to do this because *all banks hold much less cash than the amount they owe their depositors.* Moreover, this is a perfectly sound banking practice, as we shall see.

Fractional-Reserve Banking

To understand the crucial significance of *fractional-reserve banking,* as this practice is called, let's compare two situations—one where a bank must hold as reserves an amount equal to the amount it owes its depositors, another where its reserves do not have to match the amount it owes its depositors. In the first case, the bank's balance sheet might be as shown in Table 15.3, if demand deposits equal $2 million and net worth equals $500,000. The bank's loans and investments in this case are made entirely with funds put up by the owners of the bank. To see this, note that loans and investments equal $500,000, and that the bank's net worth also equals $500,000. Thus, if some of these loans are not repaid or if some of these investments lose money, the losses are borne entirely by the bank's stockholders. The depositors are protected completely because every cent of their deposits is covered by the bank's reserves.

Now let's turn to the case of fractional-reserve banking. In this case, the bank's balance sheet might be as shown in Table 15.4, if deposits equal $2 million and net worth equals $500,000. Some of the loans and investments made by the bank are not made with funds put up by the owners of the bank, but with funds deposited in the bank by depositors. Thus, though depositors deposited $2 million in the bank, the reserves are only $400,000. What happened to the remaining $1.6 million? Since the bank (in this simple case) only has two kinds of assets, loans (and investments) and reserves, the bank must have lent out (or invested) the remaining $1.6 million.

Table 15.3

BANK BALANCE SHEET: CASE WHERE RESERVES EQUAL DEMAND DEPOSITS (MILLIONS OF DOLLARS)

Assets		Liabilities and net worth	
Reserves	2.0	Demand	
Loans and		deposits	2.0
investments	0.5	Net worth	0.5
Total	2.5	Total	2.5

Table 15.4

BANK BALANCE SHEET: FRACTIONAL RESERVES (MILLIONS OF DOLLARS)

Assets		Liabilities and net worth	
Reserves	0.4	Demand	
Loans and		deposits	2.0
investments	2.1	Net worth	0.5
Total	2.5	Total	2.5

ORIGINS OF FRACTIONAL-RESERVE BANKING

The early history of banking is the story of an evolution from the first to the second situation. The earliest banks held reserves equal to the amounts they owed depositors, and were simply places where people stored their gold. But as time went on, banks began to practice fractional-reserve banking. It is easy to see how this evolution could take place. Suppose that you owned a bank of the first type. You would almost certainly be struck by the fact that most of the gold entrusted to you was not demanded on any given day. Sooner or later, you might be tempted to lend out some of the gold and obtain some interest. Eventually, as experience indicated that this procedure did not inconvenience your depositors, you and other bankers might make this practice common knowledge.

You might use several arguments to defend this practice. First, you would probably point out that none of the depositors had lost any money. (To the depositors, this would be a rather important argument.) Second, you could show that the interest you earned on the loans made it possible for you to charge depositors less for storing their gold. Consequently, you would argue that it was to the depositors' advantage (because of the savings that accrued to them) for you to lend out some of the gold. Third, you would probably argue that putting the money to work benefited the community and the economy. After all, in many cases, firms can make highly productive investments only if they can borrow the money, and by lending out your depositors' gold, you would enable such investments to be made.

LEGAL RESERVE REQUIREMENTS

Arguments of this sort have led society to permit fractional-reserve banking. In other words, a bank is allowed to hold less in reserves than the amount it owes its depositors. But what determines the amount of reserves banks hold? For example, the Bank of America, according to Table 15.2, held cash equal to about 17 percent of its total deposits. Probably it could get away with holding much less in reserves, so long as there is no panic among depositors and it makes sound loans and investments. One reason why the Bank of America held this much cash is very simple. *The Federal Reserve System requires every commercial bank (whether or not it is a member of the system) to hold a certain percentage of its deposits as reserves.* According to the 1980 financial reform act, the Fed can set this percentage between the limits of 8 and 14 percent for checkable deposits (that is, deposits subject to direct or indirect transfer by check).[3] Also, on the affirmative action of five of the seven members of the Fed's board of governors, it can impose an additional reserve requirement of up to 4 percent. And in extraordinary circumstances the Fed can for 180 days set the percentage at any level it deems necessary. These are *legal reserve requirements;* they also exist for time deposits (of businesses and nonprofit institutions), but are lower than for checkable deposits.

The Federal Reserve System in recent years has dictated that the average bank should hold about $1 in reserves for every $6 of demand deposits. Most of these reserves are held in the form of deposits by banks at their regional Federal Reserve Bank. Thus, for example, a great deal of the Bank of America's reserves are held in its deposit with the Federal Reserve Bank of San Francisco. In addition, some of any bank's reserves are held in cash on the bank's premises. However, its legal reserves are less than the "cash" entry on its balance sheet since its deposits with other banks do not count as legal reserves.

The most obvious reason why the Fed imposes these legal reserve re-

---

[3] For up to $25 million in checkable deposits, this percentage is 3 percent. Note too that *the 1980 law says that these reserve requirements apply to deposits in other thrift institutions (savings and loan associations, mutual savings banks, and credit unions), not just banks.*

quirements would seem to be to keep the banks safe, but in this case the obvious answer isn't the right one. Instead, *the most important reason for legal reserve requirements is to control the money supply*. It will take some more discussion before this becomes clear.

The Safety of the Banks

We have just argued that the reserve requirements imposed by the Federal Reserve System exceed what would be required under normal circumstances to insure the safety of the banks. To support our argument, we might cite some authorities who claim that a bank would be quite safe if it only had reserves equal to about 2 percent of its deposits. Under these circumstances it would be able to meet its depositors' everyday demands for cash. Obviously this level of reserves is much lower than the legally required level.

THE ROLE OF BANK MANAGEMENT

At the same time, one should recognize that high reserve requirements will not by themselves insure bank safety. For example, suppose that a bank lends money to every budding inventor with a scheme for producing perpetual-motion machines, and that it grants particularly large loans to those who propose to market these machines in the suburbs of Missoula, Montana. This bank is going to fail eventually, even if it holds reserves equal to 20 percent—or 50 percent, for that matter—of its demand deposits. It will fail simply because the loans it makes will not be repaid, and eventually these losses will accumulate to more than the bank's net worth. In other words, if the bank is sufficiently inept in making loans and investments, it will lose all the owners' money and some of the depositors' money besides.

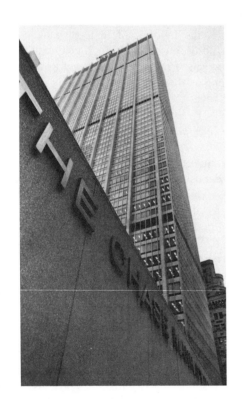

The well-managed bank must make sensible loans and investments. In addition, it must protect itself against short-term withdrawals of large amounts of money. Although much-larger-than-usual withdrawals are not very likely to occur, the bank must be prepared to meet a temporary upswing in withdrawals. One way is to invest in securities that can readily be turned into cash. For example, the bank may invest in short-term government securities that can readily be sold at a price that varies only moderately from day to day. Such securities are often referred to as *secondary reserves.*

THE ROLE OF GOVERNMENT

There can be no doubt that banks are much safer today than they were 50 or 100 years ago. The reason is that the government has put its power squarely behind the banking system. It used to be that "runs" occurred on the banks. Every now and then, depositors, frightened that their banks would fail and that they would lose some of their money, would line up at the tellers' windows and withdraw as much money as they could. Faced with runs of this sort, banks were sometimes forced to close because they could not satisfy all demands for withdrawals. Needless to say, no fractional-reserve banking system can satisfy demands for total withdrawal of funds.

Runs on banks are a thing of the past, for several reasons. One is that the government—including the Federal Deposit Insurance Corporation (FDIC), the Fed, and other public agencies—has made it clear that it will not stand by and tolerate the sorts of panics that used to occur periodically in this country. The FDIC insures the accounts of depositors in practically all banks so that, even if a bank fails, the depositor will get his money back—up to $100,000. Another reason is that the banks themselves are better managed and regulated. For example, bank examiners are sent out to look over the bankers' shoulders and see whether they are solvent. It is a far cry from the situation about 80 years ago that led to the creation of the Federal Reserve System.

Nonetheless, this does not mean that bank regulation is all that it might be. In 1984, the Continental Illinois Bank, the seventh largest bank in the U.S., required a multi-billion-dollar rescue operation by federal agencies to keep it in operation. Continental Illinois bought up more than $1 billion in loans made by Penn Square Bank of Oklahoma City. When these loans went sour (and Penn Square Bank failed), Continental's depositors became worried and began to withdraw their funds. Federal agencies tried to arrange a merger between Continental and some other bank, but no partner could be found. To keep Continental going, the FDIC put up billions of dollars and established what is essentially a new Continental Illinois Bank.

THE LENDING DECISION: A CASE STUDY

To get a better feel for the workings of a bank, let's look at an actual decision faced by Robert Swift, the assistant vice-president of the Lone Star National Bank of Houston, Texas. Mr. Swift received a call from Ralph Desmond, president of the Desmond Engineering Corporation. Mr. Desmond wanted to change his bank; he was dissatisfied with the amount he could borrow from his present bank. He wanted to borrow $30,000 from the Lone Star to pay what he owed to his present bank, pay some bills coming up, and buy some material needed to fulfill a contract. Mr. Swift asked Mr. Desmond to come to his office with various financial statements regarding the Desmond Engineering Corporation and its prospects. These included recent income statements and balance sheets, as well as a variety of other data, including information indicating how rapidly the firm collected its bills and the quality of the debts owed the firm.

Mr. Swift forwarded Mr. Desmond's loan application to the credit department of the bank for further analyses. The credit department added comments on the Desmond Engineering Corporation's solvency and prospects. Besides being secured by a mortgage on some equipment owned by the Desmond Engineering Corporation, this loan was to be personally endorsed by Mr. Desmond and another principal stockholder in the firm. Consequently, Mr. Swift obtained information on the extent and nature of the personal assets of Mr. Desmond and the other stockholder. This information was used, together with all the other data on the firm, to determine whether the bank would make the loan. After a reasonable amount of time, Mr. Swift recommended the acceptance of Mr. Desmond's loan

In recent years, the nation's commercial banks have become deregulated in a variety of ways, and they now have considerable freedom to pay whatever interest rate they like. At the same time, they (and savings and loans and savings banks) have a unique advantage over their competitors, like the money market mutual funds and the brokerage houses, because their deposits are federally insured.

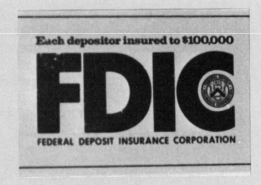

The total volume of insured deposits has grown rapidly. With the introduction by banks of new types of deposits (money market deposit accounts and Super-NOW accounts) and the elimination of ceilings on interest rates on most small time deposit accounts, investors have shifted funds out of the uninsured accounts in mutual funds and into insured deposits at the banks. Naturally, people prefer to put their money in a place where it is insured, if they can get about the same interest rate on it.

Deposit insurance dates back to the 1930s and undoubtedly has done a great deal to prevent runs on the banks. It seems very unlikely that deposit insurance will be discontinued, but there is a widespread feeling that deposit insurance has reduced the incentives for depositors to evaluate the riskiness of the banks, since their deposits are insured. Moreover, since the insurance premium charged a bank by the Federal Deposit Insurance Corporation (FDIC) is proportional to the amount of the bank's deposits (regardless of the riskiness of its assets), insured banks have an incentive to assume more risk than they otherwise would, since they do not pay higher premiums and they do obtain the higher yields that stem from riskier investments.

A number of proposals have been made to help improve matters. According to some observers, the insurance premium that the FDIC charges a particular bank should be related to the riskiness of the bank's assets. In other words, if a bank's investments are relatively risky, the FDIC should charge this bank a relatively high premium for deposit insurance. While this is an interesting suggestion, there is no simple, straightforward way to measure the riskiness of a bank's portfolio of assets.

Another proposal is that the risk exposure of large depositors should be increased. In the past, even deposits of more than $100,000 have generally been protected, because mergers have been arranged between banks that are about to fail and other healthy banks. To the FDIC, this has seemed to be the cheapest way to protect the deposits, but one consequence has been that very large depositors have little incentive to monitor the riskiness of their bank or the way it is managed. Why bother if your deposit in effect is insured, even if it does exceed $100,000?

application. In his view, Mr. Desmond had a very good chance of repaying the loan.[4]

Note two things about this decision. First, if the bank grants Mr. Desmond the loan, it will create a demand deposit for him. In other words, it will create some money. Second, the bank can do this only if it has reserves exceeding the legal reserve requirements. Both of these points are important enough to dwell on for a while.

Two Ways Banks Cannot Create Money

Genesis tells us that God created heaven and earth. Economists tell us that banks create money. To many people, the latter process is at least as mysterious as the former. Even bankers have been known to fall into serious error by claiming that they do not create money. Yet the way banks create money is a relatively simple process, which the next few sections will describe in detail. Suppose that someone receives $10,000 in newly printed currency and deposits it in his local bank. Before we see how the banks can create more than $10,000 from this deposit, we will describe two ways in which banks *cannot* create new money. Since people often jump to the conclusion that one or the other of these two processes is the correct one, it is a good idea to kill off these heresies at the outset.

CASE 1: RESERVES MUST EQUAL DEPOSITS

Suppose that ours is not a fractional-reserve banking system. In other words, assume that every bank has to maintain reserves equal to its deposits. In this case, the bank receiving the $10,000 deposit cannot create any new money. You may be inclined to think that it can be done, but it can't. To see why not, consider the changes in the bank's balance sheet, shown in Table 15.5. When the $10,000 is deposited in the bank, the bank's deposits go up $10,000. Since the bank must hold $10,000 in reserves to back up the new $10,000 deposit, it must put the $10,000 it receives from the depositor into its reserves. Thus the bank's demand deposits go up by $10,000, and its reserves go up by $10,000. Since demand deposits are on the right-hand side of the balance sheet and reserves

Table 15.5

CHANGES IN BANK BALANCE SHEET, WHERE RESERVES EQUAL DEMAND DEPOSITS
(DOLLARS)

Assets		Liabilities and net worth	
Reserves	+10,000	Demand deposits	+10,000
Loans and investments	No change	Net worth	No change
Total	+10,000	Total	+10,000

[4] This case comes from Leonard Marks and Alan Coleman, *Cases in Commercial Bank Management,* New York: McGraw Hill, 1962, pp. 168–176. However, the outcome is purely conjectural.

are on the left-hand side, the balance sheet continues to balance. *No new money is created. All that happens is that the depositor gives up $10,000 in one form of money—currency—and receives $10,000 in another form of money—a demand deposit.*[5]

CASE 2: VIOLATION OF LEGAL RESERVE REQUIREMENTS

Next, let's turn to a second way banks cannot create money. Suppose that we have a fractional-reserve banking system and that the legal reserve requirement is 16⅔ percent. In other words, the bank must hold $1 in reserves for every $6 of demand deposits. Suppose that the bank decides to take the crisp, new $10,000 in currency that is deposited and add it to its reserves, thus increasing its reserves by $10,000. Then suppose it reasons (incorrectly) that it can increase its deposits by $50,000, since it has $10,000 in additional reserves. Why $50,000? Because the $10,000 in additional reserves will support $60,000 in demand deposits; and since the person who deposited the $10,000 has a demand deposit of $10,000, this means that it can create additional demand deposits of $60,000 minus $10,000, or $50,000.

The bank will create these additional demand deposits simply by making loans or investments. Thus when a person comes in to the bank for a loan, all the banker has to do is give her a demand deposit—a checking account—that didn't exist before. In other words, the banker can say to his staff, "Establish a checking account of $50,000 for Ms. Smith. We have just lent her this amount to buy a new piece of equipment to be used in her business." At first, this whole process looks a bit like black magic, perhaps even larceny. After all, how can checking accounts be established out of thin air? But they can, and are. In essence, this is how banks create money.

WHERE IS THE ERROR?

But we prefaced this example by saying that it contains an error. The error is the supposition that the bank can create an additional $50,000 of demand deposits on the basis of the $10,000 deposit. To see why this won't work, consider the changes in the bank's balance sheet, shown in Table 15.6. After the bank received the $10,000 deposit, its demand deposits and its reserves both increased by $10,000, as shown in the first panel of Table 15.6. Then, as we noted above, the bank made a $50,000 loan and (in the process of making the loan) created $50,000 in new deposits, as shown in the second panel. So far, so good. The bank's balance sheet continues to balance—in accord with common sense and accounting (in that order). The bank's reserves are one-sixth of its demand deposits; they satisfy the legal reserve requirements established by the Fed.

Basic Idea #29: *If every bank has to maintain reserves equal to its deposits (that is, if it is not a fractional reserve system), banks cannot create new money. When a person or firm deposits a certain amount of currency in a bank, one form of money (currency) is exchanged for another form of money (demand deposit), but no new money can be created.*

[5] Note that the $10,000 in currency which the depositor gives the bank is no longer counted as money once it is given to the bank. Only currency outside the vaults of all commercial banks (as well as outside the Treasury and the Federal Reserve Banks) is included in the money supply.

For simplicity, checkable deposits other than demand deposits are ignored here and below.

Table 15.6

CHANGES IN BANK BALANCE SHEET: FRACTIONAL RESERVES (DOLLARS)

	Assets		Liabilities and net worth	
Bank receives deposit	Reserves	+ 10,000	Demand deposits	+ 10,000
	Loans and investments	No change	Net worth	No change
	Total	+ 10,000	Total	+ 10,000
Bank makes loan	Reserves	No change	Demand deposits	+ 50,000
	Loans and investments	+ 50,000	Net worth	No change
	Total	+ 50,000	Total	+ 50,000
Ms. Smith spends $50,000	Reserves	− 50,000	Demand deposits	− 50,000
	Loans and investments	No change	Net worth	No change
	Total	− 50,000	Total	− 50,000
Total effect	Reserves	− 40,000	Demand deposits	+ 10,000
	Loans and investments	+ 50,000	Net worth	No change
	Total	+ 10,000	Total	+ 10,000

So what is the problem? None, unless the money lent by the bank is spent. If the woman who received the loan—Ms. Smith—never used the money she borrowed, the bank could act this way and get away with it. But people who borrow money are in the habit of spending it; why pay interest on money one doesn't use? Even if Ms. Smith, the recipient of this loan, spent the money, the bank could act in accord with this example and get away with it if the people who received the money from Ms. Smith deposited it in this same bank. But the chances of this occurring are very small. The equipment Ms. Smith plans to buy is likely to be produced by a firm in some other city; and even if it is located in the same city, the firm may well have an account at another bank.

To see the problem that results when the loan is spent, suppose that Ms. Smith spends the $50,000 on a machine produced by the Acme Corporation, which has an account at the First National Bank of Boston. She sends the Acme Corporation a check for $50,000 drawn on our bank. When the Acme Corporation receives Ms. Smith's check, it deposits this check to its account at the First National Bank of Boston, which, using the facilities of the Federal Reserve System, presents the check to our bank for payment. Our bank must then fork over $50,000 of its cash—its reserves—to the First National Bank of Boston. Consequently, once the $50,000 check is paid, the effect on our bank's balance sheet is as shown in the third panel of Table 15.6. Taken as a whole, the bank's demand deposits have increased by $10,000, and its reserves have decreased by $40,000, as shown in the bottom panel of Table 15.6.

At this point, the error in this example is becoming clear. *If the bank was holding $1 in reserves for every $6 in demand deposits before the $10,000 deposit was made, these transactions must cause the bank to violate the legal reserve requirements.* This may be proved as follows. Suppose that, before the $10,000 deposit, our bank had $X in demand deposits and $\frac{X}{6}$ in

333

reserves. Then, after the transactions described above, it must have ($X + $10,000) in demand deposits and $\left(\$\frac{X}{6} - \$40,000 \right)$ in reserves.

Certainly, the reserves $\left(\text{which equal } \$\frac{X}{6} - \$40,000 \right)$ are now less than one-sixth of the demand deposits (which equal $X + $10,000). This must be true whatever value X has. (Try it and see.) Thus no bank can create money in this way because, if it did, it would violate the legal reserve requirements after the newly created demand deposits were used. (As we shall see later, a monopoly bank—that is, the only bank in the country—could create money like this, but monopoly banks do not exist in the United States.)

Test Yourself

1. Suppose that John Smith deposits $50,000 in newly printed currency to his account at Bank A. What is the effect on Bank A's balance sheet?

Assets (dollars)	Liabilities and net worth (dollars)
Reserves _____	Demand deposits _____
Loans and investments _____	Net worth _____
Total _____	Total _____

2. Suppose that Bank A lends the Bugsbane Music Box Company $30,000. What is the effect on Bank A's balance sheet of both the deposit described in Question 1 and this loan? Fill in the blanks below.

Assets (dollars)	Liabilities and net worth (dollars)
Reserves _____	Demand deposits _____
Loans and investments _____	Net worth _____
Total _____	Total _____

3. After the Bugsbane Music Box Company receives the $30,000 loan, it uses the money to buy a new piece of equipment from the XYZ Tool Company. The XYZ Tool Company deposits Bugsbane's check on Bank A to its account at the Bank of America. What is the total effect on Bank A's balance sheet of the deposit described in Question 1, the loan in Question 2, and the purchase described here? Fill in the blanks below.

Assets (dollars)	Liabilities and net worth (dollars)
Reserves _____	Demand deposits _____
Loans and investments _____	Net worth _____
Total _____	Total _____

4. If Bank A had no excess reserves prior to the transactions described in Questions 1, 2, and 3, and if the legal reserve requirement is that Bank A must hold $1 in reserves for every $5 in demand deposits, does Bank A have more reserves than are legally required after these transactions? If so, how much more?

How Banks Can Create Money

Now that you have learned two ways that banks *cannot* create money, let's describe how they *can* create money. Imagine the following scenario. First, suppose once again that someone deposits $10,000 of newly printed money in our bank, which we'll call Bank A. Second, suppose that Bank A lends Ms. Smith $8,333, and that Ms. Smith uses this money to purchase some equipment from Mr. Jones, who deposits Ms. Smith's check in his account at Bank B. Third, Bank B buys a bond for $6,944 from Ms. Stone, who uses the money to pay Mr. Green for some furniture. Mr. Green deposits the check to his account at Bank C. Admittedly, this is a somewhat complicated plot with a substantial cast of characters, but life is like that.

MONEY CREATION AT BANK A

The first step in our drama occurs when someone deposits $10,000 in newly printed money in Bank A. The effect of this deposit is shown in the first panel of Table 15.7: Bank A's demand deposits and its reserves both go up by $10,000. Now Bank A is far too smart to try to make a $50,000 loan, lest it wind up with less reserves than dictated by the legal reserve requirements. Instead, it makes a loan of $8,333, since this is the amount of its *excess reserves* (those in excess of legal requirements). Because of the $10,000 increase in its deposits, its legally required reserves increase by $\frac{\$10,000}{6}$, or $1,667. (Recall that $1 in reserves must be held for every $6 in deposits.) Thus, if it had no excess reserves before, *it now has excess reserves of $10,000—$1,667, or $8,333.* When Ms. Smith asks one of the loan officers of the bank for a loan to purchase equipment, the loan officer approves a loan of $8,333, not $50,000. Ms. Smith is given a checking account of $8,333 at Bank A.

How can Bank A get away with this loan of $8,333 without winding up with less than the legally required reserves? The answer is given in the rest of Table 15.7. The second panel of this table shows what happens to Bank A's balance sheet when Bank A makes the $8,333 loan and creates a new demand deposit of $8,333. Obviously, both demand deposits and loans go up by $8,333. Next, look at the third panel of Table 15.7, which shows what happens when Ms. Smith spends the $8,333 on equipment. As pointed out above, she purchases this equipment from Mr. Jones. Mr. Jones deposits

Table 15.7

CHANGES IN BANK A'S BALANCE SHEET (DOLLARS)

	Assets		Liabilities and net worth	
Bank receives deposit	Reserves	+ 10,000	Demand deposits	+ 10,000
	Loans and investments	No change	Net worth	No change
	Total	+ 10,000	Total	+ 10,000
Bank makes loan	Reserves	No change	Demand deposits	+ 8,333
	Loans and investments	+ 8,333	Net worth	No change
	Total	+ 8,333	Total	+ 8,333
Ms. Smith spends $8,333	Reserves	− 8,333	Demand deposits	− 8,333
	Loans and investments	No change	Net worth	No change
	Total	− 8,333	Total	− 8,333
Total effect	Reserves	+ 1,667	Demand deposits	+ 10,000
	Loans and investments	+ 8,333	Net worth	No change
	Total	+ 10,000	Total	+ 10,000

Ms. Smith's check to his account in Bank B which presents the check to Bank A for payment. After Bank A pays Bank B (through the Federal Reserve System), the result—as shown in the third panel—is that Bank A's deposits go down by $8,333 since Ms. Smith no longer has the deposit. Bank A's reserves also go down by $8,333 since Bank A has to transfer these reserves to Bank B to pay the amount of the check.

As shown in the bottom panel of Table 15.7, the total effect on Bank A is to increase its deposits by the $10,000 that was deposited originally and to increase its reserves by $10,000 minus $8,333, or $1,667. In other words, reserves have increased by one-sixth as much as demand deposits. This means that Bank A will meet its legal reserve requirements. To see this, suppose that before the deposit of $10,000, Bank A had demand deposits of $X and reserves of $\frac{X}{6}$. Then after the full effect of the transaction occurs on Bank A's balance sheet, Bank A's demand deposits will equal ($X + $10,000), and its reserves will equal $\left(\$\frac{X}{6} + \$\frac{10,000}{6}\right)$, since $1,667 = \frac{\$10,000}{6}$. Thus Bank A continues to hold $1 in reserves for every $6 in demand deposits, as required by the Fed.

It is important to recognize that *Bank A has now created $8,333 in new money*. To see this, note that Mr. Jones winds up with a demand deposit of this amount that he didn't have before; and this is a net addition to the money supply, since the person who originally deposited the $10,000 in currency still has his $10,000, although it is in the form of a demand deposit rather than currency.

MONEY CREATION AT BANK B

The effects of the $10,000 deposit at Bank A are not limited to Bank A. Instead, as we shall see, other banks can also create new money as a consequence of the original $10,000 deposit at Bank A. Let's begin with Bank B. Recall from the previous section that the $8,333 check made out by Ms. Smith to Mr. Jones is deposited by the latter in his account at Bank B. This is a new deposit of funds at Bank B. As pointed out in the previous section, Bank B gets $8,333 in reserves from Bank A when Bank A pays Bank B to get back the check. Thus the effect on Bank B's balance sheet, as shown in the first panel of Table 15.8, is to increase both demand deposits and reserves by $8,333.

Bank B is in much the same position as was Bank A when the latter received the original deposit of $10,000. Bank B can make loans or investments equal to its excess reserves, which are $6,944. (The way we derive $6,944 is explained in the footnote below.)[6] Specifically, it decides to buy a bond for $6,944 from Ms. Stone, and credits her checking account at Bank B for this amount. Thus, as shown in the second panel of Table 15.8, the effect of this transaction is to increase Bank B's investments by $6,944 and to increase its demand deposits by $6,944. Ms. Stone writes a check for

---

[6] Since Bank B's deposits increase by $8,333, its legally required reserves increase by $\$\frac{8,333}{6}$, or $1,389. Thus $1,389 of its increase in reserves is legally required, and the rest ($8,333—$1,389 = $6,944) is excess reserves.

Table 15.8

CHANGES IN BANK B'S BALANCE SHEET (DOLLARS)

	Assets		Liabilities and net worth	
Bank receives deposit	Reserves	+8,333	Demand deposits	+8,333
	Loans and investments	No change	Net worth	No change
	Total	+8,333	Total	+8,333
Bank buys bond	Reserves	No change	Demand deposits	+6,944
	Loans and investments	+6,944	Net worth	No change
	Total	+6,944	Total	+6,944
Mr. Green deposits money in Bank C	Reserves	−6,944	Demand deposits	−6,944
	Loans and investments	No change	Net worth	No change
	Total	−6,944	Total	−6,944
Total effect	Reserves	+1,389	Demand deposits	+8,333
	Loans and investments	+6,944	Net worth	No change
	Total	+8,333	Total	+8,333

$6,944 to Mr. Green to pay for some furniture. Mr. Green deposits the check in Bank C. Bank B's demand deposits and its reserves are decreased by $6,944 when it transfers this amount of reserves to Bank C to pay for the check. When the total effects of the transaction are summed up, Bank B, like Bank A, continues to meet its legal reserve requirements, since its increased reserves ($1,389) equal one-sixth of its increased demand deposits ($8,333).

Bank B has also created some money—$6,944 to be exact. Mr. Green has $6,944 in demand deposits that he didn't have before; and this is a net addition to the money supply since the person who originally deposited the currency in Bank A still has his $10,000, and Mr. Jones still has the $8,333 he deposited in Bank B.

THE TOTAL EFFECT OF THE ORIGINAL $8,333 IN EXCESS RESERVES

How big an increase in the money supply can the entire banking system support as a consequence of the original $8,333 of excess reserves arising from the $10,000 deposit in Bank A? Clearly, the effects of the original injection of excess reserves into the banking system spread from one bank to another, since each bank hands new reserves (and deposits) to another bank, which in turn hands them to another bank. For example, Bank C now has $6,944 more in deposits and reserves and so can create $5,787 in new money[7] by making a loan or investment of this amount. This process goes on indefinitely, and it would be impossible to describe each of the multitude of steps involved. Fortunately, it isn't necessary to do so. We can

---

[7] Why $5,787? Because it must hold $\frac{\$6,944}{6} = \$1,157$ as reserves to support the new demand deposit of $6,944. Thus it has excess reserves of $5,787, and it can create another new demand deposit of this amount.

Figure 15.2

Cumulative Expansion in Demand Deposits on the Basis of $8,333 of Excess Reserves and Legal Reserve Requirement of 16⅔ Percent *The original deposit was $10,000, which resulted in excess reserves of $8,333. In the first stage of the expansion process, Bank A created an additional $8,333. In the second stage, Bank B created an additional $6,944.*

Suppose that Bank C lent $5,787 to Mr. White, who used the money to buy a truck from Mr. Black, who deposited Mr. White's check to his account at Bank D. If so, Bank C created an additional $5,787.

Suppose that Bank D lent Ms. Cohen $4,823 which Ms. Cohen used to buy some lumber from Mr. Palucci, who deposited Ms. Cohen's check to his account at Bank E. If so, Bank D created an additional $4,823.

The process goes on until the final result is $50,000 of additional demand deposits.

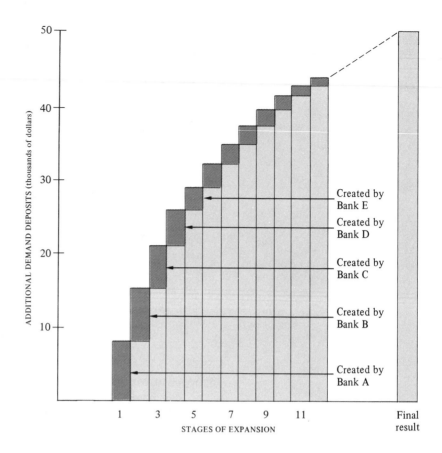

Table 15.9

INCREASE IN MONEY SUPPLY RESULTING FROM $8,333 IN EXCESS RESERVES

Source	Amount (dollars)
Created by Bank A	8,333
Created by Bank B	6,944
Created by Bank C	5,787
Created by Bank D	4,823
Created by Bank E	4,019
Created by Bank F	3,349
Created by Bank G	2,791
Created by Bank H	2,326
Created by Bank I	1,938
Created by Bank J	1,615
Created by other banks	8,075
Total	50,000

figure out the total amount of new money the entire banking system can support as a consequence of the original excess reserves at Bank A without going through all these steps.

We do this by computing how much new money each bank creates. Bank A creates $8,333, which is the amount of excess reserves provided by the $10,000 deposit. Then Bank B creates an additional $6,944, which is five-sixths of $8,333. Then Bank C creates an additional $5,787—five-sixths of $6,944 or (5/6)(5/6) $8,333, which is $(5/6)^2$ of $8,333. The amount of money created by each bank is less than that created by the previous bank, so that the total amount of new money created by the original injection of $8,333 of excess reserves—$8,333 + $6,944 + $5,787 + ... —tends to a finite limit as the process goes on and on. Elementary algebra tells us what this sum of terms will be. *When the process works itself out, the entire banking system can support $50,000 in new money as a consequence of the original injection of $8,333 of excess reserves.*[8] For a further explanation of this fact, see Figure 15.2, which describes the cumulative expansion in demand deposits. (Table 15.9 shows the amount of new demand deposits created at each stage of this process.)

[8] The proof of this is as follows. The total amount of new money supported by the $8,333 in excess reserves is $8,333 + $6,944 + $5,787 + ..., which equals $8,333 + 5/6 × $8,333 + $(5/6)^2$ × $8,333 + $(5/6)^3$ × $8,333 + ..., which equals $8,333 × $(1 + 5/6 + (5/6)^2 + (5/6)^3 + ...) = \$8,333 \times \frac{1}{1-(5/6)} = \$50,000$, since $1 + 5/6 + (5/6)^2 + (5/6)^3 + ... = \frac{1}{1-(5/6)}$.

We must note that the banking system as a whole has accomplished what we said in a previous section that an individual bank—Bank A—could not do. It has created an additional $50,000 of demand deposits on the basis of the original $8,333 in excess reserves.[9] It seems perfectly reasonable that the banking system as a whole should be able to do this, since each $1 of reserves can back up $6 in demand deposits. But for the reasons discussed in a previous section, an individual bank cannot do it, unless, of course, it is a monopoly bank. If it is, it need have no fear of losing reserves to other banks, because there are no other banks; so it can behave this way. However, banking in the United States is not monopolized.

The Effect of Excess Reserves: A General Proposition

In general, *if a certain amount of excess reserves is made available to the banking system, the banking system as a whole can increase the money supply by an amount equal to the amount of excess reserves multiplied by the reciprocal of the required ratio of reserves to deposits.* In other words, to obtain the total increase in the money supply that can be achieved from a certain amount of excess reserves, multiply the amount of excess reserves by the reciprocal of the required ratio of reserves to deposits—or, what amounts to the same thing, *divide the amount of excess reserves by the legally required ratio of reserves to deposits.* Putting it in still another way, the banking system as a whole can increase the money supply by $(1/r)$ dollars—where r is the required ratio of reserves to deposits—for every $1 in excess reserves.[10]

Let's apply this proposition to a couple of specific cases. Suppose that the banking system gains excess reserves of $10,000 and that the required ratio of reserves to deposits is $\frac{1}{6}$. To determine how much the banking system can increase the money supply, we must divide the amount of the excess reserves—$10,000—by the required ratio of reserves to deposits— $\frac{1}{6}$—to get the answer, $60,000. Now suppose that the required ratio of reserves to deposits is $\frac{1}{5}$. By how much can the banking system increase the money supply? Dividing $10,000 by $\frac{1}{5}$, we get the answer—$50,000. Note that the higher the required ratio of reserves to deposits, the smaller the amount by which the banking system can increase the money supply on the basis of a given amount of excess reserves. More will be said about this in the next chapter.

Finally, an increase in reserves generally affects a great many banks at about the same time. For expository purposes, it is useful to trace through the effect of an increase in the reserves of a single bank—Bank A in our case. But usually this is not what happens. Instead, lots of banks experience an increase in reserves at about the same time. Thus they all have excess reserves at about the same time, and they all make loans or investments at

Basic Idea #30: If a particular amount of excess reserves is made available to the banking system, it can increase the money supply by $(1/r)$ dollars for every $1 in excess reserves, where r is the required ratio of reserves to deposits. (This is only a first approximation, since it is based on some simplifying assumptions discussed below.)

---

[9] In addition, the banking system created the original $10,000 deposit, but this was not an increase in the quantity of money since $10,000 in currency in the hands of the public was exchanged for it.

[10] The total amount of money supported by $1 of excess reserves is $1 + (1 - r)$ $+ (1 - r)^2 + (1 - r)^3 + \ldots = \dfrac{1}{1 - (1 - r)} = \dfrac{1}{r}$. We reach this conclusion by the same method we used in footnote 8.

about the same time. The result is that, when the people who borrow money spend it, each bank tends both to gain and lose reserves. Thus, on balance, each bank need not lose reserves. In real life the amount of bank money often *expands simultaneously* throughout the banking system until the legally required ratio of deposits to reserves is approached.

The Effect of a Decrease in Reserves

Up to this point, we have been talking only about the effect of an increase in reserves. What happens to the quantity of money if reserves decrease?

A NUMERICAL EXAMPLE

Suppose that you draw $10,000 out of your bank and hold it in the form of currency, perhaps by sewing it in your mattress. Let us begin with the effect on your bank. Clearly, it will experience a $10,000 decrease in deposits (because of your withdrawal) and, at the same time, a $10,000 decrease in reserves. Thus, if it was holding $1 in reserves for every $6 in deposits before you withdrew the money, it now holds less than the legally required reserves. If its deposits go down by $10,000, its reserves must legally go down by $1,667, not $10,000, if the 6:1 ratio between deposits and reserves is to be maintained. To observe the legal reserve requirements, your bank must increase its reserves by $10,000 minus $1,667, or $8,333. That is, it has a *deficiency* of reserves (negative excess reserves) of $8,333. It has several ways to get this money, one being to sell securities. It may sell a municipal bond to Mrs. Cherrytree for $8,333. To pay for the bond, she writes a check on her bank, Bank Q, for the $8,333. Thus, as shown in Table 15.10, your bank's investments decrease by $8,333, and its reserves increase by $8,333 when Bank Q transfers this amount to your bank to pay for the check.

But this is not the end of the story. Because Bank Q has lost $8,333 in deposits and $8,333 in reserves, its reserves are now less than the legal minimum. To maintain the legally required reserves, its reserves should have

Table 15.10

CHANGE IN YOUR BANK'S BALANCE SHEET (DOLLARS)

	Assets		*Liabilities and net worth*	
You withdraw deposit	Reserves	−10,000	Demand deposits	−10,000
	Loans and investments	No change	Net worth	No change
	Total	−10,000	Total	−10,000
Bank sells bond and gets funds from Bank Q	Reserves	+ 8,333	Demand deposits	No change
	Loans and investments	− 8,333	Net worth	No change
	Total	No change	Total	No change
Total effect	Reserves	− 1,667	Demand deposit	−10,000
	Loans and investments	− 8,333	Net worth	No change
	Total	−10,000	Total	−10,000

gone down by $\dfrac{\$8,333}{6}$, or \$1,389—not by \$8,333. Thus Bank Q must increase its reserves by \$8,333 minus \$1,389, or \$6,944. In other words, it has a deficiency of reserves of \$6,944. To make up this deficiency, it sells a bond it holds for \$6,944. But when the person who buys the bond gives Bank Q his check for \$6,944 drawn on Bank R, Bank R loses \$6,944 in deposits and \$6,944 in reserves. Thus Bank R's reserves are now below the legal requirement. To maintain the legally required reserves, its reserves should have gone down by $\dfrac{\$6,944}{6}$, or \$1,157—not by \$6,944. So Bank R must increase its reserves by \$6,944 minus \$1,157, or \$5,787. And on and on the process goes.

Let us consider the overall effect on the money supply of the \$8,333 deficiency in reserves experienced by your bank. Bank Q's demand deposits decreased by \$8,333, Bank R's demand deposits decreased by \$6,944 (that is 5/6 of \$8,333), and so on. The total decrease in the money supply—\$8,333 + \$6,944 + . . . —tends to a finite limit as the process goes on and on. This limit is \$50,000. Thus, *when the process works itself out, the entire banking system will reduce the money supply by \$50,000 as a consequence of a \$8,333 deficiency in reserves.*

A GENERAL PROPOSITION

More generally, if the banking system has a deficiency of reserves of a certain amount, the banking system as a whole will reduce demand deposits by an amount equal to the deficiency in reserves multiplied by the reciprocal of the required ratio of reserves to deposits.

In other words, to obtain the total decrease in demand deposits resulting from a deficiency in reserves, *divide the deficiency by the legally required ratio of reserves to deposits.* Putting it another way, the banking system as a whole will reduce demand deposits by $(1/r)$ dollars—where r is the required ratio of reserves to deposits—for every \$1 deficiency in reserves. Although there is often a simultaneous contraction of money on the part of many banks, just as there is often a simultaneous expansion, this doesn't affect the result.

Let's apply this proposition to a particular case. Suppose that the banking system experiences a deficiency in reserves of \$8,333 and that the required ratio of reserves to deposits is ⅙. Applying this rule, we must divide the deficiency in reserves—\$8,333—by the required ratio of reserves to deposits—⅙—to get the answer, which is a \$50,000 reduction in demand deposits. This answer checks with the result in the previous section.

Note that the effect of a \$1 deficiency in reserves is equal in absolute terms to the effect of \$1 in excess reserves. Both result in a \$(1/r) change in demand deposits. Or, more precisely, this is the case if certain assumptions, discussed in the next sections, are true. To complete our discussion of how banks create money, we turn now to these assumptions.

Currency Withdrawals

In discussing the amount of additional demand deposits that can be created by the banking system as a result of the injection of \$8,333 of excess reserves, we made the important assumption that everyone who received the new demand deposits—from Mr. Green back to the person who originally deposited his money in Bank A—wants to keep this money in the form of demand deposits rather than currency. However, this clearly may not be the case. Some people who receive new demand deposits may choose to withdraw some part of this money as currency. For example, Mr. Green may decide to withdraw some of his new demand deposit in cash.

What effect will this withdrawal of currency have on the amount of demand deposits the banking system can create? To begin with, note that this withdrawal of currency from the entire banking system reduces the reserves of the banking system. Applying the results of the previous sec-

Example 15.1 Currency Holdings of the Public

The public is free to decide how much money it wants to hold in the form of currency (and coins) and how much it wants to hold in the form of demand deposits. Suppose that the relationship between the amount it wants to hold in currency (and coins) and the amount it wants to hold in demand deposits is as follows:

The reserve requirement is 20 percent, and commercial banks hold no excess reserves. For simplicity, assume that there are no checkable deposits other than demand deposits.

(a) If the Federal Reserve wants to reduce the quantity of money by $2 billion, how much of a decrease must occur in demand deposits? (b) To obtain this decrease in demand deposits, by how much must banks' legal reserves decline? (c) In fact, the ratio of currency (and coins) to demand deposits increased during the 1970s in the United States. Is this consistent with the above graph? (d) Some people attribute the rise in this ratio to an increase in tax evasion and the growth of the underground economy. Why?

SOLUTION

(a) The graph indicates that the public wants to hold $1 in currency (and coins) for every $3 in demand deposits. Thus, if demand deposits decrease by $1.5 billion, currency (and coin) will decrease by $0.5 billion, the total decrease in the money supply being $2.0 billion. (b) Since legal reserves equal 20 percent of demand deposits (because no excess reserves are held), legal reserves must decrease by $0.3 billion (that is, 20 percent of $1.5 billion) if demand deposits decrease by $1.5 billion. (c) No. (d) Because the underground economy tends to be based on the use of currency (which is not traceable) rather than deposits (which are traceable).

tion, this means that the banking system can create less in demand deposits than it could if the currency had not been withdrawn. Specifically, the banking system can create an amount of demand deposits equal to the amount of excess reserves *left permanently with the banking system* divided by the required ratio of reserves to demand deposits.

Similarly, in discussing how much demand deposits will be reduced as a consequence of a deficiency in reserves, we made the important assumption that everyone who buys a security from a bank pays the bank by check. But some people may pay partly or in full with currency, and this will affect how much the amount of demand deposits must be reduced by the banking system. If somebody pays in currency to one of the banks, this restores some of the reserves that the banking system lost. Thus, applying the rule set forth in the previous section, the banking system must reduce its demand deposits by less than if the bank had been paid by check.

In general, whether excess reserves are positive or negative, the change in demand deposits equals the reserves *left permanently with the banking system* divided by the required ratio of reserves to demand deposits. Thus *whether or not excess reserves have the maximum effect on demand deposits depends on how much of these reserves the public leaves in the banking system.*[11]

Excess Reserves

Another important assumption lies behind our discussion of the effects of an excess or deficiency of reserves on the amount of demand deposits. *We have assumed that no bank wants to hold excess reserves.* In other words, we have assumed that, whenever a bank has enough reserves to make a loan or investment, it will do so. Recall Bank A, which received a new deposit of $10,000. This new deposit enabled Bank A to increase its loans and investments by $8,333 without winding up with less than the legally required reserves. Thus we assumed that it would go ahead and make this much in additional loans and investments. In general, this seems to be a reasonable assumption, for the simple reason that loans and investments bring profits (in interest) into the bank while excess reserves bring none. During recent decades, banks have held relatively small amounts of excess reserves.

However, in the Great Depression of the 1930s, banks held large amounts of excess reserves. Why? Because the risks in lending and investment seemed great, and interest rates were very low. If a bank cannot find loans and investments it regards as attractive, it may decide to make no such loans or investments. After all, there isn't much profit to be made on a loan that is not repaid. Also, if interest rates are very low, the bank may feel that it isn't losing much by not lending money.

---

[11] Note too that people can convert demand deposits into time deposits, and vice versa. There are legal reserve requirements against time deposits, but they are lower than those against demand deposits. The conversion of demand deposits into time deposits will influence how much money can be supported by a certain amount of reserves. Thus the banking system can support an increase in the amount of demand deposits equal to the amount of excess reserves divided by the legally required ratio of reserves to demand deposits (no more, no less) only if there is no conversion of demand deposits into time deposits. In other words, we assume that all the demand deposits created by the banking system are converted into neither cash nor time deposits.

What difference does it make whether banks hold excess reserves? The answer is plenty. If, for example, Bank A decides to lend less than the full $8,333, this will mean that the injection of excess reserves will have a smaller effect on the amount of demand deposits than we indicated previously.[12] Similarly, if banks hold excess reserves, these reserves will offset what otherwise would be a deficiency. Thus *whether or not an injection or reduction of reserves has the maximum effect on demand deposits depends on the lending and investing policies of the bankers. If they do not lend out or invest as much as they can, the effect on demand deposits will be diminished accordingly.*

[12] Also, if a bank pays off some of its borrowings from the Fed, a $10,000 deposit may not increase its loans and investments by the full $8,333.

Test Yourself

1. "Banks do not create money. After all, they can only lend out money that they receive from depositors." Comment and evaluate.

2. Suppose that the legally required ratio of reserves to deposits is $1/5$. If the banking system's reserves shrink by $50 million, by how much will the money supply change? What assumptions are you making about excess reserves and currency withdrawals?

3. "Demand deposits are increased by banks when they call in loans and sell investments." Comment and evaluate.

4. Describe the way in which the banking system can create money if there is a single monopoly bank in the nation.

5. Suppose that the legally required ratio of reserves to deposits is $1/7$. If $100 million in excess reserves are made available to the banking system, by how much can the banking system increase the money supply? What is the answer if the legally required ratio of reserves to deposits is $1/6$ rather than $1/7$?

Summary

1. The Federal Reserve System is responsible for regulating and controlling the money supply. Established in 1913, the Federal Reserve System is composed of the member banks, 12 regional Federal Reserve Banks, and the Federal Reserve Board, which coordinates the activities of the system. The Federal Reserve is the central bank of the United States.

2. Commercial banks have two primary functions. First, they hold demand (and other checkable) deposits and permit checks to be drawn on them. Second, they lend money to firms and individuals. Most of our money supply is not coin and paper currency, but bank money—demand (and other checkable) deposits. This money is created by banks.

3. Whereas the earliest banks held reserves equal to deposits, modern banks practice fractional-reserve banking. That is, their reserves equal only a fraction of their deposits. The Federal Reserve System requires every commercial bank (and other thrift institution with checkable deposits) to hold a certain percentage of its deposits as reserves. The major purpose of these legal reserve requirements is to control the money supply.

4. Banks have become much safer in recent years, due in part to better management and regulation as well as to the government's stated willingness to insure and stand behind their deposits. However, bank failures still occur, and bank regulation is not as stringent as it might be.

5. A bank creates money by lending or investing its excess reserves. If banks had to keep reserves equal to their deposits, they could not create money. A bank cannot lend or invest more than its excess reserves, unless it is a monopoly bank, because it will wind up with less than the legally required reserves.

6. The banking system as a whole can increase its demand deposits by an amount equal to its excess reserves divided by the legally required ratio of reserves to deposits. Thus, if excess reserves in the banking system equal a certain amount, the banking system as a whole can increase demand deposits by the amount of the excess reserves divided by the legally required ratio of reserves to deposits.

7. If there is a deficiency in reserves in the banking system, the system as a whole must decrease demand deposits by the amount of this deficiency divided by the legally required ratio of reserves to deposits. Demand deposits are decreased by banks' selling securities or refusing to renew loans, just as demand deposits are increased by banks' making loans and investments.

8. Our argument so far has assumed that when excess reserves were made available to the banking system, there was no withdrawal of part of them in the form of currency, and that when deficiencies in reserves occur, no currency is deposited in banks. If such changes in the amount of currency take place, the change in demand deposits will equal the excess reserves left permanently with the banking system divided by the legally required ratio of reserves to deposits.

9. We have also assumed that the banks want to hold no excess reserves. Since banks make profits by lending money and making investments, this assumption is generally sensible. But when loans are risky and interest rates are low—for example, in the Great Depression of the 1930s—banks have been known to hold large excess reserves. Clearly, an injection of excess reserves or a deficiency of reserves will not have their full, or maximum, effect on demand deposits if the banks do not lend and invest as much as possible.

Concepts for Review

Federal Reserve System	**State banks**	**Legal reserve requirements**
Member banks	**Central banks**	**Excess reserves**
National banks	**Fractional-reserve banking**	**Simultaneous expansion**

CHAPTER 16

Monetary Policy

Like fiscal policy, monetary policy is no panacea, but it is a very important tool for stabilization of the economy. In recent years, monetary policy has been the subject of considerable controversy. For example, in early 1984, when the Federal Reserve loosened up on the money supply, some economists felt that improper monetary policy would rekindle very serious inflation in the United States, while others argued that a less restrictive monetary policy of this sort was needed to reduce unemployment. Without doubt, such controversies will continue in the future, since one thing is certain: Economists of all persuasions agree that monetary policy has a major impact on the economy.

In this chapter, we are concerned with a variety of basic questions about monetary policy. Who makes monetary policy? What sorts of tools can be employed by monetary policy makers? How does monetary policy affect our national output and the price level? What are some of the problems involved in formulating effective monetary policy? What has been the nature of monetary policy in the United States in recent decades?

The Aims of Monetary Policy

Monetary policy is the exercise of the central bank's control over the quantity of money and interest rates to promote the objectives of national economic policy. We described in Chapter 14 how the money supply influences net national product and the price level. If the economy is at considerably less than full employment, increases in the money supply tend to increase real NNP, and decreases in the money supply tend to decrease real NNP, with relatively little effect on the price level. As full employment is approached, increases in the money supply tend to affect the price level, as well as real output. Finally, once full employment is reached, increases in the money supply result primarily in increases in the price level, since real output cannot increase appreciably.

In formulating monetary policy, the government's objectives are to attain and maintain reasonably full employment without excessive inflation. In other words, when a recession seems imminent and business is soft, the monetary authorities are likely to increase the money supply and push down interest rates. That is, they will "ease credit" or "ease money," as the newspapers put it. This tends to push the aggregate demand curve to the right, thus increasing net national product. (Recall Figure 9.7.) On the other hand, when the economy is in danger of overheating and serious inflation threatens, the monetary authorities will probably rein in the money supply and push up interest rates. That is, in newspaper terms, they will "tighten credit" or "tighten money." This tends to push the aggregate demand curve to the left, thus curbing the upward pressure on the price level. (Recall Figure 9.8.)

At this point, you may be muttering to yourself, "But the aims of monetary policy are essentially the same as those of fiscal policy!" You are right. Monetary policy and fiscal policy are both aimed at promoting full employment without inflation. But they use different methods to attain this goal. Fiscal policy uses the spending and taxing powers of the government, whereas monetary policy uses the government's power over the money supply.

The Central Role of Bank Reserves

As you will recall from Chapter 14, there is a difference of view concerning the processes by which changes in the money supply affect NNP and the price level. On the one hand, monetarists use the quantity theory of money to link changes in the money supply directly to changes in nominal NNP. On the other hand, Keynesians believe that an increase (decrease) in the money supply decreases (increases) the interest rate, which in turn shifts the investment function upward (downward). This shift in the investment function tends to increase (decrease) national product.[1]

Regardless of which view is adopted, it is essential that we understand how the monetary authorities can promote their aims, since both Keynesians and monetarists acknowledge the importance of monetary policy. Economists of all persuasions would agree that a fundamental and key question is: How can the monetary authorities influence the money supply? And they would agree that the answer is: *by managing the reserves of the banking system.*

To see what this means in practice, suppose that the monetary authorities think that a recession is about to develop, and that, to prevent it, they want to increase the money supply more rapidly than they would other-

[1] Keynesians also recognize that spending by consumers and state and local governments, as well as investment, is likely to be affected by changes in the quantity of money. See Chapter 14. At this point we cannot do justice to either the Keynesian (early or modern) or monetarist views. Much of Chapter 17 and the Appendix is devoted to this subject.

wise. How can they realize this objective? By providing the banks with plenty of excess reserves. As we saw in the previous chapter, excess reserves enable the banks to increase the money supply. Indeed, we learned that if there were no desired excess reserves and no currency withdrawals, the banks could increase the money supply by $6 for every $1 of excess reserves.[2] (The ways in which the monetary authorities can increase the reserves of the banking system—and thus provide excess reserves—are discussed at length in subsequent sections.)

On the other hand, suppose that the monetary authorities smell a strong whiff of unacceptable inflation in the economic wind, and so decide to cut back on the rate of increase of the money supply. To do so, they can slow down the rate of increase of bank reserves. As we saw in the previous chapter, this will force the banks to curtail the rate of growth of their demand deposits, by easing off on the rate of growth of their loans and investments. Indeed, if the monetary authorities go so far as to reduce the reserves of the banking system, this will tend to reduce the money supply. Under the assumptions made in the previous chapter, the banks must cut back the money supply by $6 for every $1 deficiency in reserves.

Makers of Monetary Policy

Who establishes our monetary policy? Who decides that, in view of the current and prospective economic situation, the money supply should be increased (or decreased) at a certain rate? As in the case of fiscal policy, this is not a simple question to answer; many individuals and groups play an important role. Certainly, however, *the leading role is played by the Federal Reserve Board and the Federal Open Market Committee.* The chairman of the Federal Reserve Board is the chief spokesman for the Federal Reserve System. The recent chairmen—Paul A. Volcker, G. William Miller, Arthur F. Burns, and William McChesney Martin—undoubtedly have had considerable influence over monetary policy.

Although the Federal Reserve is responsible to Congress, Congress has established no clear guidelines for its behavior. Thus the Federal Reserve has had wide discretionary powers over monetary policy. But the Federal Reserve System is a huge organization, and it is not easy to figure out exactly who influences whom and who decides what. Formal actions can be taken by a majority of the board and of the Federal Open Market Committee (which is composed of the 7 members of the board plus 5 of the presidents of the 12 regional banks). However, this obviously tells only part of the story.

To get a more complete picture, it is essential to note too that many agencies and groups other than the Fed have an effect on monetary policy, although it is difficult to measure their respective influences. The Treasury

---

[2] This assumes that the legal reserve requirement is 16⅔ percent. If the legal reserve requirement were 10 percent, a $10 increase in the money supply could be supported by $1 of excess reserves. Also, as pointed out in the previous chapter, a much smaller increase in the money supply may result from a dollar of reserves if banks want to hold excess reserves and if currency is withdrawn.

frequently has an important voice in the formulation of monetary policy. The Fed must take into account the problems of the Treasury, which is faced with the task of selling huge amounts of government securities each year. Also, congressional committees hold hearings and issue reports on monetary policy and the operations of the Federal Reserve. These hearings and reports cannot fail to have some effect on Fed policy. In addition, beginning in 1975, the Congress has stipulated that the Fed must publish its long-term targets for growth in the money supply, the purpose being to establish somewhat more control over monetary policy. Finally, the president may attempt to influence the Federal Reserve Board. To keep the board as free as possible from political pressure, members are appointed for long terms—14 years—and a term expires every 2 years. But since members frequently do not serve out their full terms, a president may be able to name more than two members during each of his terms in office. (President Carter was able to name 4 members in his first few years in office.)

The Federal Reserve Banks: Their Consolidated Balance Sheet

We know from a previous section that the Federal Reserve controls the money supply largely by controlling the quantity of member bank reserves. To understand how the Federal Reserve can control the quantity of member bank reserves, one must begin by examining the consolidated balance sheet of the 12 regional Federal Reserve Banks. Such a consolidated balance sheet is shown in Table 16.1. It pertains to November 30, 1984.

As shown in Table 16.1, the assets of the Federal Reserve Banks are largely of three kinds: gold certificates, securities, and loans to commercial banks. Each is explained below.

1. Gold certificates are warehouse receipts issued by the Treasury for gold bullion. For present purposes, this item is less important than securities or loans to commercial banks.

2. The *securities* listed on the Federal Reserve Banks' balance sheet are U.S. government bonds, notes, and bills. By buying and selling these securities, the Federal Reserve exercises considerable leverage on the quantity of member bank reserves (as we shall see below).

The Federal Reserve building in Washington, DC

Table 16.1

CONSOLIDATED BALANCE SHEET OF THE 12 FEDERAL RESERVE BANKS, NOVEMBER 30, 1984 (BILLIONS OF DOLLARS)

Assets		Liabilities and net worth	
Gold certificates[a]	11	Reserves of member banks	25
Securities	158	Treasury deposits	2
Loans to commercial banks	5	Outstanding Federal Reserve notes	164
Other assets	31	Other liabilities and net worth	14
Total	205	Total	205

[a] Cash is included here too.
Source: Federal Reserve Bulletin.

3. The *loans to commercial banks* listed on the Federal Reserve Banks' balance sheet are loans of reserves that the Fed has made to commercial banks that are members of the Federal Reserve System. As pointed out in the previous chapter, the Fed can make such loans if it wants to. The interest rate charged for such loans—the discount rate—is discussed below.

According to the right-hand side of the balance sheet in Table 16.1, the liabilities of the Federal Reserve Banks are largely of three kinds: outstanding Federal Reserve notes, Treasury deposits, and reserves of member banks. Each is explained below.

1. The *outstanding Federal Reserve notes* are the paper currency that we use. Since these notes are debts of the Federal Reserve Banks, they are included among the Banks' liabilities.

2. Treasury deposits are the deposits which the U.S. Treasury maintains at the Federal Reserve banks. The Treasury draws checks on these deposits to pay its bills.

3. The *reserves of member banks* have been discussed in some detail in the previous chapter. Although these reserves are assets from the point of view of the commercial banks, they are liabilities from the point of view of the Federal Reserve Banks.

Open Market Operations

Table 16.1 shows that government securities constitute about 75 percent of the assets held by the Federal Reserve Banks. As we saw in Chapter 5, the market for government securities is huge and well developed. The Federal Reserve is part of this market. Sometimes it buys government securities, sometimes it sells them. Whether it is buying or selling—and how much—can have a heavy impact on the quantity of bank reserves. Indeed, the most important means the Federal Reserve has to control the quantity of bank reserves (and thus the quantity of excess reserves) are *open market operations,* which is the name given to the purchase and sale by the Fed of U.S. government securities in the open market.

BUYING SECURITIES

Suppose that the Federal Reserve buys $1 million worth of government securities in the open market, and that the seller of these securities is General Motors.[3] To determine the effect of this transaction on the quantity of bank reserves, let's look at the effect on the balance sheet of the Fed and on the balance sheet of the Chase Manhattan Bank, General Motors' bank.[4] In this transaction, the Fed receives $1 million in government securities and gives General Motors a check for $1 million. When General Motors deposits this check to its account at the Chase Manhattan Bank, the bank's demand deposits and reserves increase by $1 million.

Thus, as shown in Table 16.2, the left-hand side of the Fed's balance

---

[3] Large corporations often hold quantities of government securities.

[4] For simplicity, we assume that General Motors has only one bank, the Chase Manhattan Bank. Needless to say, this may not be the case, but it makes no difference to the point we are making here. We make a similar assumption regarding the investment firm of Merrill Lynch in the next section.

Table 16.2

EFFECT OF FED'S PURCHASING $1 MILLION OF GOVERNMENT SECURITIES (MILLIONS OF DOLLARS)

A. Effect on Fed's balance sheet:

Assets		Liabilities and net worth	
Government securities	+1	Member bank reserves	+1

B. Effect on balance sheet of the Chase Manhattan Bank:

Assets		Liabilities and net worth	
Reserves	+1	Demand deposits	+1

sheet shows a $1 million increase in government securities, and the right-hand side shows a $1 million increase in bank reserves. The left-hand side of the Chase Manhattan Bank's balance sheet shows a $1 million increase in reserves, and the right-hand side shows a $1 million increase in demand deposits. Clearly, *the Fed has added $1 million to the banks' reserves.* The situation is somewhat analogous to the $10,000 deposit at Bank A in the previous chapter.

SELLING SECURITIES

Suppose that the Federal Reserve sells $1 million worth of government securities in the open market. They are bought by Merrill Lynch, Pierce, Fenner, and Smith, a huge brokerage firm. What effect does this transaction have on the quantity of bank reserves? To find out, let's look at the balance sheet of the Fed and the balance sheet of Merrill Lynch's bank, which we again assume to be the Chase Manhattan. When Merrill Lynch buys the government securities from the Fed, the Fed gives Merrill Lynch the securities in exchange for Merrill Lynch's check for $1 million. When the Fed presents this check to the Chase Manhattan Bank for payment, Chase Manhattan's demand deposits and reserves decrease by $1 million.

Thus, as shown in Table 16.3, the left-hand side of the Fed's balance sheet shows a $1 million decrease in government securities, and the right-hand side shows a $1 million decrease in reserves. The left-hand side of the Chase Manhattan Bank's balance sheet shows a $1 million decrease in reserves, and the right-hand side shows a $1 million decrease in demand deposits. Clearly, *the Fed has reduced the reserves of the banks by $1 million.*

Table 16.3

EFFECT OF FED'S SELLING $1 MILLION OF GOVERNMENT SECURITIES (MILLIONS OF DOLLARS)

A. Effect on Fed's balance sheet:

Assets		Liabilities and net worth	
Government securities	−1	Member bank reserves	−1

B. Effect on balance sheet of the Chase Manhattan Bank:

Assets		Liabilities and net worth	
Reserves	−1	Demand deposits	−1

THE FEDERAL OPEN MARKET COMMITTEE

As indicated above, open market operations are the Fed's most important methods for controlling the money supply. The Federal Reserve adds to bank reserves when it buys government securities and reduces bank reserves when it sells them. Obviously, the extent to which the Federal Reserve increases or reduces bank reserves depends in an important way on the amount of government securities it buys or sells. The greater the amount, the greater the increase or decrease in bank reserves.

The power to decide on the amount of government securities the Fed should buy or sell at any given moment rests with the *Federal Open Market Committee*. This group wields an extremely powerful influence over bank reserves and the nation's money supply. Every three or four weeks, the Federal Open Market Committee meets to discuss the current situation and trends, and gives instructions to the manager of the Open Market Account at the Federal Reserve Bank of New York, who actually buys and sells the government securities.

Changes in Legal Reserve Requirements

Open market operations are not the only means the Federal Reserve has to influence the money supply. Another way is *to change the legal reserve requirements.* In other words, *the Federal Reserve Board can change the amount of reserves banks must hold for every dollar of demand deposits.* In 1934, Congress gave the Federal Reserve Board the power to set—within certain broad limits—the legally required ratio of reserves to deposits for both demand and time deposits. From time to time, the Fed uses this power to change legal reserve requirements. For example, in 1958 it cut the legally required ratio of reserves to deposits in big city banks from 17½ percent to 16½ percent, and the ratio remained there until 1968, when it was raised to 17 percent. Table 16.4 shows the legal reserve requirements in 1985. According to the 1980 financial reform act, the Fed can set the legally required ratio of reserves to deposits between the limits of 8 and 14 percent for checkable deposits. Also, on the affirmative action of five of the seven members of the Fed's board of governors, it can impose an additional re-

Table 16.4

LEGAL RESERVE REQUIREMENTS OF DEPOSITORY INSTITUTIONS, 1985

Type and size of deposits	Reserve requirements (percent of deposits)
Net transaction accounts	
Up to $28.9 million	3
Over $28.9 million	12
Nonpersonal time deposits, by original maturity	
Less than 1½ years	3
1½ years or more	0

Source: Federal Reserve *Bulletin.*

serve requirement of up to 4 percent. And in extraordinary conditions it can set the percentage at any level it deems necessary.

EFFECT OF AN INCREASE IN RESERVE REQUIREMENTS

The effect of an increase in the legally required ratio of reserves to deposits is that banks must hold larger reserves to support the existing amount of demand deposits. This in turn means that banks with little or no excess reserves will have to sell securities, refuse to renew loans, and reduce their demand deposits to meet the new reserve requirements. For example, suppose that a member bank has $1 million in reserves and $6 million in demand deposits. If the legal reserve requirement is 16 percent, it has excess reserves of $1 million minus $960,000 (.16 × $6 million), or $40,000. It is in good shape. If the legal reserve requirement is increased to 20 percent, this bank now needs $1.2 million (.20 × $6 million) in reserves. Since it only has $1 million in reserves, it must sell securities or refuse to renew loans.

Consider now what happens to the banking system as a whole. Clearly, an increase in the legally required ratio of reserves to deposits means that, with a given amount of reserves, the banking system can maintain less demand deposits than before. For example, if the banking system has $1 billion in total reserves, it can support $\frac{\$1\ \text{billion}}{.16}$, or $6.25 billion in demand deposits when the legal reserve requirement is 16 percent. But it can support only $\frac{\$1\ \text{billion}}{.20}$, or $5 billion in demand deposits when the legal reserve requirement is 20 percent. (See Table 16.5.)[5] Thus *increases in the legal reserve requirement tend to reduce the amount of demand deposits— bank money—the banking system can support.*

Table 16.5

CONSOLIDATED BALANCE SHEET OF ALL MEMBER BANKS, BEFORE AND AFTER AN INCREASE (FROM 16 TO 20 PERCENT) IN THE LEGAL RESERVE REQUIREMENT (BILLIONS OF DOLLARS)

A. Before the increase in the legal reserve requirement:

Assets		Liabilities	
Reserves	1.00	Demand deposits	6.25
Loans and investments	7.25	Net worth	2.00
Total	8.25		8.25

B. After the increase in the legal reserve requirement:

Assets		Liabilities	
Reserves	1.00	Demand deposits	5.00
Loans and investments	6.00	Net worth	2.00
Total	7.00		7.00

[5] We assume arbitrarily in Table 16.5 that the total net worth of the banks is $2 billion. Obviously, this assumption concerning the amount of total net worth makes no difference to the point we are making here. Also, for simplicity, we ignore checkable deposits other than demand deposits here and below.

EFFECT OF A DECREASE IN RESERVE REQUIREMENTS

What is the effect of a decrease in the legally required ratio of reserves to deposits? It means that banks must hold less reserves to support the existing amount of demand deposits, which in turn means that banks will suddenly find themselves with excess reserves. If the banking system has $1 billion in reserves and $5 billion in demand deposits, there are no excess reserves when the legal reserve requirement is 20 percent. But suppose the Federal Reserve lowers the legal reserve requirement to 16 percent. Now the amount of legally required reserves is $800 million ($5 billion × .16), so that the banks have $200 million in excess reserves—which means that they can increase the amount of their demand deposits. Thus *decreases in the legal reserve requirements tend to increase the amount of demand deposits—bank money—the banking system can support.*

Changes in legal reserve requirements are a rather drastic way to influence the money supply—they are to open market operations as a cleaver is to a scalpel, and so are made infrequently. For example, for about ten years—from April 1958 to January 1968—no change at all was made in legal reserve requirements for demand deposits in city banks. Nonetheless, the Fed can change legal reserve requirements if it wants to. And there can be no doubt about the potential impact of such changes. Large changes in reserve requirements can rapidly alter bank reserves and the money supply. When the Fed tightened credit in November 1978, it raised the reserve requirements for large certificates of deposit—and quickly cut bank reserves by several billions of dollars.

Changes in the Discount Rate

Still another way that the Federal Reserve can influence the money supply is through changes in the discount rate. As shown by the balance sheet of the Federal Reserve Banks (in Table 16.1), commercial banks that are members of the Federal Reserve System can borrow from the Federal Reserve when their reserves are low (if the Fed is willing). This is one of the functions of the Federal Reserve. The interest rate the Fed charges the banks for loans is called the ***discount rate,*** and the Fed can increase or decrease the discount rate whenever it chooses. Increases in the discount rate discourage borrowing from the Fed, while decreases in the discount rate encourage it.

The discount rate can change substantially and fairly often (Table 16.6). Take 1980. The discount rate was increased from 12 to 13 percent in early 1980, then reduced to 12 percent in May, 11 percent in June, and 10 percent in July, after which it was raised back up to 13 percent by December 1980. When the Fed increases the discount rate (relative to other interest rates), it makes it more expensive for banks to augment their reserves in this way; hence it tightens up a bit on the money supply. On the other hand, when the Fed decreases the discount rate, it is cheaper for banks to augment their reserves in this way, and hence the money supply eases up a bit.

The Fed is largely passive in these relations with the banks. It cannot

Basic Idea #31: The Federal Reserve influences the economy by managing the reserves of the banking system. By buying and selling U.S. government securities (open market operations), the Fed can increase or decrease the banks' reserves. Also, the Fed can change the legal reserve requirements and alter the discount rate. In this way, the Fed influences the money supply and interest rates.

Table 16.6
AVERAGE DISCOUNT RATE, 1960–84

Year	Discount rate (percent)
1960	3.53
1961	3.00
1962	3.00
1963	3.23
1964	3.55
1965	4.04
1966	4.50
1967	4.19
1968	5.17
1969	5.87
1970	5.95
1971	4.88
1972	4.50
1973	6.45
1974	7.83
1975	6.25
1976	5.50
1977	5.46
1978	7.46
1979	10.28
1980	11.77
1981	13.41
1982	11.02
1983	8.50
1984	8.80

Source: Economic Report of the President.

make the banks borrow. It can only set the discount rate and see how many banks show up at the "discount window" to borrow. Also, the Fed will not allow banks to borrow on a permanent or long-term basis. They are expected to use this privilege only to tide themselves over for short periods, not to borrow in order to relend at a profit. To discourage banks from excessive use of the borrowing privilege, the discount rate is kept relatively close to short-term market interest rates.

Most economists agree that changes in the discount rate have relatively little direct impact, and that the Fed's open market operations can and do offset easily the amount the banks borrow. Certainly changes in the discount rate cannot have anything like the direct effect on bank reserves of open market operations or changes in legal reserve requirements. *The principal importance of changes in the discount rate lies in their effects on people's expectations.* When the Fed increases the discount rate, this is generally interpreted as a sign that the Fed will tighten credit and the money supply. A cut in the discount rate is generally interpreted as a sign of easier money and lower interest rates.

Take the case in 1969 when the Federal Reserve announced an increase in the discount rate. What was the effect on the prices of stocks and bonds? They dropped sharply. Why? Because people interpreted this increase in the discount rate as a sure sign that the Fed was going to keep the money supply under tight reins to fight inflation.

Other Tools of Monetary Policy

In addition, the Federal Reserve has several other tools it can use, each of which is discussed below. These tools are generally less important than open market operations, changes in legal reserve requirements, and changes in the discount rate.

MORAL SUASION

This is a fancy term to describe various expressions of pleasure or displeasure by the Fed. In other words, the Fed tells the banks what it would like them to do or not do, and exhorts them to go along with its wishes. Banks may be asked not to "overexpand" credit. The Fed may appeal to the patriotism of the bankers, or it may make some statements that could be regarded as threats. Although the Fed does not have the power to force banks to comply with its wishes, the banks don't want to get into difficulties with the Fed. Thus moral suasion can have a definite impact, particularly for short periods. But banks are profit-oriented enterprises, and when the Fed's wishes conflict strongly with the profit motive, moral suasion may not work very well for very long.

INTEREST-RATE CEILINGS

The Fed has been able to vary the maximum interest rate commercial banks can pay on time deposits. Since the 1930s, the Fed has had the power, under *Regulation Q,* to establish a ceiling on the interest rates commercial banks can pay.[6] And the level at which this ceiling has been set has influenced the flow of funds into time deposits, savings and loan associa-

[6] During the 1930s, Congress forbade commercial banks from paying interest on demand deposits. Some people felt that many of the banks' problems in the 1920s and 1930s were due to too much competition. Hence this law. It is easy to see why bankers felt that their earnings would be improved if none of them was allowed to compete for deposits by paying interest, but this is hardly consistent with a competitive philosophy. In recent years, the situation has changed radically. For example, since the late 1970s (and particularly since the 1980 financial reform act), one can write checks on interest-bearing NOW accounts (discussed in Chapter 14).

Example 16.1   Monetary Policy and the Aggregate Demand Curve

Monetary policy has an important effect on the aggregate demand curve. As you will recall from Chapter 9, the aggregate demand curve is drawn on the assumption that the money supply is fixed.

(a) What effect does an increase in the money supply have on the aggregate demand curve? Does it shift it to the left or the right? Why? (b) Suppose that the economy is experiencing inflationary pressures. Specifically, assume that the price level is OP and the aggregate demand curve is AD_1, as shown below.

If the money supply remains fixed, in what way will these pressures work themselves out? (c) Suppose that the Fed increases the money supply to such an extent that the aggregate demand curve shifts from AD_1 to AD_2. Will the inflationary pressures subside? Will the inflation abate?

SOLUTION

(a) An increase in the money supply shifts the aggregate demand curve to the right. (A decrease in the money supply shifts the aggregate demand curve to the left.) Because an increase in the money supply lowers interest rates and increases investment, it raises aggregate demand (when the price level is held constant). (b) The price level will increase to OP_1, at which point aggregate demand and aggregate supply will be equal. (c) No. When the price level increases from OP to OP_1, there still are inflationary pressures. The price level must increase from OP_1 to OP_2, at which point aggregate demand and supply will be equal. Thus inflation does not abate after the increase in the price level to OP_1. (And so long as the Fed continues to increase the money supply at a relatively rapid rate, it will not abate.)

tions, and other financial institutions. In particular, by preventing commercial banks from paying more than a certain rate of interest on time deposits, the Fed has been able to protect the savings and loan associations, which are important sources of funds for the construction industry. In other words, the Fed could prevent the commercial banks from drawing too many deposits away from the savings and loan associations.

Because it has been aimed so directly at the construction industry, Regulation Q is often regarded as a selective credit control, not as a general tool of monetary policy. (A *selective credit control* is a control aimed at the use of credit for specific purposes.) Most economists favor the elimination of such interest ceilings on the grounds that they interfere with the functioning of free markets for funds. In 1980, the Congress passed a financial reform act phasing out Regulation Q over a six-year period.

STOCK MARKET CREDIT

Another of the Fed's tools is to vary the margin requirements for the purchase of stocks. *Margin requirements* set the maximum percentage of the price of stocks that a person can borrow. For example, in the early 1960s, you could borrow 50 percent of the cost of such securities from your broker, but in late 1972, you could borrow only 35 percent from your broker.

This is another example of a selective credit control. It may seem odd that margin requirements for the purchase of stocks were singled out for special treatment, but the severity of the stock market crash in 1929 was attributed partly to the fact that people in those days could borrow a large percentage—sometimes even 90 percent—of the value of the stock they purchased. (When stock prices slid, their small margin vanished, and unable to put up more margin, they were sold out.) Consequently, after the crash, margin requirements were imposed.

Test Yourself

1. Suppose that the Federal Reserve buys $5 million worth of government securities from U.S. Steel. Insert the effects in the blanks below.

Effects on Fed's balance sheet:

Securities _____ Member bank reserves _____

Effects on balance sheet of U.S. Steel's bank:

Reserves _____ Demand deposits _____

2. Suppose that the Federal Reserve sells $5 million worth of government securities to U.S. Steel. What is the effect on the quantity of bank reserves?

3. "When the Fed increases legal reserve requirements, it loosens credit, because the banks have more reserves." Comment and evaluate.

4. "Regulation Q interferes with the functioning of free markets, and should be abandoned. By establishing a floor under interest rates, it promotes inflation." Comment and evaluate.

5. Suppose that you have $5,000 to invest. At a restaurant you overhear someone saying that the Fed is almost certain to increase the discount rate dramatically. If this rumor is correct, do you think that you should invest now, or wait until after the increase in the discount rate? Or doesn't it matter? Be sure to explain the reasons for your preference (or lack of it) in this regard.

When Is Monetary Policy Tight or Easy?

Everyone daydreams about being powerful and important. It is a safe bet, however, that few people under the age of 21 daydream about being members of the Federal Reserve Board or the Federal Open Market Committee. Yet the truth is that the members of the board and the committee are among the most powerful people in the nation. Suppose you were appointed to the Federal Reserve Board. As a member, you would have to decide—month by month, year by year—exactly how much government securities the Fed should buy or sell, as well as whether and when changes should be made in the discount rate, legal reserve requirements, and the other instruments of Federal Reserve policy. How would you go about making your choices?

Obviously you would need lots of data. Fortunately, the Fed has a very large and able research staff to provide you with plenty of the latest information about what is going on in the economy. But what sorts of data should you look at? One thing you would want is some information on the extent to which monetary policy is inflationary or deflationary—that is, the extent to which it is *"easy"* or *"tight."* This is not simple to measure, but there is general agreement that the members of the Federal Reserve Board —and other members of the financial and academic communities—look closely at short-term interest rates and the rate of increase of the money supply.

THE LEVEL OF SHORT-TERM INTEREST RATES

As indicated in Chapter 14, Keynesians have tended to believe that changes in the quantity of money affect aggregate demand via their effects on the interest rate. High interest rates tend to reduce investment, which in turn reduces NNP. Low interest rates tend to increase investment, which in turn increases NNP. Because of their emphasis on these relationships, Keynesians tend to view monetary tightness or ease in terms of the behavior of interest rates. High interest rates are interpreted as meaning that monetary policy is tight. Low interest rates are interpreted as meaning that monetary policy is easy.

According to many economists, the *real interest rate,* not the *nominal interest rate,* is what counts in this context. The *real* interest rate is the percentage increase in *real* purchasing power that the lender receives from the borrower in return for making the loan. The *nominal* interest rate is the percentage increase in *money* that the lender receives from the borrower in return for making the loan. The crucial difference between the real rate of interest and the nominal rate of interest is that the former is *adjusted for inflation* whereas the latter is not.

Suppose that a firm borrows $1,000 for a year at 12 percent interest, and that the rate of inflation is 9 percent. When the firm repays the lender $1,120 at the end of the year, this amount of money is worth only $1,120 ÷ 1.09, or about $1,030, when corrected for inflation. Thus the real rate of interest on this loan is 3 percent, not 12 percent (the nominal rate). Why? Because the lender receives $30 in constant dollars (which is 3 percent of the amount lent) in return for making the loan. The real rate of interest is of importance in investment decisions because it measures the real cost of borrowing money.[7]

THE RATE OF INCREASE OF THE MONEY SUPPLY

As indicated in Chapter 14, monetarists have tended to link changes in the quantity of money directly to changes in NNP. Consequently, they have tended to view monetary tightness or ease in terms of the behavior of the money supply. When the money supply is growing at a relatively slow rate (much less than 4 or 5 percent per year), this is interpreted as meaning that monetary policy is tight. A relatively rapid rate of growth in the money supply (much more than 4 or 5 percent per year) is taken to mean that monetary policy is easy.

Another measure stressed by the monetarists is the **monetary base,** which by definition equals member bank reserves plus currency outside member banks. The monetary base is important because the total money supply is dependent upon—and made from—it. A relatively slow rate of growth in the monetary base (much less than 4 or 5 percent per year) is interpreted as a sign of tight money. A relatively rapid rate of growth (much more than 4 or 5 percent per year) is taken to mean that monetary policy is easy.

Should the Fed Pay More Attention to Interest Rates or the Money Supply?

We have just seen that the level of interest rates and the rate of growth of the money supply are the two principal indicators of monetary tightness or ease. Unfortunately, the Fed may not be able to control them both. To see this, suppose that the existing money supply equals $300 billion, and that the public's demand curve for money shifts upward and to the right, as shown in Figure 16.1. That is, at each level of the rate of interest, the public demands a greater amount of money than heretofore. If the interest rate remains at 12 percent, the quantity of money demanded by the public will exceed $300 billion, the existing quantity supplied. Thus the level of interest rates will rise from 12 to 14 percent, as shown in Figure 16.1. Economists who favor the use of interest rates as an indicator are likely to warn that, unless interest rates are reduced, a recession will ensue.

The Fed can push the level of interest rates back down by increasing the quantity of money. The equilibrium value of the interest rate is the one where the quantity of money demanded equals the quantity of money supplied. (Recall Chapter 14.) If the demand curve for money remains fixed at its new higher level, the Fed can push the interest rate back down to 12 percent by increasing the quantity of money to $330 billion. With this quantity of money, the equilibrium interest rate is 12 percent, as shown in Figure 16.1. However, by doing so, the Fed no longer is increas-

Basic Idea #32: To measure how tight or easy monetary policy is, economists generally look at the level of interest rates, the rate of increase of the money supply, and the rate of increase of the monetary base. Sometimes these measures point in different directions. This, together with the fact that monetary policy affects the economy with a fairly long lag, makes the Fed's job difficult.

[7] Expressed as an equation, $i_r = i_n - p$, where i_r is the real rate of interest, i_n is the nominal rate of interest, and p is the rate of inflation. In the example in the text, $i_n = 12$ percent and $p = 9$ percent; thus $i_r = 3$ percent.

Figure 16.1

Effect of a Shift in the Demand Curve for Money *If the demand curve for money shifts upward and to the right, as shown here, the equilibrium value of the interest rate will increase from 12 to 14 percent, if the quantity of money supplied remains $300 billion. (Recall from Chapter 14 that the equilibrium value of the interest rate is the one where the quantity of money demanded equals the quantity supplied.) If the Fed wants to push the equilibrium level of the interest rate back to 12 percent, it must increase the quantity of money supplied to $330 billion.*

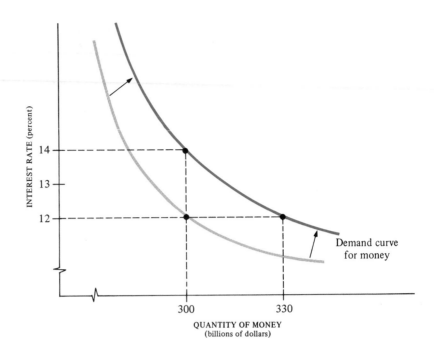

ing the money supply in accord with its previous objectives. Economists who favor the use of the rate of growth of the money supply as an indicator are likely to warn that the Fed is increasing the money supply at too rapid a rate.

Thus the Fed is faced with a dilemma. If it does not push interest rates back down to their former level, some economists will claim it is promoting recession. If it does do so, other economists will claim it is promoting inflation. Unfortunately, it is very difficult for the Fed (or anyone else) to tell exactly how much weight should be attached to each of these indicators. In the 1950s and 1960s, the Fed paid much more attention to interest rates than to the rate of increase of the money supply. In the 1970s and 1980s, due to the growing influence of the monetarists, the Fed has put more emphasis on the rate of growth of the money supply, although it continues to pay considerable attention to interest rates.

Decision Making at the Fed: A Case Study

Let's continue to assume that you have been appointed to the Federal Reserve Board, and that the economy suddenly is confronted with what seems to be a dangerously inflationary situation. What sort of action would you recommend? One appropriate action might be to sell a considerable amount of government securities, which might reduce bank reserves. You might also recommend an increase in the discount rate or even an increase in legal reserve requirements. To see how well you were doing, you would watch the variables discussed in the previous section. Specifically, you would look at the rate of increase of the money supply, as well as the rate of increase of the monetary base, and try to reduce both. At the same time you would try to increase interest rates.

Let's compare your recommendations with what the Fed really did in a similar situation. You will recall that in 1979 the inflation rate began to hit double digits. In the second quarter of 1979 the money supply began to rise sharply. Financial managers here and abroad issued statements that inflation was reaching dangerous levels. Fiscal policy was not used to curb this inflation. Consequently, much of the responsibility for fighting inflation fell to the Federal Reserve. What actions did it take?

On Saturday, October 6, 1979, the Federal Open Market Committee held a special meeting where the members were quartered in different hotels to avoid attracting public attention. Feeling that extraordinary measures were required, the committee raised reserve requirements and increased the discount rate from 11 to 12 percent, even though it was widely believed that the economy had entered a recession. At the same time, the committee indicated that it would try to reduce the rate of growth of the money supply. Some people on Wall Street called the announcement the Saturday Night Special, since it hit the financial community hard.

In the last quarter of 1979, the rate of growth of the money supply fell to about 5 percent. Interest rates rose sharply. The prime rate, which had been about 13 percent in September 1979, hit 20 percent in April 1980. However, inflationary pressures were still great. Between December 1979 and February 1980, the Consumer Price Index rose at an annual rate of 17 percent. Financial markets were demoralized. Since there was the risk of inflation getting even worse, and of interest rates therefore going through the roof, it was difficult, if not impossible, for market participants to determine what interest rate to set on new bonds. Consequently, the long-term bond market in large part suspended operations for a while.

It was hoped that the widely anticipated recession, which finally began in January 1980, would bring down the inflation rate, as well as interest rates. When asked whether monetary tightening would result in a recession, Federal Reserve Chairman Volcker is reported to have said, "yes, and the sooner the better." Apparently, policy makers felt that the most important thing was to reduce inflation, even if a slight or moderate recession ensued. In March 1980, President Carter announced a new inflation plan. The Fed's role in the new program was to tighten monetary policy further.

Clearly, the Fed did pretty much what you would have recommended. It cut down on the rate of increase of the money supply, and pushed up interest rates. Unfortunately, such actions may reduce real output (and increase unemployment), as well as cut the inflation rate. Some liberals criticized the Fed's actions on these grounds. Others, particularly conservatives, said that the Fed moved too slowly and not vigorously enough to quell inflation. In fact, inflation, while subsiding significantly, remained at historically high levels during the early 1980s. But in early 1982, it declined substantially.[8]

---

[8] Much of the material in this section is taken from T. Mayer, J. Duesenberry, and R. Aliber, *Money, Banking, and the Economy,* New York: Norton, 1981; and W. Melton, *Inside the Fed,* Homewood, Illinois: Dow Jones-Irwin, 1985.

Example 16.2　How Quickly Does Monetary Policy Work?

An enormous amount of statistical and econometric research has been carried out to determine how quickly an unanticipated recession can be combated by monetary policy. According to Robert Gordon of Northwestern University, the total lag between the occurrence of such an unanticipated slowdown in economic activity and the impact of monetary policy is about 14 months. In other words, it takes about 14 months for the Federal Reserve to become aware of the slowdown, to take the appropriate actions, and to have these actions affect real GNP.

(a) On the average, how long do you think it takes for a slowdown to be reflected in the government's economic data? (b) How long do you think it takes for the Fed to pay attention to the signal and change monetary policy? (c) Once a change has been made in the rate of increase of the money supply, how long do you think it takes until real GNP is affected? (d) What problems result from the long lag between a change in economic conditions and the impact of monetary policy?

SOLUTION

(a)–(c) According to Gordon, the lags are approximately as follows:*

Lag	Months
From slowdown to reflection in economic data	2
From reflection in economic data to change in money supply	3
From change in money supply to effect on real GNP	9
Total	14

(d) By the time the effects of the expansionary monetary policy are felt, the economy may not need additional stimulus. Suppose that you were driving a car in which the wheels responded to turns of the steering wheel with a substantial lag. The problems would be analogous to those confronting the Fed.

* R. Gordon, *Macroeconomics,* Boston: Little, Brown, 1978, p. 471.

Monetary Policy in the United States

THE NIXON AND FORD YEARS

For a more complete—and more balanced—picture of monetary policy in the United States, let's look briefly at the history of monetary policy since the late 1960s. When the Nixon administration came into office in 1969, inflation was unquestionably the nation's principal economic problem. Thus practically everyone, both Republicans and Democrats, agreed that monetary policy should be tight. In accord with this view, the Federal Reserve kept a close rein on the money supply during 1969. The result, however, was to slow the growth of national output and to increase unemployment. In August 1971, President Nixon announced his new economic policy, which entailed direct controls of wages, prices, and rents, as well as an expansionary fiscal policy. In line with the more expansionary tone of his economic policies, the president announced in early 1972 that "the Federal Reserve has taken steps to create the monetary conditions necessary for rapid economic expansion." In fact, the money supply grew by about 8 percent in 1972.

After wage and price controls were largely removed in 1973, open inflation occurred with a vengeance. In the *single month* of June 1973, wholesale prices increased by 2.4 percent. President Nixon responded by slapping a 60-day freeze on most prices (but not wages) beginning in mid-June of 1973. And the Federal Reserve, whose chairman was Arthur F. Burns (who had spent much of his professional life as an economist at Columbia University and with the National Bureau of Economic Research), tightened money considerably. On June 8, 1973, the Fed raised the discount rate to 6½ percent, its highest level since 1921.

During 1973 and 1974 the Federal Reserve cut back on the rate of increase in the money supply. During 1973 the money supply grew by about 6 percent; during 1974, it grew by about 5 percent. Interest rates reached unprecedented heights in 1974. On the average, the discount rate was almost 8 percent during the year. And the prime bank rate—the interest rate that commercial banks charge their best customers—exceeded 12 percent for a time. Many critics of the Nixon and Ford administrations charged that the Federal Reserve was taking too strong a stance in its fight against inflation.

In 1974 the United States was in a recession. During the first quarter of 1975 there was little or no growth in the money supply, but in subsequent quarters the Fed permitted the money supply to grow more rapidly, with the result that the money supply increased by about 4 percent during the year as a whole. Critics of the Fed maintained that it increased the money supply much too slowly in 1975, thus impeding the recovery.

THE CARTER YEARS

In his 1976 campaign, President Carter belabored Arthur F. Burns and the Fed on these grounds, and once Carter became president, there was speculation that he and Burns might clash. During 1977 the narrowly defined money supply (*M*-1) grew by about 7 percent, and the broadly defined money supply (*M*-2) grew by about 9 percent. Interest rates increased somewhat. Velocity increased, as it had during 1976, apparently due in part to the adoption by corporations and individuals of methods to conserve on money balances. Monetary policy in 1977 was not restrictive.

In 1978 the rate of inflation once again approached double-digit levels. As many observers predicted, President Carter did not reappoint Arthur F. Burns as chairman of the Fed; instead, the job went to G. William Miller, an industrialist. In late 1978 the Fed, led by Miller, raised the discount rate to an all-time high of 9½ percent. Some reserve requirements were also increased. The narrowly defined money supply (*M*-1) grew by about 7 percent, and the broadly defined money supply (*M*-2) grew by about 4 percent in 1978.

In August 1979 Miller resigned as Fed chairman (to become secretary of the Treasury) and was succeeded by Paul Volcker, formerly president of the Federal Reserve Bank of New York. In his first months in office, Volcker was viewed as a more determined foe of inflation than his predecessor. Interest rates were pushed to record highs. Yet the rate of inflation, which was widely regarded as the nation's number one economic problem, stubbornly remained at well above 10 percent.

THE REAGAN YEARS

During 1981, the prime rate was pushed up to about 20 percent, and the general public as well as the financial community was getting the message that the Fed meant business in its fight against inflation. The widespread expectation that inflation would continue unchecked began to disappear. During 1982, the Consumer Price Index rose by about 4 percent, which was high relative to 20 years before, but low relative to the late 1970s. The money supply grew by about 8 or 9 percent in 1982 and 1983, and interest rates fell substantially. By early 1985, the prime rate was about 11 percent.

Nonetheless, the *real* interest rate (the nominal interest rate minus the rate of inflation) remained relatively high in early 1985. Since the inflation rate was about 4 percent, the real rate of interest was 11 percent (the prime rate) minus 4 percent (the inflation rate), or 7 percent. Many economists blamed the relatively high level of the real interest rate on the huge deficits run by the federal government.

In early 1985, there was considerable public sentiment that the Fed should ease money and lower interest rates to extend the recovery, which was in its third year. At the same time, some economists were warning that inflation, while reduced, was still a potential problem.

Problems in Formulating Monetary Policy

Before attempting to evaluate the Fed's record, we must recognize the three major kinds of decisions it must continually make. First, the Fed must maintain a constant watch on the economy, checking for signs that the economy is sliding into a recession, being propelled into an inflationary boom, or growing satisfactorily. As we saw in Chapter 13, there is no foolproof way to forecast the economy's short-term movements. Recognizing the fallibility of existing forecasting techniques all too well, the Fed must nonetheless use these techniques as best it can to guide its actions.

Second, having come to some tentative conclusion about the direction in which the economy is heading, the Fed must decide to what extent it should tighten or ease money. The answer depends on the Fed's estimates of when monetary changes will take effect and the magnitude of their impact, as well as on its forecasts of the economy's future direction. Also, the answer depends on the Fed's evaluation of the relative importance of full employment and price stability as national goals. If it regards full employment as much more important than price stability, it will probably want to err in the direction of easy money. On the other hand, if it thinks price stability is at least

IS THERE AN INDEPENDENT FEDERAL RESERVE? SHOULD THERE BE?

Some say the Fed is responsible to Congress. Its enabling legislation was passed by Congress in 1913, and it could presumably be reorganized should it sufficiently rouse Congress's wrath. But Congress moves with nothing if not deliberate speed, and it seldom has sought to influence the Federal Reserve through major new legislation. The president fills vacancies on the Board of Governors, but since terms on the board run for 14 years, presidents may have to wait until their second term to appoint a majority of the board.

The Federal Open Market Committee

In fact, as knowledgeable observers often agree, there are two groups that, without appearing prominently on the organization chart, exercise considerable influence over the policies of the Fed. One is the business community—a group with a definite interest in preserving the value of a dollar. The second is the board's professional staff of senior economists. Administrations come and go, but staff economists remain, and their uniquely detailed knowledge of the workings of the Fed assure them a hearing at 20th and Constitution.

Does it matter that the Fed is a focal point for the forces in the economy who fear inflation and are willing to accept somewhat higher unemployment in the hopes prices will not rise as rapidly? It may matter less than the formal structure suggests. Virtually since its inception, the Federal Reserve has had a crop of antagonistic observers in Congress. Former Secretary of the Treasury John Connally compared one of the Fed's perennial congressional foes to a cross-eyed discus thrower. "He'll never set any records for distance but he certainly keeps the crowd on its toes."

All chairmen of the Fed—such as Paul Volcker, G. William Miller, and Arthur Burns in recent years—have been sensitive to the ultimate vulnerability of the Fed's independence, and so have been reluctant to buck administration policy too dramatically. Whether the Federal Reserve's current procedures could survive a general call for more accountability is an open question. In early 1975, Congress passed a resolution that the Federal Reserve must publish its targets for growth in the money supply. But the extent to which this really tied the Fed's hands has been by no means clear. Some critics say that the targets have been adjusted frequently to agree with the actual growth of the money supply. In 1978, the Humphrey-Hawkins Act called for annual targets for the growth in the money supply, as well as semiannual reports to Congress concerning the Fed's performance in hitting the targets. But the money supply routinely grew at rates outside the targets. In the Reagan administration, some officials have felt that the Fed's independence should be curtailed, but no such changes have been passed by Congress.

E.A.

as important as full employment, it may want to err in the direction of tight money.

Finally, once the Fed has decided what it wants to do, it must figure out how to do it. Should open market operations do the whole job? If so, how big must be the purchase or sale of government securities? Should a change be made in the discount rate, or in legal reserve requirements? How big a change? Should moral suasion be resorted to? These are the operational questions the Fed continually must answer.

In answering these questions, the Fed must reckon with two very inconvenient facts, both of which make life difficult.

1. There is often a long lag between an action by the Fed and its effect on the economy. Although the available evidence indicates that monetary policy affects some types of expenditures more rapidly than others, it is not uncommon for the bulk of the total effects to occur a year or more after the change in monetary policy.[9] Thus the Fed may act to head off an imminent recession, but find that some of the consequences of its action are not felt until later, when inflation—not recession—is the problem. Conversely, the Fed may act to curb an imminent inflation, but find that the consequences of its action are not felt until some time later, when recession, not inflation, has become the problem. In either case, the Fed can wind up doing more harm than good.

2. Experts disagree about which of the available measures—such as interest rates, the rate of increase of the money supply, or the rate of increase of the monetary base—is the best measure of how tight or easy monetary policy is. Fortunately, these measures often point in the same direction; but when they point in different directions, the Fed can be misled. During 1967-68, the Fed wanted to tighten money somewhat. Using interest rates as the primary measures of the tightness of monetary policy, it increased interest rates. However, at the same time, it permitted a substantial rate of increase in the money supply and the monetary base. By doing so, the Fed—in the eyes of many experts—really eased, not tightened money.

How Well Has the Fed Performed?

Given the difficult problems the Federal Reserve faces and the fact that its performance cannot be measured by any simple standard, it would be naïve to expect that its achievement could be graded like an arithmetic quiz. Nonetheless, just as war is too important to be left to the generals, so monetary policy is too important to be left unscrutinized to the monetary authorities. According to recent studies of Federal Reserve policy making, what have been the strengths and weaknesses of the Fed's decisions?

Forecasting. If one takes into account the limitations in existing forecasting techniques, the Fed seems to have done a reasonably good job in recent years of recognizing changes in economic conditions. As noted in previous sections, it sometimes was a bit slow to see that the economy was sinking into a recession, or that inflationary pressures were dominant. But hindsight is always much clearer than foresight (which is why Monday-

[9] Robert Gordon has estimated that it takes about 9 months for a change in the money supply to affect real GNP. See Example 16.2.

morning quarterbacks make so few mistakes—and get paid so little). Because the Fed did a creditable job of recognizing changes in economic conditions, the time interval between changes in economic conditions and changes in policy was rather short, particularly when compared with the corresponding time interval for fiscal policy.

Recognition of Lags. The Fed does not seem to have taken much account of the long—and seemingly quite variable—lags between changes in monetary policy and their effects on the economy. Instead, it simply reacted quickly to changes in business conditions. As pointed out in a previous section, such a policy can in reality be quite destabilizing. For example, the Fed may act to suppress inflationary pressures, but find that the consequences of its action are not felt until some time later when recession—not inflation—is the problem. Unfortunately, the truth is that, despite advances in knowledge in the past decade, economists do not have a firm understanding of these lags. Thus the Fed is only partly to blame.

Coordination. With a few notable exceptions, there generally seems to have been reasonably good coordination between the Federal Reserve and the executive branch (the Treasury and the Council of Economic Advisers, in particular). This is important because monetary policy and fiscal policy should work together, not march off in separate directions. The fact that the Fed and the executive branch have generally been aware of one another's views and probable actions does not mean that there has always been agreement between them. Nor does it mean that, even when they agreed, they could always point monetary and fiscal policy in the same direction. But at least the left hand had a pretty good idea of what the right hand was doing.

Measures. The Fed has been criticized for paying too much attention during the 1950s and 1960s to interest rates as measures of the tightness or looseness of monetary policy, and giving too little attention to the rate of growth of the money supply and the monetary base. During the 1970s and 1980s, however, the Fed has paid much more attention to the rate of growth of the money supply and the monetary base. Again, the fault is only partly the Fed's, since the experts cannot agree on the relative importance that should be attached to each measure. But wherever the fault, if any, may lie, the Fed's performance is bound to suffer if it acts on the basis of unreliable measures.

Emphasis. The Fed is often criticized for putting too much emphasis on preventing inflation and too little on preventing unemployment. According to various studies, it probably is true that the Fed has been more sensitive to the dangers of inflation than has the Congress or the administration. Liberals, emphasizing the great social costs of excessive unemployment, tend to denounce the Fed for such behavior. Without question, the costs of unemployment are high, as stressed in Chapter 8. Conservatives, on the other hand, argue that governments are tempted to resort to inflation in order to produce the short-term appearance of prosperity, even though the long-term effects may be undesirable. They say that, in the short run (when the next election is decided), unemployment is more likely than inflation to result in defeat at the polls. Whether you think that the Fed has put too much emphasis on restraining inflation will depend on the relative importance that you attach to reducing unemployment, on the one hand, and reducing inflation, on the other.

Should the Fed Be Governed by a Rule?

Many monetarists, led by Milton Friedman, go so far as to say that the Fed's attempts to "lean against the wind"—by easing money when the economy begins to dip and tightening money when the economy begins to get overheated—really do more harm than good. In their view, the Fed actually intensifies business fluctuations by changing the rate of growth of the money supply. Why? Partly because the Fed sometimes pays too much attention to measures other than the money supply. But more fundamentally, it is because the Fed tends to overreact to ephemeral changes, and because the effects of changes in the money supply on the economy occur with a long and highly variable lag. In their view, this lag is so unpredictable that the Fed—no matter how laudatory its intent—tends to intensify business fluctuations.

According to Professor Friedman and his followers, the Fed should abandon its attempts to "lean against the wind." *They propose that the Fed conform to a rule that the money supply should increase at some fixed, agreed-upon rate, such as 4 or 5 percent per year. The Fed's job would be simply to see that the money supply grows at approximately this rate.* The monetarists do not claim that a rule of this sort would prevent all business fluctuations, but they do claim that it would work better than the existing system. In particular, they feel that it would prevent the sorts of major depressions and inflations we have experienced in the past. Without major decreases in the money supply (such as occurred during the crash of 1929–33), major depressions could not occur. Without major increases in the money supply (such as occurred during World War II), major inflations could not occur. Of course, it would be nice if monetary policy could iron out minor business fluctuations as well, but in their view this simply cannot be done at present.

This proposal has received considerable attention from both economists and politicians. A number of studies have been carried out to try to estimate what would have happened if Friedman's rule had been used in the past. The results, although by no means free of criticism, seem to indicate that such a rule might have done better than discretionary action did in preventing the Great Depression of the 1930s and the inflation during World War II. But in the period since World War II, the evidence in favor of such a rule is less persuasive. Most economists seem to believe that it would be a mistake to handcuff the Fed to a simple rule of this sort. They think that a discretionary monetary policy can outperform Friedman's rule.

Nonetheless, the debate over rules versus discretionary action goes on, and the issues are still very much alive. Professor Friedman has been able to gain important converts, including the Federal Reserve Bank of St. Louis and members of the Joint Economic Committee of Congress. Indeed, after the Fed's "stop-go" policies of 1966–68 (when the Fed tightened money sharply in 1966 and loosened it rapidly in 1967–68), the Joint Economic Committee urged the Fed to adopt a rule of the sort advocated by Friedman. In 1968, the committee complained that its advice was not being followed, and special hearings were held. The Council of Economic Advisers and the secretary of the Treasury sided with the Fed against adopting such a rule. Some academic economists favor such a rule, others oppose it, and considerable economic research is being carried out to try to clarify and resolve the questions involved.

Test Yourself

1. "The Fed should keep interest rates low to promote prosperity. Unfortunately, however, it is dominated by bankers who like high interest rates because they increase bank profits." Comment and evaluate.

2. "The Fed is like a driver whose steering wheel takes about a minute to influence the car's wheels." Comment and evaluate.

3. Explain why the Federal Reserve may not be able to control both the level of interest rates and the rate of growth of the money supply. What problems does this cause?

4. According to economist Sherman Maisel, William McChesney Martin, former chairman of the Federal Reserve Board, felt "that the primary function of the Federal Reserve Board was to determine what was necessary to maintain a sound currency.... [To Martin] it is as immoral for a country today to allow the value of its currency to fall as it was for kings of old to clip coinage." Do you agree with Martin's views? Why or why not?

Summary

1. Monetary policy is concerned with the money supply and interest rates. Its purpose is to attain and maintain full employment without inflation. When a recession seems imminent and business is soft, the monetary authorities are likely to increase the money supply and reduce interest rates. On the other hand, when the economy is in danger of overheating and inflation threatens, the monetary authorities are likely to rein in the money supply and push up interest rates.

2. Monetary policy and fiscal policy are aimed at much the same goals, but they use different methods to promote them. One advantage of monetary policy over fiscal policy is that the lag between decision and action is relatively short. In view of the time involved in getting tax (and spending) changes enacted, this is an important point.

3. Although monetary policy is influenced by Congress, the Treasury, and other parts of the government and the public at large, the chief responsibility for the formulation of monetary policy lies with the Federal Reserve Board and the Federal Open Market Committee. To a very large extent, monetary policy operates by changing the quantity of bank reserves.

4. The most important tool of monetary policy is open market operations, which involve the buying and selling of government securities in the open market by the Federal Reserve. When the Fed buys government securities, this increases bank reserves. When the Fed sells government securities, this reduces bank reserves.

5. The Fed can also tighten or ease money by increasing or decreasing the discount rate or by increasing or decreasing legal reserve requirements. In addition, the Fed can use moral suasion.

6. As indicators of how tight or easy monetary policy is, the Fed has looked at the level of short-term interest rates, the rate of growth of the money supply, and the rate

369

of growth of the monetary base. During the 1950s and 1960s, the Fed paid most attention to the first indicator; in the 1970s and 1980s, the Fed increased the amount of attention paid to the last two.

7. The Federal Reserve is faced with many difficult problems in formulating and carrying out monetary policy. It must try to see where the economy is heading, and whether—and to what extent—it should tighten or ease money to stabilize the economy. This task is made very difficult by the fact that there is often a long—and highly variable—lag between an action by the Fed and its effect on the economy. There is also considerable disagreement over the best way to measure how tight or easy monetary policy is.

8. There has been criticism of various kinds regarding the performance of the Federal Reserve. Often, the Fed is criticized for paying too little attention to the long lags between its actions and their effects on the economy. Some monetarists, led by Milton Friedman, believe that monetary policy would be improved if discretionary policy were replaced by a rule that the Fed should increase the money supply at some fixed, agreed-on rate, such as 4 or 5 percent per year.

Concepts for Review

Monetary policy	Changes in legal	Selective credit control
Federal Reserve Board	reserve requirements	Margin requirements
Federal Open Market	Discount rate	Easy money
Committee	Moral suasion	Tight money
Open market operations	Regulation Q	Monetary base

CHAPTER 17

Controversies Over Stabilization Policy

During the past several decades, there has been a continuing controversy among economists over the effects of monetary and fiscal policy on output and employment, as well as over the kinds of public policies that should be adopted. This controversy has engaged the attention of many leading economists, and has had a major influence on the thinking of policy makers in both the public and private sectors of the economy. In previous chapters, we have discussed particular aspects of this controversy. Now we look at it in more detail. We begin by discussing the differences between the Keynesians and monetarists.[1] Then we describe the views of the rational expectations theorists and the "supply-side" economists.

At the outset, it is important to recognize that each of these groups is characterized by a great deal of disagreement. For example, Keynesians differ considerably among themselves, and so do monetarists. Moreover, as times have changed and evidence has accumulated, each group has changed its position. Thus the Keynesian views of the 1980s are not the same as those of the 1950s, and labels like neo-Keynesian or nonmonetarist are often used to represent the recent views of the Keynesians.

In the first part of this chapter, we describe the traditional differences between the Keynesians and monetarists. In particular, we discuss their disagreements over the causes of business fluctuations, the stability of the economy, the role of the interest rate, and the effects of monetary and fiscal policy. Then, in the second half of this chapter, we describe the current state

---

[1] In the Appendix to this book, we present the Keynesian-monetarist controversy in terms of a more complete model (involving *IS* and *LM* curves) than is constructed here.

of the Keynesian—monetarist debate, as well as the views of the rational expectations and supply-side economists. The latter groups have been quite influential in the late 1970s and 1980s.

Monetarists versus Keynesians: The Historical Background

The debate between the monetarists and the Keynesians has not been limited to the classroom and scholarly gatherings. It has spilled over onto the pages of the daily newspapers and aroused considerable interest in Congress and other parts of the government. At heart, the argument has been over what determines the level of output, employment, and prices. The Keynesians have put more emphasis on the federal budget than have the monetarists; the monetarists have put more emphasis on the money supply than have the Keynesians. To understand this debate, we need to know something about the recent development of economic thought. Until the Great Depression of the 1930s, the prevailing theory was that NNP, expressed in real terms, would tend automatically to its full-employment level. (Recall from Chapter 8 the classical economists' reasons for clinging to this belief.) Moreover, the prevailing theory was that the price level could be explained by the crude quantity theory of money. In other words, the price level, P, was assumed to be proportional to the quantity of money, M, because $MV = PQ$, and both Q (real NNP) and V (the velocity of money) were thought to be essentially constant.

During the Great Depression of the 1930s, this body of theory seemed inadequate to many economists. NNP was not tending automatically toward its full-employment level. And the crude quantity theory seemed to have little value. In contrast, Keynes's ideas seemed to offer the sort of theoretical guidance and policy prescriptions that were needed. Keynesians did not neglect the use of monetary policy entirely, but they felt that it played a subsidiary role. Particularly in depressions, monetary policy seemed to be of relatively little value, since "you can't push on a string." In other words, monetary policy can make money available, but it cannot insure that it will be spent. To Keynesians, fiscal policy was of central importance.

During the 1940s, 1950s, and early 1960s, the Keynesian view was definitely predominant, here and abroad. But by the mid-1960s, it was being challenged seriously by the monetarists, led by Professor Milton Friedman and his supporters. The monetarist view harked back to the pre-Keynesian doctrine in many respects. In particular, it emphasized the importance of the equation of exchange as an analytical device and the importance of the quantity of money as a tool of economic policy. The monetarist view gained adherents in the late 1960s. Partly responsible was the long delay in passing the surtax of 1968, for the reluctance of the administration to propose and of Congress to enact the new levy vividly illustrated some of the difficulties in using fiscal policy for stabilization. Even more important was the fact that the surtax, when finally enacted, failed to have the restrictive effect on NNP (in the face of expansionary monetary policy) that some Keynesians predicted.

Causes of Business Fluctuations: The Opposing Views

Monetarists and Keynesians have tended to disagree over the basic causes of business fluctuations.

The Monetarist View. As seen by monetarists, major depressions, such as that which occurred during 1929–33, are due to decreases in the money supply. Between 1929 and 1933, for example, the money supply contracted by over one-quarter. Similarly, major inflations, in their view, are due to increases in the money supply. Looking at recent developments, they assert that the inflation of the late 1960s and the middle and late 1970s has been due to the increases that occurred in the money supply.

The Keynesian View. Keynesians, on the other hand, have tended to reject the monetarist view that money is the predominant factor accounting for business fluctuations. To the Keynesians, both monetary and nonmonetary factors cause business fluctuations. Among the important nonmonetary factors are changes (other than those predicted by changes in the money supply) in investment or shifts in the consumption function. (We have discussed many of these nonmonetary factors in Chapter 13.) Thus, in explaining the severe depression of 1929–33, Keynesians emphasize the fact that investment declined by about 90 percent during this period.

The Keynesians have not denied that there is a correlation between changes in the money supply and changes in NNP, but they have argued that the monetarists tend to mix up cause and effect. The Keynesians have suggested that increases in intended spending may bring about a greater demand for money, which in turn causes the money supply to increase. Under these circumstances, the line of causation may be the opposite of that posited by the monetarists.

Stability of the Economy: The Opposing Views

Monetarists and Keynesians also tend to differ over the extent to which our economy is stable.

The Monetarist View. The monetarists are generally more inclined to believe that, if the money supply is managed properly by the government, the free-market economy will tend automatically toward full employment with reasonably stable prices. Although the monetarists are by no means unanimous in this respect, they tend to emphasize the self-regulating characteristics of a free-enterprise economy. In their view, business fluctuations must often be laid at the door of the monetary authorities, whose well-meaning attempts to stabilize the economy frequently do more harm than good.

The Keynesian View. In contrast, the Keynesians are convinced that a free-enterprise economy has relatively weak self-regulating mechanisms. Like Keynes himself, they argue that the equilibrium level of national output may remain for a long time below the level required for full employment. (See Chapter 8 for Keynes's views.) Also, they have argued that there is nothing in the modern economy to prevent considerable inflation, even if the money supply does not increase greatly. Thus, in their view, the government has a much more positive discretionary role to play in stabilizing the economy than that visualized by the monetarists.

Effects of the Interest Rate: The Opposing Views

As pointed out above, both the Keynesian and monetarist groups contain a variety of opinions; thus it is somewhat misleading to refer to *the* Keynesian view or *the* monetarist view. Further, the consensus of opinion in each group has changed over time, as new evidence and arguments have arisen. Some of the matters that were in dispute in the past are no longer major bones of contention, as we shall see below. In the past, many of the basic disagreements between the Keynesians and the monetarists have centered about the quantitative effects of the interest rate. These disagreements have been of three kinds.

Demand for Money. The first disagreement has been over the demand for money. Recall from Chapter 14 that, because the cost of holding money is the interest forgone, the quantity of money demanded goes down as the interest rate goes up—as we saw in Figure 14.3. *According to the monetarists, the quantity of money demanded is relatively insensitive to changes in the interest rate; whereas to Keynesians, it is very sensitive to such changes.* Thus, as shown in Figure 17.1, the demand curve for money, based on monetarist views, is more nearly vertical than the demand curve for money, based on Keynesian views. The reason is that monetarists have tended to put more emphasis than Keynesians on the transactions motive for holding money (where the interest rate is less important than people's incomes in determining the demand for money). On the other hand, Keynesians have tended to put greater emphasis than monetarists on other motives for holding money where the interest rate plays a major

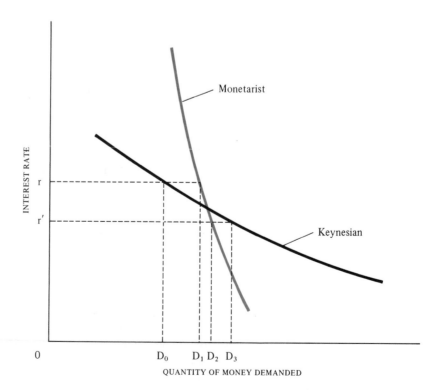

Figure 17.1

Keynesian and Monetarist Assumptions Concerning the Demand for Money
Keynesians have tended to believe that the quantity of money demanded is more sensitive to the interest rate than have monetarists. Thus, if the interest rate falls from r to r′ the quantity of money demanded increases from D₀ to D₃ under Keynesian assumptions, but only from D₁ to D₂ under monetarist assumptions.

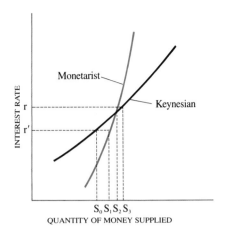

Figure 17.2

Keynesian and Monetarist Assumptions Concerning the Supply of Money *Some Keynesians have tended to believe that the supply of money is more sensitive to the interest rate than monetarists have assumed. Thus, if the interest rate falls from r to r', the supply of money drops from S_3 to S_0 under these Keynesian assumptions, but only from S_2 to S_1 under monetarist assumptions.*

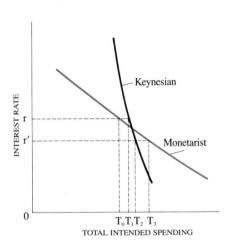

Figure 17.3

Keynesian and Monetarist Assumptions Concerning the Effect of the Interest Rate on Total Intended Spending *Some Keynesians have tended to believe that total intended spending is less sensitive to the interest rate than monetarists have assumed. Thus, if the interest rate falls from r to r', total intended spending increases from T_0 to T_3 under monetarist assumptions, but only from T_1 to T_2 under these Keynesian assumptions.*

role. Also, Keynesians have stressed that the quantity of money demanded for transactions purposes is sensitive to the interest rate.

Supply of Money. A second disagreement has been over the extent to which the supply of money is influenced by the interest rate. *Monetarists have argued that the supply of money is relatively insensitive to changes in the interest rate; whereas some Keynesians have asserted that it is quite sensitive to such changes.* In other words, monetarists have believed that the relationship between the money supply and the interest rate is nearly vertical, as shown in Figure 17.2. In their view, banks will keep few excess reserves, with the result that they are unable to vary the quantity of money in response to changes in loan demand and in interest rates. On the other hand, some Keynesians have felt that the relationship between the money supply and the interest rate is not close to vertical, as shown in Figure 17.2. Pointing to the Great Depression, they have asserted that banks may hold considerable excess reserves during depressions, and that an increase in interest rates may cause some banks to borrow more from the Fed. In their view, banks can and do increase the money supply when loan demand and interest rates are high.

Total Intended Spending. A third disagreement has been over the extent to which total intended spending is sensitive to changes in the interest rate. *According to the monetarists, total expenditure is very sensitive to changes in the interest rate; whereas to some Keynesians, it is not so sensitive to such changes.* Thus the monetarists have believed that the relationship between total intended spending and the interest rate shown in Figure 17.3 is close to horizontal, whereas some Keynesians have believed that it is closer to vertical. The reason is that the monetarists have been convinced that firms' investment decisions, as well as investment in residential housing and expenditure on consumer durable goods, depend considerably on the interest rate, whereas these Keynesians have felt that, although the interest rate has an effect, it is smaller than the monetarists assume. According to these Keynesians other factors, such as existing business conditions and business executives' expectations, have been far more important than the interest rate in determining total expenditure.

The Effect of Monetary Policy: The Opposing Views

Given the three disagreements described in the preceding section, it is easy to see why monetarists have tended to believe that monetary policy is of preeminent importance, whereas Keynesians have tended to believe that it is of lesser importance. As a first step toward understanding why this is so, it is worth emphasizing once again that *the equilibrium interest rate must be at the level where the quantity of money demanded equals the quantity of money supplied.* If the public wants to hold less money than is supplied, the interest rate will tend to decline in order to encourage people to increase the amount of money demanded. If the public wants to hold more money than is supplied, the interest rate will tend to increase in order to make people cut back on the amount of money demanded. Only if the quantity of money demanded equals the quantity of money supplied is the interest rate at its equilibrium level.

Suppose that the monetary authorities increase the money supply, with the result that the *money supply curve* (that is, the relationship between the quantity of money supplied and the interest rate in Figure 17.2) shifts to the right. Under both the Keynesian and monetarist assumptions, there will be a fall in the equilibrium interest rate, since the quantity of money supplied will exceed the quantity of money demanded at the existing interest rate. But, as shown in Figure 17.4, there will be a greater fall in the

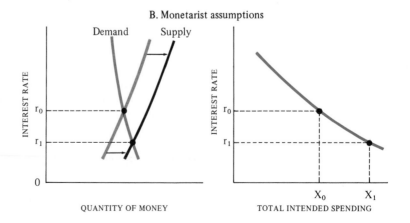

Figure 17.4

Effects of Monetary Policy under Keynesian and Monetarist Assumptions
An increase in the money supply results in a bigger drop in the interest rate, and a bigger increase in spending, under monetarist assumptions than under Keynesian assumptions.

interest rate under the monetarist assumptions (shown in panel B of Figure 17.4) than under the Keynesian assumptions (shown in panel A). Under the monetarist assumptions, the interest rate will fall to r_1, whereas under the Keynesian assumptions, it will fall to r_2.

Further, the resulting fall in the interest rate will have a greater effect on total expenditure under the monetarist assumptions than under the Keynesian assumptions. Under the monetarist assumptions, the fall in the interest rate to r_1 results in total expenditure increasing to X_1. Under the Keynesian assumptions, the fall in the interest rate to r_2 results in total expenditure increasing to X_2. Clearly, *the effect of the increase in the money supply on total expenditure is greater under the monetarist assumptions than under the Keynesian assumptions*—and it is not hard to see why monetarists have tended to emphasize the importance of monetary policy to a greater degree than Keynesians have.[2]

The Effect of Fiscal Policy: The Opposing Views

The monetarists have attacked the Keynesian view that fiscal policy works in the way described in Chapter 12.

The Monetarist View. According to the monetarists, whether the government runs a surplus or deficit has little or no long-run effect on NNP, except insofar as the government finances the surplus or deficit in a way that affects the stock of money. For example, if the government runs a deficit and finances it by borrowing from the public, the money supply will be unchanged. Thus the monetarists would argue that such a deficit has little or no long-run expansionary effect on NNP. On the other hand, if the government finances its deficit by increasing the money supply, the monetarists would expect NNP to increase, but as a result of the expansion of the money supply, not of the deficit. Thus the monetarists claim that the expansion of NNP after the tax cut of 1964 was due to considerable increases in the money supply, not to the tax cut.

Given the assumptions that they make, it is not difficult to see why the monetarists come to this conclusion. Suppose, for example, that an increase occurs in government expenditure. The result, of course, will be a shift to the right of the expenditure function in the right-hand panel of Figure 17.5B. (Note that the B panels in Figure 17.5 are the relevant ones here, since we are concerned with the monetarist assumptions.) If this function shifts from E_1 to E_2, the public will demand more money for transaction purposes, and the demand curve for money will shift to the right, as shown in the left-hand panel of Figure 17.5B. Thus the interest rate will increase to r_3. This relatively great increase in the interest rate will cut private expenditure on consumption goods and investment, and total expenditure will be X_3. (If the interest rate had not risen, total expenditure would have been X_5.) Since X_3 is not appreciably greater than X_0, the increase in government expenditure has little effect on total expenditure. Its principal effect is to substitute public for private expenditure.

---

[2] In Figure 17.4, the analysis is simplified in a number of respects. For a more complete analysis of the topics discussed in this and the following sections, see the Appendix to this book.

A. Keynesian assumptions

B. Monetarist assumptions

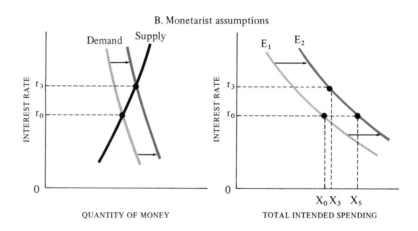

Figure 17.5

Effects of Fiscal Policy under Keynesian and Monetarist Assumptions *An increase in government expenditure results in a bigger rise in the interest rate, and a smaller increase in spending, under monetarist assumptions than under Keynesian assumptions.*

In recent years, economists have come to refer to this substitution of public for private expenditure as the ***crowding-out effect.*** More specifically, if an increase in public expenditure results in a cut in private expenditure, the public expenditure is said to crowd out the private expenditure. Under the monetarist assumptions in Figure 17.5, the rise in the interest rate caused by the increase in government expenditure reduces intended expenditure from X_5 to X_3. This reflects the crowding-out effect.

The Keynesian View. Based on their own quite different assumptions, the Keynesians conclude, of course, that fiscal policy is very effective. To see why, assume once again that an increase occurs in government expenditure, the result being a shift from E_1 to E_2 of the expenditure function in the right-hand panel of Figure 17.5A. (This time, the A panels are the relevant ones, since they contain the Keynesian assumptions.) Once again, as total expenditure rises, the public will demand more money for transactions purposes, thus increasing the interest rate. But according to the Keynesians the increase in the interest rate will be relatively small, since there will be an increase in the quantity of money supplied, and the quantity of money demanded is relatively sensitive to the interest rate. Thus the interest rate rises only to r_4, and total expenditure will be X_4. The crowding-out effect is small, since the rise in the interest rate cuts intended expenditure only from

X_6 to X_4. Since X_4 is much greater than X_0, the increase in government expenditure has a great effect on total expenditure, based on the Keynesian assumptions.

The Controversy over a Monetary Rule

The Monetarist View. Many, but not all, leading monetarists advocate the establishment of a rule to govern monetary policy. In the previous chapter, we discussed the arguments of Friedman and his supporters for such a rule.

Example 17.1   What Caused the Great Depression?

Monetarists and Keynesians have disagreed over the causes of the Great Depression of the 1930s. According to monetarists Milton Friedman and Anna Schwartz, the Great Depression was due in large measure to changes in the money supply, indicated below:

| | Money supply (billions of dollars) | |
Year	M-1	M-2
1929	26.6	46.6
1930	25.8	45.7
1931	24.1	42.7
1932	21.1	36.0
1933	19.9	32.2
1934	21.9	34.4

(a) In response to the substantial drop in NNP after 1929, the Fed, according to Friedman and Schwartz, did not undertake large-scale open market purchases until 1932. Does this policy seem correct? (b) The Friedman-Schwartz interpretation of the Great Depression has been challenged by MIT's Peter Temin, who argues that the decline in the money supply in 1929–33 was due to a shift in the demand curve for money. What might have caused such a shift? (c) If, as Temin believes, the Great Depression was due in part to a downward shift in the consumption function, would the money supply decrease?

SOLUTION

(a) Friedman and Schwartz, among others, argue that it was an incorrect policy, and that the Fed should have adopted a more expansionary policy in the early 1930s. (b) A drop in investment or a downward shift in the consumption function might have reduced NNP. The reduction in NNP would have shifted the demand curve for money to the left. (c) As pointed out in the answer to (b), a downward shift in the consumption function would reduce NNP and shift the demand curve for money to the left. The result would be a decrease in interest rates, which could reduce the money supply. For example, banks might be induced to hold more excess reserves.*

* For further discussion, see M. Friedman and A. Schwartz, *A Monetary History of the United States,* Princeton: Princeton University Press, 1963; and P. Temin, *Did Monetary Forces Cause the Great Depression?,* New York: Norton, 1976.

You will recall their charge that the Federal Reserve's monetary policies have often caused economic instability. Because of the difficulties in forecasting the future state of the economy and the fairly long and variable time lag in the effect of changes in the money supply, the Fed, in the eyes of many leading monetarists, frequently has caused excessive inflation or unemployment by its discretionary policies. According to the monetarists we would be better off with a rule stipulating that the money supply should grow steadily at a constant rate, say 4 or 5 percent per year.[3]

The Keynesian View. The Keynesians retort that such a rule would handcuff the monetary authorities and contribute to economic instability, since discretionary monetary policies are required to keep the economy on a reasonably even keel. The Keynesians grant that the Fed sometimes makes mistakes, but they assert that things would be worse if the Fed could not pursue the policies that a given set of circumstances seems to call for.

[3] When he accepted the Nobel prize in 1976, Milton Friedman jokingly said: "My monetary studies have led me to the conclusion that central banks could profitably be replaced by computers geared to provide a steady rate of growth in the quantity of money. Fortunately for me personally, and for a select group of fellow economists, the conclusion has had no practical impact ... else there would have been no Central Bank of Sweden to have established the award I am honored to receive." (The Central Bank of Sweden donated the money for the Nobel prize in economics.)

Test Yourself

1. "Keynesians are liberal activitists who want to push our society in the direction of socialism. Their emphasis on fiscal policy is a reflection of their desire to have the government purchase more and more of the national output." Comment and evaluate.

2. "Monetarists are arch-conservatives with a strong *laissez-faire* orientation. They prefer monetary policy over fiscal policy because it involves less direct interference by government in the marketplace." Comment and evaluate.

3. "The Keynesian model can easily be translated into monetarist terms, and the monetarist model can easily be translated into Keynesian terms. Thus, there really is no basic difference between the Keynesians and the monetarists." Do you agree? Why or why not?

4. "Keynesians believe that the demand curve for money is close to vertical; consequently, they feel that monetary policy has less effect on NNP than monetarists." Comment and evaluate.

The Current State of the Keynesian-Monetarist Debate

The controversy between the Keynesians and monetarists has been going on for decades. At this point, the debate no longer focuses on some of the issues that were paramount 20 years ago. At that time, the controversy centered on the choice between monetary and fiscal policy. The more partisan monetarists claimed that fiscal policy was relatively impotent; the more partisan Keynesians claimed the same regarding monetary policy. We have discussed the arguments of each side in previous sections of this chapter. During the 1970s, as more and more evidence accumulated, this issue seemed to wane in importance. At present, most monetarists concede that fiscal policy can affect output and the price level; and most Keynesians concede the same regarding monetary policy. Although it would be incorrect to say that no differences remain on this score, there seems to be a growing recognition that the differences have narrowed considerably. Thus Milton Friedman, the leading monetarist, has been quoted as saying, "We are all Keynesians now." And Franco Modigliani, a leading Keynesian (and 1985 Nobel laureate), responded in 1976 by saying, "We are all monetarists now."

During the late 1970s and early 1980s, the focus of the debate has tended to shift. Now the clash between the monetarists and the Keynesians (who in more recent years have tended to prefer other labels like neo-Keynesian or post-Keynesian or nonmonetarist) seems to be traceable largely to the following basic disagreements which continue to exist between them.

Stability of Private Spending. The monetarists believe that, if the government's economic policies did not destabilize the economy, private spending would be quite stable. One reason for this belief is the permanent-income hypothesis, discussed in Chapter 10. Personal consumption expenditures change relatively slowly as households adjust their estimates of their long-term income prospects. Keynesians, on the other hand, believe that business and consumer spending represents a substantial source of economic instability that should be offset by monetary and fiscal policy.

Flexibility of Prices. Even if intended private spending is not entirely stable, flexible prices tend to stabilize it, according to the monetarists. The Keynesians reply that prices are relatively inflexible downward, as shown by the fact that, despite widespread unemployment, prices did not decline during the late 1930s. In their view, the length of time that would be required for the economy to get itself out of a severe recession would be intolerably long. Monetarists seem more inclined than Keynesians to believe that high unemployment will cause wages and input prices to fall, shifting the aggregate supply curve downward and increasing output in a reasonable period of time.

Rules versus Activism. Monetarists believe that, even if intended private spending is not entirely stable, and if prices are not entirely flexible, an activist monetary and fiscal policy to stabilize the economy is likely to do more damage than good. As pointed out repeatedly above, they favor a rule stipulating that the monetary supply should grow steadily at a constant rate, because of the difficulties in forecasting the future state of the economy and because of the long and variable time lag in the effect of changes in the quantity of money on output and prices. The Keynesians, while admitting that monetary and fiscal policy have sometimes been destabilizing, are much more optimistic about the efficacy of such policies in the future.

To a considerable extent, the differences between the Keynesians and the monetarists stem from divergent political beliefs. The Keynesians tend to be optimistic concerning the extent to which the government can be trusted to formulate and carry out a responsible set of monetary and fiscal policies. They recognize that some politicians are willing to win votes in the next election by destabilizing the economy, but they nonetheless believe that discretionary action by elected officials will generally be more effective than automatic rules. The monetarists, on the other hand, are skeptical of the willingness of politicians to do what is required to stabilize the economy,

Basic Idea #34: It would be naive to believe that economists' views concerning economic stabilization are independent of their political views. Monetarists (generally conservative) tend to emphasize the self-regulating characteristics of a free-enterprise economy, and believe that the monetary authorities often cause business fluctuations. In contrast, Keynesians (generally liberal) think that a free-enterprise economy has relatively weak self-regulating mechanisms, and that the government should assume a more positive discretionary role.

rather than what is politically expedient. Since this aspect of the debate is difficult to resolve (in any scientific way), a complete resolution of the Keynesian-monetarist controversy is not likely any time soon. However, many other aspects of the controversy are more amenable to scientific analysis, and these aspects almost surely will be clarified substantially in the years to come.[4]

Rational Expectations: Another Element of the Current Debate

It should not be assumed that the debate between monetarists and Keynesians is the only controversy regarding stabilization policy. In recent years, there has been considerable argument over the theory of rational expectations as well.

WHAT ARE RATIONAL EXPECTATIONS?

During the 1970s, a small band of economists, led by Robert Lucas of the University of Chicago and Thomas Sargent and Neil Wallace of the University of Minnesota, formulated a theory, based on the hypothesis of *rational expectations,* that already has had a substantial impact on economic analysis and policy. Basically, what these economists assumed was that individuals and firms do not make systematic errors in forecasting the future. In other words, forecasts, *on the average,* are assumed to be correct. Of course, this does not mean that forecasters are always right. As we saw in Chapter 13, this is far from true. Instead, these economists assumed that forecasting errors are purely random.

By assuming that people's expectations are on the average correct, they also assume in effect that these expectations are formed consistently with the relevant economic model of the economy. Thus expectations are determined as part of the model and are genuinely forward-looking, rather than being based on a mechanical extrapolation of the past (as in older economic theories). Consequently, the announcement or anticipation that a particular event will occur results in immediate effects on the economy, even before the anticipated event actually occurs.[5]

CAN STABILIZATION POLICIES WORK?

Based on these assumptions, the rational expectations theorists conclude that the *government cannot use monetary and fiscal policies in the way described in previous chapters, because the models presented in those chapters do not recognize that the expectations of firms and individuals concerning their incomes, job prospects, sales, and other relevant variables are influenced by government policies.* If firms and individuals formulate their ex-

---

[4] This section has benefited from the discussion in Robert J. Gordon, *Macroeconomics,* Boston: Little, Brown, 1978.

[5] The hypothesis of rational expectations was first developed and applied by John Muth of Indiana University.

pectations rationally, they will tend to frustrate the government's attempts to use activist stabilization policies.

To illustrate what these economists are saying, suppose that the economy is in a recession and that the government, in accord with the models in Chapters 12 and 16, increases the amount that it spends on goods and services and increases the money supply. Because prices tend to move up while wages do not, profits tend to rise and firms find it profitable to expand. But this model is based on the supposition that labor is not smart enough to foresee that prices are going to go up and that labor's real wage is going to diminish. If labor does foresee this (that is, if its expectations are rational), it will insist on an increase in its money wage, which will mean that firms will not find it profitable to expand, and the government's antirecession policy will not work as expected.

UNEMPLOYMENT AND BUSINESS FLUCTUATIONS

According to the rational expectations theorists, high rates of unemployment are not evidence of a gap between actual and potential output that can be reduced; instead, output fluctuations result from random and irreducible errors. Markets are assumed to work efficiently; and firms, acting to maximize their profits, are assumed to make the best possible decisions. According to Lucas, since unemployed workers have the option of accepting pay cuts to get jobs, excess unemployment is essentially voluntary.

Fluctuations in aggregate demand are due principally to erratic and unpredictable government policy, in his view. Changes in the quantity of money induce cyclical fluctuations in the economy. But the power of policy changes to affect real NNP is limited. People come to learn the way in which policy is made, and only unanticipated government policy changes can have a substantial impact on output or employment. Once firms and individuals learn of any systematic rule for adjusting government policy to events, the rule will have no effect.

REACTIONS PRO AND CON

These views have received considerable attention, and in the late 1970s the Federal Reserve Bank of Minneapolis stated its acceptance of them. In its annual report, the bank stated,

> The [rational expectations] view conjectures that some amount of cyclical swing in production and employment is inherent in the micro-level processes of the economy that no government macro policies can, or should attempt to, smooth out. Expected additions to money growth certainly won't smooth out cycles, if the arguments in this paper are correct. Surprise additions to money growth have the potential to make matters worse. . . . One strategy that seems consistent with the significant, though largely negative, findings of rational expectations would have monetary policy focus its attention on inflation and announce, and stick to, a policy that would bring the rate of increase in the general price level to some specified low figure.[6]

Robert Lucas

---

[6] The Federal Reserve Bank of Minneapolis, *Rational Expectations—Fresh Ideas That Challenge Some Established Views of Policy Making,* Minneapolis, 1977, pp. 12–13.

Given the fact that the rational expectations theorists have challenged the core of the theory underlying current stabilization policies, it is not surprising that many economists, particularly liberals, have challenged their conclusions. Franco Modigliani, for instance, has claimed that the rational expectations model is inconsistent "with the evidence: if it were valid, deviations of unemployment from the natural rate would be small and transitory—in which case [Keynes's] *General Theory* would not have been written."[7] Since the rational expectations theory makes excess unemployment the result of purely unexpected events, one would think that unemployment would fluctuate randomly around its equilibrium level, if this theory is true. However, as we have seen, recessions often last quite a long time.

Critics also claim that the rational expectations theory neglects the inertia in wages and prices. Contracts are written for long periods of time. Workers stick with firms for considerable periods. Consequently, wages and prices do not adjust as rapidly as is assumed by the rational expectations theorists. According to the critics, most empirical analysis does not support the rational expectations model. Contrary to the theory, price movements show only slow and adaptive changes.

Only the future will tell how successful the rational expectations theorists will be in their attack on conventional doctrines, but there can be no doubt that they have caused a remarkable stir in the economics profession.[8]

Supply-Side Economics Enters the Fray

The theory of rational expectations is not the only newcomer to the scene. In the late 1970s and 1980s, *supply-side economics* also entered the fray. To a considerable extent, as we have seen, economic policy since World War II has been dominated by measures aimed at managing aggregate demand, the two traditional tools of demand management being monetary and fiscal policy. In contrast, *supply-side economics is concerned primarily with influencing aggregate supply.*

As pointed out in Chapter 9, supply-side economics really is not new. Major economists of the eighteenth and nineteenth (as well as twentieth) centuries were concerned with the stimulation of aggregate supply. But one new twist is that some people seem to believe that the emphasis in combatting inflation should be on pushing the aggregate supply curve to the right rather than on curbing the rightward movement of the aggregate demand curve.

SUPPLY-SIDE PRESCRIPTIONS

To stimulate such a rightward shift in the aggregate supply curve, *supply-siders favor the use of various financial incentives, particularly tax cuts.* In their view, the reduction of tax rates will encourage people to work longer

---

[7] F. Modligliani, "The Monetarist Controversy, or, Should We Forsake Stabilization Policies," *American Economic Review,* March 1977, p. 6.

[8] For further discussion, see S. Turnovsky, "Rational Expectations and the Theory of Macroeconomic Policy," *Journal of Economic Education,* Winter 1984.

and harder, thus increasing the level of full-employment output. Also, reduced tax rates and regulations are likely to make firms willing to make risky investments in research and new plant and equipment. Further, tax reductions are likely to cut the amount of time and resources invested in finding and exploiting tax loopholes; more would be invested in productive activities.

Supply-siders argue too that tax reductions will increase saving. By cutting taxes on income from capital, the government can increase the after-tax return to capital, and encourage saving. (Recall from Chapter 5 that this is an area of controversy.) Supply-siders emphasize that saving is a very important activity which permits and encourages investment, which in turn increases the nation's productive capacity. As pointed out in Chapter 11's discussion of the paradox of thrift, Keynes took a somewhat different view of saving, emphasizing its negative effects on aggregate demand.

There is considerable uncertainty regarding the extent to which more work, risk-taking, and saving will result from tax reductions. For example, take the case of saving. In a well-known study, Stanford's Michael Boskin found that a 10-percent increase in the real after-tax rate of return will result in an increase of 2 to 4 percent in saving per year. On the other hand, other economists, such as Phillip Howrey and Saul Hymans of the University of Michigan, have criticized Boskin's findings, and have themselves come to quite different conclusions. Although the jury is still out regarding many of the relevant points, it seems fair to say that many economists are skeptical of the claims made by the more extreme supply-siders.

THE NEED FOR DEMAND MANAGEMENT

In particular, many economists seem to question the idea that supply-side policies alone can make much of a dent in our inflation problems in any reasonable time frame. For example, suppose that we accept the supply-sider's contention that their policies would increase full-employment output substantially. In a period of two or three years, it seems doubtful that these policies could increase full-employment output enough to offset the sorts of inflationary pressures experienced in the late 1970s. Even if supply-side policies could increase the annual rate of growth of full-employment output by 0.5 percentage points (a stellar performance indeed), this would be too little to make much headway against such inflationary pressures.

Thus supply-side policies should not be viewed as a replacement for demand management. This does not mean that such policies cannot be worthwhile or important. On the contrary, it is of the utmost importance that our nation devote attention to pushing its aggregate supply curve to the right. (Chapter 19 is devoted entirely to this topic.) But it is incorrect to view such policies as adequate counter-cyclical measures. The need to influence the aggregate demand curve remains.

THE TAX CUT OF 1981 AND SUPPLY-SIDE ECONOMICS

As indicated in previous chapters, supply-side economists played an important role in formulating and arguing for the huge tax cut in 1981.

Individual income taxes were cut 25 percent across the board over three years. Corporation taxes were reduced as a consequence of an increase in the pace at which depreciation can be charged against current income. Other tax reductions were enacted as well.

The first phase of the tax cut occurred in 1981 and was discounted by the administration, because it was only 5 percent and did not prevent the recession of 1981–82. Economic policy makers in the Reagan administration, therefore, counted on the larger tax cut of 10 percent in 1982 to stimulate the economy. They argued that the Reagan Economic Recovery Program could only be judged after the successive 10 percent tax cuts in 1982 and 1983 had occurred. They were banking on the success of the successive 10 percent tax cuts to show up in a strong recovery.

In fact, there was a strong recovery in 1983 and 1984; and particularly at the beginning of 1984, the supply-siders were often more accurate than other economists in forecasting how strong it would be. However, according to many observers, this substantial increase in real NNP should have been expected on the basis of the Keynesian model described in Chapter 12. To them, the strong recovery of 1983 and 1984 was testimony to the continued usefulness of the Keynesian model, highly simplified though it is.

Also, critics of supply-side economics point out that some supply-siders claimed that the 1981 tax cut would increase output so dramatically that there would be no substantial increase in the federal deficit because output would rise sufficiently to offset the cut in tax rates. Instead, as the critics stress, the deficit for fiscal 1985 may be about $200 billion. In response to such criticisms, the supply-siders blame the Fed's tight-money policies for the fact that output did not grow as much as they expected.

Test Yourself

1. "Your preferences concerning the optimal size of the government should not influence your views concerning stabilization policy." Do you agree? Why or why not?

2. Explain why an attempt by the government to stabilize interest rates may be destabilizing.

3. Do the monetarists agree with the Keynesians' interpretation of the effects of the tax cut of 1964? If not, what is their interpretation of what happened?

4. (a) "Working hours are fixed by custom at about 40 hours per week. Cutting taxes won't affect them." Do you agree? Why or why not? (b) "Business executives are working about as hard as they can to keep their heads above water. Cutting taxes won't affect how hard they work." Do you agree? Why or why not?

Summary

1. Keynesians have tended to view the private sector of the economy as inherently unstable, and they have favored the use of fiscal policy to offset this instability. They have tended to feel that fiscal policy was more important, relative to monetary policy, than have monetarists. Keynesians have based their analysis of business fluctuations on the sorts of concepts taken up in Chapter 10 and 12.

2. Monetarists have tended to view the private sector of the economy as inherently quite stable, and they have blamed much of the economy's instability on clumsy or ill-conceived policies of the government. They have emphasized the importance of monetary policy. Monetarists have based their analysis of business fluctuations on the equation of exchange, discussed in Chapter 14.

3. Many of the disagreements between the Keynesians and monetarists have centered about the effects of changes in the interest rate. (a) Monetarists have said that the quantity of money demanded is relatively insensitive to changes in the interest rate, whereas Keynesians have said that it is sensitive to such changes. (b) Monetarists have said that the supply of money is relatively insensitive to changes in the interest rate, whereas some Keynesians have said that it is quite sensitive to such changes. (c) Monetarists have said that total expenditure is very sensitive to changes in the interest rate, whereas some Keynesians have said that it is not so sensitive to such changes. These disagreements resulted in the different views of monetarists and Keynesians concerning the relative importance of fiscal and monetary policy.

4. Many leading monetarists feel that the Federal Reserve, in its attempts to stabilize the economy, does more harm than good. They favor the establishment of a rule to govern monetary policy, an idea most Keynesians oppose.

5. During the 1970s, as more evidence accumulated, the choice between monetary and fiscal policy, which had been at the center of the debate for so long, seemed to wane in importance. At present, most monetarists concede that fiscal policy can affect output and the price level, and most Keynesians concede the same regarding monetary policy.

6. At present, the debate seems to focus on the stability of private spending, the flexibility of prices, and the desirability of rules rather than discretionary government action. Monetarists tend to feel that (a) if the government's economic policies did not destabilize the economy, private spending would be quite stable; (b) even if intended private spending is not entirely stable, flexible prices tend to stabilize it; (c) an activist monetary and fiscal policy is likely to do more harm than good.

7. Keynesians tend to feel that (a) business and consumer spending represents a substantial source of economic instability that should be offset by monetary and fiscal policy; (b) price flexibility cannot be depended on to promote economic stability in a reasonable length of time; (c) an activist monetary and fiscal policy is likely to do more good than harm.

8. According to rational expectations theorists, the government cannot use monetary and fiscal policies in the way described in previous chapters because the models presented in these chapters do not recognize that the expectations of firms and individuals concerning their incomes, job prospects, sales, and other relevant variables are influenced by government policies.

9. Supply-side economics is concerned primarily with influencing aggregate supply. To stimulate rightward shifts in the aggregate supply curve, supply-siders favor the use of various financial incentives, particularly tax cuts. Supply-side policies cannot be viewed as a replacement for demand management.

Concepts for Review

Keynesians
Monetarists

Crowding-out effect
Rational expectations
Supply-side economics

CHAPTER 18

Inflation and Anti-Inflationary Measures

Whatever their attitudes toward the controversies described in the previous chapter, policy makers in the 1970s and early 1980s found it very difficult to maintain reasonably full employment with reasonably stable prices. Inflation sometimes galloped along at close to double-digit rates even when the unemployment rate was relatively high. It was a period of considerable economic discomfort for the nation—as well as a period of discomfort for economists, since they had difficulty in coming up with any solutions that were acceptable to policy makers. In 1982–85, inflation abated somewhat; in late 1985, it was about 3 percent. But no one could say how long this would last. Between 1964 and 1982, the Consumer Price Index had tripled!

In this chapter, we take up a variety of anti-inflationary measures that have been tried or proposed, often with questionable success. Among these policies are wage and price controls, incomes policies, and tax-based incomes policies. Finally, we try to indicate where we stand in our attempts to stabilize the economy and the nature of the challenges that lie ahead.

Demand-Pull Inflation

In previous chapters, we described **demand-pull inflation,** a situation in which there is too much aggregate spending. The $C + I + G$ line is too high, resulting in inflationary pressure. Or, put in terms of the equation of exchange, $M \times V$ is too high, so that P is pushed up. Too much money is chasing too few goods. This kind of inflation stems from the demand or

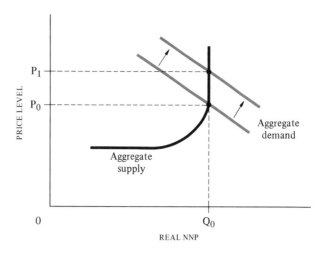

Figure 18.1

Increase in the Price Level Due to a Shift in the Aggregate Demand Curve
Major inflations during the Revolutionary and Civil Wars were due in considerable part to shifts upward and to the right in the aggregate demand curve. Such a shift results in an increase in the price level from OP_0 to OP_1. Since national output is fixed, the rise in the price level must be proportional to the increase in spending.

spending behavior of the nation's consumers, firms, and government. We have had many inflations of this kind. The major inflations during the Revolutionary War and Civil War were basically caused by demand-pull factors; and so, much more recently, was the inflation arising from the Vietnam War.

In those extreme cases in which all resources are utilized, the rise in the price level that occurs in demand-pull inflation can be viewed as a matter of arithmetic: since national output is fixed, the rise in the price level must be proportional to the increase in total spending. This is the situation shown in Figure 18.1, in which the economy is assumed to be on the vertical segment of its aggregate supply curve before the increase in aggregate demand.

Cost-Push Inflation

However, in the view of many economists, demand-pull inflation is not the only kind of inflation. There is another kind—*cost-push inflation*. The process underlying cost-push inflation is not as well understood as it should be, but, according to many economists, it works something like this. While GNP is below its potential level, costs are increased, perhaps because unions push up wages, and in an attempt to protect their profit margins, firms push up prices. These price increases affect the costs of other firms and the consumer's cost of living. As the cost of living goes up, labor feels entitled to, and obtains, higher wages to offset the higher living costs. Firms again pass on the cost increase to the consumer in the form of a price increase. This so-called *wage-price spiral* is at the heart of cost-push inflation.

One case of fairly pure cost-push inflation occurred in the late 1950s. This was a period of considerable slack in the economy. You will recall from Chapter 9 that a recession occurred in 1957–58. By 1958 6.8 percent of the labor force was unemployed. Nonetheless, wage increases took place during the late 1950s—and at a rate in excess of the rate of increase of labor productivity (output per hour of labor).[1] For example, average earnings (outside agriculture) went up by 4 percent between 1957 and 1961, while labor productivity went up by 2½ percent. Moreover, prices

[1] In a later section, we shall discuss the importance of the rate of increase of output per hour of labor. For present purposes, it is sufficient to note that the greater the rate of increase of output per hour of labor, the larger the rate of increase of cost per hour of labor that can be absorbed without an increase in cost per unit of output.

Example 18.1   The Fed and Cost-Push Inflation

Suppose that labor unions suddenly demand that their wage rate (in money, not real terms) be doubled. Since firms must increase prices if they are to be willing to produce the same output as before, the aggregate supply curve will shift upward and to the left, as shown below:

   (a) If the Federal Reserve holds the money supply at its initial level, what will happen to real output and to unemployment? (b) Will real wages double? (c) Suppose that the Federal Reserve, fearing a big rise in unemployment, increases the money supply. If the increase is large enough, can a decrease in real output be avoided? (d) If a decrease in real output is avoided in this way, what will be the effect on the price level?

SOLUTION

(a) As shown in the above diagram, the economy will move from point A to point B. Thus real output will fall from OQ_0 to OQ_1 and the decrease in real output will increase unemployment. (b) No, because the price level at point B is higher than at point A. Thus, although the money wage has doubled, the real wage has less than doubled. (c) Yes. By increasing the money supply, the Fed can push the aggregate demand curve to the right. If it pushes it far enough to the right, it can make it intersect the new aggregate supply curve at point C, where real NNP is at its original level, OQ_0. (d) The price level will rise considerably. As shown in the diagram, the price level at point C is much higher than at point A. The Fed, by enabling the cost-push action of the unions to increase the price level without resulting in additional unemployment, is said to have *accommodated* the cost-push.

increased each year—by 3 percent from 1956 to 1957, and by 2 percent from 1957 to 1958.

Certainly this seemed to be a different phenomenon than the demand-pull inflation described in previous chapters. There was no evidence that too much money was chasing too few goods. Instead, this was apparently a case of cost-push inflation. Commenting on the situation in the middle and late 1950s, the Council of Economic Advisers concluded, "The movement of wages during this period reflected in part the power exercised in labor markets by strong unions and the power possessed by large companies to pass on higher wage costs in higher prices."[2]

In some cases, increases in materials prices may play a major role in cost-push inflation. When the oil-producing countries increased the price of crude oil in 1974 and in later years like 1979, this resulted in price increases in a wide variety of products that are made (directly or indirectly) from petroleum. Because these price increases were not offset by price reductions elsewhere in the economy, the overall price level increased (and at a very rapid rate) in 1974 and 1979. Of course, the price hike for crude oil (and other materials) was by no means the sole reason for this inflation. But unquestionably it did play a noteworthy role in shifting the aggregate supply curve upward and to the left, as shown in Figure 18.2. (Recall that this was pointed out in our discussion of stagflation in Chapter 9.)

Difficulties in Distinguishing Cost-Push from Demand-Pull Inflation

Generally, it is difficult, if not impossible, to sort out cost-push inflation from demand-pull inflation. For example, an increase in aggregate demand may raise firms' demand for labor, causing workers to demand higher wages, which in turn leads firms to raise their prices. In such a case,

Figure 18.2

**Increase in the Price Level Due to a
Shift in the Aggregate Supply Curve**
*According to many economists, the
inflation of the middle and late 1970s
was due in considerable part to shifts upward and to the left in the aggregate
supply curve because of shortages and
price increases in oil and other materials.
Such a shift results in an increase in the
price level from OP to OP'.*

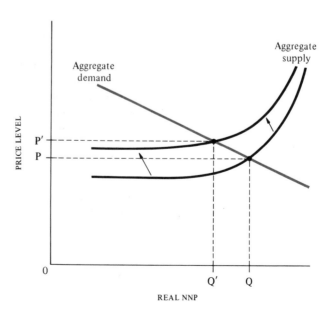

391

the inflation may be demand-pull in the sense that the ultimate cause was an increase in aggregate demand, but it is cost-push in the sense that the proximate cause of the increase in the price level was an increase in wages.

Also, it is important to note that a cost-push inflation of the sort shown in Figure 18.2 is unlikely to continue for a long period of time unless the Fed "accommodates" or "validates" it by following policies that shift the aggregate demand curve to the right. (See Example 18.1) If the aggregate demand curve does not shift, the inflation will die out. (Thus, in Example 18.1, once the economy moves from point *A* to point *B*, the inflation will be over. There will be no further increase in the price level.)

The Phillips Curve

As we have just seen, some economists believe that inflation can result from the power of labor to push up wages and the power of companies to pass on higher wage costs to consumers in the form of higher prices. What determines the rate at which labor can push up wages? If you think about it for a while, you will probably agree that *labor's ability to increase wages depends on the level of unemployment. The more unemployment, the more difficult it is for labor to increase wages.* Although perfect competition by no means prevails in the labor market, there is enough competition so that the presence of a pool of unemployed workers puts some damper on wage increases. In nonunion industries and occupations, workers are much less inclined to push for wage increases—and employers are much less inclined to accept them—when lots of people are looking for work. In unionized industries and occupations, unions are less likely to put their members through the hardship of a strike—and firms have less to lose from a strike—when business is bad and unemployment is high.

Because wages tend to be increased more rapidly when unemployment is low, one would expect the rate of increase of wages in any year to be inversely related to the level of unemployment. In a particular period of time in the United States, suppose that the rate of increase in wages tends to be related to the level of unemployment in the way shown in Figure 18.3. According to this figure, which is based on hypothetical, but reasonable, numbers, wages tend to rise by about 6 percent per year when 9 percent of the labor force is unemployed, by about 7½ percent per year when 7 percent of the labor force is unemployed, and by about 9 percent per year when 6 percent of the labor force is unemployed. *The relationship between the rate of increase of wages and the level of unemployment is known as the Phillips curve.* It was named after A. W. Phillips, the British economist who first called attention to it.

THE RELATIONSHIP BETWEEN INFLATION AND UNEMPLOYMENT

Given the Phillips curve in Figure 18.3, one can determine the relationship between the rate of inflation and the level of unemployment. If *C* is

---

[2] *1962 Annual Report of the Council of Economic Advisers,* Washington, D.C.: Government Printing Office, p. 175.

Figure 18.3
The Phillips Curve *The Phillips curve shows the relationship between the rate of increase of wages and the level of unemployment. This curve is drawn on the assumption that moderate inflation is expected.*

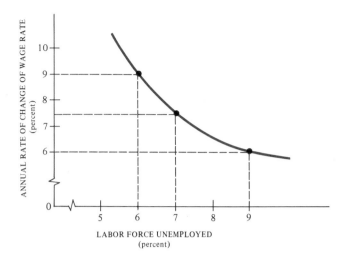

the total cost—wage and nonwage—per hour of labor, the total cost per unit of output equals $C \times H \div O$, where H is the total number of hours worked and O is total output. This says no more than that total cost per unit of output equals total cost per hour of labor times the number of hours of labor divided by the number of units of output. Thus total cost per unit of output equals total cost per hour of labor divided by output per hour of labor. (Output per hour of labor—that is, $O \div H$—is often called *labor productivity*.) Since the rate of increase of a ratio is the rate of increase of the numerator minus the rate of increase of the denominator, it follows that the *rate of increase of total cost per unit of output equals the rate of increase of total cost per hour of labor minus the rate of increase of output per hour of labor.*[3]

Suppose that the rate of increase of prices equals the rate of increase of total cost per unit of output, and that the rate of increase of total cost per hour of labor equals the rate of increase of wages. Then *the rate of increase of prices equals the rate of increase of wages minus the rate of increase of output per hour of labor.* Suppose too that the rate of increase of output per hour of labor (that is, labor productivity) is 2 percent per year. Then the rate of increase of prices equals the rate of increase of wages minus 2 percent.[4] Consequently, the relationship between the rate of increase in prices and the level of unemployment is as shown in Figure 18.4.

There is, of course, a simple relationship between the curve in Figure 18.3 and the curve in Figure 18.4. The curve in Figure 18.4 (which shows

---

[3] To see this, note that total cost per unit of output equals C (total cost per hour of labor) divided by $O \div H$ (output per hour of labor). Thus the rate of increase of total cost per unit of output equals the rate of increase of C minus the rate of increase of $O \div H$.

[4] Let p equal the rate of increase of prices, w equal the rate of increase of wages, d equal the rate of increase of output per hour of labor, a equal the rate of increase of total cost per unit of output, and b equal the rate of increase of total cost per hour of labor. The previous paragraph of the text concluded that $a = b - d$. Since we assume in this paragraph of the text that $p = a$, that $b = w$, and that $d = 2$, it follows that $p = w - 2$.

Of course, it is possible that firms will accept a lower profit rate (as a percent of sales) if they experience a decrease in demand for their products.

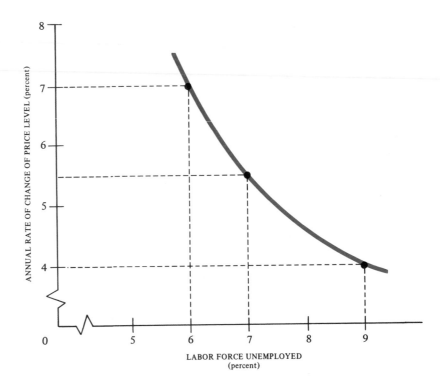

Figure 18.4

**Relationship between Unemployment
Rate and Rate of Inflation**   *This
relationship can, under the conditions
specified in the text, be deduced from the
Phillips curve.*

the relationship between *price* increases and unemployment) is always 2 percentage points below the curve in Figure 18.3 (which shows the relationship between *wage* increases and unemployment). Why? Because the rate of increase of prices—under the assumptions set forth above—always equals the rate of increase of wages minus 2 percent.

THE POLICY MENU

If the curve in Figure 18.4 remains fixed, the government is faced with a fundamental choice. It can reduce unemployment only if it is willing to accept a higher rate of inflation, and it can reduce the rate of inflation only if it is willing to accept a higher rate of unemployment. For example, in Figure 18.4, if the unemployment rate is 7 percent and the inflation rate is 5½ percent, the government will be anxious to reduce unemployment, but if it reduces it to 6 percent, the inflation rate will jump to 7 percent. It will also want to reduce inflation, but if it cuts it to 4 percent, the unemployment rate will jump to 9 percent. This poses a difficult problem for the government (and for society as a whole), since it would be desirable to reduce both inflation and unemployment.

The Instability of the Phillips Curve

During the 1960s, economists came to believe that the Phillips curve was a stable, predictable relationship. Panel A of Figure 18.5 shows the relationship between the inflation rate and the unemployment rate in the United States during 1955 to 1969. As you can see, there was a fairly close relationship between them in this period. Economists relied heavily on these data to buttress their belief that the Phillips curve really existed, and that it had the hypothesized shape. It is no exaggeration to say that the Phillips curve in Figure 18.5 (that is, the heavy line) had a major influence on both economic analysis and economic policy in the sixties.

But then something unforeseen (by most economists) occurred. *The inflation and unemployment rates in the seventies and eighties did not conform at all closely to the relationship that prevailed in the sixties.* As shown in panel B of Figure 18.5, the points for 1970 to 1984 lie far above and to the right of the relationship that prevailed earlier. In other words, holding constant the unemployment rate, the inflation rate tended to be much higher in the seventies than in the sixties. Or, holding the inflation rate constant, the unemployment rate tended to be much higher in the seventies than in the sixties. Whichever way you look at it, this departure from the earlier relationship between inflation and unemployment was bad news.

A REASON FOR INSTABILITY

Why did this departure from the earlier relationship occur? As stressed in a previous section, one reason was the shift to the left in the aggregate supply curve due to price hikes in oil, food, and raw materials. Because of this shift, both the inflation rate and the unemployment rate increased. And the rapid inflation of the seventies helped to bring on higher levels of unemployment. The oil price hikes acted like an excise tax levied on the consumer; they reduced the amount that consumers could spend on other things. The general inflation raised people's money incomes, thus pushing them into higher income tax brackets and increasing the amount they had to pay in taxes. (Similarly, the inflation swelled the paper profits of many firms, and increased their tax bills.) Because of the oil price increases and the effective increase in taxes, as well as other factors, like the decline in the stock market, consumers cut back on their spending. Thus the $C + I + G$ line was pushed downward, and the equilibrium value of NNP fell.

The Long-Run Phillips Curve

Many leading economists, like Milton Friedman and Edmund Phelps, deny that the Phillips curve exists as a stable "long-run" phenomenon. To them, the Phillips curve in Figure 18.3 is only a short-run relationship; in the long run, they believe that the Phillips curve is vertical. Thus they are not surprised that, holding constant the unemployment rate, the rate of inflation was higher in the seventies than in the sixties. In their view, expansionary monetary and fiscal policies that result in inflation will only reduce unemployment temporarily, with the result that the rate of inflation will tend to accelerate, for reasons given below. Thus they are often called *accelerationists*.

Figure 18.5
Relationship between Inflation Rate and Unemployment Rate Source: Economic Report of the President, *Washington, D.C.: Government Printing Office, 1979, 1982, and 1985.*

"NATURAL" RATE OF UNEMPLOYMENT

According to the accelerationists, there is a certain "natural" (or full-employment) rate of unemployment, which is determined by how long workers search before taking a new job. The more reluctant they are to take unattractive or low-paying jobs, the higher the "natural" rate of unemployment. Economists who stress the importance of structural unemployment argue that the "natural" rate of unemployment depends too on the rate at which changes in technology and tastes occur and the speed with which workers in declining industries can be retrained for jobs in expanding industries.

Suppose that this "natural" rate is 5½ percent, and that the government, not realizing that it is this high, uses expansionary monetary and fiscal policies to reduce unemployment to 4 percent. Because of the resulting increase in aggregate demand, the price level rises; and *if the level of money wages remains relatively constant,* firms' profits go up. Higher profits lead to expanded output and more employment. Thus the economy moves from point *C* (where it was before the government's expansionary policies) to point *D* in Figure 18.6. This movement is entirely in accord with the concept of the Phillips curve; a reduction in unemployment is gained at the expense of more inflation (6 percent rather than 4 percent).[5]

Figure 18.6

A Simplified Accelerationist Model

According to the accelerationists, expansionary monetary and fiscal policy results in a temporary reduction in the unemployment rate from 5½ to 4 percent (a movement from point C to point D). But the increase in the inflation rate (from 4 to 6 percent) results in a higher expected rate of inflation, which shifts the short-run relationship from curve 1 to curve 2. If the government persists in try-ing to reduce the unemployment rate below the natural rate of 5½ percent, all that it will achieve is a higher and higher rate of inflation. In the long run, the unemployment rate returns to the natural rate (5½ percent in this case). Thus the long-run relationship between the unemployment rate and inflation rate is vertical.

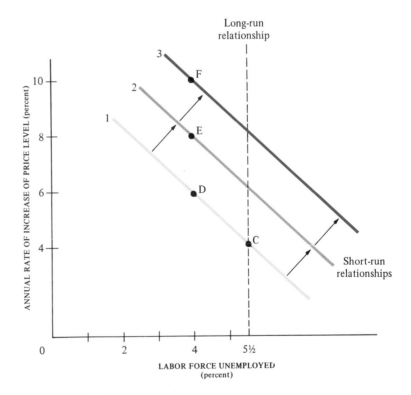

[5] To prevent confusion, note that we are not assuming that the short-run relationship between the inflation rate and the unemployment rate (curve 1 in Figure 18.6) is the same as the curve in Figure 18.4. Instead, we assume that it is below and to the left of the curve in Figure 18.4. In succeeding paragraphs, we shall show how it moves toward the position shown in Figure 18.4.

However, the accelerationists go on to argue that this movement is only temporary. To see why, it is essential to recognize that the short-run Phillips curve reflects people's expectations concerning the future rate of inflation. If people have come to expect a higher rate of inflation than in the past, this will shift the Phillips curve upward and to the right. To illustrate, let's compare two situations, one where workers and firms expect that prices will increase by 10 percent per year in the immediate future, the other where they expect no inflation at all. In the former case, unions will not be content to obtain less than a 10 percent increase in money wages, since a smaller increase would mean a cut in real wages. In the latter case, unions can afford to settle for a much more moderate increase in money wages, since none of the money wage increase is expected to be offset by inflation. Thus the rate of increase of wages is likely to be greater in the former than the latter case, if the unemployment rate is the same.

In summary, *the more inflation people expect, the further upward and out from the origin the short-run Phillips curve is likely to be. And the less inflation people expect, the further downward and close to the origin the short-run Phillips curve will be.*

According to the accelerationists, the movement from point C to point D in Figure 18.6 is only temporary because workers adjust their expectations concerning inflation. Before the government's expansionary monetary and fiscal policies were adopted, the inflation rate was 4 percent, and this was (more or less) what workers expected. The movement from point C to point D means an increase in the inflation rate to 6 percent, which the workers do not expect. Although they are fooled at first, people *adapt* their expectations; that is, the rate of inflation they expect is adjusted upward toward the new 6 percent rate. As pointed out in the previous paragraph, this increase in the expected amount of inflation will shift the short-run Phillips curve upward and out from the origin. The short-run relationship between the unemployment rate and the inflation rate will shift from curve 1 to curve 2 in Figure 18.6. Faced with this new short-run curve, the government will raise the inflation rate to 8 percent if it persists in trying to maintain the unemployment rate at 4 percent. That is, it will have to move to point E in Figure 18.6.

A SECOND TRY

Suppose that the government continues to try to maintain a 4 percent unemployment rate. Since the inflation rate increases to 8 percent as a consequence, people once more begin to adapt their expectations to the new inflation rate. Workers, trying to compensate for the higher inflation rate, ask for bigger wage increases, and firms are more willing to grant such increases because they recognize that the inflation rate has risen. Once again, the short-run Phillips curve shifts upward and outward from the origin. The short-run relationship between the unemployment rate and the inflation rate will shift from curve 2 to curve 3 in Figure 18.6. Thus the government will have increased the inflation rate to 10 percent if it persists in trying to keep the unemployment rate at 4 percent. That is, it will have to move to point F in Figure 18.6.

RECENT DEVELOPMENTS IN ECONOMICS: RATIONAL EXPECTATIONS AND CREDIBILITY IN FIGHTING INFLATION

In the previous chapter, we discussed rational expectations theories and the major impact they have had on the thinking of economists in the past decade or so. To illustrate the nature of these theories, let's consider a case where the government, rather than trying to reduce the unemployment rate (as in Figure 18.6), wants to reduce the inflation rate. Suppose that the short-run Phillips curve initially is curve 1 below, and that the government adopts a restrictive policy that moves the economy from point *A* to point *B,* with the result that the inflation rate falls from 12 percent to 10 percent. According to our argument in Figure 18.6, people will expect now that inflation will continue at 10 percent.

But such expectations would be irrational, if the public is convinced that the government really is serious about fighting inflation. Instead, people, if rational, will expect that inflation will fall further to perhaps 6 percent, because of the government's policies. This difference in expectations can be important. If people's expectations are rational, the short-run Phillips curve shifts downward much more rapidly than if people irrationally expect a 10 percent inflation rate. Specifically, it shifts to curve 3, whereas it would have shifted to curve 2 if people expected a 10 percent inflation rate. Thus it is much easier to tame inflation further, because of the change in expectations.

According to the rational expectations theorists, and many others as well, it is important that a government's anti-inflation policy be firm, consistent, and well understood. If firms, workers, and consumers are persuaded that the government will stick by its guns, and reduce inflation (even if it means heavy unemployment in the short run), they will relatively quickly moderate their wage and price demands, and inflation will soon be reduced. In other words, the credibility of a government's anti-inflationary policy is of the utmost importance. If such a policy is credible (and thus influences expectations), inflation will subside relatively quickly; if it is not credible, there may be great difficulties in bringing it down.

Without question, anti-inflation policy in the United States in the 1970s was not always credible. There was far more talk than action. In part, this was because government officials and their advisers were not convinced that people's expectations and behavior would change rapidly enough so that inflation could be licked without incurring considerable social costs (and political defeat at the polls).

398

Basic Idea #35: In the short run, there is likely to be an inverse relationship between the unemployment rate and the inflation rate. But in the long run, much, though perhaps not all, of the reduction in unemployment due to increased inflation is likely to be illusory. Thus governments that try to push the unemployment rate down to unrealistically low levels are likely to generate a lot of inflation—while failing to achieve their desired unemployment rate.

THE LONG-RUN RELATIONSHIP

If the government persists in trying to reduce the unemployment rate below the natural rate of 5½ percent, it will continually fail to do so. All that it will achieve is a higher and higher rate of inflation. Thus, according to the accelerationists, the Phillips curve really does not exist, except in the short run, and governments that believe in its existence can cause considerable mischief. It is not possible for the economy to remain permanently at any point on the short-run curves in Figure 18.6 other than at the natural rate of unemployment (5½ percent in this case). Thus the long-run relationship between the unemployment rate and the inflation rate is a vertical line, as shown in Figure 18.6.[6]

Not all economists agree with the accelerationists' view that the long-run relationship between the unemployment rate and the inflation rate is a vertical line. Some believe that, even in the long run, this relationship is inverse. However, there seems to be little doubt that the long-run relationship is a lot steeper than the short-run relationship. Thus much, though perhaps not all, of the reduction in unemployment due to increases in inflation is likely to be illusory.

[6] The available evidence seems to indicate that the natural rate of unemployment has been higher in more recent years than in the 1960s, due in considerable part to the fact that women and teenagers have been a larger percentage of the labor force than in the 1960s. (Recall our discussion of this in Chapter 8.) This increase in the natural rate of unemployment is another factor that is partly responsible for the recent stagflation, but it is by no means the whole story.

Test Yourself

1. "The inflations arising from the Revolutionary, Civil, and Vietnam wars were largely cost-push." Comment and evaluate.

2. According to Franco Modigliani, "Acceptance of the Phillips curve ... implied ... there was no longer a unique Full Employment but rather a whole family of possible equilibrium [employment] rates, each associated with a different rate of inflation."[*] Explain what he means, and indicate whether you agree or not, and why.

3. Suppose that the relationship between the annual rate of change of the wage rate and the percent of the labor force unemployed is as shown below:

Rate of change of wage rate (percent per year)	Unemployment rate (percent)
5	8
6	7
7	6
8	5

Plot the Phillips curve on a graph. Would Milton Friedman accept this curve as a long-run Phillips curve? Why or why not?

4. Suppose that output per man-hour is growing at 2 percent per year. Based on the data in Question 3, plot the relationship between the annual rate of change of the price level and the unemployment rate. State the assumptions you are making.

5. During the late 1970s, Americans began to expect higher and higher rates of inflation. Explain in detail the effects of this on the short-run relationship between the unemployment rate and the rate of inflation.

[*] F. Modigliani, "The Monetarist Controversy or, Should We Foresake Stabilization Policies," *American Economic Review,* March 1977, p. 3.

Wage and Price Controls

Still another way that the government can try to curb inflation is by adopting *wage and price controls.* During World War II—and other wartime emergencies—the government imposed controls of this sort. In other words, the government intervened directly in the market place to see that wages and prices did not increase by more than a certain amount. The economics profession has little enthusiasm for direct controls of wages and prices, for several reasons.

1. Such controls are likely to result in a distorted allocation of resources. Recall from Chapter 3 our discussion of the functions of the price system in allocating resources. Wage and price controls do not permit prices to perform these functions, and the result is inefficiency and waste.

2. Such controls are likely to be expensive to administer. For example, during the Korean War, the Economic Stabilization Agency had 16,000 employees; even so, it was difficult to prevent violation or evasion of the controls.

3. There is widespread opposition to detailed government regulation and control of this sort, on the grounds that it impairs our economic freedom. The Council of Economic Advisers undoubtedly spoke for most of the economics profession when it said in 1968,

> The most obvious—and least desirable—way of attempting to stabilize prices is to impose mandatory controls on prices and wages. While such controls may be necessary under conditions of an all-out war, it would be folly to consider them as a solution to the inflationary pressures that accompany high employment under any other circumstance. . . . Although such controls may be unfortunately popular when they are not in effect, the appeal quickly disappears once people live under them.[7]

WAGE AND PRICE CONTROLS UNDER THE NIXON ADMINISTRATION: A CASE STUDY

Despite the disadvantages of price controls, the Nixon administration adopted them in the summer of 1971. Wholesale prices were rising then at about 5 percent per year. The wage-price spiral was very much in evidence. Collective bargaining agreements were reached calling for wage increases far in excess of productivity increases, and there was no question but that firms would boost prices in an attempt to cover the resulting increase in costs. In August 1971, President Nixon froze wages and prices for a 3-month period. Then he appointed a 15-member Pay Board and a 7-member Price Commission, both of which were supervised by the government's Cost of Living Council.

The Pay Board was given the responsibility of administering wage controls, and the Price Commission was to administer price controls. In November 1971, these two bodies announced their initial policies. The Pay Board stated that pay increases had to be kept under 5.5 percent per year.

---

[7] *1968 Annual Report of the Council of Economic Advisers,* Washington, D.C.: Government Printing Office, p. 119.

A company could increase some employees' pay by more than this amount, but other employees would have to get less since total increases could not exceed this figure. The Price Commission ruled that price increases had to be kept under 2.5 percent. Both for prices and wages, exceptions could be made in some areas. Large firms were required to notify the Pay Board and Price Commission of intended wage or price increases.

From November 1971 to January 1973, this program of wage and price controls continued. Although it did not eliminate inflation, prices seemed to go up more slowly than before the freeze. (The Consumer Price Index went up by about 3 percent during 1972.) By early 1973, it appeared that controls might safely be relaxed. In January 1973, the Pay Board and the Price Commission became part of the Cost of Living Council, headed by Harvard's labor economist, John Dunlop. And controls were eliminated or relaxed for most prices and wages, with the major exceptions of the health, food, and construction industries. To a considerable extent, the Nixon administration phased out the first peacetime wage and price controls in our history.

Unfortunately, inflation occurred subsequently at a bewildering pace. During the first half of 1973, wholesale prices of farm products and processed foods and feeds rose at the unbelievable rate of 48 percent per year. At the same time, the prices of lumber, fuel, and other industrial goods rose at alarming rates. President Nixon responded by imposing a 60-day freeze on prices (but not wages), beginning in mid-June of 1973. This was only a breather, an interim measure designed to give the administration some time to deal with the serious inflationary pressures that were evident throughout the economy.

In August 1973, the administration announced that price increases could not exceed cost increases. This was the core of the new postfreeze program. But it soon became obvious that this new program was not proving effective, and that there was growing criticism and skepticism concerning price controls. In April 1974, Congress allowed the control authority to expire. This phase of the program was widely acknowledged to be a failure.

It is difficult to evaluate the effects of the wage and price controls established between 1971 and 1974. According to many observers, the price level rose, once controls were relaxed, to the level that it would have attained in any event, if there had been no controls. Thus, to these observers, the effects of the controls were short-term and largely cosmetic. (See Example 18.2.) To other observers, the controls had a significant longer-term effect. According to the Council of Economic Advisers, "regardless of the overall effect of the program, whatever contribution it may have made was probably concentrated in its first 16 months, when the economy was operating well below its potential. As various industrial sectors reached capacity operations in 1973 under the stimulus of a booming domestic and world economy, the controls system began to obstruct normal supplier-purchaser relationships, and in some cases the controls became quite unworkable."[8]

Basic Idea #36: Wage and price controls tend to result in several undesirable effects. By interfering with the functioning of the price system, they result in a distorted allocation of resources. They curtail our economic freedom, and are expensive to administer. (To a lesser extent, incomes policies may suffer from similar problems.) History indicates that wage and price controls are not a solution to the inflation problem.

[8] *1975 Annual Report of the Council of Economic Advisers,* Washington, D.C.: Government Printing Office, pp. 228–29.

Incomes Policies

As we have stressed repeatedly, the 1970s and early 1980s were a period of uncomfortably high inflation. For example, in 1980, the price level in the United States was increasing by more than 10 percent per year. Faced with such high rates of inflation, there has been considerable interest, both here and abroad, in using incomes policies to help curb inflation without cutting back on aggregate demand. According to one common definition, an *incomes policy* contains three elements:

1. An incomes policy has some targets for wages (and other forms of income) and prices for the economy as a whole. For example, the target may

---

Example 18.2   Effects of the 1971–74 Control Program

During 1971–74, the Nixon administration adopted price and wage controls. According to Northwestern's Robert Gordon, the percentage increase in the price level that would have been predicted in the absence of these controls compares as follows with the actual increase:

Period	Percent increase in price level Without controls	Actual
1971 (second quarter) to 1973 (third quarter)	11.3	7.8
1973 (third quarter) to 1975 (third quarter)	11.9	15.4

(a) If these estimates are correct, did price and wage controls have a short-term effect on the price level? (b) Did they have any long-term effect on the price level? (c) Reinforcing steel bars were subject to the controls, but the steel scrap used to make the bars was not subject to them. The price of steel scrap increased much more rapidly than the price of steel bars. What do you think was the effect on the output of steel bars? (d) Steel bars are used in construction projects. What effect do you think a shortage of steel bars would have on the construction industry?*

SOLUTION

(a) Yes. During 1971–73, the price level increased less rapidly (by about 3.5 percentage points) than would have been expected without controls. (b) No. Although the price level increased less rapidly than would have been expected without controls during 1971–73, it increased more rapidly during 1973–75. In 1973–75, the positive difference in the inflation rate over what would have been expected without controls canceled the negative difference in 1971–73. In other words, when controls were lifted, the price level jumped approximately to the level it would have reached without controls. (c) Since the profits of the bar manufacturers were reduced, they cut their output of bars. (d) It interfered with the efficient operation of construction projects. In essence, the price system was not allowed to function properly.

* For further discussion, see R. Gordon, *Macroeconomics,* 2nd ed., Little Brown, 1981, pp. 317–20.

be to stabilize the price level, or to permit the Consumer Price Index to increase by less than 2 percent per year, or to allow wage increases not exceeding a certain percentage.

2. An incomes policy gives particular firms and industries some more detailed guides for decision making on wages (and other forms of income) and prices. These guides are set in such a way that the overall targets for the entire economy will be fulfilled. For example, if the aim is price stability, these guides tell firms and unions what kinds of decisions are compatible with this target. To be useful, the guides must be specific and understandable enough to be applied in particular cases. There obviously is little point in telling firms and unions to avoid "inflationary" wage and price decisions if they don't know whether a particular decision is "inflationary" or not.

3. An incomes policy contains some mechanisms to get firms and unions to follow the guides. An incomes policy differs from price and wage controls in that it seeks to induce firms and unions to follow these guides voluntarily. But if it is to have any effect, clearly the government must be prepared to use certain forms of "persuasion" beyond moral suasion. In fact, governments sometimes have publicly condemned decisions by firms and unions that were regarded as violating the guides. Government stockpiles of materials and government purchasing policies have also been used to penalize or reward particular firms and industries. Other pressures too have been brought to bear in an attempt to induce firms to follow the established guides. Thus the difference between an incomes policy and price and wage controls is one of degree and emphasis, not a clear-cut difference in kind.

An example of an incomes policy in the United States was the so-called Kennedy-Johnson guidelines. Although earlier administrations (for example, the Eisenhower and Truman administrations) had often appealed to business and labor to limit price and wage increases, the first systematic attempt at a fairly specific incomes policy in the United States occurred during the Kennedy administration, In 1961, President Kennedy's Council of Economic Advisers issued the following wage-price guidelines:

> The general guide for noninflationary wage behavior is that the rate of increase in wage rates (including fringe benefits) in each industry be equal to the trend rate of *over-all productivity advance.* General acceptance of this guide would maintain stability of labor cost per unit of output for the economy as a whole—though not of course for individual industries. The general guide for noninflationary price behavior calls for price reduction if the industry's rate of productivity increase exceeds the over-all rate—for this would mean declining unit labor costs; it calls for an appropriate increase in price if the opposite relationship prevails; and it calls for stable prices if the two rates of productivity increase are equal. [Note once again that productivity equals output per hour of labor.][9]

To see just what this means, let's consider prices and wages in the auto industry. Suppose that labor productivity in the economy as a whole was increasing at 3.2 percent per year. Then according to the guidelines, *wages in the automobile industry should increase by 3.2 percent per year.* If labor

[9] *1962 Annual Report of the Council of Economic Advisers,* Washington, D.C.: Government Printing Office, p. 189.

productivity in the auto industry increased by 4.2 percent per year, then, if the auto makers applied this guideline, the labor cost of producing a unit of output would decrease by 1 percent per year in the auto industry (since the 3.2 percent rate of increase of wages minus the 4.2 percent rate of increase of labor productivity equals −1 percent). Thus the guidelines specified that *prices in the auto industry should decrease,* perhaps by about 1 percent per year.

The Council of Economic Advisers specified several situations where these general guidelines would have to be modified. In particular, if there was a shortage of labor in a particular industry or if an industry's wages were lower than those earned elsewhere by similar labor, higher wage increases (than specified in general) would be warranted. Or if an industry's profits were insufficient to attract needed infusions of capital, or if an industry's nonwage costs rose greatly, higher price increases than specified in general would be justified. However, the Council did not attempt to set forth detailed, quantitative provisions about the extent to which higher wages or prices would be warranted under these circumstances.

THE KENNEDY-JOHNSON GUIDELINES: CRITICISM AND
EXPERIENCE

Soon after the announcement of the Kennedy-Johnson guidelines, critics began to point out problems in them. The criticism was of several types.

Inefficiency. Some observers feared that the guidelines would result in inefficiency and waste. In a free-enterprise economy, we rely on price changes to direct resources into the most productive uses and to signal shortages or surpluses in various markets. If the guidelines were accepted by industry and labor, prices would not be free to perform this function. Of course, the guidelines specified that modifications of the general rules could be made in case of shortages, but critics of the guidelines felt that this escape hatch was too vague to be very useful.

Freedom. Many observers were concerned about the reduction in economic freedom. Of course, the guidelines were presented in the hope that they would be observed voluntarily. But a time was sure to come when they would be in serious contradiction with the interests of firms and unions. In such a situation, what would happen if the firms or unions decided not to follow them? To the extent that the government applied pressure on the firms or unions, there would certainly be a reduction in economic freedom; and to some observers, it seemed likely that the next step might well be direct government controls. Moreover, the nonlegislated character of the guidelines and the arbitrary choice of whom to pursue by the government raised important questions of a political nature.

Feasibility. Many people felt that the guidelines really were not workable. In other words, even if the public would go along with them, in many cases they would be impossible to use, because accurate and relevant data on changes in labor productivity in particular industries were often unobtainable, and the situations where exceptions were allowed were so vaguely specified.

Symptoms. Some economists felt that reliance on the guidelines was dangerous because it focused attention on symptoms rather than causes of inflation. In their view, inflation was largely the result of improper monetary and fiscal policies. In other words, the basic causes had to be laid at the government's own door. But by setting up guidelines, the government seemed to be saying that the fault lay with industry and labor. Thus some critics felt that the guidelines tended to cloud the real issues and so let the government escape responsibility for its actions.

During 1962–64 the government claimed that the guidelines were working well. To a considerable extent, this may have been because the economy still had considerable slack, as well as because of the noninflationary expectations of firms and individuals engendered by several years of relative price stability. By 1965, as labor markets tightened and prices rose in response to the Vietnam build-up (see Chapter 12), it became much more difficult to use the guidelines. Union leaders fought the guidelines tooth and nail, mainly because consumer prices were rising. In various important labor negotiations, unions demanded and got higher wage increases than the guidelines called for. For example, the airline machinists got a 4.9 percent increase in 1966. By 1968, the guideline were dead. No one was paying any attention to them.

What effect did the guidelines have? Some people claim that they had no real effect at all, while others claim that they reduced cost-push inflation in the early 1960s by a considerable amount. Since it is difficult to separate the effects of the guidelines from the effects of other factors, there is considerable dispute over the question. Considering the level of unemployment in the early 1960s, wages increased less rapidly then than in earlier or later periods. Prices too increased less rapidly during that period—holding unemployment constant—than earlier or later. But whether these developments were due to the guidelines, or to noninflationary expectations or some other factor, is very hard to say.

Perhaps the most important reason why the guidelines broke down was that they could not deal with the strong demand-pull inflation of the late 1960s. Even the strongest defenders of the guidelines are quick to point out that they are no substitute for proper monetary and fiscal policy. *If fiscal or monetary policy is generating strong inflationary pressures, such as existed in the late 1960s, it is foolish to think that guidelines can save the situation.* Perhaps they can cut down on the rate of inflation for a while; but in the long run, the dike is sure to burst. If the guidelines are voluntary, as in this case, firms and unions will ignore them, and the government will find it difficult, it not impossible, to do anything about it. *Even price and wage controls are no adequate antidote to strong inflationary pressures generated by an overly expansive fiscal or monetary policy. Such controls may deal temporarily with the symptoms of inflation, but over the long haul these inflationary pressures will have an effect.*

Tax-Based Incomes Policies

In the past ten years, a number of influential economists have proposed that tax-based incomes policies be adopted to slow the rate of inflation. Such incomes policies use the tax system or subsidies to induce firms to hold down prices and workers to hold down wages. Some tax-based incomes policies use a "carrot"; others use a "stick." To illustrate the nature

THE MEETING OF THE FEDERAL OPEN MARKET COMMITTEE ON NOVEMBER 14–15, 1983

On November 14–15, 1983, the Federal Open Market Committee met. To understand the factors influencing the committee's decisions, it is worthwhile describing this meeting in some detail. Information was presented by the staff of the Federal Reserve concerning economic conditions in the period since the committee's previous meeting on October 4, 1983. According to the latest information, real GNP was growing at a relatively rapid rate, although the pace of expansion seemed to have moderated from the annual growth rates of about 9¾ percent and 8 percent in the second and third quarters of 1983. The rate of increase of the Consumer Price Index, the rate of growth of industrial production, and the unemployment rate during August, September, and October were as follows:

Month	Percentage increase (from previous month) in Consumer Price Index	Percentage increase (from previous month) in industrial production	Un-employment rate
August	0.4	1.3	9.3
September	0.5	1.3	9.1
October	0.4	0.8	8.7

According to forecasts presented by the Federal Reserve staff, the rate of growth of real GNP would slow to a more moderate pace in 1984. The slowdown was expected to be due in part to less stimulus from inventory and housing investment, as well as a slower rate of growth of consumer spending. A fall in the unemployment rate was forecasted, but inflation was expected to remain generally moderate. These forecasts were based on the sorts of techniques described in Chapter 13.

At its previous meeting in October, the committee had decided that open market operations should be directed toward maintaining slightly less restraint on the economy. An annual rate of growth of the money supply (*M*-1) of around 7 percent was agreed upon. In fact, the money supply had grown at less than this rate during October. Interest rates generally fluctuated in a narrow range in the period since the October meeting. Long-term interest rates rose slightly, apparently in response to signs of continued strength in economic activity and to uncertainties about the prospective pattern of Treasury financing, as passage of legislation to increase the federal debt ceiling was delayed.

With this background in mind, the committee members discussed the economic situation and outlook. Based on the official account of this meeting, the discussion ran as follows:

[Some] members commented that the economic expansion had remained stronger than generally anticipated. Reports from around the country suggested increasingly widespread optimism about business conditions and a high degree of consumer confidence. While all the members expected the rate of economic growth to moderate over the year ahead, there were some differences of view with regard to the timing and likely extent of the slowdown. Some members anticipated that the slowdown might be appreciably less than projected by the staff, with unfavorable implications for inflationary pressures and the ultimate sustainability of the expansion. In support of this view, reference was made to the favorable conditions for a surge in business fixed investment created by the momentum of the expansion. In addition, it was pointed out that a highly stimulative fiscal policy remained in prospect for 1984. Thus, while the expansionary impact of housing and inventory accumulation could be expected to wane during the second year of the recovery, vigorous growth in fixed investment expenditures in conjunction with the prospective federal deficit might well sustain relatively rapid expansion in overall economic activity during the year ahead. It was also suggested that, at least for the near term, consumer spending and inventory accumulation might provide more stimulus to the economy than was generally anticipated.

Other members placed more emphasis on some elements of potential weakness in the economic outlook. It was pointed out that there was as yet no firm evidence that business fixed investment would prove to be exceptionally strong during 1984. Indeed, such investment might continue to be held down by the persistence of weak demand for the output of some traditional producers of capital equipment, and, more generally, by relatively high interest rates in the context of massive Treasury debt financings. . . .

With regard to the prospects for prices, several members questioned whether further progress could be made in containing inflationary pressures if the rate of economic expansion did not slow to a more moderate pace over the year ahead. One member observed that by late 1984, capacity utilization rates could reach levels that would tend to generate inflationary cost pressures even if unemployment were still high relative to earlier expansion periods. On the other hand, some members felt that there was little current evidence that price and wage pressures or inflationary expectations were worsening. One member also noted that the economy was still operating well below capacity and that further significant improvements in productivity, along with competitive pressures from world markets, were likely to restrain inflation during 1984.

In the Committee's discussion of policy for the period immediately ahead, all of the members found acceptable a policy directed toward maintaining the existing degree of reserve restraint. In the view of some, however, an argument could be made in favor of a small, precautionary step in the direction of firming in light of the continuing strength of the economic expansion and the associated danger of a resurgence of inflationary pressures during the year ahead. While acknowledging the risks of inflation in a rapidly expanding economy combined with large budget deficits and the relatively rapid monetary growth earlier in the year, most members saw sufficient uncertainties in the outlook to counsel against any change in reserve pressures at this time. Some members were also concerned that under the prevailing circumstances even a modest increase in restraint on reserves might have a disproportionate impact on domestic and international financial markets. The result could be an increase in domestic interest rates large enough to have damaging consequences for housing and other interest-sensitive sectors of the economy and to intensify greatly the pressures on countries with severe external debt problems.[1]

At the conclusion of the meeting, the committee decided that no change should be made in the degree of restraint on bank reserves. The committee anticipated that the money supply (M-1) would increase at an annual rate

[1] "Record of Policy Actions of the Federal Open Market Committee," *Federal Reserve Bulletin,* January 1984, pp. 25–26.

of about 5 or 6 percent and that the federal funds rate (the interest rate charged by financial institutions for lending reserves to one another, primarily on an over-night basis) would remain at 6 to 10 percent. Like most meetings of the Federal Open Market Committee (but unlike the Saturday Night Special described on p. 361), this one was hardly the stuff from which good drama is made. But to understand the workings of the economy, and the way in which public policy is formulated, it is essential that you know what goes on in the meetings of this committee, dramatic or not.

of those that use a "stick," suppose that a target of 6 percent were established for overall pay increases. If a firm's average pay increase was less than or equal to the 6 percent target, it would pay the basic corporate income tax of, say, 46 percent of its profits. But if its average pay increase exceeded the 6 percent target, it would be subject to a higher corporate income tax rate. For example, its income tax might be 51 percent of its profits if its pay increase was 7 percent, 56 percent of its profits if its pay increase was 8 percent, and so on. Clearly, the firm would be penalized for granting large pay increases. If it allowed pay increases far in excess of the target, its after-tax profits would be cut severely.

This is the kind of tax-based incomes policy proposed originally by Henry Wallich of the Federal Reserve Board and the late Sidney Weintraub of the University of Pennsylvania. Since their proposal, a number of other such schemes have been put forth. Lawrence Seidman of the University of Delaware has suggested that the tax system could be used both to penalize firms that grant large pay increases and to reward those that grant small pay increases. For example, if a firm were to keep pay increases to 5 percent (when the target is 6 percent), it would be rewarded with a lower income tax rate than if it did no better than the target. It might pay only 44 percent of its profits in income taxes, rather than the 46 percent that it would pay if it did no better than meet the 6 percent target.

In 1977, the late Arthur Okun of the Brookings Institution proposed a form of tax-based incomes policy that emphasized positive inducements for noninflationary behavior; that is, the "carrot" rather than the "stick." If a firm pledged to hold the average rate of wage increase of its employees below 6 percent and its average rate of price increase below 4 percent (except for the effects of increases in the costs of its materials and supplies), both the firm and its employees would receive a tax rebate. This proposal also received serious consideration from economists and policy makers.

Although tax-based incomes policies have attracted considerable interest and attention in the late 1970s and early and mid-1980s, they are not free of problems. For one thing, the administrative difficulties in implementing such policies are significant, according to Treasury officials and others. The job of the Internal Revenue Service would be complicated considerably if such policies were adopted, and firms might have difficulties in complying with them. Neither business nor labor has expressed enthusiasm for tax-based incomes policies. Labor leaders have been cool to them, because they feel that such policies seem to imply (unfairly, in their view) that inflation is due primarily to wage increases. They feel that such policies are an unwelcome interference with collective bargaining. Business leaders have been wary of them, because they feel that such policies would complicate wage negotiations and personnel management. Also, they fear that some firms (smaller or unincorporated businesses, in particular) may be exempt from the program, and that these firms, therefore, may be given a competitive edge.

Despite these problems, some form of tax-based incomes policy may eventually be tried, if for no other reason that it may seem preferable to other kinds of incomes policies. As Henry Wallich has put it, "Of course, nobody likes tax-based incomes policies *per se*. It is really a question of the alternatives."

Economic Stabilization: Where We Stand

Where do we stand in the struggle to achieve full employment without inflation? Clearly, we know much more than we did 40 years ago about how to use monetary and fiscal policies to attain this objective. Given the more advanced state of economics, it is very unlikely that a catastrophe like the Great Depression of the 1930s will occur again. But on the other hand, economists were overly optimistic in the mid-1960s when they talked about "fine-tuning" the economy. Our experience since then makes it clear that we have a long way to go before we understand the workings of the economy well enough to achieve continuous full employment without considerable inflation. Equally important, we have seen that, even if the advice of its economists were always correct, the government might still pursue destabilizing policies, as it did in the late 1960s.

The 1970s and 1980s have been characterized by both excessive inflation and excessive unemployment. Throughout the Western industrialized world, governments have been perplexed by this phenomenon of "stagflation." The standard economic remedies—monetary and fiscal policy—are not very effective in dealing with this combination of ailments. Although they can deal with either excessive unemployment or excessive inflation, they are not well designed to deal simultaneously with both of them.

To some economists, the answer (or at least a partial answer) is to rely more heavily on some form of incomes policy to fight inflation. But the evidence, here and abroad, seems to emphasize the problems in formulating an effective incomes policy. The unfortunate truth is that, although our understanding of the factors causing "stagflation" is more complete than the newspapers frequently imply, it is not complete enough to provide a workable cure that most economists can agree on. Until we obtain a better basic understanding of this phenomenon, the chances are that policy makers, both here and abroad, will continue to have problems with regard to economic stabilization—and that there will be a good deal of floundering. If the rate of inflation takes still another alarming upturn, it is likely that some form of wage and price controls will once again be applied in the United States. But it must be recognized that such controls have had limited success in restraining inflation more than temporarily, in the United States as in other countries.[10]

Finally, there has been a shift in emphasis in many public policy discussions by economists and others. During recent decades, the emphasis often was almost exclusively on the government's management of aggregate demand in an effort to maintain full employment. Now more attention is being given to the supply side of the economy. In part, this is due to the commodity shortages, sluggish productivity growth, and relatively low rates of capital investment in the United States during the 1970s. Some of the effects of these factors have been taken up in this chapter. Much more will be said concerning them in the next chapter.

---

[10] The Reagan administration has put less emphasis on incomes policies than did the Carter administration. As for wage and price controls, President Reagan is on record as believing that they don't "work." (See Question 4 below in "Test Yourself.") But this does not mean that such measures will not be adopted sometime in the future.

Test Yourself

1. According to Milton Friedman, "It is far better that inflation be open than that it be suppressed (by price guidelines)." Do you agree? Why or why not?

2. "The Kennedy-Johnson guidelines for noninflationary price behavior called for price reduction if an industry's rate of productivity increase exceeded the overall rate. It is unrealistic to expect price cuts of this sort." Do you agree? Why or why not?

3. "Reliance on incomes policies is dangerous because it looks at symptoms, not the basic causes of our problems." Comment and evaluate.

4. According to President Ronald Reagan, wage and price controls "didn't work when Hammurabi tried them in Babylon. They didn't work when Diocletian tried them in Rome." In this context, what does "work" mean? Why do you think they didn't "work"?

Summary

1. The Phillips curve shows the relationship between the rate of increase of wages and the level of unemployment. If the Phillips curve remains fixed, it poses an awkward dilemma for policy makers. If they reduce unemployment, inflation increases; if they reduce inflation, unemployment increases. During 1955–69, there was a fairly close relationship between the inflation rate and the unemployment rate. But then something unforeseen by most economists occurred. The inflation and unemployment rates in the seventies did not conform at all closely to the relationship that prevailed in the sixties. Both the unemployment rate and the inflation rate tended to be much higher in the seventies than in the sixties.

2. The accelerationists, led by Milton Friedman, believe that the downward-sloping Phillips curve is only a short-run relationship. In the long run, they believe that it is vertical. In their view, expansionary policies that result in inflation will only reduce unemployment temporarily, with the result that the government, if it sets out to reduce unemployment to an amount below its natural level, will have to permit higher and higher rates of inflation.

3. To reduce the inflation rate (at a given unemployment rate), governments have tried price and wage controls. Although a few economists favor such controls during peacetime, most do not agree. Such controls are likely to distort the allocation of resources, to be difficult to administer, and to run counter to our desire for economic freedom.

4. Many countries have experimented with various kinds of incomes policies. An incomes policy contains targets for prices and wages for the economy as a whole, more detailed guides for price and wage decisions in particular industries, and some mechanisms to get firms and unions to follow these guides. The Kennedy-Johnson guidelines were one form of incomes policy. Although guidelines of this sort have a short-term effect on the price level, how much effect they have in the long run is hard to say.

5. A variety of types of tax-based incomes policies has been proposed in recent years. Such policies use the tax system or subsidies to induce firms to hold down prices and workers to hold down wages. Some use a "carrot"; others use a "stick."

6. Although it is very unlikely that a catastrophe like the Great Depression will recur, our recent experience indicates that we have a long way to go before we understand the workings of the economy well enough to achieve continuous full employment without inflation. Also, even if the advice of its economists were always correct, there is no assurance that the government would always pursue policies leading toward economic stabilization.

Concepts for Review

Demand-pull inflation
Cost-push inflation
Wage-price spiral

Phillips curve
Labor productivity
Accelerationist

Wage and price controls
Incomes policies

PART FIVE

Economic Growth, Energy, and the Environment

CHAPTER 19

Economic Growth

Until fairly recently in human history, poverty was the rule, not the exception. As Sir Kenneth Clark puts it in his famous lectures on *Civilisation,*

> Poverty, hunger, plagues, disease: they were the background of history right up to the end of the nineteenth century, and most people regarded them as inevitable—like bad weather. Nobody thought they could be cured: St. Francis wanted to sanctify poverty, not abolish it. The old Poor Laws were not designed to abolish poverty but to prevent the poor from becoming a nuisance. All that was required was an occasional act of charity.[1]

Clearly, the human condition has changed considerably during the past century, at least in the industrialized nations of the world. Rising living standards have brought a decline in poverty, though by no means its disappearance. How has this increase in per capita output been achieved? This question has fascinated economists for a long time. Although we still are far from completely understanding the process of economic growth, our knowledge has increased considerably through the efforts of economic researchers, here and abroad. In this chapter, we discuss the process of economic growth in industrialized countries. A discussion of economic growth in less developed countries will be presented in Chapter 23.

---

[1] K. Clark, *Civilisation,* New York: Harper & Row, 1970.

What Is Economic Growth?

There are two common measures of the rate of *economic growth*. The first is the rate of growth of a nation's real gross national product (or net national product), which tells us how rapidly the economy's total real output of goods and services is increasing. The second is the rate of growth of *per capita* real gross national product (or net national product), which is a better measure of the rate of increase of a nation's standard of living. We shall use the second measure unless we state otherwise. Two aspects of the rate of growth of per capita real gross national product should be noted from the start.

1. *This measure is only a very crude approximation to the rate of increase of economic welfare.* For one thing, gross national product does not include one good that people prize most highly: leisure. For another, gross national product does not value at all accurately new products and improvements in the quality of goods and services, and does not allow properly either for noneconomic changes in the quality of life or for the costs of environmental pollution. Nor does gross national product take account of how the available output is distributed. Clearly, it makes a difference whether the bulk of the population gets a reasonable share of the output, or whether it goes largely to a favored few.

2. *Small differences in the annual rate of economic growth can make very substantial differences in living standards a few decades hence.* For example, per capita GNP in the United States was about $15,000 in 1984. If it grows at 2 percent per year, it will be about $20,600 (1984 dollars) in the year 2000, whereas if it grows at 3 percent per year, it will be about $24,100 (1984 dollars) in the year 2000. Thus an increase of 1 percentage point in growth rate means a $3,500 (or 17 percent) increase in per capita GNP in the year 2000. Even an increase of ¼ of 1 percentage point can make a considerable difference. If the growth rate increases from 1¾ percent to 2 percent per year, per capita GNP in the year 2000 will increase from $19,800 to $20,600. Of course, this is no more than arithmetic, but that doesn't make it any less important.

Economic Growth and the Production Possibilities Curve

To represent the process of economic growth, it is convenient to use the production possibilities curve which, as you will recall from Chapter 2, shows all efficient combinations of output an economy can produce. For example, suppose that a society produces only two goods: food and tractors. If this society has at its disposal a fixed amount of resources and if technology is fixed, the production possibilities curve (like the one in Figure 19.1) shows the maximum quantity of food that can be produced, given each amount of tractors produced.

SHIFTS OF THE PRODUCTION POSSIBILITY CURVE

A nation's potential output increases when its production possibilities curve shifts outward, as from position *A* to position *B* in Figure 19.2. This hap-

Figure 19.1
Production Possibilities Curve *The production possibilities curve shows all efficient combinations of output an economy can produce.*

Figure 19.2
Outward Shift of Production Possibilities Curve *A nation's potential output increases when its production possibilities curve shifts outward from position* A *to position* B.

pens because the society can produce (and consume) more of one good without having to produce (and consume) less of the other good. Thus its productive capacity must be greater. If the production possibilities curve shifts outward, if the economy is efficient, and if population remains constant, per capita GNP increases and economic growth occurs. Moreover, the faster the production possibilities curve shifts outward, the greater the rate of economic growth.

NO SHIFT OF THE PRODUCTION POSSIBILITY CURVE

Even if a nation's production possibilities curve does not shift outward, economic growth can occur if unemployment or inefficiency is reduced. If a nation allows some of its resources to be unemployed or underutilized because of an insufficiency of intended spending, this will cause the economy to operate at a point *inside* the production possibilities curve rather than *on* the curve. The same thing will happen if a nation allocates its resources inefficiently. Clearly, a nation can achieve some economic growth by getting closer to the production possibilities curve through a reduction in unemployment or inefficiency.

The Aggregate Production Function

A nation's potential output is directly related to the amount of resources it possesses and the extent to which they are used. These resources, or inputs, are of various kinds, including labor, capital, and land. The relationship between the amount used of each of these inputs and the resulting amount of potential output is often called the **aggregate production function.** It is analogous to the production function discussed in Chapter 6, which is the relationship between a firm's inputs and its output. However, the aggregate production function pertains to the entire economy, not a single firm.

Given that a nation's potential output depends on the amount of labor, capital, and land it uses, then the rate of growth of a nation's potential output must depend, in part at least, on the changes that occur in the amount of each of these inputs that is used. For example, if a nation invests heavily in additional capital, we would expect this to result in a substantial increase in potential output. Thus *a nation's rate of economic growth depends on the extent of the changes in the amounts of the various inputs used.* In addition, *a nation's rate of economic growth depends on the rate of technological change.* The aggregate production function is constructed on the assumption that technology is fixed. Changes in technology result in shifts in the production function, since more output is obtained from a given amount of resources.

The Law of Diminishing Marginal Returns

If a nation's land, labor, and capital increase, one would certainly expect its output to increase as well. But suppose the nation cannot increase the amount used of all of its resources at the same rate. Instead, suppose it can increase the quantity of one resource, say labor, while the amount of the other resources, like land, is held constant. In this situation, what will be the effect on output if the nation uses more and more of the resource that can be augmented? This is an important question, which occurs both in the present context and in the study of the production processes of the business firm.

To help answer it, economists have formulated the famous **law of diminishing marginal returns,** which states that, *if more and more of a resource is used, the quantities of other resources being held constant, the resulting increments of output will decrease after some point has been reached.*

To see what this means, suppose that we obtain data concerning the amounts of output resulting from the utilization of various amounts of one resource, holding constant the amounts of other resources. For example, suppose that data are obtained concerning the amounts of output resulting from various amounts of labor, holding constant the amounts of capital and land. Then suppose that we determine the *extra* amount of output resulting from the addition of each *extra* unit of labor. According to the law of diminishing marginal returns, this extra amount of output will eventually *decrease,* as more and more labor is utilized with the fixed amounts of capital and land. In other words, beyond some point, *an additional unit of labor will add less and less to total output.*

AN AGRICULTURAL EXAMPLE

To illustrate the workings of this law, consider Table 19.1, which shows the total output—or GNP—of a simple agricultural society under a set of alternative assumptions concerning the number of hours of labor used. For simplicity, we assume that this society produces only one product, corn, so that total output can be measured in bushels of corn. Also, we assume that the amount of land and capital that can be used is fixed in quantity. Column 1 in the table shows various alternative numbers of hours of labor that can be used with this fixed amount of land and capital. Column 2 shows the total output in each case.

Column 3 shows the additional output resulting from the addition of an

Table 19.1
THE LAW OF DIMINISHING MARGINAL RETURNS

(1) Hours of labor (millions)	(2) Bushels of corn (millions)	(3) Marginal product of labor (bushels per hour)	(4) Average product of labor (bushels per hour)
1	1.5		1.50
		2.0	
2	3.5		1.75
		2.5	
3	6.0		2.00
		3.0	
4	9.0		2.25
		2.0	
5	11.0		2.20
		2.0	
6	13.0		2.17
		1.0	
7	14.0		2.00
		0.0	
8	14.0		1.75

extra hour of labor; this is called the ***marginal product of labor.*** For example, if the quantity of labor is between 2 million hours and 3 million hours, the marginal product of labor is 2.5 bushels per hour of labor, because each extra hour of labor results in an extra 2.5 bushels of output.

In Table 19.1, the marginal product of labor increases as more and more labor is used, but only up to a point. Beyond 4 million hours of labor, the marginal product of labor goes down as more and more labor is used. Specifically, the marginal product of labor reaches a maximum of 3.0 bushels per hour when between 3 and 4 million hours of labor are used. Then it falls to 2.0 bushels per hour when between 4 and 5 million hours of labor are used, remains at 2.0 bushels per hour when between 5 and 6 million hours of labor are used, and falls once again to 1.0 bushel per hour when between 6 and 7 million hours of labor are used.

Thus, as predicted by the law of diminishing marginal returns, *the marginal product of labor eventually declines.* Moreover, as shown in column 4 of Table 19.1, the ***average product of labor,*** which is defined as total output per hour of labor, also falls beyond some point as more and more labor is used with a fixed amount of other resources. This too stems from the law of diminishing marginal returns.

REASONS FOR DIMINISHING RETURNS

It is easy to see why the law of diminishing marginal returns must be true. For example, imagine what would happen in the simple economy of Table 19.1 if more and more labor were applied to a fixed amount of land. Beyond a point, as more and more labor is used, the extra labor has to be devoted to less and less important tasks. If enough labor is used, it even becomes increasingly difficult to prevent the workers from getting in one another's way! For such reasons, one certainly would expect that, beyond some point, extra amounts of labor would result in smaller and smaller increments of output.

Finally, note two important things about this law. First, at least one resource must be fixed in quantity. The law of diminishing marginal returns does not apply to cases where there is a proportional increase in all resources. Second, technology is assumed to be fixed. The law of diminishing marginal returns does not apply to cases where technology changes.

Thomas Malthus and Population Growth

A nation's rate of economic growth depends on, among other things, how much the quantities of inputs of various kinds increase. To illuminate the nature of the growth process, we discuss the effect on the rate of economic growth of increasing each kind of input, holding the others constant. We begin by looking at the effects of changes in the quantity of labor. Economists have devoted a great deal of attention to the effects of population growth on the rate of economic growth. The classic work was done by Thomas Malthus (1776–1834), a British parson who devoted his life to academic research. The first professional economist, he taught at a college established by the East India Company to train its administrators—and was called "Pop" by his students behind his back. Whether "Pop" stood for population or not, Malthus's fame is based on his theories of population growth.

Malthus believed that the population tends to grow at a geometric rate. In his *Essay on the Principle of Population,* published in 1798, he pointed out the implications of such a constant rate of growth:

> If any person will take the trouble to make the calculation, he will see that if the necessities of life could be obtained without limit, and the number of people could be doubled every twenty-five years, the population which might have been produced from a single pair since the Christian era, would have been sufficient, not only to fill the earth quite full of people, so that four should stand in every square yard, but to fill all the planets of our solar system in the same way, and not only them but all the planets revolving around the stars which are visible to the naked eye, supposing each of them ... to have as many planets belong to it as our sun has.[2]

In contrast to the human population, which tends to increase at a geometric rate,[3] the supply of land can increase slowly if at all. And land, particularly in Malthus's time, was the source of food. Consequently, it seemed to Malthus that the human population was in danger of outrunning its food supply: "Taking the whole earth," he wrote, ". . . and supposing the present population to be equal to a thousand millions, the human species would increase as the numbers 1, 2, 4, 8, 16, 32, 64, 128, 256, and subsistence as 1, 2, 3, 4, 5, 6, 7, 8, 9. In two centuries, the population would be to the means of subsistence as 256 to 9; in three centuries as 4096 to 13, and in two thousand years the difference would be incalculable."[4]

A BLEAK PROSPECT

Certainly, Malthus's view of humanity's prospects was bleak, as he himself acknowledged (in a masterpiece of British understatement) when he wrote that "the view has a melancholy hue." Gone is the optimism of Adam Smith. According to Malthus, the prospect for economic progress was very limited. Given the inexorable increase in human numbers, the standard of living will be kept at a minimum level required to keep body and soul together. If it exceeds this level, the population will increase, driving the standard of living back down. On the other hand, if the standard of living is less than this level, the population will decline because of starvation. Certainly, the long-term prospects were anything but bright. Thomas Carlyle, the famous historian and essayist, called economics "the dismal science." To a considerable extent, economics acquired this bad name through the efforts of Parson Malthus.

Thomas Malthus

[2] T. Malthus, *Essay on the Principle of Population,* as quoted by R. Heilbroner, *The Worldly Philosophers,* 5th ed., New York: Simon and Schuster, 1980, p. 71. For those who would like to read more concerning the history of economic thought, Heilbroner's book is highly recommended.

[3] Of course, it does not matter to Malthus's argument whether the population doubles every 25 years or every 40 years. The important thing is that it increases at a geometric rate.

[4] T. Malthus, "The Principle of Population Growth," reprinted in E. Mansfield, *Principles of Macroeconomics: Readings, Issues, and Cases,* 4th ed. See also the full *Essay on the Principle of Population,* Philip Appleman, ed. New York: Norton, 1976, which contains critical commentary from Malthus's own time to the present.

Malthus's theory can be interpreted in terms of the law of diminishing marginal returns. Living in what was still largely an agricultural society, he emphasized the role of land and labor as resources, and assumed a relatively fixed level of technology. Since land is fixed, increases in labor—due to population growth—will eventually cause the marginal product of labor to get smaller and smaller because of the law of diminishing marginal returns. In other words, because of this law, the marginal product of labor will behave as shown in Figure 19.3, with the result that continued growth of the labor force will ultimately bring economic decline—that is, a reduction in output per worker. This happens because as the marginal product of labor falls with increases in the labor force, the

Example 19.1 "Birth Rights" and Population Control

Some observers have suggested that a nation's population might be controlled through the use of the price system. For example, the government might say that each couple should be allowed two "free births." After that, the couple would have to buy a certificate granting the right to have an additional child. The government would issue a fixed amount of certificates or "birth rights," each certificate enabling a woman to have a child. The available certificates would be sold to the highest bidders.

(a) What would the supply curve for these certificates look like? (b) Using a diagram, show how the equilibrium price of a certificate would be determined. (c) What factors would determine the location and shape of the demand curve for certificates? (d) What social, political, and religious objections can you see to such a scheme?

SOLUTION

(a) The supply curve would be a vertical line since the quantity of certificates supplied is fixed. (b) The diagram is as follows, and the equilibrium price is OP. (c) The demand curve

would be influenced by how much people want children, and how much they are willing to pay for the right to have them. (d) Obviously, many people would feel that such a program would be a major violation of their freedom, particularly since there are strong religious feelings and beliefs involved. People who wanted children and who were too poor to pay for a certificate would certainly object strenuously. There is no serious support for such a system in the United States.

Figure 19.3

Diminishing Marginal Returns and the Effect of Population Growth *According to Malthus, the labor force will tend to OP because, if output per worker exceeds OA, population will increase, and if output per worker is less than OA, starvation will reduce the population.*

Figure 19.4

Shift over Time in the Marginal Product of Labor *Technological change has shifted the marginal-product-of-labor curve to the right.*

Basic Idea #37: Holding other factors constant, rapid population growth can depress living standards because of the law of diminishing marginal returns. Beyond some point, the average product of labor (and the standard of living) will fall. However, this assumes no technological change. If technology advances greatly, as it has done, rapid population growth need not result in lower standards of living.

average product of labor will eventually fall as well—and the average product of labor is another name for output per worker.

Of course, Malthus recognized that various devices could keep the population down—war, famine, birth-control measures, among others. In fact, he tried to describe and evaluate the importance of various checks on population growth. For example, suppose that population tends to grow to the point where output per worker is at a subsistence level—just sufficient to keep body and soul together. If this is the case, and if the subsistence level of output per worker is *OA*, then the labor force will tend to equal *OP* in Figure 19.3. Why? Because, as noted above, Malthus believed that if the standard of living rises appreciably above *OA*, population will increase, thus forcing it back toward *OA*. On the other hand, if the standard of living falls below *OA*, some of the population will starve, thus pushing it back toward *OA*.

EFFECTS OF POPULATION GROWTH

Was Malthus right? Among the less developed nations of the world, his analysis seems very relevant today. During the past 40 years, the population of the less developed nations has grown very rapidly, in part because of the decrease in death rates attributable to the transfer of medical advances from the industrialized countries to the less developed countries. Between 1940 and 1970, the total population of Asia, Africa, and Oceania almost doubled. There has been a tendency for growing populations to push hard against food supplies in some of the countries of Africa, Latin America, and Asia; and the Malthusian model can explain important elements of the situation.

However, Malthus's theory seems far less relevant or correct for the industrialized countries. In contrast to his model, population has not increased to the point where the standard of living has been pushed down to the subsistence level. On the contrary, the standard of living has increased dramatically in all of the industrialized nations. The most important mistake Malthus made was to underestimate the extent and importance of technological change. Instead of remaining fixed, the marginal-product-of-labor curve in Figure 19.3 moved gradually to the right, as new methods and new products increased the efficiency of agriculture. In other words, the situation was as shown in Figure 19.4. Thus, as population increased, the marginal product of labor did not go down. Instead, technological change prevented the productivity of extra agricultural workers from falling.

Among the industrialized nations, have countries with relatively high rates of growth of population had relatively low—or relatively high—rates of economic growth? In general, there seems to be little or no relationship between a nation's rate of population increase and its rate of economic growth. Figure 19.5 plots the rate of population increase against the rate of growth of output per man-year in 11 industrialized nations between 1913 and 1959. The results suggest that there is little or no relation between them; and the relationship that exists appears to be direct rather than inverse.

420

MALTHUS AND POPULATION
GROWTH

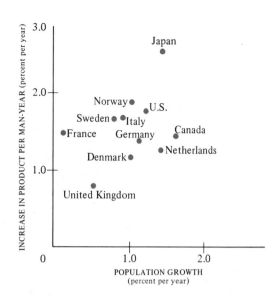

Figure 19.5

Relationship between Population Growth and Increases in National Product per Man-Year, 11 Industrialized Nations, 1913–59. *In industrialized nations, there is little or no relationship between a nation's rate of population growth and its rate of economic growth.*

Test Yourself

1. Suppose that a society produces only two goods, food and tractors, and that its production possibilities curve in 1985 and 1986 is given below:

Quantity of food (millions of tons)	Quantity of tractors (thousands of tractors)
0	9
1	8
2	7
3	5
4	3
5	0

If this society produces 4,000 tractors and 3 million tons of food in 1985 and 5,000 tractors and 3 million tons of food in 1986 (its population remaining constant), has any economic growth occurred between 1985 and 1986? If so, to what is it due?

2. Suppose that the society in Question 1 produces 6,000 tractors and 3 million tons of food in 1987 (its population remaining the same as in 1986), has any economic growth occurred between 1986 and 1987? If so, is it due entirely to a shift in the production possibilities curve? How can you tell?

3. Suppose that a society produces only one commodity, wheat, and that it has the following aggregate production function:

Hours of labor (millions)	Bushels of wheat (millions)
0	0
1	2
2	4
3	6
4	7
5	7

What is the marginal product of labor when between 1 and 2 million hours of labor are used? When between 2 and 3 million hours of labor are used? When between 4 and 5 million hours of labor are used? Do the results conform to the law of diminishing marginal returns? Why or why not?

4. Suppose that an advance in technology doubles the output that can be obtained from each amount of labor in Question 3. Under these new conditions, what is the marginal product of labor when between 1 and 2 million hours of labor are used? When between 4 and 5 million hours of labor are used? Do the results conform to the law of diminishing marginal returns? Why or why not?

5. In Question 3, suppose that the subsistence wage was 1,400 bushels of wheat. According to Malthus, what would have been the equilibrium labor force? What factors would push the labor force toward this level? What would be the effect of the technological advance in Question 4 on the equilibrium labor force?

421

David Ricardo and Capital Formation

A contemporary and good friend of Malthus's who also contributed to the theory of economic growth was David Ricardo (1772–1823). Of all the titans of economics, he is probably least known to the general public. Smith, Malthus, Marx, and Keynes are frequently encountered names. Ricardo is not, although he made many brilliant contributions to economic thought. An extremely successful stockbroker who retired at the age of 42 with a very large fortune, he devoted much of his time to highly theoretical analyses of the economic system and its workings. In contrast to Malthus, who was reviled for his pessimistic doctrines, Ricardo and his writings were widely admired in his own time. He was elected to the House of Commons and was highly respected there.

RICARDO ON INCOME DISTRIBUTION

Ricardo was concerned in much of his work with the distribution of income. Unlike Adam Smith, who paid much less attention to the conflict among classes, Ricardo emphasized the struggle between the industrialists—a relatively new and rising class in his time—and the landowners—the old aristocracy that resisted the rise of the industrial class. This clash was reflected in the struggle in Britain around 1800 over the so-called Corn Laws (*corn* being a general term covering all types of grain). Because of the increase of population, the demand for grain increased in Britain, causing the price of grain to rise greatly. This meant higher profits for the landowners. But the industrialists complained bitterly about the increase in the price of food, because higher food prices meant that they had to pay higher wages. As the price of grain increased, merchants began to import cheap grain from abroad. But the landowners, who dominated Parliament, passed legislation—the Corn Laws—to keep cheap grain out of Britain. In effect the Corn Laws imposed a high tariff or duty on grain.

According to Ricardo's analysis, the landlords were bound to capture most of the benefits of economic progress, unless their control of the price of grain could be weakened. As national output increased and population expanded, poorer and poorer land had to be brought under cultivation to produce the extra food. As the cost of producing grain increased, its price would increase too—and so would the rents of the landlords. The workers and the industrialists, on the other hand, would benefit little, if at all. As the price of grain increased, the workers would have to get higher wages—but only high enough to keep them at a subsistence level (since Ricardo agreed entirely with his friend Malthus on the population issue). Thus the workers would be no better off; and neither would the industrialists, who would wind up with lower profits because of the increase in wage rates.

Ricardo felt that the Corn Laws should be repealed and that free trade in grain should be permitted. In a beautiful piece of theoretical analysis that is still reasonably fresh and convincing 170 years after its publication, he laid out the basic principles of international trade and pointed out the benefits to all countries that can be derived by specialization and free trade. For example, suppose that England is relatively more efficient at

David Ricardo

producing textiles, and France is relatively more efficient at producing wine. Then, on the basis of Ricardo's analysis, it can be shown that each country is likely to be better off by specializing in the product it is more efficient at producing—textiles in England, wine in France—and trading this product for the one the other country specializes in producing. In Chapter 21, we shall discuss this argument in considerable detail; it is a very important part of economics.

RICARDO'S VIEW OF CAPITAL FORMATION

Let's turn to the effect on economic growth of increases in physical capital, holding other inputs and technology fixed. Ricardo constructed some interesting theories concerning the effects of capital formation—i.e., investment in plant and equipment—on economic growth. Other things held constant, a nation's output depends on the amount of plant and equipment that it has and operates. Moreover, one can draw a curve showing the marginal product of capital—the extra output that would result from an extra dollar's worth of capital—under various assumptions about the total amount of capital in existence. This curve will slope downward to the right, as shown in Figure 19.6, because of the law of diminishing marginal returns. As more and more capital is accumulated, its marginal product eventually must decrease. For example, if $100 billion is the total investment in plant and equipment (or total capital), the extra output to be derived from an extra dollar of investment is worth $A; whereas if the total investment is increased to $150 billion, the economy must resort to less productive investments, and the extra output to be derived from an extra dollar of investment is only worth $B.

The curve in Figure 19.6 leads to the conclusion that investment in plant and equipment, although it will increase the growth rate up to some point, will eventually be unable to increase it further. As more and more is invested in new plant and equipment, less and less productive projects must be undertaken. Finally, when all the productive projects have been carried out, further investment in plant and equipment will be useless. At this point—$200 billion of total capital in Figure 19.6—further investment in plant and equipment will not increase output at all.

This kind of analysis led Ricardo to the pessimistic conclusion that the economy would experience decreases in the profitability of investment in

Figure 19.6

Marginal Product of Capital *This curve shows the marginal product of capital, under various assumptions concerning the total amount of capital. For example, if there is $100 billion of capital, the marginal product of capital is $A, whereas if there is $150 billion of capital, the marginal product of capital is $B.*

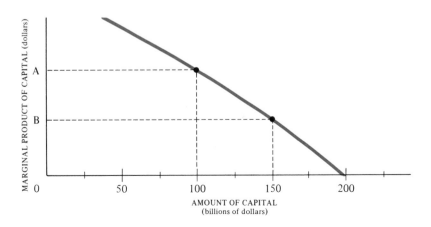

plant and equipment, and eventual termination of economic growth. Also, he expected increases in the ratio of capital to output, because he expected increases in the total amount of capital to be accompanied by decreases in the marginal product of capital.

To illustrate this, suppose that an economy's output equals $1 trillion and its total capital is $3 trillion. Suppose too that $100 billion of extra capital will result in $30 billion in extra output, another $100 billion of extra capital will result in $20 billion in extra output, and still another $100 billion in extra capital will result in $10 billion in extra output. Then the amount of capital per dollar of output will be (3,000 + 100)/(1,000 + 30) if $100 billion is invested, (3,000 + 200)/(1,000 + 50) if $200 billion is invested, and (3,000 + 300)/(1,000 + 60) if $300 billion is invested. Since the marginal product of capital is decreasing, the amount of capital per dollar of output is increasing—from 3 to 3.01 to 3.05 to 3.11.

WAS RICARDO RIGHT?

Have we seen increases in the amount of capital per dollar of output, decreases in the profitability of investment in plant and equipment, and eventual termination of economic growth? No. Ricardo, like Malthus, was led astray by underestimating the extent and impact of future changes in technology. Suppose that, because of the development of major new products and processes, lots of new opportunities for profitable investment arise. Obviously, the effect on the curve in Figure 19.6 is to shift it to the right, because there are more investment opportunities than ever before above a certain level of productivity. But if this curve shifts to the right, as shown in Figure 19.7, we may be able to avoid Ricardo's pessimistic conclusions.

To see how this can occur, note that, if X in Figure 19.7 is the relevant curve in a particular year and if $100 billion is the total amount of capital, an extra dollar of investment in plant and equipment would have a marginal product of $C. A decade later, if Y is the relevant curve and if the total amount of capital has grown to $150 billion, the marginal product of an extra dollar of investment in plant and equipment is still $C. Thus there is no reduction in the productivity of investment opportunities despite the 50 percent increase in the total amount of capital. Because of technological change and other factors, productive and profitable new investment opportunities are opened up as fast as old ones are invested in.

The history of the United States is quite consistent with this sort of shift in investment opportunities over time. Even though we have poured an enormous amount of money into new plant and equipment, we have not exhausted or reduced the productivity or profitability of investment opportunities. The rate of return on investment in new plant and equipment has not fallen. Instead, it has fluctuated around a fairly constant level during the past 70 years. Moreover, the amount of capital per dollar of output has remained surprisingly constant. It has not increased.

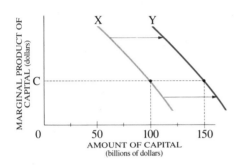

Figure 19.7
Effects of Technological Change on the Marginal Product of Capital *Technological change has shifted the marginal-product-of-capital curve to the right. (Actually, Ricardo's variable input was a combined dose of capital and labor.)*

Capital Formation and Economic Growth

To see more clearly the role of investment in the process of economic growth, let's extend the model we discussed in Chapters 10 and 11. Suppose we ignore the government and consider only the private sector of the economy. Suppose that the full-employment, noninflationary NNP this year is $1,000 billion, and that the consumption function is such that consumption expenditure is $900 billion if NNP is $1,000 billion. If intended investment this year is $100 billion, with the result that NNP is in fact $1,000 billion, *next year's full-employment NNP will increase because this year's investment will increase the nation's productive capacity.* In other words, this year's investment increases next year's full-employment NNP. The amount of the increase in full-employment NNP depends on the **capital-output ratio,** which is the number of dollars of investment (or extra capital goods) required to produce an extra dollar of output. For example, if the capital-output ratio is 2, $2 of investment is required to increase full-employment NNP by $1.

EFFECT OF INVESTMENT ON FULL-EMPLOYMENT NNP

Let's look more closely at the effect of investment on full-employment NNP. If the capital-output ratio is 2, full-employment NNP will increase by $50 billion as a consequence of the $100 billion of investment. Thus full-employment NNP next year is $1,050 billion. On the other hand, suppose that this year's investment is $200 billion rather than $100 billion, and that the consumption function is such that consumption expenditure is $800 billion rather than $900 billion if NNP is $1,000 billion. What will full-employment NNP be next year? If the capital-output ratio is 2, it will be $1,100 billion. Why? Because the $200 billion in investment will increase full-employment NNP by $100 billion—from $1,000 billion to $1,100 billion.

Thus the full-employment NNP will be larger if investment is $200 billion than if it is $100 billion. Similarly, the full-employment NNP will be larger if investment is $300 billion than if it is $200 billion. If the capital-output ratio is 2, the full-employment NNP will be $1,150 billion next year, if investment is $300 billion. Why? Because the $300 billion in investment will increase full-employment NNP by $150 billion—from $1,000 to $1,150 billion.

In general, the greater the percent of NNP that the society devotes to investment this year, the greater will be the increase in its full-employment NNP. Thus, *so long as the economy sustains noninflationary full employment and the capital-output ratio remains constant, the rate of growth of national output will be directly related to the percent of NNP devoted to investment.*[5]

SOME EVIDENCE CONCERNING THE EFFECTS OF INVESTMENT

Certainly, this result seems sensible enough. If a country wants to increase its growth rate, it should produce more blast furnaces, machine tools, and

---

[5] It can be shown that the rate of growth of NNP equals s/b, where s is the proportion of NNP that is saved (and invested), and b is the capital-output ratio, assuming that both s and b are constant and that full employment is maintained. For example, if b is 2 and $s = .10$, NNP will grow at 5 percent per year, since $.10/2 = .05$. This result is part of the so-called Harrod-Domar growth model developed by Sir Roy Harrod of Oxford and Evsey Domar of M.I.T. Although useful, this result must be used with caution since it is based on highly simplified assumptions.

Table 19.2

RATE OF GROWTH OF OUTPUT (1978–80)
AND INVESTMENT AS PERCENTAGE OF
OUTPUT (1970–77)

Nation	Rate of growth of output (percent)	Percent of output invested
	Annual average	
France	2.8	18.8
Germany	3.3	18.7
Canada	2.4	19.3
Japan	5.0	26.7
United Kingdom	1.0	17.6
United States	2.6	14.5

Source: Economic Report of the President, 1982 and Table 20.10.

plows, and less cosmetics, household furniture, and sports cars. But all this is theory. What do the facts suggest? Table 19.2 shows the rate of investment and the growth rate in six major industrialized nations of the non-Communist world in the 1970s. The investment rate was highest in Japan; so was the growth rate. The investment rates were lowest in the United States and the United Kingdom, and their growth rates were among the lowest. Of course, this does not prove that there is any simple cause-and-effect relationship between the investment rate and the growth rate, but it certainly is compatible with the view that investment influences growth.

As revealed in the historical record of the United States, between 1929 and 1947 the amount of U.S. plant and equipment increased at about the same rate as the labor force. On the other hand, between 1947 and 1965, the amount of U.S. plant and equipment increased much more rapidly than the labor force. These facts would lead one to expect that the rate of economic growth would be more rapid in the latter period; and, in keeping with the theory, this turns out to be true. Again, one must be cautious about interpreting such comparisons. Lots of other things besides the investment rate were different in 1947–65 than in 1929–47, and these other things, not the investment rate, may have been responsible for the difference in growth rates. However, it seems likely that the difference in investment rates was at least partially responsible.

The Role of Human Capital

A nation's rate of economic growth is influenced by the rate at which it invests in human capital as well as physical capital. It may seem odd to speak of *human* capital, but every society builds up a certain amount of human capital through investments in formal education, on-the-job-training, and health programs. You often hear people talk about investing in their children's future by putting them through college. For the economy as a whole, the expenditure on education and public health can also be viewed—at least partly—as an investment, because consumption is sacrificed in the present in order to make possible a higher level of per capita output in the future.

The United States invests in human capital on a massive scale. In 1960 expenditures for schools at all levels of education were about $25 billion, or about 5 percent of our gross national product. Moreover, our total investment in the education of the population—the "stock" of educational capital—has grown much more rapidly than has the stock of plant and equipment. Whereas the stock of physical capital was about 4 times as big in 1956 as in 1900, the stock of educational capital was about 8 times as big. These enormous and rapidly growing investments in human capital have unquestionably increased the productivity, versatility, and adaptability of our labor force. They have certainly made a major contribution to economic growth.

Income tends to rise with a person's education. Using this relationship to measure the influence of education on a person's productivity, some economists, notably the University of Chicago's Theodore Schultz and Gary Becker, have tried to estimate the profitability, both to society and to the person, of an investment in various levels of education. Becker has tried to estimate the rate of return from a person's investment in a college education. According to his estimates, the typical urban white male in 1950 received about a 10 percent return (after taxes) on his investment in tuition, room, books, and other college expenses (including the earnings he gave up by being in college rather than at work). This was a relatively high return—much higher, for example, than if the student (or his family) simply put the equivalent amount of money in a savings bank or in government bonds.

In more recent years, however, the return from the investment in a college education seems to have fallen considerably. For example, according to Richard Freeman of Harvard University and Herbert Hollomon of M.I.T., it declined from about 11 or 12 percent in 1969 to about 7 or 8 percent in 1974.

The Role of Technological Change

A nation's rate of economic growth depends on the rate of **technological change,** as well as on the extent to which quantities of inputs of various kinds increase. Indeed, the rate of technological change is perhaps the most important single determinant of a nation's rate of economic growth. Recall from Chapter 1 that technology is knowledge concerning the industrial and agricultural arts. Thus technological change often takes the form of new methods of producing existing products; new designs that make it possible to produce goods with important new characteristics; and new techniques of organization, marketing, and management. Two examples of technological change are new ways of producing power (for example, atomic energy) and new fibers (for example, nylon or Dacron).

We have already seen that technological change can shift the curves in both Figures 19.4 and 19.7, thus warding off the law of diminishing marginal returns. But note that new knowledge by itself has little impact. *Unless knowledge is applied, it has little effect on the rate of economic growth.* A change in technology, when applied for the first time, is called an **innovation,** and the firm that first applies it is called an **innovator.** Innovation is a key stage in the process leading to the full evaluation and utilization of a new process or product. The innovator must be willing to take the risks involved in introducing a new and untried process, good, or service; and in many cases, these risks are high. Once a change in technology has been applied for the first time, the **diffusion process**—the process by which the use of the innovation spreads from firm to firm and from use to use—begins. How rapidly an innovation spreads depends heavily on its economic advantages over older methods or products. The more profitable the use of the innovation is, the more rapidly it will spread.

Joseph Schumpeter, Harvard's distinguished economist and social theorist, stressed the important role played by innovators in the process of economic growth. In Schumpeter's view, innovators are the mainspring of economic progress, the people with the foresight to see how new things can be brought into being and the courage and resourcefulness to surmount the obstacles to change. For their trouble, innovators receive profit; but this profit eventually is whittled down by competitors who imitate the innovators. The innovators push the curves in Figures 19.4 and 19.7 to the right, and once their innovations are assimilated by the economy, other innovators may shove these curves somewhat farther to the right. For example, one innovator introduces vacuum tubes, a later innovator introduces semiconductors; one innovator introduces the steam locomotive, a later innovator introduces the diesel locomotive. This process goes on and on—and is a main source of economic growth.

THE ELECTRONIC COMPUTER: A CASE STUDY

To get a better feel for the nature of technological change and the process of innovation, let's consider one of the most important technological advances of the twentieth century—the electronic computer. Many of the basic ideas underlying the computer go back to Charles Babbage, a brilliant nineteenth-century British inventor; but not until 1946 was the first electronic computer, the ENIAC, designed and constructed. John Mauchly and J. Presper Eckert, both professors at the Moore School of Electrical Engineering at the University of Pennsylvania, were responsible for the ENIAC's design and construction. The work was supported by the U.S. Army. John von Neumann, a famous mathematician at the Institute for Advanced Study at Princeton, added the important concepts of stored programming and conditional transfer.

After the war, Mauchly and Eckert established a small firm to produce electronic computers. Their firm was acquired by Remington Rand, which in 1951 marketed the Univac I, a machine used by the Census Bureau. The International Business Machines Corporation (IBM), the leading company in office machinery and data processing, which before this had been cautious about the potential market for computers (recall Chapter 6), was spurred into action by Remington Rand's success. Once it entered the field, IBM's financial resources, strong marketing organization, and engineering strength enabled it to capture a very large share of the computer market, here and abroad. In the United States, IBM's share of the market grew to about 70 percent during the 1960s.

The electronic computer has been an extremely important stimulus to economic growth. By 1966, the total number of computers installed in the Western world exceeded 50,000 at a total value of about $20 billion. These computers have had important effects on production techniques in many industries. For example, in the chemical, petroleum, and steel industries, digital computers were an important step in the evolution of control techniques. Computers helped to determine and enforce the best conditions for process operation, as well as acting as data loggers. They could also be programmed to help carry out the complex sequence of operations required to start up or shut down a plant. They have increased production, decreased waste, improved quality control, and reduced the chance of damage to equipment. In another quite different industry, banking, computers have had an important effect too. They have made it possible to eliminate conventional machines and processes for sorting checks, balancing accounts, and computing service charges. With high-speed sorters, it is possible now to process more than 1,500 checks per minute.

Obviously, the electronic computer has enabled us to produce more output from a given amount of resources. In other words, it has enabled us to push the production possibilities curve outward, thus increasing our rate of economic growth. But it must be recognized that the process by which the computer has had this effect has by no means been simple or straightforward. Many people in many countries were involved in the development of the basic ideas. Many organizations, public and private, funded the experimental work. Firms of various types were the innovators with respect to particular aspects of the modern computer. And countless individuals and organizations had to be willing to accept, work with, and invest in computers.

Determinants of Technological Change

What determines the rate of technological change and the rate at which changes in technology are applied and spread? Clearly, *the nature and extent of a nation's scientific capability, and the size and quality of its educational system are of fundamental importance.* The first thing that must be said about the influence of a nation's scientific capability on its rate of technological change is that science and technology are two quite different things that have drawn together only recently. Until the twentieth century, it was not true that technology was built on science. Even today, many technological advances rely on little in the way of science. However, in more and more areas of the economy (such as aircraft, electronics, and chemicals), the rapid application of new technology has come to depend on a strong scientific base. Merely to imitate or adapt what others have developed, a firm in these areas needs access to high-caliber scientists.

A nation's educational system also has a fundamental influence on the rate of technological change. First, and perhaps most obviously, it determines how many scientists and engineers are graduated, and how competent they are. Clearly, the rate of technological change depends on the quantity and quality of scientific and engineering talent available in the society. Second, the educational system influences the inventiveness and adaptability of the nation's work force. Despite the closer links between technology and science, workers and independent inventors remain important sources of inventions in many areas. Third, the educational system also influences the rate of technological change and innovation via the training of managers.

Industrial managers are a key agent in the innovative process. We must emphasize that the proper management of innovation is much more than establishing and maintaining a research and development laboratory that produces a great deal of good technical output. In many industries, most important innovations are not based in any significant degree on the firms' research and development (R and D). And even when the basic idea does come from a firm's own R and D, the coupling of R and D with marketing and production is crucial. Many good ideas are not applied properly because the potential users do not really understand them, and many R and D projects are technically successful but commercially irrelevant because they were not designed with sufficient comprehension of market realities. Typically, successful technological innovations seem to be stimulated by

Basic Idea #38: The rate of technological change is probably the most important single determinant of a nation's rate of economic growth. A country's rate of technological change depends on the nature and extent of its scientific capabilities and its educational system, as well as the organization of its industries and markets. For most countries, considerable technological change can be achieved by borrowing and transferring technology from the world leaders.

429

perceived production and marketing needs, not solely by technological opportunities. In other words, most of the time it takes a market-related impetus to prompt work on a successful innovation.

In addition, *the rate of technological change depends on the organization of industry and the nature of markets.* Although a certain amount of industrial concentration may promote more rapid technological change, increases in concentration beyond a moderate level probably reduce rather than increase the rate of technological change. The rate of technological change also depends on the scale and sophistication of available markets. The scale of the market determines how many units of a new product or process are likely to be sold, which in turn influences the cost per unit of developing and introducing an innovation. Our huge domestic market has often been cited as a reason for America's technological lead over many other countries. Finally, it is extremely important to note that a country that is not a technological leader can still achieve considerable technological change by borrowing and transferring technology from the leaders.

TECHNOLOGICAL CHANGE AND LABOR PRODUCTIVITY

It is difficult to measure the rate of technological change. Perhaps the most frequently used measure is the rate of growth of labor productivity: the rate of growth of output per hour of labor. Unfortunately, this measure is influenced by lots of other factors besides the rate of technological change. Nonetheless, despite its inadequacies, it is worthwhile to look briefly at how rapidly productivity has increased in the United States over the long run. Since about 1890, the nation's real output per hour of labor increased by about 2 percent per year—and these productivity gains were widely diffused, real hourly earnings growing about as rapidly, on the average, as output per hour of labor.

As indicated in Table 19.3, the rate of growth of labor productivity slowed considerably in the 1970s and early 1980s. According to some observers, this productivity slowdown has been due in part to a decline in the rate of innovation in the United States. In their opinion, the rate of introduction of new products and processes has fallen. It is true that the patent rate has been falling since about 1969, and that direct evidence of a fall in

Table 19.3

PERCENT CHANGE IN OUTPUT PER MAN-HOUR, NONFARM BUSINESS SECTOR, U.S., 1950–84

Year	Percent change[a]	Year	Percent change[a]
1984	3.1	1966	2.5
1982	0.2	1964	3.9
1980	−0.7	1962	3.6
1978	0.6	1960	0.8
1976	3.2	1958	2.4
1974	−2.5	1956	0.3
1972	3.7	1954	1.4
1970	0.3	1952	2.3
1968	3.3	1950	6.0

[a] Percent change from the previous year.
Source: Economic Report of the President, 1985.

the rate of innovation has existed in some industries, like pharmaceuticals, where one can measure the number of major innovations that are carried out per unit of time. But in other industries, such as microelectronics, the rate of innovation seems hale and hearty.

Entrepreneurship and the Social Environment

Still another set of basic factors influencing a nation's level of potential output and its rate of economic growth is the economic, social, political, and religious climate of the nation. It is difficult, if not impossible, to measure the effect of these factors, but there can be no doubt of their importance. Some societies despise material welfare and emphasize the glories of the next world. Some societies are subject to such violent political upheavals that it is risky, if not foolish, to invest in the future. Some societies are governed so corruptly that economic growth is frustrated. And some societies look down on people engaged in industry, trade, or commerce. Obviously, such societies are less likely to experience rapid economic growth than others with a more favorable climate and conditions.

The relatively rapid economic growth of the United States was undoubtedly stimulated in part by the attitude of its people toward material gain. It is commonplace to note that the United States is a materialistic society, a society that esteems business success, that bestows prestige on the rich, that accepts the Protestant ethic (which, crudely stated, is that work is good), and that encourages individual initiative. The United States has been criticized over and over again for some of these traits—often by nations frantically trying to imitate its economic success. Somewhat less obvious is the fact that, because the United States is a young country whose people came from a variety of origins, it did not inherit many feudal components in the structure of society. This too was important.

The United States has also been characterized by great economic and political freedom, by institutions that have been flexible enough to adjust to change, and by a government that has encouraged competition in the market place. This has meant fewer barriers to new ideas. Also, the United States has for a long time enjoyed internal peace, order, and general respect for property rights. There have been no violent revolutions since the Civil War, and for many years we were protected from strife in other lands by two oceans—which then seemed much broader than they do now. All these factors undoubtedly contributed to rapid economic growth.

The American economy also seems to have been able to nurture a great many entrepreneurs and a vast horde of competent business executives. During the nineteenth century, American entrepreneurs were responsible for such basic innovations as the system of interchangeable parts, pioneered by Eli Whitney and others. In many areas, the United States gained a technological lead over other nations, which was maintained for many years. Much of this lead came from superior management as well as superior technological resources. For example, the Organization for Economic Cooperation and Development concluded in 1968 that, "In the techniques of *management,* including the management of research, and of combined technological and market forecasting, the United States appears

Robotics in U.S. industry

431

Workers have long recognized and feared technological unemployment. As long ago as the mid-1700s, a mob of worried English spinners entered James Hargreave's mill and smashed the first workable multistage frames. Although the dread of technology-induced mass unemployment is not new, it was revived in the 1980s, the new scare word being *robotics*. According to some observers, robots would result in widespread unemployment.

Do increases in the rate of technological change necessarily result in increases in aggregate unemployment? To make a long story short, the answer is *no*. To see how large-scale technological unemployment can occur—and how it can be avoided—consider the figure below, which shows the $C + I + G$ line at a particular point in time. (If you are a bit hazy about the meaning and significance of this line, review Chapter 12.) Since this line intersects the 45-degree line at point A, the equilibrium level of net national product is $400 billion. If the high-employment level of net national product is also $400 billion, the economy enjoys a high level of employment. Now suppose that there is a significant amount of technological change. What will be the result? To begin with, the advance in technology will almost certainly result in an increase in productivity. In other words, it will enable the labor force to produce more than it formerly could. Thus the high-employment level of net national product will increase —say to $450 billion. Given this increase, there will be substantial unemployment if the $C + I + G$ line stays put. If output remains the same and output per man-hour increases, fewer workers will be needed and there will be unemployment.

A. Before technological change

B. After technological change

C. After adjustments in monetary and fiscal policies

But there is no reason why the $C + I + G$ *line should remain constant.* The advance in technology itself may increase the profitability of investment, thus raising I. Moreover, the advance in technology may result in new consumer products, which prompt consumers to spend more of a given level of income, thus raising C. Suppose that, by virtue of these changes in C and I, the $C + I + G$ line shifts to $C' + I' + G'$ (shown in panel B). The new equilibrium level of net national product is $425 billion, as shown in panel B. Unfortunately, in this particular case (but not necessarily in other cases), the new equilibrium level of NNP is less than the new high-employment level of NNP. Thus, without some change in public policy, there would be some technological unemployment. But as we know, the Federal Reserve can increase I by increasing the money supply and reducing interest rates, and the government can push C upward by reducing tax rates and increase G by increasing its own expenditures. Thus there is no reason why the government cannot raise the $C + I + G$ line to the point where it intersects the 45-degree line at $450 billion. For example, the government might nudge the $C + I + G$ line up to $C'' + I'' + G''$ in panel C. And if it does this, the equilibrium level of net national product equals the high-employment level of net national product. Thus it should be possible to avoid large amounts of technological unemployment, although transitional problems obviously will remain.

to have a significant lead."[6] In the past decade, according to many observers, our technological lead has been reduced considerably. This has caused concern among American government officials and business executives.

The Gap Between Actual and Potential Output

Up to this point, our discussion of economic growth has centered on the factors that determine how rapidly a nation's potential output grows—factors like technological change, increased education, investment in plant and equipment, and increases in the labor force. Now we must examine the factors that determine how close a nation's actual output comes to its potential output. As we already know, a nation's potential output is its output under full employment. Thus, as we also know, whether or not the economy operates close to full employment is determined by the level of the $C + I + G$ line. If the $C + I + G$ line is too low, the economy will operate with considerable unemployment, and actual output will be substantially below potential output. Or, in terms of the equation of exchange, if $M \times V$ is too small, the economy will operate with considerable unemployment, and actual output will be substantially below potential output.

From previous chapters, we also know how the government can use fiscal and monetary policies to push actual output close to potential output. Cuts in tax rates, increases in government spending, incentives for private investment in plant and equipment, increases in the money supply, reductions in interest rates; all these devices can be used to push actual output closer to potential output. Such devices promote economic growth, in the sense that actual per capita output is increased. However, only so much growth can be achieved by squeezing the slack out of the economy. For example, if there is a 7 percent unemployment rate, output per capita can be increased by perhaps 6 percent simply by reducing the unemployment rate to 5 percent. *But this is a one-shot improvement.* To get any further growth, the nation must increase its potential output.

This doesn't mean that it isn't important to maintain the economy at close to full employment. On the contrary, as we stressed in Chapter 8, one of the major objectives of public policy must be full employment, and a reduction of unemployment will have a significant effect on the rate of economic growth in the short run. (Much of the economic growth in the United States in the early 1960s was caused by the transition to full employment.) But the point we are making is that, once the economy gets to full employment, no further growth can occur by this route. If a nation wants further growth, it must influence the factors responsible for the rate of growth of potential output.

---

[6] Organization for Economic Cooperation and Development, *Technology Gap: General Report,* Paris, 1968, p. 25.

433

Test Yourself

1. Suppose that a society's full-employment NNP increases between 1985 and 1986 by $100 billion. During the same period, its corporations floated $20 billion in stocks and bonds, and it invested $200 billion. What is the capital-output ratio in this society? Will the capital-output ratio in this society always be the same? Why or why not?

2. Suppose that a society's capital-output ratio is 3 and that it invests 10 percent of its NNP. If full employment is maintained, by what percentage will its NNP grow?

3. "Ricardo's pessimistic view of the prospects for economic growth stemmed from his assumptions concerning the capital-output ratio. If he had recognized that it was not fixed, he would have been closer to correct." Comment and evaluate.

4. Some studies indicate that what matters most to people is their income relative to others around them rather than the absolute level of their income. Would this fact tend to reduce the importance of growth as a means of helping the poor? Explain.

Summary

1. Economic growth is measured by the increase of per capita real gross national product, an index that does not measure accurately the growth of economic welfare, but is often used as a first approximation.

2. A nation's rate of economic growth depends on the increase in the quantity and quality of its resources (including physical and human capital) and the rate of technological change. In addition, the rate of economic growth depends on the extent to which a society maintains full employment and on the efficiency with which its resources are allocated and managed.

3. One factor that may influence a nation's rate of economic growth is the rate at which its population grows. In Malthus's view, population growth, unless checked in some way, ultimately meant economic decline, since output could not grow in proportion to the growth in population. The law of diminishing marginal returns insured that beyond some point, increases in labor, holding the quantity of land constant, would result in smaller and smaller increments of output. However, Malthus underestimated the extent and importance of technological change, which offset the law of diminishing marginal returns.

4. Another factor that determines whether per capita output grows rapidly or slowly is the rate of expenditure on new plant and equipment. Without technological change, more and more of this sort of investment would result in increases in the amount of capital per dollar of output and decreases in the profitability of investment in plant and equipment, as Ricardo pointed out. But because of technological change, none of these things has occurred. According to the available evidence, a nation's rate of economic growth seems directly related to its rate of investment in plant and equipment.

5. To a considerable extent, economic growth here and abroad has resulted from technological change. A change in technology, when applied for the first time, is called an innovation, and the firm that first applies it is called an innovator. Innovation is a key stage in the process leading to the full evaluation and utilization of a new process or product. Unless knowledge is used, it has little effect on the rate of economic growth.

6. The rate of technological change and the rate at which new technology is applied depend on a number of factors, including the nature and extent of a nation's scientific capability, the size and quality of its educational system, the quality of its managers, the attitude and structure of its firms, the organization of its industries, and the nature of its markets.

7. Another factor with an important effect on a nation's rate of economic growth is the rate at which it invests in human capital. The United States invests in human capital on a massive scale, and these enormous and rapidly growing investments have unquestionably increased the productivity, versatility, and adaptability of our labor force.

8. Still another set of basic factors influencing the rate of economic growth is the economic, social, and political climate of the nation. Some societies despise material welfare, are subject to violent political upheavals, and are governed by corrupt groups. Such societies are unlikely to have a high rate of economic growth.

9. Finally, the rate of economic growth is also affected by the extent and behavior of the gap between actual and potential GNP. However, once a nation gets to full employment, it cannot grow further by reducing this gap.

Concepts for Review

Economic growth	Marginal product of labor	Capital-output ratio
Aggregate production function	Average product of labor	Technological change
Law of diminishing marginal returns	Population growth	Innovation
	Capital formation	Innovator
		Diffusion process

CHAPTER 20

Environmental and Energy Problems

Environmental pollution and energy have been two important problems in the United States, and both are related to economic growth. According to many scientists and social observers, one of the costs of economic growth is environmental pollution. For a long time, people in the United States paid relatively little attention to the environment and what they were doing to it, but this attitude changed markedly in the last twenty years. The public became genuinely concerned about environmental problems. However, in the effort to clean up the environment, choices are not always clear, nor solutions easy. In particular, the energy crisis of the 1970s brought home the fact that a cleaner environment is not costless. Many measures that would reduce pollution would increase the demand for energy.

America's energy problems have been related only partly to environmental matters. To a considerable extent, they stem from the fact that oil reserves in this country are being depleted, and that foreign sources of oil have banded together in an international cartel which raised the price of crude oil enormously in 1974 and 1979. In this chapter, we consider the economic aspects of both environmental decay and the nation's energy needs. Our purpose is to indicate the extent of these problems, the factors that are responsible for them, and the sorts of public policies that might be adopted to help deal with them.

Our Environmental Problems

WATER POLLUTION

To see what we mean by environmental pollution, let's begin with one of the most important parts of man's environment, our water supplies. As a result of human activities, large amounts of pollutants are discharged into streams, lakes, and the sea. Chemical wastes are released by industrial plants and mines, as well as by farms and homes when fertilizers, pesticides, and detergents run off into waterways. Oil is discharged into the waters by tankers, sewage systems, oil wells, and other sources. Organic compounds enter waterways from industrial plants and farms, as well as from municipal sewage plants; and animal wastes, as well as human wastes, contribute substantially to pollution.

Obviously, we cannot continue to increase the rate at which we dump wastes into our streams, rivers, and oceans. A river, like everything else, can bear only so much. The people of Cleveland know this well. In 1969, the Cuyahoga River, which flows through Cleveland, literally caught fire, so great was its concentration of industrial and other wastes. Of course, the Cuyahoga is an extreme case, but many of our rivers, including the Hudson and the Ohio, are badly polluted. Water pollution is a nuisance and perhaps a threat.[1]

AIR POLLUTION

If clean water is vital to man's survival, so too is clean air. Yet the battle being waged against air pollution in most of our major cities has not been won. Particles of various kinds are spewed into the air by factories that utilize combustion processes, grind materials, or produce dust. Motor vehicles release lead compounds from gasoline and rubber particles worn from tires, helping to create that unheavenly condition known as smog. Citizens of Los Angeles are particularly familiar with smog, but few major cities have escaped at least periodic air pollution. No precise measures have been developed to gauge the effects of air pollution on public health and enjoyment, but some rough estimates suggest that perhaps 25 percent of all deaths from respiratory disease could be avoided by a 50 percent reduction in air pollution.

One of the most important contributors to air pollution is the combustion of fossil fuels, particularly coal and oil products: by-products of combustion comprise about 85 percent of the total amount of air pollutants in the United States. Most of these pollutants result from impure fuels or inefficient burning. Among the more serious pollutants are sulphur dioxide, carbon monoxide, and various oxides of nitrogen.

At present, the automobile is the principal source of air pollution in the United States. According to some estimates, human activities pump into the air over 200 million tons of waste each year, and automobiles can be credited with the dubious honor of contributing about 40 percent of this

[1] See *Fortune*, February 1970; D. Rohrer, D. Montgomery, M. Montgomery, D. Eaton, and M. Arnold, *The Environment Crisis*, Skokie, Ill.: National Textbook, 1970; and Environmental Protection Agency, *The Economics of Clean Water*, 1973, Washington, D.C.: Government Printing Office, 1973.

figure. Spurred on by the public interest in pollution control, some technologists have been hard at work on substitutes for the internal combustion engine. Attempts have been—and are being—made to devise economical and convenient electric and steam-driven automobiles. To date, however, these efforts have not succeeded. Thus it seems likely that in the near future at least, we shall have to rely heavily on modifications of the internal combustion engine and its fuel to reduce air pollution.[2] (More use of nonpolluting transport like bicycles and feet would help too.)

The Important Role of External Diseconomies

The reason why our economic system has tolerated pollution of the environment lies largely in the concept of external diseconomies, which we mentioned in Chapter 4. An *external diseconomy* occurs when one person's (or firm's) use of a resource damages other people who cannot obtain proper compensation. When this occurs, a market economy is unlikely to function properly. The price system is based on the supposition that the full cost of using each resource is borne by the person or firm that uses it. If this is not the case and if the user bears only part of the full costs, then the resource is not likely to be directed by the price system into the socially optimal use.

To understand why, we might begin by reviewing briefly how resources are allocated in a market economy. As we saw in Chapter 3, resources are used in their socially most valuable way because they are allocated to the people and firms who find it worthwhile to bid most for them, assuming that prices reflect true social costs. Under these circumstances, a firm that maximizes its profits will produce the socially desirable output and use the socially desirable amounts of labor, capital, and other resources. Under these circumstances, there is no problem.

PRIVATE COST ⪇ SOCIAL COST

Suppose, however, that because of the presence of external diseconomies people and firms do not pay the true social costs for resources. For example, suppose that some firms or people can use water and air for nothing, but that other firms or people incur costs as a consequence of this prior use. In this case, the *private costs* of using air and water differ from the *social costs: the price paid by the user of water and air is less than the true cost to society.* In a case like this, users of water and air are guided in their decisions by the private cost of water and air—by the prices they pay. Since they pay less than the true social costs, water and air are artificially cheap to them, so that they will use too much of these resources, from society's point of view.

Note that the divergence between private and social cost occurs if, and only if, the use of water or air by one firm or person imposes costs on other

[2] Ibid. Also, see L. Lave and E. Seskin, *Air Pollution and Human Health,* Baltimore: published for Resources for the Future by The Johns Hopkins University Press, 1977.

firms or persons. Thus, if a paper mill uses water and then treats it to restore its quality, there is no divergence between private and social cost. But when the same mill dumps harmful wastes into streams and rivers (the cheap way to get rid of its by-products), the towns downstream that use the water must incur costs to restore its quality. The same is true of air pollution. If an electric power plant uses the atmosphere as a cheap and convenient place to dispose of wastes, people living and working nearby may incur costs as a result, since the incidence of respiratory and other diseases may increase. In such cases, there may be a divergence between private and social cost.

We said above that pollution-causing activities that result in external diseconomies represent a malfunctioning of the market system. At this point, the nature of this malfunctioning should be clear. *Firms and people dump too much waste material into the water and the atmosphere. The price system does not provide the proper signals because the polluters are induced to use our streams and atmosphere in this socially undesirable way by the artificially low price of disposing of wastes in this manner. Moreover, because the polluters do not pay the true cost of waste disposal, their products are artificially cheap, so that too much is produced of them.*

Consider two examples. Electric power companies do not pay the full cost of disposing of wastes in the atmosphere. They charge an artificially low price, and the public is induced to use more electric power than is socially desirable. Similarly, since the owners of automobiles do not pay the full cost of disposing of exhaust and other wastes in the atmosphere, they pay an artificially low price for operating an automobile, and the public is induced to own and use more automobiles than is socially desirable.

Public Policy Toward Pollution

Pollution is caused by defects in our institutions, not by malicious intent, greed, or corruption. In cases where waste disposal causes significant external diseconomies, economists generally agree that government intervention may be justifiable. But how can the government intervene? Perhaps the simplest way is **direct regulation,** through the issuance of certain enforceable rules for waste disposal. For example, the government can prohibit the burning of trash in furnaces or incinerators, or the dumping of certain materials in the ocean; and make any person or firm that violates these restrictions subject to a fine, or perhaps even imprisonment. Also, the government can ban the use of chemicals like DDT, or require that all automobiles meet certain regulations for the emission of air pollutants. Further, the government can establish quality standards for air and water.

The government can also intervene by establishing effluent fees. An **effluent fee** is a fee a polluter must pay to the government for discharging waste. In other words, a price is imposed on the disposal of wastes into the environment; and the more firms or individuals pollute, the more they must pay. The idea behind the imposition of effluent fees is that they can bring the private cost of waste disposal closer to the true social costs.

Wastewater treatment plant

Basic Idea #39: A free-enterprise economy is likely to result in too much pollution because the firms and individuals who dump waste materials into the water and the atmosphere are guided by the artificially low prices they pay for disposing of wastes in this way. The true costs to society of such waste disposal are greater than the prices they pay. To remedy the situation, economists argue that polluters should be made to pay the true social costs of polluting (for example, through effluent fees).

Faced with a closer approximation to the true social costs of their activities, polluters will reduce the extent to which they pollute the environment. Needless to say, many practical difficulties are involved in carrying out this seemingly simple scheme, but many economists believe that this is the best way to deal with the pollution problem.[3]

Still another way for the government to intervene is to establish **tax credits** for firms that introduce pollution-control equipment. There are, of course, many types of equipment that a plant can introduce to cut down on pollution—for example, "scrubbers" for catching poisonous gases, and electrostatic precipitators for decreasing dust and smoke. But such pollution-control equipment costs money, and firms are naturally reluctant to spend money on purposes where the private rate of return is so low. To reduce the burden, the government can allow firms to reduce their tax bill by a certain percentage of the amount they spend on pollution-control equipment. Tax incentives of this sort have been discussed widely in recent years, and some have been adopted.

DIRECT REGULATION

Let's look more closely at the advantages and disadvantages of each of these major means by which the government can intervene to remedy the nation's pollution problems. At present we rely mostly on direct regulation of waste disposal (and the quality of the environment); and despite the many problems involved, it has undoubtedly done much good. As Allen Kneese, one of the country's top experts in this area, says about water pollution, "The control of water discharges through administrative orders regulating individual waste disposers has been a useful device and cannot be abandoned until we have a better substitute."[4]

However, economists agree that direct regulation suffers from some serious disadvantages:

1. Such regulations have generally taken the form of general, cross-the-board rules. For example, if two factories located on the same river dump the same amount of waste material into the river, such regulations would probably call for each factory to reduce its waste disposal by the same amount. Unfortunately, although this may appear quite sensible, it may in fact be very inefficient. Suppose that it is much less costly for one factory to reduce its waste disposal than for the other. In such a case, it would be more efficient to ask the factory that could reduce its wastes more cheaply to cut down more on its waste disposal than the other factory. For reasons of this sort, *pollution reductions are likely to be accomplished at more than minimum cost, if they are accomplished by direct regulation.*

2. To formulate such regulations in a reasonably sensible way, the responsible government agencies must have access to much more information than they are likely to obtain or assimilate. Unless the government agencies

---

[3] Another possibility is for the government to issue a certificate or license to pollute. The government might issue a limited number of certificates, to be auctioned off to the highest bidders.

[4] A. Kneese, "Public Policy toward Water Pollution." in E. Mansfield, *Microeconomics: Selected Readings,* 3d ed., New York: Norton, 1979.

have a detailed and up-to-date familiarity with the technology of hundreds of industries, they are unlikely to make sound rules. Moreover, unless the regulatory agencies have a very wide jurisdiction, their regulations will be evaded by the movement of plants and individuals from localities where regulations are stiff to localities where they are loose. In addition, the regulatory agencies must view the pollution problem as a whole, since piecemeal regulation may simply lead polluters to substitute one form of pollution for another. For example, New York and Philadelphia have attempted to reduce water pollution by more intensive sewage treatment. However, one result has been the production of a lot of biologically active sludge that is being dumped into the ocean—and perhaps causing problems there.

EFFLUENT FEES

The use of effluent fees is the approach most economists seem to prefer, for the following reasons. First, *it obviously is socially desirable to use the cheapest way to achieve any given reduction in pollution. A system of effluent fees is more likely to accomplish this objective than direct regulation, because the regulatory agency cannot have all the relevant information* (as we noted above), *whereas polluters, reacting in their own interest to effluent fees, will tend to use the cheapest means to achieve a given reduction in pollution.*

To see why this is the case, consider a particular polluter. Faced with an effluent fee—that is, a price it must pay for each unit of waste it discharges—the polluter will find it profitable to reduce its discharge of waste so long as the cost of doing so is less than the effluent fees it saves. Thus, if this firm can reduce its discharge of wastes relatively cheaply, it will be induced to make such a reduction by the prospect of increased profits. On the other hand, if it cannot reduce its discharge of wastes at all cheaply, it will not make such a reduction, since the costs will exceed the saving in effluent fees. Thus a system of effluent fees induces firms that can reduce waste disposal more cheaply to cut down more on their waste disposal than firms where such a reduction is more expensive. This means that a given reduction of pollution will occur at a relatively low cost.

Economists also favor effluent fees because this approach requires far less information in the hands of the relevant government agencies than does direct regulation. After all, when effluent fees are used, all the government has to do is meter the amount of pollution a firm or household produces (which admittedly is sometimes not easy) and charge accordingly. It is left to the firms and households to figure out the most ingenious and effective ways to cut down on their pollution and save on effluent fees. This too is a spur to inventive activities aimed at developing more effective ways to reduce pollution. Also, economists favor the use of effluent fees because financial incentives are likely to be easier to administer than direct regulation.

While economists tend to favor the use of effluent fees, they are not always against direct regulation. Some ways of disposing of certain types of waste are so dangerous that the only sensible thing to do is to ban them. For example, a ban on the disposal of mercury or arsenic in places where human beings are likely to consume them—and die—seems reasonable enough. In effect, the social cost of such pollution is so high that a very high penalty—imprisonment—is put on it. In addition, of course, economists favor direct regulation when it simply is not feasible to impose effluent fees—for example, in cases where it would be prohibitively expensive to meter the amount of pollutants emitted by various firms or households.

THE RUHR: A CASE STUDY[5]

Let's consider a well-known case of effluent fees in use: the Ruhr valley in West Germany. The Ruhr is one of the world's most industrialized areas. It includes about one-third of West Germany's industrialized capacity, and about 70 to 90 percent of West Germany's coal, coke, and iron and steel outputs. It contains about 10 million people and about 4,300 square miles. Water supplies in the Ruhr are quite limited. Five small rivers supply the area. The amazing amount of waste materials these rivers carry is indicated by the fact that the average annual natural low flow is less than the volume of effluent discharged into the rivers. Yet the local water authorities have succeeded in making this small amount of water serve the needs of the firms and households of this tremendous industrial area, and at the same the streams have been used for recreation. Moreover, all this has been achieved at a remarkably low cost. The success of water management in the Ruhr seems to be due in considerable part to institutional arrangements that allowed the German water managers to plan and operate a relatively efficient regional system. Collective water quality improvement measures are used. Water quality is controlled by waste treatment in over 100 plants, regulation of river flow by reservoir, and a number of oxidation lakes in the Ruhr itself.

Effluent fees are an integral part of the institutional arrangements governing water quality. The amount a firm has to pay depends upon how much waste—and what kind—it pumps into the rivers. A formula has been devised to indicate how much a polluter must pay to dispose of a particular type of waste. In simple terms, the formula bases the charge on the amount of clean water needed to dilute the effluent in order to avoid harm to fish. Using this formula, the local authorities can determine, after testing the effluent of any firm, the amount the firm should pay. Specifically, the amount depends on the amount of suspended materials that will settle out of the effluent, the amount of oxygen consumed by bacteria in a sample of effluent, the results of a potassium permanganate test, and the results of a fish toxicity test. You need not understand the nature or specific purposes of these measurements and tests. The important thing is that you understand their general aim—which is to measure roughly the amount of pollution caused by various kinds of wastes. Having made these measurements and tests, the local authorities use their formula to determine how much a firm must pay in effluent fees.

TAX CREDITS FOR POLLUTION-CONTROL EQUIPMENT

Many tax inducements to encourage firms and individuals to install pollution-control equipment have been proposed. A typical suggestion is that the

View of the Ruhr valley, Germany

[5] This section is based on A. Kneese and B. Bower, *Managing Water Quality: Economics, Technology, Institutions,* Washington, D.C.: Resources for the Future, 1968, Chapter 12.

government offer a *tax credit* equal to 20 percent of the cost of pollution-control equipment, and allow a firm to depreciate such equipment in only one to five years. In this way, the government would help defray some of the costs of the pollution-control equipment by allowing a firm that installed such equipment to pay less taxes than if no such tax inducements existed.

However, such schemes have a number of disadvantages:

1. Subsidies to promote the purchase of particular types of pollution-control equipment may result in relatively inefficient and costly reductions in pollution. After all, other methods that don't involve special pollution-control equipment—such as substituting one type of fuel for another—may sometimes be a more efficient way to reduce pollution.

2. Subsidies of this sort may not be very effective. Even if the subsidy reduces the cost to the firm of reducing pollution, it may still be cheaper for the firm to continue to pollute. In other words, subsidies of this sort make it a little less painful for polluters to reduce pollution; but unlike effluent fees, they offer no positive incentive.

3. It seems preferable on grounds of equity for the firms and individuals that do the polluting—or their customers—to pay to clean up the mess that results. Effluent fees work this way, but with tax credits for pollution-control equipment, the government picks up part of the tab by allowing the polluter to pay lower taxes. In other words, the general public, which is asked to shoulder the additional tax burden to make up for the polluters' lower taxes, pays part of the cost. But is this a fair allocation of the costs? Why should the general public be saddled with much of the bill?

Pollution-Control Programs in the United States

In recent decades, there has been considerable growth in government programs designed to control pollution. To take but one example, federal expenditures to reduce water pollution increased in the period from the mid- 1950s to 1970 from about $1 million to $300 million annually. To curb water pollution, the federal government has for years operated a system of grants-in-aid to state, municipal, or regional agencies to help construct treatment plants; and grants are made for research on new treatment methods. In addition, the 1970 Water Quality Improvement Act authorized grants to demonstrate new methods and techniques and to establish programs to train people in water control management. (The federal government has also regulated the production and use of pesticides.) The states, as well as the federal government, have played an important role in water pollution control. They have set standards for allowable pollution levels, and many state governments have provided matching grants to help municipalities construct treatment plants.

In 1969, the Congress established a new agency—the Council on Environmental Quality—to oversee and plan the nation's pollution control programs. Modeled to some extent on the Council of Economic Advisers, the Council on Environmental Quality, which has three members, is supposed to gather information on considerations and trends in the quality of the environment, review and evaluate the federal government's programs in this area, develop appropriate national policies, and conduct needed surveys and research on environmental quality. The tasks assigned to the council are obviously important ones.

In 1970, the federal government established another new agency, the Environmental Protection Agency (EPA). Working with state and local officials, this agency establishes standards for desirable air and water quality, and devises rules for attaining these goals. The 1970 Clean Air Amendments directed EPA to establish minimum ambient standards for air quality, and it set limits on the emission of carbon monoxide, hydrocarbons, and nitrous oxides from automobiles. But after a number of clashes between EPA and the auto makers, the EPA relaxed the deadlines when these limits were supposed to be met. In 1972 amendments to the Water Pollution Act authorized EPA to set up effluent standards for both privately and publicly owned plants. A stated goal of the amendments was to eliminate the discharge of pollutants into water by 1985, but, for reasons discussed in the next section, this goal was unrealistically stringent. In general, recent legislation has emphasized direct regulation, although there has been some study of the use of effluent fees. For example, the government has considered imposing a fee on the emission of sulphur oxide into the air.

Some people believe that public policy is moving too rapidly in this area: others believe that it is moving too slowly. It is not easy to determine how fast or how far we should go in attempting to reduce pollution. Those who will bear the costs of reducing pollution have an understandable tendency to emphasize (and perhaps inflate) the costs and discount the benefits of such projects. Those who are particularly interested in enjoying nature and outdoor recreation—like the Sierra Club—are understandably inclined to emphasize (and perhaps inflate) the benefits and discount the costs of such projects. Politics inevitably plays a major role in the outcome of such cases. The citizens of the United States must indicate, through the ballot box as well as the market place, how much they are willing to pay to reduce pollution. We must also decide at what level of government the relevant rules are to be made. Since many pollution problems are local, it often seems sensible to determine the appropriate level of environmental quality locally. (However, there are obvious dangers in piecemeal regulation, as pointed out above.)

How Clean Should the Environment Be?

One of the most fundamental questions about pollution control is: How clean do we want the air, water, and other parts of our environment to be? At first glance, it may seem that we should restore and maintain a pristine pure environment, but this is not a very sensible goal, since the costs of achieving it would be enormous. The Environmental Protection Agency has estimated that it would cost about $60 billion to remove 85 to 90 percent of water pollutants from industrial and municipal sources. This is hardly a trivial amount, but it is far less than the cost of achieving zero discharge of pollutants, which would be about $320 billion—a truly staggering sum.

Example 20.1   How to Reduce the Costs of Cleaning Up

According to estimates made by Allen Kneese and Charles Schultze, the cost of achieving a one-pound reduction in the amount of pollutants emitted at a petroleum refinery and a beet-sugar plant are as shown below:

(a) Suppose that it is decided that the total amount of pollutants discharged by both plants should be reduced by 50 percent. If the government decrees that each plant should cut its discharge by 50 percent, what would be the cost of a one-pound reduction at each plant? (b) Can you suggest a way in which this total reduction in pollution can be achieved more efficiently? (c) To achieve this reduction most efficiently, which plant (the petroleum refinery or the beet-sugar plant) should reduce its discharge by the greater percentage? (d) Would an effluent fee achieve this reduction at less cost than the regulation in (a)?

SOLUTION

(a) The petroleum refinery would operate at point *U*, where the cost of a one-pound reduction in pollution is 6 cents. The beet-sugar plant would operate at point *V*, where the cost of a one-pound reduction would be 1 cent. (b) Since the beet-sugar plant can reduce pollution at less cost than the petroleum refinery (1 cent per pound rather than 6 cents per pound), it should cut its pollution more and the petroleum refinery should cut its pollution less. (c) The beet-sugar plant, for the reasons given in (b). (d) Yes. If an effluent fee were established, the cost of a one-pound reduction in pollution would tend to be the same at both plants.*

* See A. Kneese and C. Schultze, *Pollution, Prices, and Public Policy,* Washington, D.C.: The Brookings Institution, 1975; and W. Baumol and W. Oates, *Economics, Environmental Policy, and the Quality of Life,* Englewood Cliffs, N.J.: Prentice-Hall, 1979.

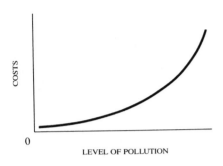

Figure 20.1

Costs to Society of Pollution *The costs to society of pollution increase with the level of pollution.*

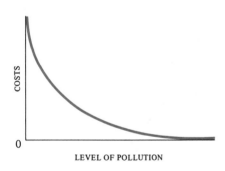

Figure 20.2

Costs to Society of Pollution Control *The more pollution is reduced, the higher are the costs to society of pollution control.*

Fortunately, however, there is no reason to aim at so stringent a goal. *It seems obvious that, as pollution increases, various costs to society increase as well.* Some of these costs were described at the beginning of this chapter. For example, we pointed out that increases in air pollution result in increased deaths, and that increases in water pollution reduce the recreational value of rivers and streams. Suppose that we could get accurate data on the cost to society of various levels of pollution. Of course, it is extremely difficult to get such data, but if we could, we could determine the relationship between the amount of these costs and the level of pollution. It would look like the hypothetical curve in Figure 20.1. The greater the level of pollution, the higher these costs will be.

But these costs are not the only ones that must be considered. *We must also take into account the costs of controlling pollution.* In other words, we must look at the costs to society of maintaining a certain level of environmental quality. These costs are not trivial, as we saw at the beginning of this section. To maintain a very low level of pollution, it is necessary to invest heavily in pollution-control equipment and to make other economic sacrifices.[6] If we could get accurate data on the cost to society of controlling pollution, we could find the relationship between the amount of these costs and the level of pollution. It would look like the hypothetical curve in Figure 20.2; the lower the level of pollution, the higher these costs will be.

A GOAL OF ZERO POLLUTION?

At this point, it should be obvious why we should not try to achieve a zero level of pollution. *The sensible goal for our society is to minimize the sum of the costs of pollution and the costs of controlling pollution.* In other words, we should construct a graph, as shown in Figure 20.3, to indicate the relationship between the sum of these two types of costs and the level of pollution. Then we should choose the level of pollution at which the sum of these two types of costs is a minimum. Thus, in Figure 20.3, we should aim for a pollution level of *A*. There is no point in trying for a lower level; such a reduction would cost more than it would be worth. For example, the cost of achieving a zero pollution level would be much more than it would be worth. Only when the pollution level exceeds *A* is the extra cost to society of the additional pollution greater than the cost of preventing it. For example, the cost of allowing pollution to increase from *A* to *B* is much greater than the cost of prevention.

It is easy to draw hypothetical curves, but not so easy actually to measure these curves. Unfortunately, no one has a very clear idea of what the curves in Figure 20.3 really look like—although we can be sure that their general shapes are like those shown there. Thus no one really knows just how clean we should try to make the environment. Under these circum-

---

[6] It is important to recognize that the costs of pollution control extend far beyond the construction of more and better water treatment plants, or the more extensive control of gas emission, or other such steps. A serious pollution-control program can put firms out of business, put people out of work, and bring economic trouble to entire communities. Further, a pollution-control system can result in a redistribution of income. For example, automobiles, electric power, and other goods and services involving considerable pollution are likely to increase in price relative to other goods and services involving little pollution. To the extent that polluting goods and services play a bigger role in the budgets of the poor than of the rich, pollution controls hurt the poor and help the rich.

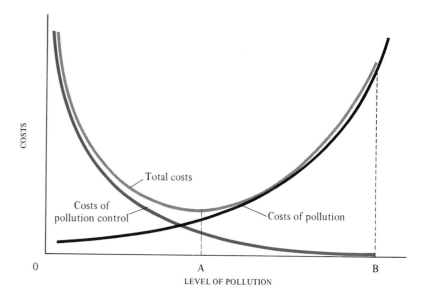

Figure 20.3
Determining Optimal Level of Pollution
The optimal level of pollution is at point
A, *since this is where the total costs are a*
minimum. Below point A, *the cost to*
society of more pollution is less than the
cost of preventing it. Above point A, *the*
cost to society of more pollution is
greater than the cost of preventing it.

stances, expert opinion differs on the nature and extent of the programs that should be carried out. Moreover, as pointed out in a previous section, political considerations and pressures enter in. But one thing is for sure: we will continue to live with some pollution—and that, for the reason just given, will be the rational thing to do.

Recent Directions of Environmental Policy

In the late seventies and early eighties, policy makers became increasingly concerned that regulatory agencies like EPA had been paying too little attention to the costs involved in reducing pollution. For example, a government study found that a relaxation of EPA's 1977 standard for water-pollution control in the steel industry *with no change in its more stringent 1983 standard* would allow savings in capital costs of $200 million. As President Carter's Council of Economic Advisers pointed out, "In making regulatory decisions on the speed of attaining standards, we should explicitly make a qualitative judgment about whether the gains from earlier attainment are worth the costs."

Going a step further, some experts, like Lester Lave and Gilbert Omenn of the Brookings Institution, have concluded from their studies that the Clean Air Act has not been very effective. In their view, "the application of pollution controls to existing plants and older cars has been limited, and costs have been excessive, largely because Congress has failed to confront [many of] the difficult issues ..."

During the 1980s, environmentalists and others charged that the Reagan administration was dismantling, or at least emasculating, EPA. Anne Gorsuch resigned in 1983 as head of EPA, as criticism of the agency continued to build. James Watt, former Secretary of the Interior, also angered environmentalists. Administration officials retorted to such criticism by claiming that they were trying to promote and restore balance between environmental objectives and economic growth.

In 1985 a political battle raged over the superfund, the fund authorized by federal legislation to clean up sites where chemical wastes have been dumped. Environmentalists wanted a fund of $10 billion; the Reagan administration proposed $5 billion. Some observers wanted the oil and chemical firms to contribute more to the fund, while these firms bitterly opposed such a move.

Test Yourself

1. Suppose that the paper industry emits wastes into rivers and streams, and that municipalities or firms downstream must treat the water to make it usable. Do the paper industry's private costs equal the social costs of producing paper? Why or why not?

2. Suppose that each ton of paper produced results in pollution that costs municipalities and firms downstream $1.00, and that a law is passed that requires the paper industry to reimburse the municipalities and firms downstream for these costs. Prior to this law, the supply curve for paper was:

Price of paper (dollars per ton)	Quantity supplied (million tons)
1.00	10.0
2.00	15.0
2.50	17.5
3.00	20.0
4.00	25.0

After the law takes effect, what will be the quantity supplied at each price?

3. In Question 2, which output—the one prevailing before the industry has to reimburse others, or the one prevailing afterward—is socially more desirable? Why?

4. If the demand curve for paper is as shown below, what will be the equilibrium output of paper before and after the paper industry has to reimburse the municipalities and firms downstream (as indicated in Question 2)?

Price of paper (dollars per ton)	Quantity demanded (million tons)
1.00	30.0
2.00	25.0
3.00	20.0
3.50	17.5
4.00	15.0

5. Suppose that the social cost (in billions of dollars) due to pollution equals $5P$, where P is the level of pollution, and that the cost (in billions of dollars) of pollution control equals $10-2P$. What is the optimal level of pollution? Is this a typical case?

Our Energy Problems

OPEC AND THE ENERGY CRISIS

During the early 1970s, even as it began to dawn on Americans that our environment was not indestructible, other urgent concerns arose about our national resources. A nation that had taken its abundant energy supplies for granted suddenly was confronted by the prospect of shortages. In late 1973, there was the Arab oil embargo; then in 1974, there was a tremendous increase in the price of imported crude oil. In September 1973, imported crude oil cost American petroleum refiners about $4.50 per barrel; a year later, it cost them about $12.50 per barrel. This great and sudden increase in the price of imported crude oil had a very substantial effect on both the national and international economy. It helped to create inflation at home, and it transferred tens of billions of dollars from the United States to the oil-producing nations. (See Figure 20.4.) Further, this big price increase was by no means the end. For example, in 1979, after Iran began cutting its oil output, the price of oil went up about 50 percent.

Why did the price of imported crude oil increase so spectacularly? Because the Organization of Petroleum Exporting Countries (OPEC) upped the price of crude oil. OPEC is an international cartel—that is, an association of national petroleum producers that gets together and sets prices for oil.[7] Formed in the early 1960s, OPEC's charter says that "members shall study and formulate a system to ensure the stabilization of prices by, among other means, the regulation of production, with due regard to the interests of the producing and the consuming nations, and to the necessity of securing a steady income to the producing countries." In the 1960s, OPEC gained strength; in the 1970s, it lowered the boom on the oil-consuming nations.

The Arab oil embargo in late 1973 called attention to another aspect of our energy problems: the fact that the United States was coming to depend to an increasing extent on foreign sources of supply of crude oil. Oil imports supplied almost one-half of domestic petroleum demand in 1977, as compared to about one-quarter in 1965. Some people worried that our national security might be imperiled by a cutoff of foreign oil.

The argument that we should try to avoid being dependent on foreign sources of oil was by no means new. Until 1973, this argument was used to justify the adoption of oil import quotas in the united States. These import quotas set a limit on the amount of foreign oil that could be imported. Many economists were opposed to these quotas because they increased the price of petroleum and petroleum products to consumers. (See Chapter 21.) Whether self-sufficiency with regard to energy is as important a goal as some policy makers seem to believe is hard to say. But the Arab oil embargo made the potential threat much more credible.

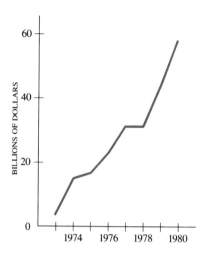

Figure 20.4

Total U.S. Payments for Crude Oil Imports, 1973–80 *Because the price of oil skyrocketed after 1973, the amount that America paid for imported oil skyrocketed too.*

ENERGY AND ECONOMIC GROWTH

Responding to the oil crises of the 1970s, U.S. policy makers proclaimed the importance of guaranteeing energy supplies that would meet the nation's growing energy demands. According to some observers, such as the authors of the *Limits to Growth,*[8] this could not be done. Why? Because there's only a finite supply of energy resources like oil and coal. If economic growth continues, the demand for these resources will increase exponentially. Eventually, according to these observers, we shall run out of such resources, with the result that both output and production will decline. Moreover, although this outcome is not around the corner, it is not so far off either. In their view, it will occur in the next 100 years.

Many people regard this as one of the most serious and fundamental of our energy problems. However, few economists accept the assumptions underlying these arguments. In the first place, economists charge that the authors of *Limits to Growth* underestimate very substantially the amount of the world's energy resources. Between 1944 and 1969, total world economic reserves of crude oil increased by about 12 times, due to producers'

[7] Although many of the oil-exporting countries are in the Middle East, OPEC also includes countries in Africa, Latin America, and other continents.

[8] D. Meadows *et al., The Limits to Growth,* New York: New American Library, 1972.

449

efforts to find and develop new sources of supply. Since annual world consumption rose about 6 times, this meant that reserves more than kept pace with oil consumption. Yet the authors of *Limits to Growth* assumed that known economic reserves of energy resources would increase only 5 times between now and the year 2100.

More fundamentally, economists charge that the authors of *Limits to Growth* do not take proper account of the workings of the price system. When the supply of a resource becomes tight, its price rises, with the result that firms have a greater financial incentive to find more of it. Also, as the price of this resource rises, firms have an incentive to develop new technology that permits less of this resource to be used. These mechanisms have resulted in the elimination of many apparent shortages in the past, and most economists tended to believe that they would play a major role in attacking our energy problems as well.

Basic Idea #40: Some people worry that before too long the world will run out of energy resources like oil. But this fails to recognize how the price system works. As the supply of such a resource becomes tight, its price rises, thus encouraging firms to find more of it and to develop ways to use less of it. History indicates that this mechanism has been powerful enough to solve many apparent prospective shortages of this kind. Don't neglect its importance.

Public Policy Toward Energy

REDUCTION OF ENERGY DEMAND

During the 1970s economists put forth a number of suggestions concerning ways to solve our energy problems. One suggestion was that we should reduce our demand for energy. Without question, there are many areas where energy could be saved with little inconvenience. One way that a reduction in energy demand could be accomplished is through the imposition of a tax on fuel. A number of economists suggested such a measure. To see how it might work, consider Figure 20.5, which shows the demand and supply curves for fuel. Without tax, the price of fuel would be OP_0, and the quantity consumed would be OQ_0.

Suppose that a tax of \$.20 per gallon[9] of fuel were imposed. If so, the supply curve would shift upward by the amount of the tax. To see why, note that, if the pretax price had to be OP_0 per gallon to induce sellers to supply OQ_0 gallons of fuel, the posttax price would have to be \$.20 higher to induce the same supply. Similarly, if the pretax price had to be OP_1 per gallon to induce sellers to supply OQ_1 gallons of fuel, the posttax price would have to be \$.20 higher to induce the same supply. The reason why the sellers require \$.20 more per gallon to supply the pretax amount is that they must pay the tax of \$.20 per gallon to the government. Thus they need the extra \$.20 to wind up with the same amount as before.

Since the tax shifts the supply curve upward by \$.20, the posttax equilibrium price and quantity are OP_2 and OQ_2, respectively. The effect of the tax on the quantity of fuel consumed is just what one would expect. It reduces fuel consumption. In Figure 20.5, the reduction is from OQ_0 to OQ_2. According to calculations by Dale Jorgensen of Harvard University and Edward Hudson of Data Resources, Inc., a tax equal to 3 percent of sales in 1985 and increasing gradually to about 15 percent in the year 2000 would result in no growth whatsoever in the quantity of energy consumed between 1985 and 2000. However, it is by no means clear that the United States

---

[9] We assume here that fuel is measured in gallons. For some fuels (like coal), this is not the case; but this simplification can easily be removed. It is used here only for convenience.

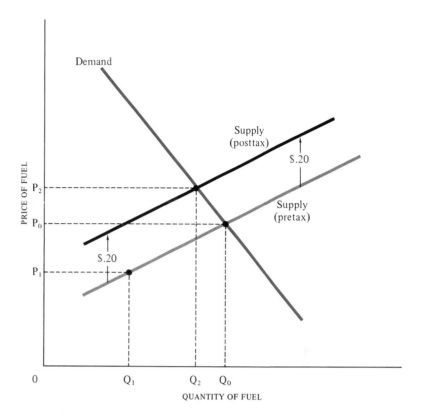

Figure 20.5
Effect of a Tax on Fuel *If a tax of $.20 per gallon is imposed on fuel, the supply curve for fuel shifts upward, as shown here. Thus the quantity of fuel consumed is cut from OQ_0 to OQ_2.*

should seek to maintain energy consumption at a constant level. For one thing, such a policy would reduce our rate of economic growth, although considerable growth would still occur.

DEVELOPMENT OF NEW ENERGY TECHNOLOGIES

Economists and others also suggested that, to avoid increased dependence on foreign oil, we might develop new technologies that can produce energy economically from our domestic resources. One important resource of this kind is shale, which is found in Colorado, Wyoming, and Utah. For many years, shale has been regarded as a promising source of synthetic oil, but so far the costs of producing oil by this route have been too high to make it economical. Also, there are many unresolved environmental problems, since it is difficult to dispose of the spent shale. In Canada, a potentially important source of synthetic oil is the tar sands located in Alberta. Here too, the costs of producing oil in this way are relatively high, but some production is occurring. In both the cases of shale and tar sands, perhaps additional investments in research and development can solve the problems that presently prevent these resources from being a more economical source of synthetic oil.

The United States has vast quantities of coal. To some extent, it might be possible to substitute our relatively plentiful coal for other fuels. However, one important problem with much of our Eastern coal is that it contains a great deal of sulphur, with the result that its combustion leads to a rise in the emission of sulphur dioxide, an important air pollutant. One way to cope with this problem is to scrub most of this chemical from power plants'

451

BUBBLES, OFFSETS, AND BANKS

Attempts to maintain an acceptable level of air quality in the United States are based on the direct regulation of individual sources of pollution. A source is defined as any installation which emits at least one pollutant; thus a single industrial plant can have several distinct sources. Each polluter is supposed to obey rules, set by the government, stipulating both the necessary amount of pollution abatement and the technology to be employed at each source. This process has proved cumbersome and time-consuming. Many studies must be made by both the regulators and the regulated. Hearings are often necessary. Moreover, for reasons discussed in this chapter, direct regulation of this sort has been inefficient. The reduction in pollution has been more costly than necessary.

In the late 1970s, the Environmental Protection Agency (EPA) began to experiment with market-like schemes for pollution control. Rather than directly controlling the behavior of each source of pollution, these schemes introduced financial incentives for firms to use their own expertise to achieve air quality levels relatively cheaply. To date, the EPA has moved very cautiously in this direction; direct regulation has not been abandoned. Only limited use of financial incentives has been approved. Three incentive schemes—bubbles, offsets, and banks—have been developed, each of which is discussed below.

The concept of a *bubble* is meant to take account of the fact that the costs of controlling pollution differ among processes within a particular plant and among plants and firms. A "bubble" is put around an entire plant or area, and it is viewed as a single source of pollution rather than several distinct sources. Regulators establish emission limits for a plant (or area) as a whole, and managers can allocate pollution abatement in any way they like as long as the overall emission target is attained. Since the managers' decisions affect their firms' profits, they have an incentive to reduce pollution in a least-cost way. The bubble concept can only be applied to existing firms, not to potential sources of pollution.

Experience with bubbles indicates that they can result in significant savings. For example, Armco Steel substituted dust-reducing actions for pollution controls in its steel-making process, the result being a saving of $20 million in capital costs and $2.5 million per year in operating costs. In Providence, Rhode Island, the New England Electric System has used different fuels at two power plants included within a bubble, and reports savings of $4 million in 2½ years. However, there are many restrictions on the use of bubbles. For example, as noted above, they can only be used by existing sources of pollution, not by new entrants.

The concept of an *offset* was developed to permit new plants to open and old ones to expand in areas that do not meet the national environmental standards, while at the same time ensuring that air quality does not get worse. Whereas bubbles apply only to existing sources of pollution, offsets apply to new sources. Offsets permit construction of new pollution sources (and enlargement of existing sources) if the resulting new emissions are *less than* the reduction in emissions from existing sources. The offset program allows firms that want to introduce new sources of pollution to negotiate with existing firms to purchase emission reductions from them. Also, firms can offset the increases in pollution stemming from their new sources by reducing the emissions from other sources that they own in the area.

The offset program began in 1977. According to EPA, there have been hundreds of offsets, most of which have occurred within a single firm. For example, in Brazoria County, Texas, Phillips Petroleum Company added new sources of pollution in order to enlarge the capacity of its refinery. The pollution from these new sources was offset by doing a more complete job of controlling hydrocarbon emissions from Phillips's existing storage tanks and other facilities. Through 1980, only 32 offsets involving negotiations between different firms had taken place, as shown in the table below. This seemed to be due in part to the bureaucratic difficulties in carrying out offsets.

The concept of a **bank** is an extension of an offset, the idea being to promote greater flexibility with regard to the timing of the trade of emission reductions. If a firm pushes its daily emissions below the mandated standards, it can hold these reductions in reserve at a clearinghouse, and it can trade them at some date in the future. In other words, it can "bank" these reductions. One advantage is that the basic offset program is made more efficient because firms that want to purchase emission reductions from other firms can find potential sellers of such reductions by consulting the clearinghouse inventory.

Bubbles, offsets, and banks are very partial steps toward the use of market incentives to help promote efficiency in pollution control. The United States is very far from having a system of marketable pollution rights. But as Robert Crandall of the Brookings Institution has put it, "We are surely closer to a system of economic incentives in air pollution control . . . than we were a decade ago, when a proposed sulfur tax disappeared without even serious legislative debate."[1]

| Pollutant | Number of offset transactions through 1980 | |
	Approved	Pending, withdrawn, or uncertain
Hydrocarbons	20	8
Total suspended particulates	8	3
Sulfur dioxide	4	1
Carbon monoxide	0	1
Nitrogen oxides	2	0
Total	32	12

Source: Wes Vivian and William Hall, "An Examination of U.S. Market Trading in Air Pollution Offsets," Institute of Public Policy Studies, University of Michigan, 1981.

[1] R. Crandall, *Controlling Industrial Pollution,* Washington, D.C.: Brookings Institution, 1983, p. 98.

Example 20.2   Oil Price Decontrol and Imports

From 1971 to early 1981, the government imposed controls on the price of crude oil. Suppose that the domestic supply and demand curves for crude oil were as shown below:

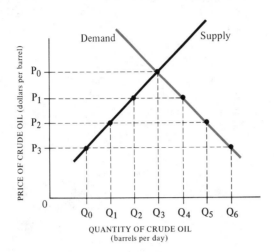

The price of imported foreign oil was OP_1 dollars per barrel. Government controls enabled buyers of crude oil to pay OP_2 dollars per barrel, but domestic suppliers received only OP_3 dollars per barrel.

(a) How much will domestic producers of crude oil supply? (b) How much will domestic buyers of crude oil demand? (c) How much crude oil will be imported? (d) If the price of crude oil were decontrolled, how much crude oil would be imported? (e) In early 1981, the price of crude oil was decontrolled. The American Petroleum Institute reported that imports of crude oil in the first six months of 1981 plunged 20 percent, to an average of 5.9 million barrels per day. Is this what would be expected, based on the above model?*

SOLUTION

(a) OQ_0 barrels per day. (b) OQ_5 barrels per day. (c) $(OQ_5 - OQ_0)$ barrels per day. (d) Under decontrol, the domestic price would have to equal the price of imported oil, OP_1. Thus the domestic producers would supply OQ_2 barrels per day, and domestic buyers would demand OQ_4 barrels per day, which means that $(OQ_4 - OQ_2)$ barrels per day would be imported. (e) Yes. The model predicts that imports will fall from $(OQ_5 - OQ_0)$ to $(OQ_4 - OQ_2)$ barrels per day under decontrol.

* See R. Leftwich and A. Sharp, *Economics of Social Issues,* Dallas: Business Publications, 1978; and "Economic Gains Tied to Ending Oil Price Curbs," *New York Times,* September 8, 1981.

flue stacks. Unfortunately, however, there does not seem to be any technology that can do this effectively and economically. Another way to cope with the problem is to convert coal to a clean gas. A number of technologies have been developed to do this, but many are still in the pilot-plant stage. Here is another area where research and development have a promising role to play.

Still another promising source of energy is the sun. Techniques for harnessing solar energy have been known for a long time. For example, flat plate collectors can be used to heat water or air, which can then be used to heat buildings. But solar energy is still very costly, and there are problems in storing it for use on cloudy days and at night. According to some experts, solar energy is potentially of great economic significance, and too little has been invested to try to develop it and reduce its cost. This is an obvious area for further research and development.

The Weakening of OPEC

During the 1980s, the power of the OPEC oil cartel was substantially reduced, for several reasons.

1. Oil consumption was reduced. Faced with the greatly increased oil prices, consumers cut back on their demand for oil. In part, this was due to the adoption of oil-saving technologies and more fuel-efficient cars. For example, a Buick Electra gets 17 miles a gallon in city driving, compared with about 10 miles that similar models got in the 1970s.

2. OPEC's share of world oil output fell. Due in part to the substantial increase in oil output by Britain, Norway, Mexico, and other non-OPEC countries, OPEC's share fell from 54 percent in 1973 to 32 percent in 1983. Countries like Britain and Norway cut oil prices, forcing OPEC producers to follow suit. In October 1984, Norway, followed by Britain, cut the price of its crude oil by $2 a barrel.

3. Some OPEC members refused to abide by the cartel agreements. In particular, Nigeria, badly needing cash, reduced its price below that set by the cartel. To help ease Nigeria's problems, other OPEC countries, such as Saudi Arabia, are reported to have allowed Nigeria to sell more oil, while cutting back their own output.

In 1983, OPEC—faced with declining demand for oil, increased competition from non-OPEC sources of oil, and price cuts within its own ranks—agreed to reduce its price from $34 to $29 a barrel. In 1984, the cartel, faced with a world oil glut and the fact that oil was trading on the world market for only about $27 a barrel, tried to muster more discipline, but without apparent success. Oil experts and analysts seemed to believe that further price declines were in the cards and that OPEC would not regain its former economic power in the foreseeable future.

However, some observers still worry about the vulnerability of the United States to oil-supply disruptions. For example, it is argued that the Soviet threat to oil-producing facilities in the Middle East is great enough to warrant the preparation of alternative energy options to supplement military contingency plans. Thus, although our energy supplies have been the subject of less worry in 1985 than in the middle and late 1970s, they continue to be the subject of some public concern.

Test Yourself

1. "A tax on fuel will reduce the quantity consumed by a greater amount if the quantity of fuel demanded is relatively insensitive to its price than if it is relatively sensitive to it." Comment and evaluate.

2. According to *Business Week,* August 19, 1985, "Falling prices have trimmed Exxon's sales, but higher profits and cash flow have fueled dividend hikes and massive share buybacks that have sent Exxon stock soaring." Interpret. Is this evidence of a crisis? If so, why?

3. During the 1970s, some economists suggested that a tax on fuel might help to solve America's energy problems. What are the disadvantages of such a tax?

4. In 1981, President Reagan decontrolled the price of oil, which had been kept below world levels by federal controls. What are the disadvantages of keeping the U.S. price of oil artificially low?

Summary

1. One of the major social issues of the 1980s is environmental pollution. To a considerable extent, environmental pollution is an economic problem. Waste disposal and other pollution-causing activities result in external diseconomies.

2. Firms and individuals that pollute the water and air (and other facets of the environment) often pay less than the true social costs of disposing of their wastes in this way. Part of the true social cost is borne by other firms and individuals, who must pay to clean up the water or air, or who must live with the consequences.

3. Because of the divergence of private from social costs, the market system does not result in an optimal allocation of resources. Firms and individuals create too much waste and dispose of it in excessively harmful ways. Because the polluters do not pay the full cost of waste disposal, their products are artificially cheap, with the result that too much is produced of them.

4. The government can intervene in several ways to help remedy the breakdown of the market system in this area. One way is to issue regulations for waste disposal and other activities influencing the environment. Another is to establish effluent fees, charges a polluter must pay to the government for discharging wastes. In recent decades, there has been considerable growth in government programs designed to control pollution.

5. It is extremely difficult to determine how clean the environment should be. Of course, the sensible goal for society is to permit the level of pollution that minimizes the sum of the costs of pollution and the costs of controlling pollution; but no one has a very clear idea of what these costs are, and to a large extent the choices must be made through the political process.

6. Another major issue has been energy. The Arab oil embargo in late 1973 and OPEC's huge price increase in early 1974 called attention to the growing dependence of the United States on foreign sources of crude oil. Billions of dollars were transferred to the oil-producing countries. A cutoff of foreign oil could disrupt our economy.

7. A variety of policy measures were proposed to help deal with our energy problems. One proposal was that we enact a tax on fuel to reduce energy demand. Another approach was to develop new energy technologies that can produce energy economically from our domestic energy resources. During the 1980s, OPEC was weakened by falling demand for oil and increased supplies. Oil prices fell, and America's energy problems seemed much less urgent.

Concepts for Review

External diseconomy	Direct regulation	Bubbles
Private costs	Effluent fees	Offsets
Social costs	Tax credits	Banks

PART SIX

International Economics

CHAPTER 21

International Trade

Practically all human beings realize that they are not islands unto themselves, and that they benefit from living with, working with, and trading with other people. Exactly the same is true of nations. They too must interact with one another, and they too benefit from trade with one another. No nation can be an island unto itself—not even the United States. To understand how the world economy functions, you must grasp the basic economic principles of international trade.

This chapter discusses many of the fundamental questions about international trade. What is the nature of American foreign trade? What are the effects of international trade? What determines the sorts of goods a nation will import or export? What are the advantages of free trade and the arguments against it? What are the social costs of tariffs and quotas, and what has been their history in the United States? What are some of the major issues regarding protectionism in the United States today? Some of these questions have occupied the attention of economists for hundreds of years; some are as current as today's newspaper.

America's Foreign Trade

America's foreign trade, although small relative to our national product, plays a very important role in our economic life. Many of our industries depend on other countries for markets or for raw materials (like coffee, tea, or tin). Our *exports*—the things we sell to other countries—amount to about 10 percent of our gross national product, which seems small relative to other countries like Germany, France, Italy, and the United Kingdom,

Table 21.1

U.S. MERCHANDISE EXPORTS, 1984

Product	Amount (billions of dollars)
Food, feed, and beverages	32
Industrial supplies and materials	63
Machinery	62
Automotive vehicles and parts	22
Aircraft	10
Other	31
Total	220

Source: Survey of Current Busness,
March 1985.

Table 21.2

PERCENT OF U.S. EXPORTS, BY AREA, 1984

Country	Percent
Japan	10
Western Europe	26
Latin America	14
Canada	24
Eastern Europe	2
Other	24
Total	100

Source: See Table 21.1.

Table 21.3

U.S. MERCHANDISE IMPORTS, 1984

Product	Amount (billions of dollars)
Food, feed, and beverages	21
Petroleum and oil products	57
Other industrial supplies and materials	67
Capital goods	60
Automotive vehicles and parts	55
Consumer goods (excluding autos)	60
Other	8
Total	328

Source: See Table 21.1.

where exports are about 15 to 20 percent of gross national product. But this is because our domestic market is so large. In absolute terms, our exports (and imports) are bigger than those of any other nation. Without question, our way of life would have to change considerably if we could not trade with other countries.

When we were a young country, we exported raw materials primarily. During the 1850s about 70 percent of our exports were raw materials and foodstuffs. But the composition of our exports has changed with time. More are now finished manufactured goods and less are raw materials. In the 1960s, about 60 percent of our exports were finished manufactured goods, and only about 20 percent were raw materials and foodstuffs. Table 21.1 shows the importance of machinery and industrial supplies in our merchandise exports. Table 21.2 indicates to whom we sell. Western Europe and Canada take about one-half of our exports, and Latin America takes over 10 percent.

What sorts of goods do we buy from abroad? About 10 percent of our *imports* are agricultural commodities like coffee, sugar, bananas, and cocoa. Almost 20 percent are petroleum and its products. But a considerable proportion is neither raw materials nor foodstuffs. Over one-half of our imports, as shown in Table 21.3, are manufactured goods like bicycles from England or color TVs from Japan. Just as we sell more to Canada and Western Europe than any other area, so we buy more from these countries too (see Table 21.4). But the pattern varies from product to product. Thus Canada is our leading foreign source for wood pulp and nonferrous metals, while Latin America is our leading source of imported coffee and sugar.

Specialization and Trade

We have discussed the extent and nature of our trade with other countries, but not *why* we trade with other countries. Do we—and our trading partners—benefit from this trade? And if so, what determines the sorts of goods we should export and import? These are very important questions, among the most fundamental in economics. The answers are by no means new. They have been well understood for considerably more than a century, due to the work of such great economists as David Hume, David Ricardo, Adam Smith, and John Stuart Mill.

WHY DO INDIVIDUALS TRADE?

As a first step, it is useful to recognize that the benefits *nations* receive through trade are essentially the same as those *individuals* receive through trade. Consider the hypothetical case of John Barrister, a lawyer, with a wife and two children. The Barrister family, like practically all families, trades continually with other families and with business firms. Since Mr. Barrister is a lawyer, he trades his legal services for money which he and his wife use to buy the food, clothing, housing, and other goods and services his family wants. Why does the Barrister family do this? What advantages does it receive through trade? Why doesn't it attempt to be self-sufficient?

Table 21.4

PERCENT OF U.S. IMPORTS, BY AREA, 1984

Country	Percent
Japan	17
Western Europe	22
Latin America	15
Canada	21
Eastern Europe	1
Other	25
Total[a]	100

Source: Table 21.1.

[a] Because of rounding errors, figures do not sum to total.

To see why the Barrister family is sensible indeed to opt for trade rather than self-sufficiency, let's compare the current situation—where Mr. Barrister specializes in the production of legal services and trades the money he receives for other goods and services—with the situation if the Barrister family attempted to be self-sufficient. In the latter case, the Barristers would have to provide their own transportation, telephone service, foodstuffs, clothing, and a host of other things. Mr. Barrister is a lawyer—a well-trained, valuable, productive member of the community. But if he were to try his hand at making automobiles—or even bicycles—he might be a total loss. Thus, if the Barrister family attempted to be self-sufficient, it might be unable to provide many of the goods it now enjoys.

WHY DO NATIONS TRADE?

Trade permits specialization, and specialization increases output. This is the advantage of trade, both for individuals and for nations. In our hypothetical case, it is obvious that, because he can trade with other families and with firms, Mr. Barrister can specialize in doing what he is good at—law. Consequently, he can be more productive than if he were forced to be a Jack-of-all-trades, as he would have to be if he could not trade with others. The same principle holds for nations. Because the United States can trade with other nations, it can specialize in the goods and services it produces particularly well. Then it can trade them for goods that other countries are especially good at producing. Thus both we and our trading partners benefit.

Some countries have more and better resources of certain types than others. Saudi Arabia has oil, Canada has timber, Japan has a skilled labor force, and so on. *International differences in resource endowments, and in the relative quantity of various types of human and nonhuman resources, are important bases for specialization.* Consider countries with lots of fertile soil, little capital, and much unskilled labor. They are likely to find it advantageous to produce agricultural goods, while countries with poor soil, much capital, and highly skilled labor will probably do better to produce capital-intensive, high-technology goods. We must recognize, however, that the bases for specialization do not remain fixed over time. Instead, as technology and the resource endowments of various countries change, the pattern of international specialization changes as well. As we saw in the previous section, the United States specialized more in raw materials and foodstuffs about a century ago than it does now.

Absolute Advantage

To clarify the benefits of trade, consider the following example. Suppose that the United States can produce 2 electronic computers or 5,000 cases of wine with 1 unit of resources. Suppose that France can produce 1 electronic computer or 10,000 cases of wine with 1 unit of resources. Given the production possibilities in each country, are there any advantages in trade between the countries? And if so, what commodity should each country export, and what commodity should each country import? Should

France export wine and import computers, or should it import wine and export computers?

To answer these questions, assume that the United States is producing a certain amount of computers and a certain amount of wine—and that France is producing a certain amount of computers and a certain amount of wine. If the United States shifts 1 unit of its resources from producing wine to producing computers, it will increase its production of computers by 2 computers and reduce its production of wine by 5,000 cases of wine. If France shifts 1 unit of resources from the production of computers to the production of wine, it will increase its production of wine by 10,000 cases and reduce its production of computers by 1 computer.

Table 21.5 shows the *net* effect of this shift in the utilization of resources on *world* output of computers and of wine. World output of computers increases (by 1 computer) and world output of wine increases (by 5,000 cases) as a result of the redeployment of resources in each country. Thus *specialization increases world output.*

Moreover, if world output of each commodity is increased by shifting 1 unit of American resources from wine to computers and shifting 1 unit of French resources from computers to wine, it follows that world output of each commodity will be increased further if each country shifts *more* of its resources in the same direction. This is because the amount of resources required to produce each good is assumed to be constant, regardless of how much is produced.

Thus, in this situation, one country—the United States—should specialize in producing computers, and the other country—France—should specialize in producing wine. This will maximize world output of both wine and computers, permitting a rise in both countries' standards of living. Complete specialization of this sort is somewhat unrealistic, since countries often produce some of both commodities, but this simple example illustrates the basic principles involved.

Table 21.5

CASE OF ABSOLUTE ADVANTAGE

| | Increase or decrease in output of: | |
	Computers	Wine (thousands of cases)
Effect of U.S.'s shifting 1 unit of resources from wine to computers	+2	− 5
Effect of France's shifting 1 unit of resources from computers to wine	−1	+ 10
Net effect	+1	+ 5

Comparative Advantage

The case just described is a very special one, since one country (France) has an absolute advantage over another (the United States) in the production of one good (wine), whereas the second country (the United States) has an absolute advantage over the first (France) in the production of another good (computers). What do we mean by the term *absolute advantage?* Country A has an **absolute advantage** over Country B in the production of a good when Country A can produce a unit of the good with less resources than can Country B. Since the United States can produce a computer with fewer units of resources than France, it has an absolute advantage over France in the production of computers. Since France requires fewer resources than the United States to produce a given amount of wine, France has an absolute advantage over the United States in the production of wine.

But what if one country is more efficient in producing both goods? If the United States is more efficient in producing both computers and wine, is there still any benefit to be derived from specialization and trade? At first glance, you are probably inclined to answer no. But if this is your inclination, you should reconsider—because you are wrong.

A NUMERICAL EXAMPLE

To see why specialization and trade have advantages even when one country is more efficient than another at producing both goods, consider the following example. Suppose the United States can produce 2 electronic computers or 5,000 cases of wine with 1 unit of resources, and France can produce 1 electronic computer or 4,000 cases of wine with 1 unit of resources. In this case, the United States is a more efficient producer of both computers and wine. Nonetheless, as we shall see, world output of both goods will increase if the United States specializes in the production of computers and France specializes in the production of wine.

Table 21.6 demonstrates this conclusion. If 2 units of American resources are shifted from wine to computer production, 4 additional computers and 10,000 fewer cases of wine are produced. If 3 units of French resources are shifted from computer to wine production, 3 fewer computers and 12,000 additional cases of wine are produced. Thus the combined effect of this redeployment of resources in both countries is to increase world output of computers by 1 computer and to increase world output of wine by 2,000 cases. Even though the United States is more efficient than France in the production of both computers and wine, world output of both goods will be maximized if the United States specializes in computers and France specializes in wine.

Basically, this is so because, although the United States is more efficient than France in the production of both goods, it has a greater advantage in computers than in wine. It is twice as efficient as France in producing computers, but only 25 percent more efficient than France in producing wine. To derive these numbers, recall that 1 unit of resources will produce 2 computers in the United States, but only 1 computer in France. Thus the United States is twice as efficient in computers. On the other hand, 1 unit of resources will produce 5,000 cases of wine in the United States, but only 4,000 cases in France. Thus the United States is 25 percent more efficient in wine.

Table 21.6

CASE OF COMPARATIVE ADVANTAGE

| | Increase or decrease in output of: | |
	Computers	Wine (thousands of cases)
Effect of U.S.'s shifting 2 units of resources from wine to computers	+4	−10
Effect of France's shifting 3 units of resources from computers to wine	−3	+12
Net effect	+1	+2

Basic Idea #41: *Trade between two countries can be mutually beneficial even if one country is more efficient at producing everything than the other country. Each country can specialize in products where it has a comparative advantage and import those where the other country has a comparative advantage. What is important in determining what a country should produce is comparative, not absolute, advantage.*

TRADE DEPENDS ON COMPARATIVE ADVANTAGE

A nation has a ***comparative advantage*** in those products where its efficiency relative to other nations is highest. Thus, in this case, the United States has a comparative advantage in the production of computers and a comparative disadvantage in the production of wine. So long as a country has a comparative advantage in the production of some commodities and a comparative disadvantage in the production of others, it can benefit from specialization and trade. A country will specialize in products where it has a comparative advantage, and import those where it has a comparative disadvantage. The point is that *specialization and trade depend on comparative, not absolute advantage*. One of the first economists to understand the full significance of this fact was David Ricardo, the English economist of the early nineteenth century.

A Geometric Representation of Comparative Advantage

The principle of comparative advantage, like so many important economic concepts, can be displayed diagrammatically. Again, we suppose that in the United States 1 unit of resources will produce 2 electronic computers or 5,000 cases of wine. Consequently, the ***production possibilities curve*** in the United States—the curve that shows the maximum number of computers that can be produced, given various outputs of wine—is the one in panel A of Figure 21.1. The United States must give up 1 computer for every additional 2,500 cases of wine that it produces; thus the slope of the American production possibilities curve is $-\dfrac{1}{2,500}$.[1]

Also, as in the previous section, we suppose that in France 1 unit of resources will produce 1 electronic computer or 4,000 cases of wine. Thus the production possibilities curve in France is as shown in panel B of Figure 21.1. France must give up 1 computer for every additional 4,000 cases of wine it produces; thus the slope of France's production possibilities curve is $-\dfrac{1}{4,000}$.

Now suppose that the United States uses all its resources to produce computers and that France uses all its resources to produce wine. In other words, the United States operates at point A on its production possibilities curve and France operates at point B on its production possibilities curve. Then suppose that the United States trades its computers for France's wine. AC in panel A of Figure 21.1 shows the various amounts of computers and wine the United States can end up with if it specializes in computers and trades them for French wine. AC is called the ***trading possibilities curve*** of the United States. The slope of AC is minus 1 times the ratio of the price of a case of wine to the price of a computer, since this ratio equals the number of computers the United States must give up to get a case of French wine. Similarly, the line BD in panel B of Figure 21.1 shows France's trading possibilities curve. That is, BD represents the various amounts of computers and wine France can wind up with if it specializes in wine and trades it for U.S. computers.

The thing to note about both panels in Figure 21.1 is that each country's trading possibilities curve—AC in panel A, BD in panel B—lies above its production possibilities curve. This means that *both countries can have more of both commodities by specializing and trading than by trying to be self-sufficient*—even though the United States is more efficient than France at producing both commodities. Thus Figure 21.1 shows what we said in the previous section: If countries specialize in products where they have a comparative advantage and trade with one another, each country can improve its standard of living.

The Terms of Trade

The ***terms of trade*** are defined as the quantity of imported goods that a country can obtain in exchange for a unit of domestic goods. Thus, in Figure 21.1, the terms of trade are measured by the ratio of the price of a

Figure 21.1

Benefits of Specialization and Trade
AC *represents the various amounts of computers and wine that the United States can end up with, if it specializes in computers and trades them for French wine. The slope of* AC *equals* − 1 *times the ratio of the price of a case of wine to the price of a computer, assumed to be* $\dfrac{1}{3,333}$. BD *represents the various amounts of computers and wine that France can wind up with, if it specializes in wine and trades for U.S. computers.* AC *lies above America's production possibilities curve and* BD *lies above France's production possibilities curve. Thus both countries can have more of both commodities by specializing and trading than by attempting to be self-sufficient.*

---

[1] As we know from Chapter 2, the production possibilities curve shows the maximum amount of one commodity that can be produced, given various outputs of the other commodity. Since the United States must give up 1/2,500 computer for each additional case of wine that it produces, the slope must be − 1/2,500.

computer to the price of a case of wine—since this ratio shows how many cases of French wine the United States can get in exchange for an American computer. In Figure 21.1, we asume that this ratio equals 3,333:1. It is important to note that this ratio must be somewhere between 2,500:1 and 4,000:1. By diverting its own resources from computer production to wine production, the United States can exchange a computer for 2,500 cases of wine. Since this is possible, it will not pay the United States to trade a computer for less than 2,500 cases of wine. Similarly, since France can exchange a case of wine for 1/4,000 of a computer by diverting its own resources from wine to computers, it clearly will not be willing to trade a case of wine for less than 1/4,000 of a computer.

But where will the price ratio lie between 2,500:1 and 4,000:1? The answer depends on *world supply and demand for the two products.* The stronger the demand for computers (relative to their supply) and the weaker the demand for wine (relative to its supply), the higher the price ratio. On the other hand, the weaker the demand for computers (relative to their supply) and the stronger the demand for wine (relative to its supply), the lower the price ratio.

Incomplete Specialization

Figure 21.1 shows that the United States should specialize completely in computers, and that France should specialize completely in wine. This result stems from the assumption that the cost of producing a computer or a case of wine is constant. If, on the other hand, the cost of producing each good increases with the amount produced, the result is likely to be incomplete specialization. In other words, although the United States will continue to specialize in computers and France will continue to specialize in wine, each country will also produce some of the other good as well. This is a more likely outcome, since specialization generally tends to be less than complete.

International Trade and Individual Markets

We have emphasized that nations can benefit by specializing in the production of goods for which they have a comparative advantage and trading these goods for others where they have a comparative disadvantage.[2]

[2] The principle of comparative advantage is useful in explaining and predicting the pattern of world trade, as well as in showing the benefits of trade. For example, consider the exports of Great Britain and the United States. Robert Stern of the University of Michigan compared British and American exports of 39 industries. In 21 of the 24 industries where our labor productivity was more than three times that of the British, our exports exceeded British exports. In 11 of the 15 industries where our labor productivity was less than three times that of the British, our exports were less than British exports. Thus, in 32 out of 39 industries, the principle of comparative advantage, as interpreted by Stern, predicted correctly which country would export more. This is a high batting average, since labor is not the only input and labor productivity is an imperfect measure of true efficiency. Moreover, as we shall see in subsequent sections, countries raise barriers to foreign trade, preventing trade from taking place in accord with the principle of comparative advantage.

465

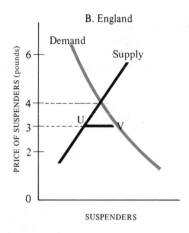

Figure 21.2

Determination of Quantity Imported and Exported under Free Trade *Under free trade, price will equal $4.20 or £3. The United States will export* XY *units, the English will import* UV *units, and* XY = UV.

But how do a nation's producers know whether they have a comparative advantage or disadvantage in the production of a given commodity? They do not call up the local university and ask the leading professor of economics (although that might not always be such a bad idea). Instead, as we shall see in this section, the market for the good provides the required signals.

To see how this works, let's consider a new (and rather whimsical) product—bulletproof suspenders. Suppose that the Mob, having run a scientific survey of gunmen and policemen, finds that most of them wear their suspenders over their bulletproof vests. As a consequence, the Mob's gunmen are instructed to render a victim immobile by shooting holes in his suspenders (thus making his trousers fall down and trip him). Naturally, the producers of suspenders will soon find it profitable to produce a new bulletproof variety, an innovation which, it is hoped, will make a solid contribution to law and order. The new suspenders are demanded only in the United States and England, since the rest of the world wear belts. The demand curve in the United States is as shown in panel A of Figure 21.2, and the demand curve in England is as shown in panel B. Suppose further that this product can be manufactured in both the United States and England. The supply curve in the United States is as shown in panel A, and the supply curve in England is as shown in panel B.

Take a closer look at Figure 21.2. Note that prices in England are expressed in pounds (£) and prices in the United States are expressed in dollars ($). This is quite realistic. Each country has its own currency, in which prices in that country are expressed. As of 1985, £1 was equal to about $1.40. In other words, you could exchange a pound note for $1.40—or $1.40 for a £1 note. For this reason, the two panels of Figure 21.2 are lined up so that a price of $2.80 is at the same level as a price of £2, $4.20 is at the same level as £3, and so on.

NO FOREIGN TRADE

To begin with, suppose that bulletproof suspenders cannot be exported or imported, perhaps because of a very high tariff (tax on imports) imposed on them in both the United States and England. (One can readily imagine members of both Congress and Parliament defending such a tariff on the grounds that a capacity to produce plenty of bulletproof suspenders is important for national defense.) If this happens, the price of bulletproof suspenders will be $2.60 in the United States and £4 in England. Why? Because, as shown in Figure 21.2, these are the prices at which each country's demand curve intersects its supply curve.

FOREIGN TRADE PERMITTED

Next, suppose that international trade in this product is permitted, perhaps because both countries eliminate the tariff. Now what will happen? Since the price is lower in the United States than in England, people can make money by sending this product from the United States to England. After all, they can buy it for $2.60 in this country and sell it for £4 (= $5.60) in England. But they will not be able to do so indefinitely. As more and more suspenders are supplied by the United States for the English market, the price in the United States must go up (to induce producers to produce the additional output) and the price in England must go down (to induce consumers to buy the additional quantity).

When an equilibrium is reached, *the price in the United States must equal the price in England.* If this did not happen, there would be an advantage in increasing American exports (if the price in England were higher) or in decreasing American exports (if the price in the United States were higher). Thus only if the prices are equal can an equilibrium exist.

At what level will this price—which is common to both countries—tend to settle? Obviously, *the price must end up at the level where the amount of the good one country wants to export equals the amount the other country wants to import.* In other words, it must settle at $4.20 or £3. Otherwise, the total amount demanded in both countries would not equal the total amount supplied in both countries. And any reader who has mastered the material in Chapter 3 knows that such a situation cannot be an equilibrium.

THE SIGNAL OF MARKET FORCES

At this point, we can see how market forces indicate whether a country has a comparative advantage or a comparative disadvantage in the production of a certain commodity. *If a country has a comparative advantage, it turns out—after the price of the good in various countries is equalized and total world output of the good equals total world demand for it—that the country exports the good under free trade and competition.* In Figure 21.2, it turns out—as we've just seen—that the United States is an exporter of bulletproof suspenders under free trade, because the demand and supply curves in the United States and England take the positions they do. The basic reason why the curves take these positions is that the United States has a comparative advantage in the production of this good. Thus, to put things in a nutshell, a nation's producers can tell (under free trade) whether they have a comparative advantage in the production of a certain commodity by seeing whether it is profitable for them to export it. If they can make a profit, they have a comparative advantage.[3]

---

[3] In reality things are not quite so simple. For one thing, high transport costs are often involved in moving goods from one country to another. These costs can impede trade in certain commodities. Also, tariffs or quotas can be enacted by governments to interfere with free trade. Much more will be said on this score in later sections.

Economies of Scale and Learning

Specialization and trade may be advantageous even if there is no difference among countries in the efficiency with which they can produce goods and services. In a case like this, although no nation has a technological advantage over any other, specialization and trade may still be of benefit, because there may be economies of scale in producing some commodities. Thus, if one country specializes in one good and another country specializes in another good, firms can serve the *combined* markets of both countries, which will make their costs *lower* than if they could only reach their domestic markets. This is a major argument for forming an international economic association like the European Common Market, discussed later in this chapter.

Another reason for specialization is that it may result in learning. It is well known that the cost of producing many articles goes down as more and more of the articles are produced. In the aircraft and machine tool industries, producers are well aware of the reduction in costs from learning. The unit costs of a new machine tool tend to be reduced by 20 percent for each doubling of cumulated output, due to improved efficiency through individual and organizational learning. If such learning is an important factor in an industry, there are advantages in having one nation's producers specialize in a certain good. Specialization can reduce costs to a lower level than if each nation tries to be self-sufficient. Longer production runs cut costs since *the more a producer makes, the lower the unit costs.*

Innovation and International Trade

International trade also arises because of technological change. Suppose that a new product is invented in the United States and an American firm begins producing and selling it in the American market. It catches on, and the American innovator decides to export the new product to Europe and other foreign markets. If the new product meets European needs and tastes, the Europeans will import it from the United States; and later, when the market in Europe gets big enough, the American firm may establish a branch plant in Europe. For a time at least, European firms do not have the technological know-how to produce the new product, which is often protected to some extent by patents.

Trade of this sort is based on a *technology gap* between countries. Consider the plastics industry. After the development of a new plastic, there generally has been a period of 15 to 25 years when the innovating country has had a decisive advantage and has been likely to lead in per capita production and exports. It has had a head start, as well as the benefits of patents and commercial secrecy. Production has been licensed to other countries, but often on a limited scale and only after a number of years. Soon after the patents expire, a different phase begins. Imitation is easier, technical know-how spreads more readily, direct technical factors lose importance, and such other factors as materials costs become much more important. Industry from other countries may challenge the innovator in export markets, and sometimes in the innovator's home market as well, although the innovating firm still benefits to some extent from its accumulated knowledge and experience and its ongoing research and development.

The United States tends to export products with a high technological component—relatively new products based on considerable research and development. If the 5 U.S. industries with the largest research programs are compared with the 14 other major industries, it turns out that the high-research industries export 4 times as much per dollar of sales as the others.[4] During the 1960s, Europeans expressed considerable concern over the technological gap between the United States and Europe. They asserted that superior know-how stemming from scientific and technical development in the United States had allowed American companies to obtain large shares of European markets in areas like aircraft, space equipment, computers, and other electronic products. More recently, our technological lead has narrowed considerably in many industries, as the Japanese, Germans, and others have upgraded their technology. Indeed, in some areas, their technology now surpasses our own. According to many observers, some American exports will be, and are being, hurt as a consequence.[5]

Multinational Firms

One of the most remarkable economic phenomena of the last 30 years has been the growth of **multinational firms**—firms that make direct investments in other countries and produce and market their products abroad. For example, Coca-Cola is produced and bottled all over the world. Most multinational firms are American, but companies like Shell in petroleum and Hoffman-La Roche in drugs are examples of foreign-based multinational firms. The available data indicate that the multinational firms have grown by leaps and bounds, and that their shipments have become a bigger proportion of international trade.

The reasons why firms have become multinational are varied. In some cases, firms have established overseas branches to control foreign sources of raw materials. In other cases, they have invested overseas in an effort to defend their competitive position. Very frequently, firms have established foreign branches to exploit a technological lead. After exporting a new product (or a cheaper version of an existing product) to foreign markets, firms have decided to establish plants overseas to supply these markets. Once a foreign market is big enough to accommodate a plant of minimum efficient size, this decision does not conflict with economies of scale. Moreover, transport costs often hasten such a decision. Also, in some

---

[4] Charles Kindleberger, *International Economics,* Homewood, Ill.: Irwin, 1968, p. 67. Also, see R. Vernon, "International Investment and International Trade in the Product Cycle," *Quarterly Journal of Economics,* May 1966; and R. Caves and R. Jones, *World Trade and Payments,* 2d ed., Boston: Little, Brown, 1977.

[5] Besides differences in technology, another reason for trade is a difference in national tastes. If Country A likes beef and Country B likes pork, it may pay both countries to produce beef and pork, and Country A may find it advantageous to import beef from Country B and Country B may find it advantageous to import pork from Country A.

cases, the only way a firm can introduce its innovation into a foreign market is through the establishment of overseas production facilities.

EFFECTS OF MULTINATIONAL FIRMS

By carrying its technology overseas, the multinational firm plays a very important role in the international diffusion of innovations. A firm with a technological edge over its competitors often prefers to exploit its technology in foreign markets through wholly owned subsidiaries rather than through licensing or other means. To some extent, this is because of difficulties in using ordinary market mechanisms to buy and sell information. The difficulties of transferring technology across organizational, as well as national, boundaries also contribute to the decision. For these and other reasons, the innovating firm may find it advantageous to transfer its technology to other countries by establishing subsidiaries abroad.

One of the most important effects of the multinational firm has been to integrate the economies of the world more closely into a worldwide system. In other words, multinational firms have tended to break down some of the barriers between nations. Besides speeding the diffusion of new technology, they have linked the capital markets of many countries and promoted the international transfer of important managerial labor.

Particularly in the less developed countries, there has been an impassioned debate over the pros and cons of the multinational firm, which sometimes is viewed with suspicion by the nation-states in which it operates. These nation-states feel that their sovereignty is threatened by the great power of the multinational firm over their national economies. And the tragedy at Bhopal, India, where thousands of people were killed in 1984 by an accident at a plant owned by a major multinational firm—Union Carbide Corporation—has caused further conflict of this sort. Also, some observers are wary of multinational firms because of the possibility that they will attain undesirable monopoly power. In addition, as we shall see in subsequent chapters, they may put undesirable stress on the international financial system.

Test Yourself

1. Suppose that the United States can produce 3 electronic computers or 3,000 cases of wine with 1 unit of resources, while France can produce 1 electronic computer or 2,000 cases of wine with 1 unit of resources. Will specialization increase world output?

2. Suppose that the United States has 100 units of resources while France has 50 units. Based on the data in Question 1, draw the production possibilities curve in each country. Without international trade, what will be the ratio of the price of an electronic computer to the price of a case of wine in each country?

3. Given the information in Questions 1 and 2, how will firms in France and the United States know whether they should produce wine or electronic computers? Must the government instruct them on this score? Why or why not?

4. Under the circumstances described in Questions 1 and 2, will each country specialize completely in the production of one or the other good? Why or why not? What factors result in incomplete specialization in the real world?

Tariffs and Quotas

WHAT IS A TARIFF?

Despite its advantages, not everyone benefits from free trade. On the contrary, the well-being of some firms and workers may be threatened by foreign competition; and they may press for a *tariff,* a tax the government imposes on imports. The purpose of a tariff is to cut down on imports in order to protect domestic industry and workers from foreign competition. A secondary reason for tariffs is to produce revenue for the government.

To see how a tariff works, consider the market for wristwatches. Suppose that the demand and supply curves for wristwatches in the United States are as shown in panel A of Figure 21.3, and that the demand and supply curves for wristwatches in Switzerland are as shown in panel B. Clearly, Switzerland has a comparative advantage in the production of wristwatches, and under free trade the price of a wristwatch would tend toward $10 in the United States and toward 25 Swiss francs in Switzerland. (Note that 1 Swiss franc is assumed to equal 40 cents.) Under free trade, the United States would import 10 million wristwatches from Switzerland.

Now if the United States imposes a tariff of $10 on each wristwatch imported from Switzerland, the imports will completely cease. Any importers who buy watches in Switzerland at the price (when there is no foreign trade) of 15 Swiss francs—which equals $6—must pay a tariff of $10; this makes their total cost $16 per watch. But this is more than the price of a watch in the United States when there is no foreign trade (which is $15). Consequently, there is no money to be made by importing watches—unless Americans can be persuaded to pay more for a Swiss watch than for an identical American watch.

THE SOCIAL COSTS OF TARIFFS

What is the effect of the tariff? The domestic watch industry receives a higher price—$15 rather than $10—than it would without a tariff. And the workers in the domestic watch industry may have more jobs and higher

Figure 21.3

Effect of a Tariff on Swiss Watches
Under free trade, price would equal $10, or 25 Swiss francs. If a tariff of $10 is imposed on each watch imported from Switzerland, there will be a complete cessation of imports. Price in the United States will increase to $15, and price in Switzerland will fall to 15 Swiss francs.

wages than without the tariff. The victim of the tariff is the American consumer, who pays a higher price for wristwatches. Thus the domestic watch industry benefits at the expense of the rest of the nation. But does the general public lose more than the watch industry gains? In general, the answer is yes. The tariff reduces the welfare of the nation as a whole.

The tariff in Figure 21.3 is a **prohibitive tariff**—a tariff so high that it stops all imports of the good in question. Not all tariffs are prohibitive. (If they were, the government would receive no revenue at all from tariffs.) In many cases, the tariff is high enough to stop some, but not all, imports; and, as you would expect, the detrimental effect of a nonprohibitive tariff on living standards is less than that of a prohibitive tariff. But this does not mean that nonprohibitive tariffs are harmless. On the contrary, they can do lots of harm to domestic consumption and living standards.

The detrimental effects of tariffs have long been recognized, even in detective stories. Thus, in the course of solving the mystery concerning the Hound of the Baskervilles, Sherlock Holmes expressed his enthusiastic approval of a newspaper editorial that read as follows:

> You may be cajoled into imagining that your own special trade or your own industry will be encouraged by a protective tariff, but it stands to reason that such legislation must in the long run ... lower the general conditions of life on this island.

Of course, Holmes considered this point elementary (my dear Watson) but worth hammering home.

WHAT IS A QUOTA?

Besides tariffs, other barriers to free trade are **quotas,** which many countries impose on the amount of certain commodities that can be imported annually. The United States sets import quotas on sugar and exerts pressure on foreigners to get them to limit the quantity of steel and textiles that they will export to us. To see how a quota affects trade, production, and prices, let's return to the market for wristwatches. Suppose the United States places a quota on the import of wristwatches: no more than 6 million wristwatches can be imported per year. Figure 21.4 shows the effect of the quota. Before it was imposed, the price of wristwatches was $10 (or 25 Swiss francs), and the United States imported 10 million wristwatches from Switzerland. The quota forces the United States to reduce its imports to 6 million.

What will be the effect on the U.S. price? The demand curve shows that, if the price is $12, American demand will exceed American supply by 6 million watches; in other words, we will import 6 million watches. Thus, once the quota is imposed, the price will rise to $12, since *this is the price that will reduce our imports to the amount of the quota.* A quota—like a tariff—increases the price of the good. (Note too that the price in Switzerland will fall to 20 francs. Thus the quota will reduce the price in Switzerland.)

Figure 21.4

Effect of a Quota on Swiss Watches
Before the quota is imposed, the price is $10, or 25 Swiss francs. After a quota of 6 million watches is imposed, the price in the United States rises to $12, and the price in Switzerland falls to 20 Swiss francs.

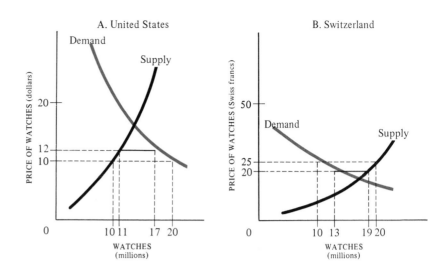

THE SOCIAL COSTS OF QUOTAS

Both a quota and a tariff reduce trade, raise prices, protect domestic industry from foreign competition, and reduce the standard of living of the nation as a whole. But most economists tend to regard quotas with even less enthusiasm than they do tariffs. Under many circumstances, a quota insulates local industry from foreign competition even more effectively than a tariff does. Foreigners, if their costs are low enough, can surmount a tariff barrier; but if a quota exists, there is no way they can exceed the quota. Moreover, a (nonprohibitive) tariff provides the government with some revenue, while quotas do not even do that. The windfall price increase from a quota accrues to the importer who is lucky enough or influential enough—or sufficiently generous with favors and bribes—to get an import license. (However, if the government auctions off the import licenses, it can obtain revenue from a quota.)

EXPORT SUBSIDIES AND OTHER NONTARIFF BARRIERS TO FREE TRADE

Finally, **export subsidies,** another means by which governments try to give their domestic industry an advantage in international competition, are also a major impediment to free trade. Such subsidies may take the form of outright cash disbursements, tax exemptions, preferential financing or insurance arrangements, or other preferential treatment for exports. Export subsidies, and other such measures, frequently lead to countermeasures. Thus, to counter foreign export subsidies, the U.S. government has imposed duties against such subsidies on goods sold here.

Other nontariff barriers to free trade include licensing requirements and unreasonable product quality standards. By granting few licenses (which are required in some countries to import goods) and by imposing unrealistically stringent product quality standards, governments discourage imports.

Arguments for Tariffs and Quotas

Given the disadvantages to society at large of tariffs and other barriers to free trade, why do governments continue to impose them? There are many reasons, some sensible, some irrational.

THE NATIONAL DEFENSE ARGUMENT

One of the most convincing arguments is the desirability of maintaining a domestic industry for purposes of *national defense.* Thus, even if the Swedes had a comparative advantage in producing airplanes, we would not allow free trade to put our domestic producers of aircraft out of business if we felt that a domestic aircraft industry was necessary for national defense. Although the Swedes are by no means unfriendly, we would not want to import our entire supply of such a critical commodity from a foreign country, where the supply might be shut off for reasons of international politics. (Recall the Arab oil embargo of 1973.)

This is a perfectly valid reason for protecting certain domestic industries, and many protective measures are defended on these grounds. To the extent that protective measures are in fact required for national defense, economists go along with them. The restrictions entail social costs (some of which were described in previous sections), but these costs may well be worth paying for enhanced national security. The trouble is that many barriers to free trade are justified on these grounds when in fact they protect domestic industries only tenuously connected with national defense. Moreover, even if there is a legitimate case on defense grounds for protecting a domestic industry, subsidies are likely to be a more straightforward and efficient way to do so than tariffs or quotas.

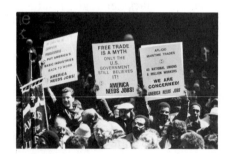

Besides national defense, there are other noneconomic reasons for protecting particular domestic industries. Some countries—Canada, for one— use a tariff to protect certain industries that they feel help them to be more independent of foreign domination and influence. Many Canadians, for understandable reasons, are intent on maintaining their traditions and values, and on resisting the penetration of American ways. Such noneconomic reasons for protection are perfectly reasonable if the nation as a whole understands the economic cost and agrees that the game is worth the candle (and if the reasons are sufficiently understood by foreigners that the measures do not provoke retaliation).

OTHER ARGUMENTS FOR TARIFFS

Besides national defense, several other arguments for tariffs or quotas can make sense.

1. Tariffs or other forms of protection can be justified to foster the growth or development of young industries. Suppose that Japan has a comparative advantage in the production of a certain semiconductor, but Japan does not presently produce this item. It may take Japanese firms several years to become proficient in the relevant technology, to engage in the learning described in a previous section and to take advantage of the relevant economies of scale. While this industry is "growing up," Japan may impose a tariff on such semiconductors, thus shielding its young industry from competition it cannot yet handle. This "infant industry" argument for tariffs has a long history; Alexander Hamilton was one of its early exponents. Needless to say, it is *not* an argument for *permanent* tariffs, since infant industries are supposed to grow up—and the sooner the better. (Moreover, a subsidy for the industry would probably be better and easier to remove than a temporary tariff, according to many economists.)

2. Tariffs sometimes may be imposed to protect domestic jobs and to reduce unemployment at home. In the short run the policy may succeed, but we must recognize that other nations are likely to retaliate by enacting or increasing their own tariffs, so that such a policy may not work very well in the long run. A more sensible way to reduce domestic unemployment is to use the tools of fiscal and monetary policy described in Chapters 12 and 16 rather than tariffs. If workers are laid off by industries that cannot compete with foreign producers, proper monetary and fiscal policy, together with retraining programs, should enable these workers to switch to other industries that can compete.

3. Tariffs sometimes may be imposed to prevent a country from being too dependent on only a few industries. Consider a Latin American country that is a major producer of bananas. Under free trade, this country might produce bananas and little else, putting its entire economy at the mercy of the banana market. If the price of bananas fell, the country's national income would decrease drastically. To promote industrial diversification, this country may establish tariffs to protect other industries—for example, certain types of light manufacturing. In a case like this, the tariff protects the country from having too many eggs—or bananas (if you want to avoid mixing a metaphor)—in a single basket.

4. Tariffs may sometimes improve a country's terms of trade—that is, the ratio of its export prices to its import prices. The United States is a major importer of bananas. If we impose a tariff on bananas, thus cutting down on the domestic demand for them (because the tariff will increase their price), the reduction in our demand is likely to reduce the price of bananas abroad. Consequently, foreign producers of bananas will really pay part of the tariff. However, other countries may retaliate; and if all countries pursue such policies, few, if any, are likely to find themselves better off.

FREQUENTLY ENCOUNTERED FALLACIES

Although, as we have just seen, tariffs can be defended under certain circumstances, many of the arguments for them frequently encountered in political oratory and popular discussions are misleading. Although no field of economics is free of popular misconceptions and fallacies, this one is particularly rich in pious inanities and thunderous *non sequiturs*.

Fallacy 1. One frequently encountered fallacy is that, if foreigners want to trade with us, they must be benefiting from the trade. Consequently, according to this argument, we must be giving them more than we get— and it must be in our interest to reduce trade. This argument is entirely erroneous in its assumption that trade cannot be beneficial to *both* trading partners. On the contrary, as we have seen, the heart of the argument for trade is that it can be mutually beneficial.

Basic Idea #42: Tariffs and quotas reduce trade, raise prices, protect domestic industry from foreign competition, and reduce the standard of living of the nation as a whole. The industries (and workers) that are protected by tariffs and quotas gain at the expense of the general public. However, national defense and "infant industry" arguments (and others) are often advanced to support tariffs and quotas.

475

Fallacy 2. Another fallacy one often encounters in polite conversation—and not-so-polite political debate—is that a tariff is required to protect our workers from low-wage labor in other countries. According to this argument, since American labor (at $8 an hour) clearly cannot compete with foreign labor (which works at "coolie" wage levels), we have no choice but to impose tariffs. If we do not, cheap foreign goods will throw our high-priced laborers out of work. This argument is wrong on two counts. First, *high wages do not necessarily mean high unit costs of production.* Because the productivity of American workers is high, unit labor costs in the United States are roughly in line with those in other countries. (Recall from Chapter 18 that unit labor cost equals the wage rate divided by labor productivity. Thus unit labor cost may be no higher here than abroad, even though the wage rate here is much higher, if labor productivity here is also much higher than abroad.) Second, *if our costs were out of line with those of other countries, there should be a change in exchange rates, which would tend to bring them back into line.* As we shall see in Chapter 22, exchange rates should move to bring our exports and imports into balance.

Fallacy 3. Still another fallacy that makes the rounds is that it is better to "buy American" because then we have both the goods that are bought and the money, whereas if we buy from foreigners we have the goods but they have the money. Like some jokes, this fallacy has an ancient lineage—and one that borders on respectability, since Abraham Lincoln is supposed to have subscribed to it. Basically, the flaw is the implicit assumption that money is somehow valued for its own sake. In reality, all foreigners can do with the money is buy some of our goods, so that really we are just swapping some of our goods for some of theirs. If such a trade is mutually advantageous, fine.

WHY SO MUCH NONSENSE?

Why do politicians (both Democrats and Republicans) sometimes utter tnese fallacies? No doubt an important reason is simply ignorance. There is no law that prevents people with little understanding of economics from holding public office. But this may not be the only reason. Special-interest groups—particular industries, unions, and regions—have a lot to gain by getting the government to enact protective tariffs and quotas. And Congress and the executive branch of the government are often sensitive to the pressures of these groups, which wield considerable political power.

Faced with a choice between helping a few powerful, well-organized groups and helping the general public—which is poorly organized and often ignorant of its own interests—politicians frequently tend to favor the special-interest groups. After all, these groups have a lot to gain and will remember their friends, while the general public—each member of which loses only a relatively small amount—will be largely unaware of its losses anyhow. Having decided to help these groups, representatives or senators may not exert themselves unduly to search out or expose the weakness in some of the arguments used to bolster their position. Thus there is the story of a well-known senator who, about to deliver a certain oration, wrote in the margin of one section of his speech: "Weak point here. Holler like hell."

Finally, it is important to recognize once again that, although the majority of citizens benefit from free trade, some are likely to be hurt by it. A reduction in the tariff on shoes is likely to hurt people who own and work in American shoe factories. If our domestic shoe industry cannot compete with foreign producers, workers will be laid off and plants will close. The result will be a considerable loss to domestic shoe producers and workers. Most people believe that society as a whole, which benefits from free trade, should help the minority that is victimized by it. To promote this objective, the United States has established "adjustment assistance" for firms or workers who, because of government agreement to reduce barriers to free trade, have suffered idleness or unemployment due to an increase in imports. Workers can enter retraining programs and can obtain allowances to help pay for moving to other jobs.

Tariffs in the United States

How high are American tariffs, now and in the past? In our early years, we were a very protectionist nation. The argument for protecting our young industry from the competition of European manufacturers was the "infant industry" argument, which, as we saw above, can be perfectly sensible. However, our own industries understandably found it advantageous to prolong their childhood for as long as possible—and to press for continuation of high tariffs. During the nineteenth century and well into the twentieth, the industrial Northeast was particularly strong in its support of tariffs. Furthermore, the Republican party, which generally held sway in American politics between the Civil War and the New Deal, favored a high tariff. Thus, as shown in Figure 21.5, the tariff remained relatively high from about 1870 until the early 1930s. With the exception of the period around World War I, average tariff rates were about 40 to 50 percent. With the enactment of the Smoot-Hawley Tariff of 1930, the tariff reached its peak—about 60 percent. Moreover, these tariff rates understate the extent to which the tariff restricted trade: Some goods were completely shut out of the country by the tariff, and do not show up in the figures.

Figure 21.5
Average American Tariff Rates *The tariff generally remained high from about 1870 to the early 1930s; in recent decades it has decreased substantially.*

477

With the Democratic victory in 1932, a movement began toward freer trade. The Trade Agreements Act of 1934 allowed the president to bargain with other countries to reduce barriers to trade. He was given the power to lower U.S. tariffs by as much as 50 percent. In 1945, he was given the power to make further tariff reductions. Between 1934 and 1948, tariff rates fell substantially, as shown in Figure 21.5. By 1948, the United States was no longer a high-tariff country; the average tariff rate was only about 10 percent.[6]

THE KENNEDY ROUND

During the 1950s, there were no further decreases in the tariff—but there were no substantial increases either. The movement toward freer trade was continued by President Kennedy in 1962, and during the 1960s, the "Kennedy Round" negotiations took place among about 40 nations in an attempt to reduce tariffs. In 1967, the United States agreed to cut tariffs by about one-third on a great many items.

The negotiations during the 1960s were prompted by the establishment of the *European Economic Community*—or *"Common Market."* The EEC was composed originally of Belgium, France, West Germany, Holland, Italy, and Luxembourg; and in the late 1970s, Britain, Denmark, and Ireland joined. When the EEC was formed, the member countries agreed to reduce the tariff barriers against one another's goods—but not against the goods of other nations, including the United States.

The formation and success of the Common Market—and the likelihood that other European countries would join—posed a problem for the United States. The Common Market is a large and rich market, with over 200 million people and a combined gross national product in the trillions of dollars. With the reduction of tariff barriers *within* the Common Market, trade *among* the members of the Common Market increased rapidly, and prices of many items were cut. But American exporters were less than ecstatic about all of this, because the members of the Common Market still maintained their tariff barriers against American goods. While the "Kennedy Round" negotiations succeeded in reducing some of the tariff barriers between the United States and the Common Market, important tariff barriers remained, particularly for agricultural products.

THE TRADE REFORM ACT AND THE TOKYO ROUND

In 1974, the Congress passed the Trade Reform Act of 1974, which enabled the president, after international negotiations, to reduce any tariff presently above 5 percent by three-fifths and to abolish any tariff presently equal to 5 percent or less. Also, the act allowed workers, firms, and communities that are hurt by import competition to obtain payments and other forms of assistance. As pointed out in a previous section, such as-

---

[6] In 1947, the United States and 22 other nations signed the *General Agreement on Tariffs and Trade* (GATT), which calls for all participating countries to meet periodically to negotiate bilaterally on tariff cuts. Any tariff cut negotiated in this way will be extended to all participating nations.

Example 21.1   The Effects of a Tariff on Shoes

The quantity of shoes demanded in the United States at each price of a pair of shoes is shown below. In addition, the quantities of shoes supplied by American producers and by foreign producers at each price are shown too.

(a) Assuming that the market for shoes is competitive, what is the equilibrium price of a pair of shoes in the United States? (b) What proportion of the U.S. market goes to foreign producers of shoes? (c) Suppose that the United States imposes a tariff of $15 per pair of shoes. How many pairs of shoes will foreign producers now supply if the price is (1) $50, (2) $55, (3) $60. (Note that a $50 price together with a $15 tariff means that the price to the foreign producer is $50 − $15, or $35.) (d) After the imposition of the tariff, what is the equilibrium price? (e) After the imposition of the tariff, what proportion of the U.S. market goes to foreign producers of shoes? (f) How much revenue does the U.S. government get from this tariff?

SOLUTION

(a) $45, since at this price U.S. supply (10 million pairs) plus foreign supply (6 million pairs) equals the quantity demanded (16 million pairs). (b) 6/16. (c) 3 million pairs (since this is what would have been supplied at a price of $35 without the tariff), 5 million pairs (since this is what would have been supplied at a price of $40 without the tariff), 6 million pairs (since this is what would have been supplied at a price of $45 without the tariff). (d) $50, since at this price U.S. supply (11 million pairs) plus foreign supply (3 million pairs) equals the quantity demanded (14 million pairs). (e) 3/14. (f) 3 million × $15, or $45 million.

sistance is a way of helping the minority of workers and firms that may be victimized by freer trade.

In 1973, over 100 nations met in Tokyo to plan a new round of trade negotiations. The aim was to make progress toward the reduction of both tariffs and nontariff barriers to trade. (In recent years, tariffs have been replaced to some extent by nontariff barriers to trade.) After over 5 years of difficult negotiations, an agreement was approved in April 1979. This agreement called for the industrial nations to reduce tariffs on thousands of goods by an average of about 33 percent during an 8-year period. It also tried to reduce export subsidies, phony technical standards for imports (used to keep out foreign goods), and barriers to international bidding for government contracts.

INCREASED PROTECTIONISM

Recent years have seen a marked increase in protectionist feelings in the United States. As Western Europe and Japan have become more formidable competitors abroad and at home, many industries have begun to press for quotas and higher tariffs. The automobile, steel, and textile industries have been among the most frequent petitioners for protection. In 1981, the Japanese agreed to limit import of Japanese autos into the U.S. to 1.68 million per year; in 1984, the ceiling was raised to 1.85 million per year, and the agreement called for the industrial nations to reduce tariffs on thousands of goods by an average of about 33 percent during an 8-year period. It also tried to reduce export subsidies, phony technical standards for imports (used to keep out foreign goods), and barriers to international bidding for government contracts.

In the mid-1980s, hundreds of petitions have been filed by industry and labor, asking the federal government to protect them from imports. In considerable part, this was due to the very strong dollar. As we shall see in the following chapter, the dollar's value relative to other currencies rose markedly from 1980 to 1983, the result being that foreign goods became much cheaper to American buyers. Also, in some industries like semiconductors, the quality of foreign goods sometimes exceeded that of American suppliers. Faced with very stiff competition from imports, American firms asked the government for protection.

As indicated in earlier sections of this chapter, the American consumer is the loser. Robert Crandall of the Brookings Institution has estimated that in 1983 the auto import quotas resulted in about a $400 per car increase in the price of U.S. cars and a $1,000 per car increase in the price of Japanese imports, the total cost to American consumers being over $4 billion in 1983 alone. According to Crandall, "The cost per job saved, therefore, was nearly $160,000 per year. Employment creation at this cost is surely not worth the candle."[7]

Most economists feel that the upsurge in protectionism in the mid-1980s

[7] R. Crandall, "Import Quotas and the Automobile Industry," *The Brookings Review,* Summer 1984, p. 16.

The EEC, born in the embers of World War II, was fathered by a desire to bind Germany to the rest of Europe. The success of the European Steel and Coal Community and the Benelux union encouraged the "Europeanists," and in 1957 the Treaty of Rome formally proclaimed the birth of a six-country free-trade area in which labor, capital, and goods were to move freely. None of this was to happen instantaneously, but the six countries—France, Germany, Italy, Belgium, the Netherlands, and Luxembourg—did agree on a timetable for the removal of centuries-old barriers and on a commission and council to manage the details of the process.

Headquarters of the European Economic Community, Brussels

There are ample statistics to tell what happened after the EEC was formed—relatively high growth rates, increased competitiveness by European firms, increases in per capita incomes, and increased membership (including Great Britain). But the flavor of this customs union comes through best by seeing what it has meant to three prototype economic people.

Nino T. was born in southern Italy, where reported unemployment has been 14 percent. If disguised unemployment were included, the rate might run as high as double that. Wages, for those with jobs, averaged about $20 per week. In 1965, he migrated to Germany to work in an automobile plant in Frankfort, where he could make $75 a week, and send back $40 to his family. He planned to stay for another two years—perhaps until he had saved enough to buy a small business.

Elizabeth C. works for a leather-goods firm in London. When Britain joined the Common Market, her chief worry was that it would mean higher food prices. Why? Because the technologically inefficient but politically powerful French farmer demanded protection from cheap American and Canadian food. Thus, while French wheat would flow freely into Great Britain, the high external tariff would now keep out North American wheat.

Richard B., an American businessman, now lives in Paris, managing the French subsidiary of a large New York-based corporation. He was moved to Paris about 20 years ago, when company officials decided that the removal of internal barriers by the EEC would allow U.S. companies to operate on the scale to which they were accustomed. To stay competitive in the European market, they decided to build production facilities inside the EEC, rather than producing in the U.S. and shipping abroad. Richard now finds himself very much at home in France, and seriously considers living out his days in Paris.

E.A.

is an unfortunate development. Although they understand that it will be difficult to beat back the protectionist tide, they hope that this upsurge of protectionist spirit will be short-lived, and that developments here and abroad will enable us and our trading partners to move closer to the realization of the benefits of free trade.

Test Yourself

1. According to Hendrik Houthakker, "Our workers get high real income not because they are protected from foreign competition, but because they are highly productive, at least in certain industries." Do you agree? Why or why not?

2. According to Richard Cooper, "Technological innovation can undoubtedly strengthen the competitive position of a country in which the innovation takes place, whether it be one which enlarges exports or displaces imports." Give examples of this phenomenon, and discuss various ways that one might measure the effects of technological innovation on a country's competitive position.

3. "The principle of comparative advantage doesn't work. The U.S. exports electronic computers to Japan and imports electronic consumer goods like TV sets from Japan." Comment and evaluate.

4. Would you favor a high tariff on imported steel if you were (a) an automobile worker, (b) a steel worker, (c) an automobile buyer, (d) a plastics worker? Explain your reasoning in each case.

Summary

1. International trade permits specialization, and specialization increases output. This is the advantage of trade, both for individuals and for nations.

2. Country A has an absolute advantage over Country B in the production of a good when Country A can produce a unit of the good with less resources than can Country B. Trade can be mutually beneficial even if one country has an absolute advantage in the production of all goods.

3. Specialization and trade depend on comparative, not absolute, advantage. A nation is said to have a comparative advantage in those products where its efficiency relative to other nations is highest. Trade can be mutually beneficial if a country specializes in the products where it has a comparative advantage and imports the products where it has a comparative disadvantage.

4. If markets are relatively free and competitive, producers will automatically be led to produce in accord with comparative advantage. If a country has a comparative advantage in the production of a certain good, it will turn out—after the price of the good in various countries is equalized and total world output of the good equals total world demand—that this country is an exporter of the good under free trade.

5. Specialization may occur because of economies of scale and learning. Also, some countries develop new products and processes, which they export to other countries until the technology becomes widely available.

6. A tariff is a tax imposed by the government on imports, the purpose being to cut down on imports in order to protect domestic industry and workers from foreign competition. Tariffs benefit the protected industry at the expense of the general public, and, in general, a tariff costs the general public more than the protected industry (and its workers and suppliers) gains.

7. Quotas are another barrier to free trade. They too reduce trade, raise prices, protect domestic industry from foreign competition, and reduce the standard of living of the nation as a whole.

8. Tariffs, quotas, and other barriers to free trade can sometimes be justified on the basis of national security and other noneconomic considerations. Moreover, tariffs and other forms of protection can sometimes be justified to protect infant industries, to prevent a country from being too dependent on only a few industries, and to carry out other national objectives. But many arguments for tariffs are fallacious.

9. In our early years, we were a very protectionist country. Our tariffs remained relatively high until the 1930s, when a movement began toward free trade. Between 1934 and 1948, our tariff rates dropped substantially. Again during the 1960s, there was a significant reduction in our tariffs. But more recently, as some of our industries (like steel) have been hit hard by imports, there has been a tendency to push for more protectionist measures. During the 1980s, the protectionist tide was very strong.

10. Although it has equaled only about 10 percent of our gross national product, foreign trade is of very considerable importance to the American economy. Many of our industries rely on foreign countries for raw materials or for markets, and our consumers buy many kinds of imported goods. In absolute terms, our exports and imports are larger than those of any other nation.

Concepts for Review

Exports	**Trading possibilities**	**Quota**
Imports	**curve**	**Export subsidy**
Absolute advantage	**Terms of trade**	**European Economic**
Comparative advantage	**Multinational firm**	**Community**
Production possibilities	**Tariff**	**(Common Market)**
curve	**Prohibitive tariff**	

Appendix: The Effects of Foreign Trade on NNP

In Chapters 10–12, we discussed how the level of net national product is determined. As a first approximation, it seemed adequate to ignore exports and imports in our discussion there. Now we must take account of exports and imports and see how they affect NNP. Recall from Chapter 7

Figure 21.6

Effects of Foreign Trade on Net National Product *The equilibrium level of NNP is at the point where the* C + I + G + X *line intersects the 45-degree line; in this case, $500 billion.*

Figure 21.7

Effect of Increase in Net Exports on Net National Product *If net exports increase from X to X', the equilibrium level of NNP increases from $500 billion to $550 billion.*

that net national product = consumption expenditure + investment + government spending + net exports, where net exports equal exports minus imports. In other words,

$$Y = C + I + G + X. \qquad (21.1)$$

where *Y* is NNP, *C* is consumption expenditure, *I* is investment, *G* is government spending, and *X* is net exports. Recall too that *the equilibrium level of NNP will be at the point where intended spending on NNP—which equals intended consumption expenditure + intended investment + government spending + intended net exports—equals NNP.*

Thus, in Figure 21.6, the equilibrium level of NNP must be $500 billion, since this is the level at which the C + I + G + X line intersects the 45-degree line. To see this, note that we are merely carrying out a straightforward extension of the analysis in Chapter 12, where we assumed that net exports were zero. Once this assumption is relaxed, intended net exports must be added to the C + I + G line to get total intended spending, and the equilibrium level of NNP is at the point where the resulting total-intended-spending line—C + I + G + X—intersects the 45-degree line.

We can also use the leakage-injection approach (described in Chapters 10 to 12) to show the effects of foreign trade on the equilibrium value of NNP. Clearly, *exports are an injection* since they add spending to the domestic flow of income and expenditure. In other words, foreign spending on American products and services results in additional output and jobs in the United States. On the other hand, *imports are a leakage* because they withdraw spending from the domestic flow of income and expenditure. In other words, they constitute a use for income other than spending on U.S. goods and services.

Once this is understood, it is clear why governments during the 1930s wanted to increase their exports and decrease their imports. Spending on net exports results in increases in NNP. If intended spending on net exports increases from *X* to *X'*, as shown in Figure 21.7, the equilibrium level of NNP increases from $500 billion to $550 billion. Moreover, *increases in spending on net exports have a multiplier effect,* which is like the multiplier effect for investment or government spending. Thus a $1 increase in intended spending on net exports results in more than a $1 increase in NNP.[8] Since governments during the 1930s wanted desperately to increase their NNP to reduce unemployment, it is clear why they tried to increase their net exports. However, all that resulted was a reduction in international trade, because of retaliatory measures.

[8] If we assume that exports, government expenditures, and tax receipts are the same at all levels of NNP, then a $1 increase in intended spending on net exports will result in an increase in equilibrium NNP of $\dfrac{1}{MPS + MPI}$ dollars, where *MPS* is the marginal propensity to save and *MPI* is the marginal propensity to import. (The *marginal propensity to import* is the proportion of an extra dollar of income that is spent on imports.) Note that the multiplier is smaller now than in the case of a closed economy (where *MPI* equals zero).

CHAPTER 22

Exchange Rates and the Balance of Payments

In late 1984, the financial pages of newspapers around the world trumpeted that the value of the dollar had reached its highest level in over a decade. (*Business Week,* for example, published a cover story on the "superdollar.") American tourists visiting other countries and U.S. importers were happy because a dollar was worth more German marks, Japanese yen, and Swiss francs. The situation was quite different from 1978, when the value of the dollar plunged, also resulting in headline news.

To understand these developments, we must consider several questions. What are exchange rates and how are they determined? How are international business transactions carried out? Should there be fixed or flexible exchange rates? What is a balance-of-payments deficit, and what is its significance? What problems have afflicted the international monetary system in recent years? These questions, which are both fundamental and timely, are taken up in this chapter.

International Transactions and Exchange Rates

Suppose you want to buy a book from a German publisher, and that book costs 20 marks. (The German currency consists of marks, not dollars.) To buy the book, you must somehow get marks to pay the publisher, since this is the currency in which the publisher deals. Or, if the publisher agrees, you might pay in dollars; but the publisher would then have to exchange the dollars for marks, since its bills must be paid in marks. Whatever happens, either you or the publisher must somehow exchange dollars for marks, since international business transactions, unlike transactions within a country, involve two different currencies.

If you decide to exchange dollars for marks to pay the German publisher, how can you make the exchange? The answer is simple. You can buy German marks at a bank, just as you might buy lamb chops at a butcher shop. Just as the lamb chops have a price (expressed in dollars), so the German marks have a price (expressed in dollars). The bank may tell you that each mark you buy will cost you $.40. This makes the *exchange rate* between dollars and marks .4 to 1, since it takes .4 dollars to purchase 1 mark (or 2½ marks to purchase 1 dollar).

In general, *the exchange rate is simply the number of units of one currency that exchanges for a unit of another currency.* The obvious question is: What determines the exchange rate? Why is the exchange rate between German marks and American dollars what it is? Why doesn't a dollar exchange for 10 marks, rather than 2½ marks? This basic question will occupy us in the next several sections.

Exchange Rates under the Gold Standard

As a starter, let's see how exchange rates were determined under the *gold standard,* which prevailed before the 1930s. *If a country was on the gold standard, a unit of its currency was convertible into a certain amount of gold.* Before World War I the dollar was convertible into one-twentieth of an ounce of gold, and the British pound was convertible into one-quarter of an ounce of gold. Thus, since the pound exchanged for 5 times as much gold as the dollar, the pound exchanged for $5. The currency of any other country on the gold standard was convertible into a certain amount of gold in the same way; and *to see how much its currency was worth in dollars, you divided the amount of gold a unit of its currency was worth by the amount of gold (one-twentieth of an ounce) a dollar was worth.*

Why did the exchange rate always equal the ratio between the amount of gold a foreign currency was worth and the amount of gold a dollar was worth? Why did the price of a British pound stay at $5 before World War I? To see why, suppose that the price (in dollars) of a pound rose above this ratio—above $5. Instead of exchanging their dollars directly for pounds, Americans would have done better to exchange them for gold and then exchange the gold for pounds. By this indirect process, Americans could have exchanged $5 for a pound, so they would have refused to buy pounds at a price above $5 per pound.

Similarly, if the price of a pound fell below $5, the British would have refused to sell pounds, since they could have obtained $5 by converting the pound into gold and the gold into dollars. Thus, *because Americans would refuse to pay more than $5, and the British would refuse to accept less, for a pound, the price of a pound had to remain at about $5.* (In practice, the pound could be a few cents above or below $5, because it costs money to transport gold in order to carry out the conversion.)

BALANCE BETWEEN EXPORTS AND IMPORTS

But what ensured that this exchange rate, dictated by the gold content of currencies, would result in a rough equality of trade between countries? If

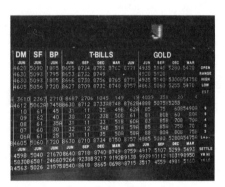

Exchange rate board showing international currencies

one pound exchanged for $5, perhaps the British might find our goods so cheap that they would import a great deal from us, while we might find their goods so expensive that we would import little from them. Under these circumstances, the British would have to ship gold to us to pay for the excess of their imports from us over their exports to us, and eventually they could run out of gold. Could this happen? If not, why not? These questions occupied the attention of many early economists. The classic answers were given by David Hume, the Scottish philosopher, in the eighteenth century.

Hume pointed out that under the gold standard a mechanism ensured that trade would be brought into balance and that neither country would run out of gold. This mechanism was as follows. If, as we assumed, the British bought more from us than we bought from them, they would have to send us gold to pay for the excess of their imports over their exports. As their gold stock declined, their price level would fall. (Recall the quantity theory of money.) As our gold stock increased, our price level would rise. Thus, because of our rising prices, the British would tend to import less from us; and because of their falling prices, we would tend to import more from them. Consequently, the trade between the two countries would tend toward a better balance. Eventually when enough gold had left Britain and entered the United States, prices here would have increased enough, and prices in Britain would have fallen enough, to put imports and exports in balance.

The Foreign Exchange Market

The gold standard is long gone; and after many decades of fixed exchange rates (discussed in a later section), the major trading nations of the world began to experiment with flexible exchange rates in early 1973. Let's consider a situation where exchange rates are allowed to fluctuate freely, like the price of any commodity in a competitive market. In a case of this sort, exchange rates—like any price—are determined by supply and demand. There is a market for various types of foreign currency—German marks, British pounds, French francs, and so on—just as there are markets for various types of meat.

In the case of the German mark, the demand and supply curves may look like those shown in Figure 22.1. The demand curve shows the amount of German marks that people with dollars will demand at various prices of a mark. The supply curve shows the amount of German marks that people with marks will supply at various prices of a mark. Since the amount of German currency supplied must equal the amount demanded in equilibrium, *the equilibrium price (in dollars) of a German mark is given by the intersection of the demand and supply curves.* In Figure 22.1, this intersection is at $.40.

THE DEMAND AND SUPPLY SIDES OF THE MARKET

Let's look in more detail at the demand and supply sides of this market. On the *demand* side are people who want to import German goods (like the book you want to buy) into the United States, people who want to

487

Figure 22.1

Determination of the Exchange Rate between Dollars and German Marks under Freely Fluctuating Exchange Rates *Under freely fluctuating exchange rates, the equilibrium price of a German mark would be $.40 if the demand and supply curves for marks are as shown here.*

Figure 22.2

Effect of Shift in Demand Curve for German Marks *Because of the demand curve's shift to the right, the equilibrium price of a German mark increases from $.40 to $.44.*

travel in Germany (where they'll need German money), people who want to build factories in Germany, and others with dollars who want German currency. The people on the *supply* side are those who want to import American goods into Germany, Germans who want to travel in the United States (where they'll need American money), people with marks who want to build factories in the United States, and others with marks who want American currency.

When Americans demand more German cameras or Rhine wine (causing the demand curve to shift upward and to the right), the price (in dollars) of the German mark will tend to increase. Thus, if the demand curve for marks shifts as shown in Figure 22.2, the result will be an increase in the equilibrium price (in dollars) of a mark from $.40 to $.44. Conversely, *when the Germans demand more American cars or computers (resulting in a shift of the supply curve downward and to the right), the price (in dollars) of the German mark will tend to decrease.*

To see why an increase in German demand for American cars or computers shifts the supply curve downward and to the right, recall that the supply curve shows the amount of marks that will be supplied at each price of a mark. Thus a shift downward and to the right in the supply curve means that more marks will be supplied at a given price (in dollars) of the mark. Given the posited increase in German demand for American goods, such a shift in the supply curve would be expected.

APPRECIATION AND DEPRECIATION OF A CURRENCY

Two terms frequently encountered in discussions of the foreign exchange market are ***appreciation*** and ***depreciation.*** When Country A's currency becomes more valuable relative to Country B's currency, Country A's currency is said to appreciate relative to that of Country B, and Country B's currency is said to depreciate relative to that of Country A. In Figure 22.2, the mark appreciated relative to the dollar and the dollar depreciated relative to the mark. This use of terms makes sense. Since the number of dollars commanded by a mark increased, the mark became more valuable relative to the dollar and the dollar became less valuable relative to the mark.

Note that such a change in exchange rates would not have been possible under the gold standard. Unless a country changed the amount of gold that could be exchanged for a unit of its currency, exchange rates were fixed under the gold standard. Sometimes governments did change the amount of gold that could be exchanged for their currencies. For example, in 1933 the United States increased the price of gold from $21 an ounce to $35 an ounce. When a country increased the price of gold, this was called a ***devaluation*** of its currency.

DETERMINANTS OF EXCHANGE RATES

In a previous section, we have seen that flexible exchange rates are determined by supply and demand. But what are some of the major factors determining the position of these supply and demand curves?

Relative Price Levels. In the long run, the exchange rate between any two currencies may be expected to reflect differences in the price levels in the two countries. (This is the so-called purchasing-power parity theory of exchange rate determination.) To see why, suppose that Germany and the United States are the only exporters or importers of automobiles, and that automobiles are the only product they export or import. If an automobile costs $4,000 in the United States and 10,000 marks in Germany, what must be the exchange rate between the dollar and the mark? Clearly, a mark must be worth .40 dollars, because otherwise the two countries' automobiles would not be competitive in the world market. If a mark were set equal to 0.60 dollars, this would mean that a German automobile would cost $6,000 (that is 10,000 times $0.60), which is far more than what an American automobile would cost. Thus foreign buyers would obtain their automobiles in the United States.

Based on this theory, one would expect that, *if the rate of inflation in Country A is higher than in Country B, Country A's currency is likely to depreciate relative to Country B's.* Suppose that costs double in the United States but increase by only 25 percent in Germany. After this burst of inflation, an automobile costs $8,000 (that is, 2 times $4,000) in the United States and 12,500 marks (that is, 1.25 times 10,000 marks) in Germany. Thus, based on the purchasing-power parity theory, the new value of the mark must be 0.64 dollars, rather than the old value of 0.40 dollars. (Why 0.64 dollars? Because this is the exchange rate that makes the new cost of an automobile in the United States, $8,000, equivalent to the new cost of an automobile in Germany, 12,500 marks.) Because the rate of inflation is higher in the United States than in Germany, the dollar depreciates relative to the mark.

Relative Rates of Growth. Although relative price levels may play an important role in the long run, other factors tend to exert more influence on exchange rates in the short run. In particular, *if one country's rate of economic growth is higher than the rest of the world, its currency is likely to depreciate.* If a country's economy is booming, this tends to increase its imports. If there is a boom in the United States, Americans will tend to import a great deal from other countries. If a country's imports tend to

Basic Idea #43: Under flexible exchange rates, the exchange rate between any two currencies will reflect differences in the price levels in the two countries. If the rate of inflation in Country A is higher than in Country B, Country A's currency is likely to depreciate relative to Country B's. Also, if one country's rate of economic growth is higher than that of the rest of the world, or if its interest rates decline, its currency is likely to depreciate.

489

grow faster than its exports, its demand for foreign currency will tend to grow more rapidly than the amount of foreign currency that is supplied to it. Consequently, its currency is likely to depreciate.

Relative Interest-Rate Levels. If the rate of interest in Germany is higher than in the United States, banks, multinational corporations, and other investors in the United States will sell dollars and buy marks in order to invest in the high-yielding Germany securities. Also, German investors (and others) will be less likely to find American securities attractive. Thus the mark will tend to appreciate relative to the dollar, since the demand curve for marks will shift to the right and the supply curve for marks will shift to the left. In general, *an increase in a country's interest rates leads to an appreciation of its currency, and a decrease in its interest rates leads to a depreciation of its currency.* In the short run, interest-rate differentials can have a major impact on exchange rates, since there is estimated to be over $100 billion in funds that are moved from country to country in response to differentials in interest rates.

THE ADJUSTMENT MECHANISM UNDER FLEXIBLE EXCHANGE RATES

Under flexible exchange rates, what insures a balance in the exports and imports between countries? The situation differs from that described by David Hume, since Hume assumed the existence of the gold standard. Under flexible exchange rates, the balance is achieved through changes in exchange rates. Suppose that for some reason Britain is importing far more from us than we are from Britain. This will mean that the British, needing dollars to buy our goods, will be willing to supply pounds more cheaply. In other words, the supply curve for British pounds will shift downward and to the right, as shown in Figure 22.3. This will cause the price of a pound to decline from P_1 dollars to P_2 dollars. Or, from Britain's point of view, the price (in pounds) of a dollar will have been bid up by the swollen demand for imports from America.

Because of the increase in the price (in pounds) of a dollar, our goods will become more expensive in Britain. Thus the British will tend to reduce their imports of our goods. At the same time, since the price (in dollars) of a pound has decreased, British goods will become cheaper in the United States, and this will stimulate us to import more from Britain. Consequently, as our currency appreciates in terms of theirs—or, to put it another way, as theirs depreciates in terms of ours—the British are induced to import less and export more. Thus there is an automatic mechanism (just as there was under the gold standard) to bring trade between countries into balance.

Figure 22.3

Adjustment Mechanism *If Britain imports more from us than we do from Britain, the supply curve for British pounds will shift downward and to the right, resulting in a decline of the price of the pound from* P_1 *to* P_2 *dollars. If Britain tries to maintain the price at* P_1 *dollars, the British government will have to exchange dollars for* $(Q_S - Q_D)$ *pounds.*

Fixed Exchange Rates

Although many economists believed that exchange rates should be allowed to fluctuate, very few exchange rates really did so in the period from the end of World War II up to 1973. Instead, *most exchange rates were fixed by government action and international agreement.* Although they may have varied slightly about the fixed level, the extent to which they were allowed to vary was small. Every now and then, governments changed the exchange rates, for reasons discussed below; but for long periods of time, they remained fixed.

If exchange rates remain fixed, the amount demanded of a foreign currency may not equal the amount supplied. Consider the situation in Figure 22.4. If *A* is the demand curve for German marks, the equilibrium price of a mark is $.40. But suppose the fixed exchange rate between dollars and marks is .35 to 1—that is, each mark exchanges for $.35. Unless the government intervenes, more German marks will be demanded at a price of $.35 per mark than will be offered. Specifically, the difference between the quantity demanded and the quantity supplied will be $Q_D - Q_S$. Unless the government steps in, a black market for German marks may develop, and the real price may increase toward $.40 per mark.

TYPES OF GOVERNMENT INTERVENTION

To maintain exchange rates at their fixed levels, governments can intervene in a variety of ways. For example, they may reduce the demand for foreign currencies by reducing defense expenditures abroad, by limiting the amount that their citizens can travel abroad, and by curbing imports from other countries. Thus, in the case depicted in Figure 22.4, the American government might adopt some or all of these measures to shift the demand curve for German marks downward and to the left. If the demand curve can be pushed from *A* to *B*, the equilibrium price of a German mark can be reduced to $.35, the fixed exchange rate. For the time being, there will no longer be any mismatch between the quantity of marks demanded and the quantity supplied.

When exchange rates are fixed, mismatches of this sort cannot be eliminated entirely and permanently. To deal with such temporary mismatches, governments enter the market and buy and sell their currencies in order to maintain fixed exchange rates. Take the case of post-World-War-II Britain. At times the amount of British pounds supplied exceeded the amount demanded. Then the British government bought up the excess at the fixed exchange rate. At other times, when the quantity demanded exceeded the amount supplied, the British government supplied the pounds desired at the fixed exchange rate. As long as the equilibrium exchange rate was close to (sometimes above and sometimes below) the fixed exchange rate, the amount of its currency the government sold at one time equaled, more or less, the amount it bought at another time.

But in some cases governments have tried to maintain a fixed exchange rate far from the equilibrium exchange rate. The British government tried during the 1960s to maintain the price (in dollars) of the pound at $2.80, even though the equilibrium price was about $2.40. The situation was as shown in Figure 22.5. Since the quantity of British pounds supplied exceeded the quantity demanded at the price of $2.80, the British government had to buy the difference. That is, it had to buy $(Q_S - Q_D)$ pounds with dollars. Moreover, it had to keep on exchanging dollars for pounds in these quantities for as long as the demand and supply curves remained in these positions. Such a situation could not go on indefinitely, since the British government eventually had to run out of dollars. How long it could

Figure 22.4
Fixed Exchange Rate *The equilibrium price of a German mark is $.40, if A is the demand curve. If $.35 is the fixed exchange rate, the U.S. government may try to shift the demand curve for marks from A to B, thus bringing the equilibrium exchange rate into equality with the fixed exchange rate.*

go on depended on how big Britain's reserves of gold and foreign currency were.

Balance-of-Payments Deficits and Surpluses

Under a system of fixed exchange rates, economists and financial analysts look at whether a country has a balance-of-payments deficit or surplus to see whether its currency is above or below its equilibrium value. What is a **balance-of-payments deficit?** What is a **balance-of-payments surplus?** It is important that both of these terms be understood.

BALANCE-OF-PAYMENTS DEFICIT

If a country's currency is *overvalued* (that is, if its price exceeds the equilibrium price), the quantity supplied of its currency will exceed the quantity demanded. Let's return to the case where the price of the British pound was set at $2.80. Under these circumstances, the quantity supplied of pounds exceeds the quantity demanded by $(Q_S - Q_D)$ pounds, as shown in Figure 22.5. This amount—$(Q_S - Q_D)$ pounds—is Britain's balance-of-payments deficit. (See Figure 22.5.) As pointed out in the previous section, it is the number of pounds that Britain's central bank, the Bank of England, must purchase. To pay for these pounds, the Bank of England must give up some of its *reserves* of foreign currencies or gold.

In a situation of this sort, there may be a "run" on the overvalued currency. Suppose that speculators become convinced that the country with the balance-of-payments deficit cannot maintain the artificially high price of its currency much longer because its reserves are running low. Because they will suffer losses if they hold on to a currency that is devalued, the speculators are likely to sell the overvalued currency (in Figure 22.5, the British pound) in very large amounts, thus causing an even bigger balance-of-payments deficit for the country with the overvalued currency. Faced with the exhaustion of its reserves, the country is likely to be forced to allow the price of its currency to fall.

Figure 22.5

Balance-of-Payments Deficit *Because the British pound is overvalued at $2.80, the quantity of pounds demanded (Q_D) is less than the quantity supplied (Q_S). The shortfall—that is, ($Q_S - Q_D$) pounds—is the balance-of-payments deficit.*

BALANCE-OF-PAYMENTS SURPLUS

If a country's currency is *undervalued* (that is, if its price is less than the equilibrium price), the quantity demanded of its currency will exceed the quantity supplied. During the early 1970s, the price of the German mark was set at $0.35, even though its equilibrium price was about $0.40. As shown in Figure 22.6, the quantity of marks demanded exceeds the quantity supplied by $(Q'_D - Q'_S)$ marks under these circumstances. This amount—$(Q'_D - Q'_S)$ marks—is Germany's balance-of-payments surplus. (See Figure 22.6.) Germany can keep the price of the mark at $0.35 only if it provides these $(Q'_D - Q'_S)$ marks in exchange for foreign currencies and gold. By doing so, it increases its reserves.

Whereas a country with an overvalued currency is likely to be forced by the reduction in its reserves to reduce the price of its currency, a country with an undervalued currency is unlikely to be forced by the increase in its reserves to increase the price of its currency. And a country with an un-

Figure 22.6

Balance-of-Payments Surplus *Because the German mark is undervalued at $.35, the quantity of marks demanded (Q'_D) is greater than the quantity supplied (Q'_S). The surplus—that is, ($Q'_D - Q'_S$) marks—is the balance-of-payments surplus.*

dervalued currency often is reluctant to increase the price of its currency because of political pressures by its exporters (and their workers) who point out that such a revaluation would make the country's goods more expensive in foreign markets and thus would reduce its exports. Consequently, when exchange rates were fixed, countries with undervalued currencies were less likely to adjust their exchange rates than countries with overvalued currencies.

MEASURING DEFICITS AND SURPLUSES

If we are given the demand and supply curves for a country's currency, it is a simple matter to determine the deficit or surplus in its balance of payments. All that we have to do is subtract the quantity demanded of the currency from the quantity supplied. However, since we do not observe these demand and supply curves in the real world, this method of determining the deficit or surplus, while fine in principle, is not practical. The available data show only the total amount of the country's currency bought and the total amount of the country's currency sold. Since each unit of the country's currency that is bought must also be sold, it is evident that the total amount bought must equal the total amount sold. Given that this is the case, how can one identify and measure a balance-of-payments deficit or surplus?

The answer lies in the transactions of the country's central bank. If the central bank's purchases or sales of currency make up for the difference between the quantity demanded and the quantity supplied, it will purchase currency if there is a balance-of-payments deficit and sell currency if there is a balance-of-payments surplus. The amount it purchases or sells measures the size of the deficit or surplus. In other words, the official transactions of this country's government with other governments are used to measure the deficit or surplus. Roughly speaking, this is how a balance-of-payments deficit or surplus has been measured. However, beginning in May 1976, the U.S. government stopped publishing figures on the deficit or surplus in our balance of payments. Under the current regime of flexible exchange rates, changes in demand and supply for foreign exchange generally show up as changes in exchange rates, rather than in the transactions of the central bank. Thus figures regarding the deficit or surplus in our balance of payments have lost much of their previous meaning.

The Balance-of-Payments Accounts

Although the U.S. government no longer calculates the deficit or surplus in our balance of payments, it does publish our **balance-of-payments accounts,** which are an important record of *the flow of payments between the United States and other countries.* There are two types of items in the balance-of-payments accounts: debit items and credit items. **Debit items** are items for which we must pay foreigners—items that use up our foreign currency. **Credit items** are items for which we are paid by foreigners—items that provide us with a stock of foreign currency. If a French importer buys an American car to sell in France, this is a credit item in the U.S. balance-of-payments accounts because a foreigner—the French importer—

Table 22.1

UNITED STATES BALANCE-OF-PAYMENTS ACCOUNTS, 1983

	Credit	Debit
	(billions of dollars)	
Current Account		
Merchandise exports	200	
Merchandise imports		261
Net travel and transportation receipts		5
Investment income (and other services)	32	
Net military transactions	1	
Unilateral transfers		9
Capital account		
Change in U.S. assets abroad		48
Change in foreign assets in U.S.	76	
Change in U.S. reserve assets		1
Change in foreign official assets in the U.S.	5	
Statistical discrepancy	9	
Total[a]	324	324

Balance on goods and services = $233 billion − $266 billion = −$33 billion
Balance on current account = $233 billion − $275 billion = −$42 billion

[a] Because of rounding, numbers may not sum to total.

must pay us for the car. On the other hand, if an American importer buys some French wine to sell in the United States, this is a debit item in the U.S. balance-of-payments accounts. We must pay the foreigner—the French winemaker—for the wine.

It is essential to understand at the outset that *the balance-of-payments accounts always balance.* The total of credit items must always equal the total of debit items, because the sum of the debit items is the total value of goods, services, and assets we received from foreigners. These goods, services, and assets must be paid for with credit items, since credit items provide the foreign currency required by foreigners. Since the debit items must be paid for by the credit items, *the sum of the credit items must equal the sum of the debit items.*

Let's consider the U.S. balance-of-payments accounts in 1983, shown in Table 22.1. Debit items are negative; credit items are positive. The entire balance-of-payments accounts are divided into two parts, the current account and the capital account, each of which is described below.

THE CURRENT ACCOUNT

The current account in Table 22.1 summarizes America's international trade in currently produced goods and services. It contains entries pertaining to six types of international transactions.

Merchandise Exports. During 1983, the United States exported about $200 billion worth of merchandise. This is a credit item since it represents payments to us by foreign purchasers of American goods.

Merchandise Imports. During 1983, the United States imported about $261 billion worth of merchandise. This is a debit item since it requires payments to manufacturers abroad.

Net Travel and Transportation Receipts. Travel and transportation services must be accounted for in the balance-of-payments accounts, since they entail payments by one country to another. When a British vessel carries our merchandise, we must pay for this service. Or when an American tourist stays at the George V Hotel in Paris, we must pay for this service—and judging from the George V's rates, pay dearly at that. You will recall from the previous section that credit items supply us with foreign currency while debit items use up our foreign currency. Thus it is clear that when foreign carriers transport our goods or people, this is a debit item, but when we carry other countries' goods or people, this is a credit item in our balance of payments. Similarly, expenditures by American tourists traveling abroad are debit items, but money spent here by foreign tourists is a credit item. Table 22.1 shows that, during 1983, the United States had a debit balance of about $5 billion with regard to travel and transportation.

Investment Income and Other Services. This item includes, among other things, the flow of profits from U.S. firms in foreign countries to their headquarters in the United States, minus the flow of profits from foreign firms in the United States to their headquarters abroad. When the Ford Motor Company's British subsidiary sends its profits home, this provides us with foreign currency, and thus is a credit item. When Ciba-Geigy's American subsidiary sends its profits to the firm's headquarters in Switzerland, this uses up our foreign currency and thus is a debit item. In addition, this item includes interest we pay foreigners for money lent to us, and interest paid to us for money we lent foreigners. Interest we pay foreigners is a debit item, since it uses up our foreign currency, while interest paid to us by foreigners is a credit item. Table 22.1 shows that, during 1983, the United States had a credit balance of about $32 billion with regard to investment income and other services.

Net Military Transactions. Besides the transactions made by private citizens, the government's transactions must be included too in our balance-of-payments accounts. The United States government supports a vast network of military bases around the world. We also engage in a host of other government activities abroad (like the Peace Corps), and all these programs affect our balance of payments. Frequently, they result in debit items since they involve payments abroad. Money spent by U.S. military authorities stationed in Wiesbaden, Germany, to buy supplies from local German companies is a debit item. However, we also earn a large amount of foreign currency by selling armaments to foreign nations; these transactions result in credit items. Table 22.1 shows that, during 1983, the United States had a credit balance of about $1 billion with regard to military transactions.

If we add up the foregoing five entries (merchandise exports, merchandise imports, net travel and transportation receipts, investment income and other services, and net military transactions), we get the so-called *balance on goods and services.* This balance, shown in Table 22.1, equaled about −$33 billion, which means that foreigners spent about $33 billion less on our goods and services than we spent on foreign goods and services.

Unilateral Transfers. This final item in the current account includes the amount that residents of the United States send abroad minus the amount that Americans residing abroad send home. If an American working in St. Louis sends part of her pay to her relatives in Italy, this is a debit item since it uses up our foreign currency. In addition, the amount that the government sends abroad for foreign aid is also counted as a unilateral transfer.

Table 22.1 shows that, during 1983, the United States had a debit balance of about $9 billion with regard to unilateral transfers.

If all six entries in the current account are totaled, we get the so-called *balance on current account*. This balance, shown in Table 22.1, equaled about −$42 billion, which means that we had a deficit of about $42 billion on current account. Any deficit of this sort must be offset by a surplus in the rest of the balance-of-payments accounts (that is, in the capital account) because, as stressed in a previous section, the total of the debit items must equal the total of the credit items.

THE CAPITAL ACCOUNT

The capital account in Table 22.1 summarizes America's international transactions associated with capital investments (but not the income from these investments, since it is included in the current account). It contains entries pertaining to four types of international transactions.

Change in U.S. Assets Abroad. When Americans buy plants in foreign countries, or purchase the securities of foreign firms, or make deposits in foreign banks, such transactions require that we use foreign currency, since we will be buying foreign assets. Thus these transactions result in debit items. During 1983, increases in U.S. *private* assets abroad resulted in a debit balance of about $43 billion, and increases in U.S. *government* assets abroad resulted in a debit balance of about $5 billion. Thus, as shown in Table 22.1, the total debit balance due to the increase in both U.S. private and government assets abroad was about $48 billion.

Change in Foreign Assets in the U.S. When Saudi Arabians buy American firms or farmland, or purchase U.S. Treasury securities, or make deposits in the Bank of America, such transactions provide us with foreign currency, since foreigners use their currency to purchase our assets. Thus these transactions result in credit items. Table 22.1 shows that, during 1983, increases in foreign assets in the U.S. resulted in a credit balance of about $76 billion.

Change in U.S. Reserve Assets. The U.S. government holds reserve assets, such as gold and foreign currencies. When we transfer some of these reserves to a foreign government, we can exchange them for dollars or foreign currencies. Thus a decrease in our reserves is a credit item. Prior to 1971, the U.S. government offset many of the debit items in its balance-of-payments accounts by transferring gold to other governments. That is, it helped to finance the deficits in its balance of payments in this way. Since 1971, the U.S. government no longer has been willing to transfer gold to foreign governments, but it has used other reserve assets such as foreign currencies. As shown in Table 22.1, there was a $1 billion increase in U.S. reserves in 1983.

Change in Foreign Official Assets in the U.S. Increases in foreign official assets in the United States are increases in dollars held by foreign governments, generally in the form of U.S. Treasury bills. Since such increases provide us in effect with foreign currency, they are credit items. For many years, they have helped in a major way to finance deficits in the U.S. balance of payments. During 1983, increases in foreign official assets in the United States resulted in a credit balance of about $5 billion.

All of the entries in both the current and capital account are subject to error. To some extent, this may be due to faulty and incomplete data collection, but a more important reason for the errors and omissions in the balance-of-payments accounts is that the United States finds it difficult to keep track of all the movements of goods, services, and money to and from other countries. Table 22.1 shows that, because of this *statistical discrepancy,* the government underestimated the credit items during 1983 by about $9 billion.

Finally, when we get down to the bottom of the balance-of-payments accounts, we find that the total of the credit items equals the total of the debit items. (Both are $324 billion.) As pointed out in a previous section, logic assures us that this equality will always prevail, since we must pay in cash or IOUs for what we get from other nations.

THE BALANCE OF TRADE

The newspapers often mention the balance of trade. The **balance of merchandise trade** refers only to a part of the balance-of-payments accounts. A nation is said to have a *favorable* balance of merchandise trade if its exports of merchandise are more than its imports of merchandise, and an *unfavorable* balance of merchandise trade if its exports of merchandise are less than its imports of merchandise. As Table 22.1 shows, the United States had an unfavorable balance of merchandise trade of about $61 billion in 1983. Until 1970, the United States generally had a favorable balance of trade, but in recent years this seldom has been the case.

Indeed, the 1983 trade deficit was a record, and it prompted considerable concern. To some extent, it was due to the strength of the dollar. Because the dollar appreciated considerably relative to other currencies in the early 1980s, American exports were expensive to foreigners and foreign imports were cheap to Americans. Also, the American economy was growing more rapidly than Europe and Japan, thus stimulating our imports.

Although the balance of merchandise trade is of interest, it tells us only part of what we want to know about a country's transactions with other countries. As shown in Table 22.1, there is much more to the balance of payments than a comparison of merchandise exports with merchandise imports. Moreover, a "favorable" balance of trade is not necessarily a good thing, since imports, not exports, contribute to a nation's standard of living.

Test Yourself

1. Suppose that the demand curve for German marks is as follows:

Quantity demanded (billions of marks)	Price (in dollars) of a mark
20	0.20
15	.30
10	.40
5	.50

Plot this demand curve on a graph. What sorts of groups, organizations, and individuals are part of the demand side of this market?

2. Suppose that the supply curve for German marks is as follows:

Quantity supplied (billions of marks)	Price (in dollars) of a mark
8	0.20
9	.30
10	.40
11	.50

Plot this supply curve on the same graph as the demand curve in Question 1. What sorts of groups, organizations, and individuals are part of the supply side of this market?

3. Based on the information in Questions 1 and 2, what is the equilibrium value of the exchange rate, if it is completely flexible? Why? Is the exchange rate between the U.S. dollar and the German mark completely flexible at present?

4. Suppose that the exchange rate is fixed, and that the price (in dollars) of a mark is set at $0.30. Based on the data in Questions 1 and 2, will the quantity of marks demanded equal the quantity supplied? What sorts of government actions will have to be taken?

Exchange Rates: Pre-World War II Experience

Now that we are familiar with a balance-of-payments deficit and surplus (and the balance-of-payments accounts), we can begin to see how various types of exchange rates have worked out. What has been our experience with the gold standard? With fixed exchange rates? With flexible exchange rates?

During the latter part of the nineteenth century, the gold standard seemed to work very well, but serious trouble developed after World War I. During the war, practically all of the warring nations went off the gold standard to keep people from hoarding gold or from sending it to neutral countries. After the war, some countries tried to re-establish the old rates of exchange. Because the wartime and postwar rates of inflation were greater in some countries than in others, under the old exchange rates the goods of some countries were underpriced and those of other countries were overpriced. According to the doctrines of David Hume, this imbalance should have been remedied by increases in the general price level in countries where goods were underpriced and by reductions in the general price level in countries where goods were overpriced. But wages and prices proved to be inflexible, and, as one would expect, it proved especially difficult to adjust them downward. When the adjustment mechanism failed to work quickly enough, the gold standard was abandoned.

During the 1930s, governments tried various schemes. This was the time of the Great Depression, and governments were trying frantically to reduce unemployment. Sometimes a government allowed the exchange rate to be flexible for a while, and when it found what seemed to be an equilibrium level, fixed the exchange rate there. Sometimes a government depreciated the value of its own currency relative to those of other countries in an attempt to increase employment by making its goods cheap to other countries. When one country adopted such policies, others retaliated, causing a reduction in international trade and lending, but little or no benefit for the country that started the fracas.

The Gold Exchange Standard

In 1944, the Allied governments sent representatives to Bretton Woods, New Hampshire, to work out a more effective system for the postwar era. It was generally agreed that competitive devaluations, such as occurred in the 1930s, should be avoided. Out of the Bretton Woods conference came the *International Monetary Fund* (IMF), which was set up to maintain a stable system of fixed exchange rates and to insure that when exchange rates had to be changed because of significant trade imbalances, disruption was minimized.

The system developed during the postwar period was generally labeled the *gold-exchange standard,* as opposed to the gold standard. Under this system, the dollar—which had by this time taken the place of the British pound as the world's key currency—was convertible (for official monetary purposes) into gold at a fixed price. And since other currencies could be converted into dollars at fixed exchange rates, other currencies were convertible indirectly into gold at a fixed price.

U.S. Balance-of-Payments Deficits, 1950–72

During the early postwar period, the gold-exchange standard worked reasonably well. However, it was not too long before problems began to develop. As noted in a previous section, when exchange rates are fixed, a U.S. balance-of-payments deficit is evidence of pressure on the dollar in foreign exchange markets. Figure 22.7 shows that, *during the period from 1950 to 1972 (the last full year when exchange rates were fixed), the United States showed a chronic deficit in its balance of payments.* This chronic deficit caused considerable uneasiness and concern, both here and abroad. Several factors were responsible for it.

Postwar Recovery of Western Europe and Japan. As the Western European and Japanese economies recovered from the devastation of World War II, they adopted new technology, and became tough competitors. To cite but one example, the Japanese were particularly adept at absorbing modern electronic technology and at producing electronic goods for civilian markets. In many areas of technology, the United States continued to enjoy a lead, but the gap seemed to be narrowing. As productivity in Western Europe and Japan rose more rapidly than ours, their costs fell relative to ours, and they were able to undersell us much more in their own markets, third markets, and sometimes even our own market.

Military and Foreign Aid. We spent enormous amounts abroad for military purposes and for foreign aid. Our military expenditures abroad were particularly high during the Vietnam War. They were about $4.5 billion in 1968 alone. Not only did this war take a heavy toll in lives and in social disruption; it also helped keep our balance of payments in deficit. Note, however, that some of our government spending abroad has involved the use of "tied" funds, which can be used only to buy American goods. Since these programs result in exports that would not otherwise be made, the elimination of some of these programs would not reduce the deficit. If the government spending were cut, the exports it financed would be cut as well.

Private Investment Abroad. American firms invested enormous amounts of money abroad. U.S. investors acquired oil refineries, assembly lines, and hundreds of other types of plants. The rate of private investment abroad increased spectacularly during the 1950s and 1960s. In the early 1950s, new American private investment abroad was about $2 billion per year; in the late 1950s over $3 billion per year; in the early 1960s, over $4 billion per year; and in the late 1960s, over $8 billion per year. The reason

Figure 22.7
Deficit or Surplus in U.S. Balance of Payments 1950–75

for this growth is fairly obvious. The markets of Western Europe (and other parts of the world) were growing rapidly and the construction of plants abroad was a profitable move. To help reduce our balance-of-payments deficit, the government introduced a voluntary program to limit such investment abroad in 1965, and made the program compulsory in 1968. (It lapsed in the 1970s.)

Inflation and Discrimination. A number of other factors, including inflation in the United States and discrimination abroad against U.S. products, also contributed to our balance-of-payments deficits. Clearly, inflation in the United States made our exports more expensive abroad. It is true that inflation in the United States was not as great as in many other countries, but in many industries, like steel, our prices rose relative to those abroad. Also, foreigners maintained various quotas, tariffs, and other devices to keep out American exports. Many of these discriminatory regulations were enacted during earlier days when such policies were more understandable than during the period under consideration.

Attempts to Eliminate the Deficits in the Early 1970s

Under a regime of fixed exchange rates, what can a country do to eliminate a balance-of-payments deficit? In general there are three routes it can take. (1) It can adjust its exchange rate. (2) It can change its price level. (3) It can adopt various kinds of controls to interfere with market forces. To illustrate each of these ways to eliminate deficits, consider the situation facing the United States in 1970. The dollar at that time was overvalued relative to other currencies, like the German mark. The situation was as shown in Figure 22.8, which contains the demand and supply curves for marks. In a free market for foreign exchange, the price (in dollars) of a German mark would have risen from the fixed exchange rate, P_F, to P_E. This would have discouraged American imports, encouraged American exports, and eliminated the U.S. balance-of-payments deficit.

Figure 22.8

"Overvaluation" of the Dollar Whereas the fixed exchange rate was only P_F dollars for a German mark, the equilibrium price was P_E dollars. Note the similarity between this diagram and Figure 22.6.

DEPRECIATE THE DOLLAR?

Thus one step the United States might have taken in 1970 to eliminate the deficit was to *depreciate the dollar.* But the United States was reluctant to depreciate its currency relative to others. Depreciation of our currency would hurt friendly nations who had been willing to hold large dollar balances. The United States wanted to discourage speculation against the dollar. And there was a chance that depreciation of the world's leading currency would seriously disrupt the entire world monetary system. Also, it must be noted that depreciation would have required the cooperation of other countries. Unless the Germans were prepared to let the mark rise in value relative to the dollar, they could stop it by also depreciating the mark.

CHANGE THE PRICE LEVEL?

A second way to eliminate the deficit was to *change the price level.* This was the sort of mechanism the gold standard used to eliminate a deficit. In a country with a chronic deficit, like the United States, the remedy would be a lowering of its general price level relative to that of other countries. This would reduce our imports and promote our exports. In contrast to the previous alternative, it would not have meant any alteration in exchange rates. However, it might well have led to a depression in the United States. Because wages and prices are very difficult to push downward, any serious attempt to reduce aggregate spending in an effort to reduce the price level would probably cut output and increase unemployment. For this reason, economists were not enthusiastic about this route to equilibrium. However, they did counsel the president to keep inflation to a minimum—for balance-of-payments reasons as well as others discussed in previous chapters. In an inflationary world, all that the United States really had to do was have a lower inflation rate than other countries, not reduce its price level.

ADOPT CONTROLS?

A third way to eliminate the deficit was to *adopt various types of controls.* For one thing, a country might impose controls over the exchange market. Thus the United States government might have required all foreign exchange received by exporters (or others) to be sold to the government, and the government might have rationed this foreign exchange among importers and others who wanted it. By so doing, the government would see that the deficit in the balance of payments was eliminated. However, this kind of scheme has many disadvantages, such as it limits freedom of choice and is difficult for the government to enforce.

Another type of government control is aimed at trade rather than the exchange markets. In this case, the government tries to influence imports and exports through quotas, tariffs, subsidies, and other such controls. The United States might have raised tariffs and imposed quotas to cut its imports, and subsidized some of its exports to increase their volume. It might also have imposed limits on the amount American tourists could spend abroad. An important difficulty with such interference with free trade is that it reduces world efficiency, as we saw in Chapter 21.

In addition, the government might have discouraged American investment abroad—and in fact it did so in various ways, including the imposition in 1963 of an "interest equalization tax" of 15 percent (later reduced to 11½ percent) on any purchase of a foreign stock or bond by an American from a foreigner. Also, in the special circumstances facing the United States, one way to eliminate the deficit in our balance of payments might have been to convince other countries to increase their share of the responsibilities for defense and foreign aid. Western Europe might have paid a larger share of the costs of maintaining a defensive shield that protects us all. The United States pressed for this for many years, with some success. Also, the United States might have tried to persuade other countries to remove discriminatory barriers to our goods. And finally, the United States might have tried to step up its rate of productivity increase and product innovation. This would have made our exports more competitive.

WHAT WAS DONE?

In fact, what did the United States do in the early 1970s to eliminate the deficit in its balance of payments? As you might expect, we adopted many of the measures described above. In 1971, we depreciated the dollar relative to all major foreign currencies. On the average, the dollar was depreciated by about 10 to 15 percent. Moreover, throughout the early 1970s a serious effort was made to contain inflation at home, and, for better or worse, some protectionist controls were established or continued. Also, the president's special assistant on international economic policy, Peter Peterson (later secretary of commerce), beat the drum for subsidies or encouragement for added research and development by American industry to make our exports more competitive in world markets.

Demise of the Bretton Woods System

As pointed out in the previous section, the dollar was depreciated relative to all major foreign currencies in 1971. And a new system of fixed exchange rates was approved by representatives of the major trading nations at a meeting at the Smithsonian Institution. Although President Nixon hailed the Smithsonian agreement as "the greatest international monetary agreement in the history of the world," events were to prove it unequal to the tasks it faced. In February 1973, scarcely more than a year after the agreement, the United States felt obliged to devalue the dollar again, as the outflow of dollars to other countries continued. Then, in March 1973, representatives of the major trading nations met in Paris to establish a system of fluctuating exchange rates, thus abandoning the Bretton Woods system of fixed exchange rates. This was a major break with the past, and one that was greeted with considerable apprehension as well as hope.

However, the major trading nations did not go so far as to establish completely flexible exchange rates. Instead, the float was to be managed. Central banks would step in to buy and sell their currency. Thus the United States agreed that "when necessary and desirable" it would support the value of the dollar. Also, some European countries decided to maintain fixed exchange rates among their own currencies, but to float jointly against other currencies.

Fixed versus Flexible Exchange Rates

Why, until 1973, did most countries fix their exchange rates, rather than allow them to fluctuate? One important reason was the feeling that flexible exchange rates might vary so erratically that it might be difficult to carry out normal trade. Thus American exporters of machine tools to Britain might not know what British pounds would be worth six months from now, when they would collect a debt in pounds. According to the proponents of fixed exchange rates, fluctuating rates would increase uncertainties for people and firms engaged in international trade and thus reduce the volume of such trade. Moreover, they argued that the harmful

THE INTERNATIONAL MONEY GAME

Q: During the early 1970s, what contributed to, or aggravated, an international monetary crisis?

A: It's not a what, but a who. In periods of international financial stress, speculators moved vast sums of money out of weak currencies into strong currencies, and forced the central banks to intervene in order to maintain orderly foreign exchange markets.

Q: Why did speculators do a thing like that?

A: Because it was very profitable.

Q: Who were the speculators?

A: Right after the war (World War II, that is), the "in" speculator was a small Swiss banker (sometimes referred to as a Gnome of Zurich). More recently, much of the speculation business was rumored to be centered in OPEC (Organization of Petroleum Exporting Countries). As long as the U.S. kept exchanging billions of U.S. dollars for oil, the shieks had plenty to speculate with.

International money desk at a Swiss bank, Zurich

Q: Were there other speculators?

A: Sure. Multinational corporations.

Q: I thought companies dealt in foreign exchange only to cover costs of their imports. Aren't they the honest merchants?

A: Some do. Most small companies deal in foreign exchange only when converting receipts from an overseas customer into dollars. But a select group of multinationals have come to be major powers in foreign exchange markets. The biggest 200 American-based MNFs (multinational firms) own huge amounts of cash, and even larger amounts of inventories and receivables. Their holdings are large even when compared with the reserves of individual nations. During the currency crises of the sixties, these MNFs learned that it was not wise to be caught in pounds sterling or dollars, and so began to move money on a large scale.

Q: By ship?

A: No, by prepayment and borrowings. For example, branches of a multinational firm continuously buy and sell from each other. If a treasurer saw an appreciation of the mark coming on, he urged the German subsidiaries to pay its sister subsidiaries as slowly as possible.

Q: It sounds unpatriotic.

A: Depends on whom you ask. The treasurer would claim enlightened profit-maximizing. Isn't that what you want a firm to do?

E.A.

effects of speculation over exchange rates would increase if exchange rates were flexible, because speculators could push a currency's exchange rate up or down, and destabilize the exchange market. Further, they argued that flexible exchange rates might promote more rapid inflation, because countries would be less affected by balance-of-payments discipline.

Many economists disagreed, feeling that flexible exchange rates would work better. They asked why flexible prices are used and trusted in other areas of the economy, but not in connection with foreign exchange. They pointed out that a country would have more autonomy in formulating its fiscal and monetary policy if exchange rates were flexible, and they claimed that speculation regarding exchange rates would not be destabilizing. But until 1973, the advocates of flexible exchange rates persuaded few of the world's central bankers and policy makers.

How Well Have Floating Exchange Rates Worked?

From 1973 to date, exchange rates have been flexible, not fixed. As noted above, there has been some intervention by central banks to keep the movement of exchange rates between broad bounds, but this intervention generally has not been very great. The result has been considerable volatility in exchange rates. The exchange rate between the dollar and the German mark has sometimes varied by 2 percent or more from one day to the next, and by 15 percent or more over a period of several months.

Unquestionably, the variations in exchange rates, some of which are erratic and without fundamental economic significance, have made international transactions more difficult. Thus Renault, the French auto manufacturer, is reported to have hesitated to launch an export drive into the U.S. market because of the erratic behavior of the dollar-franc exchange rate. However, businesses seem to have coped rather successfully with such exchange rate variation, as reflected in the following statement in late 1975 by the National Foreign Trade Council: "[Floating exchange rates have] . . . responded well to the shocks of the fast-moving developments of recent years, . . . [although] at times business has been unfavorably affected by sharp fluctuations of key currencies."

One of the greatest "shocks" of recent years was the increase in oil prices at the beginning of 1974. This sharp price increase meant that oil-importing countries suddenly had to pay unprecedented bills to the oil-producing countries, with the result that massive strain was put on the international financial system. Although the difficulties were not surmounted easily, the new system of floating exchange rates seemed to show the required resilience to overcome this crisis.

A crisis of another sort occurred in 1977 and 1978, when the value of the dollar dropped dramatically. Between September 1977 and March 1978, and again between June and October 1978, the value of the dollar fell by about 10 percent, due in part to our unfavorable balance of trade (because we pursued a more expansionary policy than our major trading partners) and to interest rates being higher abroad than here.

During the early 1980s, the dollar staged a very impressive rebound. Between 1980 and 1983, its value rose by about 50 percent. In large part, this was due to the fact that inflation in the U.S. seemed to have moderated, real interest rates here were higher than in other countries (partly the result of huge government borrowing to finance its deficits), and the rates of return from investments here seemed relatively high. This marked appreciation of the dollar hurt American exporters, since their goods became very expensive to foreigners, but it helped to keep a lid on inflation, since imported goods were relatively cheap, and many American firms could not raise their own prices very much without losing business to imported goods.

Although there is no indication that flexible exchange rates will be forsaken (and fixed exchange rates restored), some observers feel that central banks should intervene to a greater extent to influence exchange rates. In September 1985, the U.S., Britain, France, Germany, and Japan agreed to intervene to help bring down the value of the dollar.

The International Monetary Fund

Bretton Woods, New Hampshire

Having described our experience with the gold standard, fixed exchange rates, and flexible exchange rates, we must look more closely at the role of the International Monetary Fund. As pointed out above, representatives of 16 countries met in 1944 in Bretton Woods, New Hampshire, to try to establish a new international monetary system. Out of these historic conferences came a system that survived—with some crises and changes—for almost 30 years. A cornerstone of this system was the International Monetary Fund (IMF), established by 40 nations to insure reasonable stability of exchange rates. The Fund was composed initially of about $30 billion of gold and currency, contributed by the member countries. It has been enlarged greatly since then, and membership has grown to over 100 countries.

THE IMF UNDER FIXED EXCHANGE RATES

The IMF had three purposes. First, it provided a permanent mechanism for consultation by various countries on international financial problems. Second, it tried to promote the stability of exchange rates and to avoid competitive depreciation of currencies. Third, it was empowered to make temporary loans to member countries to give them time to correct disequilibria in their balances of payments, thus promoting smoother international financial adjustments.

Note that the Fund was built on a philosophy of *fixed* exchange rates. The men who met at Bretton Woods were impressed with the problems of flexible exchange rates, at least as they were used in the 1930s, and agreed that exchange rates should be reasonably stable. Of course, they recognized that from time to time changes in certain exchange rates would be required. (Among the people at Bretton Woods was John Maynard Keynes, which suggests that the conferees were hardly financial babes in the woods.) But changes in exchange rates should, they felt, be made only in response to persistent disequilibria. In this respect, the spirit behind the IMF differed substantially from the old gold standard. Whereas the IMF recognized that exchange rates should sometimes change, the gold standard emphasized exchange stability under all circumstances.

THE IMF UNDER FLEXIBLE EXCHANGE RATES

The role of the IMF in the international monetary system had to be altered considerably when flexible exchange rates were adopted. In 1976, the IMF Board of Governors adopted an amendment to the IMF Articles of Agreement. This amendment formalized a number of major changes in the functioning of the IMF. To a considerable extent, it ratified the changes that already had occurred.

Specifically, this amendment permitted each country belonging to the IMF to choose its own preferred exchange-rate arrangement. A country could allow the value of its currency to be determined entirely by supply and demand. Or it could fix the exchange rate between its currency and that of some other country. Or it could adopt some other arrangement. All that the country had to undertake to do was to foster orderly economic and financial conditions and to avoid preventing the effective adjustment of balance-of-payments problems. Although the reintroduction of a system of "stable but adjustable" exchange rates was mentioned as a possibility in the amendment, such a change would require a "high majority" of the voting power and could be vetoed by the United States (which has 20 percent of the votes).

SDRs AND GOLD

The leading Western economic powers agreed in 1968 to allow the International Monetary Fund to establish *special drawing rights (SDRs)*. These SDRs were a new kind of reserve asset, which could be used by member countries much as they used gold in the past. New SDRs can be created by a vote of 85 percent of the IMF's membership. Unlike garden-variety IMF loans, SDRs do not have to be repaid to the IMF, but their allocation among countries must be in accord with IMF quotas. SDRs are sometimes called "paper gold."

"Paper gold" is backed by nothing other than the member countries' pledge to accept it in exchange for currencies. It is much like our domestic money—which, as we know from Chapter 14, is not convertible into gold or silver. In 1970, over $3 billion worth of "paper gold" was created by the IMF. The United States received about $900 million, the United Kingdom received about $400 million, and France and Germany about $200 million each. More SDRs were issued in later years. For example, by early 1976 about $7.7 billion of SDRs had been created, of which the United States got about $2.8 billion.

The trend during the 1970s was toward a declining role for gold in the international monetary system. In 1976, it was agreed that gold would no longer be a medium of settlement in International Monetary Fund transactions. But it is still possible for countries to trade in gold. There is now a free market where anyone can buy or sell gold. The price of gold varies substantially from month to month. Since gold is viewed by many as a hedge against inflation, its price tends to rise as fears of inflation mount. While many economists favor the expanded reliance on SDRs, many of the world's bankers are suspicious of "paper gold."

International Lending

Before concluding this chapter, we must discuss international capital movements in somewhat more detail. The factors underlying international transactions with regard to goods and services are clear enough. We saw in

---

Example 22.1   Return to the Gold Standard?

Confronted by very high rates of inflation, the United States in the late 1970s and early 1980s looked hard for a remedy. To some, the answer seemed to be a return to the gold standard. In 1981, President Reagan appointed an official commission to examine the potential role of gold in the domestic and international monetary system. The commission included congressmen, senators, businessmen, and government officials, including Secretary of the Treasury Donald Regan. Many groups, including President Reagan's Council of Economic Advisers, were skeptical about the advantages of a return to the gold standard.

(a) Did the gold standard result in price stability in the United States? (b) What if we returned to the gold standard and set a price for gold that was too low? (c) What if we returned to the gold standard and set a price that was too high? (d) How could the public be reasonably sure that the gold standard, if adopted, would not be abandoned again? (e) If they couldn't be sure, does this matter?

SOLUTION

(a) No. According to the available historical evidence, the Wholesale Price Index varied as follows during 1814 to 1920:

Year	Price Level (1910–14 = 100)
1814	182
1843	75
1865	185
1889	81
1920	225

(b) As pointed out by Henry Wallich, a member of the commission, the United States would lose gold, our money supply would contract, and (if the contraction were too great), there might be very large unemployment. (c) We would have to buy large quantities of gold, our money supply would increase, and serious inflation might result. The Soviet Union and South Africa, two principal gold producers, would benefit. (d) It is hard to see how they could be sure of this. A Congress that implements a gold standard one year can terminate it the next. Even if the gold standard were put in the constitution, it could be changed. (e) Yes. For example, if the government's gold stock fell, the public might view this as meaning that the gold standard would be abandoned or that the price of gold would be increased. Thus speculators might demand gold, causing the government's gold stock to fall further, a serious recession might ensue, and there might be pressure to abandon the gold standard.*

* For further discussion, see E. Bernstein, "Back to the Gold Standard?," *Brookings Bulletin,* Fall 1980; L. Lehrman and H. Wallich, "Should We (and Could We) Return to the Gold Standard?," *New York Times,* September 6, 1981; and R. Penner, "In the Wings, the Gold Standard," *New York Times,* September 13, 1981.

the previous chapter why countries find it profitable to import and export goods and services. But we need to know more about the reasons why nations lend to one another. What factors are responsible for the fact (shown vividly in the balance-of-payments accounts in Table 22.1) that one nation invests in another?

If the world were free of political problems and nationalist fervor, the answer would be easy. Because different parts of the world are endowed with different amounts and qualities of land and other resources, and have different population densities and amounts of capital, the rate of return to be derived from investments will vary from place to place. Consequently, nations where savings rates are high and investment opportunities are relatively poor will invest their capital in nations where the investment opportunities are better.

Such international lending helps both the lender and the borrower. The lender receives a higher rate of return than it would otherwise, and the borrower gains by having more capital to work with, so that the borrower's output and wages are higher than they would be otherwise. So long as the lender receives a relatively high return from the borrowing country, there is no reason why it should ask for repayment. It may continue to lend money to the borrowing country for years and years. England, for instance, was a net lender to the United States for about a century. To pay interest to the lender, the borrowing country must sell the lender more goods than it buys, thus building up a credit in its balance of payments that it can use to finance the interest, which is a debit item.

But the world is not free of political problems and nationalist fervor. Wars occur, governments topple, devastating inflations take place, property is confiscated. Only a fool contemplates investment in another country without taking some account of these and other risks; and because these risks are present, international lending that would otherwise be profitable and beneficial—and would take place if only economic considerations were involved—is sometimes stymied. Suppose that you had $1 million to invest, and that you could invest it at 15 percent interest in a country with an unstable government, where the chances were substantial that your investment would be confiscated and that you would get back only a fraction of the $1 million. Would you make the loan? Maybe; maybe not. Unfortunately, such risks discourage many international loans that would otherwise be advantageous to both lender and borrower.

Test Yourself

1. During the 1950s and 1960s, the British government reacted to deficits in its balance of payments by adopting deflationary monetary and fiscal policies (temporarily at least). Was this sensible? Why or why not?

2. Under what circumstances would you be willing to invest $10,000 (if you had $10,000) in (a) El Salvador, (b) Poland, (c) Japan, (d) India? What interest rate would you expect? What guarantees would you expect? Why?

3. "Under floating exchange rates, reserves play a much less important role than under fixed exchange rates." What does this mean? Do you agree? Why or why not?

4. Country X has been confronted with a balance-of-payments deficit. Explain how it can eliminate this deficit by: (a) changing its exchange rate, (b) changing its price level, (c) adopting controls.

Summary

1. An important difference between international business transactions and business transactions within a country is that international business transactions involve more than one currency. The exchange rate is the number of units of one currency that exchanges for a unit of another currency.

2. Before the 1930s, many major countries were on the gold standard, which meant that their currency was convertible into a certain amount of gold, and that the relative gold content of currencies determined exchange rates.

3. From 1945 to 1973, when exchange rates became more flexible, most exchange rates were fixed by government action and international agreement. They were allowed to vary slightly, but only slightly, about the official rate.

4. If exchange rates are fixed, the amount of a foreign currency demanded may not equal the amount supplied. To maintain exchange rates at the official levels, governments enter the market and buy and sell their currencies as needed. They also intervene by curbing imports, limiting foreign travel, and other measures.

5. Under a system of fixed exchange rates, a country will have a balance-of-payments deficit if its currency is overvalued and a balance-of-payments surplus if its currency is undervalued. A balance-of-payments deficit is the difference between the quantity supplied and quantity demanded of the currency. A balance-of-payments surplus is the difference between the quantity demanded and quantity supplied of the currency.

6. The United States experienced a chronic balance-of-payments deficit during the 1950s, 1960s, and 1970s. This deficit—the result of the growing productivity of other economies, our large investments abroad, and our military and foreign aid expenditures abroad—was financed by reductions in our gold stock and by foreigners' acceptance of our short-term debt. In 1973, the system of fixed exchange rates was abandoned.

7. Under a system of flexible exchange rates, the market for foreign exchange functions like any other free market, the exchange rate being determined by supply and demand. Under such a system, exchange rates tend to move in a way that removes imbalances among countries in exports and imports. The price of a country's currency tends to fall (rise) if its inflation rate and growth rate are relatively high (low) or if its interest rate is relatively low (high).

8. A country's balance-of-payments accounts measure the flow of payments between it and other countries. Debit items result in a demand for foreign currency, whereas credit items supply foreign currency. The total of the debit items must equal the total of the credit items because the total of the debit items is the total amount of goods, services, and assets we received from foreigners, and these goods, services, and assets must be paid for with credit items.

9. The balance of merchandise trade refers only to part of the balance of payments. A nation is said to have a favorable (unfavorable) balance of merchandise trade if its exports of merchandise exceed (are less than) its imports of merchandise. During the early 1980s, the United States had a very unfavorable balance of merchandise trade.

Concepts for Review

Exchange rate
Gold standard
Appreciation
Depreciation
Devaluation of currency
Balance-of-payments
  deficit

Balance-of-payments
  surplus
Balance-of-payments
  accounts
Debit items
Credit items
Balance of
  merchandise trade

International
  Monetary Fund
Gold exchange
  standard
Special drawing
  rights (SDRs)

CHAPTER 23

The Less Developed Countries

Fresh from a raid on the well-stocked family refrigerator or comfortably placed in front of a television set, the average American finds it difficult to believe that hunger is a major problem in the world. Yet it is. The industrialized countries—like the United States, Western Europe, Japan, and the USSR—are really just rich little islands surrounded by seas of poverty in Asia, Africa, and much of Latin America. This chapter deals with the problems of these so-called "less developed countries" (LDCs): the poor countries of the world. We take up several questions. Which countries are poor and why? How badly do they need additional capital? How great is the danger of overpopulation? To what extent do they lack modern technology? How can they stimulate their rate of economic growth? What can the United States do to help them? These questions are crucial, both to the people in the less developed countries and to us.

Less Developed Countries: Definition and Characteristics

WHAT IS A LESS DEVELOPED COUNTRY?

Economics abounds with clumsy terms. A profession responsible for cross elasticity of demand and average propensity to consume cannot claim a prize for elegant language. The term *less developed country* is not a model of clarity. For a country to be less developed it must be poor, but *how* poor? Any answer has to be arbitrary. We shall define any country with a per capita income of under $3,000 (1975 dollars) as less developed. Although the

Table 23.1
COUNTRIES CLASSIFIED BY LEVEL OF PER CAPITA INCOME, 1983[A]

A. *Countries with per capita income of $3,000 or more*

Australia	Finland	Luxembourg	Sweden
Austria	France	Netherlands	Switzerland
Belgium	Germany	New Zealand	United Kingdom
Canada	Iceland	Norway	United States
Denmark	Japan	Soviet Union	

B. *Countries with per capita income of $1,000 to $2,999*

Algeria	Congo	Mexico	Paraguay
Bolivia	Jamaica	Morocco	Peru
Brazil	Korea	Nicaragua	Syria
China	Malaysia	Panama	Turkey

C. *Countries with per capita income of less than $1,000*

Afghanistan	Ethiopia	Kenya	Sudan
Bangladesh	Ghana	Madagascar	Tanzania
Burma	Haiti	Nepal	Uganda
Chad	India	Pakistan	Zaire
El Salvador	Indonesia	Sri Lanka	Zambia

[a] Where 1983 figures are not yet published, the most recent available data are used. Note that all figures are expressed in 1975 dollars.

Source: Calculations by Irving Kravis, Alan Heston, and Robert Summers, University of Pennsylvania.

$3,000 cutoff point is arbitrary, it certainly is low enough so that any country unfortunate enough to qualify is most certainly poor.[1]

Table 23.1 shows that many countries have a per capita income of under $3,000. Thus much of the world is, by this definition, less developed. Indeed, the staggering fact is that well over half of the world's population lives in the less developed countries. Indeed, hundreds of millions of people live in countries where per capita income is less than $1,000.

Imagine what life might be like if you grew up in a country with per capita income of less than $1,000 per year. Chances are that you would be illiterate. You would probably work on a farm with meager tools and little technology. You would have few possessions (and sometimes only enough food to keep body and soul together) and be likely to die young.

The unpleasant fact is that this harsh existence is the lot of a great many earth dwellers. This does not mean that the less developed countries do not have rich citizens. Indeed they do. But the rich are a tiny minority surrounded by masses of poor people. Nor does it mean that many of these people do not live in cities. Bombay is a city that is the home of over 4 million, most of them poor.

NATIONALISM, RISING EXPECTATIONS, AND A PERSISTENT GAP

It must also be recognized that many of the less developed countries have gained their political independence in recent years. Before World War II,

[1] The figures in Table 23.1 are based on the calculations of Irving Kravis, Alan Heston, and Robert Summers of the University of Pennsylvania. These figures are not comparable with many of the other per capita income figures in this book, but the differences in concept need not concern us here. The important point is that these figures are designed to be comparable from one country to another in Table 23.1.

Table 23.2

ANNUAL RATE OF GROWTH OF
INDUSTRIAL PRODUCTION, 1976–83

Less developed country	Annual growth rate
Brazil	− 0.6
Chile	2.7
India	4.4
Malaysia	5.8
Mexico	4.5
Pakistan	10.7
Philippines	5.5
South Korea	11.4
Tunisia	7.2
Zimbabwe	1.9
Average	5.3

Source: United Nations. For
Pakistan and Philippines, the data
pertain to 1976–82.

the major European powers had substantial empires. The British had colonies all over the globe. In the postwar period, many countries have achieved independence. These new countries are often fiercely nationalistic. They resent what they regard as exploitation at the hands of the former European colonists and demand power and status. Although weak individually, together they represent a force that must be reckoned with.

Moreover, because of better communications and altered religious and cultural beliefs, the expectations and demands of people in less developed countries have changed enormously. Years ago, they were more likely to accept a life of privation and want, since their eye was on the next world. Now the emphasis has shifted to this world, and to material comforts—and getting them quickly. People in less developed countries have become aware of the high standards of living in the industrialized societies, and they want to catch up as fast as they can.

Although the available data on the less developed countries are not as accurate as one would like, these countries seem to have increased their per capita output in recent years. As Table 23.2 shows, the average rate of growth of industrial production in 10 major less developed countries was about 5 percent per year during 1976–83. *But the gap between income per capita in the less developed countries and in the developed countries has not been decreasing appreciably in recent decades.* This is a disturbing fact. Apparently, the gap between rich and poor will not decrease, unless recent trends are altered.

A CLOSER LOOK AT THE LESS DEVELOPED COUNTRIES

The less developed countries vary enormously. Some, like China, are huge; others, like Paraguay, are small. Some, like Taiwan, have lots of people jammed into every square mile of land; others, like Brazil, have relatively few people spread over lots of land. Some, like Iraq, have important natural resources (notably oil); others have few resources. Some, like India, have had great civilizations many, many centuries old; others have had ruder histories. Nonetheless, although it is not easy to generalize about the less developed countries, many of them, besides suffering from relatively low productivity, have the following characteristics.

Stress on Agriculture. The less developed countries generally devote most of their resources to food production. Agriculture is by far their largest industry. This contrasts markedly with industrialized countries like the United States, where only a small percentage of output is food. Moreover, food makes up most of the goods consumed in less developed countries. They are so poor that the typical family has very little besides food, a crude dwelling, some simple clothing, and other such necessities.

Dual Economy. Many less developed countries have two economies, existing side by side. One of these is a **market-oriented economy** much like that in developed countries. This economy is generally found in the big cities, where there may be some modern manufacturing plants, as well as government agencies, wholesale and retail outlets, and services for the small number of rich people in the country. Coexisting with this relatively modern economy is a **subsistence economy** based largely on barter, innocent of all but the crudest technology and capable of producing little more—and sometimes less—than a subsistence wage for the inhabitants.

This subsistence economy often includes most of the rural areas. It has little or no capital, few decent roads, only the most rudimentary communications. Unfortunately, this is the economy in which the bulk of the population exists.

Political Problems. Some of the less developed countries have relatively weak, unstable governments. Thus the climate for long-term investment and planning is relatively poor in such countries. Moreover, some governments are controlled by a small group of wealthy citizens or by other groups with a vested interest in resisting social change. Corruption among government officials is encountered too often, and honest officials are sometimes not very well trained or experienced in their duties. To some extent these problems stem from the relative youth of many of these countries. But whatever the reasons, they hamper the effect of government on economic development.

Income Inequality. Most of the less developed countries have a relatively high degree of income inequality. Indeed, there is much more income inequality than in the industrialized countries. Typically, a few landowners or industrialists in a less developed country are rich, sometimes enormously rich. But all outside this tiny group are likely to be very poor. The middle class, so important in the industrialized countries, is very small in most less developed countries.

Barriers to Development and the Need for Capital Formation

Why are the less developed economies so poor, and what can they do to raise their income levels? These are very difficult questions, both because the answers vary from country to country and because the answers for any single country are hard to determine. A variety of factors generally is responsible for a country's poverty, and these factors are so intermeshed that it is difficult to tell which are most important. Nonetheless, certain factors stand out; among these is the lack of capital in less developed countries.

Without exception, the people in the less developed countries have had relatively little capital to work with. There have been few factories, machine tools, roads, tractors, power plants, miles of railroad, and so on. If you visited one of these countries, you would be struck by the absence of mechanical aids to production. Workers use their hands, legs, and simple tools, often as their ancestors did long ago.

There are several reasons why the less developed countries have not accumulated much capital. First, a country must usually reduce consumption to accumulate capital, but for the less developed countries, with their very low income levels, a reduction in consumption can be painful. Equally important, much of the saving that does go on in less developed countries is not utilized very effectively. Second, there are important barriers to domestic investment, such as the smallness of local markets, the lack of skilled labor, and the lack of qualified entrepreneurs (faced with the right incentives) who are willing and able to take the risks involved in carrying out investment projects. Third, fear that property will be confis-

Tobacco farming in Paraguay

Table 23.3

PERCENTAGE INCREASE OF THE
DOMESTIC PRICE LEVEL, 1970–83

Country	Percent increase
Brazil	11,442
Colombia	1,205
Egypt[a]	210
Ghana	17,307
India	189
Malaysia	20
Mexico[a]	1,617
Pakistan	61
Peru	8,480
Philippines	91
South Korea	506
Sri Lanka	243
Thailand	208
Turkey	3,525
Average	3,222

[a] The data pertain to 1970-82, not 1970-83.

Source: See Table 23.2. Note that these figures show the percentage increase over the entire period, not the average annual increase.

cated deters industrialized countries from investing in the less developed countries. As we pointed out above, many of the less developed countries are relatively young nations, filled with nationalistic fervor and fearful of becoming economically dependent. They are suspicious of foreign investment in their countries—and in some cases are quite capable of confiscating foreign-owned property. Needless to say, this does not make foreigners particularly anxious to invest in some of them.

METHODS TO INCREASE INVESTMENT

Recognizing their need for additional capital, the less developed countries have used three principal methods to increase investment. First, they have *taxed away part of the nation's resources and used them for investment purposes or made them available to private investors.* Second, they have tried to *mobilize "surplus labor" from agriculture to carry out investment projects.* Third, they have *increased government spending on investment projects without increasing taxes, thus producing inflation.* Although effective within limits, each of these methods has important limitations. Taxes may dull incentives and in any event are often evaded; "surplus labor" is difficult to transfer and utilize; and a little inflation may soon develop into a big inflation. (As shown in Table 23.3, the rate of inflation in some less developed countries has been impressive indeed.) Besides these three methods, a country can *use **foreign aid** to increase investment.* It too has its problems and limitations, but it is hard to see how many less developed countries can scrape up the capital they need without it.

Methods of this sort have enabled many less developed countries to increase the proportion of their national output devoted to capital formation. For example, Table 23.4 shows that in major LDCs the average proportion of national output devoted to capital formation was about 21 percent in

Table 23.4

GROSS FIXED CAPITAL FORMATION AS A PERCENTAGE OF NATIONAL PRODUCT, 1982[a]

Less developed countries		Developed countries	
Country	Percentage	Country	Percentage
Brazil	19	France	21
Colombia	18	Germany	21
Egypt	27	Italy	19
Ghana	3	Japan	30
India	20	United Kingdom	15
Malaysia	36	United States	15
Mexico	22	Average	20
Pakistan	15		
Peru	18		
Philippines	26		
Sri Lanka	29		
Thailand	21		
Turkey	19		
Average	21		

[a] Where 1982 figures are unavailable, these data pertain to 1981, or whatever is the latest year for which data are given.

Source: United Nations.

1982 (whereas it was less than 10 percent in 1950). This proportion is about the same as in the developed countries, where it averaged about 20 percent in 1982. Needless to say, these figures are very rough, and not too much reliance should be placed on them. But they do indicate that the less developed countries are progressing in their attempts to increase their rate of capital formation.

The Population Explosion

Another very important reason why per capita income is so low in some (but by no means all) less developed countries is that they suffer from overpopulation. Many less developed countries have sizably increased their total output. In Latin America, Africa, and Southeast Asia, it may have grown at about 5 percent per year in some recent years. If population in these areas had remained approximately constant, output per capita would also have increased at about 5 percent per year. But population has not remained constant. It has grown at almost 3 percent per year, so that output per capita has increased at only about 2 percent per year.

Table 23.5 shows the rate of population growth in a variety of less developed countries, as well as some major developed countries. The rate has been higher, without exception, in the less developed countries than in the developed ones. The most important reason is that modern methods of preventing and curing diseases have been introduced into the LDCs, thus reducing the death rate, particularly among children. It used to be that,

Table 23.5

ANNUAL RATES OF GROWTH OF POPULATION, LESS DEVELOPED AND DEVELOPED COUNTRIES, 1950–67 AND 1970–80 (PERCENTAGES)

Less developed countries			*Developed countries*		
Country	*1950–67*	*1970–80*	*Country*	*1950–67*	*1970–80*
Brazil	3.1	2.9	France	1.1	0.6
Colombia	3.2	2.8	Germany	1.2	0.1
Egypt	2.5	2.3	Italy	0.7	0.6
Ghana	2.7	2.9	Japan	1.1	1.2
India	2.2	2.1	United Kingdom	0.5	0.1
Malaysia	3.0	2.6	United States	1.6	1.1
Mexico	3.3	3.6	Average	1.0	0.6
Pakistan	2.4	3.1			
Peru	2.6	2.8			
Philippines	3.2	2.7			
South Korea	2.8	1.7			
Sri Lanka	2.5	1.7			
Taiwan	3.1	n.a.			
Thailand	3.0	2.7			
Turkey	2.7	2.4			
Average	2.8	2.6			

Source: A. Madison, *Economic Progress and Policy in Developing Countries,* New York: Norton, 1970; and United Nations.

although the birth rate in the less developed countries was higher than in the developed countries, the death rate was also higher, so that the rate of population growth was about the same in the less developed countries as in the developed ones. But in recent years, the death rate in the LDCs has been reduced by better control of malaria and other diseases, whereas the birth rate has remained high. The result has been a ***population explosion.*** Thus in parts of Latin America the population is doubling every 20 years.

This growth of sheer numbers, which recalls the work of Thomas Malthus (Chapter 19), is only part of the problem. The populations of the less developed countries also tend to be illiterate and ill-nourished. Thus they do not have the skills required to absorb much modern technology. In addition, many workers have little or nothing to do. They live with their relatives and occasionally hold a job. Although they may not be included in the official unemployment figures, they represent a case of *disguised unemployment.* In sum, the population of many less developed countries is large (relative to the available capital and natural resources), fast-growing, of relatively poor economic quality, and poorly utilized.

POLICY RESPONSES TO POPULATION PROBLEMS

The less developed countries have responded to the population explosion in at least two ways. Where birth control is opposed on religious or cultural grounds, the LDCs often concentrate on the widespread unemployment that results from population increase. The rapidly expanding labor force cannot be employed productively in agriculture; since there is already a surplus of farm labor in many LDCs, and the capital stock is not increasing rapidly enough to employ the growing numbers in industry. Governments faced with serious unemployment of this sort often are induced to *create public works programs and other projects to make jobs, even if these projects do not really promote economic growth.*

The LDCs have also responded to the population explosion by *attempting to lower the birth rate through the diffusion of contraceptive devices and other birth control techniques.* In many of the less developed countries, there is no religious barrier to the adoption of such techniques. Consider Hinduism, which does not frown on birth control. However, their adoption has been slow. One reason is the medical drawbacks of existing contraceptive devices. Also, there are obvious problems in communicating the necessary information to huge numbers of illiterate and often superstitious people. India has made considerable efforts to disseminate birth control information, but the problems have been enormous. Nonetheless, in some LDCs like South Korea, birth control programs seem to have had a noteworthy effect.

Besides trying to cope with or influence the growth rate of their populations, the LDCs have also tried to increase the economic quality of their human resources. In other words, *they have been investing in human capital.* Such an investment seems warranted; educational and skill levels in many less developed countries have been quite low. Table 23.6 shows that in 14 major less developed countries, the average percentage of public expenditure devoted to education is now about as high as in the United States. In many LDCs, the proportion of children in school is substantially higher

Table 23.6

PERCENTAGE OF TOTAL PUBLIC EXPENDITURE DEVOTED TO EDUCATION

Country	Percentage
Brazil	21
Colombia	21
Egypt	n.a.
Ghana	20
India	26
Malaysia	n.a.
Mexico	13
Pakistan	5
Peru	22
Philippines	9
South Korea	23
Sri Lanka	10
Thailand	21
Turkey	21
Average	18
United States	18

Source: See Table 23.2.

than it used to be. This is certainly a step in the right direction, although enrollment in school is only a crude measure of the quality of the labor force. In order to absorb and utilize, and eventually develop, modern technology, the LDCs must continue to invest in a more productive labor force.

Technology: A Crucial Factor

Still another very important reason why per capita income is so low in the less developed countries is that these countries use rudimentary and often backward technology. In previous chapters, we have seen that to a considerable extent the increase in per capita income in the developed countries has resulted from the development and application of new technology. Too often, the less developed countries still use the technology of their forefathers—the agricultural and manufacturing methods of long, long ago. Why is this the case? Why don't the less developed countries copy the advanced technology of the industrialized countries, following the examples of the Japanese and Russians, among others, who promoted their economic development during the twentieth century by copying Western technology?

PROBLEMS IN ADOPTING MODERN TECHNOLOGY

One barrier to the use of modern technology is lack of capital. Modern petroleum refining technology, to choose one, cannot be used without lots of capital, which the less developed countries find difficult to scrape up. But many technological improvements do not require substantial capital. Indeed, some technological improvements are capital-saving. That is, they reduce the amount of capital needed to produce a given amount of output.

A second reason why the less developed countries find it difficult to copy and use modern technology is that they lack both a skilled labor force and entrepreneurs. Imagine the difficulties in transplanting a complicated technology—for example, that involved in steel production—from the United States to a less developed country where there are few competent engineers, fewer experienced and resourceful managers, and practically no laborers with experience in the demanding work required to operate a modern steel plant.

Even more fundamental is the fact that much of our advanced Western technology is really not very well suited to circumstances in the less developed countries. Because the industrialized countries have relatively great amounts of capital and relatively little labor, they tend to develop and adopt technology that substitutes capital for labor. But this technology may not be appropriate for less developed countries where there is little capital and lots of labor. Thus *it is very important that the less developed countries pick and choose among the technologies available in the industrialized countries, and that they adapt these technologies to their own conditions.* Mindless attempts to ape the technologies used in the industrialized countries can result in waste and failure.

TECHNOLOGICAL CHANGE IN THE LDC'S

In agriculture, important technological advances have taken place in the less developed countries in recent years. In particular, new types of seeds have been developed, increasing the yields of wheat, rice, and other crops. Some of this research was supported by the Rockefeller and Ford Foundations. The resulting increase in agricultural productivity has been so impressive that many observers call it a *"green revolution."* There is no question that wheat and rice production has increased greatly in countries like Mexico, the Philippines, Iran, Sri Lanka, India, and Pakistan. Plenty of opportunity remains for improvements in livestock yields as well, but religious beliefs and traditional prejudices are sometimes an important barrier to change.

In industry, most of the new technology adopted by the less developed countries is taken from the developed countries. Very little attempt is being made to devise new technologies more appropriate to conditions in the less developed countries, both because the less developed countries do not have the engineering and scientific resources to develop them, and because such attempts have not been very successful in the past. In countries where the private sector finds it unprofitable to carry out research and development, government research institutes sometimes try to fill the void, but these institutes frequently devote too much of their limited resources to projects not closely related to economic development. In addition, productivity centers have been created in some countries to teach managers and supervisory personnel how to make better use of a new technology. Such centers have helped promote the diffusion of new technology in Mexico and Taiwan, among other countries.

Entrepreneurship and Social Institutions

Basic Idea #45: The majority of the world's population lives in countries with per capita income below $3,000. The gap between income per capita in the less developed countries and in the developed countries has not been decreasing appreciably in recent years. The LDCs need technology, capital, and a more effective allocation of resources. Some suffer from overpopulation.

Yet another important reason why per capita income is so low in the less developed countries is that they lack entrepreneurs and favorable social institutions. This point was noted in a previous section but needs more discussion. In some LDCs there is a rigid social structure. One "knows one's place" and stays in it, people distrust and resist change, and things are done in the time-honored way they have always been done (as far as anyone can remember). No wonder these countries lack entrepreneurs! The basic social and political institutions discourage entrepreneurship. Moreover, these institutions also are at least partially responsible for the ineffective utilization of savings, relatively high birth rates, and difficulties in transferring technology noted above.

The governments of many less developed countries are relatively weak and unstable. It is difficult enough for any government to give these countries an effective tax system and a rational program of public expenditures, including proper provision for the highways, public utilities, communications, and other "social overhead capital" they need. But the problems are made even more difficult when the government is weak, unstable, and perhaps somewhat corrupt. Further, the population's value systems and attitudes sometimes do little to promote economic development. Willingness to work hard, punctually, and regularly, and an awareness of the future benefits of present sacrifice are sometimes absent.

519

Lack of Natural Resources

Finally, it should also be pointed out that some of the LDCs have little in the way of natural resources. Moreover, technological change has made some of their resources less valuable, as in the case of synthetic rubber, which affected the market for natural rubber, an important natural resource of Malaya. But this is not true of all the less developed countries. Iraq and Indonesia, among others, are endowed with oil, which (as members of the OPEC cartel) they are using to try to promote their affluence. In any event, the skimpiness of natural resources in some less developed countries does not mean that they are condemned to poverty. Neither Denmark nor Switzerland is endowed with great natural resources, but both are prosperous.

The important thing is how a country uses what it has. International trade allows a country to compensate, at least in part, for its deficiencies in natural resources. Thus, although some of the less developed countries have been dealt a poor hand by Mother Nature, this lack alone does not explain their poverty. They might have been more prosperous with more natural resources; but even with what they have, they might have done much better.

There are several ways for them to use their resources more effectively. In many of the less developed countries, a peasant may farm several strips of land that are very small and distant from one another, working a small patch here and a small patch there. Obviously, this procedure is very inefficient. If these small plots could be put together into larger farms, output and productivity could be increased. In other LDCs, huge farms are owned by landlords and worked by tenant farmers. This system too tends to be inefficient, because the tenant farmers have little incentive to increase productivity (since the extra output will accrue to the landlord) and the landlords have little incentive to invest in new technology (since they often fear that the tenant farmers will not know how to use the new equipment).

Land reform is a very lively—indeed an explosive—issue in many less developed countries, and one of the issues the Communists try to exploit. Recall that agriculture is a very important part of the economy of most of the less developed countries. Thus the land is the major form of productive wealth. No wonder there is a bitter struggle in some countries over who is to own and work it.

The Role of Government

There are several opinions on the role the governments of the less developed countries should play in promoting economic growth. Some people go so far as to say that these countries would fare best if they allowed market forces to work with a minimum of government interference. But the less developed countries themselves generally seem to believe that such a free enterprise system would produce results too slowly, if at all. Thus the prevailing view in the less developed countries is that the government must intervene—and on a large scale.

Example 23.1   Economic Development with an Unlimited Labor Supply

According to a famous theory put forth by Nobel Laureate W. Arthur Lewis of Princeton University, the supply curve of unskilled labor in some less developed countries is a horizontal line, as shown below. In other words, unlimited supplies of unskilled labor are available in this country at the existing wage rate, $0W$. Suppose that the value of the marginal product of each amount of unskilled labor in this country is as shown below. For example, the value of the marginal product (which equals the price of the product times labor's marginal product) is L_1B when $0L_1$ workers are employed.

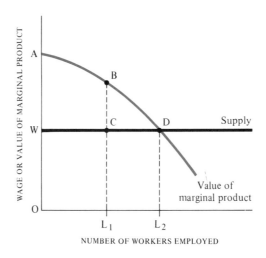

(a) How many unskilled workers will be employed in the country? (b) How much profit will be realized by hiring the $0L_1^{th}$ worker? (c) If firms invest their profit (from hiring the first, second, . . . , $0L_2^{th}$ workers) in plant and equipment, what effect will this have on the value-of-marginal-product curve? (d) If the value-of-marginal-product curve shifts, will this affect the equilibrium wage rate?

SOLUTION

(a) $0L_2$ workers, since this is the point where the supply curve intersects the value-of-marginal-product curve. So long as the value of the marginal product of an extra worker exceeds his or her wage, it pays firms to hire the extra worker. Thus extra workers will be hired up to the point where employment equals $0L_2$. (b) The profit earned from the hiring of each extra worker equals the difference between the value of this worker's marginal product and this worker's wage. Thus the profit realized by hiring the $0L_1^{th}$ worker equals L_1B minus $0W$, or CB. (c) The value-of-marginal product curve will shift to the right. With more plant and equipment, the marginal product of a particular amount of labor will increase. (d) No, because the value-of-marginal-product curve will still intersect the supply curve at a wage of $0W$.*

*For further discussion, see W. Arthur Lewis, "Economic Development with Unlimited Supplies of Labour," *The Manchester School of Economic and Social Studies,* May 1954.

In some less developed countries—China, for example—the government exercises almost complete control over the economy. Such an economy is planned. The government makes the basic decisions on what is produced, how it is produced, and who gets it. But even in the non-Communist LDCs, such as India, the government makes many decisions on what sorts of investment projects will be undertaken, and it controls foreign exchange. And, needless to say, the government has the responsibility for providing the important social overhead capital—roads, public utilities, schools, and so on —that is so badly needed.

Further, the government may also foster social and political change. As Nobel laureate Simon Kuznets has put it, "The problem of strategy is essentially the problem of how fast you can change an inadequate set of social and political institutions, without provoking a revolution internally, or losing allies and partners externally. The question is to know what institutions you want to change, and how."

Most economists would agree that the government has a very important role to play in promoting economic development. But there is a tendency to put less weight on the government's role than in the past. Experience has made it clear that some of the less developed countries are plagued by incompetent and corrupt government officials and by a plethora of bureaucratic red tape. Moreover, many governments have gone on spending sprees that have resulted in serious inflation. Even those who are very mistrustful of free markets find it difficult to put their complete faith in such governments, well-intentioned though they may be. Recent years have seen more and more emphasis on self-interest and individual action as contributors to growth. (If Adam Smith is peering down from the Great Beyond, he probably is smiling in agreement.) But this in no way denies the fact that governments have a key role to play.

Test Yourself

1. Between 1950 and 1967, the annual rate of growth of per capita national product was 5.3 percent in Taiwan, and 1.6 percent in India. Suggest as many hypotheses as you can to explain this difference.

2. In 1950, gross nonresidential investment was 9.8 percent of national product in Taiwan, and 7.4 percent of national product in India. In 1966, it was 16.7 percent of national product in Taiwan, and 13.8 percent of national product in India. Does this help to explain the difference in Question 1? Why or why not?

3. Between 1950 and 1967, the annual rate of growth of population was 3.1 percent in Taiwan and 2.2 percent in India. Does this help to explain the difference in Question 1? Why or why not?

4. Explain why the less developed countries have not adopted the advanced technology used in industrialized countries.

Balanced Growth

An important issue facing the governments of most less developed countries is the extent to which they want to maintain a balance between the agricultural and industrial sectors of the economy. That is, how much more rapidly should they expand industry than agriculture? According to some economists, less developed countries should invest heavily in industry, since the long-term trend of industrial prices is upward, relative to agricultural prices. In addition, advocates of unbalanced growth argue that the development of certain sectors of the economy will result in pressures for development elsewhere in the economy. Advocates of this approach point to the Soviet Union, which stressed industrialization in its growth strategy.

Other economists argue that industry and agriculture should be expanded at a more nearly equal rate. Successful industrial expansion requires agricultural expansion as well, because industry uses raw materials as inputs and because, as economic growth takes place, the people will demand more food. Balanced growth has other advantages. Various sectors of the economy are closely linked and an attempt to expand one sector in isolation is unlikely to succeed. Proponents of balanced growth deny that the long-term trend of industrial prices is upward, relative to agricultural prices. And to illustrate the wisdom of their approach, they cite as examples the United States and Britain, where industry and agriculture both expanded in the course of the development process.

INCREASES IN INDUSTRIALIZATION

In practically all of the 13 LDCs included in Table 23.7, industrial employment increased more rapidly than agricultural employment during the 1970s. Without question, the less developed countries expanded industry relative to agriculture. In some cases, such as India and Pakistan, it is generally agreed that more balance—more emphasis on agriculture—would have been preferable. Moreover, in many cases, the allocation of resources within industry could certainly have been improved. Countries sometimes put too

Table 23.7

AVERAGE ANNUAL RATE OF GROWTH OF PRODUCT, BY SECTOR, 1970–76

Country	Industry	Agriculture (percentage)	Wholesale and retail trade
Brazil[c]	13.8	6.2	12.3
Colombia[a]	6.3	5.4	6.1
Egypt[d]	2.8	4.0	6.6
Ghana[b]	3.0	3.6	3.2
India[b]	3.2	−0.7	2.2
Mexico	6.3	1.1	5.0
Pakistan	2.7	2.1	4.6
Peru	5.9	−0.4	6.8
Philippines	6.8	4.6	4.7
South Korea	19.3	4.9	10.7
Sri Lanka	9.1	1.7	4.5
Thailand	10.6	4.4	5.9
Turkey[a]	9.7	2.5	11.4
Average	7.7	3.0	6.5

[a] 1970–75. [b] 1970–74. [c] 1970–73. [d] 1970–71.
Source: United Nations.

much emphasis on substituting their own production—even when it is not efficient—for imports. Thus Chile prohibited the import of fully assembled cars to promote domestic production, but Chile's automobile plants have been uneconomic.

One reason why the less developed countries tend to push industrialization is that they see heavy industrialization in the wealthier countries. The United States, Western Europe, Japan, the USSR, all have lots of steel plants, oil refineries, chemical plants, and other kinds of heavy industry. It is easy for the less developed countries to jump to the conclusion that, if they want to become richer, they must become heavily industrialized too. It certainly seems sensible enough—until you think about the theory of comparative advantage. After all, if the less developed countries have a comparative advantage in areas other than heavy industry, they may do better to put more of their resources where their comparative advantage lies.

Another reason why the leaders of some less developed countries are fascinated by steel plants, airlines, and other modern industries, is that they think such industries confer prestige on their countries and themselves. Such prestige may be costly. Given their current situation, many of these countries might be well advised to invest much of their scarce resources in promoting higher productivity in agriculture, where they have a comparative advantage. We are not saying that many of these countries should not attempt to industrialize. We *are* saying that some of them have pushed industrialization too far—and that many have pushed it in uneconomic directions.

Development Planning in Less Developed Countries

The governments of many LDCs have established **development plans** to specify targets or goals for the economy. In some countries, these goals are set forth in very specific, detailed form; in others, they are more generally formulated. An important purpose of these plans is to allocate scarce resources, such as capital, in order to achieve rapid economic growth (or whatever the country's social objectives may be). Thus, in India, estimates have been made of the amount of capital that would be generated internally, as well as the capital that could be imported from abroad. Then the plan attempted to set a system of priorities for the use of this capital.

Some plans are merely window dressing, full of bold words and little else. But others are the result of careful investigation and hard work. To be useful, a plan must set realistic goals, which take proper account of the country's resources, available capital, and institutions. An unrealistically ambitious plan, if actually put in effect, is likely to lead to inflation, while a plan that is too easily satisfied is likely to mean a less than optimal rate of economic growth.

A useful plan should specify the policies to be used to reach the plan's goals, as well as the goals themselves. It should also forecast carefully how the various components of gross national product will change over time, the extent to which inflationary pressures will develop, the adequacy of the supply of foreign exchange, and the effects of the development program on various regions and parts of the population.

Planning techniques have benefited from the application of many tools of modern economic analysis, among them linear programming and input-output analysis. Linear programming can be used to determine how resources should be allocated to maximize output, and input-output analysis can determine how much capacity there must be in various industries to satisfy certain consumption targets. These modern tools have undoubt-

---

Example 23.2   The Push Toward Industrialization

Governments of less developed countries sometimes force industrialization, even though many of their people would prefer a different strategy. Suppose that a particular country's production possibilities curve is as shown below:

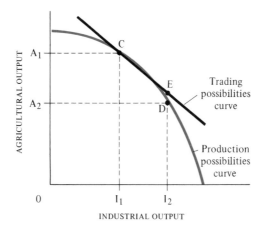

This country's government wants to increase its industrial output from $0I_1$ to $0I_2$.

(a) If its industrial output is increased in this way (and if the society remains on this production possibilities curve), what will be the cost to consumers? (b) How can the government push the society from point C to point D on the production possibilities curve? (c) Suppose that this country can trade its agricultural output for industrial goods in world markets, and that its trading possibilities curve (recall Chapter 21) is as shown above. Is there a way to reduce the cost of obtaining the extra $(0I_2 - 0I_1)$ of industrial goods? If so, what is it? (d) If the price of agricultural goods rises relative to the price of industrial goods in world markets, how will this affect the trading possibilities curve? Will it affect the cost of obtaining the extra $(0I_2 - 0I_1)$ of industrial goods? If so, how?

SOLUTION

(a) Agricultural output will have to be reduced from $0A_1$ to $0A_2$. (b) It can subsidize production of industrial goods and tax consumption of agricultural goods. Or it can intervene directly to increase industrial output and reduce agricultural output. (c) The country can move from point C to point E by trading its agricultural goods for industrial goods in world markets. Since point E lies above point D, the cost (that is, the reduction in agricultural goods) of the extra industrial goods is less than at point D. (d) It will reduce the slope of the trading possibilities curve, which will be closer to horizontal. The cost of obtaining the extra industrial goods will fall, since point E will be raised.

edly helped in formulating development plans, but their importance should not be exaggerated. It would be a great mistake to think that making a good plan is merely a job for an electronic computer.

If the plan is realistic, it can be a useful tool, but unless it is implemented properly, it will achieve very little for the economy. How well it is implemented will depend on the government's ability to marshal resources through taxation and foreign aid, to work effectively with the private sector, and to pick productive public investment projects. In some countries, like India, "the plan" has sometimes become a political symbol, but in many others, like Mexico, planning has been politically less visible. Countries where economic growth has been most rapid seem to have viewed "the plan" less as holy writ, and planning has tended to be more modest and low-keyed.

Planning in Action: The Case of India

Bokaro power station on the Konar river, India

Perhaps the best way to understand the operation of development plans is to look at the nature of a particular country's plans and how they have been fulfilled. Consider the interesting case of India, which has had a series of five-year plans.[2]

First Five-Year Plan. The First Five-Year Plan was for 1951–56. Its targets were to increase net investment in India from 5 to 6.75 percent of national income, to reduce income inequality, to cut the rate of population increase to 1 percent per year, and to lay the groundwork for a doubling of per capita output in a generation. To achieve these targets, the government relied heavily on capital formation. In particular, it sought to carry out many of the investment projects that had been discussed and planned under the British for 50 years or more. The First Five-Year Plan was accompanied by moderate growth. Per capita output grew by about 1.7 percent per year, and net investment rose from 5 to 8 percent of national income.

Second Five-Year Plan. At the beginning of 1956, the Indian Planning Commission published its Second Five-Year Plan, which called for much heavier investments—and more emphasis on investment in industry and mining, rather than agriculture and power—than the First Plan. Moreover, the Second Plan relied more heavily on deficit financing than did the First Plan, and devoted much more attention to the expansion of employment opportunities, since unemployment was a considerable problem. Unfortunately, the Second Plan ran into severe difficulties. One big problem was the loss of foreign exchange, as imports grew much more rapidly—and exports less rapidly—than expected. But perhaps more important was the fact that output did not grow as rapidly as the plan called for. By the end of the Second Five-Year Plan, all sectors of the economy, other than the service sector, were producing less than the planned targets. Nonetheless, per capita output grew about 1.8 percent per year.

---

[2] It is worthwhile emphasizing that the development strategies of *small* LDCs, because of their necessarily greater reliance on foreign trade, must be quite different from that of *large* LDCs, like India.

Inspecting maize field production during India's "green revolution"

Third Five-Year Plan. India's Third Five-Year Plan—for 1961–66—involved bigger investments and somewhat more emphasis on agriculture than the Second Plan. Responding to the fact that agricultural imports had been much higher than expected under the Second Plan, the Third Plan called for more investment in agriculture. Unfortunately, however, agricultural production during the Third Plan did not come up to expectations. Indeed, India might have experienced a serious famine in 1966 if it had not received substantial food imports from the United States. During the course of the Third Plan, India did increase the percentage of national income devoted to investment from 11 to 14 percent, but a substantial proportion of her investment was financed by foreign aid. Unfortunately, India's output grew by one-sixth, instead of the planned one-third, during the Third Plan, and there was little or no increase in per capita output.

Fourth Five-Year Plan. Although the failure of the Third Plan was due in considerable measure to India's involvement in two wars and two bad harvests, it nonetheless shook many Indians' confidence in the planning process. There was a three-year delay before the Fourth Five-Year Plan was unveiled, and its political significance was played down. The Fourth Plan shifted the emphasis to agricultural development, including irrigation and fertilizers; it stressed a large birth control program; and it called for a 5½ percent increase per year in national output, as well as further increases in investment. The Fourth Plan put somewhat more emphasis on the price system and somewhat less on detailed planning. In practice, however, the latter changes seemed to have been slow to occur.

The Late 1970s and 1980s. In 1975, when the late Prime Minister Indira Gandhi declared a national emergency, she claimed that many of the stern measures taken at that time were designed to help improve India's economic condition. She put forth a 20-Point Economic Program which emphasized the reduction of inflation, the encouragement of agriculture, and the reduction of the birth rate. Mrs. Gandhi's program of sterilization (sometimes forced) caused considerable resentment, and was one factor in her defeat at the polls in 1977. India's Janata party, which won the election over Mrs. Gandhi, promised to limit the role of centralized economic planning, and to emphasize agriculture and labor-intensive manufacturing in rural areas. In line with this objective, the Sixth Five-Year Plan, put forth in 1978, allocated 20 to 25 percent of the total investment outlay to labor-intensive industrial projects. However, many observers questioned whether the plan's targets were entirely realistic.

During the early 1980s, the Indian economy continued to experience problems. Many industrial goals were not met. India's oil import bill ate up 80 percent of its export earnings. The Indians went to the International Monetary Fund and the World Bank for massive loans. The Seventh Five-Year Plan, put forth in 1984, called for total investment of $320 billion (including $180 billion of public investment) and an annual rate of economic growth of about 5 percent. Only time will tell how much this plan will contribute to the achievement of India's economic goals.

Choosing Investment Projects in Less Developed Countries

Clearly, one of the crucial problems any less developed country must face is how the available capital should be invested. Countless investment projects could be undertaken—roads, irrigation projects, power plants, improvements in agricultural equipment, and so on. Faced with this menu of alternatives, how should a country choose?

One procedure often used is to accept projects resulting in high output per unit of capital invested. That is, projects are ranked by the ratio of the value of the output they produce to the capital they require. If a project yields $2 million worth of output per year and requires $1 million of capital, its ratio would be 2. Projects with high values of this ratio are accepted. This procedure, which is crude but sensible, is based on the correct idea that capital is the really scarce resource in many of the less developed countries. It is aimed at maximizing the output to be derived from a certain amount of capital.

However, a better technique for choosing projects is the concept of rate of return, which is used by profit-maximizing firms to choose among alternative investment opportunities. A less developed country, like a firm, can compute the rate of return from each investment opportunity. That is, it can estimate the rate of interest that will be obtained from each investment. Then it, like a firm, should choose the *projects with the highest rates of return.*[3]

In computing the rate of return from each investment project, it is necessary to attach values to the resources it uses and to the returns it produces. At first glance, it may seem adequate to use market prices of inputs and outputs as these values. Thus, if unskilled labor's market price is $.10 an hour, this would be the value attached to unskilled labor. Unfortunately, there are some important pitfalls in using market prices in this way. In particular, *market prices of inputs in the less developed countries often do not indicate social costs properly.* Although the market price of unskilled labor may be $.10 an hour, there may be lots of unskilled labor doing essentially nothing in the countryside, with the result that the social cost—the true opportunity cost—of using such labor is zero, not $.10 an hour. Moreover, *the market prices of some outputs may not indicate their social worth.* Because of tariffs and quotas, domestic prices may differ significantly from world prices, which may be closer to the appropriate price for some analyses of this sort.

Thus, when computing each project's rate of return, it is important to make proper adjustments so that inputs are valued at their social cost and outputs are valued at their social worth. This is easier said than done, but even crude adjustments in the right direction can be worthwhile.

Foreign Aid

The plight of the less developed countries is of concern to Americans, both because it is good morality and good policy to help them. From the point

Basic Idea #46: To allocate resources, an LDC, like a firm, can compute the rate of return from each investment opportunity and choose projects with relatively high rates of return. However, since market prices may be misleading, an attempt should be made to value inputs at their social cost and outputs at their social worth.

---

[3] More sophisticated criteria are presented in more advanced texts. Even for a firm, the above criterion is over-simplified, although, for important classes of problems, it generally gives the correct answer.

of view of humanitarianism, the United States and the other rich nations have a moral responsibility to help the poor nations. From the point of view of our self-interest, the promotion of growth in the less developed countries should help to preserve and encourage political and international stability and to make them more effective trading partners.

How can the United States be of help? With regard to many of their problems, we can do relatively little. But one thing that we can do is to provide badly needed capital. Responding to that need, we have given and lent a substantial amount of capital to the less developed countries in the past 25 years.

U.S. AID PROGRAMS

American financial assistance took several forms in the period after World War II. In the immediate postwar period, the primary objective was to help the populations of the war-ravaged countries and to get the European economies back on their feet. The United Nations Relief and Rehabilitation Administration (UNRRA) provided $4 billion of food, clothing, and medical services, about three-quarters of which was financed by the United States. In addition, other forms of relief, aid, and loans were extended. In all, the United States provided about $17 billion in aid between the war's end and 1948, about half in loans and about half in grants.

By the early 1950s, Europe's economy was in pretty good shape, but this did not spell the end of our foreign aid programs. On the contrary, much of our aid shifted toward the less developed nations. Table 23.8 shows the total

Table 23.8
U.S. FOREIGN ECONOMIC AND MILITARY AID PROGRAM, 1946–83

Year	Economic		Military		Total
	Loans	Grants	Loans	Grants	
		(billions of dollars)			
1946–52	8.5	22.7	–	3.8	35.0
1953–61	5.9	18.2	0.2	24.1	48.3
1962–65	8.3	8.7	0.4	8.1	25.6
1966–69	7.1	9.3	1.2	9.6	27.1
1970	1.4	2.3	0.1	3.0	6.8
1971	1.3	2.1	0.7	3.9	8.1
1972	1.6	2.3	0.6	4.8	9.2
1973	1.4	2.7	0.6	5.2	9.9
1974	1.2	2.8	1.4	3.7	9.0
1975	1.7	3.2	0.8	1.6	7.2
1976	1.8	2.1	1.4	1.3	6.6
1976TQ[a]	0.8	1.1	0.5	0.2	2.6
1977	2.1	3.5	1.4	0.8	7.8
1978	2.5	4.1	1.6	0.8	9.0
1979	1.9	5.2	5.2	1.6	13.8
1980	2.0	5.6	1.4	0.7	9.7
1981	1.5	5.8	2.5	0.7	10.6
1982	1.4	6.7	3.1	1.1	12.3
1983	1.6	7.0	3.9	1.7	14.2

[a] Transition quarter, July-September 1976. In the earlier data, the year ends June 30; in the later data, it ends September 30.
Source: Statistical Abstract of the United States.

amount the United States spent on foreign aid between 1946 and 1983. During this period, we spent about $270 billion—a huge sum by any standard. About 40 percent of these expenditures have been for military purposes, about 60 percent have been for economic purposes. No nation has ever contributed as much to the economic development of poorer countries as we have.

Much of this aid has been in the form of loans or grants that must be spent on American goods and services. Also, much of it consisted of our giving away part of what were then surplus stocks of food. (Recall the agricultural programs discussed in Chapter 4.)

In addition, the United States has established various kinds of technical assistance programs designed to help the less developed countries borrow some of our technology, administrative techniques, medical knowledge, educational methods, and so on. The emphasis frequently is on training people from the less developed countries to the point where they can teach their fellow countrymen. Often the costs of these programs are shared by United States and by the recipient of the aid. Most observers seem to believe that these technical assistance programs have been worthwhile and successful.

OTHER U.S. ASSISTANCE TO LDC'S

Some other aspects of American policy are also important, although they are not aid programs. For one thing, the United States and other developed countries can help the LDCs by reducing trade barriers, thus allowing them to increase their national incomes through trade. However, it seems unlikely that trade alone can substitute for aid, and the situation is clouded by the trade barriers the LDCs themselves have been erecting to protect their own industry. Another way that the United States can help is through private investment. American corporations have invested many billions of dollars in the less developed countries. To the less developed countries, this is a significant source of capital.

Besides providing capital, the multinational corporations have also been a source of needed technology. However, these firms have faced much more difficult problems in transmitting technology to less developed countries than to industrialized countries. Many of the techniques of the multinational firms are not very well suited to the less developed countries, with their plentiful unskilled labor, few skills, and little capital. Moreover, there is sometimes little incentive for multinational firms to adapt their products, production techniques, and marketing methods to the conditions present in developing countries. And when they do manage to make a technological transplant, its effects are often restricted to narrow segments of the economy. Still further, it should be noted that the multinational firms are often viewed with some suspicion and fear by the host governments.

CONTROVERSIES OVER FOREIGN AID

For many years, foreign aid has been a controversial subject in the United States. Many critics argue that the money could better be spent at home to alleviate domestic poverty. They claim that other industrialized countries—like Germany and Japan—should contribute a bigger share of the aid to the less developed countries. And they assert that our aid programs have not had much impact on the less developed countries so far. Liberals object to our giving aid to governments charged with serious violation of human rights. Conservatives are disturbed that some aid channeled through international organizations may go to Marxist governments.

Many suggestions have been made for ways to improve the effectiveness of our foreign aid. One prominent suggestion is that we go further in concentrating the bulk of our aid on a relatively few countries—those that really want to do what is necessary to develop, that can use the money well, and that are important from the point of view of size and international politics. Obviously adopting this suggestion means reducing aid to some other countries. Another suggestion is that, rather than impose political conditions on aid, we should give money with no strings attached. This suggestion entails a great deal more than economics. To evaluate it, one must decide what the goals of foreign aid should be. To what extent should it be aimed at raising the standard of living of the world's population, whatever the effect on the United States? To what extent should it be aimed at furthering American goals and American foreign policies? In practice, foreign aid has been bound up closely with our foreign policy. Given the political facts of life, it is difficult to see how it could be otherwise.

OTHER COUNTRIES' AID PROGRAMS

The United States has provided a large percentage of the aid that has flowed from the industrialized countries to the less developed countries, but it has by no means been the sole contributor. Other industrialized nations also have aid programs. For example, France has contributed over $2 billion per year in official development assistance and Japan and Germany have contributed over $1 billion. Moreover, the Soviet Union has formulated a significant aid program. Indeed, it is often claimed that the Russian programs have had more political effect than our own because they allow the recipient countries more freedom to build "prestige" projects like steel mills and because they make their aid look somewhat less like charity.

The World Bank

Another source of capital is the *World Bank.* In 1944, late in World War II, the major economic powers agreed to establish the International Bank for Reconstruction and Development, also known as the World Bank. Although its first loans were for postwar reconstruction, the bank's principal function now is to make long-term loans to the less developed countries—in Latin America, Asia, and elsewhere. They desperately need capital, while the rich, economically advanced countries have capital to lend. The World Bank's purpose was to channel funds from rich nations to poor, thus supplementing private investment, which was often scared off

531

by the apparent risks. More specifically, the major economic powers contributed a certain amount of money to form the bank, with each country's share determined by its economic size. About one-third of the total was put up by the United States. The Soviet Union helped organize the World Bank, but later declined to join.

Now about 40 years old, the World Bank still makes loans to people or governments with sound investment projects who have been unable to get private financing. Moreover, by floating its own bond issues it can lend money above and beyond what was originally put up by the major powers. In other words, the World Bank sells its own IOUs, which are considered safe by investors because they are guaranteed by member countries. In addition, it helps less developed countries get loans from private lenders by insuring the loans. That is, the World Bank can tell the lender that if the loan goes sour it will see that the lender is paid back.

This movement of capital from the capital-rich nations to the capital-poor nations should prove beneficial for both rich and poor. The poor countries are enabled to carry out projects that will result in economic returns high enough to pay off the lender with interest and have some net benefits left over. The rich countries are enabled to invest their capital at a higher rate of return than they could obtain at home. Thus both parties benefit, as long as the loans are economically sound.

The World Bank has established the *International Development Agency* to make "soft" loans, as well as the *International Finance Corporation,* which lends to foreign development banks. An increased percentage of the bank's financing has been channeled through these two agencies.

The bank's activities have grown substantially: in 1965, its loan authorizations were about $1 billion; in 1974, they were about $4 billion; and in 1979, its loans exceeded $10 billion. Nonetheless, despite its achievements, many economists believe that in the past the World Bank has sometimes been too conservative and that it should have been willing to take bigger risks. Since the late 1960s, when Robert McNamara (now succeeded by A. W. Clausen, former president of the Bank of America) became its head, the bank has become less conservative in this respect. By 1984, a substantial proportion of its loans were aimed at helping the LDCs with their balance-of-payments problems; and there were reports of a clash between Clausen and the Reagan administration over whether such loans should be restricted. In the administration's view, the bank should concentrate on the provision of financing for development projects.

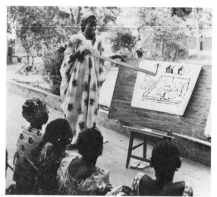

World Bank "Equal Access" program in the Upper Volta

A New International Economic Order?

Since the early 1970s, the less developed countries have been voicing their extreme displeasure with the state of the world economic system as it affects them. A special session of the UN General Assembly was called in 1975 to deal with their demands for a "new international economic order." Subsequently, many other meetings have been devoted to this topic. What the LDCs want is (1) greater control by the LDCs over their own economic destiny, (2) acceleration of their growth rate (and a narrowing of the gap in per capita income between the developed and less developed countries), and (3) a major increase in the share of the world's industrial production carried out in the LDCs. To attain these objectives, they have pressed for tariff preferences for their manufactured exports, agreements to stabilize and support their commodity prices, and the accelerated transfer of resources to them from the industrialized countries.

Tariff Preferences. To gain freer access to industrial nations' markets, the LDCs want tariff preferences for their manufactured exports; specifically, they want to be charged no tariff. This idea of preferential tariffs seems to be accepted in many industrialized countries. Consider the Trade Reform Act of 1974, which authorized the United States to join with other industrial countries in reducing tariffs to zero for many products from LDCs. But there was a catch. Items like textiles and shoes cannot be granted zero duties if they are found to be "import sensitive." In practice, how much the LDCs will get in the way of tariff preferences is hard to say.

Stabilization and Support of Commodity Prices. Most LDCs derive 80 percent or more of their foreign exchange from the sale of commodities like coffee, cocoa, and sugar. Since the price of such commodities tends to fluctuate considerably, the LDCs would like the developed countries to cooperate in the stabilization of individual commodity prices. They would like to establish commodity agreements among the countries producing a commodity, binding them not to sell at less than the agreed price. In effect, these are international cartels, like OPEC. (See p. 449.) Since such cartels generally want to raise, as well as stabilize, the price of commodities, there are obvious disadvantages to the developed countries in the establishment of such agreements.

Transfer of Resources. The LDCs would like economic aid to be increased to about 1 percent of the GNP of the donor countries. Also, they would like the developed countries to forgive at least part of the large debts they have run up in recent years. If the LDCs refuse to pay these debts, their credit standing would be undermined, and their ability to secure future loans would be impaired. Nonetheless, there is considerable worry about the possibility that some of these countries may default, and impose large losses on the commercial banks and others that have lent them money.

As one would expect, these demands for a "new international economic order" have provoked a considerable amount of controversy. Some observers have pointed out that these demands ignore the fact that, to a large extent, economic development is something that the LDCs must do for themselves, by creating the necessary political stability, social mobility, and economic incentives. Other observers are suspicious of the commodity agreements the LDCs favor, since they feel that such cartel arrangements would be relatively inefficient ways to accomplish the aims of the LDCs. Only time will tell how far the developed countries will go in trying to meet these demands of the LDCs.

Test Yourself

1. "It is always a good idea for less developed countries to substitute their own production for imports. This is the only way they can become economically independent." Comment and evaluate.

2. According to Simon Kuznets, "A substantial economic advance in the less developed countries may require modification in the available stock of material technology, and probably even greater innovations in political and social structure." What does he mean? If he is correct, what are the implications for the less developed countries? For the developed countries?

533

3. According to Hans Morgenthau, "Foreign aid for economic development has a chance to be successful only within relatively narrow limits which are raised by cultural and political conditions impervious to direct outside influence." Do you agree? If he is correct, what are the implications for the less developed countries? For the developed countries?

4. Why don't some market prices of inputs correspond closely to social costs in less developed countries? Give examples. What implications does this have for the economic analysis of investment projects in LDCs?

Summary

1. A country is defined here as a less developed country if its per capita income is less than $3,000. Well over half of the world's population live in the less developed countries, which include many of the countries in Asia, Africa, and Latin America. In recent years, there has been a great increase in the expectations and material demands of the people in these countries.

2. The less developed countries vary greatly, but they generally devote most of their resources to the production of food, are composed of two economies (one market-oriented, the other subsistence), and often have relatively weak, unstable governments and a relatively high degree of income inequality.

3. One obvious reason why income per capita is so low is that the people in the less developed countries have so little capital to work with. The less developed countries, with their low incomes, do not save much, they lack entrepreneurs, and the climate for investment (domestic or foreign) often is not good.

4. Some less developed countries suffer from overpopulation; and as total output has increased, these gains have been offset by population increases. Modern medical techniques have reduced the death rate, while the birth rate has remained high. The result is a population explosion.

5. Another very important reason why per capita income is so low in these countries is that they often use backward technology. The transfer of technology from one country to another is not as easy as it sounds, particularly when the recipient country has an uneducated population and little capital. Also, these countries lack favorable social institutions and sometimes have few natural resources.

6. An important issue facing the governments of most less developed countries is the extent to which they want to promote a balance between the agricultural and industrial sectors of the economy. Without question, the LDCs are expanding industry relative to agriculture. In some cases, such as India and Pakistan, more balance—less emphasis on industry, more on agriculture—would have been preferable. Moreover, some countries have put too much emphasis on substituting their own production for imports, even when their own production is uneconomic.

7. Many of the less developed countries have established development plans that specify targets or goals for the economy and policies designed to attain them. One criterion often used to determine whether a given investment project should be accepted or rejected is the ratio of the value of the output produced to the capital used. Only projects with high values of this ratio are accepted.

8. A more sophisticated criterion is the rate of return from the project, the method used by firms in capital budgeting. When computing each project's rate of return, it is important that inputs be valued at their social cost and that outputs be valued at their social worth.

9. The United States has been involved in a number of major aid programs to help the less developed countries. In recent years, these aid programs have come under increasing attack, because of a feeling in Congress and elsewhere that they have not been working well.

10. Besides the United States, other countries—including the Soviet Union—have carried out significant aid programs. And the World Bank has channeled major amounts of capital into the less developed countries.

Concepts for Review

Less developed country	Foreign aid	Balanced growth
Market-oriented economy	Population explosion	Development plan
Subsistence economy	Green revolution	World Bank

APPENDIX:

Digging Deeper into the Economist's Tool Box

In this final section of the book, we present important material that is sometimes considered too advanced for the elementary course. The Appendix takes up *IS* and *LM* curves, with particular reference to the Keynesian-monetarist controversy.

IS and *LM* Curves and the Keynesian-Monetarist Controversy[1]

To understand more completely the argument between the Keynesians and the monetarists, it is worthwhile to enlarge the model of national output determination in Chapters 10 to 12 to include monetary factors. The simplest extension of this sort involves the use of *IS* and *LM* curves, both of which will be discussed in detail below. These curves, originated by Oxford's Nobel laureate, Sir John Hicks, help to put the debate between the monetarists and the Keynesians into somewhat deeper perspective.

Before describing how *IS* and *LM* curves are constructed, it is important to be clear concerning the basic assumptions that are being made. First, it is assumed that the price level is fixed, and that the public has a

---

[1] To understand this appendix, the reader should be familiar with Chapters 10 to 17.

Figure A.1

Derivation of the IS Curve *If the interest rate is* i_1, *intended investment is* I_1. *If the interest rate is* i_2, *intended investment is* I_2.

If intended investment is I_1, *equilibrium NNP is* Y_1. *If intended investment is* I_2, *equilibrium NNP is* Y_2.

The IS *curve shows, for each level of the interest rate, the level of NNP that will satisfy the equilibrium condition that intended spending on output must equal NNP. Points* A *and* B *are derived in the panels above, which show that equilibrium NNP equals* Y_1 *if the interest rate is* i_1 *and* Y_2 *if the interest rate is* i_2.

fixed demand curve for real money balances, a fixed consumption function, and a fixed investment function, Second, foreign trade is ignored. Third, the money supply is fixed by the monetary authorities, and does not vary with NNP or the interest rate. Fourth, tax rates are fixed, and fiscal policy takes the form of varying government expenditure.

THE *IS* CURVE: DEFINITION AND DERIVATION

The IS *curve shows, for each possible level of the interest rate, the level of NNP that will satisfy the equilibrium condition that intended spending on output must equal NNP.* (If this equilibrium condition is a bit hazy, review Chapter 10.) This equilibrium condition is equivalent to saying that the public must be spending the intended amount relative to its income. (We put a great deal of stress on this equilibrium condition in Chapter 10.) To construct the *IS* curve, it is essential to recognize two things. First, the level of intended investment is inversely related to the interest rate. (In other words, for reasons described in Chapter 10, the higher the rate of interest, the lower the amount of intended investment, as shown in panel A of Figure A.1.) Second, the level of intended investment (as well as consumption and government expenditure) will determine the equilibrium level of NNP. (See panel B of Figure A.1.) Thus, since the interest rate determines the level of intended investment, and the level of intended investment determines the equilibrium level of NNP, there will be a relationship between the level of the interest rate and the equilibrium level of NNP. This relationship is the *IS* curve, shown in panel C of Figure A.1.

To see more precisely what the *IS* curve is, it is useful to derive some points on such a curve. Let's derive two points—*A* and *B*—on the *IS* curve in panel C of Figure A.1. To derive point *A,* note that, if the interest rate is i_1, intended investment will be I_1, according to panel A of Figure A.1. And if intended investment is I_1, total intended spending at each level of NNP will be as shown by the $C + I_1 + G$ line in panel B of Figure A.1, with the result that the equilibrium level of NNP will be Y_1. Thus, if the interest rate is i_1, the equilibrium level of NNP is Y_1—which explains the coordinates of point *A.*

To explain point *B,* note that if the interest rate is i_2, intended investment will be I_2, according to panel A of Figure A.1. And if intended

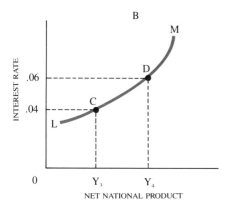

Figure A.2

Derivation of the LM Curve *Holding constant the interest rate,* i, *the quantity of money demanded increases as NNP increases. Holding constant NNP, the quantity of money demanded increases as the interest rate decreases. If* i = .04 *and NNP* = Y₃, *the quantity of money demanded equals $1 trillion. If* i = .06 *and NNP* = Y₄, *the quantity of money demanded equals $1 trillion. These correspond to points C and D in panel* B.

The LM curve shows, for each possible level of the interest rate, the level of NNP that will satisfy the equilibrium condition that the quantity of money demanded equal the supply of money. Points C and D are derived in panel A.

investment is I_2, total intended spending at each level of NNP will be as shown by the $C + I_2 + G$ line in panel B of Figure A.1, with the result that the equilibrium level of NNP will be Y_2. Thus, if the interest rate is i_2, the equilibrium level of NNP is Y_2—which explains the coordinates of point *B*.

Note that *the IS curve slopes downward to the right*. That is, the lower the interest rate, the higher the level of NNP on the *IS* curve. For example, when the interest rate fell from i_1 to i_2 in Figure A.1, panel A, intended investment increased from I_1 to I_2. And when intended investment rose from I_1 to I_2, the equilibrium level of NNP increased from Y_1 to Y_2, as shown in panel B of Figure A.1. More generally, since the level of intended investment is inversely related to the interest rate, but directly related to the equilibrium level of NNP, it follows that the interest rate must be inversely related to the level of NNP on the *IS* curve.

THE *LM* CURVE: DEFINITION AND DERIVATION

The LM curve shows, for each possible level of the interest rate, the level of NNP that will satisfy the equilibrium condition that the public be satisfied to hold the existing quantity of money. Chapter 14 stressed the importance of this equilibrium condition. Clearly, the quantity of money demanded for transactions purposes is dependent upon the value of NNP. Further, the quantity of money demanded is dependent on the rate of interest. Thus, as stressed in Chapter 14, the total quantity of money demanded by the public is dependent both on the value of NNP and on the interest rate.

More specifically, the total quantity of money demanded by the public is *directly* related to the value of NNP and *inversely* related to the interest rate. (Recall the discussion in Chapter 14.) As NNP increases (and incomes rise), people want to keep more money on hand to carry out the larger volume of transactions. Thus the quantity of money demanded by the public is directly related to the value of NNP (as shown in panel A of Figure A.2). On the other hand, the higher the interest rate, the more costly it is to hold money (because the more interest is forgone by holding money rather than buying bonds or other securities). Thus the higher the interest rate, the smaller the amount of money that is demanded. In other words, the quantity of money demanded by the public is inversely related to the interest rate. (This is shown in panel A of Figure A.2 by the fact that, if NNP is held constant, the quantity of money demanded increases as *i* decreases.)

Let's derive two points, *C* and *D*, on the *LM* curve, shown in panel B of Figure A.2. Recall that any *LM* curve is based on the supposition that the money supply is *fixed*, and that the money supply must be just equal to the quantity of money demanded (for an equilibrium to occur). The *LM* curve in panel B of Figure A.2 shows, for each interest rate, the value of NNP that will result in the public's demanding this fixed amount of money, say $1 trillion. If the relationships in panel A of Figure A.2 hold, the quantity of money demanded will equal $1 trillion if the interest rate is 4 percent and NNP is Y_3. Thus, if the interest rate is 4 percent, NNP (on this *LM* curve) must be Y_3—which explains the coordinates of point *C*.

Panel A of Figure A.2 shows that the quantity of money demanded will also equal $1 trillion if the interest rate is 6 percent and the NNP is Y_4. Thus, if the interest rate is 6 percent, NNP (on this *LM* curve) must be Y_4—which explains the coordinates of point *D*.

Note that to maintain the quantity of money demanded equal to the fixed money supply ($1 trillion in this case), an increase in the interest rate must be accompanied by an increase in NNP. Why? Because, holding NNP constant, an increase in the interest rate will reduce the quantity of money demanded, as shown in panel A of Figure A.2. Thus, unless NNP is increased, the quantity of money demanded will be less than the fixed money supply. To bring it back into equality with the fixed money supply, and thus to maintain the equilibrium on which the *LM* curve is based, NNP must be increased. Similarly, a decrease in the interest rate must be accompanied by a decrease in NNP, if the quantity of money demanded is to equal the fixed money supply. For these reasons, *the* LM *curve slopes upward to the right.* That is, the higher the interest rate, the higher the level of NNP that satisfies the equilibrium condition underlying the *LM* curve.

THE EQUILIBRIUM LEVEL OF NNP

As pointed out in an earlier section, a full-scale equilibrium requires *both* that households and firms be spending the intended amounts relative to their incomes *and* that they be satisfied to hold the existing amount of money. In other words, both the equilibrium condition underlying the *IS* curve and the equilibrium condition underlying the *LM* curve must be satisfied. For this to be so, the equilibrium combination of NNP and interest rate must be at a point lying both on the *IS* curve (which means that it satisfies the equilibrium condition underlying this curve) and on the *LM* curve (which means that it satisfies the equilibrium condition underlying this curve).

If we plot the IS *and* LM *curves on the same diagram, as in Figure A.3, the equilibrium combination of NNP and interest rate must therefore be the one that is given by the intersection of the two curves.* Only this combination lies on both curves, and thus satisfies both equilibrium conditions. For example, in Figure A.3, the equilibrium level of NNP must be Y_5, and the equilibrium level of the interest rate must be i_5. This is the only combination of NNP and interest rate that will satisfy both equilibrium conditions, given that the money supply, the public's demand curve for money, its consumption function, its investment function, and government expenditures (and taxes) remain fixed.

EFFECTS OF FISCAL POLICY ON THE *IS* CURVE

The IS *curve will shift to the right if government expenditures increase or taxes decrease.* The reason why these factors shift the *IS* curve to the right is that, holding the interest rate constant, each of these factors increases the level of NNP that satisfies the equilibrium condition underlying the *IS* curve.

To see why this is so, take as an example the effect of a $10 billion increase in government expenditures in Figure A.1. Before the increase

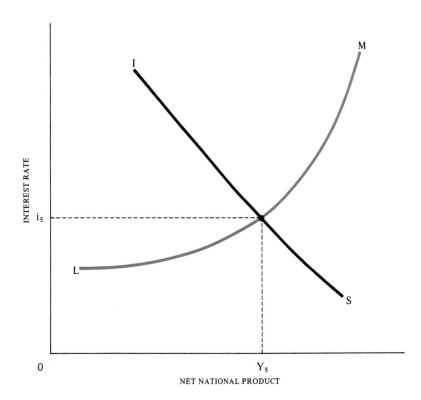

Figure A.3

Determination of Equilibrium NNP and Interest Rate *The equilibrium level of NNP (and of the interest rate) must be at the intersection of the IS and LM curves. The equilibrium NNP equals Y_5, and the equilibrium interest rate equals i_5.*

occurs, what is the equilibrium level of NNP corresponding to an interest rate of i_1? As we saw in Figure A.1, it is Y_1. But after the increase occurs, it is no longer Y_1. Due to the increased government expenditure, the $C + I + G$ line in panel B of Figure A.1 is raised from $C + I_1 + G$ to $C + I_1 + (G + 10)$, as shown in Figure A.4. Thus the equilibrium level of

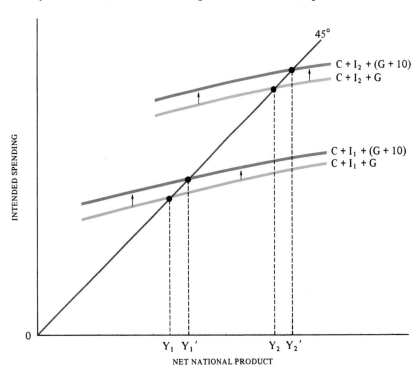

Figure A.4

Effect of a \$10 Billion Increase in Government Expenditures on IS Curve *If government expenditures are increased by \$10 billion, and the interest rate is i_1, equilibrium NNP increases from Y_1 to Y_1'. If the interest rate is i_2, it increases from Y_2 to Y_2'. Since the level of NNP on the IS curve corresponding to any level of the interest rate is increased, the effect of the increase in government expenditures must be to shift the IS curve to the right.*

A5

NNP is increased to Y_1', as shown in Figure A.4. Similarly, if the interest rate is i_2, the equilibrium level of NNP is increased from Y_2 to Y_2'. Since the level of NNP on the *IS* curve corresponding to each level of the interest rate is increased, the effect of the increase in government expenditure is to shift the *IS* curve to the right.

EFFECTS OF MONETARY POLICY ON THE *LM* CURVE

The LM *curve will shift to the right if the monetary authorities increase the money supply, and it will shift to the left if they decrease the money supply.* To see why, consider first an increase in the money supply. Under such circumstances, if the interest rate stays the same, NNP must increase in order to bring the quantity of money demanded into equality with the new money supply. Why? Because the quantity of money demanded, if it is to equal the new money supply, must increase, and an increase in NNP will be required to produce such an increase in the quantity of money demanded. Thus, since the level of NNP where this equality holds (the interest rate being unchanged) is greater than before, the effect of the increase in the money supply must be to shift the *LM* curve to the right.

Next, consider a decrease in the money supply. If the interest rate stays the same, NNP must decrease in order to bring the quantity of money demanded into equality with the new money supply. Why? Because decreases in NNP will decrease the quantity of money demanded, which is required if the quantity of money demanded is to equal the diminished money supply. Thus, since the level of NNP where this equality holds (the interest rate being unchanged) is smaller than before, the effect of the decrease in the money supply must be to shift the *LM* curve to the left.

EFFECTS OF FISCAL POLICY ON NNP

To understand the difference between Keynesian and monetarist views concerning the effects of fiscal policy on NNP, it is useful to consider three alternative assumptions:

1. Let's assume that the economy is operating at a point where *the* LM *curve is neither close to being vertical nor close to being horizontal.* Under these circumstances, what are the effects of an expansionary fiscal policy (that is, an increase in government expenditures or a cut in taxes)? Since it shifts the *IS* curve to the right, an expansionary fiscal policy will increase both NNP and the interest rate, if the *LM* curve has such a shape. Panel A of Figure A.5 shows that this is the case. A shift to the right of the *IS* curve (such as from I_1S_1 to $I_1'S_1'$) increases both NNP (from Y_6 to Y_7) and the interest rate (from i_6 to i_7).

2. Let's assume that the economy is operating at a point where *the* LM *curve is close to being vertical.* Indeed, to make things simple, let's assume that it is vertical. If so, an expansionary fiscal policy results in an increase in the interest rate, but no increase in NNP. For example, in panel B of Figure A.5, a shift to the right of the *IS* curve (such as from I_2S_2 to $I_2'S_2'$) increases the interest rate (from i_8 to i_9), but not NNP. This is the so-called *classical range* of the *LM* curve, where fiscal policy cannot increase NNP.

3. Let's assume that the economy is operating at a point where *the* LM

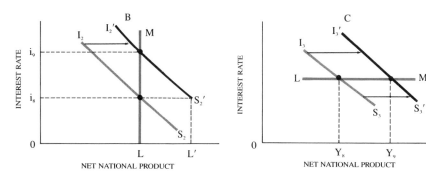

Figure A.5

Effects of Fiscal Policy *An expansionary fiscal policy shifts the IS curve to the right. If the LM curve is upward sloped (as in panel A), the result of an expansionary fiscal policy will be an increase in both NNP and the interest rate. If the LM curve is vertical (as in panel B), the result will be an increase in the interest rate, but no increase in NNP. If the LM curve is horizontal (as in panel C), the result will be an increase in NNP, but no increase in the interest rate. The monetarists have tended to believe that the LM curve is close to vertical, whereas the Keynesians have tended to believe that it is closer to horizontal.*

curve is horizontal (or nearly so). If so, an expansionary fiscal policy results in an increase in NNP, but no increase in the interest rate. For example, in panel C of Figure A.5, a shift to the right of the *IS* curve (such as from $I_3 S_3$ to $I_3' S_3'$) increases NNP (from Y_8 to Y_9), but not the interest rate. This is sometimes called the *liquidity-trap range*.

Although both a perfectly vertical and a perfectly horizontal *LM* curve are polar extremes, they are useful in indicating the differences that have existed between the monetarists and the Keynesians. *The monetarists have tended to believe that the LM curve is close to vertical, whereas the Keynesians have tended to believe that it is much closer to horizontal.* (Why? Because of the differences in their assumptions, indicated in Figures 17.1 to 17.3.) Given their different views concerning the shape of the *LM* curve, it is easy to see why they have come to quite different conclusions concerning the effects of fiscal policy on NNP. Clearly, the monetarists, based on their assumptions, have tended to conclude that fiscal policy has less impact on NNP than the Keynesians have been willing to accept.[2]

EFFECTS OF MONETARY POLICY ON NNP

To understand the difference between Keynesian and monetarist views concerning the effects of monetary policy on NNP, it is useful to consider three alternative assumptions:

1. Let's assume that the economy is operating at a point where the IS *curve is neither close to being horizontal nor close to being vertical.* Under these circumstances, what are the effects of an expansionary monetary policy (that is, an increase in the money supply)? Since it shifts the *LM* curve to the right, an expansionary monetary policy will increase NNP and reduce the interest rate, if the *IS* curve has this shape. Panel A of Figure A.6 shows that this is the case. A shift to the right of the *LM* curve (from $L_1 M_1$ to $L_1' M_1'$) increases NNP (from Y_{10} to Y_{11}) and reduces the interest rate (from i_{10} to i_{11}).

2. Let's assume that the economy is operating at a point where *the* IS

[2] The crowding-out effect, cited earlier in Chapter 17, is measured by the difference between (1) the equilibrium value of NNP if the interest rate remained at its original level, and (2) the equilibrium level of NNP at the new interest rate. In panel A of Figure A.5, the crowding-out effect equals $Y_6' - Y_7$; in panel B, it equals $L' - L$; and in panel C, it equals zero. If the crowding-out effect is zero, the effect on NNP of government expenditure conforms to the simple multiplier given in Chapter 12.

Figure A.6
Effects of Monetary Policy *An increase
in the money supply shifts the* LM *curve
to the right. If the* IS *curve is downward
sloped (as in panel A), an increase in the
money supply will increase NNP and
reduce the interest rate. If the* IS *curve is
horizontal (as in panel B), it will increase
NNP, but have no effect on the interest
rate. If the* IS *curve is vertical (as in
panel C), it will reduce the interest rate,
but have no effect on NNP. The monetarists have tended to believe that the* IS
*curve is close to horizontal, whereas
some Keynesians have tended to believe
that it is closer to vertical.*

curve is horizontal (or very nearly so). If so, expansionary monetary policy results in an increase in NNP, but little or no decrease in the interest rate. For example, in panel B of Figure A.6, a shift to the right of the *LM* curve (from L_2M_2 to $L_2'M_2'$) increases NNP (from Y_{12} to Y_{13}) but does not reduce the interest rate.

3. Let's assume that the economy is operating at a point where *the* IS *curve is close to being vertical.* If so, an expansionary monetary policy results in a decrease in the interest rate, but little or no increase in NNP. For example, in panel C of Figure A.6, a shift to the right of the *LM* curve (from L_3M_3 to $L_3'M_3'$) decreases the interest rate (from i_{12} to i_{13}) but does not affect NNP.

Although both a perfectly horizontal and a perfectly vertical *IS* curve are polar extremes, they are useful in indicating the differences between the monetarists and the Keynesians. *Some Keynesians have believed that the* IS *curve is close to vertical, whereas the monetarists have believed that it is closer to horizontal.* (Why? Because of the differences in their assumptions, indicated in Figures 17.1 to 17.3.) Given their different views concerning the shape of the *IS* curve, it is easy to see why they have come to different conclusions concerning the effects of monetary policy on NNP. Clearly, the monetarists, based on their assumptions, have tended to conclude that monetary policy has a greater impact on NNP than the Keynesians have been willing to accept.

Brief Answers to Odd-Numbered Test-Yourself Questions*

Chapter 1 (p. 8)

1. (a) Iron ore that is still in the ground is included in land. (b) The 747 is capital. (c) These inventories are capital, as explained on p. 6. (d) Unless the University owns the telephone, it is not part of the university's capital, but it is capital to the telephone company.

3. Yes, use of the catalyst alters the relationship between inputs of crude oil and the refined oil output. By making the refining process more efficient, the catalyst allows a larger volume of refined oil to be gleaned from a barrel of crude oil. The services of engineers and scientists, as well as research laboratories, were used to obtain the invention.

Chapter 1 (p. 16)

1. Preparing the meal costs the family $25.00, assuming that Ms. Harris could see patients during that hour.

3. The $1,000 figure is correct because the remaining cost of room and board must be met whether the student goes to college or works instead.

---

* The answers provided here are meant only to be brief guides, not complete or exhaustive treatments. Many were contributed by Michael Claudon of Middlebury College, who is responsible for the *Instructor's Manual* accompanying this book.

Chapter 2 (p. 23)

1. 2 million bushels generates $2 million; 1 million bushels generates $2 million. No, I would produce 1 million bushels since I can sell it for as much as I can get for 2 million bushels.

3. The demand curve in Figure 2.2 shifts to the right when preferences change in favor of playing tennis.

Chapter 2 (p. 35)

1. (a) No. (b) Yes. (c) The combination of 20 million tons of food and 6 million tractors is inside the curve. Contributory factors: unemployment, inefficiency, or bad weather.

3. Yes, it is on the new curve. The horizontal intersection is 24 million tons, and the vertical one is 60 million tractors.

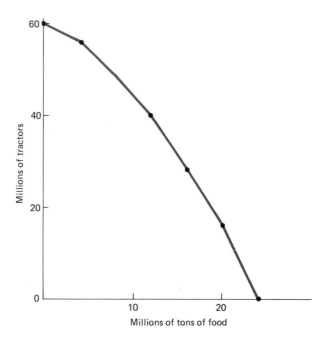

5. This statement is true. Of course, it is also important to note that not all individuals have the same number of votes, because of income inequality.

Chapter 3 (p. 47)

1. This is a direct relationship. Supply curves are generally direct relationships.

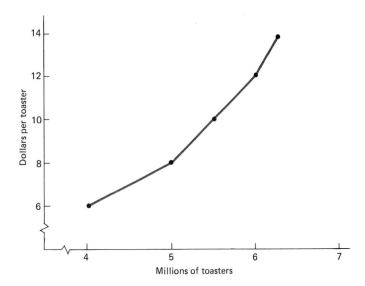

3. No, quantity demanded will exceed quantity supplied. Black markets and queues may arise. If black markets develop, the price may rise above the official price of $8. Such a ceiling might be introduced as part of an anti-inflationary program or to help the poor.

5. Equilibrium price = $3.33, and equilibrium quantity = 6.67 million pounds.

Chapter 3 (p. 61)

1. The toaster demand curve shifts: (a) right; (b) right; (c) left; (d) right; (e) no shift.

3. The impact on price is ambiguous. Equilibrium quantity rises.

5. The demand for beets and beet growers' profits rise. The opposite happens for string beans. Bean growers spy beet growers' high profits and plant beets instead of beans. Beet supply rises and string bean supply falls.

Chapter 4 (p. 75)

1. It is very difficult in many cases to know whether a certain activity can be performed better by government than private citizens can do for themselves. But the first half of this chapter indicates a number of areas where most economists believe the government has legitimate functions.

3. You can consume the services provided by national defense without depriving me of also doing so simultaneously. A rifle is not a public good; the hallmark of a public good is that it can be consumed collectively or jointly.

5. Such activities result in external economies.

Chapter 4 (p. 83)

1. The socially optimal output of paper is less than *OQ*. The supply curve reflecting true social costs lies to the left of the one shown because the latter neglects part of the social cost of paper production.

3. Government programs supported prices of dairy and grain farmers. The result has been excess supply of dairy and grain products, and huge government purchases of the excesses to support prices. Federal government programs have not solved the problem. See the section of the text on "Evaluation of Government Farm Programs."

5. The essential point here is one shared by many government programs, be they protective tariffs or farm subsidies. The benefits of the programs are concentrated on a relatively small and highly organized group of people, while the programs' costs are spread across the population at large.

Chapter 5 (p. 97)

1. The government should build the road from A to B since its benefits exceed its costs. The numbers imply that the cost of the road between B and C exceeds its benefits. The cost equals $15 million − $10 million = $5 million, while the benefit equals $22 million − $20 million = $2 million.

3. No. It is impossible to tell in which sector the inefficiency exists. The nonattainment of potential production might result from inefficiency in either sector.

Chapter 5 (p. 106)

1.

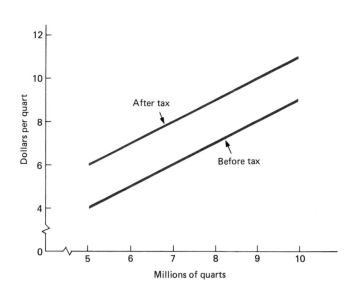

3. The equilibrium price of gin is $6 per quart both before and after the tax. None of the tax is passed on to the consumer.

Chapter 6 (p. 118)

1. The new olefins plant is not a firm; it is part of Exxon, which is a firm. A proprietorship is unlikely to build such a plant due to a lack of resources.

3. (a) and (b) are false because neither the University of Texas nor Massachusetts General Hospital are run to make profits. (c) is false because many firms are individual proprietorships with only one owner. (d) is false because many stockholders or partners do not participate in the management of the firms of which they are part owners.

5. Bondholders are not owners of the corporation, but stockholders are. Bondholders have lent money to the corporation at an agreed-upon interest rate, whereas stockholders' returns are based upon the profitability of the corporation they own.

Chapter 6 (p. 128)

1. All but (h).

3. Column 1: $700,000; Column 2: $1,100,000 and $2,000,000. The owners owe $1,600,000. The owners have contributed $400,000. The difference between current assets and fixed assets is the length of time before they will be converted into cash.

Chapter 7 (p. 140)

1. The figures are 1,000 for 1974, 1,200 for 1976, 1,820 for 1978, 2,400 for 1980, and 1,600 for 1986.

3. No. If GNP is used to gauge the net social value of economic output, pollution's costs should be subtracted from the market value of the goods produced.

Chapter 7 (p. 148)

1. GNP = $1,900 millions; NNP = $1,800 millions.

3. GNP = $93 millions, the sum of all items except for transfer payments.

5. Inventories represent goods that can be sold without drawing upon the economy's current productive capacity. Ignoring inventory increases excludes the value of these goods from the GNP calculation, even though they were produced during the year.

Chapter 8 (p. 163)

1. (i) Unemployment benefits are temporary, and averaged only about $120 per week in 1982. (ii) Unemployed workers involve an opportunity cost to the country in the form of the goods and services that these workers could produce.

3. Frictionally unemployed people have left one job (often voluntarily) and have not as yet begun a new one. Structural unemployment occurs when jobs are available for qualified workers, but the unemployed do not have the necessary qualifications. Cyclical unemployment occurs when, because of an insufficiency of aggregate demand, there are more people looking for work than there are jobs. The government should not attempt to reduce all types of unemployment to zero because severe inflation would be likely to result.

Chapter 8 (p. 173)

1. The point is that there may be tradeoffs between inflation and unemployment, and that full-employment policy should take inflation into consideration as well.

3. About 7 years.

5. Recessions tend to reduce inflation substantially. There are lots of excess capacity and unemployed resources, which put a damper on price increases.

Chapter 9 (p. 186)

1. A leftward shift in the aggregate supply curve, combined with a rightward shift in the aggregate demand curve, that kept their intersection at the same output level, would result in a constant real output but a higher price level.

3. Q falls by \$2 billion from \$18 billion to \$16 billion.

5. The principal effect will be on the aggregate supply curve, which will shift upward and to the left. All other things equal, the result will be a higher price level and a lower real output level.

Chapter 9 (p. 192)

1. No, they tend to be caused by massive shifts to the left of the aggregate demand curve.

3. No, business cycles are movements around trend lines of this sort. Such trends are not business cycles; they are longer-term movements.

5. Policies that increase savings and investment, enhance R and D activity, and increase labor productivity will tend to shift the U.S. aggregate supply curve rightward. If we want to increase output without inflation, such a shift may be desirable.

Chapter 10 (p. 204)

1. The marginal propensity to consume = the average propensity to consume = 0.9 in this example. The consumption function has been assumed to pass through the origin. In this example, the marginal propensity to consume is unrelated to the income distribution, which is unrealistic since different socioeconomic groups have different spending and savings habits.

3. The marginal propensity to consume is not constant. The average propensity to consume falls as disposable income rises.

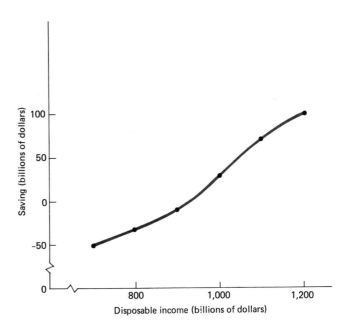

5. (a) Decrease (especially inventory investment); (b) increase; (c) increase; (d) decrease; (e) increase.

Chapter 10 (p. 215)

1. Equilibrium NNP = $500 billion. (*Note:* There is the implicit assumption that disposable income = NNP, i.e., that taxes are zero.) No, equilibrium NNP may not be full-employment NNP.

3. When NNP = $800 billions, intended saving ($330 billion) is substantially greater than intended investment ($140 billion). If NNP = $800 billions, the difference between intended investment and intended (= actual) saving becomes unintended inventory investment.

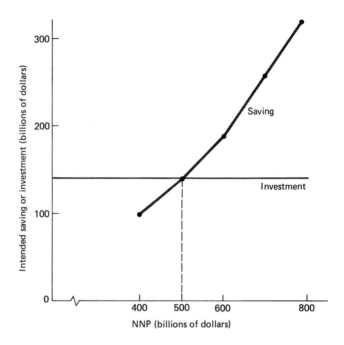

5. Intended saving equals intended investment, since this is an equilibrium. Thus saving equals $100 billion, and the average propensity to save is ⅓. Consequently, the consumption function is:

$$C = \frac{2}{3}D,$$

where C is consumption expenditure and D is disposable income.

Chapter 11 (p. 224)

1. NNP will increase by $2 billion, from $500 billion to $502 billion.

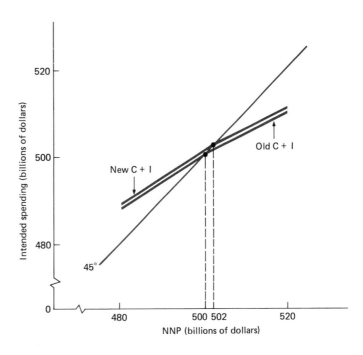

3. Multiplier = 1 ÷ .2 = 5.

5. The marginal propensity to save equals 0.25, and the multiplier is 4.

Chapter 11 (p. 232)

1. (a) Lower; (b) raise; (c) lower; (d) increase; (e) temporary increase.

3. It will shift downward, since consumers want to save $50 billion less at each level of disposable income.

5. Since the marginal propensity to save must be ⅓, the marginal propensity to consume must be ⅔.

Chapter 12 (p. 251)

1. $600 billion.

3. From top to bottom, the figures are: 500; 625; 750; 875; 1,000.

5. You cannot tell, since all you can conclude is that NNP is less than $500 billion. But if the consumption function is a straight line at all levels of disposable income, taxes will equal $75 billion and government spending will equal $50 billion, so the government will have a $25 billion surplus.

Chapter 12 (p. 264)

1. The balanced-budget multiplier indicates the influence on equilibrium NNP of an extra dollar of government spending that is financed by a one dollar increase in lump sum taxes. A simultaneous increase in both government expenditure and taxes by one dollar raises equilibrium NNP by one dollar according to the balanced-budget multiplier.

3. While it has obvious limitations, the full-employment budget has been of use to both Democratic and Republican administrations.

Chapter 13 (p. 280)

1. 1981: 0. 1982: $90,000. 1983: $90,000. 1984: $30,000. 1985: $15,000. 1986: 0.

3. If consumers acted upon their optimism and actually began to buy more autos and appliances, the consumption function might shift to the right, thus increasing NNP (and having a multiplier effect). The sales rate would increase, which, by the accelerator principle, might increase expenditures on equipment and inventory investment.

Chapter 13 (p. 292)

1. Economic cycles are not so regular that one can use them alone to forecast accurately.

3. Consumption rises by $6.52 billion in 1985–86, and by $6.53 billion in each subsequent year. Consumption levels ($ billions) for 1985 to 1989: 111.4, 117.9, 124.4, 131.0, 137.5.

5. If the estimate of $G + I = \$700$ billion + $10 billion, the $2 trillion forecast will be in error by $28.6 billion.

Chapter 14 (p. 306)

1. The paper content of a dollar has little value. Money derives value from its ability to be exchanged for goods and services, because it is a unit of account, and because it acts as a store of value.

3. Time deposits can be transformed into a medium of exchange, currency, by savings withdrawal. They represent a store of value. But the traditional argument against including them in the money supply has been that, in most instances, you could not pay directly for anything with them.

Chapter 14 (p. 317)

1. Yes, according to $MV = PQ$, V must increase by 10 percent. If people and firms conserve on the use of cash because of higher interest rates or the use of new technologies and payment methods, velocity will increase.

3. (a) Keynesian model: Changes in the money supply influence total spending through interest rates.

(b) Crude quantity theory: The quantity of money affects the price level, but not real output, thereby influencing nominal NNP.

(c) Sophisticated quantity theory: Nominal NNP is proportional to the quantity of money. In some formulations, velocity is a function of other variables like the interest rate.

Chapter 15 (p. 334)

1. Reserves, demand deposits, total assets and total liabilities rise by $50,000. Loans and investments and net worth are unchanged.

3. New balance sheet:

Assets		Liabilities	
Reserves	$20,000	Demand deposits	$50,000
Loans	$30,000	Net worth	0
Total	$50,000	Total	$50,000

Chapter 15 (p. 344)

1. The loans made by banks within the limits of reserve requirements do create money.

3. No, calling in loans and selling investments increases the bank's reserves. It does not increase demand deposits.

5. If the reserve ratio is 1/7, the system can support an additional $700 million with $100 million in excess reserves. If the reserve requirement is 1/6, $100 million in excess reserves can support a $600 million increase in the money supply.

Chapter 16 (p. 357)

1. All entries should be +$5 million.

3. No, increasing reserve requirements reduces excess reserves, but does nothing to total member bank reserves.

5. You probably should wait to invest as a dramatic increase in the discount rate is likely to mean higher interest rates and lower bond prices.

Chapter 16 (p. 369)

1. Keeping interest rates low in no way guarantees prosperity. In fact, such a policy could lead to serious inflation at times when the economy is becoming overheated.

3. The answer should focus on the material included in the section on "Should the Fed Pay More Attention to Interest Rates or the Money Supply?"

Chapter 17 (p. 380)

1. While some Keynesians may be social activists, Keynesians' preference for fiscal policy has sprung from the view that aggregate demand management is necessary for stabilizing the economy, and that fiscal policy is relatively effective at achieving this goal.

3. Although it is true that one model can be translated into the other, this does not mean that the two models are the same. As indicated in the text, they are not the same.

Chapter 17 (p. 386)

1. Whatever the size of the government, it should be possible to establish policies to move in the direction of economic stabilization.

3. No, monetarists argue that the expansionary monetary policy pursued during this period was more important than the tax cut in causing the boom that followed.

Chapter 18 (p. 399)

1. These three inflations are classic examples of demand-pull inflation.

3. The plot shows a downward-sloping Phillips curve. Friedman would reject it as a long-run Phillips curve since it is not vertical.

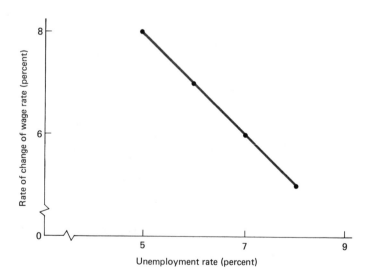

Chapter 18 (p. 411)

1. The response should include a discussion of the objections to guidelines in the section in the text on "The Kennedy-Johnson Guidelines: Criticism and Experience," as well as their possible short-term benefits.

3. To the extent that the basic causes lie with monetary or fiscal policy, this may be true.

Chapter 19 (p. 421)

1. Yes, there was an increase in output per capita. The economy was operating inside its production possibilities curve in 1985, and on its production possibilities curve in 1986.

3. 2 bushels per hour; 2 bushels per hour; zero. The law of diminishing marginal returns sets in beyond 3 million hours of labor input.

5. The equilibrium labor force occurs where the annual average product of labor is 1,400 bushels. The factors responsible are described in Figure 19.3 of the text. The technological advance would increase the equilibrium labor force.

Chapter 19 (p. 434)

1. The capital-output ratio is 2. No, this ratio can change; its value depends on technological change, among other things.

3. Ricardo did not assume that the capital-output ratio was fixed. He believed that it would increase.

Chapter 20 (p. 448)

1. No, the private costs are less than the social costs because of the required downstream water treatment.

3. The output prevailing after the industry has to reimburse others is more desirable, because it reflects the social costs of paper manufacture.

5. The total cost equals $10 - 2P + 5P = 10 + 3P$. Thus it is minimized when $P = 0$. No.

Chapter 20 (p. 456)

1. The statement is incorrect. The tax raises the price, and therefore has a greater influence on consumption the greater is the sensitivity of demand to price.

3. One disadvantage of such a fuel tax is that it might reduce our rate of economic growth.

Chapter 21 (p. 470)

1. Yes, since the domestic opportunity cost of a computer is 1,000 cases of wine in the United States and 2,000 cases in France. The United States has a comparative advantage in computers, and France has one in producing wine. The United States is three times as efficient as France in computers, but only 50 percent more efficient in wine production.

3. No, forces of supply and demand will set the price of each good in world markets so that U.S. firms will find it profitable to make and export computers, while French firms will find it profitable to make and export wine.

Chapter 21 (p. 482)

1. Yes, protection is likely to reduce, not increase, a country's standard of living. On the other hand, a country's standard of living tends to be directly related to its productivity.

3. The United States may have a comparative advantage in computers, but not in TV sets.

Chapter 22 (p. 497)

1. Demanders of marks include buyers of German exports, foreign tourists in Germany, and foreign buyers of German financial assets.

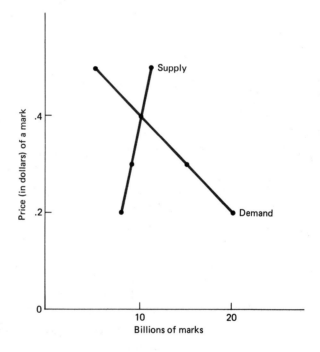

3. $.40 per mark, since at this exchange rate the quantity of marks demanded equals the quantity supplied. In recent years, there has been considerable flexibility in exchange rates, as described on pp. 487.

Chapter 22 (p. 508)

1. One way to reduce a deficit is to keep inflation to a minimum. One possible problem is that policies designed to accomplish this may induce a recession.

3. The market, through changing exchange rates, tends to erase payments imbalances within a flexible exchange rate system. Reserves are required to maintain fixed exchange rates in the face of payments imbalances.

Chapter 23 (p. 522)

1. Hypotheses might include differential savings, investment, population growth, and literacy rates, a more poorly developed capital market in India, and sociological and cultural differences between the two countries.

3. No, not in the sense that population growth has been higher in India than Taiwan. In fact, the opposite was true.

Chapter 23 (p. 533)

1. No. For example, consider the case of Chile, cited on p. 524.

3. The point here is that cultural differences among nations greatly influence the countries' abilities, and even their will, to generate rapid economic development. Obviously, they also set limits on what both the developed countries and the LDCs themselves can do effectively to promote development.

Glossary of Terms

Absolute advantage the ability of one country to produce a good or service more cheaply than another country.

Aggregate demand curve a curve, slopping downward to the right, that shows the level of real national output that will be demanded at various economy-wide price levels.

Aggregate production function the relationship between the amount used of each of the inputs available in the economy and the resulting amount of potential output, i.e., the most output that existing technology permits the economy to produce from various quantities of all available inputs.

Aggregate supply curve a curve, sloping upward to the right, that shows the level of real national output that will be supplied at various economy-wide price levels.

Alternative cost the value of what certain resources could have produced had they been used in the best alternative way; also called **opportunity cost.**

Antitrust laws legislation (such as the Sherman Act, the Clayton Act, and the Federal Trade Commission Act) intended to promote competition and control monopoly.

Appreciation of currency an increase in the value of one currency relative to another.

Automatic stabilizers structural features of the economy that tend by themselves to stabilize national output, without the help of new legislation or government policy measures.

Average product of an input total output divided by the amount of input used to produce this amount of output.

Average product of labor total output per unit of labor.

Average propensity to consume the fraction of total disposable income that is spent on consumption; equal to personal consumption expenditure divided by disposable income.

Balance-of-payments deficit the difference between the quantity supplied and the quantity demanded of a currency when the currency is overvalued (i.e., priced above its equilibrium price).

Balance-of-payments surplus the difference between the quantity demanded and the quantity supplied of a currency when the currency is undervalued (i.e., priced below its equilibrium price).

Balance sheet an accounting statement showing the nature of a firm's assets, the claims by creditors on those assets, and the value of the firm's ownership at a certain point in time.

Balanced budget a budget in which tax revenues cover government expenditures.

Base year a year chosen as a reference point for comparison with some later or earlier year.

Bond a debt (generally long-term) of a firm or government.

Budget a statement of the government's anticipated expenditures and tax revenues for a fiscal year.

Budget deficit a budget in which tax revenues fall short of government expenditures.

Budget surplus a budget in which tax revenues exceed government expenditures.

$C + I + G$ **line** a curve showing total intended spending (the sum of intended consumption expenditure, investment expenditure, and government expenditure) at various levels of net national product; for simplicity, net exports are omitted.

Capital resources (such as factory buildings, equipment, raw materials, and inventories) that are created within the economic system for the purpose of producing other goods.

Capital consumption allowance the value of the capital (i.e., the plant, equipment, and structures) that is worn out in a year; also called **depreciation.**

Capital formation investment in plant and equipment.

Capital goods output consisting of plant and equipment that are used to make other goods.

Capital-output ratio the ratio of the total capital stock to annual national output.

Capitalism an economic system characterized by private ownership of the tools of production; freedom of choice and of enterprise whereby consumers and firms can pursue their own self-interest; competition for sales among producers and resource owners; and reliance on the free market.

Central bank a government-established agency that controls the supply of money and supervises the country's commercial banks; the central bank of the United States is the Federal Reserve.

Commercial banks financial institutions that hold demand and other checkable deposits and permit checks to be written on them, and lend money to firms and individuals.

Common stock certificate of ownership of a corporation. Holders of common stock are owners of the corporation.

Comparative advantage the law that states that a nation should produce and export goods where its efficiency *relative to other nations* is highest; specialization and trade depend on comparative, not absolute advantage.

Compensation of employees the wages and salaries paid by firms and government agencies to the suppliers of labor, including supplementary payments for employee benefits (such as payments into public and private pension and welfare funds).

Constant dollar amounts amounts measured in base-year dollars (i.e., according to the purchasing power of the dollar in some earlier year), in order to express value in a way that corrects for changes in the price level.

Consumer an individual or household that purchases the goods and services produced by the economic system.

Consumer goods output consisting of items that consumers purchase, such as clothing, food, and drink.

Consumer Price Index a measure of U.S. inflation, calculated by the Bureau of Labor Statistics, originally intended to measure changes in the prices of goods and services purchased by urban wage earners and clerical workers; in 1978, expanded to cover all urban consumers.

Consumption function the relationship between consumption spending and disposable income, i.e., the amount of consumption expenditure that will occur at various levels of disposable income.

Corporate profits the net income of corporations (i.e., corporate profits before income taxes), including dividends received by the stockholders, retained earnings, and the amount paid by corporations as income taxes.

Corporation a fictitious legal person separate and distinct from the stockholders who own it, governed by a board of directors elected by the stockholders.

Council of Economic Advisers a group established by the Employment Act of 1946, whose function is to help the president formulate and assess the economic policies of the government.

Creeping inflation an increase in the general price level of a few percent per year that gradually erodes the value of money.

Crowding-out effect the tendency for an increase in public sector expenditure to result in a cut in private sector expenditure.

Crude quantity theory of money and prices the theory that if the velocity of circulation of money remains constant and real net national product remains fixed at its full-employment level, it follows from the equation of exchange that the price level will be proportional to the money supply.

Cyclical unemployment joblessness that occurs because of business cycle fluctuations.

Deflating the conversion of values expressed in current dollars into values expressed in constant dollars, in order to correct for changes in the price level.

Demand curve for money a curve representing the quantity of money that will be demanded at various interest rates (holding net national product constant).

Demand deposits checking accounts; bank deposits subject to payment on demand.

Demand-pull inflation an increase in the general price level that occurs when there is too much aggregate spending, too much money chasing too few goods; also called **demand-induced inflation.**

Depreciation the value of the capital (i.e., plant, equipment, and structures) that is worn out in a year; also called a **capital consumption allowance.**

Depreciation of currency a decrease in the value of one currency relative to another.

Depression a period when national output is well below its potential (i.e., full-employment) level; a severe recession.

Devaluation of currency under the gold standard, a decrease in the value of a currency as a consequence of an increase in the price of gold.

Diffusion process the process by which the use of an innovation spreads from firm to firm and from use to use.

Direct regulation government issue of enforceable rules concerning the conduct of firms.

Discount rate the interest rate the Federal Reserve charges for loans to commercial banks.

Discretionary fiscal policy government tax and spending programs that supplement the effects of the automatic stabilizers in managing the economy.

Disposable income the total amount of income people can keep after personal taxes.

Easy monetary policy a monetary policy that increases the money supply substantially and reduces interest rates.

Economic profits the excess of a firm's profits over what it could make in other industries.

Economic resources resources that are scarce and thus command a nonzero price.

Economics the study of how resources are allocated among alternative uses to satisfy human wants.

Effluent fee a fee that a polluter must pay to the government for discharging waste.

Equation of exchange a way of restating the definition of the velocity of circulation of money, such that the amount received for the final goods and services during a period equals the amount spent on those final goods and services during the same period (that is, $MV = PQ$).

Equilibrium a situation in which there is no tendency for change.

Equilibrium level of net national product the value of national output at which the flow of income generated by this level of output results in a level of spending precisely sufficient to buy this level of output.

Equilibrium price a price that shows no tendency for change, because it is the price at which the quantity demanded equals the quantity supplied; the price toward which the actual price of a good always tends to move.

Exchange rate the number of units of one currency that can purchase a unit of another currency.

Excise tax a tax imposed on each unit sold of a particular product, such as cigarettes or liquor.

Expansion the phase in the business cycle after the trough during which national output rises.

Exports the goods and services that a nation sells to other nations.

External diseconomy an uncompensated cost to one person or firm resulting from the consumption or output of another person or firm.

External economy an uncompensated benefit to one person or firm resulting from the consumption or output of another person or firm.

Federal Open Market Committee (FOMC) a group, composed of the seven members of the Federal Reserve Board plus five presidents of Federal Reserve Banks, which makes decisions concerning the purchase and sale of government securities, in order to control bank reserves and the money supply.

Federal Reserve Board the Board of Governors of the Federal Reserve System, composed of seven members appointed by the president for 14-year terms, whose function is to promote the nation's economic welfare by supervising the operations of the U.S. money and banking system.

Federal Reserve System a system established by Congress in 1913 that includes the member banks (commercial banks), the twelve Federal Reserve Banks, and the seven-member Board of Governors of the Federal Reserve System.

Final goods and services goods and services that are destined for the ultimate user (such as flour purchased for family consumption).

Firm an organization that produces a good or service for sale in an attempt to make a profit.

45-degree line a line that contains all points where the amount on the horizontal axis equals the amount on the vertical axis.

Fractional-reserve banking the practice whereby banks hold less cash than the amount they owe their depositors.

Free resources resources (such as air) that are so abundant that they can be obtained without charge.

Frictional unemployment temporary joblessness, such as that occurring among people who have quit jobs, people looking for their first job, and seasonal workers.

Full employment the minimum level of joblessness that the economy could achieve without undesirably high inflation, recognizing that there will always be some frictional and structural unemployment.

Full-employment budget the difference between tax revenues and government expenditures that would result if the economy were operating at full employment.

Functional finance a budgetary policy whereby the government's budget is set to promote the socially optimal combination of unemployment and inflation, even if this means that the budget is unbalanced over considerable periods of time.

Gold exchange standard an exchange rate system developed after World War II, under which the dollar was directly convertible into gold at a fixed price, and other currencies, since they could be converted into dollars at fixed exchange rates, were thus indirectly convertible into gold at a fixed price.

Gold standard a method of exchange rate determination prevailing until the 1930s, under which currencies were convertible into a certain amount of gold.

Government purchases federal, state, and local government spending on final goods and services, excluding transfer payments.

Gross national product (GNP) the value of the total amount of final goods and services produced by the economy during a period of time; this value can be measured either by the expenditure on the final goods and services, or by the income generated by the output.

Gross private domestic investment all additions to the nation's stock of investment goods, i.e., all investment spending by firms, including purchases of tools, equipment, and machinery, all construction expenditures, and the change in total inventories.

Imports the goods and services that a nation buys from other nations.

Income statement an accounting statement showing a firm's sales, costs, and profits during a particular period (often a quarter or a year).

Income tax a federal, state, or local tax imposed on personal income and corporate profits.

Incomes policy a policy to control inflation that sets some targets for wages and prices in the economy as a whole; gives particular firms and industries detailed guides for making wage and price decisions; and provides some inducements for firms and unions to follow these guidelines.

Indirect business taxes taxes (such as general sales taxes, excise taxes, and customs duties) that are imposed not directly on the business itself but on its products or services, and hence are treated by firms as costs of production.

Inflation an increase in the general level of prices economy-wide.

Innovation the first commercial application of a new technology.

Innovator a firm that is first to apply a new technology.

Input any resource used in the production process.

Interest the payment of money by borrowers to suppliers of money capital.

Interest rate the annual amount that a borrower must pay for the use of a dollar for a year.

Intermediate good a good that is not sold to the ultimate user, but is used as an input in producing final goods and services (such as flour to be used in manufacturing bread).

IS curve a curve showing, for each level of the interest rate, the level of NNP that will satisfy the equilibrium condition that intended spending on output must equal NNP.

Keynesians economists who share many of the beliefs of John Maynard Keynes. His principal tenet was that a capitalist system does not automatically tend toward a full-employment equilibrium (due in part to the rigidity of wages). Keynesians tend to believe that a free-enterprise economy has weak self-regulating mechanisms that should be supplemented by activist fiscal (and other) policies.

Labor human effort, both physical and mental, used to produce goods and services.

Labor force the number of people employed plus the number of those unemployed (i.e., actively looking for work and willing to take a job if one were offered).

Labor productivity the average amount of output that can be obtained for every unit of labor.

Laffer curve a curve representing the relationship between the amount of income tax revenue collected by the government and the marginal tax rate, i.e., how much revenue will be collected at various marginal tax rates.

Land natural resources, including minerals as well as plots of ground, used to produce goods and services.

Law of diminishing marginal returns the principle that if equal increments of a given input are added (the quantities of other inputs being held constant), the resulting increments of product obtained from the extra unit of input (i.e., the marginal product) will begin to decrease beyond some point.

Law of increasing cost the principle that as more and more of a good is produced, the production of each additional unit of the good is likely to entail a larger and larger opportunity cost.

Legal reserve requirements regulations, imposed by the Federal Reserve System in order to control the money supply, requiring banks (and other institutions) to hold a certain fraction of deposits as reserves.

Liabilities the debts of a firm.

LM curve a curve showing, for each level of the interest rate, the level of NNP that will satisfy the equilibrium condition that the public be satisfied to hold the existing quantity of money.

Long run the period of time during which all of a firm's inputs are variable, i.e., during which the firm could completely change the resources used in the production process.

M-1 narrowly defined money supply, which includes coins, currency, demand deposits, and other checkable deposits.

M-2 broadly defined money supply, which includes savings deposits, small time deposits, money market mutual fund balances, and money market deposit accounts, as well as the components of the narrowly defined money supply, M-1 (coins, currency, demand deposits, and other checkable deposits).

Marginal cost the addition to total cost resulting from the addition of the last unit of output.

Marginal product of an input the addition to total output that results from the addition of an extra unit of input (the quantities of all other inputs being held constant).

Marginal product of labor the additional output resulting from the addition of an extra unit of labor.

Marginal propensity to consume the fraction of an extra dollar of disposable income that is spent on consumption.

Marginal propensity to save the fraction of an extra dollar of disposable income that is saved.

Marginal tax rate the proportion of an extra dollar of income that must be paid in taxes.

Market a group of firms and individuals that are in touch with each other in order to buy or sell some good or service.

Market demand curve a curve, usually sloping downward to the right, showing the relationship between a product's price and the quantity demanded of the product.

Market demand curve for labor a curve showing the relationship between the price of labor and the total amount of labor demanded in the market.

Market supply curve a curve, usually sloping upward to the right, showing the relationship between a product's price and the quantity supplied of the product.

Market supply curve for labor a curve showing the relationship between the price of labor and the total amount of labor supplied in the market.

Member banks the commercial banks (all of the national banks and many of the larger state banks) that belong to the Federal Reserve System.

Model a theory composed of assumptions that simplify and abstract from reality, from which conclusions or predictions about the real world are deduced.

Monetarists economists generally sharing the belief that business cycle fluctuations are due largely to changes in the money supply. Many monetarists think that a free-enterprise economy has effective self-regulating mechanisms that activist fiscal and monetary policies tend to disrupt. Some monetarists, like Milton Friedman, advocate a rule for stable growth in the money supply of 3 to 5 percent per year.

Monetary base the reserves of Federal Reserve member banks plus currency outside of the member banks.

Monetary policy the exercise of the central bank's control over the quantity of money and the level of interest rates in order to promote the objectives of national economic policy.

Money anything that serves as a medium of exchange and a standard and store of value; the unit in which the prices of goods and services are measured.

Money income income measured in current dollars (i.e., actual money amounts).

Monopoly a market structure (such as

those for public utilities) in which there is only one seller of a product.

Moral suasion the Federal Reserve's practice of exhorting member banks to go along with its wishes, in the absence of any actual power to force the banks' compliance.

Multinational firm a firm that makes direct investments in other countries, and produces and markets its products abroad.

National banks commercial banks chartered by the federal government.

National debt the amount owed by the government. To cover the difference between its expenditures and its tax revenues, the government sells bonds, notes, and other forms of IOUs.

National income the total amount of income paid out (or owed) by employees, approximately equal to gross national product minus indirect business taxes and depreciation.

Near-money assets (such as government bonds) that can be converted into cash, though not quite as easily as time and savings accounts.

Net exports the amount spent by foreigners on a nation's goods and services (exports) minus the amount a nation spends on foreign goods and services (imports).

Net national product (NNP) gross national product minus depreciation. (Depreciation equals the value of the plant, equipment, and structures that are worn out during the relevant period of time.)

Nominal expressed in current dollars (i.e., actual money amounts).

Normative economics economic propositions about what ought to be, or about what a person, organization, or nation ought to do.

Open market operations the purchase and sale of U.S. government securities on the open market by the Federal Reserve in order to control the quantity of bank reserves.

Opportunity cost the value of what certain resources could have produced had they been used in the best alternative way; also called **alternative cost.**

Overvaluation of currency the setting of a currency's price above the equilibrium price.

Partnership a form of business organization whereby two or more people agree to own and conduct a business, with each party contributing some proportion of the capital and/or labor and receiving some proportion of the profit or loss.

Peak the point in the business cycle where national output is highest relative to its potential (i.e., full-employment) level.

Perfect competition a market structure in which there are many sellers of identical products, where no one seller or buyer has control over the price, where entry is easy, and where resources can switch readily from one use to another. Many agricultural markets have many of the characteristics of perfect competition.

Personal consumption expenditures the spending by households on durable goods, nondurable goods, and services.

Phillips curve a curve representing the relationship between the rate of increase in wages and the level of unemployment.

Positive economics descriptive statements, propositions, and predictions about the economic world that are generally testable by an appeal to the facts.

Potential gross national product the total amount of goods and services that could have been produced had the economy been operating at full capacity or full employment.

Precautionary demand for money the demand for money because of uncertainty about the timing and size of future disbursements and receipts.

Price index the ratio of the value of a set of goods and services in current dollars to the value of the same set of goods and services in constant dollars.

Price supports price floors imposed by the government on a certain good.

Price system a system under which every good and service has a price, and which in a purely capitalistic economy carries out the basic functions of an economic system (determining what goods and services will be produced, how the output will be produced, how much of it each person will receive, and what the nation's growth of per capita income will be).

Primary inputs resources (such as labor and land) that are produced outside of the economic system.

Private cost the price paid by the individual user for the use of a resource.

Product market a market where products are bought and sold.

Production function the relationship between the quantities of various inputs used per period of time and the maximum quantity of output that can be produced per period of time, i.e., the most output that existing technology permits the firm to produce from various quantities of inputs.

Production possibilities curve a curve showing the combinations of amounts of various goods that a society can produce with given (fixed) amounts of resources.

Profit the difference between a firm's revenue and its costs.

Progressive tax a tax whereby the rich pay a larger proportion of their income for the tax than do the poor.

Prohibitive tariff a tariff so high that it prevents imports of a good.

Property tax a tax imposed on real estate and/or other property.

Proprietors' income the net income of unincorporated businesses (i.e., proprietorships and partnerships).

Proprietorship a firm owned by a single individual.

Prosperity a period when national output is close to its potential (i.e., full-employment) level.

Public goods goods and services that can be consumed by one person without diminishing the amount of them that others can consume. Often there is no way to prevent citizens from consuming public goods whether they pay for them or not.

Public sector the governmental sector of the economy.

Quota a limit imposed on the amount of a commodity that can be imported annually.

Rate of return the annual profit per dollar invested that business can obtain by building new structures, adding new equipment, or increasing their inventories; the interest rate earned on the investment in a particular asset.

Rational expectations theory the theory put forth by Robert Lucas, Thomas Sargent, and others that markets clear quickly and expectations are rational. Under these circumstances, predictable macroeconomic policies may not influence real output or unemployment.

Real expressed in constant dollars.

Real income income measured in constant dollars (i.e., the amount of goods and services that can be bought with the income).

Recession the phase in the business cycle after the peak during which national output falls.

Regressive tax a tax whereby the rich pay a smaller proportion of their income for the tax than do the poor.

Resource market a market where resources are bought and sold.

Resources inputs used to produce goods and services.

Retained earnings the total amount of profit that the stockholders of a corporation have reinvested in the business, rather than withdrawing as dividends.

Runaway inflation a very rapid increase in the general price level that wipes out practically all of the value of money.

Sales tax a tax imposed on the goods consumers buy (with the exception, in some states, of food and medical care).

Saving the process by which people give up a claim on present consumption goods in order to receive consumption goods in the future.

Saving function the relationship between total saving and disposable income, i.e., the total amount of saving that will occur at various levels of disposable income.

Say's Law the principle that the production of a certain amount of goods and services results in the generation of an amount of income precisely sufficient to buy that output.

Short run the period of time during which at least one of a firm's inputs (generally its plant and equipment) is fixed.

Special drawing rights (SDRs) a reserve asset established since 1968 by the International Monetary Fund, which member countries can use to exchange for other currencies, much as they used gold in the past.

Stagflation a simultaneous combination of high unemployment and high inflation.

State banks commercial banks chartered by the states.

Structural unemployment joblessness that occurs when new goods or new technologies call for new skills, and workers with older skills cannot find jobs.

Supply-side economics a set of propositions concerned with influencing the aggregate supply curve through the use of financial incentives such as tax cuts.

Tariff a tax imposed by the government on imported goods (designed to cut down on imports and thus protect domestic industry and workers from foreign competition).

Tax avoidance legal steps taken by taxpayers to reduce their tax bill.

Tax evasion misreporting of income or other illegal steps taken by taxpayers to reduce their tax bill.

Technological change new methods of producing existing products, new designs that make it possible to produce new products, and new techniques of organization, marketing, and management.

Technology society's pool of knowledge concerning how goods and services can be produced from a given amount of resources.

Terms of trade the ratio of an index of export prices to an index of import prices.

Tight monetary policy a monetary policy that restrains or reduces the money supply and raises interest rates.

Total revenue a firm's total dollar sales volume.

Trading possibilities curve a curve showing the various combinations of products that a nation can get if it specializes in one product and trades that specialty for foreign goods.

Transactions demand for money the holding of money in cash or in checking accounts in order to pay for final goods and services; the higher the level of NNP, the greater the quantity of money demanded for transactions purposes.

Transfer payments payments made by the government or private business to individuals who do not contribute to the production of goods and services in exchange for them.

Trough the point in the business cycle where national output is lowest relative to its potential (i.e., full-employment) level.

Undervaluation of currency the setting of a currency's price below the equilibrium price.

Unemployment according to the definition of the Bureau of Labor Statistics, joblessness among people who are actively looking for work and would take a job if one were offered.

Unemployment rate the number of people who are unemployed divided by the number of people in the labor force.

Value-added the amount of value added by a firm or industry to the total worth of a product.

Variable input a resource used in the production process (such as labor or raw material) whose quantity can be changed during the particular period under consideration.

Velocity of circulation of money the rate at which the money supply is used to make transactions for final goods and services, i.e., the average number of times per year that a dollar is used to buy the final goods and services produced by the economy. It equals NNP divided by the money supply.

Wage and price controls limits imposed by the government on the amount by which wages and prices can increase, in order to reduce the inflation rate at a given unemployment rate.

Wage-price spiral a series of steps whereby higher wage demands by workers prompt firms to raise their prices to consumers, which in turn raises the general cost of living and prompts workers to make yet higher wage demands.

Wage rate the price of labor.

Photograph Credits

Bureau of Land Management (6, 68); U.S. Department of Labor (6); Sperry New Holland (7); Warder Collection (13, 30, 51, 158, 163, 253, 368, 418, 422, 465, 486); Free-Lance Photo Guild, photo by Kerwin B. Roche (33); photo by Amanda Adams (40); photos by Jeremy Townsend (58, 113, 202, 330); Food and Drug Administration (66); Official U.S. Coast Guard Photo (68); U.S. Air Force Photo (73); AP/Wide World (75); Caterpillar Tractor Company (76); U.S. Congressional Budget Office (87); Project Double Discovery Summer Math Class—Neville Dowe, Teacher—Courtesy Upward Bound and Talent Search of Columbia University (88); Internal Revenue Service (96); Department of Treasury (105); IBM (110, 428); Wide World (115); Edward C. Topple, NYSE Photographer (116); Copyright Gilles Peress, Magnum Photos (153); New York Public Library (160); Sheffield City Museums (161); Courtesy of the New York Historical Society (162); Courtesy of British Airways (172); Billie B. Shaddix/The White House (249); U.S. Senate (254); Jack Kightlinger/The White House (255); Courtesy of U.S. Senator Patrick Moynihan (256); U.S. Government Printing Office (257); White House Photo (258, left and right); The Norwegian Information Service (275); The Bank of America (323); Chase Manhattan Bank (328); Vermont National Bank (329); Federal Reserve (349, 365); Courtesy of Robert Lucas (383); General Motors (431); National Archives, photo by Joseph Sterling (439); E. I. Du Pont de Nemours & Co. (440); German Information Center (442, 481); Burt Glinn/Magnum Photos (468); The Picture Group (474); Copyright by Christian Baur, Photograph basel Missionsstr 10 (503); International Monetary Fund (505); United Nations (514, 519, 526, 527); World Bank photo by Ray Witlin (532).

Index

Definitions of terms appear on pages set in **boldface** type.